Ford Vans

Automotive Repair Manual

by Ralph Rendina, Robert Maddox and John H Haynes

Member of the Guild of Motoring Writers

Models covered:

E-150, E-250 and E-350 Econoline Vans with 4.2L V6, 4.9L inline six-cylinder, 5.0L, 5.8L and 7.5L OHV V8, 4.6L, 5.4L OHC V8 and 6.8L OHC V10 gasoline engines

1992 through 2005

Does not include diesel engine information or commercial-chassis vehicles

(2J5 - 36094)

ABCDE
FGHI

Haynes Publishing Group
Sparkford Nr Yeovil
Somerset BA22 7JJ England

Haynes North America, Inc
861 Lawrence Drive
Newbury Park
California 91320 USA

Acknowledgements

Technical writers contributing to this project are Ed Scott and Rob Maddox.

A book in the Haynes Automotive Repair Manual Series

Printed in the U.S.A.

ISBN-13: 978-1-56392-629-7
ISBN-10: 1-56392-629-6

Library of Congress Control Number 2006922608

Contents

Haynes mechanic, author and photographer with E-250 Van

About this manual

Its purpose

The purpose of this manual is to help you get the best value from your vehicle. It can do so in several ways. It can help you decide what work must be done, even if you choose to have it done by a dealer service department or a repair shop; it provides information and procedures for routine maintenance and servicing; and it offers diagnostic and repair procedures to follow when trouble occurs.

We hope you use the manual to tackle the work yourself. For many simpler jobs, doing it yourself may be quicker than arranging an appointment to get the vehicle into a shop and making the trips to leave it and pick it up. More importantly, a lot of money can be saved by avoiding the expense the shop must pass on to you to cover its labor and overhead costs. An added benefit is the sense of satisfaction and accomplishment that you feel after doing the job yourself.

Using the manual

The manual is divided into Chapters. Each Chapter is divided into numbered Sections, which are headed in bold type between horizontal lines. Each Section consists of consecutively numbered paragraphs.

At the beginning of each numbered Section you will be referred to any illustrations which apply to the procedures in that Section. The reference numbers used in illustration captions pinpoint the pertinent Section and the Step within that Section. That is, illustration 3.2 means the illustration refers to Section 3 and Step (or paragraph) 2 within that Section.

Procedures, once described in the text, are not normally repeated. When it's necessary to refer to another Chapter, the reference will be given as Chapter and Section number. Cross references given without use of the word "Chapter" apply to Sections and/or paragraphs in the same Chapter. For example, "see Section 8" means in the same Chapter.

References to the left or right side of the vehicle assume you are sitting in the driver's seat, facing forward.

Even though we have prepared this manual with extreme care, neither the publisher nor the author can accept responsibility for any errors in, or omissions from, the information given.

NOTE

A **Note** provides information necessary to properly complete a procedure or information which will make the procedure easier to understand.

CAUTION

A **Caution** provides a special procedure or special steps which must be taken while completing the procedure where the Caution is found. Not heeding a Caution can result in damage to the assembly being worked on.

WARNING

A **Warning** provides a special procedure or special steps which must be taken while completing the procedure where the Warning is found. Not heeding a Warning can result in personal injury.

Introduction

The models covered by this manual are conventional front-engine, rear-wheel drive vehicles. They are available in various Gross Vehicle Weight Rating classifications; ranging from the 1/2-ton E-150 model to the 3/4-ton E-250 and 1-ton E-350 models.

Engine options include the 4.2L (256 cu. in.) V6 engine, the 4.9L (300 cu. in.) inline six-cylinder engine, the 4.6L (281 cu. in.), the 5.0L (302 cu. in.), the 5.4L (329 cu. in.), the 5.8L (351 cu. in.), the 7.5L (460 cu. in.) V8 engines and the 6.8L (415 cu. in.) V10 engines. The fuel system on all engines is a computer controlled multi-port fuel-injected system.

Power from the engine is transferred through an automatic transmission to the differential mounted in the solid rear axle assembly by a tubular driveshaft incorporating universal joints. Axles inside the assembly carry power from the differential to the rear wheels. Transmission types include a heavy-duty 3-speed model and several different 4-speed models, with fourth gear being an overdrive ratio. Some 4-speed automatics utilize computer controlled electronic shifting capabilities. Some 2004 and later models with 6.8L V10 engines have an optional TorqShift 5-speed automatic overdrive transmission.

Suspension is independent twin I-beam in the front, with coil springs and radius arms used to locate the knuckle assembly at each wheel. The rear suspension features semi-elliptical leaf springs. All models use hydraulic shock absorbers at each corner. Power steering is standard on all models.

The brakes are disc at the front and drum at the rear. Some late models are equipped with rear disc brakes. All models use hydraulic brakes assisted by a vacuum booster. Some models are equipped with an Anti-lock Braking System (ABS).

Vehicle identification numbers

Modifications are a continuing and unpublicized process in vehicle manufacturing. Since spare parts lists and manuals are compiled on a numerical basis, the individual vehicle numbers are necessary to correctly identify the component required.

Vehicle Identification Number (VIN)

This very important identification number is stamped on a plate attached to the dashboard inside the windshield on the driver's side of the vehicle (see illustration). The VIN also appears on the Vehicle Certificate of Title and Registration. It contains information such as where and when the vehicle was manufactured, the model year and the body style.

VIN engine and model year codes

Two particular important pieces of information found in the VIN are the engine code and the model year code. Counting from the left, the engine code letter designation is the 8th digit and the model year code designation is the 10th digit.

On the models covered by this manual the engine codes are:

2	4.2L V6
Y	4.9L inline 6
W	4.6L (Romeo) V8
6	4.6L (Windsor) V8
N	5.0L V8
H	5.8L V8
L	5.4L V8
G	7.5L V8
S or 5	6.8L V10

The Vehicle Identification Number (VIN) is visible through the driver's side windshield

The Certification label is located on the driver's side door pillar

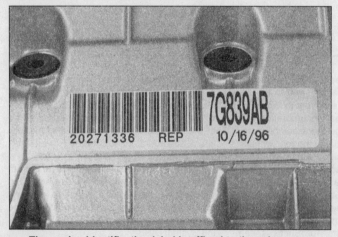

The engine identification label is affixed to the valve cover

The differential identification tag is bolted to the differential cover

The VECI label is located near the radiator support

On the models covered by this manual the model year codes are:

5	2005
4	2004
3	2003
2	2002
1	2001
Y	2000
X	1999
W	1998
V	1997
T	1996
S	1995
R	1994
P	1993
N	1992

Vehicle Certification Label

The Vehicle Certification Label is attached to the driver's side door pillar **(see illustration)**. Information on this label includes the name of the manufacturer, the month and year of production, the Gross Vehicle Weight Rating (GVWR), the Gross Axle Weight Rating (GAWR) and other vehicle specific information.

Engine identification numbers

Labels containing the engine code, engine number and build date can be found on the valve cover **(see illustration)**. The engine number is also stamped onto a machined pad on the external surface of the engine block.

Transmission identification numbers

The automatic transmission ID number is affixed to a label on the right side of the case.

Differential identification numbers

The differential ID number is stamped on a tag which is bolted to the differential cover **(see illustration)**.

Vehicle Emissions Control Information (VECI) label

This label is found in the engine compartment **(see illustration)**. See Chapter 6 for more information on this label.

Booster battery (jump) starting

Observe the following precautions when using a booster battery to start a vehicle:

a) Before connecting the booster battery, make sure the ignition switch is in the Off position.
b) Turn off the lights, heater and other electrical loads.
c) Your eyes should be shielded. Safety goggles are a good idea.
d) Make sure the booster battery is the same voltage as the dead one in the vehicle.
e) The two vehicles MUST NOT TOUCH each other.
f) Make sure the transmission is in Neutral (manual transaxle) or Park (automatic transaxle).
g) If the booster battery is not a maintenance-free type, remove the vent caps and lay a cloth over the vent holes.

Connect the red jumper cable to the positive (+) terminals of each battery.

Connect one end of the black cable to the negative (-) terminal of the booster battery. The other end of this cable should be connected to a good ground on the engine block **(see illustration)**. Make sure the cable will not come into contact with the fan, drivebelts or other moving parts of the engine.

Start the engine using the booster battery, then, with the engine running at idle speed, disconnect the jumper cables in the reverse order of connection.

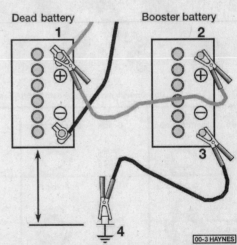

Make the booster battery cable connections in the numerical order shown (note that the negative cable of the booster battery is NOT attached to the negative terminal of the dead battery)

Buying parts

Replacement parts are available from many sources, which generally fall into one of two categories - authorized dealer parts departments and independent retail auto parts stores. Our advice concerning these parts is as follows:

Retail auto parts stores: Good auto parts stores will stock frequently needed components which wear out relatively fast, such as clutch components, exhaust systems, brake parts, tune-up parts, etc. These stores often supply new or reconditioned parts on an exchange basis, which can save a considerable amount of money. Discount auto parts stores are often very good places to buy materials and parts needed for general vehicle maintenance such as oil, grease, filters, spark plugs, belts, touch-up paint, bulbs, etc. They also usually sell tools and general accessories, have convenient hours, charge lower prices and can often be found not far from home.

Authorized dealer parts department: This is the best source for parts which are unique to the vehicle and not generally available elsewhere (such as major engine parts, transmission parts, trim pieces, etc.).

Warranty information: If the vehicle is still covered under warranty, be sure that any replacement parts purchased - regardless of the source - do not invalidate the warranty!

To be sure of obtaining the correct parts, have engine and chassis numbers available and, if possible, take the old parts along for positive identification.

Maintenance techniques, tools and working facilities

Maintenance techniques

There are a number of techniques involved in maintenance and repair that will be referred to throughout this manual. Application of these techniques will enable the home mechanic to be more efficient, better organized and capable of performing the various tasks properly, which will ensure that the repair job is thorough and complete.

Fasteners

Fasteners are nuts, bolts, studs and screws used to hold two or more parts together. There are a few things to keep in mind when working with fasteners. Almost all of them use a locking device of some type, either a lockwasher, locknut, locking tab or thread adhesive. All threaded fasteners should be clean and straight, with undamaged threads and undamaged corners on the hex head where the wrench fits. Develop the habit of replacing all damaged nuts and bolts with new ones. Special locknuts with nylon or fiber inserts can only be used once. If they are removed, they lose their locking ability and must be replaced with new ones.

Rusted nuts and bolts should be treated with a penetrating fluid to ease removal and prevent breakage. Some mechanics use turpentine in a spout-type oil can, which works quite well. After applying the rust penetrant, let it work for a few minutes before trying to loosen the nut or bolt. Badly rusted fasteners may have to be chiseled or sawed off or removed with a special nut breaker, available at tool stores.

If a bolt or stud breaks off in an assembly, it can be drilled and removed with a special tool commonly available for this purpose. Most automotive machine shops can perform this task, as well as other repair procedures, such as the repair of threaded holes that have been stripped out.

Flat washers and lockwashers, when removed from an assembly, should always be replaced exactly as removed. Replace any damaged washers with new ones. Never use a lockwasher on any soft metal surface (such as aluminum), thin sheet metal or plastic.

Fastener sizes

For a number of reasons, automobile manufacturers are making wider and wider use of metric fasteners. Therefore, it is important to be able to tell the difference between standard (sometimes called U.S. or SAE) and metric hardware, since they cannot be interchanged.

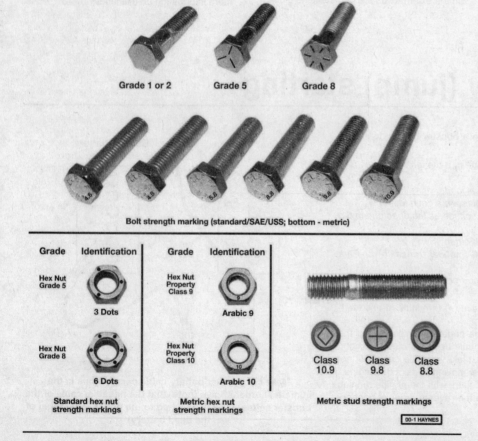

Grade 1 or 2   Grade 5   Grade 8

Bolt strength marking (standard/SAE/USS; bottom - metric)

Grade	Identification
Hex Nut Grade 5	3 Dots
Hex Nut Grade 8	6 Dots

Standard hex nut strength markings

Grade	Identification
Hex Nut Property Class 9	Arabic 9
Hex Nut Property Class 10	Arabic 10

Metric hex nut strength markings

Class 10.9   Class 9.8   Class 8.8

Metric stud strength markings

00-1 HAYNES

Metric thread sizes	Ft-lbs	Nm
M-6	6 to 9	9 to 12
M-8	14 to 21	19 to 28
M-10	28 to 40	38 to 54
M-12	50 to 71	68 to 96
M-14	80 to 140	109 to 154

Pipe thread sizes		
1/8	5 to 8	7 to 10
1/4	12 to 18	17 to 24
3/8	22 to 33	30 to 44
1/2	25 to 35	34 to 47

U.S. thread sizes		
1/4 - 20	6 to 9	9 to 12
5/16 - 18	12 to 18	17 to 24
5/16 - 24	14 to 20	19 to 27
3/8 - 16	22 to 32	30 to 43
3/8 - 24	27 to 38	37 to 51
7/16 - 14	40 to 55	55 to 74
7/16 - 20	40 to 60	55 to 81
1/2 - 13	55 to 80	75 to 108

Standard (SAE and USS) bolt dimensions/ grade marks

G   Grade marks (bolt strength)
L   Length (in inches)
T   Thread pitch (number of threads per inch)
D   Nominal diameter (in inches)

Metric bolt dimensions/grade marks

P   Property class (bolt strength)
L   Length (in millimeters)
T   Thread pitch (distance between threads in millimeters)
D   Diameter

All bolts, whether standard or metric, are sized according to diameter, thread pitch and length. For example, a standard 1/2 - 13 x 1 bolt is 1/2 inch in diameter, has 13 threads per inch and is 1 inch long. An M12 - 1.75 x 25 metric bolt is 12 mm in diameter, has a thread pitch of 1.75 mm (the distance between threads) and is 25 mm long. The two bolts are nearly identical, and easily confused, but they are not interchangeable.

In addition to the differences in diameter, thread pitch and length, metric and standard bolts can also be distinguished by examining the bolt heads. To begin with, the distance across the flats on a standard bolt head is measured in inches, while the same dimension on a metric bolt is sized in millimeters (the same is true for nuts). As a result, a stan- dard wrench should not be used on a metric bolt and a metric wrench should not be used on a standard bolt. Also, most standard bolts have slashes radiating out from the center of the head to denote the grade or strength of the bolt, which is an indication of the amount of torque that can be applied to it. The greater the number of slashes, the greater the strength of the bolt. Grades 0 through 5 are commonly used on automobiles. Metric bolts have a property class (grade) number, rather than a slash, molded into their heads to indi- cate bolt strength. In this case, the higher the number, the stronger the bolt. Property class numbers 8.8, 9.8 and 10.9 are commonly used on automobiles.

Strength markings can also be used to distinguish standard hex nuts from metric hex nuts. Many standard nuts have dots stamped into one side, while metric nuts are marked with a number. The greater the number of dots, or the higher the number, the greater the strength of the nut.

Metric studs are also marked on their ends according to property class (grade). Larger studs are numbered (the same as met- ric bolts), while smaller studs carry a geomet- ric code to denote grade.

It should be noted that many fasteners, especially Grades 0 through 2, have no dis- tinguishing marks on them. When such is the case, the only way to determine whether it is standard or metric is to measure the thread pitch or compare it to a known fastener of the same size.

Standard fasteners are often referred to as SAE, as opposed to metric. However, it should be noted that SAE technically refers to a non-metric fine thread fastener only. Coarse thread non-metric fasteners are referred to as USS sizes.

Since fasteners of the same size (both standard and metric) may have different strength ratings, be sure to reinstall any bolts, studs or nuts removed from your vehicle in their original locations. Also, when replacing a fastener with a new one, make sure that the new one has a strength rating equal to or greater than the original.

Tightening sequences and procedures

Most threaded fasteners should be tight- ened to a specific torque value (torque is the twisting force applied to a threaded compo- nent such as a nut or bolt). Overtightening the fastener can weaken it and cause it to break, while undertightening can cause it to even- tually come loose. Bolts, screws and studs, depending on the material they are made of and their thread diameters, have specific torque values, many of which are noted in the Specifications at the beginning of each Chap- ter. Be sure to follow the torque recommen- dations closely. For fasteners not assigned a specific torque, a general torque value chart is presented here as a guide. These torque values are for dry (unlubricated) fasteners threaded into steel or cast iron (not alumi- num). As was previously mentioned, the size and grade of a fastener determine the amount of torque that can safely be applied to it. The figures listed here are approximate for Grade 2 and Grade 3 fasteners. Higher grades can tolerate higher torque values.

Fasteners laid out in a pattern, such as cylinder head bolts, oil pan bolts, differential cover bolts, etc., must be loosened or tight- ened in sequence to avoid warping the com- ponent. This sequence will normally be shown in the appropriate Chapter. If a specific pat- tern is not given, the following procedures can be used to prevent warping.

Initially, the bolts or nuts should be assembled finger-tight only. Next, they should be tightened one full turn each, in a criss- cross or diagonal pattern. After each one has been tightened one full turn, return to the first

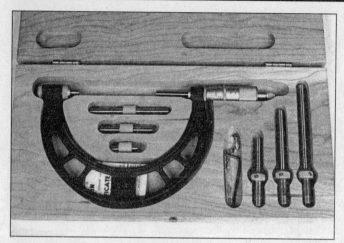

Micrometer set

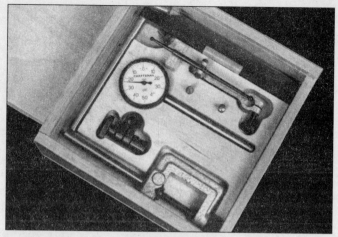

Dial indicator set

one and tighten them all one-half turn, following the same pattern. Finally, tighten each of them one-quarter turn at a time until each fastener has been tightened to the proper torque. To loosen and remove the fasteners, the procedure would be reversed.

Component disassembly

Component disassembly should be done with care and purpose to help ensure that the parts go back together properly. Always keep track of the sequence in which parts are removed. Make note of special characteristics or marks on parts that can be installed more than one way, such as a grooved thrust washer on a shaft. It is a good idea to lay the disassembled parts out on a clean surface in the order that they were removed. It may also be helpful to make sketches or take instant photos of components before removal.

When removing fasteners from a component, keep track of their locations. Sometimes threading a bolt back in a part, or putting the washers and nut back on a stud, can prevent mix-ups later. If nuts and bolts cannot be returned to their original locations, they should be kept in a compartmented box or a series of small boxes. A cupcake or muffin tin is ideal for this purpose, since each cavity can hold the bolts and nuts from a particular area (i.e. oil pan bolts, valve cover bolts, engine mount bolts, etc.). A pan of this type is especially helpful when working on assemblies with very small parts, such as the carburetor, alternator, valve train or interior dash and trim pieces. The cavities can be marked with paint or tape to identify the contents.

Whenever wiring looms, harnesses or connectors are separated, it is a good idea to identify the two halves with numbered pieces of masking tape so they can be easily reconnected.

Gasket sealing surfaces

Throughout any vehicle, gaskets are used to seal the mating surfaces between two parts and keep lubricants, fluids, vacuum or pressure contained in an assembly.

Many times these gaskets are coated with a liquid or paste-type gasket sealing

compound before assembly. Age, heat and pressure can sometimes cause the two parts to stick together so tightly that they are very difficult to separate. Often, the assembly can be loosened by striking it with a soft-face hammer near the mating surfaces. A regular hammer can be used if a block of wood is placed between the hammer and the part. Do not hammer on cast parts or parts that could be easily damaged. With any particularly stubborn part, always recheck to make sure that every fastener has been removed.

Avoid using a screwdriver or bar to pry apart an assembly, as they can easily mar the gasket sealing surfaces of the parts, which must remain smooth. If prying is absolutely necessary, use an old broom handle, but keep in mind that extra clean up will be necessary if the wood splinters.

After the parts are separated, the old gasket must be carefully scraped off and the gasket surfaces cleaned. Stubborn gasket material can be soaked with rust penetrant or treated with a special chemical to soften it so it can be easily scraped off. A scraper can be fashioned from a piece of copper tubing by flattening and sharpening one end. Copper is recommended because it is usually softer than the surfaces to be scraped, which reduces the chance of gouging the part. Some gaskets can be removed with a wire brush, but regardless of the method used, the mating surfaces must be left clean and smooth. If for some reason the gasket surface is gouged, then a gasket sealer thick enough to fill scratches will have to be used during reassembly of the components. For most applications, a non-drying (or semi-drying) gasket sealer should be used.

Hose removal tips

Warning: *If the vehicle is equipped with air conditioning, do not disconnect any of the A/C hoses without first having the system depressurized by a dealer service department or a service station.*

Hose removal precautions closely parallel gasket removal precautions. Avoid scratching or gouging the surface that the hose mates against or the connection may

leak. This is especially true for radiator hoses. Because of various chemical reactions, the rubber in hoses can bond itself to the metal spigot that the hose fits over. To remove a hose, first loosen the hose clamps that secure it to the spigot. Then, with slip-joint pliers, grab the hose at the clamp and rotate it around the spigot. Work it back and forth until it is completely free, then pull it off. Silicone or other lubricants will ease removal if they can be applied between the hose and the outside of the spigot. Apply the same lubricant to the inside of the hose and the outside of the spigot to simplify installation.

As a last resort (and if the hose is to be replaced with a new one anyway), the rubber can be slit with a knife and the hose peeled from the spigot. If this must be done, be careful that the metal connection is not damaged.

If a hose clamp is broken or damaged, do not reuse it. Wire-type clamps usually weaken with age, so it is a good idea to replace them with screw-type clamps whenever a hose is removed.

Tools

A selection of good tools is a basic requirement for anyone who plans to maintain and repair his or her own vehicle. For the owner who has few tools, the initial investment might seem high, but when compared to the spiraling costs of professional auto maintenance and repair, it is a wise one.

To help the owner decide which tools are needed to perform the tasks detailed in this manual, the following tool lists are offered: *Maintenance and minor repair, Repair/overhaul* and *Special.*

The newcomer to practical mechanics should start off with the *maintenance and minor repair* tool kit, which is adequate for the simpler jobs performed on a vehicle. Then, as confidence and experience grow, the owner can tackle more difficult tasks, buying additional tools as they are needed. Eventually the basic kit will be expanded into the *repair and overhaul* tool set. Over a period of time, the experienced do-it-yourselfer will assemble a tool set complete enough for most repair and

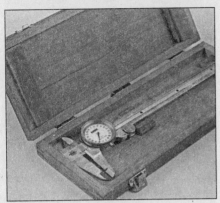

Dial caliper

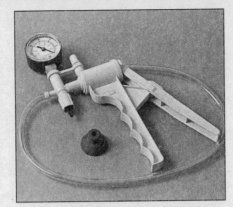

Hand-operated vacuum pump

Timing light

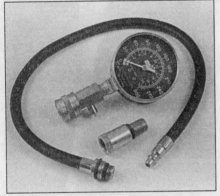

Compression gauge with spark plug hole adapter

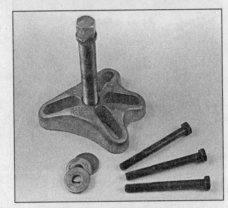

Damper/steering wheel puller

General purpose puller

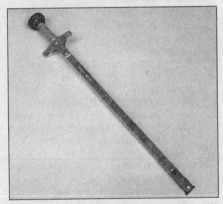

Hydraulic lifter removal tool

Valve spring compressor

Valve spring compressor

Ridge reamer

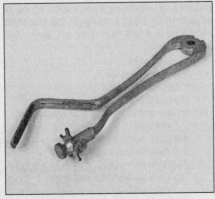

Piston ring groove cleaning tool

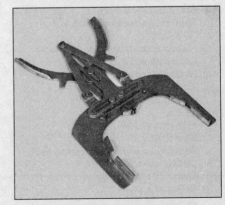

Ring removal/installation tool

Ring compressor

Cylinder hone

Brake hold-down spring tool

Torque angle gauge

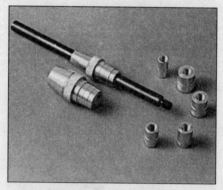

Clutch plate alignment tool

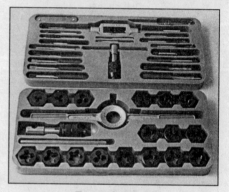

Tap and die set

overhaul procedures and will add tools from the special category when it is felt that the expense is justified by the frequency of use.

Maintenance and minor repair tool kit

The tools in this list should be considered the minimum required for performance of routine maintenance, servicing and minor repair work. We recommend the purchase of combination wrenches (box-end and open-end combined in one wrench). While more expensive than open end wrenches, they offer the advantages of both types of wrench.

> Combination wrench set (1/4-inch to 1 inch or 6 mm to 19 mm)
> Adjustable wrench, 8 inch
> Spark plug wrench with rubber insert
> Spark plug gap adjusting tool
> Feeler gauge set
> Brake bleeder wrench
> Standard screwdriver (5/16-inch x 6 inch)
> Phillips screwdriver (No. 2 x 6 inch)
> Combination pliers - 6 inch
> Hacksaw and assortment of blades
> Tire pressure gauge
> Grease gun
> Oil can
> Fine emery cloth
> Wire brush
> Battery post and cable cleaning tool
> Oil filter wrench
> Funnel (medium size)
> Safety goggles
> Jackstands (2)
> Drain pan

Note: *If basic tune-ups are going to be part of routine maintenance, it will be necessary to purchase a good quality stroboscopic timing light and combination tachometer/dwell meter. Although they are included in the list of special tools, it is mentioned here because they are absolutely necessary for tuning most vehicles properly.*

Repair and overhaul tool set

These tools are essential for anyone who plans to perform major repairs and are in addition to those in the maintenance and minor repair tool kit. Included is a comprehensive set of sockets which, though expensive, are invaluable because of their versatility, especially when various extensions and drives are available. We recommend the 1/2-inch drive over the 3/8-inch drive. Although the larger drive is bulky and more expensive, it has the capacity of accepting a very wide range of large sockets. Ideally, however, the mechanic should have a 3/8-inch drive set and a 1/2-inch drive set.

> Socket set(s)
> Reversible ratchet
> Extension - 10 inch
> Universal joint
> Torque wrench (same size drive as sockets)
> Ball peen hammer - 8 ounce
> Soft-face hammer (plastic/rubber)
> Standard screwdriver (1/4-inch x 6 inch)
> Standard screwdriver (stubby - 5/16-inch)
> Phillips screwdriver (No. 3 x 8 inch)

> Phillips screwdriver (stubby - No. 2)
> Pliers - vise grip
> Pliers - lineman's
> Pliers - needle nose
> Pliers - snap-ring (internal and external)
> Cold chisel - 1/2-inch
> Scribe
> Scraper (made from flattened copper tubing)
> Centerpunch
> Pin punches (1/16, 1/8, 3/16-inch)
> Steel rule/straightedge - 12 inch
> Allen wrench set (1/8 to 3/8-inch or 4 mm to 10 mm)
> A selection of files
> Wire brush (large)
> Jackstands (second set)
> Jack (scissor or hydraulic type)

Note: *Another tool which is often useful is an electric drill with a chuck capacity of 3/8-inch and a set of good quality drill bits.*

Special tools

The tools in this list include those which are not used regularly, are expensive to buy, or which need to be used in accordance with their manufacturer's instructions. Unless these tools will be used frequently, it is not very economical to purchase many of them. A consideration would be to split the cost and use between yourself and a friend or friends. In addition, most of these tools can be obtained from a tool rental shop on a temporary basis.

This list primarily contains only those tools and instruments widely available to the public, and not those special tools produced by the vehicle manufacturer for distribution to dealer service departments. Occasionally, references to the manufacturer's special tools are included in the text of this manual. Generally, an alternative method of doing the job without the special tool is offered. However, sometimes there is no alternative to their use. Where this is the case, and the tool cannot be purchased or borrowed, the work should be turned over to the dealer service department or an automotive repair shop.

Valve spring compressor
Piston ring groove cleaning tool
Piston ring compressor
Piston ring installation tool
Cylinder compression gauge
Cylinder ridge reamer
Cylinder surfacing hone
Cylinder bore gauge
Micrometers and/or dial calipers
Hydraulic lifter removal tool
Balljoint separator
Universal-type puller
Impact screwdriver
Dial indicator set
Stroboscopic timing light (inductive pick-up)
Hand operated vacuum/pressure pump
Tachometer/dwell meter
Universal electrical multimeter
Cable hoist
Brake spring removal and installation tools
Floor jack

Buying tools

For the do-it-yourselfer who is just starting to get involved in vehicle maintenance and repair, there are a number of options available when purchasing tools. If maintenance and minor repair is the extent of the work to be done, the purchase of individual tools is satisfactory. If, on the other hand, extensive work is planned, it would be a good idea to purchase a modest tool set from one of the large retail chain stores. A set can usually be bought at a substantial savings over the individual tool prices, and they often come with a tool box. As additional tools are needed, add-on sets, individual tools and a larger tool box can be purchased to expand the tool selection. Building a tool set gradually allows the cost of the tools to be spread over a longer period of time and gives the mechanic the freedom to choose only those tools that will actually be used.

Tool stores will often be the only source of some of the special tools that are needed, but regardless of where tools are bought, try to avoid cheap ones, especially when buying screwdrivers and sockets, because they won't last very long. The expense involved in replac-

ing cheap tools will eventually be greater than the initial cost of quality tools.

Care and maintenance of tools

Good tools are expensive, so it makes sense to treat them with respect. Keep them clean and in usable condition and store them properly when not in use. Always wipe off any dirt, grease or metal chips before putting them away. Never leave tools lying around in the work area. Upon completion of a job, always check closely under the hood for tools that may have been left there so they won't get lost during a test drive.

Some tools, such as screwdrivers, pliers, wrenches and sockets, can be hung on a panel mounted on the garage or workshop wall, while others should be kept in a tool box or tray. Measuring instruments, gauges, meters, etc. must be carefully stored where they cannot be damaged by weather or impact from other tools.

When tools are used with care and stored properly, they will last a very long time. Even with the best of care, though, tools will wear out if used frequently. When a tool is damaged or worn out, replace it. Subsequent jobs will be safer and more enjoyable if you do.

How to repair damaged threads

Sometimes, the internal threads of a nut or bolt hole can become stripped, usually from overtightening. Stripping threads is an all-too-common occurrence, especially when working with aluminum parts, because aluminum is so soft that it easily strips out.

Usually, external or internal threads are only partially stripped. After they've been cleaned up with a tap or die, they'll still work. Sometimes, however, threads are badly damaged. When this happens, you've got three choices:

1) *Drill and tap the hole to the next suitable oversize and install a larger diameter bolt, screw or stud.*
2) *Drill and tap the hole to accept a threaded plug, then drill and tap the plug to the original screw size. You can also buy a plug already threaded to the original size. Then you simply drill a hole to the specified size, then run the threaded plug into the hole with a bolt and jam nut. Once the plug is fully seated, remove the jam nut and bolt.*
3) *The third method uses a patented thread repair kit like Heli-Coil or Slimsert. These easy-to-use kits are designed to repair damaged threads in straight-through*

holes and blind holes. Both are available as kits which can handle a variety of sizes and thread patterns. Drill the hole, then tap it with the special included tap. Install the Heli-Coil and the hole is back to its original diameter and thread pitch.

Regardless of which method you use, be sure to proceed calmly and carefully. A little impatience or carelessness during one of these relatively simple procedures can ruin your whole day's work and cost you a bundle if you wreck an expensive part.

Working facilities

Not to be overlooked when discussing tools is the workshop. If anything more than routine maintenance is to be carried out, some sort of suitable work area is essential.

It is understood, and appreciated, that many home mechanics do not have a good workshop or garage available, and end up removing an engine or doing major repairs outside. It is recommended, however, that the overhaul or repair be completed under the cover of a roof.

A clean, flat workbench or table of comfortable working height is an absolute necessity. The workbench should be equipped with a vise that has a jaw opening of at least four inches.

As mentioned previously, some clean, dry storage space is also required for tools, as well as the lubricants, fluids, cleaning solvents, etc. which soon become necessary.

Sometimes waste oil and fluids, drained from the engine or cooling system during normal maintenance or repairs, present a disposal problem. To avoid pouring them on the ground or into a sewage system, pour the used fluids into large containers, seal them with caps and take them to an authorized disposal site or recycling center. Plastic jugs, such as old antifreeze containers, are ideal for this purpose.

Always keep a supply of old newspapers and clean rags available. Old towels are excellent for mopping up spills. Many mechanics use rolls of paper towels for most work because they are readily available and disposable. To help keep the area under the vehicle clean, a large cardboard box can be cut open and flattened to protect the garage or shop floor.

Whenever working over a painted surface, such as when leaning over a fender to service something under the hood, always cover it with an old blanket or bedspread to protect the finish. Vinyl covered pads, made especially for this purpose, are available at auto parts stores.

Jacking and towing

Jacking

Warning: *The jack supplied with the vehicle should only be used for changing a tire or placing jackstands under the frame. Never work under the vehicle or start the engine while this jack is being used as the only means of support.*

The vehicle should be located on level ground. Place the shift lever in Park. Block the wheel diagonally opposite the wheel being changed. Set the parking brake.

Remove the spare tire and jack from stowage. Remove the wheel cover (if equipped) with the tapered end of the lug nut wrench by inserting and twisting the handle and then prying against the back of the wheel cover. Loosen, but do not remove, the lug nuts (one-half turn is sufficient).

Place the jack under the axle nearest the wheel being changed. There is a right and left jacking point on each axle **(see illustration)**.

Turn the jack handle clockwise until the tire clears the ground. Remove the lug nuts and pull the wheel off. Replace it with the spare.

Install the lug nuts with the beveled edges facing in. Tighten them snugly. Don't attempt to tighten them completely until the vehicle is lowered or it could slip off the jack. Lower the vehicle. Remove the jack and tighten the lug nuts in a criss-cross pattern **(see illustration)**.

Install the wheel cover and be sure it's snapped into place all the way around.

Stow the tire, jack and wrench. Unblock the wheels.

Towing

As a general rule, the vehicle should be towed with the rear wheels off the ground. If they can't be raised, either place them on a dolly or disconnect the driveshaft from the differential. When a vehicle is towed with the rear wheels raised, the steering wheel must be clamped in the straight ahead position with a special device designed for use during towing The ignition key must be in the OFF position, since the steering lock mechanism isn't strong enough to hold the front wheels straight while towing.

Vehicles equipped with an automatic transmission can be towed from the front only with all four wheels on the ground, provided that speeds don't exceed 35 mph and the distance is not over 50 miles. Before towing, check the transmission fluid level (see Chapter 1). If the level is below the HOT line on the dipstick, add fluid or use a towing dolly. Release the parking brake, put the transmission in Neutral and place the ignition key in the OFF position. There's no distance limitation when towing with either the rear wheels off the ground or the driveshaft disconnected, but don't exceed 50 mph.

Equipment specifically designed for towing should be used. It should be attached to the main structural members of the vehicle, not the bumpers or brackets.

Safety is a major consideration when towing and all applicable state and local laws must be obeyed. A safety chain system must be used at all times. Remember that power steering and power brakes will not work with the engine off.

Front jacking locations - 2WD models

Rear jacking location - all models

Automotive chemicals and lubricants

A number of automotive chemicals and lubricants are available for use during vehicle maintenance and repair. They include a wide variety of products ranging from cleaning solvents and degreasers to lubricants and protective sprays for rubber, plastic and vinyl.

Cleaners

Carburetor cleaner and choke cleaner is a strong solvent for gum, varnish and carbon. Most carburetor cleaners leave a dry-type lubricant film which will not harden or gum up. Because of this film it is not recommended for use on electrical components.

Brake system cleaner is used to remove brake dust, grease and brake fluid from the brake system, where clean surfaces are absolutely necessary. It leaves no residue and often eliminates brake squeal caused by contaminants.

Electrical cleaner removes oxidation, corrosion and carbon deposits from electrical contacts, restoring full current flow. It can also be used to clean spark plugs, carburetor jets, voltage regulators and other parts where an oil-free surface is desired.

Demoisturants remove water and moisture from electrical components such as alternators, voltage regulators, electrical connectors and fuse blocks. They are non-conductive and non-corrosive.

Degreasers are heavy-duty solvents used to remove grease from the outside of the engine and from chassis components. They can be sprayed or brushed on and, depending on the type, are rinsed off either with water or solvent.

Lubricants

Motor oil is the lubricant formulated for use in engines. It normally contains a wide variety of additives to prevent corrosion and reduce foaming and wear. Motor oil comes in various weights (viscosity ratings) from 0 to 50. The recommended weight of the oil depends on the season, temperature and the demands on the engine. Light oil is used in cold climates and under light load conditions. Heavy oil is used in hot climates and where high loads are encountered. Multi-viscosity oils are designed to have characteristics of both light and heavy oils and are available in a number of weights from 5W-20 to 20W-50.

Gear oil is designed to be used in differentials, manual transmissions and other areas where high-temperature lubrication is required.

Chassis and wheel bearing grease is a heavy grease used where increased loads and friction are encountered, such as for wheel bearings, balljoints, tie-rod ends and universal joints.

High-temperature wheel bearing grease is designed to withstand the extreme temperatures encountered by wheel bearings in disc brake equipped vehicles. It usually contains molybdenum disulfide (moly), which is a dry-type lubricant.

White grease is a heavy grease for metal-to-metal applications where water is a problem. White grease stays soft under both low and high temperatures (usually from -100 to +190-degrees F), and will not wash off or dilute in the presence of water.

Assembly lube is a special extreme pressure lubricant, usually containing moly, used to lubricate high-load parts (such as main and rod bearings and cam lobes) for initial start-up of a new engine. The assembly lube lubricates the parts without being squeezed out or washed away until the engine oiling system begins to function.

Silicone lubricants are used to protect rubber, plastic, vinyl and nylon parts.

Graphite lubricants are used where oils cannot be used due to contamination problems, such as in locks. The dry graphite will lubricate metal parts while remaining uncontaminated by dirt, water, oil or acids. It is electrically conductive and will not foul electrical contacts in locks such as the ignition switch.

Moly penetrants loosen and lubricate frozen, rusted and corroded fasteners and prevent future rusting or freezing.

Heat-sink grease is a special electrically non-conductive grease that is used for mounting electronic ignition modules where it is essential that heat is transferred away from the module.

Sealants

RTV sealant is one of the most widely used gasket compounds. Made from silicone, RTV is air curing, it seals, bonds, waterproofs, fills surface irregularities, remains flexible, doesn't shrink, is relatively easy to remove, and is used as a supplementary sealer with almost all low and medium temperature gaskets.

Anaerobic sealant is much like RTV in that it can be used either to seal gaskets or to form gaskets by itself. It remains flexible, is solvent resistant and fills surface imperfections. The difference between an anaerobic sealant and an RTV-type sealant is in the curing. RTV cures when exposed to air, while an anaerobic sealant cures only in the absence of air. This means that an anaerobic sealant cures only after the assembly of parts, sealing them together.

Thread and pipe sealant is used for sealing hydraulic and pneumatic fittings and vacuum lines. It is usually made from a Teflon compound, and comes in a spray, a paint-on liquid and as a wrap-around tape.

Chemicals

Anti-seize compound prevents seizing, galling, cold welding, rust and corrosion in fasteners. High-temperature ant-seize, usually made with copper and graphite lubricants, is used for exhaust system and exhaust manifold bolts.

Anaerobic locking compounds are used to keep fasteners from vibrating or working loose and cure only after installation, in the absence of air. Medium strength locking compound is used for small nuts, bolts and screws that may be removed later. High-strength locking compound is for large nuts, bolts and studs which aren't removed on a regular basis.

Oil additives range from viscosity index improvers to chemical treatments that claim to reduce internal engine friction. It should be noted that most oil manufacturers caution against using additives with their oils.

Gas additives perform several functions, depending on their chemical makeup. They usually contain solvents that help dissolve gum and varnish that build up on carburetor, fuel injection and intake parts. They also serve to break down carbon deposits that form on the inside surfaces of the combustion chambers. Some additives contain upper cylinder lubricants for valves and piston rings, and others contain chemicals to remove condensation from the gas tank.

Miscellaneous

Brake fluid is specially formulated hydraulic fluid that can withstand the heat and pressure encountered in brake systems. Care must be taken so this fluid does not come in contact with painted surfaces or plastics. An opened container should always be resealed to prevent contamination by water or dirt.

Weatherstrip adhesive is used to bond weatherstripping around doors, windows and trunk lids. It is sometimes used to attach trim pieces.

Undercoating is a petroleum-based, tar-like substance that is designed to protect metal surfaces on the underside of the vehicle from corrosion. It also acts as a sound-deadening agent by insulating the bottom of the vehicle.

Waxes and polishes are used to help protect painted and plated surfaces from the weather. Different types of paint may require the use of different types of wax and polish. Some polishes utilize a chemical or abrasive cleaner to help remove the top layer of oxidized (dull) paint on older vehicles. In recent years many non-wax polishes that contain a wide variety of chemicals such as polymers and silicones have been introduced. These non-wax polishes are usually easier to apply and last longer than conventional waxes and polishes.

Conversion factors

Length (distance)

Inches (in)	X	25.4	= Millimeters (mm)	X 0.0394	= Inches (in)
Feet (ft)	X	0.305	= Meters (m)	X 3.281	= Feet (ft)
Miles	X	1.609	= Kilometers (km)	X 0.621	= Miles

Volume (capacity)

Cubic inches (cu in; in^3)	X	16.387	= Cubic centimeters (cc; cm^3)	X 0.061	= Cubic inches (cu in; in^3)
Imperial pints (Imp pt)	X	0.568	= Liters (l)	X 1.76	= Imperial pints (Imp pt)
Imperial quarts (Imp qt)	X	1.137	= Liters (l)	X 0.88	= Imperial quarts (Imp qt)
Imperial quarts (Imp qt)	X	1.201	= US quarts (US qt)	X 0.833	= Imperial quarts (Imp qt)
US quarts (US qt)	X	0.946	= Liters (l)	X 1.057	= US quarts (US qt)
Imperial gallons (Imp gal)	X	4.546	= Liters (l)	X 0.22	= Imperial gallons (Imp gal)
Imperial gallons (Imp gal)	X	1.201	= US gallons (US gal)	X 0.833	= Imperial gallons (Imp gal)
US gallons (US gal)	X	3.785	= Liters (l)	X 0.264	= US gallons (US gal)

Mass (weight)

Ounces (oz)	X	28.35	= Grams (g)	X 0.035	= Ounces (oz)
Pounds (lb)	X	0.454	= Kilograms (kg)	X 2.205	= Pounds (lb)

Force

Ounces-force (ozf; oz)	X	0.278	= Newtons (N)	X 3.6	= Ounces-force (ozf; oz)
Pounds-force (lbf; lb)	X	4.448	= Newtons (N)	X 0.225	= Pounds-force (lbf; lb)
Newtons (N)	X	0.1	= Kilograms-force (kgf; kg)	X 9.81	= Newtons (N)

Pressure

Pounds-force per square inch (psi; lbf/in^2; lb/in^2)	X	0.070	= Kilograms-force per square centimeter (kgf/cm^2; kg/cm^2)	X 14.223	= Pounds-force per square inch (psi; lbf/in^2; lb/in^2)
Pounds-force per square inch (psi; lbf/in^2; lb/in^2)	X	0.068	= Atmospheres (atm)	X 14.696	= Pounds-force per square inch (psi; lbf/in^2; lb/in^2)
Pounds-force per square inch (psi; lbf/in^2; lb/in^2)	X	0.069	= Bars	X 14.5	= Pounds-force per square inch (psi; lbf/in^2; lb/in^2)
Pounds-force per square inch (psi; lbf/in^2; lb/in^2)	X	6.895	= Kilopascals (kPa)	X 0.145	= Pounds-force per square inch (psi; lbf/in^2; lb/in^2)
Kilopascals (kPa)	X	0.01	= Kilograms-force per square centimeter (kgf/cm^2; kg/cm^2)	X 98.1	= Kilopascals (kPa)

Torque (moment of force)

Pounds-force inches (lbf in; lb in)	X	1.152	= Kilograms-force centimeter (kgf cm; kg cm)	X 0.868	= Pounds-force inches (lbf in; lb in)
Pounds-force inches (lbf in; lb in)	X	0.113	= Newton meters (Nm)	X 8.85	= Pounds-force inches (lbf in; lb in)
Pounds-force inches (lbf in; lb in)	X	0.083	= Pounds-force feet (lbf ft; lb ft)	X 12	= Pounds-force inches (lbf in; lb in)
Pounds-force feet (lbf ft; lb ft)	X	0.138	= Kilograms-force meters (kgf m; kg m)	X 7.233	= Pounds-force feet (lbf ft; lb ft)
Pounds-force feet (lbf ft; lb ft)	X	1.356	= Newton meters (Nm)	X 0.738	= Pounds-force feet (lbf ft; lb ft)
Newton meters (Nm)	X	0.102	= Kilograms-force meters (kgf m; kg m)	X 9.804	= Newton meters (Nm)

Vacuum

Inches mercury (in. Hg)	X	3.377	= Kilopascals (kPa)	X 0.2961	= Inches mercury
Inches mercury (in. Hg)	X	25.4	= Millimeters mercury (mm Hg)	X 0.0394	= Inches mercury

Power

Horsepower (hp)	X	745.7	= Watts (W)	X 0.0013	= Horsepower (hp)

Velocity (speed)

Miles per hour (miles/hr; mph)	X	1.609	= Kilometers per hour (km/hr; kph)	X 0.621	= Miles per hour (miles/hr; mph)

Fuel consumption*

Miles per gallon, Imperial (mpg)	X	0.354	= Kilometers per liter (km/l)	X 2.825	= Miles per gallon, Imperial (mpg)
Miles per gallon, US (mpg)	X	0.425	= Kilometers per liter (km/l)	X 2.352	= Miles per gallon, US (mpg)

Temperature

Degrees Fahrenheit = (°C x 1.8) + 32   Degrees Celsius (Degrees Centigrade; °C) = (°F - 32) x 0.56

*It is common practice to convert from miles per gallon (mpg) to liters/100 kilometers (l/100km), where mpg (Imperial) x l/100 km = 282 and mpg (US) x l/100 km = 235

DECIMALS to MILLIMETERS

Decimal	mm	Decimal	mm
0.001	0.0254	0.500	12.7000
0.002	0.0508	0.510	12.9540
0.003	0.0762	0.520	13.2080
0.004	0.1016	0.530	13.4620
0.005	0.1270	0.540	13.7160
0.006	0.1524	0.550	13.9700
0.007	0.1778	0.560	14.2240
0.008	0.2032	0.570	14.4780
0.009	0.2286	0.580	14.7320
		0.590	14.9860
0.010	0.2540		
0.020	0.5080		
0.030	0.7620		
0.040	1.0160	0.600	15.2400
0.050	1.2700	0.610	15.4940
0.060	1.5240	0.620	15.7480
0.070	1.7780	0.630	16.0020
0.080	2.0320	0.640	16.2560
0.090	2.2860	0.650	16.5100
		0.660	16.7640
0.100	2.5400	0.670	17.0180
0.110	2.7940	0.680	17.2720
0.120	3.0480	0.690	17.5260
0.130	3.3020		
0.140	3.5560		
0.150	3.8100		
0.160	4.0640	0.700	17.7800
0.170	4.3180	0.710	18.0340
0.180	4.5720	0.720	18.2880
0.190	4.8260	0.730	18.5420
		0.740	18.7960
0.200	5.0800	0.750	19.0500
0.210	5.3340	0.760	19.3040
0.220	5.5880	0.770	19.5580
0.230	5.8420	0.780	19.8120
0.240	6.0960	0.790	20.0660
0.250	6.3500		
0.260	6.6040		
0.270	6.8580	0.800	20.3200
0.280	7.1120	0.810	20.5740
0.290	7.3660	0.820	21.8280
		0.830	21.0820
0.300	7.6200	0.840	21.3360
0.310	7.8740	0.850	21.5900
0.320	8.1280	0.860	21.8440
0.330	8.3820	0.870	22.0980
0.340	8.6360	0.880	22.3520
0.350	8.8900	0.890	22.6060
0.360	9.1440		
0.370	9.3980		
0.380	9.6520		
0.390	9.9060	0.900	22.8600
0.400	10.1600	0.910	23.1140
0.410	10.4140	0.920	23.3680
0.420	10.6680	0.930	23.6220
0.430	10.9220	0.940	23.8760
0.440	11.1760	0.950	24.1300
0.450	11.4300	0.960	24.3840
0.460	11.6840	0.970	24.6380
0.470	11.9380	0.980	24.8920
0.480	12.1920	0.990	25.1460
0.490	12.4460	1.000	25.4000

FRACTIONS to DECIMALS to MILLIMETERS

Fraction	Decimal	mm	Fraction	Decimal	mm
1/64	0.0156	0.3969	33/64	0.5156	13.0969
1/32	0.0312	0.7938	17/32	0.5312	13.4938
3/64	0.0469	1.1906	35/64	0.5469	13.8906
1/16	0.0625	1.5875	9/16	0.5625	14.2875
5/64	0.0781	1.9844	37/64	0.5781	14.6844
3/32	0.0938	2.3812	19/32	0.5938	15.0812
7/64	0.1094	2.7781	39/64	0.6094	15.4781
1/8	0.1250	3.1750	5/8	0.6250	15.8750
9/64	0.1406	3.5719	41/64	0.6406	16.2719
5/32	0.1562	3.9688	21/32	0.6562	16.6688
11/64	0.1719	4.3656	43/64	0.6719	17.0656
3/16	0.1875	4.7625	11/16	0.6875	17.4625
13/64	0.2031	5.1594	45/64	0.7031	17.8594
7/32	0.2188	5.5562	23/32	0.7188	18.2562
15/64	0.2344	5.9531	47/64	0.7344	18.6531
1/4	0.2500	6.3500	3/4	0.7500	19.0500
17/64	0.2656	6.7469	49/64	0.7656	19.4469
9/32	0.2812	7.1438	25/32	0.7812	19.8438
19/64	0.2969	7.5406	51/64	0.7969	20.2406
5/16	0.3125	7.9375	13/16	0.8125	20.6375
21/64	0.3281	8.3344	53/64	0.8281	21.0344
11/32	0.3438	8.7312	27/32	0.8438	21.4312
23/64	0.3594	9.1281	55/64	0.8594	21.8281
3/8	0.3750	9.5250	7/8	0.8750	22.2250
25/64	0.3906	9.9219	57/64	0.8906	22.6219
13/32	0.4062	10.3188	29/32	0.9062	23.0188
27/64	0.4219	10.7156	59/64	0.9219	23.4156
7/16	0.4375	11.1125	15/16	0.9375	23.8125
29/64	0.4531	11.5094	61/64	0.9531	24.2094
15/32	0.4688	11.9062	31/32	0.9688	24.6062
31/64	0.4844	12.3031	63/64	0.9844	25.0031
1/2	0.5000	12.7000	1	1.0000	25.4000

Safety first!

Regardless of how enthusiastic you may be about getting on with the job at hand, take the time to ensure that your safety is not jeopardized. A moment's lack of attention can result in an accident, as can failure to observe certain simple safety precautions. The possibility of an accident will always exist, and the following points should not be considered a comprehensive list of all dangers. Rather, they are intended to make you aware of the risks and to encourage a safety conscious approach to all work you carry out on your vehicle.

Essential DOs and DON'Ts

DON'T rely on a jack when working under the vehicle. Always use approved jackstands to support the weight of the vehicle and place them under the recommended lift or support points.

DON'T attempt to loosen extremely tight fasteners (i.e. wheel lug nuts) while the vehicle is on a jack - it may fall.

DON'T start the engine without first making sure that the transmission is in Neutral (or Park where applicable) and the parking brake is set.

DON'T remove the radiator cap from a hot cooling system - let it cool or cover it with a cloth and release the pressure gradually.

DON'T attempt to drain the engine oil until you are sure it has cooled to the point that it will not burn you.

DON'T touch any part of the engine or exhaust system until it has cooled sufficiently to avoid burns.

DON'T siphon toxic liquids such as gasoline, antifreeze and brake fluid by mouth, or allow them to remain on your skin.

DON'T inhale brake lining dust - it is potentially hazardous (see *Asbestos* below).

DON'T allow spilled oil or grease to remain on the floor - wipe it up before someone slips on it.

DON'T use loose fitting wrenches or other tools which may slip and cause injury.

DON'T push on wrenches when loosening or tightening nuts or bolts. Always try to pull the wrench toward you. If the situation calls for pushing the wrench away, push with an open hand to avoid scraped knuckles if the wrench should slip.

DON'T attempt to lift a heavy component alone - get someone to help you.

DON'T rush or take unsafe shortcuts to finish a job.

DON'T allow children or animals in or around the vehicle while you are working on it.

DO wear eye protection when using power tools such as a drill, sander, bench grinder, etc. and when working under a vehicle.

DO keep loose clothing and long hair well out of the way of moving parts.

DO make sure that any hoist used has a safe working load rating adequate for the job.

DO get someone to check on you periodically when working alone on a vehicle.

DO carry out work in a logical sequence and make sure that everything is correctly assembled and tightened.

DO keep chemicals and fluids tightly capped and out of the reach of children and pets.

DO remember that your vehicle's safety affects that of yourself and others. If in doubt on any point, get professional advice.

Asbestos

Certain friction, insulating, sealing, and other products - such as brake linings, brake bands, clutch linings, torque converters, gaskets, etc. - may contain asbestos. Extreme care must be taken to avoid inhalation of dust from such products, since it is hazardous to health. If in doubt, assume that they do contain asbestos.

Fire

Remember at all times that gasoline is highly flammable. Never smoke or have any kind of open flame around when working on a vehicle. But the risk does not end there. A spark caused by an electrical short circuit, by two metal surfaces contacting each other, or even by static electricity built up in your body under certain conditions, can ignite gasoline vapors, which in a confined space are highly explosive. Do not, under any circumstances, use gasoline for cleaning parts. Use an approved safety solvent.

Always disconnect the battery ground (-) cable at the battery before working on any part of the fuel system or electrical system. Never risk spilling fuel on a hot engine or exhaust component. It is strongly recommended that a fire extinguisher suitable for use on fuel and electrical fires be kept handy in the garage or workshop at all times. Never try to extinguish a fuel or electrical fire with water.

Fumes

Certain fumes are highly toxic and can quickly cause unconsciousness and even death if inhaled to any extent. Gasoline vapor falls into this category, as do the vapors from some cleaning solvents. Any draining or pouring of such volatile fluids should be done in a well ventilated area.

When using cleaning fluids and solvents, read the instructions on the container carefully. Never use materials from unmarked containers.

Never run the engine in an enclosed space, such as a garage. Exhaust fumes contain carbon monoxide, which is extremely poisonous. If you need to run the engine, always do so in the open air, or at least have the rear of the vehicle outside the work area.

If you are fortunate enough to have the use of an inspection pit, never drain or pour gasoline and never run the engine while the vehicle is over the pit. The fumes, being heavier than air, will concentrate in the pit with possibly lethal results.

The battery

Never create a spark or allow a bare light bulb near a battery. They normally give off a certain amount of hydrogen gas, which is highly explosive.

Always disconnect the battery ground (-) cable at the battery before working on the fuel or electrical systems.

If possible, loosen the filler caps or cover when charging the battery from an external source (this does not apply to sealed or maintenance-free batteries). Do not charge at an excessive rate or the battery may burst.

Take care when adding water to a non maintenance-free battery and when carrying a battery. The electrolyte, even when diluted, is very corrosive and should not be allowed to contact clothing or skin.

Always wear eye protection when cleaning the battery to prevent the caustic deposits from entering your eyes.

Household current

When using an electric power tool, inspection light, etc., which operates on household current, always make sure that the tool is correctly connected to its plug and that, where necessary, it is properly grounded. Do not use such items in damp conditions and, again, do not create a spark or apply excessive heat in the vicinity of fuel or fuel vapor.

Secondary ignition system voltage

A severe electric shock can result from touching certain parts of the ignition system (such as the spark plug wires) when the engine is running or being cranked, particularly if components are damp or the insulation is defective. In the case of an electronic ignition system, the secondary system voltage is much higher and could prove fatal.

Troubleshooting

Contents

This Section provides an easy reference guide to the more common problems that may occur during the operation of your vehicle. Various symptoms and their probable causes are grouped under headings denoting components or systems, such as Engine, Cooling system, etc. They also refer to the Chapter and/or Section that deals with the problem.

Remember that successful troubleshooting isn't a mysterious art practiced only by professional mechanics, it's simply the result of knowledge combined with an intelligent, systematic approach to a problem. Always use a process of elimination starting with the simplest solution and working through to the most complex - and never overlook the obvious. Anyone can run the gas tank dry or leave the lights on overnight, so don't assume that you're exempt from such oversights.

Finally, always establish a clear idea why a problem has occurred and take steps to ensure that it doesn't happen again. If the electrical system fails because of a poor connection, check all other connections in the system to make sure they don't fail as well. If a particular fuse continues to blow, find out why - don't just go on replacing fuses. Remember, failure of a small component can often be indicative of potential failure or incorrect functioning of a more important component or system.

Engine

1 Engine will not rotate when attempting to start

1 Battery terminal connections loose or corroded. Check the cable terminals at the battery; tighten cable clamp and/or clean off corrosion as necessary (see Chapter 1).
2 Battery discharged or faulty. If the cable ends are clean and tight on the battery posts, turn the key to the On position and switch on the headlights or windshield wipers. If they won't run, the battery is discharged.
3 Automatic transmission not engaged in park (P) or Neutral (N).
4 Broken, loose or disconnected wires in the starting circuit. Inspect all wires and connectors at the battery, starter solenoid and ignition switch (on steering column).
5 Starter motor pinion jammed in driveplate ring gear. Remove starter (Chapter 5) and inspect pinion and driveplate (Chapter 2).
6 Starter solenoid faulty (Chapter 5).
7 Starter motor faulty (Chapter 5).
8 Ignition switch faulty (Chapter 12).
9 Engine seized. Try to turn the crankshaft with a large socket and breaker bar on the pulley bolt.

2 Engine rotates but will not start

1 Fuel tank empty.
2 Battery discharged (engine rotates slowly).
3 Battery terminal connections loose or corroded.
4 Fuel not reaching fuel injectors. Check for clogged fuel filter or lines and defective fuel pump. Also make sure the tank vent lines aren't clogged (Chapter 4).
5 Faulty distributor components. Check the cap and rotor (Chapter 1).
6 Low cylinder compression. Check as described in Chapter 2.
7 Water in fuel. Drain tank and fill with new fuel.
8 Defective ignition coil (Chapter 5).
9 Dirty or clogged fuel injector(s) (Chapter 4).
10 Wet or damaged ignition components (Chapters 1 and 5).
11 Worn, faulty or incorrectly gapped spark plugs (Chapter 1).
12 Broken, loose or disconnected wires in the starting circuit (see previous Section).
13 Loose distributor (if equipped). Turn the distributor body as necessary to start the engine, then adjust the ignition timing as soon as possible (Chapter 5).
14 Broken, loose or disconnected wires at the ignition coil or faulty coil (Chapter 5).
15 Timing chain failure or wear affecting valve timing (Chapter 2).
16 Fuel injection or engine control systems failure (Chapters 4 and 6).
17 Defective MAF sensor.

3 Starter motor operates without turning engine

1 Starter pinion sticking. Remove the starter (Chapter 5) and inspect.
2 Starter pinion or driveplate teeth worn or broken. Remove the inspection cover and inspect.

4 Engine hard to start when cold

1 Battery discharged or low. Check as described in Chapter 1.
2 Fuel not reaching the fuel injectors. Check the fuel filter, lines and fuel pump (Chapters 1 and 4).
3 Defective spark plugs (Chapter 1).
4 Defective engine coolant temperature sensor (Chapter 6).
5 Fuel injection or engine control systems malfunction (Chapters 4 and 6).

5 Engine hard to start when hot

1 Air filter dirty (Chapter 1).

2 Fuel not reaching the fuel injection (see Section 4). Check for a vapor lock situation, brought about by clogged fuel tank vent lines.
3 Bad engine ground connection.
4 Defective stator in the distributor (Chapter 5).
5 Fuel injection or engine control systems malfunction (Chapters 4 and 6).

6 Starter motor noisy or engages roughly

1 Pinion or driveplate teeth worn or broken. Remove the inspection cover on the left side of the engine and inspect.
2 Starter motor mounting bolts loose or missing.

7 Engine starts but stops immediately

1 Loose or damaged wire harness connections at distributor, coil or alternator.
2 Intake manifold vacuum leaks. Make sure all mounting bolts/nuts are tight and all vacuum hoses connected to the manifold are attached properly and in good condition (see Chapters 2 and 4).
3 Insufficient fuel pressure (see Chapter 4).
4 Fuel injection or engine control systems malfunction (Chapters 4 and 6).

8 Engine 'lopes' while idling or idles erratically

1 Vacuum leaks. Check mounting bolts at the intake manifold for tightness. Make sure that all vacuum hoses are connected and in good condition. Use a stethoscope or a length of fuel hose held against your ear to listen for vacuum leaks while the engine is running. A hissing sound will be heard. A soapy water solution will also detect leaks. Check the intake manifold gasket surfaces.
2 Leaking EGR valve or plugged PCV valve (see Chapters 1 and 6).
3 Air filter clogged (Chapter 1).
4 Fuel pump not delivering sufficient fuel (Chapter 4).
5 Leaking head gasket. Perform a cylinder compression check (Chapter 2).
6 Timing chain worn (Chapter 2).
7 Camshaft lobes worn (Chapter 2).
8 Valves burned or otherwise leaking (Chapter 2).
9 Ignition timing out of adjustment (Chapter 5).
10 Ignition system not operating properly (Chapters 1 and 5).
11 Fuel injection or engine control systems malfunction (Chapters 4 and 6).

9 Engine misses at idle speed

1 Spark plugs faulty or not gapped properly (Chapter 1).
2 Faulty spark plug wires (Chapter 1).
3 Wet or damaged distributor components (Chapter 1).
4 Short circuits in ignition, coil or spark plug wires.
5 Sticking or faulty emissions systems (see Chapter 6).
6 Clogged fuel filter and/or foreign matter in fuel. Remove the fuel filter (Chapter 1) and inspect.
7 Vacuum leaks at intake manifold or hose connections. Check as described in Section 8.
8 Incorrect idle speed (Chapter 4).
9 Low or uneven cylinder compression. Check as described in Chapter 2.
10 Fuel injection or engine control systems malfunction (Chapters 4 and 6).

10 Excessively high idle speed

1 Sticking throttle linkage (Chapter 4).
2 Vacuum leaks at intake manifold or hose connections. Check as described in Section 8.
3 Fuel injection or engine control systems malfunction (Chapters 4 and 6).

11 Battery will not hold a charge

1 Alternator drivebelt defective or not adjusted properly (Chapter 1).
2 Battery cables loose or corroded (Chapter 1).
3 Alternator not charging properly (Chapter 5).
4 Loose, broken or faulty wires in the charging circuit (Chapter 5).
5 Short circuit causing a continuous drain on the battery.
6 Battery defective internally.

12 Alternator light stays on

1 Fault in alternator or charging circuit (Chapter 5).
2 Alternator drivebelt defective or not properly adjusted (Chapter 1).

13 Alternator light fails to come on when key is turned on

1 Faulty bulb (Chapter 12).
2 Defective alternator (Chapter 5).
3 Fault in the printed circuit, dash wiring or bulb holder (Chapter 12).

14 Engine misses throughout driving speed range

1 Fuel filter clogged and/or impurities in the fuel system. Check fuel filter (Chapter 1) or clean system (Chapter 4).
2 Faulty or incorrectly gapped spark plugs (Chapter 1).
3 Incorrect ignition timing (Chapter 5).
4 Cracked distributor cap, disconnected distributor wires or damaged distributor components (Chapter 1).
5 Defective spark plug wires (Chapter 1).
6 Emissions system components faulty (Chapter 6).
7 Low or uneven cylinder compression pressures. Check as described in Chapter 2.
8 Weak or faulty ignition coil (Chapter 5).
9 Weak or faulty ignition system (Chapter 5).
10 Vacuum leaks at intake manifold or vacuum hoses (see Section 8).
11 Dirty or clogged fuel injector(s) (Chapter 4).
12 Leaky EGR valve (Chapter 6).
13 Fuel injection or engine control systems malfunction (Chapters 4 and 6).

15 Hesitation or stumble during acceleration

1 Ignition system not operating properly (Chapter 5).
2 Dirty or clogged fuel injector(s) (Chapter 4).
3 Low fuel pressure. Check for proper operation of the fuel pump and for restrictions in the fuel filter and lines (Chapter 4).
4 Fuel injection or engine control systems malfunction (Chapters 4 and 6).

16 Engine stalls

1 Idle speed incorrect (Chapter 4).
2 Fuel filter clogged and/or water and impurities in the fuel system (Chapter 1).
3 Damaged or wet distributor cap and wires.
4 Emissions system components faulty (Chapter 6).
5 Faulty or incorrectly gapped spark plugs (Chapter 1). Also check the spark plug wires (Chapter 1).
6 Vacuum leak at the intake manifold or vacuum hoses. Check as described in Section 8.
7 Fuel injection or engine control systems malfunction (Chapters 4 and 6).

17 Engine lacks power

1 Incorrect ignition timing (Chapter 5).
2 Excessive play in distributor shaft (if

equipped). At the same time check for faulty distributor cap, wires, etc. (Chapter 1).
3 Faulty or incorrectly gapped spark plugs (Chapter 1).
4 Air filter dirty (Chapter 1).
5 Faulty ignition coil (Chapter 5).
6 Brakes binding (Chapters 1 and 10).
7 Automatic transmission fluid level incorrect, causing slippage (Chapter 1).
8 Fuel filter clogged and/or impurities in the fuel system (Chapters 1 and 4).
9 EGR system not functioning properly (Chapter 6).
10 Use of sub-standard fuel. Fill tank with proper octane fuel.
11 Low or uneven cylinder compression pressures. Check as described in Chapter 2.
12 Vacuum leak at intake manifold or vacuum hoses (check as described in Section 8).
13 Dirty or clogged fuel injector(s) (Chapters 1 and 4).
14 Fuel injection or engine control systems malfunction (Chapters 4 and 6).
15 Restricted exhaust system (Chapter 4).

18 Engine backfires

1 EGR system not functioning properly (Chapter 6).
2 Ignition timing incorrect (Chapter 5).
3 Vacuum leak (refer to Section 8).
4 Damaged valve springs or sticking valves (Chapter 2).
5 Vacuum leak at the intake manifold or vacuum hoses (see Section 8).

19 Engine surges while holding accelerator steady

1 Vacuum leak at the intake manifold or vacuum hoses (see Section 8).
2 Restricted air filter (Chapter 1).
3 Fuel pump or pressure regulator defective (Chapter 4).
4 Fuel injection or engine control systems malfunction (Chapters 4 and 6).

20 Pinging or knocking engine sounds when engine is under load

1 Incorrect grade of fuel. Fill tank with fuel of the proper octane rating.
2 Ignition timing incorrect (Chapter 5).
3 Carbon build-up in combustion chambers. Remove cylinder head(s) and clean combustion chambers (Chapter 2).
4 Incorrect spark plugs (Chapter 1).
5 Fuel injection or engine control systems malfunction (Chapters 4 and 6).
6 Restricted exhaust system (Chapter 4).

21 Engine diesels (continues to run) after being turned off

1   Idle speed too high (Chapter 4).
2   Ignition timing incorrect (Chapter 5).
3   Incorrect spark plug heat range (Chapter 1).
4   Vacuum leak at the intake manifold or vacuum hoses (see Section 8).
5   Carbon build-up in combustion chambers. Remove the cylinder head(s) and clean the combustion chambers (Chapter 2).
6   Valves sticking (Chapter 2).
7   EGR system not operating properly (Chapter 6).
8   Fuel injection or engine control systems malfunction (Chapters 4 and 6).
9   Check for causes of overheating (Section 27).

22 Low oil pressure

1   Improper grade of oil.
2   Oil pump worn or damaged (Chapter 2).
3   Engine overheating (refer to Section 27).
4   Clogged oil filter (Chapter 1).
5   Clogged oil strainer (Chapter 2).
6   Oil pressure gauge not working properly (see Chapter 2E, Section 2).

23 Excessive oil consumption

1   Loose oil drain plug.
2   Loose bolts or damaged oil pan gasket (Chapter 2).
3   Loose bolts or damaged front cover gasket (Chapter 2).
4   Front or rear crankshaft oil seal leaking (Chapter 2).
5   Loose bolts or damaged valve cover gasket (Chapter 2).
6   Loose oil filter (Chapter 1).
7   Loose or damaged oil pressure switch (Chapter 2).
8   Pistons and cylinders excessively worn (Chapter 2).
9   Piston rings not installed correctly on pistons (Chapter 2).
10   Worn or damaged piston rings (Chapter 2).
11   Intake and/or exhaust valve oil seals worn or damaged (Chapter 2).
12   Worn valve stems or guides.
13   Worn or damaged valves/guides (Chapter 2).
14   Faulty or incorrect PCV valve allowing too much crankcase airflow.

24 Excessive fuel consumption

1   Dirty or clogged air filter element (Chapter 1).
2   Incorrect ignition timing (Chapter 5).
3   Incorrect idle speed (Chapter 4).

4   Low tire pressure or incorrect tire size (Chapter 10).
5   Inspect for binding brakes.
6   Fuel leakage. Check all connections, lines and components in the fuel system (Chapter 4).
7   Dirty or clogged fuel injectors (Chapter 4).
8   Fuel injection or engine control systems malfunction (Chapters 4 and 6).
9   Thermostat stuck open or not installed.
10   Improperly operating transmission.

25 Fuel odor

1   Fuel leakage. Check all connections, lines and components in the fuel system (Chapter 4).
2   Fuel tank overfilled. Fill only to automatic shut-off.
3   Charcoal canister filter in Evaporative Emissions Control system clogged (Chapter 1).
4   Vapor leaks from Evaporative Emissions Control system lines (Chapter 6).

26 Miscellaneous engine noises

1   A strong dull noise that becomes more rapid as the engine accelerates indicates worn or damaged crankshaft bearings or an unevenly worn crankshaft. To pinpoint the trouble spot, remove the spark plug wire from one plug at a time and crank the engine over. If the noise stops, the cylinder with the removed plug wire indicates the problem area. Replace the bearing and/or service or replace the crankshaft (Chapter 2).
2   A similar (yet slightly higher pitched) noise to the crankshaft knocking described in the previous paragraph, that becomes more rapid as the engine accelerates, indicates worn or damaged connecting rod bearings (Chapter 2). The procedure for locating the problem cylinder is the same as described in Paragraph 1.
3   An overlapping metallic noise that increases in intensity as the engine speed increases, yet diminishes as the engine warms up indicates abnormal piston and cylinder wear (Chapter 2). To locate the problem cylinder, use the procedure described in Paragraph 1.
4   A rapid clicking noise that becomes faster as the engine accelerates indicates a worn piston pin or piston pin hole. This sound will happen each time the piston hits the highest and lowest points in the stroke (Chapter 2). The procedure for locating the problem piston is described in Paragraph 1.
5   A metallic clicking noise coming from the water pump indicates worn or damaged water pump bearings or pump. Replace the water pump with a new one (Chapter 3).
6   A rapid tapping sound or clicking sound that becomes faster as the engine speed

increases indicates "valve tapping." This can be identified by holding one end of a section of hose to your ear and placing the other end at different spots along the valve cover. The point where the sound is loudest indicates the problem valve. If the pushrod and rocker arm components are in good shape, you likely have a collapsed valve lifter. Changing the engine oil and adding a high viscosity oil treatment will sometimes cure a stuck lifter problem. If the problem persists, the lifters, pushrods and rocker arms must be removed for inspection (see Chapter 2).
7   A steady metallic rattling or rapping sound coming from the area of the timing chain cover indicates a worn, damaged or out-of-adjustment timing chain. Service or replace the chain and related components (Chapter 2).

Cooling system

27 Overheating

1   Insufficient coolant in system (Chapter 1).
2   Drivebelt defective or not adjusted properly (Chapter 1).
3   Radiator core blocked or radiator grille dirty and restricted (Chapter 3).
4   Thermostat faulty (Chapter 3).
5   Cooling fan not functioning properly (Chapter 3).
6   Radiator cap not maintaining proper pressure. Have cap pressure tested by gas station or repair shop.
7   Ignition timing incorrect (Chapter 5).
8   Defective water pump (Chapter 3).
9   Improper grade of engine oil.
10   Inaccurate temperature gauge (Chapter 12).

28 Overcooling

1   Thermostat faulty (Chapter 3).
2   Inaccurate temperature gauge (Chapter 12).

29 External coolant leakage

1   Deteriorated or damaged hoses. Loose clamps at hose connections (Chapter 1).
2   Water pump seals defective. If this is the case, water will drip from the weep hole in the water pump body (Chapter 3).
3   Leakage from radiator core or header tank. This will require the radiator to be professionally repaired (see Chapter 3 for removal procedures).
4   Leakage from the coolant expansion tank.
5   Engine drain plugs or water jacket freeze

plugs leaking (see Chapters 1 and 2).
6   Leak from coolant temperature switch (Chapter 3).
7   Leak from damaged gaskets or small cracks (Chapter 2).

30   Internal coolant leakage

Note: *Internal coolant leaks can usually be detected by examining the oil. Check the dipstick and inside the rocker arm cover for water deposits and an oil consistency like that of a milkshake.*
1   Leaking cylinder head gasket. Have the system pressure tested or remove the cylinder head (Chapter 2) and inspect.
2   Cracked cylinder bore or cylinder head. Dismantle engine and inspect (Chapter 2).
3   Loose cylinder head bolts (tighten as described in Chapter 2).

31   Abnormal coolant loss

1   Overfilling system (Chapter 1).
2   Coolant boiling away due to overheating (see causes in Section 27).
3   Internal or external leakage (see Sections 29 and 30).
4   Faulty radiator cap. Have the cap pressure tested.
5   Cooling system being pressurized by engine compression. This could be due to a cracked head or block or leaking head gasket(s).

32   Poor coolant circulation

1   Inoperative water pump. A quick test is to pinch the top radiator hose closed with your hand while the engine is idling, then release it. You should feel a surge of coolant if the pump is working properly (Chapter 3).
2   Restriction in cooling system. Drain, flush and refill the system (Chapter 1). If necessary, remove the radiator (Chapter 3) and have it reverse flushed or professionally cleaned.
3   Loose water pump drivebelt (Chapter 1).
4   Thermostat sticking (Chapter 3).
5   Insufficient coolant (Chapter 1).

33   Corrosion

1   Excessive impurities in the water. Soft, clean water is recommended. Distilled or rainwater is satisfactory.
2   Insufficient antifreeze solution (refer to Chapter 1 for the proper ratio of water to antifreeze).
3   Infrequent flushing and draining of system. Regular flushing of the cooling system

should be carried out at the specified intervals as described in (Chapter 1).

Automatic transmission

Note: *Due to the complexity of the automatic transmission, it's difficult for the home mechanic to properly diagnose and service. For problems other than the following, the vehicle should be taken to a reputable mechanic.*

34   Fluid leakage

1   Automatic transmission fluid is a deep red color, and fluid leaks should not be confused with engine oil which can easily be blown by air flow to the transmission.
2   To pinpoint a leak, first remove all built-up dirt and grime from the transmission. Degreasing agents and/or steam cleaning will achieve this. With the underside clean, drive the vehicle at low speeds so the air flow will not blow the leak far from its source. Raise the vehicle and determine where the leak is located. Common areas of leakage are:
a)   *Fluid pan: tighten mounting bolts and/or replace pan gasket as necessary (Chapter 1).*
b)   *Rear extension: tighten bolts and/or replace oil seal as necessary.*
c)   *Filler pipe: replace the rubber oil seal where pipe enters trans-mission case.*
d)   *Transmission oil lines: tighten fittings where lines enter trans-mission case and/or replace lines.*
e)   *Vent pipe: transmission overfilled and/or water in fluid (see checking procedures, Chapter 1).*
f)   *Speedometer connector: replace the O-ring where speedometer cable enters transmission case.*

35   General shift mechanism problems

Chapter 7 deals with checking and adjusting the shift linkage on automatic transmissions. Common problems which may be caused by out of adjustment linkage are:
a)   *Engine starting in gears other than P (park) or N (Neutral).*
b)   *Indicator pointing to a gear other than the one actually engaged.*
c)   *Vehicle moves with transmission in P (Park) position.*

36   Transmission will not downshift with the accelerator pedal pressed to the floor

Chapter 7 deals with adjusting the throttle valve cable to enable the transmission to downshift properly.

37   Engine will start in gears other than Park or Neutral

Chapter 7 deals with adjusting the Neutral start switch installed on automatic transmissions.

38   Transmission slips, shifts rough, is noisy or has no drive in forward or Reverse gears

1   There are many probable causes for the above problems, but the home mechanic should concern himself only with one possibility; fluid level.
2   Before taking the vehicle to a shop, check the fluid level and condition as described in Chapter 1. Add fluid, if necessary, or change the fluid and filter if needed. If problems persist, have a professional diagnose the transmission.

Driveshaft

Note: *Refer to Chapter 8, unless otherwise specified, for service information.*

39   Leaks at front of driveshaft

Defective transmission seal. See Chapter 7 for replacement procedure. As this is done, check the splined yoke for burrs or roughness that could damage the new seal. Remove burrs with a fine file or whetstone.

40   Knock or clunk when transmission is under initial load (just after transmission is put into gear)

1   Loose or disconnected rear suspension components. Check all mounting bolts and bushings (Chapters 7 and 10).
2   Loose driveshaft bolts. Inspect all bolts and nuts and tighten them securely.
3   Worn or damaged universal joint bearings (Chapter 8).
4   Worn sleeve yoke and mainshaft spline.

41   Metallic grating sound consistent with vehicle speed

Pronounced wear in the universal joint bearings. Replace U-joints or driveshaft, as necessary.

42   Vibration

Note: *Before blaming the driveshaft, make sure the tires are perfectly balanced and perform the following test.*
1   Install a tachometer inside the vehicle to monitor engine speed as the vehicle is driven.

Drive the vehicle and note the engine speed at which the vibration (roughness) is most pronounced. Now shift the transmission to a different gear and bring the engine speed to the same point.

2   If the vibration occurs at the same engine speed (rpm) regardless of which gear the transmission is in, the driveshaft is NOT at fault since the driveshaft speed varies.

3   If the vibration decreases or is eliminated when the transmission is in a different gear at the same engine speed, refer to the following probable causes:

a)   *Bent or dented driveshaft. Inspect and replace as necessary.*

b)   *Undercoating or built-up dirt, etc. on the driveshaft. Clean the shaft thoroughly.*

c)   *Worn universal joint bearings. Replace the U-joints or driveshaft as necessary.*

d)   *Driveshaft and/or companion flange out of balance. Check for missing weights on the shaft. Remove driveshaft and reinstall 180-degrees from original position, then recheck. Have the driveshaft balanced if problem persists.*

e)   *Loose driveshaft mounting bolts/nuts.*

f)   *Worn transmission rear bushing (Chapter 7).*

43   Scraping noise

Make sure there is nothing, such as an exhaust heat shield, rubbing on the driveshaft.

Axle and differential

Note: *For differential servicing information, refer to Chapter 8, unless otherwise specified.*

44   Noise - same when in drive as when vehicle is coasting

1   Road noise. No corrective action available.

2   Tire noise. Inspect tires and check tire pressures (Chapter 1).

3   Front wheel bearings loose, worn or damaged (Chapter 1).

4   Insufficient differential oil (Chapter 1).

5   Defective differential.

45   Knocking sound when starting or shifting gears

Defective or incorrectly adjusted differential.

46   Noise when turning

Defective differential.

47   Vibration

See probable causes under Driveshaft. Proceed under the guidelines listed for the driveshaft. If the problem persists, check the rear wheel bearings by raising the rear of the vehicle and spinning the wheels by hand. Listen for evidence of rough (noisy) bearings. Remove and inspect (Chapter 8).

48   Oil leaks

1   Pinion oil seal damaged (Chapter 8).

2   Axleshaft oil seals damaged (Chapter 8).

3   Differential cover leaking. Tighten mounting bolts or replace the gasket as required.

4   Loose filler plug on differential (Chapter 1).

5   Clogged or damaged breather on differential.

Brakes

Note: *Before assuming a brake problem exists, make sure the tires are in good condition and inflated properly, the front end alignment is correct and the vehicle is not loaded with weight in an unequal manner. All service procedures for the brakes are included in Chapter 9, unless otherwise noted.*

49   Vehicle pulls to one side during braking

1   Defective, damaged or oil contaminated brake pad or lining on one side. Inspect as described in Chapter 1. Refer to Chapter 9 if replacement is required.

2   Excessive wear of brake pad or lining material, disc or drum on one side. Inspect and repair as necessary.

3   Loose or disconnected front suspension components. Inspect and tighten all bolts securely (Chapters 1 and 10).

4   Defective front brake caliper assembly. Remove caliper and inspect for stuck piston or damage.

5   Brake lining adjustment needed. Inspect automatic adjusting mechanism for proper operation.

6   Scored or out of round disc or drum.

7   Loose front brake caliper mounting bolts.

8   Incorrect wheel bearing adjustment.

50   Noise (high-pitched squeal)

1   **Front brake pads worn out. This noise comes from the wear sensor rubbing against the disc. Replace pads with new ones immediately!**

2   Glazed or contaminated pads.

3   Dirty or scored rotor.

4   Bent support plate.

51   Excessive brake pedal travel

1   Partial brake system failure. Inspect entire system (Chapter 1) and correct as required.

2   Insufficient fluid in master cylinder. Check (Chapter 1) and add fluid - bleed system if necessary.

3   Air in system. Bleed system.

4   Excessive lateral rotor play.

5   Brakes out of adjustment. Check the operation of the automatic adjusters.

6   Defective proportioning valve. Replace valve and bleed system.

7   Defective master cylinder.

52   Brake pedal feels spongy when depressed

1   Air in brake lines. Bleed the brake system.

2   Deteriorated rubber brake hoses. Inspect all system hoses and lines. Replace parts as necessary.

3   Master cylinder mounting nuts loose. Inspect master cylinder bolts (nuts) and tighten them securely.

4   Master cylinder faulty.

5   Incorrect shoe or pad clearance.

6   Defective check valve. Replace valve and bleed system.

7   Clogged reservoir cap vent hole.

8   Deformed rubber brake lines.

9   Soft or swollen caliper seals.

10   Poor quality brake fluid. Bleed entire system and fill with new approved fluid.

53   Excessive effort required to stop vehicle

1   Power brake booster not operating properly.

2   Excessively worn linings or pads. Check and replace if necessary.

3   One or more caliper pistons seized or sticking. Inspect and rebuild as required.

4   Brake pads or linings contaminated with oil or grease. Inspect and replace as required.

5   Worn or damaged master cylinder or caliper assemblies. Check particularly for frozen pistons.

54   Pedal travels to the floor with little resistance

Little or no fluid in the master cylinder reservoir caused by leaking caliper piston(s) or loose, damaged or disconnected brake lines. Inspect entire system and repair as necessary.

55 Brake pedal pulsates during brake application

1   Wheel bearings damaged, worn or out of adjustment (Chapter 1).
2   Caliper not sliding properly due to improper installation or obstructions. Remove and inspect.
3   Rotor not within specifications. Remove the rotor and check for excessive lateral run-out and parallelism. Have the rotors resurfaced or replace them with new ones. Also make sure that all rotors are the same thickness.
4   Out of round rear brake drums. Remove the drums and have them turned or replace them with new ones.

56 Brakes drag (indicated by sluggish engine performance or wheels being very hot after driving)

1   Pushrod adjustment incorrect at the brake pedal or power booster.
2   Obstructed master cylinder compensator. Disassemble master cylinder and clean.
3   Master cylinder piston seized in bore. Overhaul master cylinder.
4   Caliper assembly in need of overhaul.
5   Brake pads or shoes worn out.
6   Piston cups in master cylinder or caliper assembly deformed. Overhaul master cylinder.
7   Rotor not within specifications.
8   Parking brake assembly will not release.
9   Clogged brake lines.
10   Wheel bearings out of adjustment (Chapter 1).
11   Brake pedal height improperly adjusted.
12   Wheel cylinder needs overhaul.
13   Improper shoe to drum clearance. Adjust as necessary.

57 Rear brakes lock up under light brake application

1   Tire pressures too high.
2   Tires excessively worn (Chapter 1).
3   Defective power brake booster.
4   Rear axle seal(s) leaking contaminating brake lining(s) with rear axle lubricant (Chapter 8).

58 Rear brakes lock up under heavy brake application

1   Tire pressures too high.
2   Tires excessively worn (Chapter 1).
3   Front brake pads contaminated with oil, mud or water. Clean or replace the pads.
4   Front brake pads excessively worn.
5   Defective master cylinder or caliper assembly.

Suspension and steering

Note: All service procedures for the suspension and steering systems are included in Chapter 10, unless otherwise noted.

59 Vehicle pulls to one side

1   Tire pressures uneven (Chapter 1).
2   Defective tire (Chapter 1).
3   Excessive wear in suspension or steering components (Chapter 1).
4   Front end alignment incorrect.
5   Front brakes dragging. Inspect as described in Section 71.
6   Wheel bearings improperly adjusted (Chapter 1).
7   Wheel lug nuts loose.

60 Shimmy, shake or vibration

1   Tire or wheel out of balance or out of round.
2   Loose, worn or out of adjustment wheel bearings (Chapter 1).
3   Shock absorbers and/or suspension components worn or damaged (see Chapter 10).

61 Excessive pitching and/or rolling around corners or during braking

1   Defective shock absorbers. Replace as a set.
2   Broken or weak leaf springs and/or suspension components.
3   Worn or damaged stabilizer bar or bushings.

62 Wandering or general instability

1   Improper tire pressures.
2   Incorrect front end alignment.
3   Worn or damaged steering linkage or suspension components.
4   Improperly adjusted steering gear.
5   Out-of-balance wheels.
6   Loose wheel lug nuts.
7   Worn rear shock absorbers.
8   Fatigued or damaged rear leaf springs.

63 Excessively stiff steering

1   Lack of fluid in the power steering fluid reservoir, where appropriate (Chapter 1).
2   Incorrect tire pressures (Chapter 1).
3   Lack of lubrication at balljoints (Chapter 1).
4   Front end out of alignment.
5   Steering gear out of adjustment or lacking lubrication.
6   Improperly adjusted wheel bearings.
7   Worn or damaged steering gear.
8   Interference of steering column with turn signal switch.

9   Low tire pressures.
10   Worn or damaged balljoints.
11   Worn or damaged steering linkage.

64 Excessive play in steering

1   Loose wheel bearings (Chapter 1).
2   Excessive wear in suspension bushings (Chapter 1).
3   Steering gear improperly adjusted.
4   Incorrect front end alignment.
5   Steering gear mounting bolts loose.
6   Worn steering linkage.

65 Lack of power assistance

1   Steering pump drivebelt faulty or not adjusted properly (Chapter 1).
2   Fluid level low (Chapter 1).
3   Hoses or pipes restricting the flow. Inspect and replace parts as necessary.
4   Air in power steering system. Bleed system.
5   Defective power steering pump.

66 Steering wheel fails to return to straight-ahead position

1   Incorrect front end alignment.
2   Tire pressures low.
3   Steering gears improperly engaged.
4   Steering column out of alignment.
5   Worn or damaged balljoint.
6   Worn or damaged steering linkage.
7   Improperly lubricated idler arm.
8   Insufficient oil in steering gear.
9   Lack of fluid in power steering pump.

67 Steering effort not the same in both directions (power system)

1   Leaks in steering gear.
2   Clogged fluid passage in steering gear.

68 Noisy power steering pump

1   Insufficient oil in pump.
2   Clogged hoses or oil filter in pump.
3   Loose pulley.
4   Improperly adjusted drivebelt (Chapter 1).
5   Defective pump.

69 Miscellaneous noises

1   Improper tire pressures.
2   Insufficiently lubricated balljoint or steering linkage.
3   Loose or worn steering gear, steering linkage or suspension components.

4   Defective shock absorber.
5   Defective wheel bearing.
6   Worn or damaged suspension bushings.
7   Damaged leaf spring.
8   Loose wheel lug nuts.
9   Worn or damaged rear axleshaft spline.
10   Worn or damaged rear shock absorber mounting bushing.
11   Incorrect rear axle endplay.
12   See also causes of noises at the rear axle and driveshaft.

70   Excessive tire wear (not specific to one area)

1   Incorrect tire pressures.

2   Tires out of balance.
3   Wheels damaged. Inspect and replace as necessary.
4   Suspension or steering components worn (Chapter 1).
5   Front end alignment incorrect.
6   Lack of proper tire rotation routine. See Routine Maintenance Schedule, Chapter 1.

71   Excessive tire wear on outside edge

1   Incorrect tire pressure.
2   Excessive speed in turns.
3   Front end alignment incorrect.

72   Excessive tire wear on inside edge

1   Incorrect tire pressure.
2   Front end alignment incorrect.
3   Loose or damaged steering components (Chapter 1).

73   Tire tread worn in one place

1   Tires out of balance.
2   Damaged or buckled wheel. Inspect and replace if necessary.
3   Defective tire.

Chapter 1
Tune-up and routine maintenance

Contents

Specifications

Note: *Listed here are manufacturer recommendations at the time this manual was written. Manufacturers occasionally upgrade their fluid and lubricant specifications, so check with your local auto parts store for current recommendations.*

Recommended lubricants and fluids

Engine oil	
Type	API "certified for gasoline engines"
Viscosity	See accompanying chart
Power steering fluid type	
Models through 2000	Premium power steering fluid
2001 and later models	MERCON automatic transmission fluid
Brake fluid type	DOT 3 heavy duty brake fluid

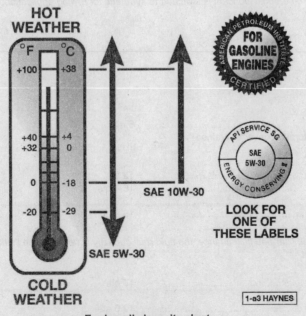

Engine oil viscosity chart

1-a3 HAYNES

Recommended lubricants and fluids (continued)

Automatic transmission fluid type	
1992 through 1997	MERCON automatic transmission fluid
1998 and later	
E4OD and 4R100	MERCON automatic transmission fluid
4R70W	MERCON V automatic transmission fluid
TorqShift 5-speed automatic (2004 and later)	MERCON SP
Coolant type	
1992 through 2000	Ethylene glycol-based antifreeze meeting current manufacturer's Specifications
2001 and 2002	
Models sold in Oregon	F5FZ-19549-CC
All other models	Ethylene glycol-based antifreeze meeting current standards (green color)
2003 and later models	Motorcraft premium coolant (yellow color)
Front wheel bearing grease	NLGI No. 2 lithium base grease containing polyethylene and molybdenum disulfide
Caliper slide rail grease	Disc brake caliper slide rail grease
Chassis grease	NLGI No. 2 lithium base grease containing polyethylene and molybdenum disulfide
Differential lubricant	
1992 through 1995	API GL-5 SAE 90 hypoid gear lubricant*
1996	SAE XY 80W-90 QL gear lubricant*
1997 through 1999	
Model 60, 70 axles	SAE XY 80W-90 QL gear lubricant*
Ford 8.8 and 9.75 inch	SAE 75W-140 GL-synthetic gear lubricant*
2000 through 2002	
Ford 9.75 inch and Model 60 axles	SAE 75W-140 GL-synthetic gear lubricant*
Ford 8.8 inch and Model 70 axles	SAE XY 80W-90 QL gear lubricant*
2003	
Visteon axles (E-150 models)	"Fuel-efficient" high-performance synthetic 70W-90
Dana 9.75 axles	SAE hypoid gear oil
2004	
Visteon axles (E-150 models)	SAE 75W-90 "fuel efficient" high-performance rear axle lube
Dana 9.75 axles	SAE 75W-140 synthetic rear axle lubricant
Dana (limited-slip)	SAE 90W hypoid gear lubricant*
2005	
Visteon axles (E-150 models)	SAE synthetic 75W-140 rear axle lubricant
Dana 9.75 axles	SAE 80W-90 premium rear axle lubricant
Dana (limited slip)	SAE 90W hypoid gear lubricant*

For Traction-Lok axles (limited slip) add friction modifier when lubricant is changed
  1992 through 1996 models add 4 oz.
  1997 through 1999 models.
    Model 60 add 6 oz. (add 4 oz. If differential lubricant is switched to synthetic for towing applications)
    Model 70 add 6 oz
    Ford 8.8 and 9.75 inch add 4 oz.
  2000 and later models
    Model 60 add 7 oz.
    Model 70 add 5.5 oz
    Ford 8.8 and 9.75 inch add 4 oz.

Capacities (approximate)

Engine oil (with filter change)	6 qts
Automatic transmission (capacity with torque converter drained)*	
1992 through 1995	12 qts
1996 and later	
C6	12 qts.
4R100	16.4 qts.
4R70W	13.9 qts.
E4OD	15.9 qts.
TorqShift 5-speed (2004 and later)	17.5

* *For normal maintenance pan removal, filter and fluid change, the fluid refill capacity is far less than listed. Measure the amount of fluid drained to arrive at an approximate refill amount.*

Cooling system*	
4.9L engine	17 qts
5.0L engine	
Without air conditioning	19.6 qts
With air conditioning	20 qts

5.8L engine
    Without air conditioning .... 19.8 qts
    With air conditioning .... 20.2 qts
7.5L engine .... 23.6 qts
4.2L engine
    Without rear heating .... 23.2 qts
    With rear heating .... 25.4 qts
4.6L engine
    Models to 2001
        Without rear heating .... 23.2 qts
        With rear heating .... 25.4 qts
    2002 and later models
        Without rear heating .... 23.7 qts
        With rear heating .... 25.7 qts
5.4L and 6.8L engines
    Without rear heating .... 29 qts
    With rear heating .... 31 qts
Fuel tank
    138 inch wheelbase .... 35 gallons
    158 inch wheelbase .... 37 gallons
    176 inch wheelbase .... 37 gallons
    158 inch wheelbase E-Super Duty .... 55 gallons
    176 inch wheelbase E-Super Duty .... 55 gallons

* *Capacity may vary +/- 15% due to equipment variations. Most service refills take only 80% of listed capacity because some coolant remains in the engine.*

Brakes

Disc brake pad thickness (minimum)
    Single piston 1/16-inch
    Dual piston 1/32-inch
Drum brake shoe lining thickness (minimum)
    Bonded linings .... 1/16-inch above metal shoe
    Riveted linings .... 1/32-inch above rivet heads

Ignition system

Spark plug
    Pushrod engines
        4.9L.. Motorcraft BSF-44C or equivalent
        5.0L and 7.5L .... Motorcraft ASF-42C or equivalent
        5.8L.. Motorcraft ASF-32C or equivalent
        4.2L
            1997 .... Motorcraft AWSF-42EE or equivalent
        1998 through 2000.. Motorcraft AGSF-34-EE or equivalent

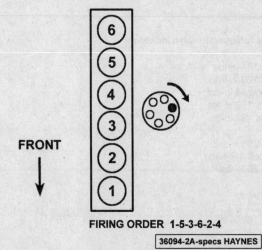

FIRING ORDER 1-5-3-6-2-4

36094-2A-specs HAYNES

Cylinder location and distributor rotation (4.9L engine)

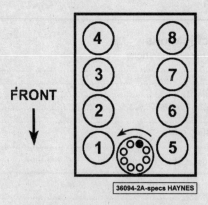

36094-2A-specs HAYNES

**Cylinder location and distributor rotation
(5.0L, 5.8L and 7.5L engines)**

Firing order
1994 through 1996 5.0L and all 5.8L: 1-3-7-2-6-5-4-8
1992 and 1993 5.0L and all 7.5L: 1-5-4-2-6-3-7-8

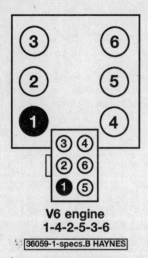

V6 engine
1-4-2-5-3-6

36059-1-specs.B HAYNES

**Cylinder and coil terminal locations
(4.2L engine)**

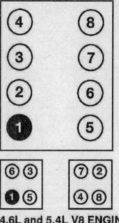

4.6L and 5.4L V8 ENGINE
1-3-7-2-6-5-4-8

**Cylinder location and coil pack arrangement (4.6L, 5.4L and 6.8L engines) - Note that
some models are equipped with coil-over-plug assemblies mounted on each cylinder**

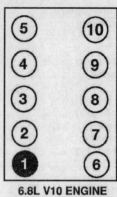

6.8L V10 ENGINE
1-6-5-10-2-7-3-8-4-9

36059-1-specs.C HAYNES

Ignition system (continued)
2001 through 2003
  Cylinders 1 through 3 .... Motorcraft AGSF-34 EG or equivalent
  Cylinders 4 through 6 .... Motorcraft AGSF-34 E or equivalent
Overhead camshaft engines
  4.6L
    Models through 2003 .... Motorcraft AWSF-32P or equivalent
    2004 and later .... Motorcraft AGSF-33P or equivalent
  5.4L and 6.8L
    1997 through 1999 .... Motorcraft AWSF-22E or equivalent
    2000 through 2003 .... Motorcraft AWSF-22W or equivalent
    2004 and later .... Motorcraft AGSF-22WM or equivalent
  Gap
    4.9L, 5.8L and 7.5L 0.044-inch
    5.0L 0.054-inch
    4.2L, 4.6L, 5.4L and 6.8L 0.054-inch
Ignition timing
  1992 through 1996 .... 10 degrees BTDC at idle with SPOUT disconnected
  1997 and later .... 10 degrees BTDC (base timing - not adjustable)

Fuel system
Idle speed .... Not adjustable

Torque specifications   **Ft-lbs** (unless otherwise indicated)
Automatic transmission pan bolts
  C6 .... 96 to 144 in-lbs
  AOD .... 72 to 120 in-lbs
  E4OD .... 120 to 144 in-lbs
  4R70W .... 108 to 132 in-lbs
  4R100 .... 108 to 132 in-lbs
Front hub adjusting nut
  Step 1 .... 17 to 25
  Step 2 .... Back off 1/2-turn
  Step 3 .... 22 to 25 in-lbs
Spark plugs
  4.2L engine .... 132 in-lbs
  4.9L engine .... 15 to 20
  4.6L, 5.0L, 5.4L, 5.8L and 6.8L engines .... 84 to 168 in-lbs
Wheel lug nuts
  E-150 100
  E-250, E-350 140

Maintenance schedule

The following maintenance intervals are based on the assumption that the vehicle owner will be doing the maintenance or service work, as opposed to having a dealer service department do the work. Although the time/mileage intervals are loosely based on factory recommendations, most have been shortened to ensure, for example, that such items as lubricants and fluids are checked/changed at intervals that promote maximum engine/driveline service life. Also, subject to the preference of the individual owner interested in keeping his or her vehicle in peak condition at all times, and with the vehicle's ultimate resale in mind, many of the maintenance procedures may be performed more often than recommended in the following schedule. We encourage such owner initiative.

Because severe duty use necessitates more frequent maintenance, a separate schedule is included for vehicles used for other than normal use as outlined in the schedule. When the vehicle is new it should be serviced initially by a factory authorized dealer service department to protect the factory warranty. In many cases the initial maintenance check is done at no cost to the owner (check with your dealer service department for more information).

Normal driving conditions

Every 250 miles or weekly, whichever comes first

Check the engine oil level (Section 3)
Check the engine coolant level (Section 3)
Check the brake fluid level (Section 3)
Check the windshield washer fluid level (Section 3)
Check the tires and tire pressures (Section 4)
Perform owner safety checks (Section 5)

Every 3,000 miles or 3 months, whichever comes first

All items listed above, plus . . .
Change the engine oil and replace the oil filter (Section 6)
Check the power steering fluid level (Section 7)
Check the automatic transmission fluid level (Section 8)

Every 6,000 miles or 6 months, whichever comes first

All items listed above, plus . . .
Check/service the battery (Section 12)
Inspect/replace the windshield wiper blades (Section 27)
Rotate the tires and check air pressure (Section 9)
Inspect exhaust system for leaks, damage or loose parts. Remove any debris trapped by the exhaust system shielding (Section 23)

Every 15,000 miles or 12 months, whichever comes first

All items listed above, plus . . .
Replace fuel filter (Section 21)
Inspect disc brake system, lubricate caliper slide rails (Section 25)
Inspect drum brake system, hoses and lines (Section 25)
Check parking brake system for damage and correct operation (Section 25)
Check the differential lubricant level (Section 17)
Inspect the drivebelt (Section 11)
Inspect the underhood hoses (Section 10)
Inspect the fuel system (Section 20)
Inspect engine cooling system hoses and clamps; check coolant strength (Section 22)
Inspect/lubricate automatic transmission shift linkage (Section 15)
Inspect/lubricate steering linkage, suspension, driveshaft U-joint (if equipped with grease fittings) (Section 15) (Section 24)

Every 30,000 miles or 24 months, whichever comes first

All items listed above, plus . . .
Change automatic transmission fluid (Section 8)**
Lubricate throttle valve (TV) cable ends and lever ball studs (AOD automatic transmission only) (Section 15)
Replace the spark plugs (Section 13)
Replace the distributor cap and rotor (Section 14)
Replace the air filter (Section 18)*
Replace the crankcase ventilation filter (Section 18)
Check/lubricate the front wheel bearings (Section 26)
Service the cooling system (drain, flush and refill) (Section 28)***

Every 60,000 miles or 48 months, whichever comes first

All items listed above, plus . . .
Replace the drivebelt (Section 11)
Replace the PCV valve (Section 19)
Replace the spark plug wires (Section 13)

Every 100,000 miles or 72 months, whichever comes first

All items listed above, plus . . .
Change the differential lubricant (Section 17)

*Replace more often if the vehicle is driven in dusty areas
**If the vehicle is operated in continuous stop and go driving or in mountainous areas, change at 15,000 miles
*******Caution:*** *Beginning in 2001, some models are equipped with red, long life coolant. Do not mix green-colored ethylene glycol coolant and red-colored coolant because doing so will cause cooling system damage. Read the warning label in the engine compartment for additional information.*

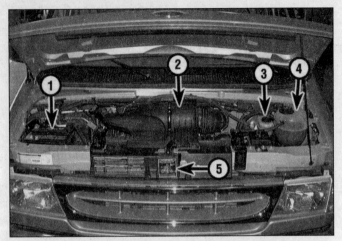

**Engine compartment routine maintenance items -
typical 1997 and later V8 and V10 models**

1   Battery
2   Air filter housing
3   Brake fluid reservoir
4   Coolant expansion tank
5   Drivebelt diagram

**Engine compartment with access cover removed -
typical 1997 and later V8 and V10 models**

1   Access to left bank spark plugs
2   Access to right bank spark plugs

1   Introduction

This Chapter is designed to help the home mechanic maintain his or her vehicle with the goals of maximum performance, economy, safety and reliability in mind.

Included is a master maintenance schedule, followed by procedures dealing specifically with each item on the schedule. Visual checks, adjustments, component replacement and other helpful items are included. Refer to the accompanying illustrations of the engine compartment and the underside of the vehicle for the locations of various components. Servicing the vehicle, in accordance with the mileage/time maintenance schedule and the step-by-step procedures will result in a planned maintenance program that should produce a long and reliable service life. Keep in mind that it is a comprehensive plan, so maintaining some items but not others at specified intervals will not produce the same results.

As you service the vehicle, you will discover that many of the procedures can - and should - be grouped together because of the nature of the particular procedure you're performing or because of the close proximity of two otherwise unrelated components to one another.

For example, if the vehicle is raised for chassis lubrication, you should inspect the exhaust, suspension, steering and fuel systems while you're under the vehicle. When you're rotating the tires, it makes good sense to check the brakes since the wheels are already removed. Finally, let's suppose you have to borrow or rent a torque wrench. Even if you only need it to tighten the spark plugs, you might as well check the torque of as many critical fasteners as time allows.

The first step in this maintenance program is to prepare yourself before the actual work begins. Read through all the procedures you're planning to do, then gather up all the parts and tools needed. If it looks like you might run into problems during a particular job, seek advice from a mechanic or an experienced do-it-yourselfer.

2   Tune-up general information

The term tune-up is used in this manual to represent a combination of individual operations rather than one specific procedure.

If, from the time the vehicle is new, the routine maintenance schedule is followed closely and frequent checks are made of fluid levels and high wear items, as suggested throughout this manual, the engine will be kept in relatively good running condition and the need for additional work will be minimized.

More likely than not, however, there will be times when the engine is running poorly due to a lack of regular maintenance. This is even more likely if a used vehicle, which has not received regular and frequent maintenance checks, is purchased. In such cases, an engine tune-up will be needed outside of the regular maintenance intervals.

The first step in any tune-up or diagnostic procedure to help correct a poor running engine is a cylinder compression check. A compression check (see Chapter 2, Part E) will help determine the condition of internal engine components and should be used as a guide for tune-up and repair procedures. If, for instance, a compression check indicates serious internal engine wear, a conventional tune-up will not improve the performance of the engine and would be a waste of time and money. Because of its importance, the compression check should be done by someone with the right equipment and the knowledge to use it properly.

The following procedures are those most often needed to bring as generally poor running engine back into a proper state of tune.

Minor tune-up

Clean, inspect and test the battery (see Section 12)
Check all engine related fluids (see Section 3)
Check and adjust the drive belts (see Section 11)
Replace the spark plugs (see Section 13)
Inspect the spark plug wires (see Section 13)
Check the PCV valve (see Section 19)
Check the air filter (see Section 18)
Check the cooling system (see Section 22)
Check all underhood hoses (see Section 10)

Major tune-up

All items listed under minor tune-up, plus . . .
Check the ignition system (see Chapter 5)
Check the charging system (see Chapter 5)
Check the fuel system (see Chapter 4)
Replace the spark plug wires (see Section 13)

3   Fluid level checks (every 250 miles or weekly)

Refer to illustrations 3.4a, 3.4b, 3.6, 3.9, 3.15
Note: *The following are fluid level checks to be done on a 250 mile or weekly basis. Additional fluid level checks can be found in specific maintenance procedures which follow. Regardless of intervals, be alert to fluid leaks under the vehicle which would indicate a fault to be corrected immediately.*

3.4a Remove the dipstick, wipe it clean, then reinsert it all the way before withdrawing it for an accurate oil level check

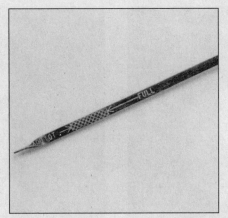

3.4b If the oil level is below the ADD line, add oil to bring the level up to the FULL mark; don't overfill the crankcase

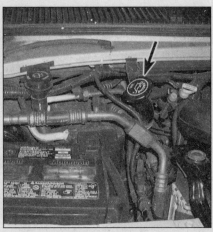

3.6 To add oil, remove the oil filler cap

1   Fluids are an essential part of the lubrication, cooling, brake and windshield washer systems. Because the fluids gradually become depleted and/or contaminated during normal operation of the vehicle, they must be periodically replenished. See *recommended lubricants and fluids* at the beginning of this Chapter before adding fluid to any of the following components. **Note:** *The vehicle must be on level ground when fluid levels are checked.*

Engine oil

2   Engine oil is checked with a dipstick, which is located on the side of the engine (refer to the underhood illustration at the front of this Chapter for dipstick location). The dipstick extends through a metal tube down into the oil pan.

3   The engine oil should be checked before the vehicle has been driven, or about 15 minutes after the engine has been shut off. If the oil is checked immediately after driving the vehicle, some of the oil will remain in the upper part of the engine, resulting in an inaccurate reading on the dipstick.

4   Pull the dipstick out of the tube **(see illustration)** and wipe all of the oil away from the end with a clean rag or paper towel. Insert the clean dipstick all the way back into the tube and pull it out again. Note the oil at the end of the dipstick. At its highest point, the oil should be above the ADD mark, in the SAFE range **(see illustration)**.

5   It takes one quart of oil to raise the level from the ADD mark to the FULL mark on the dipstick. Do not allow the level to drop below the ADD mark or oil starvation may cause engine damage. Conversely, overfilling the engine (adding oil above the FULL or MAX mark) may cause oil fouled spark plugs, oil leaks or oil seal failures.

6   To add oil, remove the filler cap **(see illustration)**. After adding oil, wait a few minutes to allow the level to stabilize, then pull the dipstick out and check the level again. Add more oil if required. Install the filler cap and tighten it by hand only.

7   Checking the oil level is an important preventive maintenance step. A consistently low oil level indicates oil leakage through damaged seals, defective gaskets or past worn rings or valve guides. The condition of the oil should also be noted. If the oil looks milky in color or has water droplets in it, the cylinder head gasket(s) may be blown or the head(s) or block may be cracked. The engine should be repaired immediately. Whenever you check the oil level, slide your thumb and index finger up the dipstick before wiping off the oil. If you see small dirt or metal particles clinging to the dipstick, the oil should be changed (see Section 6).

Engine coolant

Warning: *Do not allow antifreeze to come in contact with your skin or painted surfaces of the vehicle. Rinse off spills immediately with plenty of water. Antifreeze is highly toxic if ingested. Never leave antifreeze lying around in an open container or in puddles on the floor; children and pets are attracted by it's sweet smell and may drink it. Check with local authorities about disposing of used antifreeze. Many communities have collection centers which will see that antifreeze is disposed of safely.*

Caution: *Beginning in 2001, some models are equipped with red, long life coolant. Do not mix green-colored ethylene glycol coolant and red-colored coolant because doing so will cause cooling system damage. Read the warning label in the engine compartment for additional information.*

8   All vehicles covered by this manual are equipped with a pressurized coolant recovery system. A white plastic coolant reservoir or expansion tank located at the front of the engine compartment is connected by a hose to the radiator filler neck. If the engine overheats on 1996 and earlier models, coolant escapes through a valve in the radiator cap and travels through the hose into the reservoir. As the engine cools, the coolant is auto-matically drawn back into the cooling system to maintain the correct level. On 1997 and later models there is no radiator cap. Instead, the cap on the expansion tank is pressurized. The tank is part of the cooling system, and coolant flows through it whenever the engine is running. The cap should only be removed when the engine is off and cold.

9   The coolant level in the reservoir/expansion tank should be checked regularly. **Warning:** *Do not remove the radiator or expansion tank cap to check the coolant level when the engine is warm! The level in the reservoir/expansion tank varies with the temperature of the engine. When the engine is cold, the coolant level should be at or slightly above the COLD FULL mark on the reservoir/expansion tank. Once the engine has warmed up, the level should be at or near the FULL HOT mark. If it isn't, remove the cap (allow the engine to cool first on 1997 and later models)* **(see illustration)** *and add a 50/50 mixture of ethylene glycol based antifreeze and water. Don't use rust inhibitors or additives.*

3.9 With the engine cool, remove the cap from the expansion tank and add a 50/50 mixture of ethylene glycol based antifreeze and water to bring the coolant to the correct level

3.15 Check the fluid level in the master cylinder by looking through the translucent reservoir

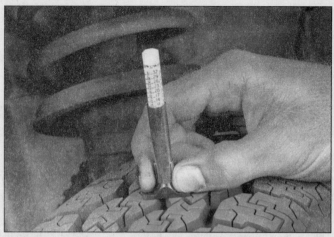

4.2 Use the tread depth gauge indicator to monitor tire wear -they are available at auto parts stores and service stations and are relatively inexpensive

10   Drive the vehicle and recheck the coolant level. If only a small amount of coolant is required to bring the system up to the proper level, water can be used. However, repeated additions of water will dilute the antifreeze and water solution. In order to maintain the proper ratio of antifreeze and water, always top up the coolant level with the correct mixture. An empty plastic milk jug or bleach bottle makes an excellent container for mixing coolant.

11   If the coolant level drops consistently, there may be a leak in the system. Inspect the radiator, hoses, filler cap, drain plugs and water pump (see Section 22). If no leaks are noted, have the radiator or expansion tank cap pressure tested by a service station.

12   If you have to remove the radiator cap, wait until the engine has cooled completely, then wrap a thick cloth around the cap and turn it to the first stop. If coolant or steam escapes, let the engine cool down longer, then remove the cap.

13   Check the condition of the coolant as well. It should be relatively clear. If it's brown or rust colored, the system should be drained, flushed and refilled. Even if the coolant appears to be normal, the corrosion inhibitors wear out, so it must be replaced at the specified intervals.

Brake fluid

Warning: *Brake fluid can harm your eyes and damage painted surfaces, so use extreme caution when handling or pouring it. Do not use brake fluid that has been standing open or is more than one year old. Brake fluid absorbs moisture from the air, which can cause a dangerous loss of brake effectiveness. Use only the specified type of brake fluid. Mixing different types (such as DOT 3 or 4 and DOT 5) can cause brake failure.*

14   The brake master cylinder is mounted at the left (driver's side) rear corner of the engine compartment.

15   The brake fluid level is checked by looking through the plastic reservoir mounted on the master cylinder. The fluid level should be between the MAX and MIN lines on the reservoir **(see illustration)**. If the fluid level is low, wipe the top of the reservoir and the cap with a clean rag to prevent contamination of the system as the cap is removed. Top up with the recommended brake fluid, but do not overfill.

16   While the reservoir cap is off, check the master cylinder reservoir for contamination. If rust deposits, dirt particles or water droplets are present, the system should be drained and refilled by a dealer service department or repair shop.

17   After filling the reservoir to the proper level, make sure the cap is seated to prevent fluid leakage and/or contamination.

18   The fluid level in the master cylinder will drop slightly as the disc brake pads wear. A very low level may indicate worn brake pads or linings. Check the brakes for wear (see Section 25).

19   If the brake fluid level drops consistently, check the entire system for leaks immediately. Examine all brake lines, hoses and connections, along with the calipers, wheel cylinders and master cylinder (see Section 25).

20   When checking the fluid level, if you discover one or both reservoirs empty or nearly empty, the brake hydraulic system should be checked for leaks and bled (see Chapter 8).

Windshield washer fluid

21   Fluid for the front windshield washer system is stored in a plastic reservoir in the engine compartment. To add fluid, open the filler tube cap, add fluid and close the cap.

22   In milder climates, plain water can be used in the reservoir, but it should be kept no more than 2/3 full to allow for expansion if the water freezes. In colder climates, use windshield washer system antifreeze, available at any auto parts store, to lower the freezing point of the fluid. This comes in concentrated or pre-mixed form. If you purchase concentrated antifreeze, mix the antifreeze with water in accordance with the manufacturer's directions on the container. **Caution:** *Do not use cooling system antifreeze - it will damage the vehicle's paint.*

4   Tire and tire pressure checks (every 250 miles or weekly)

Refer to illustrations 4.2, 4.3, 4.4a, 4.4b and 4.8

1   Periodic inspection of the tires may save you the inconvenience of being stranded with a flat tire. It can also provide you with vital information regarding possible problems in the steering and suspension systems before major damage occurs.

2   Tires are equipped with 1/2-inch wide bands that will appear when tread depth reaches 1/16-inch, at which point the tires can be considered worn out. Tread wear can be monitored with a simple, inexpensive device known as a tread depth indicator **(see illustration)**.

3   Note any abnormal tire wear **(see illustration)**. Tread pattern irregularities such as cupping, flat spots and more wear on one side that the other are indications of front end alignment and/or balance problems. If any of these conditions are noted, take the vehicle to a tire shop or service station to correct the problem.

4   Look closely for cuts, punctures and embedded nails or tacks. Sometimes a tire will hold air pressure for a short time or leak down very slowly after a nail has embedded itself in the tread. If a slow leak persists, check the valve stem core to make sure it is tight **(see illustration)**. Examine the tread for an object that may have embedded itself in the tire or for a "plug" that may have begun to leak (radial tire punctures are repaired with a plug that is installed in the puncture). If a puncture is suspected, it can be easily verified by spraying a solution of soapy water onto the puncture **(see illustration)**. The soapy solution will bubble if there is a leak. Unless the

UNDERINFLATION

CUPPING

OVERINFLATION

**INCORRECT TOE-IN
OR EXTREME CAMBER**

Cupping may be caused by:
- Underinflation and/or mechanical irregularities such as out-of-balance condition of wheel and/or tire, and bent or damaged wheel.
- Loose or worn steering tie-rod or steering idler arm.
- Loose, damaged or worn front suspension parts.

**FEATHERING DUE
TO MISALIGNMENT**

4.3 This chart will help you determine the condition of the tires, the probable cause(s) of abnormal wear and the corrective action necessary

puncture is unusually large, a tire shop or service station can usually repair the tire.

5   Carefully inspect the inner sidewall of each tire for evidence of brake fluid leakage. If you see any, inspect the brakes immediately.

6   Correct air pressure adds miles to the life span of the tires, improves mileage and enhances overall ride quality. Tire pressure cannot be accurately estimated by looking at a tire, especially if it's a radial. A tire pressure gauge is essential. Keep an accurate gauge in the glove compartment. The pressure gauges attached to the nozzles of air hoses at gas stations are often inaccurate.

7   Always check tire pressure when the tires are cold. Cold, in this case, means the vehicle has not been driven over a mile in the three hours preceding a tire pressure check. A pressure rise of four to eight pounds is not uncommon once the tires are warm.

8   Unscrew the valve cap protruding from the wheel or hubcap and push the gauge firmly onto the valve stem **(see illustration)**. Note the reading on the gauge and compare the figure to the recommended tire pressure shown in your owner's manual or on the tire placard on the passenger side door or door pillar. Be sure to reinstall the valve cap to keep dirt and moisture out of the valve stem mechanism. Check all four tires and, if necessary, add enough air to bring them to the recommended pressure.

9   Don't forget to keep the spare tire inflated to the specified pressure (refer to your owner's manual or the placard attached to the door pillar).

4.4a If a tire loses air on a steady basis, check the valve core first to make sure it's snug (special inexpensive wrenches are commonly available at auto parts stores)

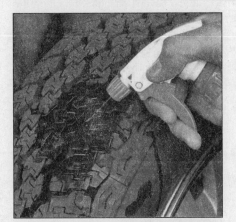

4.4b If the valve core is tight, raise the corner of the vehicle with the low tire and spray a soapy water solution onto the tread as the tire is turned slowly - leaks will cause small bubbles to appear

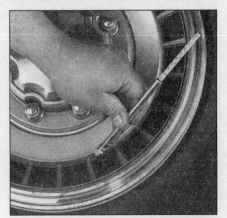

4.8 To extend the life of the tires, check the pressure at least once a week with an accurate tire gauge (don't forget the spare tire!)

5 Owner safety checks (every 250 miles or weekly)

1 Most of these checks can be easily performed while the vehicle is being driven, simply by paying attention to the specified items. The checks are intended to make the vehicle owner aware of potential safety problems before they occur.

2 Check the seat belts for wear, fraying and cuts. Make sure the buckles latch securely and that the automatic retractors function correctly. Do not try to repair seat belts; always replace them if any problems are found.

3 Make sure the ignition key cannot be removed when the transmission is in any gear other than Park. Make sure the steering column locks when the key is removed from the ignition. It may be necessary to rotate the steering wheel slightly to lock the steering column.

4 Check the parking brake. The easiest way to do this is to park on a steep hill, set the parking brake and note whether it keeps the vehicle from rolling.

5 Also check the automatic transmission Park mechanism. Place the transmission in Park, release the parking brake and note whether the transmission holds the vehicle from rolling. If the vehicle rolls while in Park, the transmission should be taken to a qualified shop for repairs.

6 Note whether the automatic transmission shift indicator shows the proper gear. If it doesn't, refer to Chapter 7 for linkage adjustment procedures.

7 Make sure the vehicle starts only in Park or Neutral. If it starts in any other gear, refer to Chapter 7 for switch adjustment procedures.

8 Make sure the brakes do not pull to one side while stopping. The brake pedal should feel firm, but excessive effort should not be required to stop the vehicle. If the pedal sinks too low, if you have to pump it more than once to get a firm pedal, or if pedal effort is too high, refer to Chapter 9 for repair procedures. A squealing sound from the front brakes may be caused by the pad wear indicators. Refer to Chapter 9 for pad or brake shoe replacement procedures.

9 Rear view mirrors should be clean and undamaged. They should hold their position when adjusted.

10 Sun visors should hold their position when adjusted. They should remain securely out of the way when lifted off the windshield.

11 Make sure the defroster blows heated air onto the windshield. If it doesn't, refer to Chapter 3 for heating system service.

12 The horn should sound with a clearly audible tone every time it is operated. If not, refer to Chapter 12.

13 Make sure the windows are clean and undamaged.

14 Turn on the lights, then walk around the vehicle and make sure they all work. Check headlights in both the high beam and low beam positions. Check the turn indicators for

one side of the vehicle, then for the other side. If possible, have an assistant watch the brake lights while you push the pedal. If no assistant is available, the brake lights can be checked by backing up to a wall or garage door, then pressing the pedal. There should be three distinct patches of red light when the brake pedal is pressed.

15 Make sure door locks operate smoothly when the key is turned. Lubricate locks if necessary with lock lubricant, available at most auto parts stores. Make sure all latches hold securely.

6 Engine oil and filter change (every 3,000 miles or 3 months)

Refer to illustrations 6.2, 6.7, 6.12 and 6.16

1 Frequent oil changes are the most important preventive maintenance procedures that can be done by the home mechanic. As engine oil ages, it becomes diluted and contaminated, which leads to premature engine wear.

2 Make sure that you have all the necessary tools before you begin this procedure **(see illustration)**. You should also have plenty of rags or newspapers handy for mopping up oil spills.

3 Start the engine and allow it to reach normal operating temperature, oil and sludge will flow more easily when warm. If new oil, a filter or tools are needed, use the vehicle to go get them and warm up the engine oil at the same time. Park on a level surface and shut off the engine when it's warmed up. Remove the oil filler cap from the valve cover.

4 Access to the oil drain plug and filter will be improved if the vehicle can be lifted on a hoist, driven onto ramps or supported by jackstands. **Warning:** *DO NOT work under a vehicle supported only by a bumper, hydraulic or scissors-type jack - always use jackstands!*

5 Raise the vehicle and support it on jackstands. Make sure it is safely supported!

6 If you haven't changed the oil on this vehicle before, get under it and locate the drain plug and the oil filter. The exhaust components will be hot as you work, so note how they are routed to avoid touching them.

7 Being careful not to touch the hot exhaust components, position a drain pan under the plug in the bottom of the engine. Clean the area around the plug, then remove the plug **(see illustration)**. It's a good idea to wear an old glove while unscrewing the plug the final few turns to avoid being scalded by hot oil. It will also help to hold the drain plug against the threads as you unscrew it, then pull it away from the drain hole suddenly. This will place your arm out of the way of the hot oil, as well as reducing the chances of dropping the drain plug into the drain pan.

8 It may be necessary to move the drain pan slightly as oil flow slows to a trickle. Inspect the old oil for the presence of metal particles.

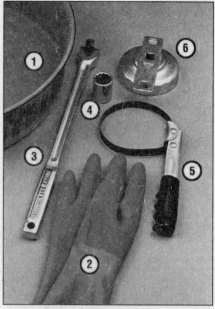

6.2 The tools required to change the engine oil and filter

1 **Drain pan** - *It should be fairly shallow in depth, but wide to prevent spills*

2 **Rubber gloves** - *When removing the drain plug and filter, you will get oil on your hands (the gloves help prevent burns)*

3 **Breaker bar** - *Sometimes the oil drain plug is tight and the long breaker bar is needed to loosen it*

4 **Socket** - *To be used with the breaker bar or a ratchet (must be the correct size to fit the drain plug - six-point preferred)*

5 **Filter wrench** - *This is metal band-type wrench, which requires clearance around the filter to be effective*

6 **Filter wrench** - *This type fits on the bottom of the filter and can be turned with a ratchet or breaker bar (different size wrenches are available for different type of filters)*

6.7 Use a proper size wrench or socket to remove the drain plug and avoid rounding it off

6.12 The oil filter is usually on very tight and will require a special oil filter wrench to remove it - DO NOT use the wrench to tighten the filter

6.16 Lubricate the oil filter seal with clean engine oil before installing the filter on the engine

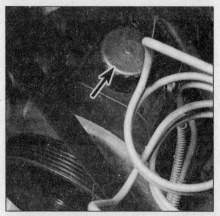

7.2 Typical location of power steering pump cap (arrow) (1992 through 1996 model shown)

9   After all the oil has drained, wipe off the drain plug with a clean rag. Any small metal particles clinging to the plug would immediately contaminate the new oil.

10   Reinstall the plug and tighten it securely, but don't strip the threads.

11   Move the drain pan into position under the oil filter.

12   Loosen the oil filter by turning it counterclockwise with a filter wrench (**see illustration**). Any standard filter wrench will work.

13   Sometimes the oil filter is screwed on so tightly that it can't be loosened. If it is, punch a metal bar or long screwdriver directly through it, as close to the engine as possible, and use it as a T-bar to turn the filter. Be prepared for oil to spurt out of the filter canister as it's punctured.

14   Once the filter is loose, use your hands to unscrew it from the block. Just as the filter is detached from the block, immediately tilt the open end up to prevent oil inside the filter from spilling out. Drain residual oil from the filter into the drain pan, then place the filter in a resealable plastic bag prior to discarding it.

15   Using a clean rag, wipe off the mounting surface on the block. Also, make sure that the old seal doesn't remain stuck to the mounting surface.

16   Compare the old filter with the new one to make sure they are the same type. Smear some clean engine oil on the rubber seal of the new filter and screw it into place (**see illustration**). Over-tightening the filter will damage the seal, so don't use a filter wrench. Most filter manufacturers recommend tightening the filter by hand only. Normally, they should be tightened 3/4-turn after the seal contacts the block, but be sure to follow the directions on the filter or container.

17   Remove all tools and materials from under the vehicle, being careful not to spill the oil in the drain pan, then lower the vehicle.

18   Add new oil to the engine through the oil filler cap in the rocker arm cover. Use a funnel to prevent oil from spilling onto the top of the engine. Pour five quarts of fresh oil into the engine. Wait a few minutes to allow the oil

to drain into the pan, then check the level on the dipstick (see Section 3 if necessary). If the oil level is in the SAFE range, install the filler cap.

19   Start the engine and run it for about a minute. While the engine is running, look under the vehicle and check for leaks at the oil pan drain plug and around the oil filter. If either one is leaking, stop the engine and tighten the plug or filter slightly. Protect your hands as the oil filter may be hot already.

20   Wait a few minutes, then recheck the level on the dipstick. Add oil as necessary to bring the level into the SAFE range.

21   During the first few trips after an oil change, make it a point to check frequently for leaks and proper oil level.

22   The old oil drained from the engine cannot be reused in its present state and should be discarded. Oil reclamation centers, auto repair shops and gas stations will normally accept the oil, which can be recycled. After the oil has cooled, it can be drained into a container (plastic jugs, bottles, milk cartons, etc.) for transport to an authorized disposal site.

7   Power steering fluid level check (every 3,000 miles or 3 months)

Refer to illustrations 7.2 and 7.5

1   Check the power steering fluid level periodically to avoid steering system problems, such as damage to the pump. **Caution:** *DO NOT hold the steering wheel against either stop (extreme left or right turn) for more than five seconds. If you do, the power steering pump could be damaged.*

2   The power steering pump, located at the left (driver's side) front corner of the engine on all models, is equipped with a twist-off cap with an integral fluid level dipstick (**see illustration**).

3   Park the vehicle on level ground and apply the parking brake.

4   Run the engine until it has reached normal operating temperature. With the engine

at idle, turn the steering wheel back-and-forth several times to get any air out of the steering system. Shut the engine off, remove the cap by turning it counterclockwise, wipe the dipstick clean and reinstall the cap (make sure it is seated).

5   Remove the cap again and note the fluid level. It must be between the two lines designating the FULL HOT range (**see illustration**) (be sure to use the proper temperature range on the dipstick when checking the fluid level - the FULL COLD lines on the reverse side of the dipstick are only usable when the engine is cold). **Note:** *1997 through 2001 models are equipped with a power steering oil reservoir mounted on the left side radiator support. Unscrew the cap and follow the same procedure as early models to check the fluid level.*

6   Add small amounts of fluid until the level is correct. **Caution:** *Do not overfill the pump. If too much fluid is added, remove the excess with a clean syringe or suction pump.*

7   Check the power steering hoses and connections for leaks and wear (see Section 10).

8   Check the condition and tension of the serpentine drivebelt (see Section 11).

7.5 Check the power steering fluid level with the engine at normal operating temperature - fluid should not go above the Full Hot mark

8   Automatic transmission fluid check/change (check every 3,000 miles or 3 months - change every 30,000 miles or 24 months)

Caution: *The use of transmission fluid other than the type listed in this Chapter's Specifications could result in transmission malfunctions or failure.*

Fluid level check

Refer to illustrations 8.5 and 8.6

1   The automatic transmission fluid should be carefully maintained. Low fluid level can lead to slipping or loss of drive, while overfilling can cause foaming and loss of fluid. Either condition can cause transmission damage.

2   Since transmission fluid expands as it heats up, the fluid level should only be checked when the transmission is warm (at normal operating temperature). If the vehicle has just been driven over 20 miles (32 km), the transmission can be considered warm. **Caution:** *If the vehicle has just been driven for a long time at high speed or in city traffic, in hot weather, or if it has been pulling a trailer, an accurate fluid level reading cannot be obtained. Allow the transmission to cool down for about 30 minutes. You can also check the transmission fluid level when the transmission is cold. If the vehicle has not been driven for over five hours and the fluid is about room temperature (70 to 95-degrees F), the transmission is cold. However, the fluid level is normally checked with the transmission warm to ensure accurate results.*

3   Immediately after driving the vehicle, park it on a level surface, set the parking brake and start the engine. While the engine is idling, depress the brake pedal and move the selector lever through all the gear ranges, beginning and ending in Park.

4   Locate the automatic transmission dipstick tube in the engine compartment. On some models, it is necessary to remove the rear panel of the air filter housing to access the dipstick.

5   With the engine still idling, pull the dipstick away from the tube **(see illustration)**, wipe it off with a clean rag, push it all the way back into the tube and withdraw it again, then note the fluid level.

6   If the transmission is cold, the level should be in the room temperature range on the dipstick (between the two half-circles); if it's warm, the fluid level should be in the operating temperature range (within the cross-hatched area) **(see illustration)**. If the level is low, slowly add the specified automatic transmission fluid through the dipstick tube - use a clean funnel to prevent spills.

7   Add just enough of the recommended fluid to fill the transmission to the proper level. It takes about one pint to raise the level from the low mark to the high mark when the fluid is hot, so add the fluid a little at a time and keep checking the level until it's correct.

8   The condition of the fluid should also be checked along with the level. If the fluid is black or a dark reddish-brown color, or if it smells burned, it should be changed. If you are in doubt about its condition, purchase some new fluid and compare the two for color and smell.

Fluid change

Refer to illustrations 8.14, 8.15, 8.16, 8.17 and 8.18

9   At the specified intervals, the transmission fluid should be drained and replaced. Since the fluid will remain hot long after driving, perform this procedure only after the engine has cooled down completely.

10   Before beginning work, purchase the specified quantity of transmission fluid (see *Recommended lubricants and fluids* at the front of this Chapter), a new filter and gasket. Never reuse the old filter or gasket!

11   Other tools necessary for this job include jackstands to support the vehicle in a raised position, a drain pan capable of holding at least eight quarts, newspapers and clean rags.

12   Raise the vehicle and support it securely on jackstands. DO NOT crawl under the vehi-

8.5 Make sure the area around the transmission dipstick is clean, then pull it out of the tube

cle when it is supported only by a jack! Place the drain pan beneath the transmission.

13   Loosen, but do not remove, all transmission pan bolts.

14   Carefully pry the transmission pan loose with a screwdriver. Let the pan hang down so the fluid can drain **(see illustration)**. Don't damage the pan or transmission gasket surfaces or leaks could develop.

15   With the drain pan in place, remove the mounting bolts from the rear and both sides of the transmission fluid pan **(see illustration)**. Drain as much fluid as possible from the pan.

16   Remove the front pan bolts, pan and gasket. Carefully clean the gasket surface of the transmission to remove all traces of the old gasket and sealant **(see illustration)**. **Note:** *Upon initial service, many of the transmissions from 1997 and later will have a plastic plug lying in the bottom of the pan. This plug was used to keep out contamination while on the assembly line. Discard the factory installed dust plug.*

17   Remove the old filter from the transmission **(see illustration)**. If the filter seal did not come out with the filter, remove it from the transmission being careful not to gouge the seal bore. **Note:** *On most 2000 and later*

8.6 Maintain the transmission fluid at the proper level on the dipstick

8.14 Remove the bolts around the rear and sides of the transmission pan . . .

8.15 . . . and let the front of the pan hang down and drain

8.16 Discard the factory installed dust plug. This plug will be in the pan if this is the first time the fluid has been changed

8.17 Pull straight down on the filter to remove it

models, the transmission fluid filter can be replaced every other fluid change. Some models have an inline external transmission fluid filter, which should be changed at every fluid change interval.

18 Install a new seal and filter **(see illustration)**.

19 Drain the fluid from the transmission pan, clean it with solvent and dry it with compressed air.

20 Make sure the gasket surface on the transmission pan is clean, then install a new gasket. Put the pan in place against the transmission and install the bolts. Working around the pan, tighten each bolt a little at a time until the torque listed in this Chapter's Specifications is reached. Don't overtighten the bolts! **Note:** On 2000 and later models, the fluid pan gasket is reusable if it isn't damaged during pan removal.

21 Lower the vehicle and add automatic transmission fluid through the filler tube. **Caution:** Refer to the Specifications at the front of this Chapter for the correct type of transmission fluid. Use of the wrong type or the wrong amount can cause transmission damage. Transmission capacities are listed with the torque converter drained. Since the torque converter cannot be drained without removing the transmission from the vehicle, it is best to

measure the amount drained for an approximate refill amount.

22 With the transmission in Park and the parking brake set, run the engine at a fast idle, but don't race it.

23 Move the gear selector through each range and back to Park. Check the fluid level. Add fluid if needed to reach the correct level.

24 Check under the vehicle for leaks after the first few trips.

9 Tire rotation (every 6,000 miles or 6 months)

Refer to illustration 9.2

1 The tires should be rotated at the specified intervals and whenever uneven wear is noticed. Since the vehicle will be raised and the tires checked anyway, check the brakes also (see Section 25).

2 Radial tires must be rotated in a specific pattern **(see illustration)**. If your vehicle is equipped with a temporary or compact spare, don't include it in the rotation pattern.

3 Refer to the information in Jacking and towing at the front of this manual for the proper procedure to follow when raising the vehicle and changing a tire.

4 The vehicle must be raised on a hoist or supported on jackstands to get all four tires off the ground. Make sure the vehicle is safely supported! If the brakes are to be checked, release the parking brake after the vehicle is supported.

5 After the rotation procedure is finished, check and adjust the tire pressures as necessary and be sure to tighten the lug nuts to the torque listed in this Chapter's Specifications.

10 Underhood hose check and replacement (every 15,000 miles or 12 months)

Warning: Replacement of air conditioning hoses must be left to a dealer service department or air conditioning shop that has the equipment to depressurize the system safely and properly recover the refrigerant. Never disconnect air conditioning hoses or components until the system has been depressurized.

General

1 High temperatures under the hood, and engine cover, can cause deterioration of the rubber and plastic hoses used for engine, accessory and emission systems operation. Periodic inspection should be made for cracks, loose clamps, material hardening and leaks.

2 Information specific to the cooling system can be found in Section 22.

3 Most (but not all) hoses are secured to the fitting with clamps. Where clamps are used, check to be sure they haven't lost their tension, allowing the hose to leak. If clamps aren't used, make sure the hose has not expanded and/or hardened where it slips over the fitting, allowing it to leak.

8.18 Install a new seal on the transmission filter

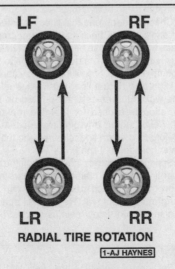

9.2 Tire rotation pattern

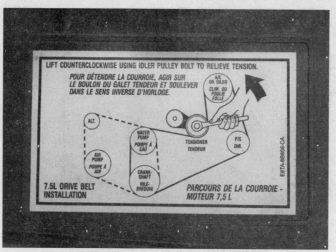

11.2 The belt's pathway is illustrated in a decal on the radiator support

PCV system hose

4   To reduce hydrocarbon emissions, crank-case blow-by gas is vented through the PCV valve to the intake manifold via a neoprene hose on most models. The blow-by gases mix with incoming air in the intake manifold before being burned in the combustion chambers.

5   Check the PCV hose for cracks, leaks and other damage. Disconnect it from the valve cover and the intake manifold and check the inside for obstructions. If it's clogged, clean it out with solvent.

Vacuum hoses

6   It's quite common for vacuum hoses, especially those in the emissions system, to be color coded or identified by colored stripes molded into them. Various systems require hoses with different wall thickness, collapse resistance and temperature resistance. When replacing hoses, be sure the new ones are made of the same material. A number of hoses connect to a vacuum fitting on the intake manifold.

7   Often the only effective way to check a hose is to remove it completely from the vehicle. If more than one hose is removed, be sure to label the hoses and fittings to ensure correct installation.

8   When checking vacuum hoses, be sure to include any plastic T-fittings in the check. Inspect the fittings for cracks and the hose where it fits over each fitting for distortion, which could cause leakage.

9   A small piece of vacuum hose can be used as a stethoscope to detect vacuum leaks. Hold one end of the hose to your ear and probe around vacuum hoses and fittings, listening for the "hissing" sound characteristic of a vacuum leak. **Warning:** *When probing with the vacuum hose stethoscope, be careful not to come into contact with moving engine components such as the drivebelt, cooling fan, etc.*

Fuel hoses

Warning: *Gasoline is extremely flammable, so take extra precautions when you work on any part of the fuel system. Don't smoke or allow open flames or bare light bulbs near the work area, and don't work in a garage where a gas-type appliance (such as a water heater or a clothes dryer) is present. Since gasoline is carcinogenic, wear fuel-resistant gloves when there's a possibility of being exposed to fuel, and, if you spill any fuel on your skin, rinse it off immediately with soap and water. Mop up any spills immediately and do not store fuel-soaked rags where they could ignite. The fuel system is under constant pressure, so, if any fuel lines are to be disconnected, the fuel pressure in the system must be relieved first (see Chapter 4). When you perform any kind of work on the fuel system, wear safety glasses and have a Class B type fire extinguisher on hand.*

10   The fuel lines are usually under pressure, so if any fuel lines are to be disconnected be prepared to catch spilled fuel.

11   Check all neoprene fuel lines for deterioration and chafing. Check especially for cracks in areas where the hose bends and just before fittings, such as where a hose attaches to the fuel pump, fuel filter or fuel injection system.

12   High quality fuel line, usually identified by the word Fluoroelastomer printed on the hose, should be used for fuel line replacement. Never, under any circumstances, use unreinforced vacuum line, clear plastic tubing or water hose for fuel lines.

13   Spring-type clamps are commonly used on fuel lines. These clamps often lose their tension over a period of time, and can be "sprung" during removal. Replace all spring-type clamps with screw clamps whenever a hose is replaced.

Metal lines

14   Sections of metal line are often used for fuel line between the fuel pump and fuel injec-tion system. Check carefully to make sure the line isn't bent, crimped or cracked.

15   If a section of metal fuel line must be replaced, use seamless steel tubing only, since copper and aluminum tubing do not have the strength necessary to withstand the vibration caused by the engine.

16   Check the metal brake lines where they enter the master cylinder and brake propor-tioning unit (if used) for cracks in the lines and loose fittings. Any sign of brake fluid leakage calls for an immediate thorough inspection of the brake system.

Nylon fuel lines

17   Nylon fuel lines are used at several points in fuel injection systems. These lines require special materials and methods for repair. Refer to Chapter 4 for details.

Power steering hoses

18   Check the power steering hoses for leaks, loose connections and worn clamps. Tighten loose connections. Worn clamps or leaky hoses should be replaced.

---

11   Drivebelt check, adjustment and replacement (check every 15,000 miles or 12 months - replace every 60,000 miles or 48 months)

Refer to illustrations 11.2, 11.3, 11.5a and 11.5b

1   The accessory drivebelt is located at the front of the engine. The single serpentine belt drives the water pump, alternator, power steering pump and air conditioning compres-sor. The condition and tension of the drivebelt is critical to the operation of the engine and accessories. Excessive tension causes bear-ing wear, while insufficient tension produces slippage, noise, component vibration and belt failure. Because of their composition and the high stress to which they are subjected, drive

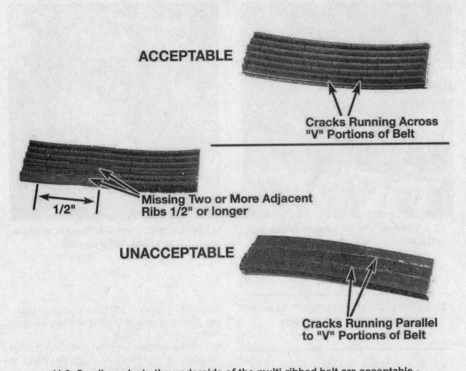

ACCEPTABLE

**Cracks Running Across
"V" Portions of Belt**

1/2"

**Missing Two or More Adjacent
Ribs 1/2" or longer**

UNACCEPTABLE

**Cracks Running Parallel
to "V" Portions of Belt**

**11.3 Small cracks in the underside of the multi-ribbed belt are acceptable -
lengthwise cracks, or missing pieces that can cause the belt to
make noise, are cause for replacement**

winding path it follows between various drive, accessory and idler pulleys **(see illustration)**.

3   With the engine off, open the hood and locate the drivebelt at the front of the engine. With a flashlight, check the belt for separation of the plies from each side of the core, a severed core, separation of the ribs, torn or worn ribs. Also check for fraying and glazing, which gives the belt a shiny appearance. Small cracks in the rib side of multi-ribbed belts are acceptable, as are small sections missing from the ribs. If a multi-ribbed belt has lost sections bigger than 1/2-inch (13 mm) from two adjacent ribs, or if the missing sections cause belt noise, the belt should be replaced **(see illustration)**. Both sides of the belt should be inspected, which means you'll have to twist it to check the underside. Use your fingers to feel the belt where you can't see it. If any of the above conditions are evident, replace the belt as described below.

Adjustment

4   Tension is set by an automatic tensioner. Manual adjustment is not required. To verify that belt tensioner is working properly and the belt has not stretched beyond use; check the belt length indicator mark on the drive belt tensioner. The belt length indicator mark must fall between the minimum and maximum marks on the belt tensioner **(see illustration)**. Replace the belt if the belt mark is not within the belt tensioner marks.

Replacement

5   To replace a serpentine belt, rotate the tensioner to lift it off the belt **(see illustrations)**. Slip the belt off the pulleys.

belts stretch and continue to deteriorate as they get older. As a result, they must be periodically checked. The serpentine belt has an automatic tensioner and requires no adjustment for the life of the belt.

Check

2   These vehicles use a single multi-ribbed belt to drive all of the accessories. This is known as a "serpentine" belt because of the

11.5a To release the tension on the belt on 1992 through 1996 models, place a wrench on the pulley center bolt (arrow) and rotate the pulley counterclockwise

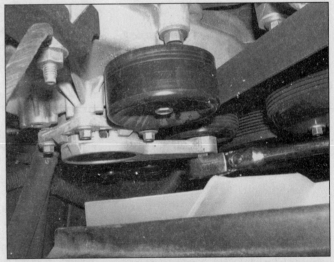

11.5b To release tension on the belt on 2000 and later models, insert a ratchet into the square drive on the tensioner arm and rotate the tension (clockwise on some models, counterclockwise on later models) - there are many variations depending on engine size, A/C equipped, etc., so be sure to refer to the belt diagram on the vehicle

12.1 Tools and materials required for battery maintenance

1   **Face shield/safety goggles** - When removing corrosion with a brush, the acidic particles can easily fly up into your eyes
2   **Baking soda** - A solution of baking soda and water can be used to neutralize corrosion
3   **Petroleum jelly** - A layer of this on the battery posts will help prevent corrosion
4   **Battery post/cable cleaner** - This wire brush cleaning tool will remove all traces of corrosion from the battery posts and cable clamps
5   **Treated felt washers** - Placing one of these on each post, directly under the clamps, will help prevent corrosion
6   **Puller** - Sometimes the cable clamps are very difficult to pull off the posts, even after the nut/bolt has been completely loosened. This tool pulls the clamp straight up and off the post without battery damage
7   **Battery post/cable cleaner** - Here is another cleaning tool which is a slightly different version of number 4 above, but it does the same thing
8   **Rubber gloves** - Another safety item to consider when servicing the battery; remember that's acid in the battery!

6   Hold the tensioner in the released position. Install a new belt and make sure it is routed correctly **(see illustration 11.2)**. Be sure the ribs of the new belt engage the pulley ribs correctly. Release the tensioner, but do not allow it to snap back on to the belt as may damage the tensioner.

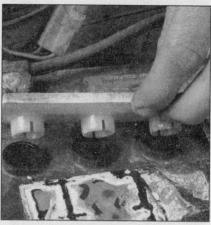

12.4 Remove the cell caps to check the water level in the battery - if the level is low, add distilled water only

12   Battery check, maintenance and charging (every 6,000 miles or 6 months)

Refer to illustrations 12.1, 12.4, 12.8a, 12.8b, 12.8c and 12.8d

Check and maintenance

Warning: *Certain precautions must be followed when checking and servicing the battery. Hydrogen gas, which is highly flammable, is always present in the battery cells, so keep lighted tobacco and all other flames and sparks away from it. The electrolyte inside the battery is actually dilute sulfuric acid, which will cause injury if splashed on your skin or in your eyes. It will also ruin clothes and painted surfaces. When removing the battery cables, always detach the negative cable first and hook it up last!*

1   Battery maintenance is an important procedure which will help ensure that you are not stranded because of a dead battery. Several tools are required for this procedure **(see illustration)**.
2   Before servicing the battery, always turn the engine and all accessories off and disconnect the cable from the negative terminal of the battery.
3   A sealed (sometimes called maintenance free) battery is standard equipment. The cell caps cannot be removed, no electrolyte checks are required and water cannot be added to the cells. However, if an aftermarket battery has been installed and it is a type that requires regular maintenance, the following procedures can be used.
4   Check the electrolyte level in each of the battery cells **(see illustration)**. It must be above the plates. There's usually a split-ring indicator in each cell to indicate the correct level. If the level is low, add distilled water only, then install the cell caps. **Caution:** *Overfilling the cells may cause electrolyte to spill*

12.8a Battery terminal corrosion appears as light, fluffy powder

over during periods of heavy charging, causing corrosion and damage to nearby components.
5   If the positive terminal and cable clamp on your vehicle's battery is equipped with a rubber protector, make sure that it's not torn or damaged. It should completely cover the terminal.
6   The external condition of the battery should be checked periodically. Look for damage such as a cracked case.
7   Check the tightness of the battery cable clamps to ensure good electrical connections and inspect the entire length of each cable, looking for cracked or abraded insulation and frayed conductors.
8   If corrosion (visible as white, fluffy deposits) is evident, remove the cables from the terminals, clean them with a battery brush and reinstall them **(see illustrations)**. Corrosion can be kept to a minimum by installing specially treated washers available at auto parts stores or by applying a layer of petroleum jelly or grease to the terminals and cable clamps after they are assembled.
9   Make sure that the battery carrier is in good condition and that the hold-down clamp bolt is tight. If the battery is removed (see Chapter 5 for the removal and installation procedure), make sure that no parts remain in the bottom of the carrier when it's reinstalled. When reinstalling the hold-down clamp, don't overtighten the bolt.
10   Corrosion on the carrier, battery case and surrounding areas can be removed with a solution of water and baking soda. Apply the mixture with a small brush, let it work, then rinse it off with plenty of clean water.
11   Any metal parts of the vehicle damaged by corrosion should be coated with a zinc-based primer, then painted.
12   Additional information on the battery and jump starting can be found in Chapter 5 and the front of this manual.

12.8b Removing the cable from a battery post with a wrench - sometimes a special battery puller is required for this procedure if corrosion has caused deterioration of the nut hex (always remove the ground cable first and hook it up last!)

12.8c Regardless of the type of tool used on the battery posts, a clean, shiny surface should be the result

12.8d When cleaning the cable clamps, all corrosion must be removed (the inside of the clamp is tapered on the post, so don't remove too much material)

Charging

Warning: *When batteries are being charged, hydrogen gas, which is very explosive and flammable, is produced. Do not smoke or allow open flames near a charging or recently charged battery. Wear eye protection when near the battery during charging. Also, make sure the charger is unplugged before connecting or disconnecting the battery from the charger.*

13 Remove all of the cell caps (if equipped) and cover the holes with a clean cloth to prevent spattering electrolyte. Disconnect the negative battery cable and hook the battery charger leads to the battery posts (positive to positive, negative to negative), then plug in the charger. Make sure it is set at 12-volts if it has a selector switch.

14 If you're using a charger with a rate higher than two amps, check the battery regularly during charging to make sure it doesn't overheat. If you're using a trickle charger, you can safely let the battery charge overnight after you've checked it regularly for the first couple of hours.

15 If the battery has removable cell caps, measure the specific gravity with a hydrometer every hour during the last few hours of the charging cycle. Inexpensive hydrometers are available from auto parts stores, follow the instructions with the hydrometer. Consider the battery charged when there's no change in the specific gravity reading for two hours and the electrolyte in the cells is gassing (bubbling) freely. The specific gravity reading from each cell should be very close to the others. If not, the battery probably has a bad cell(s).

16 Some batteries with sealed tops have built-in hydrometers on the top that indicate the state of charge by the color displayed in the hydrometer window. Normally, a bright-colored hydrometer indicates a full charge and a dark hydrometer indicates the battery

needs charging. Check the battery manufacturer's instructions to be sure you know what the colors mean.

17 If the battery has a sealed top and no built-in hydrometer, you can hook up a voltmeter across the battery terminals to check the charge. A fully charged battery should read 12.6-volts or higher.

18 Further information on the battery and jump starting can be found in Chapter 5 and at the front of this manual.

---

13 Spark plug and wire check and replacement (every 30,000 miles or 24 months)

Note: *Spark plug replacement is recommended every 30,000 miles or 24 months while spark plug wire replacement is recommended every 60,000 miles or 48 months.*

Spark plugs

Refer to illustrations 13.2, 13.5a, 13.5b, 13.6a, 13.6b, and 13.10.

1 Vehicles equipped with the pushrod engines (4.2L, 4.9L, 5.0L, 5.8L and 7.5L) have the spark plugs located on the sides of the engine. Vehicles equipped with OHC engines (4.6L, 5.4L and 6.8L) have the spark plugs located at the top of the engine.

2 In most cases, the tools necessary for spark plug replacement include a spark plug socket which fits into a ratchet (spark plug sockets are padded inside to prevent damage to the porcelain insulators on the new plugs and to hold the plugs in the socket during removal and installation), various extensions and a gap gauge to check and adjust the gaps on the new plugs **(see illustration)**. A special plug wire removal tool is available for separating the wire boots from the spark plugs, but it isn't absolutely necessary. A torque wrench should be used to tighten the new plugs.

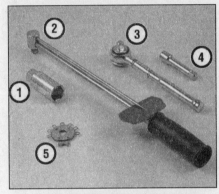

13.2 Tools required for changing spark plugs

1 *Spark plug socket - This socket has a special rubber boot inside to protect the spark plug porcelain insulator*
2 *Torque wrench - Although not mandatory, use of a torque wrench will ensure the plugs are tightened properly*
3 *Ratchet - Standard hand tool for use with the spark plug socket*
4 *Extension - Depending on the model and accessories, you may need an extension and universal joint to reach one or more plugs*
5 *Spark plug gap gauge - This tool is essential for checking and adjusting the spark plug electrode gap*

3 The best approach when replacing the spark plugs is to purchase the new ones in advance, adjust them to the proper gap and replace the plugs one at a time. When buying the new spark plugs, be sure to obtain the correct type for your particular engine. This information can usually be found on the Vehicle Emission Control Information label located under the hood, in the vehicle owner's manual and in this Chapter's Specifications. If differences exist between the plug specified on the

emissions label and in the owner's manual, assume the emissions label is correct.

4   Allow the engine to cool completely before attempting to remove any of the plugs. While you are waiting for the engine to cool, check the new plugs for defects and adjust the gaps.

5   The gap is checked by inserting the proper thickness gauge between the electrodes at the tip of the plug (see illustration). The gap between the plugs should be the same as the one specified on the Vehicle Emissions Control Information label or in this Chapter's Specifications. The gauge wire should just slide between the electrodes with a slight amount of drag. If the gap is incorrect, use the adjuster on the gauge body to bend the curved side electrode slightly until the specified gap is obtained (see illustration). If the side electrode is not exactly over the center electrode, bend it with the adjuster until it is. Check for cracks in the porcelain insulator (if any are found, the plug should not be used).

6   With the engine cool, remove the spark plug wire from one spark plug. Pull only on the boot at the end of the wire - do not pull on the wire. A plug wire removal tool should be used if available (see illustration). On 2000 and later models, the overhead cam engines are equipped with individual coils, which must be removed first to access the spark plugs. These models do not have secondary spark plug wires (see illustration).

7   If compressed air is available, use it to blow any dirt or foreign material away from the spark plug hole. A common bicycle pump will also work. The idea here is to eliminate the possibility of debris falling into the cylinder as the spark plug is removed.

8   Place the spark plug socket over the plug and remove it from the engine by turning in a counterclockwise direction.

9   Compare the spark plug to those shown on the inside back cover of this manual to get an indication of the general running condition of the engine.

13.5a Spark plug manufacturers recommend using a wire type feeler gauge when checking the gap - if the wire does not slide between the electrodes with a slight drag, adjustment is required

13.5b To adjust the gap, bend the side electrode only, as indicated by the arrows, and be very careful not to crack or chip the porcelain insulator surrounding the center electrode

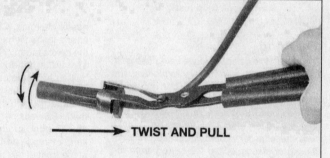

13.6a When removing the spark plug wires, pull only on the boot and twist it back-and-forth

TWIST AND PULL

10   Thread one of the new plugs into the hole until you can no longer turn it with your fingers, then tighten it to the torque listed in this Chapter's Specifications. It's a good idea to slip a short length of rubber hose over the end of the plug to use as a tool to thread it into place (see illustration). The hose will grip the plug well enough to turn it, but will start to slip if the plug begins to cross-thread in the hole - this will prevent damaged threads and the

accompanying repair costs.

11   Before pushing the spark plug wire onto the end of the plug, inspect it following the procedures outlined below.

12   Attach the plug wire to the new spark plug, again using a twisting motion on the boot until it is seated on the spark plug.

13   Repeat the procedure for the remaining spark plugs, replacing them one at a time to prevent mixing up the spark plug wires.

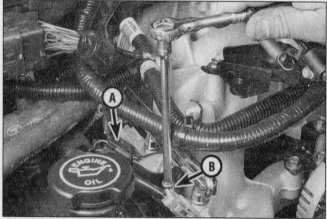

13.6b On some later models, the coil pack must be removed to access the spark plugs - disconnect the electrical connector (A) and remove the coil pack retaining screw (B) - pull straight up and out to remove the coil pack

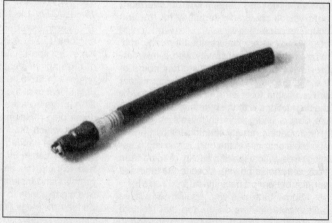

13.10 A length of snug-fitting rubber hose will save time and prevent damaged threads when installing the spark plugs

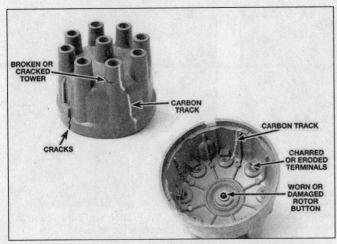

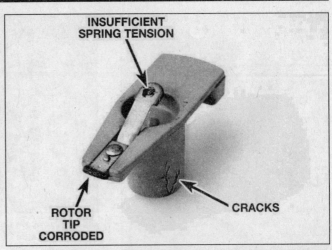

14.1 Shown here are some of the common defects to look for when inspecting the distributor cap (if in doubt about its condition, install a new one)

14.2 Check the rotor for cracks and carbon tracks and make sure the center terminal spring tension is adequate - if the rotor tip is burned or corroded, install a new rotor

Spark plug wires

Note 1: *Every time a spark plug wire is detached from a spark plug, the distributor cap or the coil, silicone dielectric compound (a white grease available at auto parts stores) should be applied to the inside of each boot before reconnection to seal out moisture and ensure a good electrical connection. Use a small standard screwdriver to coat the entire inside surface of each boot with a thin layer of the compound.*

Note 2: *2000 and later engines have individual coils for each spark plug and do not have secondary plug wires.*

14   The spark plug wires should be checked and, if necessary, replaced at the same time new spark plugs are installed.

15   The easiest way to identify bad wires is to make a visual check while the engine is running. In a dark, well-ventilated garage, start the engine and look at each plug wire. Be careful not to come into contact with any moving engine parts. If there is a break in the wire, you will see arcing or a small spark at the damaged area. If arcing is noticed, make a note to obtain new wires.

16   The spark plug wires should be inspected one at a time, beginning with the spark plug for the number one cylinder (the cylinder closest to the radiator on the right-side bank on V-8 models), to prevent confusion. Clearly label each original plug wire with a piece of tape marked with the correct number. The plug wires must be reinstalled in the correct order to ensure proper engine operation.

17   Disconnect the spark plug wire from the first spark plug. A removal tool can be used **(see illustration 13.6)**, or you can grab the wire boot, twist it slightly and pull the wire free. Do not pull on the wire itself, only on the rubber boot.

18   Push the wire and boot back onto the end of the spark plug. It should fit snugly. If it doesn't, detach the wire and boot once more and use a pair of pliers to carefully crimp the metal connector inside the wire boot until it does.

19   Using a clean rag, wipe the entire length of the wire to remove built-up dirt and grease.

20   Once the wire is clean, check for burns, cracks and other damage. Do not bend the wire sharply or you might break the conductor.

21   Disconnect the wire from the distributor. Again, pull only on the rubber boot. Check for corrosion and a tight fit. Replace the wire in the distributor.

22   Inspect each of the remaining spark plug wires, making sure that each one is securely fastened at the distributor and spark plug when the check is complete.

23   If new spark plug wires are required, purchase a set for your specific engine model. Pre-cut wire sets with the boots already installed are available. Remove and replace the wires one at a time to avoid mix-ups in the firing order.

14   Distributor cap and rotor check and replacement (every 30,000 miles or 24 months)

Refer to illustrations 14.1 and 14.2

Note: *This maintenance procedure applies only to vehicles equipped with the TFI-IV ignition system (1992 through 1996 models).*

1   Remove the mounting screws and detach the cap from the distributor. Check it for cracks, carbon tracks and worn, burned or loose terminals **(see illustration)**.

2   Check the rotor for cracks and carbon tracks. make sure the center terminal spring tension is adequate and look for corrosion and wear on the rotor tip **(see illustration)**.

3   Replace the cap and rotor if damage or defects are found.

4   When installing a new cap, remove the wires from the old cap one at a time and attach them to the new cap in exactly the same location. Do not simultaneously remove all the wires from the old cap or firing order mix-ups may occur.

15   Automatic transmission shift cable linkage, throttle valve (TV) cable ends and lever ball lubrication (every 6,000 miles or 6 months)

Refer to illustration 15.3

1   Open the hood and locate the shift cable pivot point on the steering column. Also locate the cable end and pivot point on the transmission lever (raise the vehicle and support it securely on jackstands, if necessary).

2   Clean the cable ends and pivot points.

3   Carefully pry the cable end off the pivot point and lubricate the pivot point with multi-purpose grease **(see illustration)**.

4   On models so equipped, carefully pry the cable end off the throttle valve (TV) cable ends and lever ballstud, then lubricate the stud with multi-purpose grease. Reconnect the cable.

15.3 Lubricate the shift cable pivot (arrow)

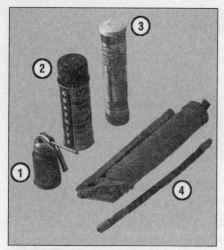

16.1 Materials required for chassis and body lubrication

1   *Engine oil - Light engine oil in a can like this can be used for door and hood hinges*
2   *Graphite spray - Used to lubricate lock cylinders*
3   *Grease - Grease, in a variety of types and weights, is available for use in a grease gun. Check specifications for your requirements.*
4   *Grease gun - A common grease gun, shown with a detachable hose and nozzle, is needed for chassis lubrication. After use, clean it thoroughly!.*

16.6a Lubricate the tie-rod ends (one on each side of the vehicle) . . .

16.6b . . . the Pitman arm connection to the steering linkage . . .

16.6c . . . and the steering linkage cross rod

16.13 After the cover is removed, carefully pry the linkage from the stud (arrow), grease the stud and reconnect the linkage

16   Chassis lubrication (every 6,000 miles or 6 months)

Refer to illustrations 16.1, 16.6a, 16.6b, 16.6c and 16.13

1   Refer to Recommended lubricants and fluids at the front of this Chapter to obtain the necessary grease, etc. You'll also need a grease gun **(see illustration)**. Occasionally plugs will be installed rather than grease fittings. If so, grease fittings will have to be purchased and installed.
2   Look under the vehicle and locate the grease fittings or plugs in the tie-rod ends. If there are plugs, remove them and buy grease fittings, which will thread into the component. A dealer or auto parts store will be able to supply the correct fittings. Straight, as well as angled, fittings are available.
3   For easier access under the vehicle, raise it with a jack and place jackstands under the frame. Make sure the vehicle is safely supported - DO NOT crawl under the vehicle when it is supported only by the jack! If the wheels are to be removed at this interval for tire rotation or brake inspection, loosen the lug nuts slightly while the vehicle is still on the ground.
4   Before beginning, force a little grease out of the nozzle to remove any dirt from the end of the gun. Wipe the nozzle clean with a rag.

5   With the grease gun and plenty of clean rags, crawl under the vehicle.
6   Wipe the tie-rod end grease fitting nipple clean and push the nozzle firmly over it. Squeeze the trigger on the grease gun to force grease into the component **(see illustrations)**. They should be lubricated until the rubber seal is firm to the touch. Don't pump too much grease into the fitting as it could rupture the seal. If grease escapes around the grease gun nozzle, the nipple is clogged or the nozzle is not completely seated on the fitting. Resecure the gun nozzle to the fitting and try again. If necessary, replace the fitting with a new one.
7   Wipe the excess grease from the components and the grease fitting. Repeat the procedure for the remaining fitting(s).
8   Open the hood and smear a little chassis grease on the hood latch mechanism. Have an assistant pull the hood release lever from inside the vehicle as you lubricate the cable at the latch.
9   Lubricate all the hinges (door, hood, etc.) with engine oil to keep them in proper working order.
10   The key lock cylinders can be lubricated with spray graphite or silicone lubricant, which is available at auto parts stores.
11   Lubricate the door weatherstripping with silicone spray. This will reduce chafing and retard wear.

12   Lubricate the parking brake linkage. Note that two different types of grease are required. Use multi-purpose grease on the linkage, adjuster assembly and connectors; use speedometer cable lubricant on parts of the cable that touch other parts of the vehicle. Lubricate the cable twice, once with the parking brake set and once with it released.
13   On models so equipped, remove the protective cover from the throttle lever ballstud. Carefully unsnap the throttle linkage from the ballstud **(see illustration)**. Lubricate the ballstud with multi-purpose grease, then reconnect the linkage and install the protective cover.

17   Differential lubricant level check and change (check every 6,000 miles or 6 months - change every 100,000 miles or 72 months)

Refer to illustrations 17.2a, 17.2b, 17.3, 17.7, 17.8, 17.11a, 17.11b and 17.12

Level check

1   The differential has a check/fill plug which must be removed to check the lubricant

17.2a The check/fill plug for the differential is located either on the front of the differential housing...

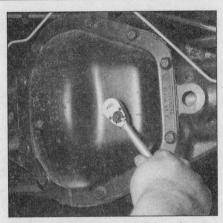

17.2b ... or in the cover plate at the rear - use a 3/8-inch drive ratchet wrench to loosen it

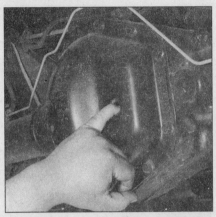

17.3 Reach into the filler hole with a little finger to check the lubricant level

17.7 A suction pump can be used to remove the old lubricant from the differential

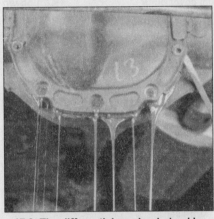

17.8 The differential can be drained by removing the cover if you don't have a suction pump

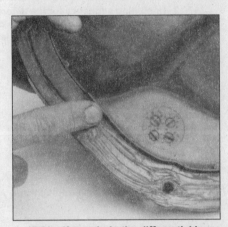

17.11a If you drain the differential by removing the cover, apply a thin film of RTV sealant to the differential cover just before installation ...

17.11b ... then apply a thick bead all around the inside edge of the cover inboard of the bolt holes

level. If the vehicle is raised to gain access to the plug, be sure to support it safely on jackstands -DO NOT crawl under the vehicle when it's supported only by the jack!

2   Remove the lubricant check/fill plug from the differential (**see illustrations**). Use a 3/8-inch drive ratchet and short extension without a socket to unscrew the plug from the rear differential.

3   Use your little finger as a dipstick to make sure the lubricant level is even with the bottom of the plug hole (**see illustration**). If not, use a syringe to add the recommended lubricant until it just starts to run out of the opening. On some models a tag is located in the area of the plug which gives information regarding lubricant type, particularly on models equipped with a limited slip differential.

4   Install the plug and tighten it securely.

Lubricant change

5   If it is necessary to change the differential lubricant, remove the check/fill plug, then drain the differential. Some differentials can be drained by removing the drain plug, while on others it's necessary to remove the cover

plate on the differential housing. As an alternative, a hand suction pump can be used to remove the differential lubricant through the filler hole. If you remove the cover plate, obtain a tube of silicone sealant to be used when reinstalling the differential cover.

6   If equipped with a drain plug, remove the plug and allow the differential lubricant to drain completely. After the lubricant has drained, install the plug and tighten it securely.

7   If a suction pump is being used, insert the flexible hose (**see illustration**). Work the hose down to the bottom of the differential housing and draw the lubricant out.

8   If the differential is being drained by removing the cover plate, remove all of the bolts except the two near the top. Loosen the remaining two bolts and use them to keep the cover loosely attached. Allow the lubricant to drain into the pan, then completely remove the cover (**see illustration**).

9   Using a lint-free rag, clean the inside of the cover and the accessible areas of the differential housing. As this is done, check for chipped gears and metal particles in the lubricant, indicating that the differential should be more thoroughly inspected and/or repaired.

10   Clean all old gasket material from the cover and differential housing.

11   Apply a thin film of RTV sealant to the cover mating surface, then run a thick bead all the way around inside the cover bolt holes (**see illustrations**).

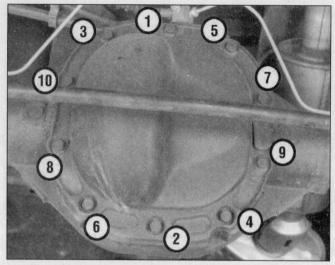

17.12 Tightening sequence for the differential cover bolts - don't overtighten the bolts, or the cover may be distorted, causing it to leak

18.2 Loosen the clamp(s) and disconnect the inlet and outlet tube(s) and hose(s)

12   Place the cover on the differential housing and install the bolts. Tighten the bolts securely in a criss-cross pattern (see illustration). Don't overtighten them or the cover may be distorted and leaks may develop.
13   On all models, use a hand pump, syringe or funnel to fill the differential housing with the specified lubricant until it's level with the bottom of the plug hole.
14   Install the check/fill plug and tighten it securely.

18   Air filter and crankcase ventilation filter replacement (every 30,000 miles or 24 months)

1   Purchase new filter elements for the air cleaner and the crankcase ventilation system.

1992 through 1996 models
Refer to illustrations 18.2 and 18.6
2   Loosen the clamp(s) and disconnect the inlet and the outlet tube(s) from the air cleaner cover (see illustration).
3   On 4.9L engines, loosen the clamp and disconnect the Exhaust Air Supply Pump inlet tube from the air cleaner cover.
4   Disconnect the PCV hose from the air outlet tube, then, if equipped, disconnect the electrical connector from the mass air flow (MAF) sensor.
5   Remove the cover retaining screws or unhook the clamps. Disengage the cover tabs from the slots and lift the cover off.
6   Remove the filter elements (see illustration).
7   Wipe the inside of the air cleaner housing with a clean cloth. If it's necessary to

remove the housing, squeeze the air inlet hose and push it out of the housing. Remove the mounting bolts and lift the housing out.
8   Place the new filter elements in the housing. If the air element is marked TOP be sure the marked side faces up.
9   Reinstall the cover and retaining screws or hook the clamps. Don't overtighten the screws!
10   Reconnect the air outlet tube(s), the Exhaust Air Supply Pump inlet tube (4.9L engine) and electrical connector.

1997 and later models
Refer to illustrations 18.11, 18.12 and 18.13
11   Remove the mounting screws and separate the air cleaner inlet tube assembly from the radiator support near the front of vehicle (see illustration).

18.6 Lift the cover off and remove the filter element from the housing

18.11 Remove the air filter inlet assembly from
the radiator support

18.12 Release the clamp and separate the cover
from the air filter housing

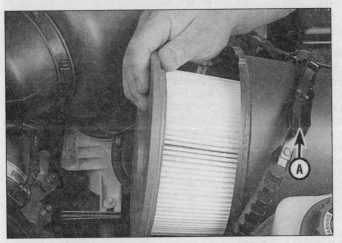

18.13 Remove the air filter from the housing

19.1 The PCV valve is located on the valve cover (1992 through
1996 models shown)

12 Release the clamp and separate the cover from the air filter housing (see illustration).

13 Access the air filter and remove it from the air filter housing (see illustration).

14 Installation is the reverse of removal.

19 Positive Crankcase Ventilation (PCV) valve check and replacement (every 60,000 miles or 48 months)

Refer to illustrations 19.1, 19.2a and 19.2b

Note: To maintain the efficiency of the PCV system, clean the hoses and check the PCV valve at the intervals recommended in the maintenance schedule. For additional information on the PCV system, refer to Chapter 6.

1 Locate the PCV valve (see illustration).

2 To check the valve, first remove it from the valve cover. Shake the valve (see illustrations). It should rattle, indicating that it is not clogged with deposits. If the valve does not rattle, replace it with a new one. If it does rattle, reinstall it.

3 Start the engine and allow it to idle, then disconnect the PCV hose. If vacuum is felt, the PCV valve system is working properly (see Chapter 6 for additional PCV system information).

4 If no vacuum is felt, the oil filler cap, hoses or valve cover gasket may be leaking or the PCV valve may be bad. Check for vacuum leaks at the valve, filler cap and all hoses.

5 Check the rubber grommet for cracks and distortion. If it's damaged, replace it.

6 If the valve is clogged, the hose is also probably plugged. Remove the hose and clean with solvent.

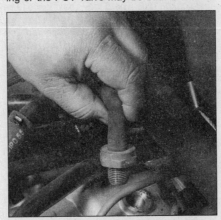

19.2a Shake the valve to test it - if it
doesn't rattle, the valve is stuck and
should be replaced (1992 through
1996 models shown)

19.2b PCV valve on a late model
(1997 and later) shown

7   After cleaning the hose, inspect it for damage, wear and deterioration. Make sure it fits snugly on the fittings.

8   If necessary, install a new PCV valve. **Note:** *The elbow (if equipped) is not part of the PCV valve. A new valve will not include the elbow. The original must be transferred to the new valve. If a new elbow is purchased, it may be necessary to soak it in warm water for up to an hour to slip it onto the new valve. Do not attempt to force the elbow onto the valve or it will break.*

9   Install the PCV system hose. Make sure that the PCV valve and hose are secure.

20   Fuel system check (every 15,000 miles or 12 months)

Warning: *Gasoline is extremely flammable, so take extra precautions when you work on any part of the fuel system. Don't smoke or allow open flames or bare light bulbs near the work area, and don't work in a garage where a gas-type appliance (such as a water heater or a clothes dryer) is present. Since gasoline is carcinogenic, wear fuel-resistant gloves when there's a possibility of being exposed to fuel, and, if you spill any fuel on your skin, rinse it off immediately with soap and water. Mop up any spills immediately and do not store fuel-soaked rags where they could ignite. The fuel system is under constant pressure, so, if any fuel lines are to be disconnected, the fuel pressure in the system must be relieved first (see Chapter 4). When you perform any kind of work on the fuel system, wear safety glasses and have a Class B type fire extinguisher on hand.*

1   If you smell gasoline while driving or after the vehicle has been sitting in the sun, inspect the fuel system immediately.

2   Remove the fuel filler cap and inspect it for damage and corrosion. The gasket should have an unbroken sealing imprint. If the gasket is damaged or corroded, install a new cap.

3   Inspect the fuel feed and return lines for cracks. Make sure that the connections between the fuel lines and the fuel injection system and between the fuel lines and the in-line fuel filter are tight.

4   Since some components of the fuel system - the fuel tank and some of the fuel feed and return lines, for example - are underneath the vehicle, they can be inspected more easily with the vehicle raised on a hoist. If that's not possible, raise the vehicle and support it on jackstands.

5   With the vehicle raised and safely supported, inspect the gas tank and filler neck for punctures, cracks or other damage. The connection between the filler neck and the tank is particularly critical. Sometimes a rubber filler neck will leak because of loose clamps or deteriorated rubber. Inspect all fuel tank mounting brackets and straps to be sure the tank is securely attached to the vehicle. **Warning:** *Do not, under any circumstances,*

21.1 The inline fuel filter is mounted in the frame rail

try to repair a fuel tank (except rubber components). A welding torch or any open flame can easily cause fuel vapors inside the tank to explode.

6   Carefully check all rubber hoses and metal or nylon lines leading away from the fuel tank. Check for loose connections, deteriorated hoses, crimped lines and other damage. Repair or replace damaged sections as necessary (see Chapter 4).

21   Fuel filter replacement (every 15,000 miles or 12 months)

Refer to illustrations 21.1 and 21.5
Warning: *Gasoline is extremely flammable, so take extra precautions when you work on any part of the fuel system. Don't smoke or allow open flames or bare light bulbs near the work area, and don't work in a garage where a gas-type appliance (such as a water heater or a clothes dryer) is present. Since gasoline is carcinogenic, wear fuel-resistant gloves when there's a possibility of being exposed to fuel, and, if you spill any fuel on your skin, rinse it off immediately with soap and water. Mop up any spills immediately and do not store fuel-soaked rags where they could ignite. The fuel system is under constant pressure, so, if any fuel lines are to be disconnected, the fuel pressure in the system must be relieved first (see Chapter 4). When you perform any kind of work on the fuel system, wear safety glasses and have a Class B type fire extinguisher on hand.*

1   The fuel filter is mounted within the frame rail **(see illustration)**. Obtain a new fuel filter before starting. **Warning:** *Use only the approved fuel filter and O-rings for your specific vehicle. Never substitute hose clamps for the approved fittings on nylon fuel lines. The system operates under high pressure and the failure to do so may result in vehicle damage or personal injury.*

2   Relieve the fuel system pressure (see Chapter 4). Disconnect the cable from the negative battery terminal.

3   Secure the front of the vehicle with jack-

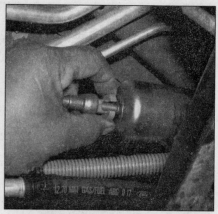

21.5 Use a special fuel line disconnect tool to uncouple the fuel line and fuel filter

stands. Position the front end of the vehicle higher than the rear to prevent fuel siphoning. Remove the gas cap, then reinstall it after relieving the fuel system pressure.

4   Inspect the hose fittings at both ends of the filter to see if they're clean. If more than a light coating of dust is present, clean the fittings before proceeding.

5   Disconnect the push-connect fittings from the filter **(see illustration)**. Refer to Chapter 4 for additional information on fuel line disconnect tools.

6   Note which way the arrow on the filter is pointing - the new filter must be installed the same way. Loosen the clamp screw and detach the filter from the bracket.

7   Install the new filter in the bracket with the arrow pointing in the right direction and tighten the clamp screw securely.

8   Carefully connect the inlet and outlet hoses to the filter (see Chapter 4).

9   Clean-up any spilt fuel. Connect the negative battery cable. Start the engine and check for fuel leaks.

22   Cooling system check (every 15,000 miles or 12 months)

Caution: *Beginning in 2001, some models are equipped with red, long life coolant. Do not mix green-colored ethylene glycol coolant and red-colored coolant because doing so will cause cooling system damage. Read the warning label in the engine compartment for additional information.*
Refer to illustrations 22.3, 22.4a and 22.4b

1   Many major engine failures can be attributed to a faulty cooling system. If the vehicle is equipped with an automatic transmission, the cooling system also plays an important role in prolonging transmission life because it cools the fluid.

2   The engine should be cold for the cooling system check, so perform the following procedure before the vehicle is driven for the day or after it has been shut off for at least three hours.

3   Remove the radiator cap (1992 through 1996) or expansion tank cap (1997 and later)

22.3 The radiator cap seal (arrow) and the sealing surfaces in the radiator filler neck should be checked for built-up corrosion - the radiator cap should be replaced if the seal is brittle or deteriorated

(see illustration) and clean it thoroughly, inside and out, with clean water. Also clean the filler neck on the radiator/expansion tank. The presence of rust or corrosion in the filler neck means the coolant should be changed (see Section 28). The coolant inside the radiator/expansion tank should be relatively clean and transparent. If it's rust colored, drain the system and refill with new coolant.

4   Carefully check the radiator hoses and smaller diameter heater hoses **(see illustration)**. Inspect each coolant hose along its entire length, replacing any hose which is cracked, swollen or deteriorated. Cracks will show up better if the hose is squeezed. Pay close attention to hose clamps that secure the hoses to cooling system components. Hose clamps can pinch and puncture hoses, resulting in coolant leaks. **Note:** *1997 and later model are equipped with a heater hose that is located under the intake manifold and connected to the water pump* **(see illustration)**. *If this hose develops a leak, the coolant will run down the back of the engine. Refer to Chapter 2D for intake manifold removal and installation.*

5   Make sure all hose connections are tight. A leak in the cooling system will usually show up as white or rust colored deposits on the area adjoining the leak. If wire-type clamps are used on the hoses, it may be a good idea to replace them with screw-type clamps.
6   Carefully clean the front of the radiator and air conditioning condenser with compressed air, if available, or a soft brush. Remove all bugs, leaves, etc. embedded in the fins. Be extremely careful not to damage the cooling fins or cut your fingers on them.
7   If the coolant level has been dropping consistently and no leaks are detectable, have the radiator cap and cooling system pressure checked at a service station.

---

23 Exhaust system check (every 6,000 miles or 6 months)

Refer to illustration 23.4
1   With the engine cold (at least three hours after the vehicle has been driven), check the complete exhaust system from the engine to end of the tailpipe. Ideally, the inspection should be done with the vehicle on a hoist to permit unrestricted access. If a hoist isn't available, raise the vehicle and support it securely on jackstands.
2   Check the exhaust pipes and connections for evidence of leaks, severe corrosion and damage. Make sure that all brackets and hangers are in good condition and are tight.
3   At the same time, inspect the underside of the body for holes, corrosion, open seams, etc. which may allow exhaust gases to enter the passenger compartment. Seal all body openings with silicone or body putty.
4   Rattles and other noises can often be traced to the exhaust system, especially the mounts, hangers and heat shields. Try to move the pipes, muffler and catalytic converter **(see illustration)**. If the components can come in contact with the body or suspension parts, secure the exhaust system with new mounts.

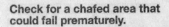
Check for a chafed area that could fail prematurely.

Check for a soft area indicating the hose has deteriorated inside.

Overtightening the clamp on a hardened hose will damage the hose and cause a leak.

Check each hose for swelling and oil-soaked ends. Cracks and breaks can be located by squeezing the hose.

22.4a Hoses, like drive belts, have a habit of failing at the worst possible time - to prevent the inconvenience of a failed radiator or heater hose, inspect them carefully as shown here

22.4b A leak in the engine heater hose means the intake manifold will have to be removed for hose replacement - coolant coming out the back of the engine is the symptom

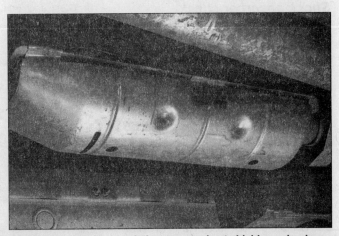

23.4 Make sure the catalytic converter heat shields are in place

24.10 To check the suspension balljoints, try to move the lower edge of the front tire in-and-out while watching/feeling for movement at the top of the tire

24.11a To check the steering gear and idler arm mounts and tie-rod connections for play, grasp the front tire like this and try to move it back-and-forth . . .

5   Check the running condition of the engine by inspecting inside the end of the tail-pipe. The exhaust deposits here are an indication of engine state-of-tune. If the pipe is black and sooty or coated with white deposits, the engine may need a tune-up, including a thorough fuel system inspection.

---

24   Steering and suspension check (every 15,000 miles or 12 months)

Refer to illustrations 24.10, 24.11 and 24.11b

Note: *The steering linkage and suspension components should be checked periodically. Worn or damaged suspension and steering linkage components can result in excessive and abnormal tire wear, poor ride quality and vehicle handling and reduced fuel economy. For detailed illustrations of the steering and suspension components, refer to Chapter 10.*

Shock absorber check

1   Park the vehicle on level ground, turn the engine off and set the parking brake. Check the tire pressures.
2   Push down at one corner of the vehicle, then release it while noting the movement of the body. It should stop moving and come to rest in a level position with one or two bounces.
3   If the vehicle continues to move up-and-down or if it fails to return to its original position, a worn or weak shock absorber is probably the reason.
4   Repeat the above check at each of the three remaining corners of the vehicle.
5   Raise the vehicle and support it on jack-stands.
6   Check the shock absorbers for evidence of fluid leakage. A light film of fluid is no cause for concern. Make sure that any fluid noted is from the shocks and not from any other

source. If leakage is noted, replace the shocks as a set.
7   Check the shock absorbers to be sure that they are securely mounted and undamaged. Check the upper mounts for damage and wear. If damage or wear is noted, replace the shock absorbers as a set.
8   If the shock absorbers must be replaced, refer to Chapter 10 for the procedure.

Steering and suspension check

9   Visually inspect the steering system components for damage and distortion (see Chapter 10). Look for leaks and damaged seals, boots and fittings.
10   Clean the lower end of the steering knuckle. Have an assistant grasp the lower edge of the tire and move the wheel in-and-out **(see illustration)** while you look for movement at the steering knuckle-to-axle arm balljoints. If there is any movement, the balljoint(s) must be replaced.
11   Grasp each front tire at the front and rear

edges, push in at the front, pull out at the rear and feel for play in the steering linkage **(see illustrations)**. If any freeplay is noted, check the steering gear mounts and the tie-rod balljoints for looseness. If the steering gear mounts are loose, tighten them. If the tie-rods are loose, the balljoints may be worn (check to make sure the nuts are tight). Additional steering and suspension system illustrations can be found in Chapter 10.

Front wheel bearing check

12   Refer to Section 26 for the wheel bearing check, repack and adjustment procedure.

---

25   Brake system check (every 15,000 miles or 12 months)

Refer to illustrations 25.7a, 25.7b, 25.11, 25.15a, 25.15b, 25.17
Warning: *Dust produced by lining wear and deposited on brake components is hazardous to your health. DO NOT blow it out with com-*

24.11b . . . if play is noted, check the steering gear mounts and make sure that they're tight; look for looseness at the tie-rod ends (arrow) and the steering linkage

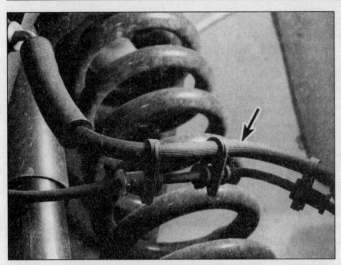

25.7a The brake hoses at the front the vehicle (arrow) should be inspected and replaced if they show any defects

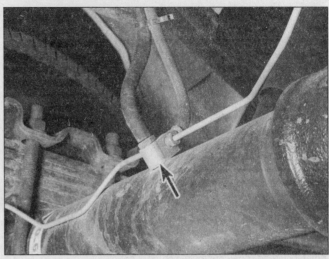

25.7b The rear brake hose meets the metal brake lines at the junction block on the rear axle housing (arrow) - they should also be inspected and replaced if they show any defects

pressed air and DO NOT inhale it! DO NOT use gasoline or solvents to remove the dust. Brake system cleaner should be used to flush the dust into a drain pan. After the brake components are wiped with a damp rag, dispose of the contaminated rag(s) and brake cleaner in a covered and labeled container. Try to use non-asbestos replacement parts whenever possible.

Note: *In addition to the specified intervals, the brake system should be inspected each time the wheels are removed or a malfunction is indicated. Because of the obvious safety considerations, the following brake system checks are some of the most important maintenance procedures you can perform on your vehicle.*

Symptoms of brake system problems

1   The disc brakes have built-in wear indicators which should make a high-pitched squealing or scraping noise when they're worn to the replacement point. When you hear this noise, replace the pads immediately or expensive damage to the brake discs could result.

2   Any of the following symptoms could indicate a potential brake system defect. The vehicle pulls to one side when the brake pedal is depressed, the brakes make squealing or dragging noises when applied, brake travel is excessive, the pedal pulsates and brake fluid leaks are noted (usually on the inner side of the tire or wheel). If any of these conditions are noted, inspect the brake system immediately.

Brake lines and hoses

Note: *Steel tubing is used throughout the brake system, with the exception of flexible, reinforced hoses at the front wheels and as connectors at the rear axle. Periodic inspection of these lines is very important.*

3   Park the vehicle on level ground and turn the engine off.

4   Remove the wheel covers. Loosen, but do not remove, the lug nuts on all four wheels.

5   Raise the vehicle and support it securely on jackstands.

6   Remove the wheels (see *Jacking and towing* at the front of this book, or refer to your owner's manual, if necessary).

7   Check all brake lines and hoses for cracks, chafing of the outer cover, leaks, blisters and distortion. Check the brake hoses at front and rear of the vehicle for softening, cracks, bulging, or wear from rubbing on other components (**see illustrations**). Check all threaded fittings for leaks and make sure

the brake hose mounting bolts and clips are secure.

8   If leaks or damage are discovered, they must be fixed immediately. Refer to Chapter 9 for detailed brake system repair procedures.

Disc brakes

9   If it hasn't already been done, raise the vehicle and support it securely on jackstands. Remove the front wheels.

10   The disc brake calipers, which contain the pads, are now visible. Each caliper has an outer and an inner pad - all pads should be checked.

11   Note the pad thickness by looking through the inspection hole in the caliper (**see illustration**). If the lining material is 1/16-inch thick or less on a single piston caliper, or 1/32-inch thick or less on a dual piston caliper, or if it is tapered from end-to-end, the pads should be replaced (see Chapter 9). Keep in mind

25.11 The lining thickness of the front disc brake pads (arrows) can be checked through the caliper inspection hole

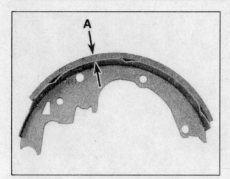

25.15a The lining thickness of the rear brake shoes (A) is measured from the surface of the lining to the metal shoe

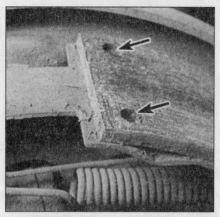

25.15b On riveted brake linings, the measurement is taken from the top of the rivet heads (arrows) to the surface of the lining material

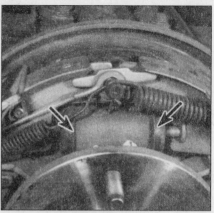

25.17 Carefully peel back the rubber boots (arrows) and check the wheel cylinders for leakage

that the lining material is riveted or bonded to a metal plate or shoe - the metal portion is not included in this measurement.

12   Check the condition of the brake disc. Look for score marks, deep scratches and overheated areas (they will appear blue or discolored). If damage or wear is noted, the disc can be removed and resurfaced by an automotive machine shop or replaced with a new one. Refer to Chapter 9 for more detailed inspection and repair procedures.

13   Remove the calipers without disconnecting the brake hoses (see Chapter 9). Lubricate the caliper slide rails and the inner pad slots on the steering knuckles with special caliper slide grease.

Drum brakes

14   Refer to Chapter 9 and remove the rear brake drums.

15   Note the thickness of the lining material **(see illustration)** on the rear brake shoes and look for signs of contamination by brake fluid or grease. If the lining material is within 1/16-inch of the recessed rivets **(see illustration)** or metal shoes, replace the brake shoes with new ones. The shoes should also be replaced if they are cracked, glazed (shiny lining surfaces), or contaminated with brake fluid or grease. See Chapter 9 for the replacement procedure.

16   Check the shoe return and hold-down springs and the adjusting mechanism to make sure they are installed correctly and in good condition. Deteriorated or distorted springs, if not replaced, could allow the linings to drag and wear prematurely.

17   Check the wheel cylinders for leakage by carefully peeling back the rubber boots **(see illustration)**. Slight moisture behind the boots is acceptable. If brake fluid is noted behind the boots or if it runs out of the wheel cylinder, the wheel cylinders must be overhauled or replaced (see Chapter 9).

18   Check the drums for cracks, score marks, deep scratches and hard spots, which will appear as small discolored areas. If imperfections cannot be removed with emery cloth, the drums must be resurfaced by an automotive machine shop (see Chapter 9 for more detailed information).

19   Refer to Chapter 9 and install the brake drums.

20   Install the wheels and lower the vehicle. Tighten the lug nuts to the torque listed in this Chapter's Specifications.

Parking brake

Note: *The parking brake cable and linkage should be periodically lubricated (see Section 16). This maintenance procedure helps prevent the parking brake cable from binding and adversely affecting the operation of the parking brake.*

21   The easiest, and perhaps most obvious, method of checking the parking brake is to park the vehicle on a steep hill with the parking brake set and the transmission in Neutral. If the parking brake doesn't prevent the vehicle from rolling, check the cables, parking brake pedal assembly and adjust the rear brakes (see Chapter 9). The parking brake is self-adjusting and there are no provisions for adjustment.

26   Front wheel bearing check, repack and adjustment (every 30,000 miles or 24 months)

Refer to illustrations 26.1, 26.8, 26.9, 26.15 and 26.16

1   In most cases the front wheel bearings will not need servicing until the brake pads are changed. However, the bearings should be checked whenever the front of the vehicle is raised for any reason. Several items, including a torque wrench and special grease, are required for this procedure **(see illustration)**.

2   With the vehicle securely supported on jackstands, spin each wheel and check for noise, rolling resistance and freeplay.

3   Move the wheel in-and-out on the spindle **(see illustration 24.11a)**. If there's any noticeable movement, the bearings should be checked and then repacked with grease or replaced if necessary.

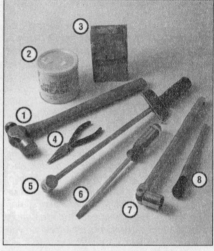

26.1 Tools and materials needed for front wheel bearing maintenance

1   *Hammer - A common hammer will do just fine*

2   *Grease - High-temperature grease that is formulated specifically for front wheel bearings should be used*

3   *Wood block - If you have a scrap piece of 2x4, it can be used to drive the new seal into the hub*

4   *Needle-nose pliers - Used to straighten and remove the cotter pin in the spindle*

5   *Torque wrench - This is very important in this procedure; if the bearing is too tight, the wheel won't turn freely- if it's too loose, the wheel will "wobble" on the spindle. Either way, it could mean extensive damage.*

6   *Screwdriver - Used to remove the seal from the hub (a long screwdriver would be preferred)*

7   *Socket/breaker bar - Needed to loosen the nut on the spindle if it's extremely tight*

8   *Brush - Together with some clean solvent, this will be used to remove old grease from the hub and spindle*

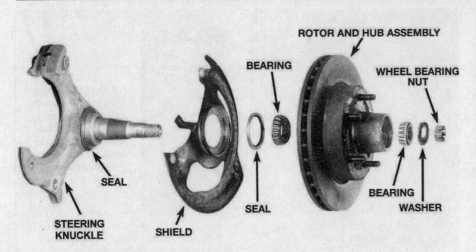

26.8 An exploded view of the front wheel bearing components

26.9 Pull out on the hub to dislodge the outer bearing

4   Remove the wheel.

5   Remove the brake caliper (see Chapter 9) and hang it out of the way on a piece of wire. **Warning:** *DO NOT allow the brake caliper to hang by the rubber hose! On some later models, the caliper mounting bracket must also be removed* (see Chapter 9).

6   Pry the grease cap out of the hub with a screwdriver or hammer and chisel.

7   Straighten the bent ends of the cotter pin, then pull the cotter pin out of the retaining nut and spindle. Discard the cotter pin and use a new one during reassembly.

8   Remove the retaining nut, the adjusting nut and bearing retainer washer from the end of the spindle (**see illustration**)

9   Pull the hub/rotor assembly out slightly, then push it back into its original position. This should force the outer bearing off the spindle enough so it can be removed (**see illustration**).

10   Pull the hub/rotor off the spindle.

11   Use a screwdriver to pry the grease seal out of the rear of the hub. As this is done, note how the seal is installed.

12   Remove the inner wheel bearing from the hub.

13   Use solvent to remove all traces of old grease from the bearings, inside of the hub and spindle. A small brush may prove helpful; however make sure no bristles from the brush embed themselves inside the bearing rollers. Allow the parts to air dry.

14   Carefully inspect the bearings for cracks, heat discoloration, worn rollers, etc. Check the bearing races inside the hub for wear and damage. If the bearing races are defective, the hubs should be taken to a machine shop with the facilities to remove the old races and press new ones in. Note that the bearings and races come as matched sets and new bearings should never be installed on old races.

15   Use high-temperature front wheel bearing grease to pack the bearings. Work the grease completely into the bearings, forcing it between the rollers, cone and cage from the back side (**see illustration**).

16   Apply a thin coat of grease to the spindle

at the outer bearing seat, inner bearing seat, shoulder and seal seat (**see illustration**).

17   Put a small quantity of grease inboard of each bearing race inside the hub. Using your finger, form a dam at these points to provide extra grease availability and to keep thinned grease from flowing out of the bearing.

18   Place the grease-packed inner bearing into the rear of the hub and put a little more grease outward of the bearing.

19   Position the new seal in the same direction as noted during removal. Place a new seal over the inner bearing and tap the seal evenly into place with a hammer and wood block until it's flush with the hub.

20   Carefully place the hub/rotor assembly onto the spindle and push the grease-packed outer bearing into position.

21   Install the bearing retainer washer and adjusting nut. Tighten the nut only slightly.

22   Spin the hub in a forward direction to seat the bearings and remove any grease or burrs which could cause excessive bearing play later.

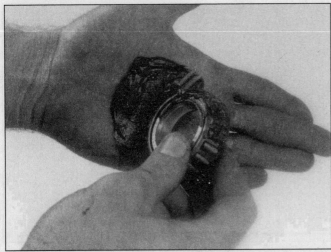

26.15 Pack each wheel bearing by working the grease into the rollers from the back side

26.16 Apply a thin coat of grease to the spindle, particularly where the seal rides

23   While spinning the hub counterclockwise, tighten the adjusting nut to the specified torque (Step 1 in this Chapter's Specifications).

24   Loosen the adjusting nut 1/2-turn, no more.

25   Tighten the adjusting nut to the specified torque (Step 3 in this Chapter's Specifications).

26   Install the nut retainer, then install a new cotter pin through the hole in the spindle and retainer nut. If the holes don't line up, don't turn the adjusting nut. Instead, remove the nut retainer and try it in a different position. The notches in the nut retainer are offset for this purpose. Keep trying the nut retainer in different positions until the holes line up, then install the cotter pin.

27   Bend the ends of the cotter pin until they're flat against the nut. Cut off any extra length which could interfere with the grease cap.

28   Install the grease cap, tapping it into place with a hammer.

29   Install the caliper (see Chapter 9).

30   Install the wheel and tighten the lug nuts securely, but not to the final torque.

31   Check the bearings in the manner described earlier in this Section.

32   Lower the vehicle, then tighten the lug nuts to the torque listed in this Chapter's Specifications.

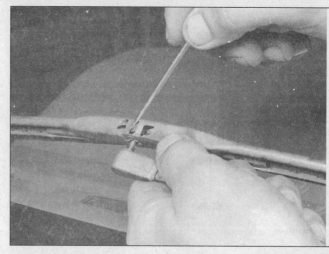

27.6   On 1992 through 1994 models, press down on the spring with a screwdriver blade as shown to release the wiper blade assembly from the arm

---

27   Windshield wiper blade check and replacement (every 6,000 miles or 6 months)

---

1   Road film can build up on the wiper blades and affect their efficiency, so they should be washed regularly with a mild detergent solution.

Check

2   The windshield wiper and blade assembly should be inspected periodically. Even if you don't use your wipers, the sun and elements will dry out the rubber portions, causing them to crack and break apart. If inspection reveals hardened or cracked rubber, replace the wiper blades. If inspection reveals nothing unusual, wet the windshield, turn the wipers on, allow them to cycle several times, then shut them off. An uneven wiper pattern across the glass or streaks over clean glass indicate that the blades should be replaced.

3   The operation of the wiper mechanism can loosen the fasteners, so they should be checked and tightened, as necessary, at the same time the wiper blades are checked (see Chapter 12 for further information regarding the wiper mechanism).

Wiper blade replacement
Refer to illustrations 27.6, 27.7a and 27.7b

4   Park the wiper blades in a convenient position to be worked on. To do this, run the wipers, then turn the ignition key to Off when the wiper blades reach the desired position.

5   Lift the blade slightly from the windshield.

6   On 1992 through 1994 models, insert a small screwdriver into the release spring at the center of the blade and push down on the spring. While pressing down with the screwdriver, pull the wiper blade off the wiper arm **(see illustration)**.

7   On 1995 and later models, push the release pin to release the blade, unhook the wiper arm from the blade **(see illustrations)** and take the blade off.

8   Slide the new blade onto the wiper arm hook until the blade locks. Make sure the spring lock secures the blade to the pin.

Wiper element replacement
Refer to illustration 27.12

9   Insert a screwdriver blade between the wiper blade and element. Twist the screwdriver clockwise while pressing in and down to separate the element from the end retaining claw.

10   Slide the element out of the remaining retaining claws.

11   Starting at either end of the blade, slide a new element into the second retaining claw (not the one closest to the end of the blade). Slide it through the other retaining claws until it reaches the end of the blade.

12   Bend the element and slide it back into

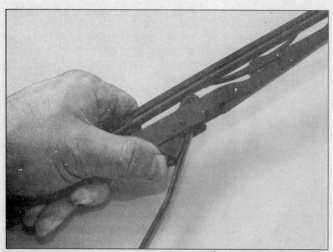

27.7a   On 1995 and later models, push the release pin . . .

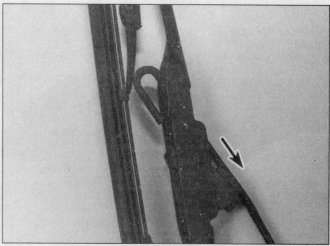

27.7b   . . . and pull the wiper blade in the direction of the arrow to separate it from the arm

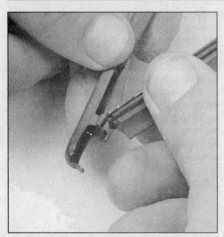

27.12 To install an element, slide it into three of the retaining claws, then bend it back and slide it into the retaining claw at the end of the blade

28.4a The radiator drain (arrow) is located on the bottom of the radiator (1997 and later shown)

28.4b Connect a length of rubber hose to the drain and let it drain into the pan

the claw at the end of the blade **(see illustration)**.

28 Cooling system servicing (draining, flushing and refilling) (every 30,000 miles or 24 months)

Refer to illustrations 28.4a, 28.4b, 28.5a and 28.5b

Warning: *Do not allow antifreeze to come in contact with your skin or painted surfaces of the vehicle. Rinse off spills immediately with plenty of water. Antifreeze is highly toxic if ingested. Never leave antifreeze lying around in an open container or in puddles on the floor; children and pets are attracted by it's sweet smell and may drink it. Check with local authorities about disposing of used antifreeze. Many communities have collection centers which will see that antifreeze is disposed of safely.*

Caution: *Beginning in 2001, some models are equipped with red, long life coolant. Do not mix green-colored ethylene glycol coolant and red-colored coolant because doing so will cause cooling system damage. Read the warning label in the engine compartment for additional information.*

1   Periodically, the cooling system should be drained, flushed and refilled to replenish the antifreeze mixture and prevent formation of rust and corrosion, which can impair the performance of the cooling system and cause engine damage. When the cooling system is serviced, all hoses and the radiator cap should be checked and replaced if necessary.

Draining

2   Apply the parking brake and block the wheels. If the vehicle has just been driven, wait several hours to allow the engine to cool down before beginning this procedure.

3   Once the engine is completely cool, remove the radiator or expansion tank cap.

4   Move a large container under the radiator drain to catch the coolant **(see illustration)**. Attach a 3/8-inch diameter hose to the drain fitting to direct the coolant into the container **(see illustration)**, then open the drain fitting (a pair of pliers may be required to turn it).

5   Move the large container under the engine block and remove the block drain plug(s), if they're accessible, and allow the coolant in the block to drain **(see illustrations)**.

6   While the coolant is draining, check the condition of the radiator hoses, heater hoses and clamps (see Section 10 if necessary).

7   Replace any damaged clamps or hoses (see Chapter 3 for detailed replacement procedures).

Flushing

8   Once the system is completely drained, flush the radiator with fresh water from a

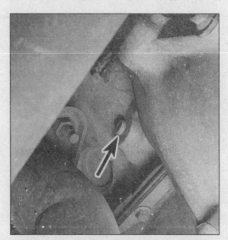

28.5a Location of the left side engine block drain plug on a V8 engine (arrow) (the plug on the right side is obscured by the starter) (1992 through 1996 models shown)

garden hose until the water runs clear at the drain. The flushing action of the water will remove sediments from the radiator but will not remove rust and scale from the engine and cooling tube surfaces.

9   These deposits can be removed by the chemical action of a cooling system cleaner. Follow the procedure outlined in the manufacturer's instructions. If the radiator is severely corroded, damaged or leaking, it should be removed (see Chapter 3) and taken to a radiator repair shop.

10   The heater core should be back flushed whenever the cooling system is flushed. To do this, disconnect the heater return hose from the thermostat housing or engine. Slide a female garden hose fitting into the heater hose and secure it with a clamp. This will allow you to attach a garden hose securely.

11   Attach the end of a garden hose to the fitting you installed in the heater hose.

12   Disconnect the heater inlet hose and position it to act as a drain.

28.5b Coolant block drain plugs (arrow) are generally located one to two inches above the oil pan - there is one on each side of the engine block (1997 and later models shown)

13   Turn the water on and off several times to create a surging action through the heater core. Then turn the water on full force and allow it to run for approximately five minutes.

14   Turn off the water and disconnect the garden hose from the female fitting. Remove the fitting from the heater return hose, then reconnect the hoses to the engine.

15   Remove the overflow hose from the coolant recovery reservoir (1996 and earlier models only). Drain the reservoir and flush it with clean water, then reconnect the hose.

Refilling

16   Close and tighten the radiator drain. Install and tighten the block drain plug(s).

17   Place the heater temperature control in the maximum heat position.

18   Slowly add new coolant (a 50/50 mixture of water and antifreeze) to the radiator or expansion tank until it is full. On 1996 and earlier models, add coolant to the reservoir up to the lower mark.

19   Leave the radiator or expansion tank cap off and run the engine in a well-ventilated area until the thermostat opens (coolant will begin flowing through the radiator and the upper radiator hose will become hot).

20   Turn the engine off and let it cool. Add more coolant mixture to bring the coolant level back up to the lip on the radiator filler neck.

21   Squeeze the upper radiator hose to expel air, then add more coolant mixture if necessary. Replace the radiator or expansion tank cap.

22   Start the engine, allow it to reach normal operating temperature and check for leaks.

Chapter 2 Part A
4.9L inline six-cylinder engine

Contents

Specifications

General

Displacement	4.9 liters (300 cubic inches)
Bore and stroke	4.00 x 3.98 inches
Cylinder numbering, front to rear	1-2-3-4-5-6
Firing order	1-5-3-6-2-4

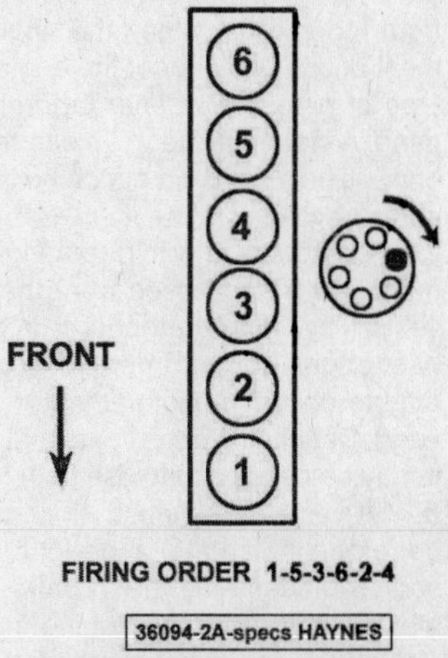

Camshaft lobe lift

Intake	0.249 inch
Exhaust	0.249 inch

Torque specifications

	Ft-lbs (unless otherwise indicated)
Timing cover bolts	12 to 18
Cylinder head bolts	
1988 through 1995	
Step 1	55
Step 2	65
Step 3	85
1996 only	
Step 1	45 to 55
Step 2	Tighten an additional 80 to 100 degrees
Crankshaft vibration damper bolt	130 to 150
Exhaust manifold-to-cylinder head bolts	22 to 32
Flywheel/flexplate-to-crankshaft bolts	75 to 85
Upper intake manifold-to-lower intake manifold bolts	12 to 18
Lower intake manifold-to-cylinder head bolts	22 to 32
Intake manifold-to-exhaust manifold nuts	28 to 32
Oil filter insert-to-cylinder block/adapter	20 to 35
Oil filter adapter-to-cylinder block	40 to 50
Oil pump pick-up tube-to-pump bolts	10 to 15
Oil pan drain plug	15 to 25
Oil pan-to-cylinder block bolts	15 to 18
Oil pump-to-cylinder block bolts	10 to 15
Oil inlet tube-to-main bearing cap	22 to 32
Pulley-to-damper bolt	35 to 50
Rocker arm stud nut or bolt	17 to 23

FRONT

FIRING ORDER 1-5-3-6-2-4

36094-2A-specs HAYNES

Cylinder location and distributor rotation diagram

Torque specifications (continued)

	Ft-lbs (unless otherwise indicated)
Valve cover bolts	72 to 108 in-lbs
Pushrod cover bolts	18 to 27 in-lbs
Camshaft thrust plate bolts	12 to 18
Engine mount-to-chassis bracket	57 to 74
Engine mount-to-block bolts	50 to 68

1   General information

The in-line six-cylinder engine block is made of cast iron. The crankshaft, which is supported by seven main bearings, is cast of nodular iron and the pistons are of aluminum alloy with integral steel struts. The rocker arms are of the ball-pivot, stud-mounted design, employing positive-stop studs. The lifters (tappets) are hydraulic and self-adjusting and rotators are employed on the exhaust valves. There is no timing chain or belt, the camshaft is driven by helical gears, with the camshaft gear made of phenolic material.

2   Repair operations possible with the engine in the vehicle

1   Many major repair operations can be accomplished without removing the engine from the vehicle. Clean the engine compartment and the exterior of the engine with some type of pressure washer before any work is done. A clean engine will make the job easier and will help keep dirt out of the internal areas of the engine.

2   Components within the engine compartment can be accessed from the front of the vehicle by lifting the hood or from inside the passenger compartment by removing the engine cover (refer to Chapter 11 if necessary). Depending upon the extent of the repair, it may be necessary to use both methods.

3   If vacuum, exhaust, oil or coolant leaks develop, indicating a need for gasket or seal replacement, the repairs can generally be made with the engine in the vehicle. The intake and exhaust manifold gaskets, oil pan gasket and cylinder head gasket are all accessible with the engine in place.

4   Exterior engine components as well as some internal components can be checked and serviced with the engine in the vehicle. Refer to this Chapter's table-of-contents for these operations and components. In addition, the water pump (refer to Chapter 3), the starter motor, the alternator, the distributor (refer to Chapter 5) and the fuel injection system (refer to Chapter 4) can be removed for repair with the engine in place.

5   Some component checks such as camshaft lobe lift measurement, timing gear wear, and piston ring/cylinder head condition (compression check) can also be performed while the engine is installed.

6   Since the cylinder head can be removed without pulling the engine, valve component servicing can also be accomplished with the engine in the vehicle.

7   In extreme cases caused by a lack of necessary equipment, repair or replacement of piston rings, pistons, connecting rods and rod bearings is possible with the engine in the vehicle. However, this practice is not recommended because of the cleaning and preparation work that must be done to the components involved.

3   Top Dead Center (TDC) for number 1 piston - locating

Refer to illustration 3.7

1   Top Dead Center (TDC) is the highest point in the cylinder that each piston reaches as it travels up-and-down when the crankshaft turns. Each piston reaches TDC on the compression stroke and again on the exhaust stroke, but TDC generally refers to piston position on the compression stroke.

2   Positioning the piston(s) at TDC is an essential part of many procedures such as rocker arm removal, timing gear replacement and distributor removal.

3   Before beginning this procedure, be sure to disable the ignition system. On 1992 through 1996 models (TFI-IV ignition systems), disconnect the coil wire from the distributor cap and ground it to prevent damage to the coil (see Chapter 5). On distributorless ignition systems, disconnect the primary lead from the coil pack (DIS ignition systems) or the individual coil assemblies (COP ignition systems) at the spark plugs (see Chapter 5).

4   In order to bring any piston to TDC, the crankshaft must be turned using one of the following methods. When looking at the front of the engine, normal crankshaft rotation is clockwise. **Warning:** *Before beginning this procedure, be sure to place the transmission in Park.*

a) *The preferred method is to turn the crankshaft with a large socket and breaker bar attached to the pulley bolt threaded into the front of the crankshaft. Apply pressure onto the bolt in a clockwise direction only. Never turn the bolt counterclockwise.*

b) *A remote starter switch, which may save some time, can also be used. Attach the switch leads to the small ignition switch terminal and the positive (red) battery cable terminal on the starter solenoid (mounted near the battery). Once the piston is close to TDC, use a socket and breaker bar as described above.*

c) *If an assistant is available to turn the ignition switch to the START position in short bursts, you can get the piston close to TDC without a remote starter switch. Use a socket and breaker bar as described in Paragraph a) to complete the procedure.*

5   Place your finger partially over the number 1 spark plug hole and rotate the crankshaft using one of the methods described above until air pressure is felt at the spark plug hole. Air pressure felt at the spark plug hole indicates that the cylinder has started the compression stroke. Once the compression stroke has begun, TDC for the number one cylinder is obtained when the piston reaches the top of the cylinder on the compression stroke.

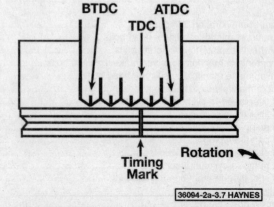

3.7 Details of the timing scale and timing mark on the crankshaft vibration damper

36094-2a-3.7 HAYNES

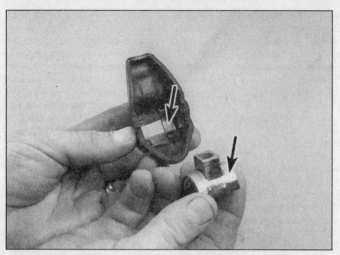

5.3 Check for wear on the rocker arm and fulcrum contact areas

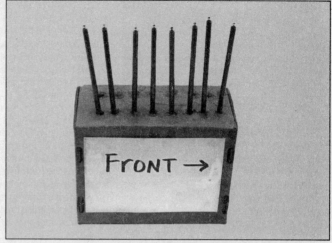

5.4 Keep the pushrods in order or mark them if they are to be re-installed so that they can be replaced in their original positions - a cardboard box such as the one shown can be used to identify and store pushrods in order

6   Rotate the crankshaft until the rotor is pointing directly to the chalk mark. **Note:** *This step will only apply to 1992 through 1996 models with the TFI-IV ignition system.*

7   To bring the piston to the top of the cylinder, continue to turn the crankshaft until the timing marks on the vibration damper align with the timing marks on the front cover. The timing marks are located on the crankshaft pulley and the scale on the timing chain cover. The timing mark line should indicate close to 0-degrees (TDC) **(see illustration)**. If not, turn the crankshaft until it does.

8   When the rotor is pointing at the number one spark plug wire terminal in the distributor cap and the 0-degree timing marks are aligned, the number one piston is at TDC on the compression stroke.

9   After the number one piston has been positioned at TDC on the compression stroke, TDC for any of the remaining cylinders can be located by turning the crankshaft clockwise 120-degrees at a time and following the firing order of the engine. **Note:** *120 degrees applies only to the 4.9L and 4.2L engines. All V8 engines are designed at 90 degrees for each cylinder and V10 engines are designed at 72-degrees.*

4   Valve cover and pushrod cover - removal and installation

Removal

Valve cover

1   Remove the PCV valve from the top of the valve cover (see Chapter 6).

2   Disconnect the clean air vent tube from the valve cover mounted oil filler cap or filter assembly (see Chapter 6).

3   Disconnect the inlet air hose and accelerator cable from the throttle body. Remove the throttle cable bracket and position the

cable and bracket out of the way.

4   Mark and disconnect any wires or hoses connected to the upper intake manifold. Remove the upper intake manifold (see Section 10).

5   Remove the retaining screws holding the valve cover to the cylinder head. Inspect bolts for worn or damaged seals under the head of the bolts and replace, if necessary.

6   Remove the valve cover from the cylinder head and clean the old gasket from the mating surfaces.

Pushrod cover

7   Remove the distributor cap from the distributor.

8   Remove the ignition coil and bracket from the side of the engine (see Chapter 5).

9   Remove the retaining bolts for the pushrod cover on left side of the engine.

10   Remove the pushrod cover from the side of the engine and clean the old gasket from the cover and engine block.

Installation

Valve cover

11   Place a new gasket on the cylinder head making sure the tabs of the gasket face down, towards the head. No sealant is required.

12   Install the valve cover on the cylinder head, making sure that the bolt holes line up and the gasket seals evenly all around the head.

13   Install the valve cover retaining bolts and tighten them to the torque listed in this Chapter's Specifications.

14   The remainder of installation is the reverse of removal.

Pushrod cover

15   Install a new gasket on the pushrod cover. Use RTV sealant on the gasket to keep it positioned, if necessary.

16   Place the pushrod cover on the engine

and tighten the retaining bolts to the torque listed in this Chapter's Specifications.

17   The remainder of installation is the reverse of removal.

Either cover

18   After the engine has been started, run it until it reaches normal operating temperature. Check the pushrod cover and/or valve cover for leaks.

5   Rocker arms and pushrods - removal and installation

Refer to illustrations 5.3 and 5.4

Removal

1   Remove the valve cover (see Section 6).

2   Remove the rocker arm bolt, fulcrum seat and rocker arm from each cylinder. Keep them in order or mark them, if they are to be re-installed, so they can be replaced in their original positions.

3   Inspect the rocker arms and fulcrums for wear **(see illustration)**.

4   To remove the pushrods, pull them straight up through the cylinder head and out of the lifter pocket. Keep them in order or mark them, if they are to be re-installed, so that they can be replaced in their original positions **(see illustration)**.

5   Inspect the pushrods as described in Chapter 2, Part E.

Installation

6   Apply engine oil or assembly lube to the top of the valve stem.

7   Apply assembly lube to the rocker arm fulcrum seat and the fulcrum seat socket in the rocker arm.

8   Install the pushrod (with lubricant applied to both ends).

6.7 Use the recommended puller to remove the vibration damper - if a puller that applies force to the outer edge is used, the damper will be damaged

9 Install the fulcrum guide (if equipped), rocker arm, fulcrum seat and bolt. Tighten the bolt to the torque listed in this Chapter's Specifications.

10 If components were replaced, check the valve clearance (see Chapter 2, Part E). If necessary, install a longer or shorter pushrod.

11 Replace the valve cover and gasket (see Section 6).

---

6 Timing cover and gears - removal and installation

Note: *The following procedure requires the use of a gear puller and gear installation tools.*

Removal

Refer to illustrations 6.7 and 6.31

Cover

1 Drain the cooling system (see Chapter 3).

2 Remove the fan shroud and the radiator (see Chapter 3).

3 Remove the fan and pulley (see Chapter 3).

4 Remove the power steering pump (see Chapter 10) and air conditioning compressor (see Chapter 3) from the engine bracket and position them to the side of the engine compartment. **Note:** *Don't disconnect the hoses from these accessories.* Remove the bracket from the engine to gain access to the timing cover bolts.

5 Remove any alternator support brackets from the timing cover, if necessary, to gain access to the timing cover bolts (see Chapter 5).

6 Remove the pulley from the crankshaft damper, then remove the large bolt and washer from the crankshaft nose. It may be necessary to prevent the crankshaft from rotating by wedging a screwdriver between the teeth on the starter ring gear and the block.

7 Remove the vibration damper using a vibration damper puller **(see illustration)**.

8 Remove the front oil pan attaching bolts and loosen the first six pan bolts on each side of the pan to allow the pan to droop slightly under a light downward force.

9 Remove the timing cover attaching bolts.

10 Remove the cover and scrape the old gasket from the mating surfaces of the cover and the engine block.

11 Remove the crankshaft oil seal by pushing it out of the front cover with a suitably sized drift. Be careful not to damage the front cover while performing this operation.

12 Remove any chemical sealants from the seal bore of the cover. Check the bore carefully for anything that would prevent the new seal from seating properly in the cover.

Timing gears

13 Before removing the gears, the camshaft endplay, timing gear backlash and timing gear runout should be inspected (see Chapter 2, Part E). If measurements indicate worn components, replace as required during reassembly.

14 Turn the crankshaft and/or camshaft until the timing marks of both gears can be aligned.

15 Use a two-jaw puller to remove the gear from the camshaft. **Note:** *This operation can also be done with camshaft out of engine during camshaft removal (see section 7).* **Caution:** *If the head, valves and pistons remain in the engine while the gears are being installed, do not turn either the crankshaft or camshaft prior to gear installation. Serious internal engine damage can result from rotating either assembly independent of the other. If the camshaft begins to turn by itself, remove the valve cover and loosen the rocker arm bolts two or three turns.*

16 Using a bolt-type puller, remove the timing gear from the crankshaft. **Note:** *Most steering wheel pullers can be used.*

Installation

Timing gears

17 Align the key before installing the camshaft drive gear onto the camshaft. **Note:** *If camshaft endplay was excessive during the wear checks, install an appropriately sized thrust plate prior to gear installation. If backlash was excessive, be sure to install new timing gears.*

18 Install the gear on the camshaft using a special tool. **Note:** *If the crankshaft gear is still installed, make sure the timing marks are correctly aligned prior to gear engagement.* An alternative is to use a bolt that will fit the threaded hole in the end of the camshaft. Put a nut and large flat washer on the bolt. Thread the bolt into the camshaft with the gear in place. Hold the bolt stationary and turn the nut down the bolt to push the gear into place on the camshaft. Remove the bolt and nut combination after the cam gear is in place.

19 Install the crankshaft key and gear using

a special installation tool or a large deep socket to drive the gear onto the crankshaft. Make sure the timing marks on both gears are correctly aligned prior to gear engagement. Adjust camshaft **slightly** if necessary to align. **Caution:** *If the head, valves and pistons remain in the engine while the gears are being installed, do not turn either the crankshaft or camshaft prior to gear installation. Serious internal engine damage can result from rotating either assembly independent of the other.* **Note:** *If the rocker arm nuts or bolts were loosened, tighten them to the torque listed in this Chapter's Specifications, then install the valve cover.*

20 Install the crankshaft oil slinger in front of the crankshaft drive gear. Note that the cupped side faces away from the engine.

Cover

21 Coat the outside edge of the new crankshaft oil seal with grease and install the seal in the cover using an appropriate drive tool. Make sure the seal is seated completely in the bore.

22 If the oil pan is still on the engine, cut the old front oil pan seal flush at the cylinder block-to-pan junction. Remove the old seal.

23 Clean all gasket surfaces on the valve cover, block and oil pan.

24 If the oil pan is in place, cut and install a new pan seal so that it is flush with the engine block-to-oil pan junction.

25 Align the pan seal locating tabs with the holes in the oil pan. Make sure the seal tabs pull all the way through so that the seal is completely seated. Apply RTV sealant to the block and pan mating surfaces (particularly to the corner junctions of the block, oil pan and cover).

26 Position the cover over the end of the crankshaft and onto the cylinder block. Start the cover and pan retaining screws by hand.

27 Slide an alignment tool over the end of the crankshaft to make sure the cover is located correctly before tightening the retaining bolts. If no alignment tool is available, temporarily install the crankshaft vibration damper to serve as a guide.

28 Tighten the retaining bolts, first for the cover and then the oil pan, to the torque values listed in this Chapter's Specifications. Remove the alignment tool if used.

29 Lubricate the nose of the crankshaft, the inner hub of the vibration damper and the seal surface with engine oil.

30 Apply RTV sealant to the inside keyway of the damper hub.

31 Align the damper keyway with the key on the crankshaft and install the damper using an installation tool **(see illustration)**.

32 Install the bolt and washer retaining the damper and tighten it to the torque listed in this Chapter's Specifications. Install the pulley on the damper and tighten the bolts to the torque listed in this Chapter's Specifications.

33 The remainder of installation is reverse of removal.

34 Fill the engine with oil if the oil has been drained (see Chapter 1).

6.31 Align the damper keyway with the key on the crankshaft, then use a damper installation tool to press the damper into place

7.3a The lifters in an engine that has accumulated many miles may have to be removed with a special tool

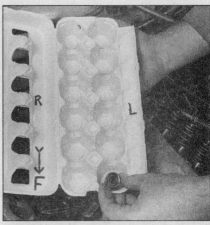

7.3b Keep the lifters in order or mark them if they are to be re-installed so they can be installed in their original positions - an old egg carton works well

35   Start the engine and allow it to reach normal operating temperature. Check for leaks of any type. Check the ignition timing (see Chapter 5).

7   Lifters and camshaft - removal and installation

Refer to illustrations 7.3a, 7.3b, 7.9 and 7.10

Removal

Lifters

1   Remove the valve cover and pushrod cover (see Section 4).
2   Remove the applicable rocker arm(s) and pushrod(s) for the lifter(s) to be removed (see Section 5). If the camshaft is to be removed, remove all of the lifters.
3   Remove the valve lifter(s) with a retrieval tool **(see illustration)**. Keep them in order or mark them, if they are to be re-installed, so they can be replaced in their original positions **(see illustration)**.
4   Inspect the lifters as described in Chapter 2, Part E. If no further disassembly is required, proceed to Step 21.

Camshaft

5   Position the engine at TDC compression for the number one cylinder (see Section 3) and remove the distributor (see Chapter 5).
6   Remove the valve lifters as described in this Section.
7   Remove the timing cover (see Section 6).
8   Prior to removing camshaft, check camshaft endplay, lobe lift and timing gears for wear (see Section 8 of this Chapter and Chapter 2, Part E). If measurements indicate worn components, replace as required during reassembly.
9   Check the timing marks - they should be directly adjacent to each other. If not, turn the crankshaft until they are **(see illustration)**.
10   Remove the camshaft thrust plate retaining bolts **(see illustration)**.
11   Pull the camshaft from the engine block,

7.9 Proper alignment of the camshaft and crankshaft timing marks

7.10 The camshaft thrust plate retaining bolts are accessible through the two openings in the camshaft gear

being careful that the lobes do not catch on the camshaft bearings. **Caution:** *Do not rotate the engine until re-installation is complete.*
12   Inspect the camshaft and bearings as described in Chapter 2, Part E. If your measurements indicate worn components, replace parts as required during reassembly.
13   If required for gear or camshaft replacement, remove the gear from the camshaft (see Section 6).

Installation

Camshaft

14   If removed, install the camshaft gear onto the camshaft (see Section 6). If a new timing gear is installed, replacement of the corresponding crankshaft timing gear is also recommended. **Note:** *If camshaft endplay was excessive during wear checks, install an appropriately-sized thrust plate prior to gear installation.*
15   Apply camshaft installation lubricant to all of the camshaft lobes and journals **(see illustration)**.
16   Install the camshaft into the engine mak-

ing sure the mark on the camshaft gear is aligned with the mark on the crankshaft gear. Be careful not to nick or damage the camshaft bearings. Install the thrust plate bolts.

7.15 Be sure to apply moly-based grease or camshaft installation lube to the cam lobes and bearing journals before installing the camshaft

8.4 To measure cam lobe lift, secure a dial indicator to the head next to the valve (one at a time) and position the indicator plunger directly above and in line with the pushrod - rotate crankshaft and measure lift

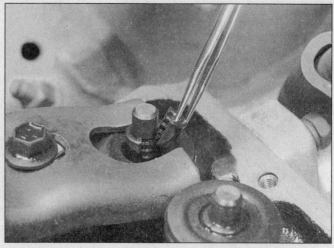

9.8 Compress the valve spring and remove the keepers with a small magnet, a pair of needle-nose pliers or tweezers

17   Tighten the camshaft thrust plate bolts to the torque listed in this Chapter's Specifications.
18   The remainder of installation is reverse of removal.
19   Start the engine and check for leaks.
20   Adjust the ignition timing as described in Chapter 5.

Lifters

21   Lubricate the bottom of the lifters with engine assembly lube and install them. If the original lifters are to be used, install them in their original bores.
22   The remainder of installation is reverse of removal.

8   Camshaft lobe lift - check

Refer to illustration 8.4

1   To determine the extent of cam lobe wear, the lobe lift should be checked prior to camshaft removal.
2   Remove the valve cover (see Section 4).
3   Position the number one piston at TDC on the compression stroke (see Section 3).
4   Beginning with the valves for the number one cylinder, remove the rocker arms (see Section 5), mount a dial indicator on the engine and position the plunger in-line with and resting on the first pushrod **(see illustration)**.
5   Zero the dial indicator, then very slowly turn the crankshaft in the normal direction of rotation. The dial indicator needle will begin to move as the cam ramps up. Continue rotating until the indicator needle stops and begins to move in the opposite direction. The point at which the highest reading is noted indicates maximum cam lobe lift. Record the indicator reading.
6   After recording the first measurement, again reposition the piston at TDC on the

compression stroke for the same cylinder.
7   Move the dial indicator to the other number one cylinder pushrod and repeat the check. Be sure to record the results for each valve.
8   Repeat the same check for the remaining valves. Since each piston must be at TDC on the compression stroke for this procedure, work from cylinder-to-cylinder following the firing order sequence, turning the engine 120-degrees each time.
9   After the check is complete, compare the results to the values listed in this Chapter's Specifications. If camshaft lobe lift is less than specified, cam lobe wear has occurred and a new camshaft should be installed. Further camshaft specifications are in Chapter 2E.

9   Valve springs, retainers and seals - replacement

Refer to illustrations 9.8, 9.9, 9.14 and 9.16
Note: *Broken valve springs and defective valve stem seals can be replaced without removing the cylinder head. Two special tools and a compressed air source are normally required to perform this operation, so read through this Section carefully and rent or buy the tools before beginning the job.*

Removal

1   Remove the valve cover from the cylinder head (see Section 4).
2   Remove the spark plug from the cylinder with the defective valve component. If all of the valve stem seals are being replaced, remove all of the spark plugs.
3   Turn the crankshaft until the piston in the affected cylinder is at top dead center on the compression stroke (refer to Section 3 for instructions). If you're replacing all of the valve stem seals, begin with cylinder number one and work on the valves for one cylinder at

a time. Move from cylinder-to-cylinder following the firing order sequence.
4   Thread an adapter into the spark plug hole and connect an air hose from a compressed air source to it. Most auto parts stores can supply the air hose adapter. **Note:** *Many cylinder compression gauges utilize a screw-in fitting that may work with your air hose quick-disconnect fitting.*
5   Remove the rocker arm mounting bolt, the rocker arm/fulcrum and the pushrod (see Section 5) for the valve with the defective part. If all of the valve stem seals are being replaced, all of the rocker arms and pushrods should be removed (be sure to keep them in order).
6   Apply compressed air to the cylinder. **Warning:** *The piston may be forced down by compressed air, causing the crankshaft to turn suddenly. If the wrench used when positioning the number one piston at TDC is still attached to the bolt in the crankshaft nose, it could cause damage or injury when the crankshaft moves. The valves should be held in place by the air pressure. If the valve faces or seats are in poor condition, leaks may prevent the air pressure from retaining the valves, in this case the cylinder head will have to be removed and a valve job performed.*
7   Stuff shop rags into the cylinder head oil return holes to prevent parts or debris from falling into the engine, then use a valve-spring compressor to compress the spring. **Note:** *Several different types of tools are available for compressing the valve springs with the head in place. One type grips the lower spring coils and presses on the retainer as the knob is turned, while the other type, used in this procedure, utilizes the rocker arm mounting stud or bolt for leverage. Both types work well, but the lever type is less expensive.*
8   Remove the keepers with a small pair of needle-nose pliers, a magnet or forceps **(see illustration).**

9.9 Remove the old valve stem seals - be sure that you don't scratch, nick or otherwise damage the valve stems

9.14 A deep socket and hammer can be used to seat the new seals on the valve guides

9.16 Apply a small dab of grease as shown to help hold the valve keepers in place during valve spring retainer installation

9   Remove the spring retainer and valve spring and set them aside. Using a pair of pliers, remove the valve stem seal **(see illustration)** and discard it. **Note:** *Watch for the presence of a spring shim(s) under the spring or on the spring seat and make sure it is installed prior to retainer re-installation.*

10   Wrap a rubber band or tape around the top of the valve stem so the valve won't fall into the combustion chamber, then release the air pressure.

11   Inspect the valve stem for damage. Rotate the valve in the guide and check the end for eccentric movement, which would indicate that the valve is bent.

12   Move the valve up-and-down in the guide and make sure it doesn't bind. If the valve stem binds, the valve is bent or the guide is damaged. In either case, the head will have to be removed for repair.

13   Reapply air pressure to the cylinder to retain the valve in the closed position, then remove the tape or rubber band from the valve stem.

Installation

14   Lubricate the valve stem with engine oil and install a new valve stem seal. Use a deep socket and a hammer to seat the seal squarely on the valve guide **(see illustration)**.

15   Place the valve spring in position, then install the retainer.

16   Compress the valve spring assembly and carefully install the keepers in the grooves in the valve stem. Apply a small dab of grease to the inside of each keeper to hold it in place, if necessary **(see illustration)**.

17   Remove the pressure from the spring tool and make sure the keepers are seated.

18   Disconnect the air hose and remove the adapter from the spark plug hole.

19   Refer to Section 7 and install the rocker arm and pushrod.

20   If you are replacing all of the seals, repeat the procedure for each valve assembly. Remember, the piston for each cylinder must be positioned at TDC before removing the valve keepers.

21   Install the spark plug(s) and hook up the wire(s).

22   Install the valve cover (Section 4).

23   Start and run the engine, then check for oil leaks and unusual sounds coming from the valve cover area.

10   Manifolds - removal and installation

Warning: *Gasoline is extremely flammable, so take extra precautions when you work on any part of the fuel system. Don't smoke or allow open flames or bare light bulbs near the work area, and don't work in a garage where a gas-type appliance (such as a water heater or clothes dryer) is present. Since gasoline is carcinogenic, wear fuel-resistant gloves when there's a possibility of being exposed to fuel, and, if you spill any fuel on your skin, rinse it off immediately with soap and water. Mop up any spills immediately and do not store fuel-soaked rags where they could ignite. The fuel system is under constant pressure, so if any fuel lines are to be disconnected, the fuel pressure in the system must be relieved first (see Chapter 4 for more information). When you perform any kind of work on the fuel system, wear safety glasses and have a Class B type fire extinguisher on hand.*

Removal

Upper intake manifold

1   Disconnect the EGR, the TPS, the IAC valve and EGR transducer harness connectors (see Chapter 6).

2   Label and disconnect the EGR valve vacuum line, the throttle body vacuum lines and other upper intake manifold vacuum lines that may be present.

3   Working on the underside of the upper intake manifold, disconnect the PCV fitting.

4   Remove the air cleaner outlet duct (see Chapter 4).

5   Remove the lines from the fuel rail (see Chapter 4).

6   Disconnect the accelerator cable from

the throttle body (see Chapter 4).

7   Disconnect the EGR valve tube at the exhaust manifold and EGR valve (see Chapter 6).

8   Disconnect the upper intake manifold support bracket.

9   Remove the upper intake manifold mounting bolts. Lift the upper intake manifold and throttle body as a complete assembly.

Lower intake manifold and exhaust manifold

10   Remove the fuel rail and injectors from the lower intake manifold (see Chapter 4).

11   Label and disconnect the lower intake manifold vacuum hoses, thermactor bypass valve and tube assembly, and any other electrical connectors that may be present.

12   Disconnect the exhaust pipe from the exhaust manifold and support it out of the way.

13   Remove the bolts (and nuts if equipped) retaining the intake and exhaust manifolds to the cylinder head. Lift the manifold assemblies away from the engine.

14   Clean all traces of old gasket material from the mating surfaces of the manifolds and cylinder head. If new manifolds are to be installed, remove the nuts connecting the intake manifold to the exhaust manifold.

Installation

Lower intake manifold and exhaust manifold

Refer to illustration 10.18

15   Install new studs in the exhaust manifold for the inlet pipe. **Note:** *This step is not absolutely necessary if the studs are in good condition, however, it is recommended in order to prevent future problems.*

16   Install a new intake/exhaust manifold-to-cylinder head gasket.

17   Place the exhaust manifolds, front and rear, onto cylinder head. Connect them onto the cylinder head with lock washers and nuts. Tighten the nuts finger tight.

18   Place the intake manifold assembly against the mating surface of the cylinder

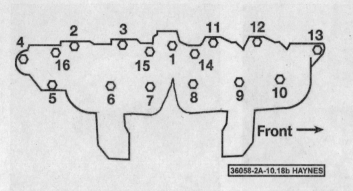

10.18 Intake and exhaust manifold bolt tightening sequence

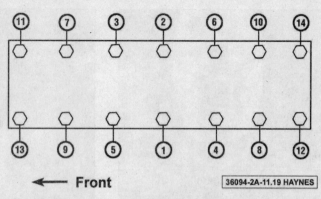

11.19 Cylinder head bolt TIGHTENING sequence

head, making sure that the gaskets are positioned correctly. Install the attaching washers, bolts and nuts finger tight and make sure everything is positioned and aligned correctly. Tighten the nuts and bolts in the proper sequence **(see illustration)** to the torque values listed in this Chapter's Specifications **Note:** *Use an intake/exhaust manifold gasket if the original manifolds are equipped with them. However, if the exhaust manifold is changed with an updated part, install it without an exhaust manifold gasket(s). Check with a dealer parts department or qualified auto parts store.*

19   Attach a new gasket to the exhaust pipe and fasten the pipe to the exhaust manifold. Tighten the nuts securely.

20   The remainder of installation is reverse of removal.

Upper intake manifold

21   Install a new intake manifold gasket onto the lower intake manifold. Be sure the gasket surface is clean of all gasket material. Use the lower intake manifold dowels to position the gasket.

22   Install the upper intake manifold and throttle body assembly onto the lower intake manifold.

23   Tighten the bolts to the torque listed in the beginning of this Chapter's Specifications.

24   Install the upper intake manifold brace.

25   install the EGR valve tube (see Chapter 6).

26   Install the accelerator cable and cruise control cable, if equipped.

27   Installation is the reverse of removal.

11   Cylinder head - removal and installation

Refer to illustration 11.19

Removal

1   Disconnect the negative cable from the battery.

2   Drain the cooling system (see Chapter 3).

3   Disconnect the upper radiator hose from the thermostat outlet (see Chapter 3).

4   Remove the heater hose at the coolant outlet elbow (see Chapter 3).

5   Mark the wires leading to the coil and disconnect them. Remove the coil bracket attaching bolt. Secure the coil and bracket out of the way (see Chapter 5).

6   Remove any power accessory brackets attached to the cylinder head. **Note:** *It is not necessary to disconnect refrigerant hoses or power steering hoses.*

7   Remove the manifolds (see Section 10).

8   Remove the valve cover (see Section 4).

9   Loosen the rocker arm bolts or stud nuts so the rocker arms can be rotated to one side.

10   Remove the pushrods (see Section 5). A numbered box or rack will keep them properly organized.

11   Disconnect the spark plug wires at the spark plugs (see Chapter 1) and any sensor electrical connectors that would interfere with removal.

12   Remove the cylinder head retaining bolts, in sequence, using the reverse order of the tightening sequence. Use a helper if available and pry the cylinder head up off of the engine block. The cylinder head is heavy, and removal is easiest from inside the vehicle with the engine cover off. **Caution:** *Do not wedge any tools between the cylinder head and block gasket mating surfaces - pry only on casting protrusions.*

13   Secure the head on a workbench or cylinder head holding device.

14   Inspect the cylinder head as outlined in Chapter 2, Part E. **Note:** *New and rebuilt cylinder heads are commonly available for engines at dealer parts departments and auto parts stores. Due to the fact that some specialized tools are necessary for the dismantling and inspection of the head, and replacement parts may not be readily available, it may be more practical and economical for the home mechanic to purchase a replacement head and install it. Another alternative, at this point, is to take the cylinder head to an automotive machine shop or shop specializing in cylinder heads and exchange it or leave your head for the overhaul process.*

15   Replace or service the cylinder head as required (see Chapter 2E).

Installation

16   Make sure the cylinder head and cylinder block mating surfaces are clean, flat and prepared for the new cylinder head gasket (see Chapter 2 Part E for the inspection procedures). Clean the exhaust manifold and exhaust pipe gasket surfaces.

17   Position the gasket over the dowel pins on the cylinder block, making sure that it is facing the right direction and that the correct surface is exposed. Gaskets are often marked 'front' and 'this side up' to aid in installation.

18   Using another person as a helper, carefully lower the cylinder head into place on the block. Take care not to move the head sideways or to scrape it across the surface as it can dislodge the gasket and/or damage the mating surfaces.

19   Coat the cylinder head retaining bolts with a light coat of engine oil and thread the bolts into the block. Tighten the bolts to the torque listed in this Chapter's Specifications using the tightening sequence shown in the accompanying illustration **(see illustration)**. Work up to the final torque in three steps to avoid warping the head.

20   The remaining steps are the reverse of the removal procedure.

21   Refill radiator with coolant (see Chapter 3).

22   Start the engine and allow it to reach operating temperature. Check for leaks. **Note:** *Some gasket manufacturers recommend re-tightening the cylinder head bolts after the engine has cooled down. Check the instructions furnished with the gasket kit to determine if this is necessary.*

12   Oil pan - removal and installation

Note: *This procedure is for removal and installation of the oil pan with the engine in the vehicle only. If the engine has been removed for an overhaul, use only Step 10 and Steps 15 through 26.*

Removal

1   Disconnect the negative battery cable from the battery (see Chapter 1).

2   Drain the cooling system (see Chapter 3) and engine oil (see Chapter 1).
3   Remove the radiator (see Chapter 3). **Note:** *This operation is required so that the radiator is not damaged by the engine when it is raised from its mounts.*
4   Raise the vehicle and support it securely on jackstands. Disconnect the starter cable at the starter (see Chapter 5).
5   Remove the starter (see Chapter 5).
6   Remove the engine front insulator-to-support bracket retaining nuts and washers (see Section 16).
7   Raise the front of the engine with a jack. Place a thick wooden block between the jack and the oil pan to serve as a cushion.
8   Place one inch wood blocks between the front support insulators and the support brackets.
9   Lower the engine onto the spacer blocks and remove the jack.
10   Remove the oil pan attaching bolts.
11   Lower the pan to the crossmember.
12   Remove the oil pump pick-up tube-to-oil pump retaining bolts and washers.
13   Remove the oil pump pick-up tube and allow it to rest in the oil pan.
14   Remove the oil pan from the vehicle. It may be necessary to rotate the crankshaft so the counterweights clear the pan.
15   Clean all gaskets from the mating surfaces of the engine block and the pan.
16   Remove the rear main bearing cap-to-oil pan seal.
17   Remove the timing cover-to-oil pan seal.

Installation

18   Clean all mating surfaces and seal grooves.
19   Install new oil pan-to-front cover oil seals.
20   Install a new rear main bearing cap-to-oil pan seal.
21   Install a new pan gasket. Apply a thin, even coat of RTV sealant to both sides of the gasket.
22   Make sure the tabs of the front and rear seal fit properly into the mating slots on the oil pan side seals. A small amount of RTV sealant at each mating junction will help prevent any leaks from these critical spots.
23   Clean the pick-up tube and screen assembly and place it in the oil pan.
24   Position the oil pan underneath the engine.
25   Lift the pick-up tube and screen assembly from the oil pan and secure it to the oil pump with a new gasket. Tighten the retaining bolts to the torque listed in this Chapter's Specifications.
26   Attach the oil pan to the engine block and install the retaining bolts. Tighten the bolts to the torque listed in this Chapter's Specifications, starting from the center and working out in each direction. **Note:** *Some models have oil pan flange reinforcing strips that go between the pan bolts and the block.*
27   Raise the engine with a jack and a block

14.6 Using a seal removal tool to pry out the crankshaft front oil seal

of wood underneath the oil pan and remove the wood spacers previously installed under the support brackets.
28   Lower the engine to the correct installed position and install the washers and nuts on the insulator studs. Tighten the nuts to the torque listed in this Chapter's Specifications.
29   Install the starter (see Chapter 5).
30   Lower the vehicle.
31   Install the radiator (see Chapter 3).
32   Fill the cooling system with coolant (see Chapter 1) and check for leaks.
33   Fill the engine crankcase with oil (see Chapter 1) and connect the negative battery cable.
34   Start the engine and check carefully for leaks at the oil pan gasket sealing surfaces. **Note:** *When the battery has been disconnected, some unusual driveability symptoms may be present until the vehicle is driven ten miles and the computer "relearns." (see Chapter 6).*

13   Oil pump - removal and installation

1   Remove the oil pan as described in Section 12.
2   Remove the bolts retaining the oil pump to the block.
3   Remove the oil pump assembly.
4   Clean the mating surfaces of the oil pump and the block.
5   Inspect the oil pump as described in Chapter 2, Part E.
6   Before installation, prime the pump by filling the inlet opening with oil and rotating the pump shaft until the oil spurts out of the outlet.
7   Attach the oil pump to the engine block using the retaining bolts.
8   Tighten the bolts to the torque listed in this Chapter's Specifications.
9   Install the oil pan (see Section 12).

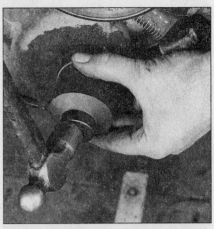

14.8 If you're very careful, you can use a large socket to drive the new seal into the timing cover

14   Crankshaft oil seals - replacement

Crankshaft front oil seal

Refer to illustrations 14.6 and 14.8
Note: *The following operation requires a special tool for proper seal installation.*
1   Drain the cooling system (see Chapter 3).
2   Remove the fan shroud and the radiator (see Chapter 3).
3   Remove the fan and pulley (see Chapter 3).
4   Remove the large bolt and washer from the crankshaft nose. It may be necessary to prevent the crankshaft from rotating by wedging a screwdriver between the teeth on the starter ring gear and the block.
5   Remove the vibration damper **(see illustration 6.7)**.
6   Using a seal remover tool, remove seal from timing cover **(see illustration)**.
7   Clean out the recess in the cover.
8   Coat the outer edge of the new seal with engine oil and install it using a seal driver. As an alternative, a large socket or piece of pipe can be used to push the new seal in **(see illustration)**. However, use extreme caution as the seal can be damaged easily with this method. Drive in the seal until it is fully seated in the recess. Make sure the spring is properly positioned within the seal.
9   Lubricate the nose of the crankshaft, the inner hub of the vibration damper and the seal surface with engine oil.
10   Apply RTV sealant to the inside keyway of the damper hub.
11   Align the damper keyway with the key on the crankshaft and install the damper using an installation tool **(see illustration 6.31)**.
12   Install the bolt and washer retaining the damper and tighten it to the torque listed in this Chapter's Specifications.
13   The remainder of installation is the reverse of removal.
14   Fill the engine with oil, if the oil has been drained (see Chapter 1).

15   Start and operate the engine at a fast idle and check for leaks of any type.

Rear main oil seal

16   Disconnect the negative battery cable from the battery, then remove the starter (see Chapter 5).

17   Remove the transmission (Chapter 7).

18   Remove the driveplate (see Section 15).

19   Use an awl to punch two holes in the oil seal. Punch the holes on opposite sides of the crankshaft, just above the bearing cap-to-engine block junction.

20   Thread a sheet metal screw into each punched hole.

21   Use two large screwdrivers or small pry-bars and pry against both screws at the same time to remove the seal. A wood block placed against the engine will provide additional leverage. **Caution:** *Be very careful when performing this operation that you do not damage the oil seal contact surfaces on the crankshaft.*

22   Clean the oil recess in the rear of the engine block and the main bearing cap surface of the crankshaft.

23   Inspect, clean and, using crocus cloth, polish the oil seal contact surfaces of the crankshaft. If the area in which the seal rides is grooved or otherwise damaged, the new seal will leak.

24   Coat the outer diameter of the new seal with a light film of engine oil.

25   Coat the crankshaft surface with a light film of engine oil.

26   Start the seal into the cavity in the back of the engine with the seal lip facing the engine and install it with a special seal driver tool. Make sure that the seal is driven in squarely until the tool contacts the block.

27   The remainder of installation is the reverse of removal. If the engine oil was drained, refill the crankcase (see Chapter 1). Start the engine and check for leaks. **Note:** *When the battery has been disconnected,* some unusual driveability symptoms may be present until the vehicle is driven ten miles and the computer "relearns." (see Chapter 6).

---

15   Driveplate - removal, inspection and installation

---

1   Remove the transmission (see Chapter 7).

2   Mark the relationship of the driveplate to the crankshaft to ensure installation in the same position.

3   To keep the crankshaft from turning, wedge a large screwdriver or prybar between the ring gear teeth and the engine block (it must be positioned so that as the crankshaft moves, the tool bears against the block). Make sure that the tool is not pushing against the oil pan.

4   Remove the driveplate retaining bolts from the crankshaft flange.

5   Remove the driveplate from the crankshaft by it pulling straight back. If it's stuck, wiggle it from side-to-side.

6   Inspect the driveplate for cracks and warpage. If the driveplate is cracked, it must be replaced with a new one.

7   Installation is the reverse of removal. The retaining bolts should be coated with a thread-locking compound and tightened in a criss-cross pattern to the torque listed in this Chapter's Specifications.

---

16   Engine mounts - check and replacement

---

1   Engine mounts seldom require attention, but broken or deteriorated mounts should be replaced immediately or the added strain placed on the driveline components may cause damage.

Check

2   During the check, the engine must be raised slightly to remove the weight from the mounts.

3   Raise the vehicle and support it securely on jackstands, then position the jack under the engine oil pan. Place a large block of wood between the jack head and the oil pan, then carefully raise the engine just enough to take the weight off the mounts.

4   Check the mounts to see if the rubber is cracked, hardened or separated from the metal plates. Sometimes the rubber will split right down the center. Rubber preservative should be applied to the mounts to slow deterioration.

5   Check for relative movement between the mount plates and the engine, transmission or frame/body (use a large screwdriver or prybar to attempt to move the mounts). If excess movement is noted, new mount isolators will be required.

Replacement (front mounts)

6   Raise the vehicle and place it securely on jackstands.

7   Place a wood block and a jack under the engine.

8   Remove the upper and lower nut and washer assemblies from the insulator assembly.

9   Raise the engine just enough to allow clearance for the removal of the mount insulator and heat shield if equipped. **Warning:** *DO NOT place any part of your body under the engine when it's supported only by a jack.*

10   Installation is reverse of removal. Tighten the fasteners to the torque listed in this Chapter's Specifications.

Replacement (rear mount)

11   For the rear (transmission) mount replacement procedure, see Chapter 7.

Chapter 2 Part B
4.2L V6 engine

Contents

Specifications

General

Displacement	4.2 liters (256 cubic inches)
Cylinder numbers (front-to-rear)	
Left (driver's) side	4-5-6
Right side	1-2-3
Firing order	1-4-2-5-3-6

Camshaft and lifters

Lobe lift	
Intake	0.245 inch
Exhaust	0.259 inch
Lobe wear limit	0.005 inch
Endplay	0.001 to 0.006 inch
Journal diameter (all)	2.0515 to 2.0505 inches
Cam bearing inside diameter	2.0535 to 2.0525 inches
Journal-to-bearing (oil) clearance	
Models through 2002	0.002 inch
2003 and later	0.001 to 0.003 inch
Journal runout limit	0.002 inch
Journal out-of-round limit	0.001 inch

Oil pump

Gear backlash	0.008 to 0.0012 inch
Gear radial clearance	0.002 to 0.0055 inch
Gear height (housing to gear tops)	0.0004 to 0.0033 inch

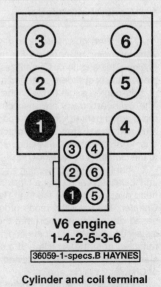

**V6 engine
1-4-2-5-3-6**

36059-1-specs.B HAYNES

**Cylinder and coil terminal
locations – 4.2L V6 engine**

Torque specifications*

Ft-lbs (unless otherwise indicated)

Camshaft sprocket bolt	30 to 36
Camshaft thrust plate bolts	72 to 120 in-lbs
Balance shaft thrust plate bolts	72 to 120 in-lbs
Timing chain cover-to-block bolts	
1997 through 1999	15 to 22
2000 and later	
Bolt number 12 **(see illustration 10.18)**	89 in-lbs
All others	
Step 1	16
Step 2	Tighten an additional 90 degrees
Water pump-to-timing chain cover bolts	15 to 22
Oil pan-to-block bolts	
Step 1	36 to 44 in-lbs
Step 2	80 to 106 in-lbs
Oil pan-to-transmission bolts	29 to 38
Oil pump and filter body to front cover	
8-mm bolts	15 to 22
6-mm bolts	71 to 97 in-lbs
Cylinder head bolts (oiled)	
Step 1	14
Step 2	29
Step 3	36
Step 4	Loosen 3 turns (DO NOT loosen all the bolts at the same time, from this point on work on one bolt at a time) (see Section 7)
Step 5	
Long bolts	30 to 36
Short bolts	15 to 22
Step 6 (all bolts)	Tighten an additional 175 to 185-degrees
Rocker arm fulcrum bolts	23 to 29
Upper intake-to-lower intake manifold bolts	
Step 1	53 in-lbs
Step 2	89 in-lbs
Lower intake manifold-to-cylinder head bolts	
Step 1	44 in-lbs
Step 2	89 in-lbs
Exhaust manifold bolts	15 to 22
Crankshaft pulley-to-vibration damper bolts	20 to 28
Upper intake manifold-to-lower intake manifold bolts	89 in-lbs
Valve cover bolts	71 to 102 in-lbs
Vibration damper bolt	103 to 117
Driveplate mounting bolts	54 to 64

Note: Refer to Part E for additional specifications.

1   General information

This Part of Chapter 2 is devoted to in-vehicle repair procedures for the 4.2L V6 engine. This engine design utilizes a cast-iron block with six cylinders arranged in a V-shape at a 90-degree angle between the two banks. The cylinder heads are also cast-iron and the block-mounted camshaft operates push-rods and rocker arms for valve actuation. The engine also features a balance shaft geared to the camshaft in the block.

All information concerning engine removal and installation and engine block and cylinder head overhaul can be found in Part E of this Chapter. The following repair procedures are based on the assumption that the engine is installed in the vehicle. If the engine has been removed from the vehicle and mounted on a stand, many of the steps outlined in this Part of Chapter 2 will not apply.

The Specifications included in this Part of Chapter 2 apply only to the procedures contained in this Part. Part E of Chapter 2 contains the Specifications necessary for cylinder head and engine block rebuilding.

2   Repair operations possible with the engine in the vehicle

Many major repair operations can be accomplished without removing the engine from the vehicle.

Clean the engine compartment and the exterior of the engine with some type of pressure washer before any work is done. It will make the job easier and help keep dirt out of the internal areas of the engine.

Components within the engine compartment can be accessed from the front of the vehicle by lifting the hood or from inside the passenger compartment by removing the engine cover (refer to Chapter 11 if necessary). Depending upon the extent of the repair, it may be necessary to use both methods.

If vacuum, exhaust, oil or coolant leaks develop, indicating a need for gasket or seal replacement, the repairs can generally be made with the engine in the vehicle. The intake and exhaust manifold gaskets, timing cover gasket, oil pan gasket, crankshaft oil seals and cylinder head gaskets are all accessible with the engine in place.

Exterior engine components, such as the intake and exhaust manifolds, the oil pan (and the oil pump), the water pump, the starter motor, the alternator, and the fuel system components can be removed for repair with the engine in place.

Since the cylinder heads can be removed without pulling the engine, valve component servicing can also be accomplished with the engine in the vehicle. Replacement of the timing chain and sprockets is also possible with the engine in the vehicle.

In extreme cases caused by a lack of necessary equipment, repair or replacement of piston rings, pistons, connecting rods and

3.1 Turn the crankshaft clockwise until the zero on the vibration damper scale is directly opposite the pointer

rod bearings is possible with the engine in the vehicle. However, this practice is not recommended because of the cleaning and preparation work that must be done to the components involved.

3   Top Dead Center (TDC) for number one piston - locating

Refer to illustration 3.1

1   Follow the procedure described in Chapter 2, Part A but use the timing marks as shown in the accompanying illustration **(see illustration)**.

2   After the number one piston has been positioned at TDC on the compression stroke, TDC for any of the remaining cylinders can be located by turning the crankshaft and following the firing order (refer to the Specifications). Divide the crankshaft pulley into three equal sections with chalk marks at three points, each indicating 120-degrees of crankshaft rotation. Rotating the engine 120- degrees past TDC #1 will put the engine at TDC for cylinder no. 4.

4   Valve covers - removal and installation

Removal

Refer to illustrations 4.2 and 4.5

1   Disconnect the cable from the negative battery terminal.

2   Note their locations, then detach the spark plug wire clips from the valve cover studs **(see illustration)**.

3   Detach the spark plug wires from the plugs (see Chapter 1). Position the wires out of the way. Remove the engine-lifting bracket.

4   On some vehicles with cruise control, it may be necessary to disconnect the servo linkage at the throttle body and remove the servo bracket.

5   If you're removing the left (driver's side) valve cover, detach the oil fill cap and crankcase vent tube **(see illustration)**. On 2001 and later models, remove the air intake assembly and remove the oil filler and unbolt the dipstick extension tube.

6   If you're removing the right (passenger's side) valve cover, position the air cleaner duct out of the way (see Chapter 4) and remove the ignition coils (see Chapter 5) and EGR tube (see Chapter 6). On 2001 and later models, disconnect the differential pressure feedback sensor and position the wiring harness out of the way.

7   Remove the valve cover bolts/nuts **(see illustration 4.5)**, then detach the cover from the cylinder head. **Note:** *If the cover is stuck to the cylinder head, bump one end with a wood block and a hammer to jar it loose. If that doesn't work, try to slip a flexible putty knife between the cylinder head and cover to break the gasket seal. Don't pry at the cover-to-cylinder head joint or damage to the sealing surfaces may occur (leading to oil leaks in the future). Some valve covers are made of plastic - be extra careful when tapping or pulling on them. On some models, the valve cover bolts stay with the valve cover. Do not attempt to remove them completely.*

Installation

8   The mating surfaces of each cylinder head and valve cover must be perfectly clean when the covers are installed. Use a gasket scraper to remove all traces of sealant and old gasket material, then clean the mating surfaces with lacquer thinner or acetone. If there's sealant or oil on the mating surfaces when the cover is installed, oil leaks may develop.

9   Clean the mounting bolt threads with a die to remove any corrosion and restore damaged threads. Make sure the threaded holes in the cylinder head are clean - run a tap into them to remove corrosion and restore damaged threads. Apply a small amount of light oil to the bolt threads.

10   The gaskets should be mated to the covers before the covers are installed. Make sure the tabs on the gaskets(s) engage in the slots in the cover(s). On engines that don't have gaskets, apply a 3/16-inch bead of RTV sealant to the cover flange, inside of the bolt holes.

11   Carefully position the cover on the cylinder head and install the bolts/nuts.

12   Tighten the bolts in three or four steps to the torque listed in this Chapter's Specifications. Plastic valve covers are easily damaged, so don't overtighten the bolts!

13   The remaining installation steps are the reverse of removal.

14   Start the engine and check carefully for oil leaks as the engine warms up.

5   Rocker arms and pushrods - removal, inspection and installation

Removal

Refer to illustrations 5.2 and 5.4

1   Refer to Section 4 and detach the valve cover(s) from the cylinder head(s).

2   Beginning at the front of one cylinder head, remove the rocker arm fulcrum bolts

4.2 Remove the spark plug wire clips (arrow)

4.5 Detach the crankcase vent tube (A) - B indicates two of the valve cover bolts

5.2 The rocker arm fulcrum bolts (arrow) may not have to be completely removed in all cases - loosen them several turns and see if the rocker arms can be pivoted out of the way to allow pushrod removal

5.4 A perforated cardboard box can be used to store the pushrods to ensure that they are reinstalled in their original locations - note the label indicating the front of the engine

(see illustration). Store them separately in marked containers to ensure that they will be reinstalled in their original locations. **Note:** *If the pushrods are the only items being removed, loosen each bolt just enough to allow the rocker arms to be rotated to the side so the pushrods can be lifted out.*

3   Lift off the rocker arms and fulcrums. Store them in the marked containers with the bolts (they must be reinstalled in their original locations).

4   Remove the pushrods and store them separately to make sure they don't get mixed up during installation **(see illustration)**.

Inspection

Refer to illustration 5.7

5   Check each rocker arm for wear, cracks and other damage, especially where the pushrods and valve stems contact the rocker arm faces.

6   Make sure the hole at the pushrod end of each rocker arm is open.

7   Check each rocker arm pivot area and fulcrum for wear, cracks and galling **(see illustration)**. If the rocker arms are worn or damaged, replace them with new ones and use new fulcrums as well.

8   Inspect the pushrods for cracks and excessive wear at the ends. Roll each pushrod across a piece of plate glass to see if it's bent (if it wobbles, it's bent).

Installation

9   Lubricate the lower end of each pushrod with clean engine oil or moly-base grease and install them in their original locations. Make sure each pushrod seats completely in the lifter.

10   Apply moly-base grease to the ends of the valve stems and the upper ends of the pushrods before positioning the rocker arms and fulcrums.

11   Apply moly-base grease to the fulcrums to prevent damage to the mating surfaces before engine oil pressure builds up. Set the rocker arms and guides in place, then install

the fulcrums and bolts. Tighten the rocker arm bolts to Specifications.

12   Install the valve covers.

13   The remainder of installation is the reverse of removal.

---

6   Valve springs, retainers and seals - replacement

Refer to illustrations 6.4, 6.8, 6.9 and 6.16

Note: *Broken valve springs and defective valve stem seals can be replaced without removing the cylinder heads. Two special tools and a compressed air source are normally required to perform this operation, so read through this Section carefully and rent or buy the tools before beginning the job.*

1   Refer to Section 4 and remove the valve cover from the affected cylinder head. If all of the valve stem seals are being replaced, remove both valve covers.

2   Remove the spark plug from the cylinder which has the defective component. If all of the valve stem seals are being replaced, all of the spark plugs should be removed.

3   Turn the crankshaft until the piston in the affected cylinder is at Top Dead Center on

the compression stroke (refer to Section 3 for instructions). If you're replacing all of the valve stem seals, begin with cylinder number one and work on the valves for one cylinder at a time. Move from cylinder-to-cylinder following the firing order sequence (see this Chapter's Specifications).

4   Thread an adapter into the spark plug hole **(see illustration)** and connect an air hose from a compressed air source to it. Most auto parts stores can supply the air hose adapter. **Note:** *Many cylinder compression gauges utilize a screw-in fitting that may work with your air hose quick-disconnect fitting.*

5   Remove the bolt, fulcrum and rocker arm for the valve with the defective part and pull out the pushrod. If all of the valve stem seals are being replaced, all of the rocker arms and pushrods should be removed (refer to Section 5).

6   Apply compressed air to the cylinder. **Warning:** *The piston may be forced down by compressed air, causing the crankshaft to turn suddenly. If the wrench used when positioning the number one piston at TDC is still attached to the bolt in the crankshaft nose, it could cause damage or injury when the crankshaft moves.*

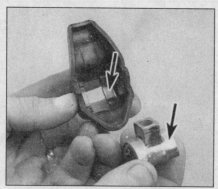

5.7 Check for wear on the rocker arm and fulcrum contact areas (arrows)

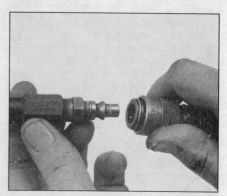

6.4 This is what the air hose adapter that threads into the spark plug hole looks like - they're commonly available from auto parts stores

6.8 Once the spring is depressed, the keepers can be removed with a small magnet or needle-nose pliers (a magnet is preferred to prevent dropping the keepers)

6.9 The seal can be pulled off the guide with a pair of pliers

6.16 Apply a small dab of grease to each keeper as shown here before installation - it'll keep them in place on the valve stem as the spring is released

7   The valves should be held in place by the air pressure.

8   Stuff shop rags into the cylinder head holes above and below the valves to prevent parts and tools from falling into the engine, then use a valve spring compressor to compress the spring. Remove the keepers with small needle-nose pliers or a magnet (see illustration). Note: *A couple of different types of tools are available for compressing the valve springs with the cylinder head in place. One type, shown here, grips the lower spring coils and presses on the retainer as the knob is turned, while the other type utilizes the rocker arm bolt for leverage. Both types work very well, although the lever type is usually less expensive.*

9   Remove the spring keepers, retainer and spring, then remove the valve guide seal (see illustration). Note: *If air pressure fails to hold the valve in the closed position during this operation, the valve face or seat is probably damaged. If so, the cylinder head will have to be removed for additional repair operations.*

10   Wrap a rubber band or tape around the top of the valve stem so the valve won't fall into the combustion chamber, then release the air pressure.

11   Inspect the valve stem for damage. Rotate the valve in the guide and check the end for eccentric movement, which would indicate that the valve is bent.

12   Move the valve up-and-down in the guide and make sure it doesn't bind. If the valve stem binds, either the valve is bent or the guide is damaged. In either case, the cylinder head will have to be removed for repair.

13   Reapply air pressure to the cylinder to retain the valve in the closed position, then remove the tape or rubber band from the valve stem.

14   Lubricate the valve stem with engine oil, then install a new guide seal.

15   Install the spring in position over the valve.

16   Install the valve spring retainer. Compress the valve spring and carefully position the keepers in the groove. Apply a small dab

of grease to the inside of each keeper to hold it in place (see illustration).

17   Remove the pressure from the spring tool and make sure the keepers are seated.

18   Disconnect the air hose and remove the adapter from the spark plug hole.

19   Refer to Section 5 and install the rocker arm(s) and pushrod(s).

20   Install the spark plug(s) and hook up the wire(s).

21   Refer to Section 4 and install the valve cover(s).

22   Start and run the engine, then check for oil leaks and unusual sounds coming from the valve cover area.

7   Intake manifold (upper and lower) - removal and installation

1   Relieve the fuel pressure and remove the air duct assembly and the engine cover (see Chapter 4).

2   Disconnect the negative cable from the battery.

3   Drain the cooling system (see Chapter 1).

Upper intake manifold
Refer to illustrations 7.10, 7.12a and 7.12b

4   Remove the accelerator cable (see Chapter 4) and cruise control cable (if equipped) from the throttle body. On models so equipped, remove the plastic splash shield over the throttle linkage first.

5   Disconnect the electrical connectors for the throttle position sensor (TPS), the idle air control (IAC) valve and the EGR valve position sensor (see Chapter 6).

6   Clearly label and then disconnect the vacuum lines from the upper intake manifold, the EGR valve and the fuel pressure regulator.

7   Disconnect the EGR tube from the upper intake manifold (lower intake on later models) and the exhaust manifold (see Chapter 6).

8   Remove the upper intake manifold brace, if applicable.

9   Remove the PCV tube from the upper intake manifold and the valve cover (see Chapter 6).

10   Remove the upper intake manifold mounting bolts (see illustration).

11   Remove the upper intake manifold and throttle body as a complete unit from the lower

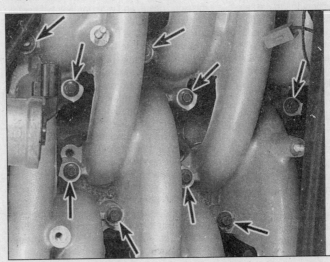

7.10 Remove the upper intake manifold mounting bolts (arrows) (not all bolts are visible) (1997 through 1999 models shown)

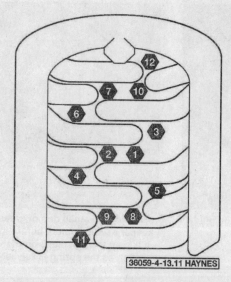

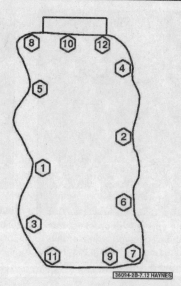

7.12a Upper intake manifold mounting bolt tightening sequence (1997 through 1999 models)

7.12b Upper intake manifold mounting bolt tightening sequence (2000 and later models)

7.13 Disconnect the two electrical connectors (arrows) on the IMRC solenoids at the back of the intake manifold

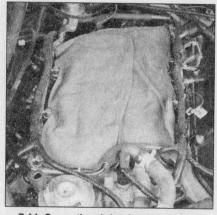

7.14 Cover the air intake with a shop towel to prevent debris from falling into the engine

7.15 Disconnect the lines and vacuum hose at the EGR valve (arrow)

intake manifold.

12   Installation is the reverse of removal. Be sure to clean and inspect the mounting faces of the lower intake manifold and the upper intake manifold before positioning the gaskets onto the lower intake manifold mounting face. The use of alignment studs may be helpful. Install the upper intake manifold and throttle body as a single unit. Be sure to follow the correct bolt tightening sequence **(see illustrations)** and torque specification listed at the beginning of this Chapter.

Lower intake manifold

Refer to illustrations 7.13, 7.14, 7.15, 7.16, 7.17, 7.18, 7.19, 7.22, 7.23 and 7.26

13   Disconnect the IMRC vacuum and electrical connectors, the fuel lines, fuel pressure regulator and injector connectors **(see illustration)**.

14   Cover the air intake passages with a shop towel **(see illustration)**. Disconnect the upper radiator hose and heater hoses from the intake manifold fittings.

15   Disconnect the EGR valve vacuum hose and the EGR tube fitting at the EGR valve **(see illustration)**.

16   Label and disconnect the vacuum and emissions hoses and wire harness connectors attached to the intake manifold **(see illustration)**. On 2001 and later models, remove the eight bolts and the intake manifold spacer from the lower intake manifold, which is in the lower half of the plenum, then the lower intake bolts are accessible.

17   Loosen the intake manifold mounting bolts in 1/4-turn increments until they can be removed by hand **(see illustration)**. Not all bolts are easily noticed; there are 14 in all, six long ones and eight short ones. Keep track of which ones go where.

18   The intake manifold will probably be stuck to the cylinder heads and force may be required to break the gasket seal. A prybar can be positioned under the cast-in lug **(see illustration)** to pry up the front of the intake manifold, but make sure all bolts have been removed first! **Caution:** *Don't pry between the*

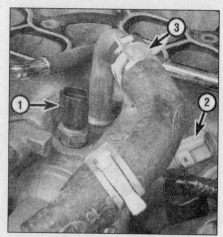

7.16 Label and disconnect the hoses and wiring

1   *Engine Coolant Temperature sensor*
2   *Coolant temperature sending unit*
3   *Coolant hose*

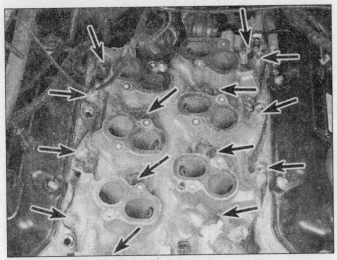

7.17 Remove the intake manifold mounting bolts (arrows)

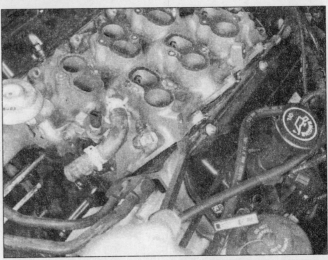

7.18 Pry against a casting protrusion to break the intake manifold loose

7.19 After covering the lifter valley, use a gasket scraper to remove all traces of sealant and old gasket material from the cylinder head and intake manifold mating surfaces

engine block and intake manifold or the cylinder heads and intake manifold or damage to the gasket sealing surfaces may occur, leading to vacuum and oil leaks.

19 Use a plastic gasket scraper to remove all traces of sealant and old gasket material **(see illustration)**, then clean the mating surfaces with lacquer thinner or acetone. If there's old sealant or oil on the mating surfaces when the manifold is installed, oil or vacuum leaks may develop. When working on the cylinder heads and block, cover the lifter valley with shop rags to keep debris out of the engine. Use a vacuum cleaner to remove any gasket material that falls into the intake ports in the cylinder heads. **Caution:** *The mating surfaces of the cylinder heads, engine block and manifold must be perfectly clean when the manifold is installed. Gasket removal solvents in aerosol cans are available at most auto parts stores and may be helpful when removing old gasket material that's stuck to the cylinder heads and manifold (since the manifold is made of aluminum, aggressive scraping can cause damage). Be sure to follow directions printed on the container.*
20 Use a tap of the correct size to chase the threads in the bolt holes, then use com-

pressed air (if available) to remove the debris from the holes. **Warning:** *Wear safety glasses or a face shield to protect your eyes when using compressed air!* Remove excessive carbon deposits and corrosion from the exhaust and coolant passages in the cylinder heads and manifold.
21 Make a final inspection of the gasket surfaces before installing the manifold.
22 Apply a 1/8-inch wide bead of RTV sealant to the front and rear of the block surface and install the rubber front and rear manifold seals **(see illustration)**. **Note:** *This sealant sets up in 15 minutes. Do not take longer to install and tighten the manifold once the sealant is applied, or leaks may occur.*
23 Apply a small dab of RTV at the four corners where the side gaskets will fit against the end seals. Position the side gaskets on the cylinder heads, over the alignment studs. The upper side of each gasket will have a TOP or THIS SIDE UP label stamped into it to ensure correct installation **(see illustration)**.
24 Make sure all intake port openings, cool-

7.22 Install the rubber end seals over a thin bead of RTV sealant, then apply a thin bead on top (arrow)

7.23 Apply a dab of RTV sealant to the corners where the engine block, cylinder heads and intake manifold converge, then position the side gaskets in place and apply an additional bead of RTV sealant where the end seals and intake manifold gaskets meet (arrow)

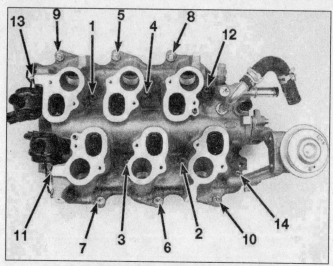

7.26 Intake manifold bolt tightening sequence

8.5 From below, remove the two exhaust
Y-pipe-to-manifold nuts (arrows)

8.7 Remove the nut (arrow) and pull the oil dipstick tube out

8.8 Remove the exhaust manifold bolts and studs
(left side shown, right side similar)

ant passage holes and bolt holes are aligned correctly.

25   Carefully set the manifold in place while the sealant is still wet. **Caution:** *Don't disturb the gaskets. Make sure the end seals haven't been disturbed.*

26   Lightly oil the manifold bolts, install them and tighten to the torque listed in this Chapter's Specifications, following the recommended sequence **(see illustration)**. Work up to the final torque in three steps. Reinstall the manifold spacer with a new gasket, then install the upper manifold with its new gasket.

27   The remaining installation steps are the reverse of removal. Start the engine and check carefully for oil and coolant leaks at the intake manifold joints.

8   Exhaust manifolds - removal and installation

Removal
Refer to illustrations 8.5, 8.7 and 8.8
1   Disconnect the negative battery cable

from the battery and remove the engine cover.

2   Raise the vehicle and support it securely on jackstands.

3   Disconnect the oxygen sensor electrical connector (see Chapter 6).

4   Working under the vehicle, apply penetrating oil to the exhaust Y-pipe-to-manifold studs and nuts (they're usually rusty).

5   Remove the nuts holding the exhaust Y-pipe to the exhaust manifolds **(see illustration)**. In extreme cases you may have to heat them with a propane or acetylene torch in order to loosen them.

Right (passenger's side) manifold
6   Disconnect the right-hand oxygen sensor, then disconnect the EGR tube from the manifold (see Chapter 6) and remove the exhaust Y-pipe bolts (see Chapter 4).

Left (driver's side) manifold
7   Remove the nut holding the oil dipstick tube support at the front of the manifold, then pull the dipstick tube up and out of the oil pan **(see illustration)**. Disconnect the left-hand

oxygen sensor (see Chapter 6), then remove the exhaust Y-pipe bolts (see Chapter 4).

Both manifolds
8   Remove the mounting bolts and separate the exhaust manifold(s) from the cylinder head **(see illustration)**. Note the locations of the bolts and studs, and remove the old gaskets.

Installation
9   Check the exhaust manifold for cracks and make sure the bolt threads are clean and undamaged. The exhaust manifold and cylinder head mating surfaces must be clean before the manifolds are reinstalled - use a gasket scraper to remove all carbon deposits and old gasket material. **Note:** *If the exhaust manifold is being replaced with a new one, remove the oxygen sensor. Clean the threads of the oxygen sensor with a wire brush and coat the threads with high-temperature antiseize compound before transferring the sensor to the new exhaust manifold.*

10   Position the exhaust manifold and new gasket on the cylinder head and install the

9.8 Remove the bolts and nuts (arrows) until the compressor and power steering pump steel bracket can be moved aside, away from the LH cylinder head

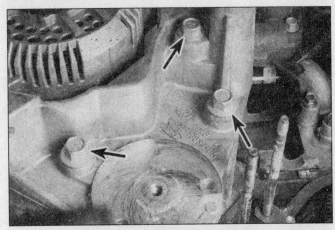

9.9 Remove the bolts/nuts (arrows) holding the compressor/ alternator bracket to the RH head idler pulley (shown removed)

mounting bolts and studs. **Note:** *Exhaust manifold warpage is possible on some V6 engines. If the manifold is warped slightly, install the pilot bolts first. Sometimes it's necessary to elongate (with a round file) some holes in the exhaust manifolds to start the bolts - but never file out the pilot bolt holes!*

11 When tightening the mounting bolts, tighten the center pair first, the front pair, then the rear pair, and be sure to use a torque wrench. Tighten the bolts in three equal steps until the torque listed in this Chapter's Specifications is reached.

12 The remaining installation steps are the reverse of removal.

13 Start the engine and check for exhaust leaks.

9 Cylinder heads - removal and installation

Caution: *The engine must be completely cool when the cylinder heads are removed. Failure to allow the engine to cool off could result in cylinder head warpage.*

Removal

1 Disconnect the cable from the negative battery terminal. Refer to Chapter 1 and drain the cooling system, including removing the engine block drain plugs.

2 Remove the valve covers (see Section 4).

3 Remove the pushrods and rocker arms (see Section 5).

4 Remove the upper intake manifold and the lower intake manifold (see Section 7).

5 Unbolt the exhaust manifold (see Section 8) for the head(s) being removed.

Left (driver's side) cylinder head

Refer to illustration 9.8

6 Unbolt the power steering reservoir and tie it aside in an upright position. Leave the hoses connected (see Chapter 10).

7 Remove the drivebelts (see Chapter 1).

8 Remove the air conditioning compressor/

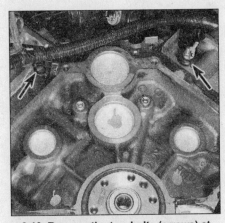

9.10 Remove the two bolts (arrows) at the back of the heads holding the wiring harness (transmission removed for clarity)

power steering pump bracket from the head and position the assembly out of the way (see Chapter 3). DO NOT disconnect the hoses! **(see illustration)**.

Right cylinder head

Refer to illustration 9.9

9 On 2001 and later models, remove the ignition coil pack and the drivebelt idler pulley. Disconnect the alternator wiring (see Chapter 5). Unbolt the alternator bracket **(see illustration)**. **Note:** *The bracket can be left in place, with just the upper bolt in place, loose enough to allow the steel bracket to be swung out of the way. For removal of the aluminum compressor/alternator mount, remove all the bolts/studs.*

Both cylinder heads

Refer to illustrations 9.10 and 9.11

10 Loosen the cylinder head bolts in 1/4-turn increments until they can be removed by hand. Work from bolt-to-bolt in a pattern that's the reverse of the tightening sequence. **Note:** *Head bolts should not be reused. Remove the bolts and discard them -* **new bolts must be used** *when installing the cylinder head(s).*

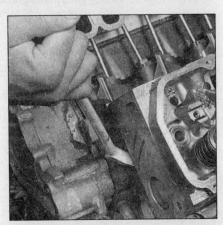

9.11 Using a prybar, carefully lever it against a casting protrusion to lift the cylinder head and break the gasket seal

Note: *At the back of the cylinder heads, near the firewall, remove the bolts holding the wiring harness to each head* **(see illustration)**.

11 Lift the cylinder head(s) off the engine. If resistance is felt, DO NOT pry between the cylinder head and engine block as damage to the mating surfaces will result. To dislodge the cylinder head, place a wood block against the end of it and strike the wood block with a hammer or place a prybar against a casting protrusion **(see illustration)**. Store the cylinder heads on blocks of wood to prevent damage to the gasket sealing surfaces. **Caution:** *Do not slide the heads across the floor or workbench, the aluminum is easily gouged.*

12 Cylinder head disassembly and inspection procedures are covered in detail in Chapter 2, Part E.

Installation

Refer to illustrations 9.14, 9.16 and 9.19

13 The mating surfaces of the cylinder heads and engine block must be perfectly clean when the cylinder heads are installed. Use a gasket scraper to remove all traces of carbon and old gasket material, then clean the mating surfaces with lacquer thinner or

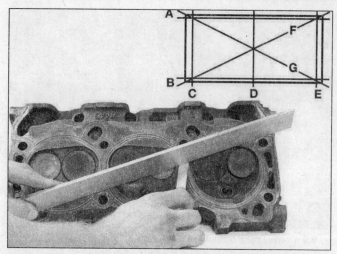

9.14 Check the cylinder head and block surfaces for flatness with a straightedge - if a feeler gauge in excess of the Specification fits under it, have the head machined

9.16 Locating dowels (arrows) are used to position the gaskets on the engine block - make sure the mark (circled) is correctly oriented

acetone. If there's oil on the mating surfaces when the cylinder heads are installed, the gaskets may not seal correctly and leaks may develop. When working on the engine block, cover the lifter valley with shop rags to keep debris out of the engine. Use a vacuum cleaner to remove any debris that falls into the valley or intake ports.

14   Check the engine block and cylinder head mating surfaces for nicks, deep scratches and other damage. If damage is slight, it can be removed with a file - if it's excessive, machining may be the only alternative. Do not use a rotary abrasive tool or wire brush on the aluminum cylinder heads. Use a straightedge and feeler gauges to check for warpage **(see illustration)**. If the warpage is beyond Specifications, have the head machined at an automotive machine shop.

15   Use a tap of the correct size to chase the threads in the cylinder head bolt holes. Dirt, corrosion, sealant and damaged threads will affect torque readings.

16   Position the new gasket(s) over the dowel pins in the engine block **(see illustration)**. Make sure it's facing the right way.

17   Carefully position the cylinder head(s) on the engine block without disturbing the gasket(s).

18   Before installing the new cylinder head bolts, lightly oil the threads.

19   Install the bolts (long bolts inside, short bolts outside row) and tighten them finger tight. Follow the recommended sequence and tighten the bolts, in the recommended steps, to the torque listed in this Chapter's Specifications **(see illustration)**. **Caution:** *When following the torque sequence for the V6 engine, at Step 4, do not loosen all the bolts at the same time or the gasket will not seal properly. Loosen the first bolt in the sequence, tighten it to the final torque (see Steps 5 and 6) then go on to the next bolt in sequence, loosening and tightening the bolts until the sequence is completed.*

20   The remaining installation steps are the reverse of removal.

21   Change the engine oil and filter (Chap-

ter 1), then start the engine and check carefully for oil and coolant leaks.

10   Timing chain cover - removal and installation

Removal

Refer to illustrations 10.3, 10.7, 10.8, 10.9a and 10.9b

1   Refer to Chapter 1 and drain the cooling system. Refer to Chapter 3 and remove the fan, fan shroud and water pump. Disconnect the radiator and heater hoses.

2   Drain the engine oil and remove the oil filter (Chapter 1).

3   Remove the crankshaft pulley and vibration damper (see Section 16). Loosen the bolt on the belt idler and swing it aside **(see illustration)**. It isn't necessary to remove the idler.

4   Unbolt and remove all accessory brackets attached to the timing chain cover. When unbolting the power steering pump (see Sec-

9.19 Cylinder head bolt tightening sequence

10.3 Loosen the bolt on the idler assembly and swing the idler out of the way of the cover

10.7 Remove this Allen bolt (arrow) from the bottom left of the front cover (oil filter and pump shown removed)

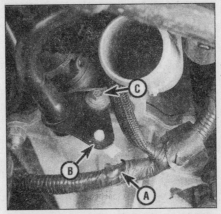

10.8 Pry the wiring harness clip (A) out of the heater tube mount (B), then remove the bolt (C) and pull the tube out

10.9a Gently tap the timing chain cover loose with a soft-face hammer

tion 9), tie it aside with the hoses still connected. On air-conditioned models, remove the compressor/power steering pump assembly and bracket, (see Section 9).

5   Position the number one piston at TDC on the compression stroke (Section 3), then disconnect the electrical connector at the camshaft position sensor and remove the camshaft position sensor, (see Chapter 6). Also disconnect the knock sensor and crankshaft position sensor electrical connectors (see Chapter 6).

6   Remove the front oil pan bolts (see Section 14).

7   Remove the socket-head bolt (**see illustration**).

8   Disconnect the two heater hoses, then unbolt the heater outlet tube and pull it out (**see illustration**). **Note:** *Pry the wiring harness clip out of the hole in the heater tube bracket.*

9   Remove the bolts and separate the timing chain cover from the engine block. If it's stuck, tap it gently with a soft-face hammer (**see illustrations**). *Caution: DO NOT use excessive force or you may crack the cover. If the cover is difficult to remove, double*

check to make sure all of the bolts have been removed.

Installation

Refer to illustrations 10.10, 10.12, 10.16 and 10.18

10   Use a gasket scraper to remove all traces of old gasket material and sealant from the cover, oil pan and engine block, then clean them with lacquer thinner or acetone (**see illustration**).

11   The oil pump is mounted in the timing chain cover and driven by the intermediate shaft, which is driven by the camshaft position sensor. See Section 15 for oil pump information.

12   Inspect the gear and intermediate shaft inside the cover (**see illustration**).

13   While the cover is off the engine, it's a good idea to install a new crankshaft front seal (see Section 16).

14   Lubricate the front crankshaft oil seal lip with engine oil.

15   Apply a small bead or RTV sealant along the oil pan-to-block joints.

16   Install the timing chain cover gasket on the block and press it into place. Then again

10.9b Timing chain cover bolt and stud locations (arrows)

apply a small bead of RTV sealant to the block-to-pan joints and along the front edge of the oil pan (**see illustration**).

17   Slide the timing chain cover onto the engine. The dowel pins will position it correctly. Don't damage the seal and make sure the gasket remains in place.

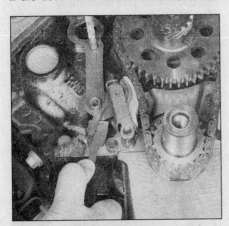

10.10 Scrape the old gasket and sealant from the block and cover, then clean the surfaces thoroughly

10.12 While the cover is off, inspect the camshaft position sensor driven gear (A) and the shaft (B)

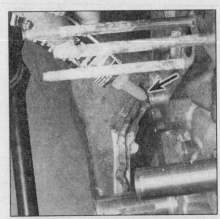

10.16 With the new cover gasket on the engine, apply a small bead of RTV sealant along the pan-to-cover flange, and a small bead on each side (arrow) where the pan, cover and block meet

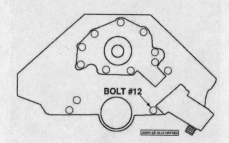

10.18 Location of the timing chain cover bolt number 12 on 2000 and later models (see the specifications at the front of this Chapter for the various bolt torque values)

11.4 Install a dial indicator to measure timing chain deflection - use a short length of vacuum hose to hold the plunger on the pushrod (rocker arm removed), or set the indicator on the pushrod end of the rocker arm

11.14a Align the timing marks on the crankshaft and camshaft sprockets (arrows) before removing the sprockets from the shafts

18   Install the bolts finger tight. Tighten them to the torque listed in this Chapter's Specifications **(see illustration)** only after the water pump has been installed (some of the water pump bolts also hold the timing chain cover in place). **Note:** *When installing the water pump, be sure to coat the threads of the water pump bolt with sealant* (see Chapter 3).
19   Install the oil pan bolts (Section 14).
20   Install the remaining parts in the reverse order of removal.
21   Add engine oil and coolant (Chapter 1).
22   Run the engine and check for leaks.

11   Timing chain and sprockets - inspection, removal and installation

Inspection

Refer to illustration 11.4
1   Disconnect the negative battery cable from the battery.
2   Refer to Section 3 and position the number one piston several degrees before TDC on the compression stroke.
3   Remove the right valve cover (Section 4).
4   Attach a dial indicator to the cylinder

head with the plunger in-line with and resting on the pushrod side of the rocker arm **(see illustration)**.
5   Remove the timing chain cover (see Section 10).
6   Temporarily remove the timing chain and sprockets to remove the chain tensioner (see below).
7   Temporarily install the timing chain and sprockets without the tensioner and slip the timing chain cover and vibration damper in place to provide timing marks.
8   Turn the crankshaft clockwise until the number one piston is at TDC (Section 3). This will take up the slack on the right side of the chain.
9   Zero the dial indicator.
10   Slowly turn the crankshaft counterclockwise until the slightest movement is seen on the dial indicator. Stop and note how far the number one piston has moved away from TDC by looking at the ignition timing marks.
11   If the mark has moved more than 6 degrees, install a new timing chain and sprockets.

Removal

Refer to illustrations 11.14a, 11.14b, 11.15, 11.16 and 11.17
12   Position the number one piston at TDC on the compression stroke (Section 3).
13   Remove the timing chain cover (Section 10). Try to avoid turning the crankshaft during vibration damper removal.
14   Make sure the crankshaft, camshaft and balance shaft sprocket timing marks are aligned **(see illustrations)**. If they aren't, install the vibration damper bolt and use it to turn the crankshaft clockwise until all marks are aligned. **Note:** *When all marks are aligned, the crankshaft keyway is straight up, the camshaft keyway is straight down, and the balance shaft keyway is straight up.*
15   Remove the camshaft sprocket mounting bolt and camshaft position sensor drive gear **(see illustration)**. **Caution:** *Do not allow the crankshaft to be turned from TDC while removing the camshaft sprocket bolt.*
16   Compress the timing chain tensioner with a screwdriver and insert a drill, punch or Allen wrench as a retaining pin to hold it in the retracted position **(see illustration)**.
17   Pull the camshaft sprocket/chain off the

11.14b When the marks are aligned for TDC, the balance shaft keyway (arrow) will point straight up

11.15 Remove the camshaft sprocket bolt without turning the engine

11.16 Compress the timing chain tensioner with a screwdriver and insert a pin punch as a retaining pin

11.17 Remove the camshaft sprocket and chain from the camshaft

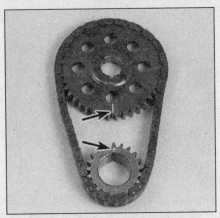

11.20 Assemble the chain and both sprockets so the marks (arrows) are aligned, then slip the assembly onto the crankshaft and camshaft

11.22 Align the keyway (arrow) on the camshaft position sensor drive gear with the Woodruff key on the camshaft

camshaft **(see illustration)**. Note: *The crankshaft sprocket will slide off with the chain and camshaft sprocket.*

18   If you intend to remove the tensioner assembly, remove the two bolts holding it to the block.

Installation

Refer to illustrations 11.20 and 11.22

19   Turn the crankshaft until the key is facing up (12 o'clock position).
20   Drape the chain over the camshaft sprocket and turn the sprocket until the timing mark faces down (6 o'clock position). Position the chain over the camshaft and crankshaft sprockets with their timing marks aligned, then slip both sprockets onto the camshaft and crankshaft **(see illustration)**.
21   When correctly installed, a straight line should pass through the center of the balance shaft gear, the camshaft, the camshaft timing mark (in the 6 o'clock position), the crankshaft timing mark (in the 12 o'clock position) and the center of the crankshaft **(see illustrations 11.14a and 11.14b)**. DO NOT proceed until the valve timing is correct!
22   Install the camshaft position sensor drive gear **(see illustration)**.
23   Apply a non-hardening thread locking compound to the threads and install the camshaft sprocket bolt. Tighten the bolt to the torque listed in this Chapter's Specifications.
24   Remove the retaining pin from the timing chain tensioner. Reinstall the remaining parts in the reverse order of removal.

12   Valve lifters - removal, inspection and installation

Removal

Refer to illustrations 12.3a, 12.3b, 12.4a and 12.4b

1   Remove the upper intake plenum (Chapter 4) and lower intake manifold (Section 7).
2   Remove the rocker arms and pushrods (Section 5).
3   Before removing the lifters, arrange to store them in a clearly labeled box to ensure

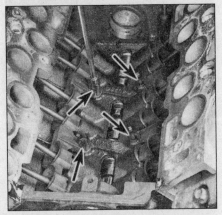

12.3a Remove the lifter guide retainer bolts (arrows)

that they're reinstalled in their original locations. Remove the lifter guide plates **(see illustrations)**.
4   There are several ways to extract the lifters from the bores. Special tools designed to grip and remove lifters are manufactured by many tool companies and are widely available **(see illustration)**, but may not be needed in every case. On newer engines without a

12.4a If the lifters are difficult to remove, you may have to remove them with a special puller . . .

12.3b Be sure to store the lifters in an organized manner to make sure they're reinstalled in their original locations

lot of varnish buildup, the lifters can often be removed with a small magnet **(see illustration)** or even with your fingers. A machinist's scribe with a bent end can be used to pull the lifters out by positioning the point under the retainer ring in the top of each lifter. On later engines, the roller lifters are retained in position by a tappet guide on each side (one guide

12.4b . . . or you may be able to remove the lifters with a magnet

for each bank of the engine). When the guides are removed, the lifters are easy to grasp and remove. **Caution:** *Don't use pliers to remove the lifters unless you intend to replace them with new ones (along with the camshaft). The pliers may damage the precision machined and hardened lifters, rendering them useless.* On engines with a lot of sludge and varnish, work the lifters up and down, using carburetor cleaner spray to loosen the deposits.

Inspection

Refer to illustrations 12.6 and 12.7

5   Clean the lifters with solvent and dry them thoroughly without mixing them up.

6   Check each lifter wall and pushrod seat for scuffing, score marks and uneven wear. If the lifter walls are damaged or worn (which isn't very likely), inspect the lifter bores in the engine block as well. If the pushrod seats **(see illustration)** are worn, check the pushrod ends.

7   Check the roller carefully for wear and damage and make sure they turn freely without excessive play **(see illustration)**.

8   If any lifters are found to be defective, they can be replaced with new ones without having to replace the camshaft (unlike conventional, non-roller lifters), but if the camshaft is being replaced due to high mileage, all the lifters should be replaced as well.

Installation

9   The original lifters, if they're being reinstalled, must be returned to their original locations. Coat them with moly-base grease or engine assembly lube.

10   Install the lifters in the bores.

11   Install the guide plates and guide retainer.

12   Install the pushrods and rocker arms.

13   Install the intake manifold and valve covers.

14   Change the engine oil and filter (see Chapter 1).

---

13   Camshaft, balance shaft and bearings - removal, inspection and installation

Camshaft lobe lift check

1   In order to determine the extent of cam lobe wear, the lobe lift should be checked prior to camshaft removal. Refer to Section 4 and remove the valve covers. The rocker arms must also be removed (Section 5), but leave the pushrods in place.

2   Position the number one piston at TDC on the compression stroke (see Section 3).

3   Beginning with the number one cylinder, mount a dial indicator on the engine and position the plunger in-line with and resting on the first pushrod **(see illustration 8.4 in Chapter 2, Part A)**.

4   Zero the dial indicator, then very slowly turn the crankshaft in the normal direction of rotation until the indicator needle stops and

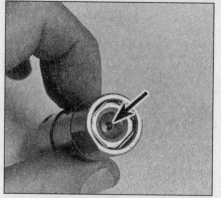

12.6 Inspect the pushrod seat (arrow) in the top of each lifter for wear

13.11 Slide the balance shaft drive gear (arrow) from the camshaft

begins to move in the opposite direction. The point at which it stops indicates maximum cam lobe lift.

5   Record this figure for future reference, then reposition the piston at TDC on the compression stroke.

6   Move the dial indicator to the remaining number one cylinder pushrod and repeat the check. Be sure to record the results for each valve.

7   Repeat the check for the remaining valves. Since each piston must be at TDC on the compression stroke for this procedure, work from cylinder-to-cylinder following the firing order sequence (see Section 3).

8   After the check is complete, compare the results to the Specifications. If camshaft lobe lift is less than specified, cam lobe wear has occurred and a new camshaft should be installed.

Removal

Refer to illustrations 13.11, 13.12 and 13.13

9   Refer to the appropriate Sections and remove the pushrods, the valve lifters and the timing chain and camshaft sprocket. The radiator should be removed also (Chapter 3). You also may have to remove the air conditioning condenser and the grille as well, but wait and see if the camshaft can be pulled out of the engine.

12.7 The roller must turn freely - check for wear and excessive play as well

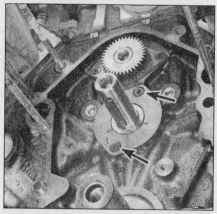

13.12 T-30 Torx screws (arrows) retain the camshaft thrust plate - remove the thrust plate and spacer (at center of plate)

10   Check the camshaft end play with a dial indicator aligned with the front of the camshaft. Insert the camshaft sprocket bolt and use it to pull the camshaft fore and aft. If the play is greater than specified, replace the thrust plate with a new one when the camshaft is reinstalled.

11   Slide the larger balance shaft drive gear from the end of the camshaft **(see illustration)**.

12   Remove the camshaft thrust plate bolts. A T-30 Torx bit is required. Remove the thrust

13.13 Carefully guide the camshaft out of the engine block to avoid nicking the bearings with the lobes

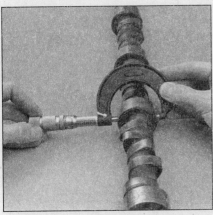

13.15 The camshaft bearing journal diameters are checked to pinpoint excessive wear and out-of-round conditions

13.17 Remove the balance shaft thrust plate bolts (arrows)

13.18 Guide the balance shaft out with one hand supporting the shaft inside the engine's valley

plate and the spacer ring **(see illustration)**.
13 Carefully pull the camshaft out. Support the cam so the lobes don't nick or gouge the bearings as it's withdrawn **(see illustration)**.

Inspection

Refer to illustration 13.15
14 After the camshaft has been removed, clean it with solvent and dry it, then inspect the bearing journals for uneven wear, pitting and evidence of seizure. If the journals are damaged, the bearing inserts in the engine block are probably damaged as well. Both the camshaft and bearings will have to be replaced. Replacement of the camshaft bearings requires special tools and techniques which place it beyond the scope of the home mechanic. The engine block will have to be removed from the vehicle and taken to an automotive machine shop for this procedure.
15 Measure the bearing journals with a micrometer **(see illustration)** to determine whether they are excessively worn or out-of-round.
16 Inspect the camshaft lobes for heat discoloration, score marks, chipped areas, pitting and uneven wear. If the lobes are in good condition and if the lobe lift measurements are as specified, you can reuse the camshaft.

Balance shaft

Refer to illustrations 13.17 and 13.18
17 Remove the bolts holding the balance shaft thrust plate **(see illustration)**.
18 Carefully guide the balance shaft out of the block **(see illustration)**. **Note:** *There is very little to go wrong with the balance shaft or its bearings, which are pressed into the front and rear of the block like camshaft bearings. If abnormal wear is noticed on either bearings or the front and rear balance shaft journals, the bearings must be replaced at an automotive machine shop, and a new balance shaft installed. The balance shaft gear can be replaced without replacing the balance shaft, but requires a machine shop press to replace it or the thrust plate on the balance shaft.*

19 When reinstalling the balance shaft, lubricate the front and rear journals and the back of the thrust plate with camshaft installation or engine assembly lube, and line the gear's keyway at the 12 o'clock position. Torque the thrust plate bolts to Specifications.

Installation

Refer to illustrations 13.20 and 13.21
20 Lubricate the camshaft bearing journals and cam lobes with camshaft installation lube **(see illustration)**.
21 Slide the camshaft into the engine. Support the cam near the engine block and be careful not to scrape or nick the bearings. Align the camshaft keyway straight down (6 o'clock position) and the balance shaft drive gear (on the camshaft) should align perfectly with the smaller gear on the balance shaft. Align their marks **(see illustration)**.
22 Apply moly-base grease or engine assembly lube to both sides of the thrust plate, then position it on the engine block with the oil grooves in (against the engine block). Install the bolts and tighten them to the torque listed in this Chapter's Specifications.
23 Refer to the appropriate Sections and

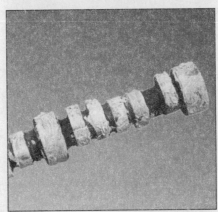

13.20 Apply camshaft installation lube to the camshaft lobes and journals prior to installation

install the lifters, pushrods, rocker arms, timing chain/sprocket, timing chain cover and valve covers.
24 The remaining installation steps are the reverse of removal.
25 Before starting and running the engine, change the oil and install a new oil filter (see Chapter 1).

---

14 Oil pan - removal and installation

Removal

Refer to illustrations 14.10 and 14.11
1 If the vehicle is equipped with air suspension, turn the switch OFF before raising the vehicle.
2 Disconnect the cable from the negative battery terminal.
3 Remove the oil dipstick.
4 Refer to Chapter 1 and drain the engine oil and remove the oil filter.
5 Remove the oil cooler, if equipped, from the engine block.
6 Raise the vehicle and place it securely on jackstands.

13.21 Align the marks (arrows) on the balance shaft drive gear on the camshaft (A) and the balance shaft driven gear (B) above it

14.10 Remove the two oil pan-to-transmission bolts (arrows)

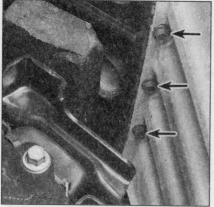

14.11 Remove the pan-to-engine bolts (arrows indicate three) - note block of wood between engine and mount

14.15 Press the new rear rubber seal onto the rear main cap and place a dab of RTV on each side (arrows)

7   Remove the engine mount through-bolts (see Section 18).

8   Raise the engine about two inches with either an overhead support fixture or a crane attached to the lifting eyes on the top of the engine. **Caution:** *Do not use a jack under the oil pan itself, it is cast aluminum and can be damaged easily.* **Note:** *On 2001 and later models, the engine must be raised 13 inches to allow oil pan removal. This requires that the upper intake manifold and manifold spacer be removed first to provide clearance (see Section 7).*

9   Disconnect the electrical connector from the low oil level sensor located in the oil pan if so equipped.

10   Remove the oil pan-to-transmission bolts **(see illustration)**.

11   Remove the oil pan-to-engine bolts **(see illustration)**.

12   Remove the oil pan. It may be necessary to break the seal of the pan with a thin putty knife, but do not pry between the pan and block or the pan's sealing edge could be gouged, leading to oil leaks later. Empty any residual oil from the oil pan, and clean it out with solvent.

Installation

Refer to illustration 14.15

13   Use a gasket scraper or putty knife to remove all traces of old gasket material and sealant from the pan and engine block. Remove the rubber seals at the rear main cap and clean any sealant residue with lacquer thinner.

14   Clean the mating surfaces with lacquer thinner or acetone. Make sure the bolt holes in the engine block are clean.

15   Use a dab of gasket adhesive to hold the rear rubber seals in the rear main cap, using a small screwdriver to force the new seal tightly into the groove **(see illustration)**. Stick the side gaskets in place on the engine block with a few dabs of adhesive and tuck the front and rear tabs into the slots in the ends of the front and rear rubber seals. Apply a dab of RTV sealant to the four corners where the side gaskets meet the end seals.

16   Make two alignment dowels by cutting off

the heads of two long bolts that fit the holes in the block. Slot the ends of the "studs" with a hacksaw and install one at the front of the block and one at the rear.

17   Apply a bead of RTV sealant on the block and front cover, and a small dab at each corner of the rubber rear seal. **Caution:** *The oil pan must be installed within 15 minutes or the sealant will "kick off" and must be cleaned off and new sealer applied.*

18   Carefully position the pan against the engine block and install the bolts finger tight. When all of the pan-to-engine bolts are started, tighten the bolts to the torque listed in this Chapter's Specifications in two steps, removing the two alignment studs and replacing them with pan bolts. Start at the rear of the pan and work out toward the front. After the pan-to-engine bolts are tightened, install and tighten the pan-to-transmission bolts.

19   The remaining steps are the reverse of removal. **Caution:** *Don't forget to refill the engine with oil and install a new oil filter before starting it* (see Chapter 1).

20   Start the engine and check carefully for oil leaks at the oil pan. Drive the vehicle and check again.

15 Oil pump - removal and installation

Refer to illustrations 15.3, 15.11, 15.12a, 15.12b and 15.13

Note: *If there is insufficient oil pressure, see Chapter 2, Part E for oil pressure testing.*

1   The oil pump is mounted externally on the timing chain cover.

2   Detach the oil filter (Chapter 1).

3   Detach the cover and O-ring, then remove the gears from the cavity in the timing chain cover **(see illustration)**. Discard the O-ring.

4   Clean and inspect the oil pump cavity. If the oil pump gear pocket in the timing chain cover is damaged or worn, replace the timing chain cover.

15.3 After the filter is removed, the oil pump cover bolts are accessible (arrows)

5   Remove all traces of gasket material from the oil pump cover, then check it for warpage with a straightedge and feeler gauges. If it's warped more than 0.0016-inch, replace it with a new one.

6   To remove the pressure relief valve, first detach the timing chain cover from the engine (Section 10). Drill a hole in the plug **(see illustration 10.14)**, then pry it out or remove it with a slide hammer and screw adapter. Remove the spring and valve from the bore.

7   Remove all metal chips from the bore and the valve, then check them carefully for wear, score marks and galling. If the bore is worn or damaged, a new timing chain cover will be required. The valve should fit in the bore with no noticeable side play or binding.

8   If the spring appears to be fatigued or collapsed, replace it with a new one.

9   Apply clean engine oil to the valve and install it in the bore, small end first. Insert the spring, then install a new plug. Carefully tap it in until it's 0.010-inch below the machined surface of the cover.

10   Intermediate shaft removal and installation is covered in Section 10.

11   The oil pump pickup tube is inside the oil pan. For access, remove the oil pan (see Section 14). Remove the pick-up tube nut and the

15.11 To detach the oil pickup tube, remove the nut and bolts (arrows)

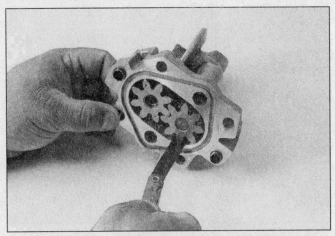

15.12a Measure the clearance between the rotor tips and the pump housing and compare to the Specifications

15.12b Put a straightedge across the pump body and measure the clearance above the gears

15.13 Install a new O-ring (arrow) lubricated with clean oil before reinstalling the oil pump

16.4a Mark the pulley and vibration damper (marks A) before removing the four bolts (arrows) - the large vibration damper bolt in the center is usually very tight, so use a six-point socket and a breaker bar to loosen it

two mounting bolts (see illustration). When reinstalling it, replace the gasket at the front.

12   Using feeler gauges, measure the clearance between the rotors and the pump housing, and the clearance over the rotors (see illustrations).

13   Installation is the reverse of removal. **Caution:** *Fill the oil pump with clean engine oil before installation.* Install a new cover O-ring and tighten the bolts to the torque listed in this Chapter's Specifications in a criss-cross pattern (see illustration). Use a new pick-up tube gasket and tighten the mounting bolts securely.

16   Crankshaft oil seals - replacement

Front seal - timing chain cover in place

Refer to illustrations 16.4a, 16.4b, 16.5, 16.6, 16.8 and 16.10

1   Disconnect the cable from the negative battery terminal.

2   Remove the electric cooling fan/shroud assembly (see Chapter 3).

3   Remove the drivebelts (see Chapter 1).

4   Mark the crankshaft pulley and vibration damper so they can be reassembled in the same relative position. This is important, since the damper and pulley are initially balanced as a unit. Unbolt and remove the pulley (see illustrations).

5   Remove the bolt from the front of the crankshaft, then use a puller to detach the vibration damper (see illustration). **Caution:** *Don't use a puller with jaws that grip the outer edge of the damper. The puller must be the*

16.4b While the damper is off, inspect the crankshaft position sensor ring; if it is damaged, remove the four bolts (arrows) and replace it

16.5 Use the recommended puller to remove the vibration damper - if a puller that applies force to the outer edge is used, the damper will be damaged!

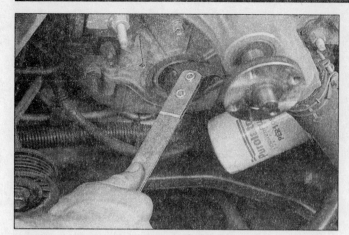

16.6 Use a screwdriver or seal removal tool (shown) to work the seal out of the timing chain cover - be very careful not to damage the cover or nick the crankshaft!

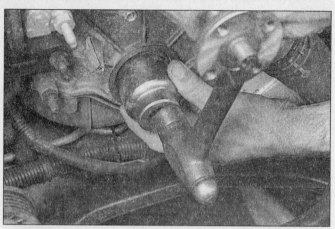

16.8 Clean the bore, then apply a small amount of oil to the outer edge of the new seal and drive it squarely into the opening with a large socket and a hammer - don't damage the seal in the process and make sure it's completely seated

type shown in the illustration that utilizes bolts to apply force to the damper hub only. Clean the crankshaft nose and the seal contact surface on the vibration damper with lacquer thinner or acetone. Leave the Woodruff key in place in the crankshaft keyway. **Note:** *The damper-to-crankshaft bolt is very tight. Have an assistant hold the driveplate from turning while removing the bolt, or hold the damper with a special strap wrench designed for this purpose.*

6   Carefully remove the seal from the cover with a screwdriver or seal removal tool **(see illustration)**. Be careful not to damage the cover or scratch the wall of the seal bore. If the engine has accumulated a lot of miles, apply penetrating oil to the seal-to-cover joint and allow it to soak in before attempting to remove the seal.

7   Check the seal bore and crankshaft, as well as the seal contact surface on the vibration damper for nicks and burrs. Position the new seal in the bore with the open end of the seal facing IN. A small amount of oil applied to the outer edge of the new seal will make installation easier.

8   Drive the seal into the bore with a large socket and hammer until it's completely seated **(see illustration)**. Select a socket that's the same outside diameter as the seal (a section of pipe can be used if a socket isn't available).

9   Apply moly-base grease or clean engine oil to the seal contact surface of the vibration damper and coat the keyway (groove) with a thin layer of RTV sealant.

10   Install the damper on the end of the crankshaft. The keyway in the damper bore must be aligned with the Woodruff key in the crankshaft nose. If the damper can't be seated by hand, tap it into place with a soft-face hammer **(see illustration)** or slip a large washer over the bolt, install the bolt and tighten it to press the damper into place. Remove the large washer, then install the bolt and tighten it to the torque listed in this Chapter's Specifications.

11   Install the remaining parts removed for access to the seal.

12   Start the engine and check for leaks at the seal-to-cover joint.

Front seal - timing chain cover removed

Refer to illustration 16.15

13   Use a punch or screwdriver and hammer to drive the seal out of the cover from the back side. Support the cover as close to the seal bore as possible. Be careful not to distort the cover or scratch the wall of the seal bore. If the engine has accumulated a lot of miles, apply penetrating oil to the seal-to-cover joint on each side and allow it to soak in before attempting to drive the seal out.

14   Clean the bore to remove any old seal material and corrosion. Support the cover on blocks of wood and position the new seal in the bore with the open end of the seal facing IN. A small amount of oil applied to the outer edge of the new seal will make installation easier - don't overdo it!

15   Drive the seal into the bore with a large socket and hammer until it's completely seated **(see illustration)**. Select a socket that's the same outside diameter as the seal (a section of pipe can be used if a socket isn't available).

16.10 A soft-face hammer can be used to tap the vibration damper onto the crankshaft - don't use a steel hammer!

16.15 The new seal can also be driven in carefully with the cover off the engine - be sure to support the cover from below with a wood block to prevent damage to the cover

16.17 If you're very careful not to damage the crankshaft or the seal bore, the rear seal can be pried out with a screwdriver - normally a special puller is used for this procedure

17.2 Make an alignment mark (arrow) on the driveplate and crankshaft

Rear main seal

Refer to illustration 16.17

16   Refer to Chapter 7 and remove the transmission, then detach the driveplate and the rear cover plate from the engine (Section 17).

17   The old seal can be removed by prying it out with a screwdriver (see illustration) or by making one or two small holes in the seal flange with a sharp pick, then using a screw-in type slide-hammer puller. Be sure to note how far the seal is recessed into the bore before removing it; the new seal will have to be recessed an equal amount. **Caution:** *Be very careful not to scratch or otherwise damage the crankshaft or the bore in the housing or oil leaks could develop!*

18   Clean the crankshaft and seal bore with lacquer thinner or acetone. Check the seal contact surface very carefully for scratches and nicks that could damage the new seal lip and cause oil leaks. If the crankshaft is damaged, the only alternative is a new or different crankshaft.

19   Make sure the bore is clean, then apply a thin coat of engine oil to the outer edge of the new seal. Apply multi-purpose grease to the seal lips. The seal must be pressed squarely into the bore, a special seal installation tool is highly recommended. Hammering it into place is not recommended. If you don't have access to the special tool, you may be able to tap the seal in with a large section of pipe and a hammer. If you must use this method, be very careful not to damage the seal or crankshaft! And work the seal lip carefully over the end of the crankshaft with a blunt tool such as the rounded end of a socket extension.

20   Reinstall the engine rear cover plate, the driveplate and the transmission.

17   Driveplate - removal and installation

Refer to illustrations 17.2 and 17.3

1   Raise the vehicle and support it securely

17.3 Insert a prybar through a hole to keep the crankshaft from turning when loosening/tightening the bolts

on jackstands, then refer to Chapter 7 and remove the transmission. If it's leaking, now would be a very good time to replace the front pump seal/O-ring.

2   Look for factory paint marks that indicate driveplate-to-crankshaft alignment. If they aren't there, use a center-punch or paint to make alignment marks on the driveplate and crankshaft to ensure correct alignment during reinstallation (see illustration).

3   Remove the bolts that secure the drive-plate to the crankshaft (see illustration). If the crankshaft turns, wedge a screwdriver through the starter opening to jam the drive-plate.

4   Remove the driveplate from the crank-shaft. **Warning:** *The ring gear teeth may be sharp, so wear gloves to protect your hands.*

5   Clean and inspect the mating surfaces of the driveplate and the crankshaft. If the crank-shaft rear seal is leaking, replace it before reinstalling the driveplate.

6   Position the driveplate against the crank-shaft. Be sure to align the marks made during removal. Note that some engines have an alignment dowel or staggered bolt holes to ensure correct installation. Before installing the bolts, apply Teflon thread sealant to the threads.

7   Prevent the driveplate from turning as

you tighten the bolts to the torque listed in this Chapter's Specifications.

8   The remainder of installation is the reverse of the removal procedure.

18   Engine mounts - check and replacement

1   Engine mounts seldom require attention, but broken or deteriorated mounts should be replaced immediately or the added strain placed on the driveline components may cause damage or wear.

Check

2   During the check, the engine must be raised slightly to remove the weight from the mounts.

3   Raise the vehicle and support it securely on jackstands, then position a jack under the engine oil pan. Place a large wood block between the jack head and the oil pan, then carefully raise the engine just enough to take the weight off the mounts. **Warning:** *DO NOT place any part of your body under the engine when it's supported only by a jack!*

4   Check the mounts to see if the rubber is cracked, hardened or separated from the

18.9 Remove the engine mount through-bolts (A) - B indicates one of the mount-to-block bolts (left side shown here)

18.11 Remove the remaining bolts (arrows) holding the mount to the engine - front of left mount shown here

metal plates. Sometimes the rubber will split right down the center. Rubber preservative should be applied to the mounts to slow deterioration.

5   Check for relative movement between the mount plates and the engine or frame (use a large screwdriver or pry bar to attempt to move the mounts). If movement is noted, lower the engine and tighten the mount fasteners.

Replacement

Refer to illustrations 18.9 and 18.11

6   Disconnect the cable from the negative battery terminal.

7   Detach the air cleaner duct.
8   Support the engine from above, using an engine support fixture or overhead crane. Take a slight amount of weight off the engine.
9   Remove the engine mount through-bolts **(see illustration)**.
10   Raise the engine high enough to clear the brackets. Do not force the engine up too high. If it touches anything before the mounts are free, remove the part for clearance.
11   Unbolt the mount from the engine block and remove it from the vehicle **(see illustration)**. **Note:** *On vehicles equipped with self-locking nuts and bolts, replace them with new ones whenever they are disassembled.*

Prior to assembly, remove hardened residual adhesive from the engine block holes with an appropriate-size bottoming tap.

12   Attach the new mount to the engine block and install the bolts and stud/nuts in the appropriate locations. Tighten the fasteners securely.
13   Lower the engine into place. Install the through bolts and tighten them to Specifications.
14   Complete the installation by reinstalling all parts removed to gain access to the mounts.

Chapter 2 Part C
5.0L, 5.8L and 7.5L OHV V8 engines

Contents

Specifications

General

Displacement

5.0L	302 cubic inches
5.8L	351 cubic inches
7.5L	460 cubic inches

Cylinder numbering, front to rear

Right bank	1-2-3-4
Left bank	5-6-7-8

Firing order

1992 and 1993 5.0L and 7.5L engines	1-5-4-2-6-3-7-8
1994 through 1996 5.0L and all 5.8L engines	1-3-7-2-6-5-4-8

Camshaft lobe lift

5.0L and 5.8L engines

Intake

5.0L

1992 through 1995	0.2375 inch
1996	0.2637 inch

5.8L

1992 through 1995	0.2780 inch
1996	0.2637 inch

Exhaust

5.0L

1992 through 1995	0.2474 inch
1996	0.2801 inch

5.8L

1992 through 1995	0.2830 inch
1996	0.2801 inch
Maximum allowable lift loss	0.0050 inch

7.5L engine

Intake	0.2520 inch
Exhaust	0.2780 inch
Maximum allowable lift loss	0.0050 inch

Torque specifications

	Ft-lbs (unless otherwise indicated)
Camshaft sprocket bolt	40 to 45
Camshaft thrust plate screws	108 to 144 in-lbs
Timing cover bolts	15 to 21
Cylinder head bolts	
5.0L engine	
1992 through 1995	
Step 1	55 to 65
Step 2	65 to 72
1996	
Step 1	25 to 35
Step 2	45 to 55
Step 3	Turn an additional 90 degrees
5.8L engine	
Step 1	85
Step 2	95
Step 3	105 to 112
7.5L engine	
Step 1	70 to 80
Step 2	100 to 110
Step 3	130 to 140
Crankshaft vibration damper bolt	70 to 90
Driveplate bolts	75 to 85
Intake manifold (lower) bolts	
1992 through 1995	
3/8-inch bolts	22 to 30
5/16-inch bolts	19 to 25
1996	
5.0L and 5.8L engines	
Step 1	60 to 120 in-lbs
Step 2	23 to 25
7.5L engines	
Step 1	96 to 144 in-lbs
Step 2	12 to 22
Step 3	22 to 35
Intake manifold (upper) bolts	12 to 18
Exhaust manifold bolts	
5.0L and 5.8L engines	18 to 24
7.5L engine	24 to 30
Oil pick-up tube-to-oil pump bolts	12 to 18
Oil pick-up tube-to-main bearing cap bolt	22 to 32
Oil pump-to-block bolt	22 to 32
Oil pan bolts	
1/4-inch bolts	84 to 108 in-lbs
5/16-inch bolts	108 to 132 in-lbs
Crankshaft pulley-to-damper bolts	35 to 50
Rocker arm bolts	18 to 25
Valve cover bolts	
5.0L and 5.8L engines	132 to 168 in-lbs
7.5L engine	72 to 108 in-lbs

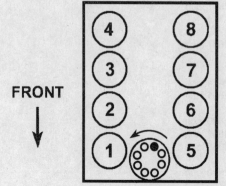

FRONT

Cylinder location and distributor rotation

Firing order

1994 through 1996 5.0L and all 5.8L: 1-3-7-2-6-5-4-8
1992 and 1993 5.0L and all 7.5L: 1-5-4-2-6-3-7-8

36094-2A-specs HAYNES

1   General information

Several V8s of various displacements are covered by this manual. All are gasoline fueled with overhead valves actuated by hydraulic lifters and have crankshafts supported by five main bearings.

'Family' engine groupings include the 5.0L (302 cubic inch) models, the 5.8L (351 cubic inch) and the 7.5L (460 cubic inch) model.

All of these engines are three-point mounted, with two side mounts at the front and one crossmember mount underneath the transmission. The engines can be removed from the vehicle with a normal amount of preparatory work when overhaul or other major operations are necessary.

2   Repair operations possible with the engine in the vehicle

Many major repair operations can be accomplished without removing the engine from the vehicle. Clean the engine compartment and the exterior of the engine with some type of pressure washer before any work is done. A clean engine will make the job easier and will help keep dirt out of the internal areas of the engine.

Components within the engine compartment can be accessed from the front of the vehicle by lifting the hood or from inside the passenger compartment by removing the engine cover (refer to Chapter 11 if necessary). Depending upon the extent of the repair, it may be necessary to use both methods.

If vacuum, exhaust, oil or coolant leaks develop, indicating a need for gasket or seal replacement, the repairs can generally be made with the engine in the vehicle. The intake and exhaust manifold gaskets, oil pan gasket and cylinder head gasket are all accessible with the engine in place.

Exterior engine components as well as some internal components can be checked and serviced with the engine in the vehicle. Refer to this Chapter's Table of Contents for these operations and components. In addition, the water pump (see Chapter 3), the starter motor, the alternator, the distributor (see Chapter 5) and the fuel injection system (see Chapter 4) can be removed for repair with the engine in place.

Some component checks such as camshaft lobe lift measurement, timing chain wear, and piston ring/cylinder head condition (compression check) can also be performed while the engine is installed.

Since the cylinder head can be removed without pulling the engine, valve component servicing can also be accomplished with the engine in the vehicle.

In extreme cases caused by a lack of necessary equipment, repair or replacement of piston rings, pistons, connecting rods and rod bearings is possible with the engine in the vehicle. However, this practice is not recommended because of the cleaning and preparation work that must be done to the components involved.

3   Top Dead Center (TDC) for number 1 piston - locating

Refer to illustration 3.1

Follow the procedure described in Chapter 2, Part A, but use the timing marks as shown in the accompanying illustration **(see illustration)**.

4   Valve covers - removal and installation

Refer to illustrations 4.8 and 4.10

Removal

1   Remove the air cleaner and intake duct assembly (see Chapter 4).

2   Remove the crankcase ventilation hoses

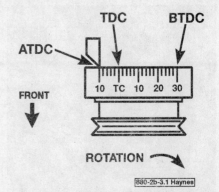

3.1 Details of the timing marks and stationary pointer

and lines where applicable (see Chapter 6).

3   Disconnect the spark plug wires. Mark them so they can be installed in their original locations.

4   If necessary, remove the air injection valves and hoses and position them out of the way (see Chapter 6).

5   On some models it is necessary to remove the air conditioning compressor for clearance (see Chapter 3). Unbolt the air conditioning compressor and position it aside. **Warning:** *The air conditioning system is under pressure. Don't disconnect the hoses.*

6   Remove the upper intake manifold (see Section 10) from the lower intake manifold.

7   Mark and detach any vacuum hoses, electrical connectors or wiring harnesses that would interfere with removal of the valve cover(s).

8   Remove the valve cover retaining bolts **(see illustration)**.

9   Remove the valve covers. If a cover sticks, knock it loose with a hammer and a block of wood. If it is still stuck, carefully pry the cover off, but be very careful not to distort the sealing surface of the cover.

10   Remove all old gasket material and sealant from the valve cover and cylinder head gasket surfaces **(see illustration)**.

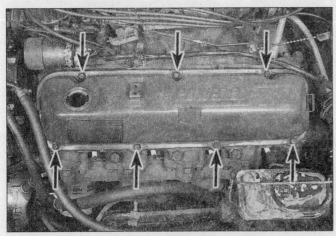

4.8 The valve cover is held in place with several bolts (arrows)

4.10 Being careful not to damage the mating surface of the head, carefully remove the valve cover gasket with a gasket scraper or putty knife

5.4 Loosen the nut or bolt (arrow) and pivot the rocker arm to the side to remove the pushrod

6.20 Correct alignment of the crankshaft and the camshaft sprocket timing marks (arrows)

6.22 Once the camshaft sprocket bolt has been removed, pull both sprockets and the chain from their shafts

Installation

11   Make sure the gasket surfaces of the valve covers are flat and smooth, particularly around the bolt holes. Use a hammer and a block of wood to flatten them out if they are deformed.

12   Attach a new valve cover gasket to the cover. Notice that there are tabs provided in the cover to retain the gasket. It may be necessary to apply RTV sealant to the corners of the cover to retain the gasket there.

13   Install the valve cover onto the cylinder head, making sure that the bolt holes are aligned correctly.

14   Install the valve cover retaining bolts finger tight.

15   Tighten the retaining bolts, a little at a time, to the torque listed in this Chapter's Specifications. **Caution:** *Do not overtighten the bolts or the valve covers will warp and the gaskets will be pushed out of position, resulting in leaks.*

16   The remainder of the installation procedure is the reverse of removal.

17   Start the engine and run it until it reaches normal operating temperature, then check for leaks.

---

5   Rocker arms and pushrods - removal and installation

Refer to illustration 5.4

Removal

1   Remove the valve covers as described in Section 7.

2   If you're removing the rocker arms, remove the rocker arm fulcrum bolts **(see illustration 5.2 in Chapter 2, Part A).**

3   Remove the oil deflectors (if equipped), fulcrums, fulcrum guides (if equipped) and the rocker arms. Keep the rocker arms and fulcrums in order so that they may be installed in their original positions and orientation.

4   If only the pushrods are being removed, loosen the fulcrum retaining bolts and rotate

the rocker arms out of the way of the pushrods. Simply lift the pushrods from their holes in the cylinder head **(see illustration)**. Keep the pushrods in order so that they may be installed in their original positions and orientation.

5   Inspect the rocker arms and pushrods as described in Chapter 2, Part E.

Installation

6   Apply engine oil or assembly lube to the top of the valve stem and the pushrod guide in the cylinder head.

7   Apply engine oil to the rocker arm fulcrum seat and the fulcrum seat socket in the rocker arm.

8   Install the pushrods in the correct positions, with lubricant applied to both ends.

9   Install the fulcrum guides (if equipped), rocker arms, fulcrums, oil deflectors (if equipped) and fulcrum bolts.

10   Tighten the fulcrum bolts to the torque listed in this Chapter's Specifications.

11   If components were replaced, check the valve clearances (see Chapter 2, Part E). If necessary, install a longer or shorter pushrod.

12   Install the valve covers as described in Section 4.

13   Start the engine and check for oil leaks.

---

6   Timing cover and chain - removal and installation

Timing chain wear - quick check

1   Using a breaker bar and a socket on the crankshaft vibration damper bolt, rotate the crankshaft until the timing marks on the pulley indicate TDC (see Section 3).

2   Rotate the crankshaft counterclockwise about 30-degrees, then slowly and smoothly bring the crank back up to TDC. Do not pass the 0-degree mark. If TDC is passed, repeat steps 1 and 2.

3   Remove the distributor cap from the distributor (if not already done) (see Chapter 5). **Note:** *It is not necessary to remove the spark plug wires for this operation.*

4   While observing the distributor rotor for movement, slowly rotate the crankshaft counterclockwise again, stopping as soon as any rotor movement is noted.

5   Check the timing marks and record the number of degrees before TDC is indicated on the scale.

6   If the check indicates that over five degrees of crankshaft movement is required before any rotor movement is noted, the timing chain is probably stretched and requires replacement.

7   Replace the timing chain and sprockets as required.

Removal

Refer to illustrations 6.20 and 6.22

8   Remove the radiator (see Chapter 3).

9   Remove the water pump (see Chapter 3).

10   Remove the bolts and washers retaining the crankshaft pulley to the vibration damper. Remove the crankshaft pulley.

11   Remove the large bolt and washer retaining the vibration damper to the crankshaft.

12   Remove the vibration damper **(see illustration 6.7 in Chapter 2, Part A).**

13   Remove the damper key and crankshaft pulley spacer if equipped.

14   Remove the oil pan-to-timing cover bolts.

15   Remove the retaining bolts holding the timing cover to the engine block.

16   Use a thin bladed knife or similar tool to cut the oil pan seal flush with the engine block mating surface, inserting the thin blade between the cover and the block at the block/pan/cover joint area.

17   Remove the timing cover.

18   Stuff shop rags into the opening at the front of the oil pan to keep out gasket material or other debris, and remove the circular rubber seal from the front of the pan.

19 Check the timing chain deflection (see Chapter 2, Part E). If the deflection exceeds the Specifications, the timing chain and sprockets will need replacement with new parts.

20 If the timing chain and sprockets are being removed, turn the engine until the timing marks are aligned (see illustration).

21 Remove the camshaft sprocket retaining bolt and washer.

22 Slide the timing chain and sprockets forward and off of the camshaft and crankshaft as an assembly (see illustration). Warning: *Do not rotate the crankshaft or the camshaft while the timing chain is removed or damage to valvetrain or pistons may result.*

23 Remove the timing cover gasket. Clean all residual gasket material from the cover, oil pan and block.

24 Remove the crankshaft front oil seal from the timing cover.

Installation

25 Coat the outside edge of the new crankshaft oil seal with engine oil and install the seal in the cover using an appropriate drive tool. Make sure the seal is seated completely in the bore.

26 Assemble the timing chain and sprockets so the timing marks are in alignment (see illustration 6.20).

27 Install the chain and sprockets onto the camshaft and crankshaft as an assembly. Make sure that the timing marks remain in proper alignment during the installation procedure.

28 Install the camshaft sprocket retaining bolt and washer. Tighten the retaining bolt to the torque listed in this Chapter's Specifications. Lubricate the timing chain and sprockets with engine oil.

29 Cut and position the required forward sections of new oil pan gaskets to the exposed flanges of the oil pan. Glue the pieces down with contact cement.

30 Apply sealant at the corners of the mating surfaces.

31 Install a new rubber seal at the front of the pan and secure it to the pan with contact cement.

32 Coat the gasket surfaces of the cover with sealant and install a new gasket. Coat the mating surface on the block with sealant.

33 Position the timing cover on the block. Use care when installing the cover to avoid damaging the front seal or dislocating any gaskets.

34 Install the cover alignment tool if available to position the cover properly. If no alignment tool is available, you will have to use the crankshaft pulley to position the seal. It may be necessary to force the cover down slightly to compress the oil pan seal. This can be done by inserting a punch through the bolt holes.

35 Coat the threads of the bolts with RTV sealant and install the bolts.

36 While holding the cover in alignment, tighten the cover bolts and then the oil pan-to-front cover retaining bolts to the torque values listed in this Chapter's Specifications.

7.6 The lifters in an engine that has accumulated many miles may have to be removed with a special tool - be sure to store the lifters in an organized manner to make sure they're reinstalled in their original locations

37 Remove the alignment tool or punch.

38 Apply a thin coat of grease to the vibration damper seal contact surface.

39 Install the crankshaft spacer, if equipped.

40 Install the Woodruff key onto the crankshaft and slide the vibration damper into position.

41 Install the damper using an installation tool (see illustration 6.31 in Chapter 2, Part A).

42 Install the vibration damper retaining bolt and washer. Tighten the bolt to the torque listed in this Chapter's Specifications. Note: *This bolt may be used to push the damper onto the crankshaft if the proper installation tool is not available.*

43 Attach the crankshaft pulley to the damper and install the pulley retaining bolts.

44 The remainder of the installation procedure is the reverse of removal. Make sure that all bolts are tightened securely. If any coolant entered the oil pan when separating the timing chain cover from the block, the crankcase oil should be drained and the oil filter removed. Install a new oil filter and refill the crankcase with the proper grade and amount of oil (see Chapter 1).

45 Start and run the engine at a fast idle and check for coolant and oil leaks.

46 Check the engine idle speed and ignition timing (see Chapter 5).

---

7 Lifters and camshaft - removal and installation

Refer to illustrations 7.6, 7.14 and 7.17

Removal

Lifters

1 Remove the upper and lower intake manifold (see Section 10).

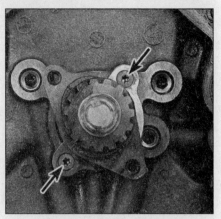

7.14 Some models use T-30 Torx screws to retain the camshaft thrust plate (arrows)

2 Remove the valve covers (see Section 4).

3 Loosen the rocker arm nuts and rotate the rocker arms to the side (see Section 5).

4 Remove the pushrods.

5 Remove the valve lifters from the engine with a magnet if there is no varnish build up or wear on them. Keep the lifters in order so they can be returned to their original bores.

6 If the lifters are stuck in their bores, you will have to obtain a special tool designed for grasping lifters internally and work them out (see illustration).

7 Inspect the lifters as described in Chapter 2, Part E. If no further disassembly is required, proceed to Step 22.

Camshaft

8 Rotate the engine to TDC compression for the number one cylinder (see Section 3) and remove the distributor (see Chapter 5).

9 Remove the valve lifters as described in this Section.

10 Remove the radiator and condenser (if equipped) (see Chapter 3).

11 Remove the timing cover (see Section 6).

12 Prior to removing the camshaft, check the camshaft endplay, lobe lift and timing chain for wear (see Chapter 2, Part A and Chapter 2, Part E). If measurements indicate worn components, replace as required during reassembly.

13 Remove the timing chain and sprockets (see Section 6).

14 Remove the bolts securing the camshaft thrust plate to the engine block (see illustration).

15 Carefully withdraw the camshaft from the engine block, being careful that the lobes do not catch on the camshaft bearings (they can scrape and damage them easily). Note: *Do not rotate the engine until re-installation is complete.*

16 Perform camshaft and bearing inspections (see Chapter 2, Part E). If measurements indicate worn components, replace as required during reassembly.

7.17 Be sure to apply camshaft installation lube or engine assembly lube to the lobes and journals prior to installation

Installation
Camshaft

17   Lubricate the camshaft journals and lobes with camshaft installation lube **(see illustration)**.
18   Slide the camshaft into position, being careful not to scrape or nick the bearings.
19   Install the camshaft thrust plate. Tighten the thrust plate bolts to the torque listed in this Chapter's Specifications. **Note:** *If camshaft endplay was excessive during wear checks, install an appropriately-sized thrust plate prior to sprocket installation.*
20   Check the camshaft endplay (see Chapter 2, Part E).
21   If the endplay is excessive, check the spacer for correct installation before it is removed. If the spacer is installed correctly, replace the thrust plate. Notice that the thrust plate has a groove on it; it should face in on all engines.

Lifters

22   Lubricate the bottom of the lifters with engine assembly lube and install them into their original bores (if the same lifters are being installed).
23   The remainder of installation is the reverse of removal.
24   Start the engine and check for oil and fuel leaks.
25   Adjust the ignition timing as described in Chapter 5.

8   Camshaft lobe lift measurement

Follow the procedure described in Chapter 2, Part A, but note that it will be necessary to remove both valve covers as described in Section 4 of this Chapter and use the specifications listed at the front of this Chapter.

9   Valve springs, retainers and seals - replacement

Follow the procedure described in Chapter 2, Part A. **Note:** *On the 7.5L engine, intake and exhaust valve seals are different and are*

not interchangeable. Intake seals are identified by the marking IN and exhaust seals by the marking EX.

10   Intake manifold (upper and lower) - removal and installation

1   Relieve the fuel pressure and remove the air cleaner and duct assembly (see Chapter 4).
2   Disconnect the negative cable from the battery.
3   Drain the cooling system (see Chapter 1).

Removal
Upper intake manifold

4   Remove the accelerator cable (see Chapter 4) and cruise control cable (if equipped) from the throttle body.
5   Disconnect the electrical connectors for the throttle position sensor (TPS), the idle air control (IAC) valve and the EGR valve position sensor (see Chapter 6).
6   Clearly label and then disconnect the vacuum lines from the upper intake manifold, the EGR valve and the fuel pressure regulator.
7   Remove the coolant lines from the throttle body. **Note:** *On 7.5L engines, it will be necessary to remove the oil fill pipe and engine cover.*
8   Disconnect the EGR tube from the upper intake manifold and the exhaust manifold (see Chapter 6).
9   Remove the bolts or nuts from the EGR transducer bracket and separate the EGR transducer from the manifold.
10   Remove the upper intake manifold brace.
11   Remove the PCV tube from the upper intake manifold and the valve cover (see Chapter 6).
12   Remove the upper intake manifold mounting bolts
13   Remove the upper intake manifold and throttle body as a complete unit from the lower intake manifold.

Lower intake manifold

14   Remove the upper intake manifold (see Steps 4 through 13).
15   Remove the distributor (see Chapter 5).
16   Label and disconnect all electrical harness connectors from lower intake manifold sensors and attached solenoids.
17   Label and disconnect any vacuum hoses from the lower intake manifold.
18   Disconnect the fuel supply and return lines from the fuel rail and disconnect the fuel injector electrical connectors (see Chapter 4).
19   Remove the secondary air injection system from the manifolds (see Chapter 6).
20   Remove the upper radiator hose from the thermostat housing.
21   Remove the heater bypass and outlet hoses from the intake manifold.

22   Remove the coil/solenoid bracket assembly and position it out of the way (see Chapter 5).
23   Remove the bolts retaining the intake manifold to the cylinder heads.
24   Remove the intake manifold. **Note:** *It may be necessary to pry the intake manifold away from the cylinder heads but be careful to avoid damaging the mating surfaces.*
25   Clean the mating surfaces of the intake manifold and cylinder heads. Take care not to get any material down into the intake ports.
26   Remove the end gaskets from the top of the engine block.
27   Remove the oil gallery splash pan from the engine (if so equipped).

Installation
Lower intake manifold

Refer to illustrations 10.31, 10.36a and 10.36b
Caution: *The mating surfaces of the cylinder heads, block and manifold must be perfectly clean when the manifold is installed. Gasket removal solvents in aerosol cans are available at most auto parts stores and may be helpful when removing old gasket material that's stuck to the heads and manifold (since the manifold is made of aluminum, aggressive scraping can cause damage!) Be sure to follow directions printed on the container.*
Note: *The manufacturer recommends the use of guide pins when installing the manifold. To make these, buy four extra manifold bolts. Cut the heads off the bolts, then grind a taper and cut a screwdriver slot in the cut ends.*
28   If the manifold was disassembled, reassemble it. Use electrically conductive sealant on the temperature sending unit threads. Use a new EGR valve gasket.
29   Use a gasket scraper to remove all traces of sealant and old gasket material, then clean the mating surfaces with lacquer thinner or acetone. If there's old sealant or oil on the mating surfaces when the manifold is installed, oil or vacuum leaks may develop. When working on the heads and block, cover the lifter valley with shop rags to keep debris out of the engine. Use a vacuum cleaner to remove any gasket material that falls into the intake ports in the heads.
30   Use a tap of the correct size to chase the threads in the bolt holes, then use compressed air (if available) to remove the debris from the holes. **Warning:** *Wear safety glasses or a face shield to protect your eyes when using compressed air!* Remove excessive carbon deposits and corrosion from the exhaust and coolant passages in the heads and manifold.
31   Apply a 1/8-inch wide bead of RTV sealant to the four corners where the manifold, block and heads converge **(see illustration)**. **Note:** *This sealant sets up in 10 minutes. Do not take longer to install and tighten the manifold once the sealant is applied, or leaks may occur.*
32   Apply a small amount of contact adhesive, or equivalent, to the manifold gasket

10.31 Apply RTV-type sealant to the corners where the heads meet the block when installing the intake manifold gaskets

mating surface on each cylinder head. Position the gaskets on the cylinder heads. The upper side of each gasket will have a TOP or THIS SIDE UP label stamped into it to ensure correct installation.

33 Position the end seals on the block, then apply a 1/8-inch wide bead of RTV sealant to the four points where the end seals meet the heads.

34 Make sure all intake port openings, coolant passage holes and bolt holes are aligned correctly. Use locating pins if necessary.

35 Carefully set the manifold in place while the sealant is still wet. **Caution:** *Don't disturb the gaskets and don't move the manifold fore-and-aft after it contacts the seals on the block. Make sure the end seals haven't been disturbed.* After the manifold is in place, run a finger around the seal area to make sure that the seals are in place. If the seals are not in place, remove the manifold and reposition the seals.

36 Install the intake manifold retaining bolts. If locating pins were used, start the other

manifold bolts in place before removing the locators. Tighten the bolts in the sequence shown **(see illustrations)** in three steps, to the torque listed in this Chapter's Specifications.

37 Install the remaining components in the reverse order of removal.

38 Refill the cooling system (see Chapter 1).

39 Start and run the engine and allow it to reach operating temperature. After it has reached operating temperature, check carefully for leaks.

40 Check the ignition timing and adjust it, if necessary (see Chapter 5).

Upper intake manifold

41 Installation is the reverse of removal. Be sure to clean and inspect the mounting faces of the lower intake manifold and the upper intake manifold before positioning the gaskets onto the lower intake manifold mounting face. The use of alignment studs may be helpful. Install the upper intake manifold and throttle body as a single unit. Be sure to tighten the bolts to the torque specification listed at the beginning of this Chapter.

11 Exhaust manifold - removal and installation

1 If you're removing the right-side manifold, remove the air cleaner and intake duct.

2 On the right-side manifold, remove the upper intake manifold-to-exhaust manifold support bracket (5.0L and 5.8L engines only).

3 On the right-side manifold, remove the engine and/or transmission dipstick tube bracket(s) as applicable.

4 Also on the right-side manifold, remove the EGR tube (5.8L engine only).

5 On the left side manifold, remove the EGR tube (7.5L engine only).

6 On the left side manifold, remove the engine oil dipstick tube bracket if equipped.

7 On either manifold, remove the thermal reactor manifold, if equipped.

8 Disconnect the retaining bolts holding the exhaust pipe(s) to the exhaust manifold(s) (see Chapter 4).

9 Remove the spark plug wires and heat shields.

10 Remove the exhaust manifold retaining bolts, lifting eyes and nuts. **Note:** *Keep track of parts location and bolt lengths so they may be reinstalled in their original positions.*

11 Remove the exhaust manifold.

12 Clean the mating surfaces of the exhaust manifold and the cylinder head.

13 Clean the mounting flange of the exhaust manifold and the exhaust pipe.

Installation

14 Apply graphite grease to the mating surface of the exhaust manifold and cylinder head.

15 Position the exhaust manifold on the head and install the attaching bolts. Tighten the bolts to the torque listed in this Chapter's Specifications in three steps, working from the center to the ends.

16 Install the spark plug heat shields and lifting eyes.

17 The remainder of installation is the reverse of removal.

18 Start the engine and check for exhaust leaks.

12 Cylinder heads - removal and installation

Caution: *The engine must be completely cool before beginning this operation.*

Removal

1 Disconnect the cable from the negative terminal of the battery.

2 If the left cylinder head is being removed, remove the air conditioning compressor/power steering bracket at the front of the engine, complete with accessories. If

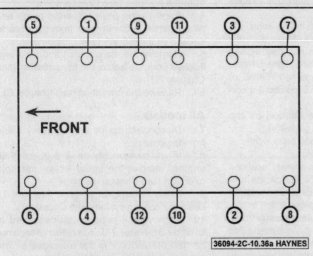

10.36a Intake manifold bolt tightening sequence - 5.0L and 5.8L engines

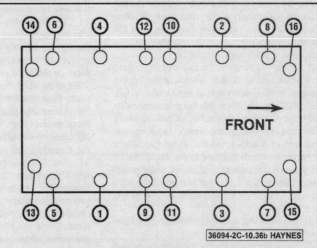

10.36b Intake manifold bolt tightening sequence - 7.5L engine

12.18 Be certain that the cylinder head gaskets are positioned with the correct side up - note the FRONT designation (arrow)

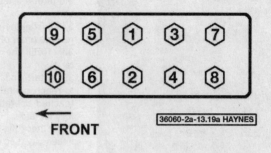

12.21 Cylinder head bolt TIGHTENING sequence

necessary, remove the compressor from the bracket. **Warning:** *The air conditioning system is under high pressure. Do not disconnect the hoses, as serious injury or damage to the system will result.*

3   If the left cylinder head is being removed, remove the oil dipstick and tube assembly and speed control bracket, if equipped.

4   If the right cylinder head is being removed, disconnect the alternator wiring harness and air pump hoses.

5   Remove the alternator/air pump bracket from the front of the engine, complete with accessories.

6   Remove the intake manifold (see Section 10).

7   Remove the valve cover(s) (see Section 4).

8   Remove the rocker arms and pushrods (see Section 5).

9   Remove exhaust manifold(s) (see Section 11).

10   If equipped, disconnect thermactor air supply tubes from rear of head.

11   Loosen the cylinder head retaining bolts by reversing the order shown in the tightening sequence diagram **(see illustration 12.21)**, then remove the bolts from the heads. Keep them in order so they can be installed in their original locations.

12   Carefully remove the cylinder head from the block, using care to avoid damaging the gasket mating surfaces. If resistance is felt, DO NOT pry between the head and block as damage to the mating surfaces will result. To dislodge the head, place a wood block against the end of it and strike the wood block with a hammer. Store the heads on wood blocks to prevent damage to the gasket sealing surfaces. **Note:** *On 7.5L engines, you may want to use a hoist or an assistant, as the heads are heavy.*

13   Inspect the cylinder head and components.

14   Be sure to check the cylinder head and block deck for flatness (see Chapter 2, Part E).

Installation

Refer to illustrations 12.18 and 12.21

15   The mating surfaces of the cylinder heads and block must be perfectly clean when the heads are installed. Use a gasket scraper to remove all traces of carbon and old gasket material, then clean the mating surfaces with lacquer thinner or acetone. If there's oil on the mating surfaces when the heads are installed, the gaskets may not seal correctly and leaks may develop. When working on the block, cover the lifter valley with shop rags to keep debris out of the engine. Use a vacuum cleaner to remove any debris that falls into the cylinders.

16   Check the block and head mating surfaces for nicks, deep scratches and other damage. If damage is slight, it can be removed with a file - if it's excessive, machining may be the only alternative.

17   Use a tap of the correct size to chase the threads in the head bolt holes. Mount each bolt in a vise and run a die down the threads to remove corrosion and restore the threads. Dirt, corrosion, sealant and damaged threads will affect torque readings.

18   Position the new gasket(s) over the locating dowels in the block. Make sure it's facing the correct direction and that all bolt and coolant passage holes are aligned. **Note:** *Most gaskets will either be marked FRONT or TOP to be sure the gasket is positioned correctly* **(see illustration)**.

19   Carefully position the head(s) on the block without disturbing the gasket(s).

20   Before installing the head bolts, lightly oil the threads on all of the bolts.

21   Install the bolts in their original locations and tighten them finger tight. Follow the recommended sequence and tighten the bolts, in two or three steps, to the torque listed in this Chapter's Specifications **(see illustration)**. **Note:** *Once the bolts have been tightened to the correct final torque it is not necessary to re-tighten the bolts after extended operation. However, the bolts may be checked and re-tightened if desired.*

22   The remaining installation steps are the reverse of removal.

23   Change the engine oil and filter (see Chapter 1), then start the engine and check carefully for oil and coolant leaks.

24   Check and adjust the ignition timing (see Chapter 5). **Note:** *When the battery has been disconnected, some unusual driveability symptoms may be present until the vehicle is driven a few miles and the computer "relearns."*

13   Oil pan - removal and installation

Refer to illustrations 13.17, 13.23 and 13.24

Removal

7.5L models only

1   Remove the oil dipstick tube and bracket.

2   Disconnect the throttle body linkages, wiring and vacuum hoses to allow the engine to be raised (see Chapter 4).

3   Remove the fuel supply and return lines from the fuel rails (see Chapter 4).

4   Remove the power steering pump and air conditioning compressor from their brackets and tie them aside (see Chapter 3).

5   Remove the manual shift and kickdown linkage from the automatic transmission (see Chapter 7).

6   Remove the driveshaft (see Chapter 8).

All models

7   Disconnect the negative battery cable from the battery.

8   If you're working on a 5.0L or 5.8L engine, remove the upper intake manifold (plenum) (see Chapter 4).

9   Drain the engine oil (see Chapter 1). Drain the cooling system (see Chapter 3).

10   Remove the radiator (as described in Chapter 3). **Note:** *This operation is required so that the radiator is not damaged by the engine when it is raised from its mounts.*

11   Raise the vehicle and support it securely on jack stands.

13.17 Place wood blocks between the engine mount and frame brackets

12   Remove the engine front insulator-to-support bracket retaining nuts and washers (see Section 17).

13   Disconnect the exhaust pipes from exhaust manifolds to allow the engine to be raised (see Chapter 4).

14   Place a wooden block between the jack and the oil pan and raise the front of the engine with a jack. **Caution:** *Verify that all cables, wiring and hoses between engine and vehicle have enough slack to avoid damage.*

15   On all engines except the 7.5L, raise the engine only far enough to facilitate pan removal.

16   On the 7.5L engine, raise the engine until the transmission bellhousing contacts the floorpan (minimum of four inches).

17   Place wood blocks between the front engine mounts and the support brackets to maintain the engine in the raised position **(see illustration)**.

18   Lower the engine onto the spacer blocks and remove the jack.

19   Remove the oil pan attaching bolts.

20   Lower the pan to the crossmember.

21   On 5.0 and 5.8L engines, remove the oil pump inlet-tube-to-oil pump retaining bolts and washers and inlet tube support-brace fastener (see Section 16). Let inlet tube drop into the pan.

22   On the 7.5L engine, remove the entire pump from the block (see Section 14). Let the pump and pickup drop into the pan.

23   Remove the oil pan from the vehicle. It may be necessary to rotate the crankshaft so the counterweights clear the pan **(see illustration)**.

24   Clean all gasket material from the mating surfaces of the engine block and the pan **(see illustration)**.

Installation

25   Apply a thin, even coat of RTV sealant to both sides of the gasket(s). A small amount of RTV sealant at each mating junction will help prevent any leaks from these critical spots. Install the gaskets and seals on the pan.

26   On 5.0L and 5.8L engines, clean the oil pump pick-up tube and screen assembly and place it in the oil pan.

27   On the 7.5L engine, clean the inlet tube screen and prime the oil pump (see Section 14). Place the primed pump and pick-up tube in the oil pan.

28   Position the oil pan underneath the engine.

29   On 5.0 and 5.8L engines, lift the inlet tube and screen assembly from the oil pan and secure it to the oil pump with a new gasket. Tighten the retaining bolts to the torque listed in this Chapter's Specifications.

30   On the 7.5L engine, install the pump and pickup tube to the block (see Section 14).

31   Attach the oil pan to the engine block and install the retaining bolts. Tighten the bolts to the torque listed in this Chapter's Specifications, starting from the center and working out in each direction.

32   Raise the engine with a jack and a block of wood underneath the oil pan and remove the wood spacers previously installed under the support brackets.

33   Lower the engine to the correct installed position and connect the engine mounts (see Section 17).

34   The remainder of installation is the reverse of removal.

35   Fill the cooling system with coolant and check for leaks.

36   Fill the engine with oil (see Chapter 1) and connect the negative battery cable.

37   Start the engine and check carefully for leaks at the oil pan gasket sealing surfaces. **Note:** *When the battery has been disconnected, some unusual driveability symptoms may be present until the vehicle is driven a few miles and the computer "relearns."*

14 Oil pump - removal and installation

1   Remove the oil pan as described in Section 13.

2   Remove the bolts retaining the oil pump and support brace to the block.

3   Remove the oil pump and pick-up tube assembly.

4   Clean the mating surfaces of the oil pump and the block.

5   Inspect the oil pump as described in Chapter 2, Part E.

6   Before installation, prime the pump by filling the inlet opening with oil and rotating the pump shaft until the oil spurts out of the outlet.

7   Attach the oil pump to the engine block using the two retaining bolts.

8   Tighten the bolts to the torque listed in this Chapter's Specifications.

9   Install the oil pan (see Section 13).

15 Crankshaft oil seals - replacement

Refer to illustrations 15.7, 15.9, 15.23 and 15.26

Front oil seal

1   Drain the cooling system (see Chapter 1).

2   Remove the fan shroud and the radiator (see Chapter 3).

3   Remove the fan and pulley (see Chapter 3).

4   On 7.5L engines, remove the remaining drivebelt.

5   Remove the large bolt and washer from

13.23 Slip the oil pan out, turning it slightly to clear the driveplate

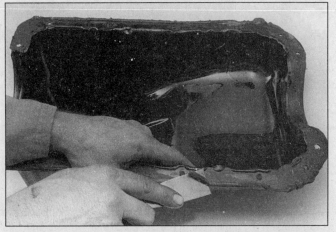

13.24 Scrape away all traces of gasket material and sealant, then clean the gasket surfaces with lacquer thinner or acetone

15.7 A chisel and hammer must be used to work the seal out of the timing chain cover - be very careful not to damage the cover or nick the crankshaft!

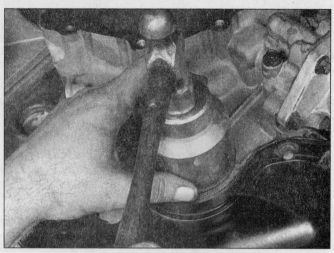

15.9 Drive the seal squarely into the bore with a large socket and hammer - don't damage the seal and make sure it's completely seated

the crankshaft nose. It may be necessary to prevent the crankshaft from rotating by putting the transmission in gear (if the engine is still in the vehicle) or by holding the driveplate or crankshaft flange with a suitable tool (if the engine is out of the vehicle).

6   Remove the vibration damper using a suitable puller **(see illustration 6.7** in Chapter 2, Part A).

7   Remove the seal from the timing cover with seal remover tool, or equivalent, or by carefully tapping it out with a chisel and hammer **(see illustration)**. Tap the chisel in as a wedge at several points around the seal.

8   Clean out the recess in the cover.

9   Coat the outer edge of the new seal with motor oil and install it using the special tool. As an alternative, a large socket or piece of pipe can be used to drive the new seal in **(see illustration)**. However, use extreme caution as the seal can be damaged easily with this

method. Drive in the seal until it is fully seated in the recess. Make sure that the spring is properly positioned within the seal.

10   Lubricate the nose of the crankshaft, the inner hub of the vibration damper and the seal surface with engine oil.

11   Apply RTV sealant to the inside keyway of the damper hub.

12   Align the damper keyway with the key on the crankshaft and install the damper using an installation tool **(see illustration 6.31 in Chapter 2, Part A)**.

13   Install the bolt and washer retaining the damper and tighten it to the torque listed in this Chapter's Specifications.

14   The remainder of installation is the reverse of removal.

15   Fill the engine with oil (if the oil has been drained) and coolant (see Chapter 1).

16   Start and operate the engine at a fast idle and check for leaks of any type.

Rear main oil seal

One-piece rear main oil seal (5.0L and 5.8L engines)

17   See Chapter 2, Part A for the procedure, but use a seal installation tool, or equivalent, and use the driveplate bolt torque specification listed in this Chapter.

Two-piece rear main oil seal (7.5L engine)

Removal

18   Drain the engine oil and follow the procedure in Section 13 to remove the oil pan.

19   Loosen all the main bearing cap bolts, but only enough to lower the crank a very small amount (less than 1/32-inch).

20   Remove the rear main bearing cap.

21   The upper portion of the rear seal will remain in the block, but with 3/8-inch sticking out on one end. Being careful not to nick the

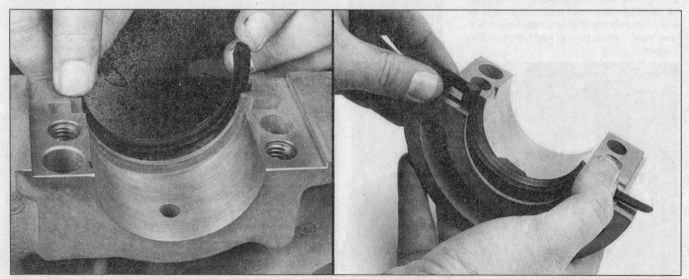

15.23 Insert the upper half of the two-piece seal with 3/8-inch sticking out and stagger the bottom half correspondingly in the cap (make sure the seal lips face the front of the engine)

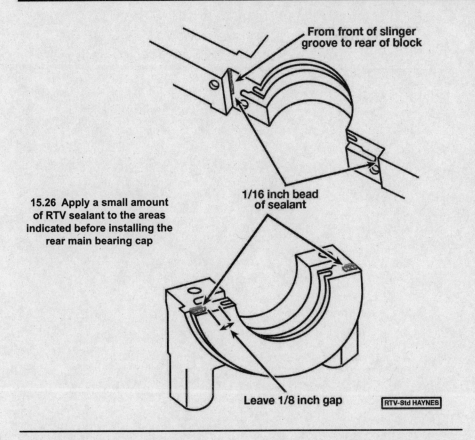

From front of slinger groove to rear of block

15.26 Apply a small amount of RTV sealant to the areas indicated before installing the rear main bearing cap

1/16 inch bead of sealant

Leave 1/8 inch gap

RTV-Std HAYNES

crankshaft, Use a seal removing tool, or insert a small sheetmetal screw into the exposed seal and pull on the screwhead with locking pliers.

22   Clean the cap and block areas thoroughly with lacquer thinner.

23   Dip the new seal halves in clean engine oil and install one into the block, leaving 3/8-inch sticking out on one side.

24   Tighten the other four main bearing caps to the torque listed in Chapter 2, Part E Specifications.

25   Install the other half in the rear main bearing cap, with 3/8-inch sticking up from the side of the cap opposite where the upper half sticks out.

26   Apply RTV sealant to the cap and where the corners of the block where the cap seats **(see illustration)**, install the rear main bearing cap and tighten the bolts to the torque listed in Chapter 2, Part E Specifications.

27   The remainder of the installation is the reverse of the disassembly procedure.

16   Driveplate - removal, inspection and installation

Refer to the procedure described in Chapter 2, Part A, but use the torque values listed in this Chapter's Specifications.

17   Engine mounts - removal and installation

1   Engine mounts seldom require attention, but broken or deteriorated mounts should be replaced immediately or the added strain placed on the driveline components may cause damage.

2   For the check and replacement procedure, refer to Chapter 2, Part A.

Notes

Chapter 2 Part D
4.6L, 5.4L, 6.8L V8 and V10 OHC engines

Contents

Specifications

General

Displacement

4.6L	4.6 liters (281 cubic inches)
5.4L	5.4 liters (329 cubic inches)
6.8L	6.8 liters (415 cubic inches)

Bore and stroke

4.6L	3.554 X 3.546 inches
5.4L	3.554 X 4.168 inches
6.8L	3.554 X 4.168 inches

Cylinder numbers (front to rear)

V8 engines

Right side	1-2-3-4
Left (driver's) side	5-6-7-8

V10 engines

Right side	1-2-3-4-5
Left (driver's) side	6-7-8-9-10

Firing order

V8 engines	1-3-7-2-6-5-4-8
V10 engines	1-6-5-10-2-7-3-8-4-9

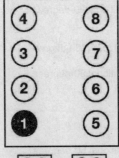

4.6L and 5.4L V8 ENGINE
1-3-7-2-6-5-4-8

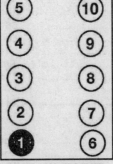

6.8L V10 ENGINE
1-6-5-10-2-7-3-8-4-9

Cylinder location and coil pack arrangement - Note that later models are equipped with coil-over-plug assemblies mounted on each cylinder

36059-1-specs.C HAYNES

Camshaft

Lobe lift	
4.6L, intake and exhaust	0.259 inch
5.4L	
Models through 2002	
Exhaust	
Left side	0.260 inch
Right side	0.259 inch
Intake	0.259 inch
2003 and later	
Intake and exhaust	0.256 inch
6.8L	
Models through 2001	
Exhaust	0.260 inch
Intake	0.259 inch
2002 through 2004, intake and exhaust	0.259 inch
2005	
Exhaust	0.295 inch
Intake	0.280 inch
Allowable lobe lift loss	0.004 inch
Endplay	
4.6L	0.001 to 0.006 inch
5.4L	0.001 to 0.007 inch
6.8L	0.001 to 0.007 inch
Journal diameter (all)	
Models through 2000	1.060 to 1.061 inches
2001 and later	1.061 to 1.062 inches
Bearing inside diameter (all)	1.062 to 1.063 inches
Journal-to-bearing (oil) clearance	
Standard	0.001 to 0.003 inch
Service limit	0.005 inch maximum

Torque specifications

	Ft-lbs (unless otherwise indicated)
Balance shaft journal cap bolts (6.8L engine only)	71 to 106 in-lbs
Camshaft sprocket bolts	
4.6L and 5.4L engines	
M10 bolt	
Step 1	30
Step 2	Tighten an additional 90-degrees
M12 bolts	
Models through 2004	41 to 55
2005	
Step 1	40
Step 2	Tighten an additional 90-degrees
6.8L engines	41 to 55
Camshaft caps to cylinder head	71 to 106 in-lbs
Drivebelt idler and tensioner bolts	15 to 22
Cylinder head bolts	
Step 1	28 to 31
Step 2	Tighten an additional 90-degrees
Step 3	Tighten an additional 90-degrees
Crankshaft pulley-to-crankshaft bolt	
Step 1	66
Step 2	Loosen one full turn (360-degrees)
Step 3	34 to 39
Step 4	Tighten an additional 90-degrees
Valve cover bolts	71 to 106 in-lbs
Oil pan-to-engine block bolts	
Step 1	18 in-lbs
Step 2	15
Step 3	
Models through 2000	Tighten an additional 60-degrees
2001 and later	Tighten an additional 90-degrees
Exhaust manifold-to-cylinder head nuts	17 to 20
Exhaust manifold-to-cylinder head studs	89 to 115 in-lbs
Driveplate mounting bolts	54 to 64
Intake manifold-to-cylinder head bolts	
Step 1	18 in-lbs
Step 2	15 to 22

Intake manifold lower section-to-intake manifold bolts	
Step 1	18 in-lbs
Step 2	71 to 106 in-lbs
Oil filter adapter bolts	15 to 22
Oil cooler-to-filter adapter nut	30 to 40
Oil pump-to-engine block mounting bolts	71 to 106 in-lbs
Oil pick-up tube-to-main bearing cap nut	15 to 22
Oil pick-up tube-to-oil pump bolts	71 to 106 in-lbs
Timing chain cover-to-engine block bolts	**Ft-lbs** (unless otherwise indicated)
4.6L Romeo engines	18
All other engines	
Bolts 1 through 5	15 to 22
Bolts 6 through 15	30 to 41
Timing chain cover-to oil pan bolts	
Step 1	15
Step 2	Additional turn of 60 degrees
Timing chain guides	71 to 107 in-lbs
Timing chain tensioners	15 to 20
Engine mount-to-engine block bolts	39 to 53
Engine mount through-bolts	50 to 68

1 General information

This Part of Chapter 2 is devoted to in-vehicle repair procedures for the 4.6L, 5.4L, 6.8L Single Overhead Cam (SOHC) V8 and V10 engines. All engines are of the same "modular" design, the 5.4L engine has a longer stroke for more displacement. The 6.8L V10 engine is designed with 2 banks with five cylinders per bank. All engines have aluminum heads, iron blocks, a single camshaft for each cylinder head, and two valves per cylinder. All information concerning engine removal and installation and engine block and cylinder head overhaul can be found in Part E of this Chapter.

There are two versions of the V8, depending on where it was produced; the Romeo (Romeo, Michigan plant) and the Windsor (Windsor, Ontario, Canada), with minor differences in some of the components and procedures. It's important when working on the engine to know which engine you have. The REP (Romeo Engine Plant) 4.6L has 11 bolts on the left and right valve cover, while the WEP (Windsor Engine Plant) 4.6L and 5.4L has 13 bolts on the left valve cover and 14 bolts on the right valve cover. The engines can also be identified from the VIN number of the vehicle. The eighth place in the VIN is the engine identification, with the letter W designating the 4.6L Romeo, the number 6 designating the 4.6L Windsor engines and the letter L designating the 5.4L Windsor engine. 1997 through 1999 models are equipped with a 4.6L Windsor, 5.4L Windsor engine or 6.8L V10 engine. 2000 models are equipped with Romeo 4.6L engines, 4.6L Windsor engines, 5.4L Windsor engines or 6.8L V10 engines. 2001 models do not offer the 4.6L Windsor engine.

The 6.8L V10 engine is designed similarly to the 5.4L V8 engine. The 6.8L V10 cylinders and pistons are designed with the exact same bore and stroke as the 5.4L V8 with the addition of two cylinders at the rear of the engine block. The timing chains and components are also similar. The 6.8L engine is also designed with a balance shaft in the left cylinder head, timed from the camshaft, to smooth out engine pulsation.

The following repair procedures are based on the assumption that the engine is installed in the vehicle. If the engine has been removed from the vehicle and mounted on a stand, many of the steps outlined in this Part of Chapter 2 will not apply.

The Specifications included in this Part of Chapter 2 apply only to the procedures contained in this Part. Part E of Chapter 2 contains the Specifications necessary for cylinder head and engine block rebuilding.

2 Repair operations possible with the engine in the vehicle

Many major repair operations can be accomplished without removing the engine from the vehicle.

If possible, clean the engine compartment and the exterior of the engine with some type of pressure washer before any work is started. It will make the job easier and help keep dirt out of the internal areas of the engine.

Components within the engine compartment can be accessed from the front of the vehicle by lifting the hood or from inside the passenger compartment by removing the engine cover (refer to Chapter 11 if necessary). Depending upon the extent of the repair, it may be necessary to use both methods.

If vacuum, exhaust, oil or coolant leaks develop, indicating a need for gasket or seal replacement, the repairs can generally be made with the engine in the vehicle. The intake and exhaust manifold gaskets, timing cover gasket, oil pan gasket, crankshaft oil seals and cylinder head gaskets are all accessible with the engine in place.

Exterior engine components, such as the intake and exhaust manifolds, the oil pan, the water pump, the starter motor, the alternator and the fuel system components can be removed for repair with the engine in place.

Since the cylinder heads can be removed without pulling the engine, valve component servicing can also be accomplished with the engine in the vehicle. Replacement of the timing chain and sprockets and oil pump is also possible with the engine in the vehicle.

In extreme cases caused by a lack of necessary equipment, repair or replacement of piston rings, pistons, connecting rods and rod bearings is also possible with the engine in the vehicle. However, this practice is not recommended because of the cleaning and preparation work that must be done to the components involved.

3 Top Dead Center (TDC) for number one piston - locating

Refer to illustration 3.1

Refer to Chapter 2, Part A for the TDC locating procedure, but use the illustration provided with this Section for the appropri-

3.1 When placing the engine at Top Dead Center (TDC), align the notch in the crankshaft pulley (arrow) with the TDC indicator on the timing chain cover

4.6 Remove the bolts around the perimeter of the valve cover (arrows)

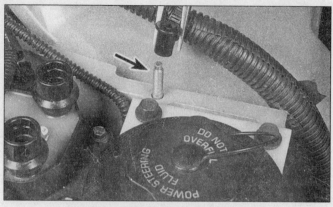

4.16 Detach the wiring harness from the valve cover studs (arrow)

ate reference marks and the following exceptions:

a) *Disable the ignition system by disconnecting the primary electrical connectors at the ignition coil pack/modules (see Chapter 5).*

b) *Remove the spark plugs and install a compression gauge in the number one cylinder. Turn the crankshaft clockwise with a socket and breaker bar as described in Chapter 2A.*

c) *When the piston approaches TDC, compression will be noted on the compression gauge. Continue turning the crankshaft until the notch in the crankshaft pulley is aligned with the TDC mark on the front cover* **(see illustration)**. *At this point number one cylinder is at TDC on the compression stroke.*

4   Valve covers - removal and installation

Removal

Note: *The valve cover bolts are connected to the valve covers. Do not attempt to remove them from the covers, just loosen them until they are free of the cylinder head.*

4.6L engine

Left valve cover

Refer to illustration 4.6

1   Disconnect the cable from the negative battery terminal. Remove the engine cover.
2   Remove the air cleaner and intake duct (see Chapter 4).
3   Disconnect the PCV hose and pull the wiring harness from the studs on the valve cover.
4   On Romeo built engines, remove the DPFE EGR sensor (see Chapter 6). Also, remove the EGR tube from the exhaust manifold and the intake manifold (see Chapter 6).
Note: *Some models will have two additional metal tubes linking the EGR tube with the DPFE sensor. Use caution when disconnecting the metal fittings from the DPFE sensor to avoid twisting or bending the metal tubes.*
5   On Windsor built engines, remove the

EGR tube from the EGR valve and exhaust manifold (see Chapter 6). **Note:** *Some models will have two additional metal tubes linking the EGR tube with the EGR valve. Use caution when disconnecting the metal fittings from the EGR valve to avoid twisting or bending the metal tubes.*
6   Loosen the valve cover bolts and remove the cover **(see illustration)**. If it's stuck, tap it with a hammer and block of wood. On 2005 models, remove the nut securing the engine oil dipstick tube bracket to the valve cover.

Right valve cover

7   Disconnect the cable from the negative battery terminal.
8   Remove the air cleaner and intake duct (see Chapter 4).
9   Remove the PCV valve and hose from the valve cover.
10   Remove the oil filler tube from the valve cover.
11   Remove the nuts retaining the wiring harness to the valve cover studs and separate the harness from the top of the engine.
12   Loosen the valve cover bolts and remove the valve cover. If it's stuck tap it with a hammer and block of wood.

5.4L and 6.8L engines

Left valve cover

Refer to illustration 4.16

13   Disconnect the cable from the negative battery terminal.
14   On 6.8L engines, remove the intake manifold (see Section 11).
15   Remove the air cleaner and intake duct (see Chapter 4).
16   Disconnect the PCV hose and pull the wiring harness from the studs on the valve cover **(see illustration)**.
17   Remove the EGR tube from the exhaust manifold and the intake manifold (see Chapter 6). **Note:** *Some models will have two additional metal tubes linking the EGR tube with the EGR valve. Use caution when disconnecting the metal fittings from the EGR valve to avoid twisting or bending the metal tubes.*
18   Pull the harness away from the valve cover to allow enough room to get the cover out. On 2005 models, remove the bolt secur-

ing the oil dipstick tube to the engine and move the tube out of the way.
19   Loosen the valve cover bolts and remove the valve cover. If it's stuck, tap it with a hammer and block of wood.

Right valve cover

20   Follow Steps 7 through 11 for the right valve cover on the 4.6L engine.
21   On 6.8L engines, remove the intake manifold (see Section 11).
22   Disconnect the electrical connectors on the fuel injectors (see Chapter 4) and the ignition coils (see Chapter 5).
23   Remove the A/C compressor connector (see Chapter 3) and the crankshaft position sensor connector (see Chapter 6). On 2001 and later 5.4L engines, disconnect the radio interference capacitor (near the oil dipstick tube).
24   Pull the harness away from the valve cover to allow enough room to get the cover out **(see illustration 4.16)**.
25   Loosen the valve cover bolts and remove the valve cover. If it's stuck, tap it with a hammer and block of wood.

Installation - all models

Refer to illustration 4.28

26   The mating surfaces of each cylinder

4.28 Apply a dab of RTV sealant to the mating joints (arrows) between the timing cover and the cylinder head before installing the valve cover

5.3 Have an assistant hold the crankshaft and use a breaker bar and socket to remove the crankshaft pulley bolt (arrow)

5.4 Remove the crankshaft pulley with a puller that bolts to the crankshaft pulley hub

5.5 Inspect the crankshaft pulley for signs of damage or excessive wear

1   *Oil seal surface*
2   *Woodruff keyway*

head and valve cover must be perfectly clean when the valve covers are installed. Remove all traces of sealant, and clean the mating surfaces with lacquer thinner or acetone. If there's old sealant or oil on the mating surfaces when the valve cover is installed, oil leaks may develop.

27   The valve cover gaskets should be mated to the valve covers with gasket adhesive before the valve covers are installed. Make sure the gasket is pushed all the way into the groove in the valve cover.

28   At the mating joint (two spots per cylinder head) between the timing chain cover and cylinder head, apply a dab of RTV sealant before installing the valve cover **(see illustration)**.

29   Carefully position the valve cover on the cylinder head and install the nuts and bolts. **Note:** *Install the covers within five minutes of applying the RTV sealant.*

30   Tighten the fasteners in two steps to the torque listed in this Chapter's Specifications. Wait two minutes between the first and the second round of tightening. On all except Romeo 4.6L engines, tighten the bolts/nuts in a sequence starting in the center and working alternately toward each end of the valve cover. On Romeo 4.6L models, tighten the upper row of bolts first, then the lower row, from rear to front. **Caution:** *Be careful with the plastic valve covers; don't over-tighten the bolts!*

31   The remaining installation steps are the reverse of removal.

32   Start the engine and check for oil leaks as the engine warms up.

5   Crankshaft pulley - removal and installation

Removal

Refer to illustrations 5.3 and 5.4

1   Remove the air cleaner and air intake duct (see Chapter 4).

2   Refer to Chapter 3 and remove the cooling fan and shroud. Remove the accessory drivebelt (see Chapter 1).

3   Remove the driveplate inspection cover (see Chapter 7) and with the help of an assistant, wedge a large screwdriver into the starter ring gear teeth to prevent the crankshaft from turning. Remove the large center bolt from the crankshaft pulley with a breaker bar and socket **(see illustration)**.

4   Using a suitable puller, detach the crankshaft pulley **(see illustration)**. Leave the Woodruff key in place in the crankshaft keyway. **Caution:** *Don't use a puller with jaws that grip the outer edge of the crankshaft pulley. The puller must be the type shown in the illustration that utilizes bolts to apply force to the crankshaft pulley hub only.*

Installation

Refer to illustration 5.5

5   Lubricate the oil seal contact surface of the crankshaft pulley hub **(see illustration)** with multi-purpose grease or clean engine oil. Apply a dab of RTV sealant to the front end of the keyway in the crankshaft pulley before installation.

6   Install the crankshaft pulley on the end of the crankshaft. The keyway in the crankshaft pulley must be aligned with the Woodruff key in the crankshaft. If the crankshaft pulley cannot be seated by hand, slip the large washer over the bolt, install the bolt and tighten it to pull the crankshaft pulley into place. Now loosen the bolt one full turn, then tighten the bolt to the torque listed in this Chapter's Specifications.

7   The remaining installation steps are the reverse of removal.

8   Check the oil level. Run the engine and check for oil leaks.

6   Timing chain cover - removal and installation

Removal

Refer to illustrations 6.9 and 6.11

1   Disconnect the cable from the negative battery terminal.

2   Drain the engine oil and remove the oil filter (see Chapter 1).

3   Remove the drivebelt and the water pump pulley. Remove the crankshaft pulley (see Section 5).

4   Refer to Section 4 and remove both valve covers.

5   Drain the cooling system (see Chapter 1). Refer to Chapter 3 and remove the radiator and water pump.

6   From below, remove the four front oil pan bolts (see Section 14) that secure the bottom section of the timing chain cover.

7   Disconnect the electrical connectors to the camshaft sensor and the crankshaft sensor (see Chapter 6).

8   Remove the bolts securing the power steering pump to the engine (see Chapter 10). **Note:** *The front lower bolt on the power steering pump will not come all the way out.* Position the pump aside and secure it out of the way.

9   Unbolt and remove the drivebelt tensioner assembly from the right side of the timing cover **(see illustration)**.

6.9 Remove the bolts (arrows) and the drivebelt tensioner assembly from the right side

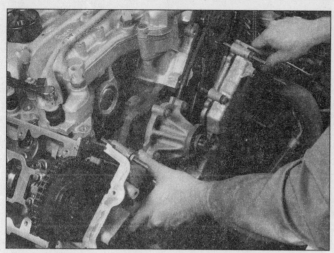

6.11 Separate the timing chain cover from the engine, using a soft-faced hammer if necessary to break the gasket seal

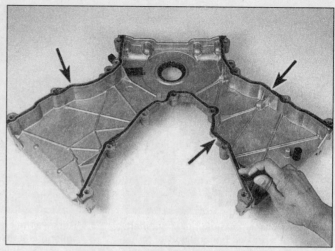

6.13 Install three new gaskets (arrows) into the grooves in the back of the timing chain cover

10   Remove the timing chain cover-to-engine block bolts and the four oil pan-to-timing chain cover bolts from underneath. Including the oil pan bolts, there are 19 bolts to be removed from the timing chain cover. Note the locations of studs and different length bolts so they can be reinstalled in their original locations.

11   Separate the timing chain cover from the engine block **(see illustration)**. If it's stuck, tap it gently with a soft-face hammer to break the gasket bond. **Caution:** *DO NOT use excessive force or you may crack the cover. If the cover is difficult to remove, make sure all of the bolts have been removed.*

Installation

Refer to illustrations 6.13, 6.14 and 6.16

12   Clean the mating surfaces of the timing chain cover, engine block and cylinder heads to remove all traces of old gasket material, oil and dirt. Final cleaning should be with lacquer thinner or acetone. **Warning:** *Be careful when cleaning any of the aluminum components. Use of a metal scraper could cause scratches or gouges that could lead to an oil leak later.*

13   Install the three new gaskets to the backside of the timing chain cover **(see illustration)**.

14   Apply a 1/8-inch bead of RTV sealant to the junctions of the oil pan-to-engine block and the cylinder head-to-engine block **(see illustration)**. Apply a small dab of RTV where the timing chain cover and engine block meet at the valve cover surface.

15   Lubricate the timing chains and the lip of the crankshaft front oil seal with clean engine oil.

16   Install the timing chain cover on the engine, within five minutes of applying the RTV sealant. Position the bottom/front edge of the timing chain cover flush with the front edge of the oil pan and "tilt" the top of the cover into place against the engine. Do not press the cover straight in against the engine or the sealant may be scraped off the front of the oil pan and cause a leak. Tighten the timing chain cover-to-engine block bolts in the recommended sequence **(see illustration)**, to the torque and sequence listed in this Chapter's Specifications. Tighten the timing

chain cover-to-oil pan bolts to the specified torque as well.

17   Install the remaining parts in the reverse order of removal.

18   Add the proper type and quantity of engine oil and coolant (see Chapter 1). Run the engine and check for leaks.

7   Timing chains, tensioners and sprockets - removal, inspection and installation

Caution: *At no time, once the timing chain(s) have been removed, can the crankshaft or the camshafts be rotated. If moved, damage to the valves and/or pistons can occur. Special tools are necessary to prevent the camshafts from moving when the timing chain is removed. Read through the entire procedure and obtain the necessary tools before proceeding.*

Note: *Because this is an "interference" engine design, if the chain has broken, there will be damage to the valves and/or pistons and will require removal of the cylinder heads.*

6.14 Apply a small bead of RTV sealant to the mating junctions of the oil pan-to-engine block and cylinder head-to-engine block

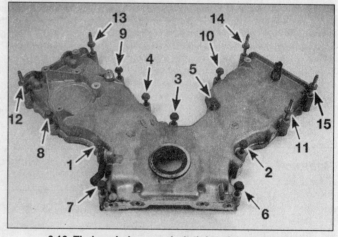

6.16 Timing chain cover bolt tightening sequence

7.3 All of the engines covered in this Chapter have two long timing chains with two main tensioners (arrows)

7.4 The crankshaft sensor tooth wheel has a specific direction to be installed - look for the word "rear" stamped in it (arrow)

Removal

Refer to illustrations 7.3 and 7.4

1   Disconnect the cable from the negative battery terminal.

2   Position the number one cylinder on TDC (see Section 3), and remove the spark plugs (see Chapter 1).

3   Remove the valve covers (see Section 4) and the timing chain cover (see Section 6). Two long timing chains connect the crankshaft to the camshafts **(see illustration)**.

4   Remove the crankshaft position sensor toothed-wheel **(see illustration)** by sliding it off the end of the crankshaft nose. Note the stamped word "rear" on the wheel to be sure it's reinstalled in the correct direction.

5.4L, 6.8L and 4.6L Windsor-built engines

Refer to illustrations 7.6a and 7.6b

5   On 6.8L V10 engines, mark the balance shaft caps to ensure that they're installed in the correct position, then remove the cap bolts, the caps and the balance shaft.

6   Install the camshaft and crankshaft

7.6a On Windsor-built engines, use this crankshaft positioning tool - the side hole (arrow) fits over the dowel on the right side of the engine

retaining tools **(see illustrations)**. Because of different methods of retaining the camshaft sprockets on the WEP and REP engines, different tools are required for each version. The tools lock the camshafts in position to prevent any movement of the camshafts in either direction, due to valve spring pressure, when the timing chains are removed. **Caution:** *The camshaft(s) MUST be retained exactly at TDC. If the valve timing is off when the timing*

chain(s) are reinstalled, severe engine damage could result.

4.6L Romeo-built engine

Refer to illustrations 7.7a and 7.7b

7   When positioning the engine at TDC for number 1 piston, look at the keyways on the camshaft sprockets. Use a square to insure that each keyway is at 90-degrees to the valve cover mounting surface of the cylinder head **(see illustration)**. Then install the camshaft position tool on the rear of the camshafts **(see illustration)**.

7.6b Each Windsor camshaft should be locked in TDC position with the camshaft holding tool, which bolts onto the camshaft between the second and third (from the front) camshaft retaining caps - the "legs" fit against the valve cover mounting surface on the cylinder head

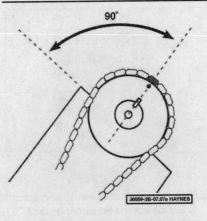

7.7a Both camshaft keyways on the 4.6L Romeo-built engine must be perpendicular to the valve cover mounting surface of the heads

7.7b The camshaft positioning tool for the 4.6L Romeo engine and adapters installs over the rear of the camshaft at TDC

7.8a To remove the timing chain tensioner, remove the two bolts from the tensioner (arrows) . . .

All models

Refer to illustrations 7.8a, 7.8b and 7.10

8   Remove the right side timing chain tensioner **(see illustrations)**.

9   Remove the right timing chain from the crankshaft and camshaft sprockets, by slipping the chain off the camshaft sprocket and pulling the crankshaft sprocket off with the chain.

10   Remove the stationary guide **(see illustration)**. **Note:** *The appearance of the chain guides is different between the WEP and REP engines, but the procedure and fasteners are the same.*

11   Remove the left side timing chain tensioner. Lift the chain off the camshaft sprocket and remove the chain along with the crankshaft sprocket.

12   Remove the left side stationary guide.

13   If the camshaft sprockets are to be replaced, remove the camshaft sprocket bolt and large washer from the camshafts (REP engines), then pull the camshaft sprockets off. On WEP engines, use a two-bolt puller to remove the camshaft sprockets. **Note:** *Note the location and direction of any spacers on the crankshaft or camshafts, but do not remove the spacers unless necessary.*

Inspection

Refer to illustrations 7.15a and 7.15b

14   Inspect the individual sprocket teeth and keyways for wear and damage. Check the chain for cracked plates, pitted or worn rollers. Check the wear surface of the chain guides for wear and damage. Replace any excessively worn or defective parts with new ones.

Caution: *If excessive plastic material is missing from the chain guides, the oil pan should be removed and cleaned of all debris (see Section 14). Check the oil pick-up tube and screen. Replace the assembly if it is clogged.*

15   Check the primary tensioners for proper operation:

a) *Release the plunger lock* **(see illustration)** *and make sure the piston moves freely.*

b) *Submerge the tensioner in a can of oil or solvent, remove from the fluid and depress the plunger to make sure the oil feed oil is not plugged* **(see illustration)**. **Note:** *Also inspect the oil feed hole in the engine block to be certain it's not plugged.*

Installation

Refer to illustration 7.17

16   Install the stationary chain guides, for both sides, and tighten the bolts to the torque listed in this Chapter's Specifications.

17   If removed, install the left crankshaft sprocket on the crankshaft with the shoulder of the sprocket facing forward. When the two sprockets are placed correctly the hubs will be

7.8b . . . and detach the guide assembly from the dowel at the opposite end

7.10 The stationary chain guide is removed by removing the bolts (arrows) at the mount plate

7.15a To fully retract the primary tensioner, release the plunger lock (arrow) and push the plunger into the tensioner body

7.15b Check the tensioner oil feed hole (arrow) to be sure it's not plugged by debris

7.17 When both are installed, the two crankshaft sprockets should align like this; here the left sprocket is installed with its shoulder forward, and the right sprocket (in hand) is ready to install with its shoulder (arrow) toward the other sprocket

7.21a When installing the timing chain, align one of the bright links in the timing chain with the dimple on the camshaft sprocket (arrows) - sprocket should also align with the keyway in the camshaft

7.21b Align the bright link at the lower end of the chain with the alignment mark on the crankshaft sprocket (it should be at 6 o'clock) then bolt the camshaft sprocket to the camshaft - both chains are aligned here

facing each other and there will be the maximum space possible between the two sprockets **(see illustration)**. For now, only install the inner (left chain) crankshaft sprocket, with its shoulder forward. **Note:** *On later models, the sprocket is one-piece and installs with the flange forward.*

18   The two timing chains should each have two bright or colored links. The links separate the chain in two equal halves. If no colored links are present, lay the chain down, make a paint mark on a link, then count links and make another paint mark halfway around the chain. Refer to Step 10 and reinstall both stationary chain guides. **Note:** *The longer bolts are the ones that hold the guide to the cylinder head, the shorter ones go to the engine block.*

5.4L, 6.8L and 4.6L Windsor-built engines
Refer to illustrations 7.21a and 7.21b

19   Loosen the camshaft holding tools just enough to permit minor movement of the camshafts for alignment. Using a camshaft positioning tool, available at most auto parts stores, or a two-pin spanner that catches two of the camshaft sprocket holes, turn the left camshaft until the timing mark on the sprocket is at 12 o'clock (viewed from the front of the engine). Turn the right sprocket until its mark is at 11 o'clock, then retighten both camshaft holding tools.

20   Install the inner crankshaft sprocket with the shoulder facing out, if not already done **(see illustration 7.17)**.

21   Install the left timing chain, aligning the bright link with the dimple on the camshaft sprocket **(see illustration)**. Loop the timing chain under the crankshaft sprocket and align the bright link with the alignment mark on the crankshaft sprocket. The timing marks on the crankshaft sprocket should be in the 6 o'clock position **(see illustration)**. **Note:** *The slack side of the chain (towards the water pump) must be below the dowel pin on the block.*

22   Install the right side chain and crankshaft sprocket (with its shoulder facing in) as above, but its slack side (the bottom run of the chain) should be above the dowel on the block. **Note:** *If necessary to achieve exact alignment of the chains and sprockets, move the camshaft sprockets slightly by loosening the holding tools.*

23   On 6.8L V10 engines, install the balance shaft on the left cylinder head, align the index mark on the balance shaft with the camshaft gear tooth mark **(see illustration 9.19)**, install the balance shaft bearing caps and then tighten the cap bolts to the torque listed in this Chapter's Specifications.

4.6L Romeo-built engine

24   Install the camshaft sprocket spacers (if removed before) and bolt on the camshaft sprockets, tightening the bolts to the torque listed in this Chapter's Specifications. Make sure the sprocket keyways are aligned with the camshaft keys before forcing the sprockets on or installing the bolt.

25   Install the left timing chain, aligning its colored link to the mark on the crankshaft sprocket and to the mark on the camshaft sprocket. Install the right timing chain and its crankshaft sprocket. When both chains are installed and all colored links and marks are aligned, the keyways of the camshaft sprockets should be at a 90-degree angle to the valve cover mounting surface of the cylinder heads **(see illustration 7.17)**. Remember, the shoulders on the crankshaft sprockets must face each other.

All models
Refer to illustration 7.26

26   The steps for installing the timing chain tensioners/guides are the same for both sides, either side can be done first. Before assembling the tensioner with the chain guide, compress the tensioner and lock it in this position with a straightened paper clip, Allen wrench or

drill bit **(see illustration)**.

27   Remove the slack from the chain by hand, and install the moveable guide assembly to the engine block and install the tensioner in the retracted position. Tighten the bolts to the torque listed in this Chapter's Specifications. Repeat for the other chain.

28   Remove the paper clip and apply pressure against the tensioner chain guide so the tensioner fully extends against the chain guide and all slack is removed from the chain.

29   Recheck all the timing marks to make sure they are still in alignment **(see illustration 7.21b)**.

30   Remove the camshaft positioning tools and retaining tools.

31   Slowly rotate the crankshaft in the normal direction of rotation (clockwise) at least two revolutions and again bring the engine to TDC. If you feel any resistance, stop and find out why. Check all alignment marks to verify that everything is properly assembled.

32   The remainder of installation is the reverse of removal.

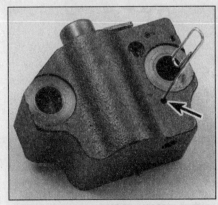

7.26 Lock the timing chain tensioner in the fully retracted position by placing a paper clip into the hole in the tensioner body (arrow)

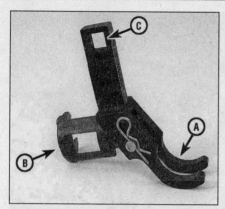

8.3a The special valve spring compressor hooks under the camshaft at (A), pushes on the valve spring retainer at (B), and is operated by a 1/2-inch drive breaker bar placed at (C)

8.3b Compress the valve spring until you can slip the rocker arm out - keep the rocker arms and lash adjusters matched to their original location

8.4 Pull the lash adjuster straight up and out of the cylinder head

8 Rocker arms and valve lash adjusters - removal, inspection and installation

There are two methods of removing the rocker arms and lash adjusters on these engines. The method recommended by the manufacturer accomplishes the removal of the camshaft roller followers without the removal of the camshaft(s) by using two special tools specified by the manufacturer: a valve spring spacer and a valve spring compressor, which are made specifically for these overhead cam engines and are available at some auto parts stores that carry special tools, or can be ordered from specialty tool dealers. The valve spring compressor uses the camshaft as a pivot point and, with a ratchet or bar attached, pushes down on the spring to release tension on the cam follower. The spring spacer keeps the spring from collapsing too far and hitting the valve stem seal. The alternative method requires the removal of the camshaft (see Section 9) in order to remove the cam fol-

lowers. Either method will achieve the same results, but it is much easier using the special tools, if they can be located.

Removal
Refer to illustrations 8.3a, 8.3b and 8.4

1 Remove the valve cover(s) (see Section 4).

2 Because of the interference design of these modular engines, the pistons must be positioned off TDC before compressing the valve springs to remove the rocker arms or lash adjusters. For whatever cylinder you are removing the rocker arms from, remove the spark plug and insert a plastic pen (hold onto it) to see how far the piston is from the top of its travel. If necessary, turn the crankshaft until the pen indicates the pistons are down at least an inch or two from TDC.

3 Install valve spring compressor and compress the spring enough to remove the rocker arm **(see illustrations)**. Camshaft rocker arms and hydraulic lash adjusters MUST be reinstalled with the same camshaft lobe that they were removed from. Label and store all components to avoid confusion during reassembly. **Caution:** *A valve spring spacer should be inserted into the coils of the spring before compressing it. If the spacer isn't in place between one of the valve spring coils, the spring can be compressed too far and the valve seal may be damaged.*

4 Remove the hydraulic lash adjuster

(see illustration). If there are many miles on the vehicle, the adjusters may have become varnished and difficult to remove. Apply a little penetrating oil around the lash adjuster to help loosen the varnish. **Note:** *Keep the rocker arm and lash adjuster for each valve together in a marked plastic sandwich bag.*

Inspection
Refer to illustrations 8.5 and 8.7

5 Inspect each adjuster carefully for signs of wear or damage. The areas of possible wear are the ball tip that contacts the cam follower and the sides of the adjuster that contact the bore in the cylinder head **(see illustration)**. Since the lash adjusters can become clogged as mileage increases, we recommend replacing them if you're concerned about their condition or if the engine is exhibiting valve "tapping" noises.

6 A thin wire or paper clip can be placed in the oil hole to move the plunger and make sure it's not stuck. **Note:** *The lash adjuster must have no more than 1/16-inch of total plunger travel.* It's recommended that if replacement of any of the adjusters is necessary, that the entire set be replaced. This will avoid the need to repeat the repair procedure as the others require replacement in the future.

7 Inspect the rocker arms for signs of wear or damage. The areas of wear are the ball socket that contacts the lash adjuster and the roller where the follower contacts the camshaft **(see illustration)**.

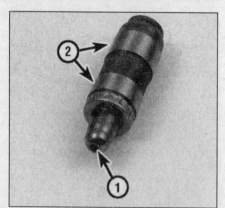

8.5 Inspect the lash adjuster for signs of excessive wear or damage, such as pitting, scoring or signs of overheating (bluing or discoloration), where the tip contacts the camshaft follower (1) and the side surfaces that contact the lifter bore in the cylinder head (2)

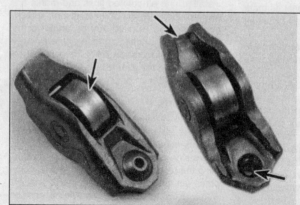

8.7 Check the roller surface (arrow) of the rocker arms and the areas where the valve stem and lash adjuster contact the rocker (arrows at right)

9.3 Camshaft end play can be checked by setting up a dial indicator off the front of the camshaft and prying the camshaft gently forward and back

9.4 REP engines have two "camshaft cap clusters" (rather than individual bearing caps like the WEP engines), that hold the camshaft in place on the cylinder head. Note the position of the two different bolts (arrows)

Installation

8 Before installing the lash adjusters, bleed as much air as possible out of them. Stand the adjusters upright in a container of oil. Use a thin wire or paper clip to work the plunger up and down. This "primes" the adjuster and removes most of the air. Leave the adjusters in the oil until ready to install.

9 Lubricate the valve stem tip, rocker arm, and lash adjuster bore with clean engine oil.

10 Install the lash adjusters and, with the valve spring depressed as in Step 3, install each rocker arm.

11 The remainder of installation is the reverse of the removal procedure.

12 When re-starting the engine after replacing the adjusters, the adjusters will normally make some "tapping" noises, until all the air is bled from the lash adjusters. After the engine is warmed-up, raise the speed from idle to 3,000 rpm for one minute. Stop the engine and let it cool down. All of the noise should be gone when it is restarted.

9 Camshaft(s) - removal, inspection and installation

Removal

Refer to illustrations 9.3 and 9.4

1 Remove the valve covers (see Sec-tion 4), and the timing chain cover (see Section 6). **Note:** *On the 6.8L V10 engine, it will be necessary to remove the intake manifold from the engine.*

2 Remove the timing chains, camshaft sprockets and spacers (see Section 7). **Caution:** *Don't mix up the sprockets; they are marked as RB (right bank) and LB (left bank), and must go back on the appropriate cam-shaft.*

3 Measure the thrust clearance (endplay) of the camshaft(s) with a dial indicator **(see illustration)**. If the clearance is greater than the value listed in this Chapter's Specifica-tions, replace the camshaft and/or the cyl-der head.

4 There are two designs for holding the camshaft journals. On Windsor-built engines, there are individual camshaft caps at each journal, while Romeo-built engines have two "camshaft cap clusters" for each camshaft. The configuration of the two cap clusters are different and must be placed in their original locations. Mark the camshaft cap clusters with a front and rear indication, for both the left and right cylinder heads. **Note:** *Two bolts used on one of the camshaft cap clusters are different than the others* **(see illustration)***; be sure they go back in the same locations on reassembly.*

5 Refer to Section 6 for removal of the front cover and Section 7 for removal of the timing chains. **Note:** *While the timing chains are off, the crankshaft must not be turned or valve-to-piston interference could result.*

6 On 6.8L engines, remove the balance shaft journal bolts and lift the balance shaft from each cylinder head.

7 Remove the caps and lift the camshaft off the cylinder head. You may have to tap lightly under the camshaft caps to jar them loose. Don't mix up the camshafts or any of the components. They must all go back on the same positions, and on the same cylin-der head they were removed from. **Note:** *It's IMPORTANT to loosen the bearing cap bolts only 1/4-turn at a time, following the reverse of the tightening sequence* **(see illustra-tions 9.16a, 9.16b and 9.16c)***, until they can be removed by hand.*

8 Repeat this procedure for removal of the remaining camshaft.

Inspection

Refer to illustrations 9.9a, 9.9b, 9.10a, 9.10b, 9.10c, 9.11a, 9.11b and 9.13

9 Visually examine the cam lobes and bearing journals for score marks, pitting, gall-ing and evidence of overheating (blue, discol-ored areas). Look for flaking of the hardened surface of each lobe **(see illustrations)**.

9.9a Areas to look for excessive wear or damage on the camshafts are the bearing surfaces and the camshaft lobes (arrows)

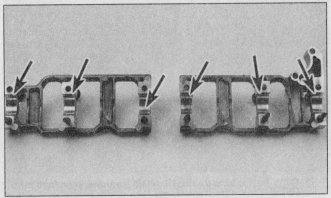

9.9b Inspect the bearing surfaces of the camshaft bearing caps (arrows) for signs of excessive wear, damage or overheating

9.10a Measuring the camshaft bearing journal diameter

9.10b Measure the camshaft lobe at its greatest dimension . . .

9.10c . . . and subtract the camshaft lobe diameter at its smallest dimension to obtain the lobe lift specification

9.11a Lay a strip of Plastigage on each of the camshaft journals

9.11b Compare the width of the crushed Plastigage to the scale on the envelope to determine the oil clearance

c) Lay a strip of Plastigage on each journal **(see illustration)**.

d) Install the camshaft bearing caps.

e) Tighten the cap bolts, a little at a time, to the torque listed in this Chapter's Specifications. **Note:** *Don't turn the camshaft while the Plastigage is in place.*

f) Remove the bolts and detach the caps.

g) Compare the width of the crushed Plastigage (at its widest point) to the scale on the Plastigage envelope **(see illustration)**.

h) If the clearance is greater than specified, and the diameter of any journal is less than specified, replace the camshaft. If the journal diameters are within specifications but the oil clearance is too great, the cylinder head is worn and must be replaced.

12   Scrape off the Plastigage with your fingernail or the edge of a credit card - don't scratch or nick the journals or bearing surfaces.

13   Finally, be sure to check the timing chain tensioner oil feed tube and reservoir before installing the cam caps **(see illustration)**.

10   Using a micrometer, measure the diameter of each camshaft journal and the lift of each camshaft lobe **(see illustrations)**. Compare your measurements with the Specifications listed at the front of this Chapter, and if the diameter of any one of these is less than specified, replace the camshaft.

11   Check the oil clearance for each camshaft journal as follows:

a) *Clean the bearing surfaces and the camshaft journals with lacquer thinner or acetone.*

b) *Carefully lay the camshaft(s) in place in the cylinder head. Don't install the rocker arms or lash adjusters and don't use any lubrication.*

9.13 Oil is delivered to the timing chain tensioner by a feed tube and reservoir in the cylinder head

1   Tensioner oil feed tube   *2   Reservoir*

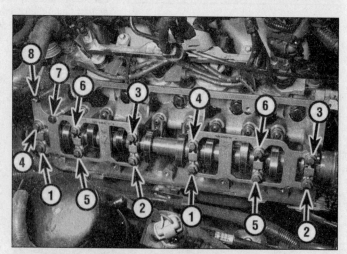

9.16a Camshaft cap cluster bolt tightening sequence, 4.6L Romeo engines - notice that each cap is tightened separately and has its own sequence

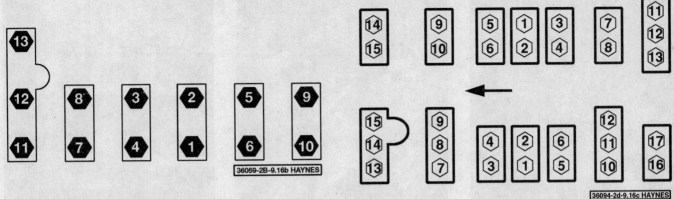

9.16b Camshaft cap tightening sequence - 4.6L and 5.4L Windsor engines

9.16c Camshaft cap tightening sequence - 6.8L engines

It must be absolutely clean and free of all obstructions or it will affect the operation of the timing chain tensioner.

Installation

Refer to illustrations 9.16a, 9.16b, 9.16c and 9.19

14   If the lash adjusters and/or camshaft followers have been removed, install them in their original locations (see Section 8).

15   Apply moly-base grease or camshaft installation lube to the camshaft lobes and bearing journals, then install the camshaft(s).

16   Install the camshaft caps in the correct locations, and loosely install all the bolts. Refer to Section 7 to align the camshaft sprockets before tightening the cap bolts. Following the correct bolt-tightening sequence **(see illustrations)**, tighten the bolts in 1/4-turn increments to the torque listed in this Chapter's Specifications.

17   Reinstall the camshaft positioning and retaining tools (see Section 7) to set the camshafts at TDC before reinstalling the timing chain(s).

18   Install the timing chain(s), tensioners and timing chain cover (see Section 7).

19   On 6.8L engines, install the balance shaft on the left cylinder head. Be sure to align the index mark on the balance shaft with the camshaft gear tooth mark **(see illustration)**. Tighten the balance shaft bearing cap bolts to the torque listed in this Chapter's Specifications. Start with the front (timing chain side) cap bolts and work towards the rear.

20   The remainder of installation is the reverse of the removal procedure.

10   Valve springs, retainers and seals - removal and installation

Broken valve springs and/or defective valve stem seals can be replaced without removing the cylinder heads. There is a method described in Section 8, using a tool recommended by the manufacturer, which accomplishes the removal of the valve springs and seals without the removal of the camshafts. The alternative method uses a more commonly available tool, but will require the removal of the camshaft (see Section 9) in order to remove the valve spring. Either method will achieve the same results, but it is much easier using the manufacturer's recommended procedure, if the correct tools can be located.

In either repair procedure, a compressed air source is normally required to perform this operation, so read through this Section carefully and rent or buy the tools before beginning the job.

Removal

Refer to illustration 10.4

1   Remove the valve cover (see Section 4).

2   Remove the spark plug from the cylinder with the defective component. If all of the valve stem seals are being replaced, remove all the spark plugs.

3   Turn the crankshaft until the piston in the affected cylinder is at Top Dead Center (TDC) on the compression stroke (see Section 3). If you're replacing all of the valve stem seals, begin with cylinder number one and work on the valves for one cylinder at a time. Move from cylinder-to-cylinder following the firing order sequence (see this Chapter's Specifications).

4   Thread an air hose adapter into the spark plug hole **(see illustration)** and connect an air hose from a compressed air source to it. Most auto parts stores can supply the air hose adapter. **Note:** *Many cylinder compression gauges utilize a screw-in fitting that may work with your air hose quick-disconnect fitting.*

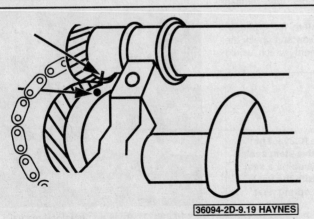

9.19 Camshaft and balance shaft alignment marks (arrows) on the 6.8L V10 engine

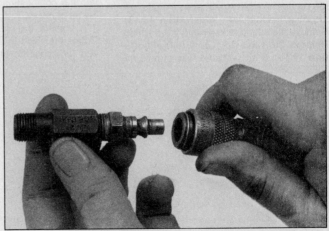

10.4 This is the air hose adapter that threads into the spark plug hole - they're commonly available from auto parts stores

10.12 Installation of a valve spring compressor more commonly available at local automotive parts stores (the camshaft must be removed for the use of this type of valve spring compressor)

10.13 Once the spring is compressed, remove the keepers with a needle-nose pliers or a magnet, as shown here

10.15 Use pliers to firmly grasp the old seal and pull it off the valve guide

5   Apply compressed air to the cylinder. **Warning:** *The piston may be forced down by compressed air, causing the crankshaft to turn suddenly. If the wrench used when positioning the number one piston at TDC is still attached to the bolt in the crankshaft nose, it could cause damage or injury when the crankshaft moves.*

6   The valves should be held in place by the air pressure.

7   Stuff shop rags into the cylinder head holes above and below the valves to prevent parts and tools from falling into the engine.

Method using special tools

8   Install a valve spacer, available at most auto parts stores. **Caution:** *If the spacer isn't in place between one of the valve coils, the spring can be compressed too far, possibly damaging the valve seal.*

9   Compress the spring and remove the rocker arm (see Section 8). Rocker arms and hydraulic lash adjusters MUST be reinstalled with the same camshaft lobe that they were removed from. Label and store all components to avoid confusion during reassembly.

10   Keeping the spring compressed, remove the keepers with small needle-nose pliers or a magnet **(see illustration 10.13)**. Remove the spring retainer and valve spring. Remove the valve stem seal **(see illustration 10.15)**. If air pressure fails to hold the

valve in the closed position during this operation, the valve face and/or seat is probably damaged. If so, the cylinder head will have to be removed for additional repair operations.

Alternative procedure

Refer to illustrations 10.12, 10.13 and 10.15

11   Remove the camshaft(s) (see Section 9).

12   Install the commonly available clamp-type valve spring compressor **(see illustration)**.

13   Compress the spring and remove the keepers with small needle-nose pliers or a magnet **(see illustration)**.

14   Remove the spring retainer and valve spring.

15   Remove the stem seal **(see illustration)**. If air pressure fails to hold the valve in the closed position during this operation, the valve face and/or seat is probably damaged. If so, the cylinder head will have to be removed for additional repair operations.

Installation

Refer to illustrations 10.20a, 10.20b and 10.22

16   Wrap a rubber band or tape around the top of the valve stem so the valve won't fall into the combustion chamber, then release the air pressure.

17   Inspect the valve stem for damage. Rotate the valve in the guide and check the end for eccentric movement, which would

indicate that the valve is bent.

18   Move the valve up-and-down in the guide and make sure it doesn't bind. If the valve stem binds, either the valve is bent or the guide is damaged. In either case, the cylinder head will have to be removed for repair.

19   Reapply air pressure to the cylinder to retain the valve in the closed position, then remove the tape or rubber band from the valve stem.

20   Lubricate the valve stem with engine oil and install a new seal **(see illustration)**. There is a special tool for the installation of the valve seal. If the tool isn't available, a socket that will fit over the seal and is deep enough to make contact with the seat **(see illustration)**, can be used to carefully tap the new seal into place. **Caution:** *The valve seal used on these engines is a combination seal and spring seat. Never place a valve spring directly against the aluminum cylinder head (without a seal/spring seat) - the hardened spring would damage the cylinder head.*

21   Make sure the garter spring on the seal is still in place, and install the spring in position over the valve.

22   Install the valve spring retainer. Compress the valve spring and carefully position the keepers in the groove. Apply a small dab of grease to the inside of each keeper to hold

10.20a The valve stem seals combine a seal with the valve spring seat

10.20b There is a special valve seal installation tool available, but a deep socket that fits over the seal can be used to gently tap the seal into place

10.22 Apply a small dab of grease to each keeper as shown here before installation - it'll hold them in place on the valve stem as the spring is released

it in place if necessary **(see illustration)**.

23   Remove the pressure from the spring tool and make sure the keepers are seated.

24   Disconnect the air hose and remove the adapter from the spark plug hole.

25   If the camshaft(s) were removed, reinstall them at this time (see Section 9).

26   Install the spark plug(s) and connect the wire(s).

27   The remaining installation steps are the reverse of removal.

28   Start and run the engine, then check for oil leaks and unusual sounds coming from the valve cover area.

11   Intake manifold - removal and installation

Note: *The intake manifold is designed as a two piece unit. The lower section of the intake manifold can only be accessed after the intake manifold has been removed from the engine. The lower section of the intake manifold contains the intake manifold tuning valve. Refer to Chapter 4 for additional information.*

Removal

1   Disconnect the cable from the negative battery terminal. Relieve the fuel system pressure (see Chapter 4).

2   Drain the cooling system and remove the drivebelt (see Chapter 1).

3   Disconnect the radiator hose from the thermostat housing and remove the thermostat housing (see Chapter 3). The thermostat housing bolts also retain the intake manifold.

4   Remove the air cleaner and outlet tube (see Chapter 4).

5   Label and disconnect all vacuum lines connected to the intake manifold. On 2001 and later models, disconnect the fuel pressure sensor vacuum hose and electrical connector.

6   Remove the PCV and canister purge hoses from the valve covers (see Section 4).

7   Refer to Chapter 4 for the following procedures: disconnect the accelerator cable, speed control linkage (if so equipped), electrical connectors at the throttle body, fuel injectors, fuel rails, and disconnect and plug the fuel supply and return lines.

8   Refer to Chapter 5 and disconnect the ignition wire brackets, boots and wires and set them out of the way. On later models, remove the individual coils over each spark plug. **Note:** *Pull the spark plug wire separators from their mounts on the valve cover studs and lay the wires out of the way.*

9   Refer to Chapter 6 for the following procedures: disconnect the idle air control valve, differential pressure feedback transducer and hoses, engine vacuum regulator sensor and EGR valve-to-exhaust manifold pipe.

10   Disconnect the alternator electrical connectors and remove the alternator (see Chapter 5).

11   Remove the bolts retaining the alternator bracket to the intake manifold (see Chapter 5).

12   Disconnect the ignition coils (see Chapter 5).

13   Disconnect the electrical connectors from the camshaft sensor, coolant temperature sending unit, air charge temperature sensor, throttle positioner and idle speed control solenoid (see Chapter 6). **Note:** *On 2005 models, the throttle body does not have an accelerator cable. The electronic throttle body has a large electrical connector - to disconnect it, pull out the red clip first.*

14   Disconnect the heater hose at the manifold, then unbolt the heater hose tube from the back of the engine.

15   Pull the engine wiring harness off the valve cover and intake studs and away from the intake manifold. On 2001 and later models, remove the mounting bolts/nuts and remove the throttle body.

16   Unbolt the power steering reservoir bracket and set the pump aside (see Chapter 10).

17   Unbolt the bracket supporting the power brake booster hose at the left-rear of the engine.

18   Loosen the intake manifold bolts and nuts in 1/4-turn increments, following the reverse order of the tightening sequence **(see illustrations 11.27a and 11.27b)**, until they can be removed by hand.

19   Lift the intake manifold from the cylinder heads and disconnect the intake manifold tuning valve from the lower section, if necessary. The manifold may be stuck to the cylinder heads and force may be required to break the gasket seal. A prybar can be used to pry up the manifold, but make sure all bolts and nuts have been removed first! **Caution:** *Don't pry between the engine block and manifold or the cylinder heads, or damage to the gasket sealing surface may occur, leading to vacuum and oil leaks. Pry only at the manifold protrusion.*

20   Remove the intake manifold gaskets and clean all traces of gasket or sealant material from the sealing surfaces of the cylinder heads and intake manifold.

Lower section of intake manifold

Refer to illustrations 11.23a and 11.23b

21   Remove the bolts that retain the lower section of the intake manifold. These bolts are located on the interior portion of the upper intake manifold **(see illustrations 11.23a and 11.23b)**. Follow the reverse of the tightening sequence.

22   Clean all traces of old gasket material from the mating surfaces of the manifolds. Be sure to install a new gasket.

23   Installation is the reverse of removal. Tighten the bolts to the torque listed in this Chapter's Specifications. Follow the correct tightening sequence **(see illustrations)**.

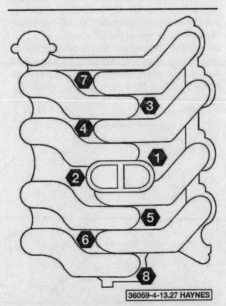

11.23a Intake manifold lower section tightening sequence - V8 engines

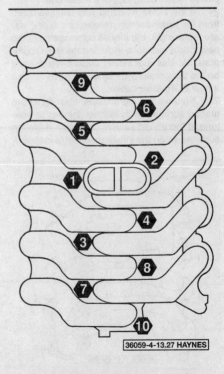

11.23b Intake manifold lower section tightening sequence - V10 engines

11.27 Check the condition of the water pump hose (arrow) and replace it if necessary - REP engine shown

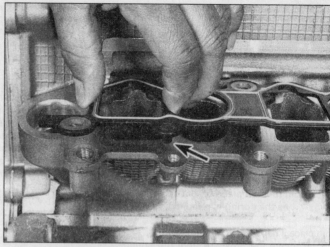

11.28 Install the new intake manifold gaskets to the cylinder head, aligning the plastic pins (arrow) to their holes in the cylinder head

Installation

Refer to illustrations 11.27, 11.28, 11.30a and 11.30b

Caution: *The mating surfaces of the cylinder heads, engine block and intake manifold must be perfectly clean. Gasket removal solvents in aerosol cans are available at most auto parts stores and may be helpful when removing old gasket material that's stuck to the cylinder heads and intake manifold. Since the cylinder heads are aluminum and the intake manifold is aluminum or plastic, aggressive scraping can cause damage! Be sure to follow directions printed on the container, and use only a plastic-tipped scraper, not a metal one.*

24   If the intake manifold was disassembled from the lower section, reassemble it or if you are replacing it, transfer all components to the new intake manifold, including the IMRC components. Use electrically conductive sealant on the temperature sending unit threads. Use a new EGR valve gasket.

25   Remove the old gaskets, then clean the mating surfaces with lacquer thinner or acetone. If there's old sealant or oil on the mating surfaces when the intake manifold is installed,

oil or vacuum leaks may develop.

26   When working on the cylinder heads and engine block, cover the open engine areas with shop rags to keep debris out of the engine. Use a vacuum cleaner to remove any gasket material that falls into the intake ports in the cylinder heads.

27   Use a tap of the correct size to chase the threads in the bolt holes, then use compressed air (if available) to remove the debris from the holes. **Warning:** *Wear safety glasses or a face shield to protect your eyes when using compressed air!* Remove excessive carbon deposits and corrosion from the exhaust and coolant passages in the cylinder heads and intake manifold. **Note:** *If the vehicle has many miles on it, replace the water pump hose (normally hidden by the intake manifold) before replacing the manifold* (see illustration). *On REP engines, the hose is retained by a clamp, and a metal tube and nut are used on WEP engines. On WEP engines, replace the O-ring at the tube nut.*

28   Install the gaskets on the cylinder heads (see illustration). Make sure all alignment tabs, intake port openings, coolant passage holes and bolt holes are aligned correctly.

The gasket that goes on the cylinder head will have projecting plastic pins to align it with holes in the cylinder head.

29   Carefully set the intake manifold in place. Don't disturb the gaskets and don't move the manifold fore-and-aft after it contacts the gaskets on the engine block.

30   Install the intake manifold bolts and, following the recommended tightening sequence (see illustrations), tighten them to the torque listed in this Chapter's Specifications. Replace the O-ring seal on the thermostat housing. Install the thermostat housing and tighten the bolts to the torque listed in Chapter 3 Specifications.

31   The remaining installation steps are the reverse of removal. Use a new gasket when installing the throttle body. Start the engine and check carefully for oil and coolant leaks.

12   Exhaust manifolds - removal and installation

Removal

Refer to illustrations 12.5, 12.6a and 12.6b

1   Disconnect the cable from the negative battery terminal.

2   Remove the nut and move the power brake booster vacuum hose support bracket.

3   Raise the vehicle and support it securely on jackstands. **Warning:** *Some models covered by this manual are equipped with an air suspension system. Always disconnect the electrical power to the suspension system before lifting or towing (see Chapter 10). Failure to perform this procedure may result in unexpected shifting or movement of the vehicle, which could cause personal injury.* Remove the inner splash shield from the fenderwell.

4   Working under the vehicle, apply penetrating oil to the exhaust pipe-to-manifold studs and nuts (they're usually corroded or rusty). Also apply some to the EGR pipe fitting on the left exhaust manifold.

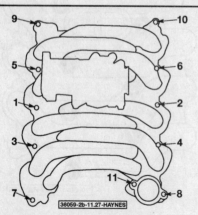

11.30a Intake manifold bolt tightening sequence - V8 engines

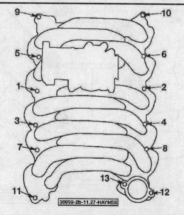

11.30b Intake manifold bolt tightening sequence - V10 engines

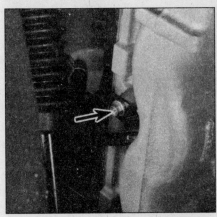

12.5 Remove the nut (arrow) securing the oil dipstick tube

12.6a Disconnect the EGR tube (arrow) from the left exhaust manifold

5   Remove the nuts retaining the exhaust pipes to the manifolds. On the left side, remove the nut and bracket securing the oil dipstick tube **(see illustration)**.

6   Remove the EGR pipe fitting from the left exhaust manifold. And on later models, remove the EGR tube from the vehicle. Remove the eight mounting nuts from each manifold **(see illustrations)**. **Note:** *The exhaust manifold nuts are difficult to access. You'll need a flex-socket and various-length 3/8-inch drive or 1/4-inch drive extensions to reach all the bolts.*

Installation

7   Check the exhaust manifolds for cracks. Make sure the bolt threads are clean and undamaged. The exhaust manifold and cylinder head mating surfaces must be clean before the exhaust manifolds are reinstalled - use a gasket scraper to remove all carbon deposits.

8   Position a new gasket in place and slip the exhaust manifold over the studs on the cylinder head. Install the mounting nuts.

9   When tightening the mounting nuts, tighten one top row bolt and its opposite on the bottom row, working from the center of the manifold out toward each end of the manifold.

10   The remaining installation steps are the reverse of removal. When reconnecting the EGR tube to the left manifold, use a slight amount of anti-seize compound on the threads.

12.6b Remove the exhaust manifold nuts (three are shown here on the left manifold)

11   Start the engine and check for exhaust leaks.

---

13 Cylinder heads - removal and installation

Caution: *The engine must be completely cool when the cylinder heads are removed. Failure to allow the engine to cool off could result in cylinder head warpage.*

Note 1: *Cylinder head removal is a difficult and time-consuming job requiring several special tools. Read through the procedure and obtain the necessary tools before beginning.*

Note 2: *On 2003 and later models, the manufacturer recommends removing the engine from the vehicle to remove the cylinder heads (see Chapter 2, Part E).*

Removal

1   Disconnect the negative battery cable and drain the cooling system (see Chapter 1).

2   Remove the valve covers (see Section 4) and the intake manifold (see Section 11).

3   Remove the exhaust manifolds (see Section 12).

4   Remove the timing chain cover (see Section 6).

5   The cylinder heads can be removed with the camshafts, rocker arms and lash adjust-

ers in place. Remove the timing chains, tensioners and guides (see Section 7). **Caution:** *Use the required camshaft retaining fixtures to lock the camshafts and leave the tools in place.*

6   If the cylinder head is to be completely overhauled, refer to Section 8 and remove the rocker arms, and Section 9 for removal of the camshafts.

7   Following the reverse of the tightening sequence **(see illustration 13.18a)**, use a breaker bar to remove the cylinder head bolts. Loosen the bolts in sequence 1/4-turn at a time.

8   Use a pry bar at the corners of the cylinder head-to-engine block mating surface to break the cylinder head gasket seal. Do not pry between the cylinder head and engine block in the gasket sealing area.

9   Lift the cylinder head(s) off the engine. If resistance is felt, place a wood block against the end and strike the wood block with a hammer. **Caution:** *The cylinder heads are aluminum - store them on wood blocks to prevent damage to the gasket sealing surfaces.*

10   Remove the cylinder head gasket(s). Before removing, note which gasket goes on which side (they are different and cannot be interchanged).

11   Cylinder head disassembly and inspection procedures are covered in detail in Chapter 2, Part E.

Installation

Refer to illustrations 13.15, 13.16, 13.18a, 13.18b and 13.18c

Caution: *New cylinder head bolts must be used for reassembly. Failure to use new bolts may result in cylinder head gasket leakage and engine damage.*

12   The mating surfaces of the cylinder heads and engine block must be perfectly clean when the cylinder heads are installed. Use liquid silicone-gasket remover on the gasket surfaces and scrape the head and block with a plastic scraper only or the gasket surfaces could be damaged. Use a gasket scraper to remove all traces of carbon and old gasket material, then clean the mating surfaces with lacquer thinner or acetone. If there's oil on the mating surfaces when the cylinder heads are installed, the gaskets may not seal correctly and leaks may develop. When working on the engine block, cover the open areas of the engine with shop rags to keep debris out during repair and reassembly. Use a vacuum cleaner to remove any debris that falls into the cylinders. **Caution:** *Do not use abrasive wheels or sharp metal scrapers on the heads or block surface, use a plastic scraper and chemical gasket remover, or the head gasket surfaces could have future leaks.*

13   Check the engine block and cylinder head mating surfaces for nicks, deep scratches and other damage.

14   Use a tap of the correct size to chase the threads in the cylinder head bolt holes. Dirt, corrosion, sealant and damaged threads will affect torque readings.

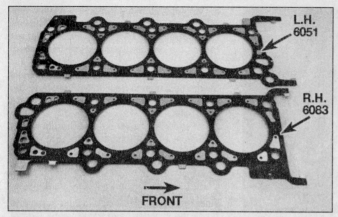

13.15 Identify the left and right cylinder head gaskets, the shapes are different and cannot be interchanged

13.16 Position the gaskets on the correct cylinder banks, then push them down over the alignment dowels (arrows)

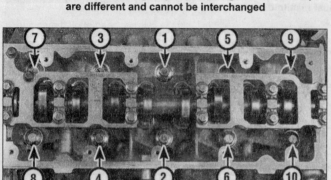

13.18a Cylinder head bolt tightening sequence for V8 engines - 4.6L Romeo engine shown but the V8 Windsor engines similar

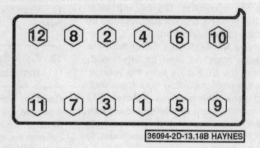

36094-2D-13.18B HAYNES

13.18b Cylinder head bolt tightening sequence for V10 engines

15   Make sure the new gaskets are installed on the correct cylinder banks **(see illustration)**. They are not interchangeable.

16   Position the new gasket(s) over the alignment dowels **(see illustration)** in the engine block.

17   If the cylinder heads are being installed with the camshafts in place, make sure the camshafts are back in their original TDC positions **(see Sections 7 and 9)** before placing the cylinder heads on the engine block. **Caution:** *If the camshafts aren't in the position described, damage may result to either the*

13.18c Mark each cylinder head bolt with a paint stripe (arrows) and using a breaker bar and socket, tighten the bolts in sequence the additional 1/4-turn (90-degrees)

pistons and/or valve train parts.

18   Carefully position the cylinder heads on the engine block without disturbing the gaskets. Install NEW cylinder head bolts (the cylinder head bolts are torque-to-yield design and cannot be reused). Following the recommended sequence **(see illustrations)**, tighten the cylinder head bolts, in three steps, to the torque listed in this Chapter's Specifications. **Note:** *The method used for the cylinder head bolt tightening procedure is referred to as "torque-angle" or "torque-to-yield" method. Follow the procedure exactly.* Tighten the bolts in the first step using a torque wrench, then use a breaker bar and a special torque-angle adapter (available at most auto parts stores) to tighten the bolts the required angle. If the adapter is not available, mark each bolt with a paint stripe to aid in the torque angle process **(see illustration)**.

19   The remaining installation steps are the reverse of removal.

20   Change the engine oil and filter (Chapter 1), then start the engine and check carefully for oil and coolant leaks.

14   Oil pan - removal and installation

Removal
Refer to illustration 14.13

1   Disconnect the negative battery cable

from the battery.

2   Remove the air cleaner and intake duct (see Chapter 4).

3   Refer to Chapter 1 and drain the engine oil and remove the oil filter.

4   Refer to Chapter 3 and remove the engine cooling fan assembly and shroud.

5   Remove the throttle body from the intake manifold (see Chapter 4). On 2001 and later models, refer to Section 11 and remove the intake manifold.

6   Remove the vapor management valve (see Chapter 6).

7   Remove the transmission tube nut, located at the back of the right cylinder head, and position the tube aside.

8   Raise the vehicle and support it securely on jackstands.

9   Remove the nuts from the front engine mounts.

10   Remove the driveplate inspection cover from the transmission bellhousing.

11   Carefully position two floor jacks under the right and left oil pan rails and raise the engine. **Caution 1:** *Raise the engine slowly while observing the location of the intake manifold if not removed already. Do not allow the intake manifold to contact the vehicle or damage to the throttle body may occur.* **Caution 2:** *Do not position the floorjack onto the oil pan or it will be severely damaged.* **Note:** *It is preferable to use two screw jacks to lift the*

14.13 Remove the bolts from around the perimeter of the oil pan (arrows indicate four) and lower the pan to the frame crossmember

14.17 Apply a bead of RTV sealant at the junctions of the front cover-to-engine block and the rear seal retainer-to-engine block (arrows) before installing the oil pan

engine because of the narrow lifting pad. The manufacturer recommends raising the engine from above, using an engine support cradle or crane.

12   If using jacks from below, place two large blocks of wood between the engine mounts and the lower engine mount brackets after the engine is raised. Lower the engine onto the blocks. Note that the engine must be raised 10.25 inches.

13   Remove the oil pan mounting bolts **(see illustration)**.

14   Carefully separate the oil pan from the engine block. Don't pry between the engine block and oil pan or damage to the sealing surfaces may result and oil leaks could develop. Instead, dislodge the oil pan with a large rubber mallet or a wood block and a hammer. The oil pan will come down only so far. Reach in between the engine and the oil pan and remove the two bolts and one nut securing the oil pump pickup tube, then remove the oil pickup with the oil pan. **Note:** The oil pan gasket is reusable if care is taken in oil pan removal.

Installation

Refer to illustrations 14.17 and 14.18

15   Use a plastic gasket scraper or putty knife to remove all traces of old gasket material and sealant from the pan and engine block. **Caution:** *Be careful not to gouge the oil pan or block, or oil leaks could develop later.*

16   Clean the mating surfaces with lacquer thinner or acetone. Make sure the bolt holes in the engine block are clean.

17   Apply a bead of RTV sealant to the four corner seams where the rear seal retainer meets the engine block, and the front cover meets the engine block **(see illustration)**.

18   Carefully position the oil pan against the engine block and install the bolts finger tight. Make sure the gaskets haven't shifted, then tighten the bolts to the torque listed in this Chapter's Specifications **(see illustration)**. Start at the center of the oil pan and work out toward the ends in a spiral pattern.

19   The remaining steps are the reverse of removal. **Caution:** *Don't forget to refill the*

engine with oil before starting it (see Chapter 1).

20   Start the engine and check carefully for oil leaks at the oil pan. Drive the vehicle and check again.

15   Oil pump - removal and installation

Refer to illustrations 15.3, 15.5 and 15.6
Note: *The oil pump is available as a complete replacement unit only. No service parts or repair specifications are available from the manufacturer.*

Removal

1   Raise the vehicle and support it securely on jackstands.

2   Drain the engine oil (see Chapter 1).

3   Unbolt and lower the oil pan as described in Section 14. It's not necessary to completely remove the oil pan. Remove the two bolts that attach the oil pump pick-up tube to the oil pump **(see illustration)**.

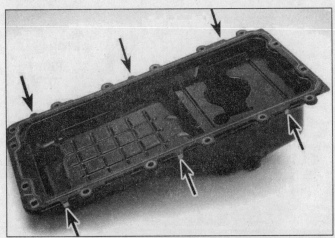

14.18 Place the gasket on the oil pan, the locating tabs (arrows) on each side of the gasket will keep the gasket aligned during installation

15.3 Remove the two bolts (arrows) retaining the pickup tube to the oil pump

4   Remove the timing chain cover, timing chains, chain guides and crankshaft sprockets (see Sections 6 and 7).
5   Remove the four oil pump mounting bolts **(see illustration)** and separate the pump from the engine block.

Installation

6   Inspect the O-ring gasket on the pick-up tube **(see illustration)**. If it's damaged, replace it.
7   Install the oil pump to the engine and tighten the bolts to the torque listed in this Chapter's Specifications. **Note:** *Prime the oil pump prior to installation. Pour clean oil into the pick-up port and turn the pump by hand.*
8   The remainder of installation is the reverse of removal procedure.
9   Fill the engine with the correct type and quantity of oil. Start the engine and check for leaks.

16   Driveplate - removal and installation

Removal

Refer to illustration 16.4
1   Disconnect the cable from the negative battery terminal.
2   Raise the vehicle and support it securely on jackstands.
3   Refer to Chapter 7 and remove the transmission.
4   Look for factory paint marks that indicate driveplate-to-crankshaft alignment. If they aren't there, scribe or paint marks on the driveplate and crankshaft to ensure correct alignment during reassembly **(see illustration)**.
5   Remove the bolts that secure the driveplate to the crankshaft. Insert a screwdriver or punch through one of the holes in the driveplate to keep the crankshaft from turning while loosening the driveplate bolts.
6   Remove the driveplate from the crank-

15.5 Remove the four oil pump mounting bolts (arrows) and oil pump from the engine block

shaft. Be sure to support it while removing the last bolt. **Warning:** *The teeth on the driveplate may be sharp. Be sure to hold it with gloves or rags.* After the driveplate is removed, there is a sheetmetal reinforcement/mounting plate that is located between the engine block and the driveplate. It doesn't need to be removed, unless necessary.

Installation

Refer to illustration 16.7
7   If removed, be sure the reinforcement plate is installed as shown **(see illustration)**, so it is correctly positioned for the starter installation.
8   Clean and inspect the mating surfaces of the driveplate and the crankshaft. If the crankshaft rear seal is leaking, replace it before reinstalling the driveplate (see Section 19).
9   Check for cracked, broken or missing ring gear teeth. If any of these conditions are found, replace the driveplate.
10   Install the driveplate to the engine, aligning the marks made during removal. Note that some engines have an alignment dowel or staggered bolt holes to ensure correct installation. Before installing the bolts, apply Teflon

15.6 Before bolting the pickup tube back into the oil pump, inspect the O-ring (arrow) and replace it if necessary

thread sealant to the threads.
11   Prevent the driveplate from turning as you tighten the bolts to the torque listed in this Chapter's Specifications.
12   The remainder of installation is the reverse of the removal procedure.

17   Crankshaft oil seals - replacement

Front seal

Refer to illustrations 17.4 and 17.6
1   Disconnect the negative battery cable.
2   Remove the drivebelt (Chapter 1) and fan/shroud assembly (Chapter 3).
3   Remove the crankshaft pulley (see Section 5).
4   Carefully remove the seal from the cover with a seal removal tool **(see illustration)**. If a seal removal tool is not available, carefully use a screwdriver. If the timing cover is removed, use a chisel or small punch and hammer to drive the seal out of the cover from the back side. Support the cover as close to the seal bore as possible with two wood blocks. Be

16.4 Make an alignment mark (arrow), if not already on the driveplate, to reassure proper reassembly

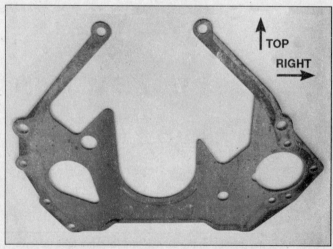

16.7 If the reinforcement plate is removed, for any reason, it should be reinstalled in the direction shown here

17.4 Using a special seal removal tool or screwdriver, remove the crankshaft front oil seal, being very careful not to scratch the crankshaft during seal removal

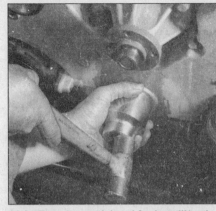

17.6 There is special tool for installing the front oil seal into the timing chain cover, but if the tool is unavailable a large socket or section of tubing (the same diameter as the seal) can be used to drive the seal into place

17.15 Remove the eight bolts (arrows) and separate the seal retainer from the engine block

careful not to damage the cover or scratch the wall of the seal bore.

5   Check the seal bore and crankshaft, as well as the seal contact surface on the crankshaft pulley for nicks and burrs. Position the new seal in the bore with the open end of the seal facing IN. A small amount of engine oil applied to the outer edge of the new seal will make installation easier.

6   Drive the seal into the bore with a large socket and hammer until it's completely seated **(see illustration)**. If the cover is removed, support the cover on wood blocks. Select a socket that's the same outside diameter as the seal (a section of pipe can be used if a socket isn't available).

7   Lubricate the lip of the seal with clean engine oil and install the crankshaft pulley on the end of the crankshaft. The keyway in the crankshaft pulley bore must be aligned with the Woodruff key in the crankshaft nose. **Note:** *Before reinstalling the crankshaft pulley, apply as small dab of RTV sealant to the front end of the crankshaft key groove.*

8   If the crankshaft pulley can't be seated by hand, tap it into place with a soft-face hammer, or install the bolt and washer and tighten it to press the crankshaft pulley into place.

9   Tighten the crankshaft pulley bolt to the torque listed in this Chapter's Specifications.
10   Install the drivebelt.
11   Install the remaining parts removed for access to the seal.
12   Start the engine and check for leaks.

Rear seal

Refer to illustrations 17.15, 17.16, 17.17 and 17.18

13   Disconnect the cable from the negative battery terminal. Raise the vehicle and support it securely on jackstands. Refer to Chapter 7 and remove the transmission.
14   Remove the driveplate and the rear cover plate from the engine (Section 16).
15   Remove the bolts, detach the seal retainer **(see illustration)** and clean off all the old gasket and/or sealant material from both the engine block and the seal retainer.
16   Support the seal and retainer assembly on wood blocks and drive the old seal out from the back side with a punch and hammer **(see illustration)**.
17   Drive the new seal into the retainer with a wood block **(see illustration)**.

18   Clean the crankshaft and seal bore with lacquer thinner or acetone. Check the seal contact surface on the crankshaft very carefully for scratches or nicks that could damage the new seal lip and cause oil leaks **(see illustration)**. If the crankshaft is damaged, the only alternative is a new or different crankshaft.
19   Lubricate the crankshaft seal journal and the lip of the new seal with engine oil.
20   Place a 1/16-inch wide bead of anaerobic sealant on either the engine block or the seal retainer.
21   Install the oil seal retainer by slowly and carefully pushing the seal onto the crankshaft. The seal lip is stiff, so work it onto the crankshaft with a smooth object such as the end of a socket extension as you push the retainer against the engine block.
22   Install and tighten the retainer bolts to the torque listed in this Chapter's Specifications.
23   Reinstall the engine rear cover plate, driveplate and the transmission.
24   The remaining steps are the reverse of removal.
25   Check the oil level and add if necessary, run the engine and check for oil leaks.

17.16 Support the seal retainer on two wood blocks and drive out the old seal with a blunt punch and hammer

17.17 Support the seal retainer and drive the new seal into the housing with a wood block (be careful not to cock the seal in the bore while installing)

17.18 Inspect the seal contact surface on the crankshaft (arrow) for signs of excessive wear or grooves

18   Engine mounts - check and replacement

Check

Refer to illustration 18.4

1   Engine mounts seldom require attention, but broken or deteriorated mounts should be replaced immediately or the added strain placed on the driveline components may cause damage or wear.

2   During the check, the engine must be raised slightly to remove the weight from the mounts.

3   Raise the vehicle and support it securely on jackstands, then position a jack under the engine oil pan. Place a large wood block between the jack head and the oil pan, then carefully raise the engine just enough to take the weight off the mounts.

4   Check the mounts to see if the rubber is cracked, hardened or separated from the metal plates **(see illustration)**. Sometimes the rubber will split right down the center.

5   Check for relative movement between the mount plates and the engine or frame (use a large screwdriver or pry bar to attempt to move the mounts). If movement is noted, lower the engine and tighten the mount fasteners.

6   Rubber preservative should be applied to the mounts to slow deterioration.

Replacement

Refer to illustrations 18.11 and 18.12

7   Disconnect the negative battery cable.

8   Refer to Chapter 3 and remove the engine cooling fan assembly and shroud.

9   Attach an engine support fixture to the engine lifting eyes adjacent to the exhaust manifolds. **Note:** *Many equipment rental yards rent the engine support fixture. If a support fixture isn't available, a floor jack and block of wood, positioned under the oil pan, can be used.*

10   Raise the vehicle and support it securely on jackstands.

11   Take some of the weight off the engine mounts then remove the engine mount through-bolts **(see illustration)**.

12   Raise the engine a little at a time watching for interference with any engine compartment components. When the engine is raised about two inches, remove the bolts retaining

18.4 Inspect the engine mount components for cracked rubber insulators (arrow), missing bolts or cracked metal brackets

the mount to the engine block **(see illustration)**.

13   Installation is the reverse of removal. Tighten the bolts to the torque listed in this Chapter's Specifications.

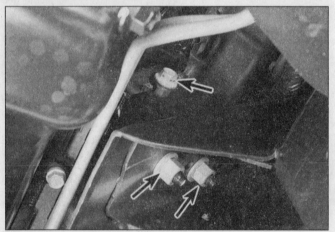

18.11 With the engine raised slightly, remove the mount through-bolt (upper arrow) - lower arrows indicate nuts to remove if the lower bracket is to be replaced

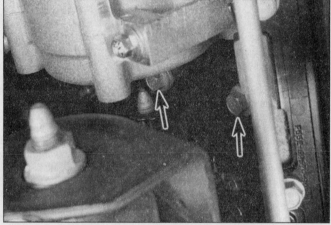

18.12 There are three bolts holding the mount to the block (arrows indicate two; there is one more at the other end of the mount)

Chapter 2 Part E
General engine overhaul procedures

Contents

Specifications

4.9L inline six-cylinder engine

General

Displacement	300 cubic inches
Bore and stroke	4.00 x 3.98 inches
Compression pressure	Lowest cylinder must be within 75-percent of highest cylinder
Oil pressure (at 2000 rpm, normal operating temperature)	40 to 60 psi

Engine block

Cylinder bore	
Diameter	4.000 to 4.0048 inches
Taper limit	0.010 inch
Out-of-round limit	0.005 inch
Deck warpage limit	0.003 inch per 6 inches, or 0.006 inch overall

Pistons and rings

Piston diameter	
Coded red	3.9982 to 3.9988 inches
Coded blue	3.9994 to 4.0000 inches
Oversize available	0.003 inch
Piston-to-cylinder bore clearance	0.0010 to 0.0018 inch
Piston ring-to-groove side clearance	
Standard	
Top ring	0.0019 to 0.0036 inch
2nd ring	0.002 to 0.004 inch
Oil ring	Snug fit in groove
Service limit	0.002 inch maximum increase in clearance
Piston ring end gap	
Top ring	0.010 to 0.020 inch
2nd ring	0.010 to 0.020 inch
Oil ring	
1992 through 1995	0.015 to 0.055 inch
1996	0.010 to 0.035 inch
Piston pin diameter (standard)	
1992 through 1995	0.9749 to 0.9754 inch
1996	0.9754 to 0.9757 inch
Piston pin-to-piston clearance	
Over 8500 GVW	0.0002 to 0.0004 inch
Under 8500 GVW	0.0003 to 0.0005 inch
Piston pin-to-connecting rod clearance	Interference fit

4.9L inline six-cylinder engine (continued)

Crankshaft and connecting rods

Main journal
    Diameter.. 2.3982 to 2.3990 inches
    Taper limit .... 0.0005 inch per inch
    Out-of-round limit .... 0.0006 inch
    Runout limit .... 0.002 inch
Main bearing oil clearance
    Standard .... 0.0008 to 0.0015 inch
    Service limit .... 0.0028 inch
Connecting rod journal
    Diameter.. 2.1228 to 2.1236 inches
    Taper limit .... 0.0006 inch per inch
    Out-of-round limit .... 0.0006 inch
Connecting rod bearing oil clearance
    Standard .... 0.0008 to 0.0015 inch
    Service limit .... 0.0024 inch
Connecting rod side clearance
    Standard .... 0.006 to 0.013 inch
    Service limit .... 0.018 inch
Crankshaft endplay
    Standard .... 0.004 to 0.008 inch
    Service limit .... 0.012 inch

Camshaft

Bearing journal
    Diameter.. 2.017 to 2.018 inches
    Journal runout .... 0.008 inch max
Bearing oil clearance
    Standard .... 0.001 to 0.003 inch
    Service limit .... 0.006 inch
Lobe lift
    Intake .... 0.249 inch
    Exhaust .... 0.249 inch
Runout limit .... 0.008 inch
Endplay
    Standard .... 0.001 to 0.007 inch
    Service limit .... 0.009 inch
Cam gear-to-crankshaft gear backlash .... 0.004 to 0.100 inch
Cam gear runout limit (assembled) .... 0.005 inch
Crankshaft gear runout limit (assembled) .... 0.005 inch

Cylinder head and valve train

Head warpage limit.. 0.003 inch per 6 inches or 0.006 in overall
Valve seat angle 45-degrees
Valve seat width
    Intake .... 0.060 to 0.080 inch
    Exhaust .... 0.070 to 0.090 inch
Valve seat runout limit .... 0.002 inch
Valve face angle 44-degrees
Valve face runout limit .... 0.002 inch
Valve margin width .... 1/32 inch minimum
Valve stem diameter - standard
    Intake .... 0.3416 to 0.3423 inch
    Exhaust .... 0.3416 to 0.3423 inch
Valve guide diameter
    Intake .... 0.3433 to 0.3443 inch
    Exhaust .... 0.3433 to 0.3443 inch
Valve stem-to-guide clearance
    Intake
        Standard .... 0.0010 to 0.0027 inch
        Service limit .... 0.0055 inch
    Exhaust
        Standard .... 0.0010 to 0.0027 inch
        Service limit .... 0.0055 inch
Valve spring free length
    Intake .... 1.96 inches
    Exhaust .... 1.78 inches

Valve spring installed height
    Intake .... 1.61 to 1.67 inches
    Exhaust .... 1.44 to 1.50 inches
Valve spring out-of-square limit .... 0.078 inch
Valve clearance (collapsed lifter gap)... 0.125 to 0.175 inch
Lifter diameter .... 0.8740 to 0.8745 inch
Lifter bore diameter .... 0.8752 to 0.8767 inch
Lifter-to-bore clearance
    Standard .... 0.0007 to 0.0027 inch
    Service limit .... 0.005 inch
Pushrod runout limit .... 0.015 inch

Oil pump
Outer race-to-housing clearance... 0.001 to 0.013 inch
Rotor assembly end clearance.. 0.004 inch max
Rotor tip clearance .... 0.012 inch max
Driveshaft-to-housing bearing clearance.. 0.0015 to 0.0030 inch
Relief valve clearance .... 0.0015 to 0.0030 inch

Torque specifications*
                                                  Ft-lbs (unless otherwise indicated)
Connecting rod nuts .... 40 to 45
Main bearing cap bolts .... 60 to 70

*__Note:__ *Refer to Part A for additional torque specifications*

4.2L V6 engine
General
Displacement.. 4.2 liters (256 cubic inches)
Bore and stroke .... 3.81 x 3.74 inches
Compression pressure .... Lowest cylinder must be within 75-percent of highest cylinder
Oil pressure (at 2000 rpm, normal operating temperature) .... 40 to 60 psi

Engine block
Cylinder bore
    Diameter.. 3.8139 inches
    Taper limit... 0.002 inch
    Out-of-round limit .... 0.002 inch
Deck warpage limit .... 0.003 inch per 6 inches, or 0.006 inch overall

Valves and related components
Seat angle 44.5-degrees
Seat width.. 0.060 to 0.080 inch
Minimum valve margin width .... 1/32 inch
Stem diameter
    Through 2002
        Intake.. not available
        Exhaust... 0.3418 to 0.3410 inch
    2003
        Intake.. 0.2738 to 0.2751 inch
        Exhaust... 0.2728 to 0.2741 inch
Stem-to-guide clearance
    Intake .... 0.0008 to 0.0027 inch
    Exhaust .... 0.0018 to 0.0037 inch
Valve spring
    Free length... 1.99 inches
    Installed height... 1.566 to 1.637 inches
Valve lifter
    Lifter-to-bore clearance
        Standard .... 0.0007 to 0.0027 inch
        Service limit .... 0.005 inch

Crankshaft and connecting rods
Connecting rod journal
    Diameter.. 2.3103 to 2.3111 inches
    Out-of-round limit .... 0.0012 inch
    Taper limit... 0.0006 inch per inch
    Bearing oil clearance .... 0.0010 to 0.0027 inch
Connecting rod side clearance (endplay).. 0.0047 to 0.0193 inch

4.2L V6 engine (continued)

Crankshaft and connecting rods (continued)

Main bearing journal
    Diameter* .... 2.5190 to 2.5198 inches
    Out-of-round limit .... 0.0012 inch
    Taper limit.. 0.0006 inch per inch
Main bearing oil clearance .... 0.0010 to 0.0025 inch
Crankshaft endplay .... 0.00003 to 0.00787 inch

* Note: *The crankshaft journals can't be machined more than 0.010 inch under the standard dimension.*

Pistons and rings

Piston diameter .... 3.810 inches
Piston-to-bore clearance limit... 0.0007 to 0.0017 inch
Piston ring end gap
    Top compression ring .... 0.009 to 0.016 inch
    Second compression ring .... 0.039 to 0.064 inch
    Oil ring .... 0.0059 to 0.0064 inch
Piston ring side clearance .... 0.0012 to 0.0031 inch

Torque specifications*   Ft-lbs

Main bearing cap stud/bolts
    Step 1... 37
    Step 2... Rotate an additional 120 degrees
Connecting rod cap nuts
    Step 1... 29
    Step 2... Rotate an additional 90 degrees

*Note: *Refer to Chapter 2, Part B for additional torque specifications.*

5.0L and 5.8L V8 engines

General

Displacement
    5.0L... 302 cu. in.
    5.8L... 351 cu. in.
Bore and stroke
    5.0L... 4.00 x 3.00 inches
    5.8L... 4.00 x 3.50 inches
Compression pressure .... Lowest cylinder must be at least 75-percent of highest cylinder
Oil pressure (at 2000 rpm, normal operating temperature)
    5.0L... 40 to 60 psi
    5.8L... 40 to 65 psi

Engine block

Cylinder bore
    Diameter
        5.0L... 4.0000 to 4.0012 inches
        5.8L... 4.0000 to 4.0048 inches
    Taper limit.. 0.010 inch
    Out-of-round limit .... 0.005 inch
Deck warpage limit .... 0.003 inch per 6 inch or 0.006 inch overall

Pistons and rings

Piston diameter
    5.0L
        Coded red
            1992 through 1995 .... 3.9989 to 3.9995 inches
            1996 .... 3.9987 to 3.9993 inches
        Coded blue
            1992 through 1995 .... 4.0001 to 4.0007 inches
            1996 .... 3.9999 to 4.0005 inches
    5.8L
        Coded red.. 3.9978 to 3.9984 inches
        Coded blue
            1992 through 1995 .... 3.9990 to 3.9996 inches
            1996 .... not available
Oversizes available .... 0.003 inch
Piston-to-bore clearance
    5.0L... 0.0014 to 0.0022 inch
    5.8L... 0.0015 to 0.0023 inch

Piston ring-to-groove clearance
    Top and bottom compression
        5.0L .... 0.0013 to 0.0033 inch
        5.8L .... 0.0020 to 0.0040 inch
    Oil .... Snug fit in groove
    Service limit (compression rings only) .... 0.002 inch max increase in clearance
Piston ring end gap
    Top compression .... 0.010 to 0.020 inch
    Bottom compression
        5.0L .... 0.018 to 0.028 inch
        5.8L .... 0.010 to 0.020 inch
    Oil .... 0.010 to 0.040 inch
Piston pin diameter (standard) .... 0.9119 to 0.9124 inch
Piston pin-to-piston clearance
    5.0L .... 0.0002 to 0.0004 inch
    5.8L .... 0.0003 to 0.0005 inch
Piston pin-to-connecting rod bushing clearance .... Interference fit

Crankshaft and connecting rods

Main bearing journal
    Diameter
        5.0L .... 2.2482 to 2.2490 inches
        5.8L .... 2.9994 to 3.0002 inches
    Taper limit - max per inch .... 0.0005 inch
    Out-of-round limit .... 0.0006 inch
    Runout .... 0.002 inch
    Runout service limit .... 0.005 inch
Main bearing oil clearance
    Standard .... 0.0004 to 0.0015 inch
    Service limit .... 0.0004 to 0.0021 inch
Connecting rod journal
    Diameter
        5.0L .... 2.1228 to 2.1236 inches
        5.8L .... 2.3103 to 2.3111 inches
    Taper limit - max per inch .... 0.0006 inch
    Out-of-round limit .... 0.0006 inch
Connecting rod bearing oil clearance
    5.0L .... 0.0007 to 0.0024 inch
    5.8L .... 0.0008 to 0.0025 inch
Connecting rod side clearance
    Standard .... 0.010 to 0.020 inch
    Service limit .... 0.023 inch
Crankshaft endplay
    Standard .... 0.004 to 0.008 inch
    Service limit .... 0.012 inch

Camshaft

Bearing journal diameter
    5.0L
        No. 1 .... 2.0805 to 2.0815 inches
        No. 2 .... 2.0655 to 2.0665 inches
        No. 3 .... 2.0505 to 2.0515 inches
        No. 4 .... 2.0355 to 2.0365 inches
        No. 5 .... 2.0205 to 2.0215 inches
    5.8L
        No. 1 .... 2.0815 inches
        No. 2 .... 2.0665 inches
        No. 3 .... 2.0515 inches
        No. 4 .... 2.0365 inches
        No. 5 .... 2.0215 inches
Bearing oil clearance
    Standard .... 0.001 to 0.003 inch
    Service limit .... 0.006 inch
Endplay
    Standard .... 0.001 to 0.007 inch
    Service limit .... 0.009 inch
Timing chain deflection limit .... 1/2 inch

Cylinder heads and valve train

Head warpage limit .... 0.003 inch per 6 inches or 0.006 inch total
Valve seat angle 45-degrees

5.0L and 5.8L V8 engines (continued)

Cylinder heads and valve train (continued)

Valve seat width..	0.060 to 0.080 inch
Valve seat runout limit	0.002 inch
Valve face angle	44-degrees
Valve face runout limit	0.002 inch
Valve margin width	1/32 inch min.
Valve stem diameter	
Intake	0.3415 to 0.3423 inch
Exhaust	0.3410 to 0.3418 inch
Valve guide diameter	0.3433 to 0.3443 inch
Valve stem-to-guide clearance	
Intake	
Standard	0.0010 to 0.0027 inch
Service limit	0.0055 inch
Exhaust	
Standard	0.0015 to 0.0032 inch
Service limit	0.0055 inch
Valve spring free length	
Intake	2.06 inches
Exhaust	1.88 inches
Valve spring installed height	
Intake	1.75 to 1.81 inches
Exhaust	1.58 to 1.64 inches
Valve spring out-of-square limit	0.078 inch
Valve clearance (collapsed lifter gap)	
5.0L	0.091 to 0.151 inch
5.8L	
1992 through 1994	0.123 to 0.172 inch
1995 and 1996	0.091 to 0.151 inch
Lifter diameter	0.8740 to 0.8745 inch
Lifter bore diameter	0.8752 to 0.8767 inch
Lifter-to-bore clearance	
Standard	0.0007 to 0.0027 inch
Service limit	0.005 inch
Pushrod runout limit	0.015 inch

Oil pump

Outer race-to-housing clearance	
5.0L	0.001 to 0.013 inch
5.8L	0.001 to 0.003 inch
Rotor assembly end clearance	0.004 inch max
Rotor tip clearance	0.012 inch max
Driveshaft-to-housing clearance...	0.0015 to 0.0030 inch

Torque specifications*

Ft-lbs

Connecting rod cap nuts	
5.0L	19 to 24
5.8L	40 to 45
Main bearing cap bolts	
5.0L	60 to 70
5.8L	95 to 105

*Note: Refer to Part C for additional torque specifications.

7.5L V8 engines

General

Displacement..	460 cu. in.
Bore and stroke	4.36 x 3.85 inches
Compression pressure	Lowest cylinder must be at least 75-percent of highest cylinder
Oil pressure (at 2000 rpm, normal operating temperature)	40 to 88 psi

Engine block

Cylinder bore	
Diameter..	4.3600 to 4.3636 inches
Taper limit...	0.010 inch
Out-of-round	
Maximum	0.0015 inch
Service limit	0.0050 inch
Deck warpage limit	0.003 inch per 6 inches or 0.006 inch overall

Pistons and rings

Piston diameter
  Coded red
    1992 through 1994 .... 4.3577 to 4.3583 inches
    1995 and 1996... 4.3585 to 4.3595 inches
  Coded blue
    1992 through 1994 .... 4.3589 to 4.3595 inches
    1995 and 1996... 4.3595 to 4.3605 inches
  Oversizes available .... 0.003 inch
Piston-to-bore clearance
  1992 through 1994 .... 0.0022 to 0.0030 inch
  1995 and 1996 .... 0.0014 to 0.0022 inch
Piston ring-to-groove clearance
  Compression - top and bottom
    1992 through 1994 .... 0.0025 to 0.0045 inch
    1995 and 1996... 0.0012 to 0.0022 inch
  Oil .... Snug fit in groove
  Service limit... 0.002 inch max increase in clearance
Piston ring end gap
  Compression - top and bottom................................ 0.010 to 0.020 inch
  Oil... 0.010 to 0.035 inch
Piston pin diameter (standard)
  1992 through 1994 .... 1.0398 to 1.0403 inches
  1995 and 1996 .... 1.0401 to 1.0406 inches
Piston pin-to-piston clearance .... 0.0002 to 0.0005 inch
Piston pin-to-connecting rod bushing clearance .... Interference fit

Crankshaft and connecting rods

Main journal
  Diameter... 2.9994 to 3.0002 inches
  Taper limit - max per inch .... 0.0005 inch
  Out of round limit.. 0.0006 inch
  Runout limit
    Standard .... 0.002 inch
    Service limit .... 0.005 inch
Main bearing oil clearance
  1992 through 1994
    Standard .... 0.0008 to 0.0015 inch
    Service limit .... 0.0008 to 0.0026 inch
  1995 and 1996
    Standard
      Cap 1... 0.0004 to 0.0022 inch
      Cap 2, 3, 4, 5... 0.0009 to 0.0027 inch
    Service limit .... 0.0004 to 0.0027 inch
Connecting rod journal
  Diameter... 2.4992 to 2.5000 inches
  Taper limit- max per inch .... 0.0006 inch
  Out-of-round limit .... 0.0006 inch
Connecting rod bearing oil clearance
  Desired... 0.0008 to 0.0015 inch
  Allowable.. 0.0008 to 0.0025 inch
Connecting rod side clearance
  Standard .... 0.010 to 0.020 inch
  Service limit.. 0.023 inch
Crankshaft endplay
  Standard .... 0.004 to 0.008 inch
  Service limit.. 0.012 inch

Camshaft

Bearing journal diameter (all) .... 2.1238 to 2.1248 inches
Bearing oil clearance
  Standard .... 0.001 to 0.003 inch
  Service limit.. 0.006 inch
Endplay
  Standard .... 0.001 to 0.006 inch
  Service limit.. 0.009 inch
Timing chain deflection limit .... 0.500 inch

Cylinder heads and valve train

Head warpage limit... 0.003 inch per 6 inches or 0.006 inch overall
Valve seat angle 45-degrees

7.5L V8 engines (continued)

Cylinder heads and valve train (continued)

Valve seat width	0.060 to 0.080 inch
Valve seat runout limit	0.002 inch
Valve face angle	44-degrees
Valve face runout limit	0.002 inch
Valve margin width	1/32 inch
Valve stem diameter	0.3415 to 0.3423 inch
Valve guide diameter	0.3433 to 0.3443 inch
Valve stem-to-guide clearance	
Standard	0.0010 to 0.0027 inch
Service limit	0.0055 inch
Valve spring free length	2.06 inches
Valve spring installed height	
1992 through 1994	1.77 to 1.82 inches
1995 and 19961994	1.78 to 1.84 inches
Valve spring out-of-square limit	0.078 inch
Vale clearance (collapsed lifter gap)	
Allowable	0.075 to 0.175 inch
Desired	0.100 to 0.150 inch
Lifter diameter	0.8740 to 0.8745 inch
Lifter bore diameter	0.8752 to 0.8767 inch
Lifter-to-bore clearance	
Standard	0.0007 to 0.0027 inch
Service limit	0.005 inch
Pushrod runout limit	0.015 inch

Oil pump

Outer race-to-housing clearance	0.001 to 0.013 inch
Rotor assembly end clearance	0.004 inch max
Rotor tip clearance	0.012 inch max
Driveshaft-to-housing clearance	0.0015 to 0.0030 inch

Torque specifications*

Ft-lbs

Connecting rod nuts	41 to 50
Main bearing cap bolts	95 to 105

*Note: *Refer to Part C for additional torque specifications*

4.6L and 5.4L V8 engines

General

Displacement	
4.6L	4.6 liters (281 cubic inches)
5.4L	5.4 liters (329 cubic inches)
Bore and stroke	
4.6L	3.554 X 3.546 inches
5.4L	3.554 X 4.168 inches
Compression pressure	Lowest cylinder must be at least 15-percent of highest cylinder (100 psi minimum)
Oil pressure (at 1500 rpm, normal operating temperature)	
4.6L	20 to 45 psi
5.4L	40 to 70 psi

Engine block

Cylinder bore diameter	3.554 inches
Out-of-round	
Standard	0.0006 inch
Service limit	0.0008 inch
Taper	0.0002 inch maximum
Deck warpage limit	0.003 inch per 6 inch or 0.006 inch overall

Valves and related components

Valve arrangement (front-to-rear)	
Left cylinder head	E-I-E-I-E-I-E-I
Right cylinder head	I-E-I-E-I-E-I-E
Intake valve	
Seat angle	45 degrees
Seat width	0.0748 to 0.0827 inch
Seat runout limit	0.0010 inch maximum (total indicator reading)

Stem diameter (standard)

Models through 2000 .... 0.2746 to 0.2750 inch
2001 and later .... 0.2746 to 0.2754 inch
Valve stem-to-guide clearance .... 0.0008 to 0.0027 inch
Valve face angle .... 45.5 degrees
Valve face runout limit .... 0.002 inch maximum

Exhaust valve

Seat angle .... 45 degrees
Seat width .... 0.0748 to 0.0827 inch
Seat runout limit .... 0.0010 inch maximum (total indicator reading)

Stem diameter (standard)

Models through 2000 .... 0.2740 to 0.2736 inch
2001 and later .... 0.2736 to 0.2744 inch
Valve stem-to-guide clearance .... 0.0018 to 0.0037 inch
Valve face angle .... 45.5 degrees
Valve face runout limit .... 0.0020 inch maximum

Valve spring

Free length
4.6L .... 1.951 inches
5.4L
Models through 2001 .... 1.078 inches
2002 and later .... 2.100 inches
Out-of-square limit .... 2 degrees maximum

Installed height

Models through 2001 .... 1.576 inches
2002 and later .... 1.677 inches

Pressure, intake and exhaust
4.6L
Valve open... 132 lbs at 1.104 inches
Valve closed .... 55 lbs at 1.576 inches
5.4L
Models through 2001
Valve open... 142 to 157 lbs at 1.104 inches
Valve closed .... 61 to 68 lbs at 1.576 inches
2002 and later
Valve open... 170.8 lbs at 1.133 inches
Valve closed .... 67.9 lbs at 1.675 inches
Valve spring pressure service limit................................. 10 percent pressure loss at 1.104 inches

Hydraulic lash adjuster (lifter)

Diameter (standard) .... 0.6299 to 0.6304 inch
Lifter-to-bore clearance
Standard .... 0.0007 to 0.0027 inch
Service limit .... 0.0006 inch maximum
Collapsed tappet gap - desired .... 0.0335 to 0.0177 inch
Rocker arm ratio (roller cam followers) 1.75:1

Crankshaft and connecting rods

Crankshaft

Endplay
4.6L.. 0.0051 to 0.012 inch
5.4L.. 0.0029 to 0.0148 inch
Runout to rear face of block (standard) .... 0.002 inch

Connecting rods

Connecting rod journal
Diameter .... 2.0877 to 2.0883 inches
Bearing oil clearance
4.6L .... 0.0011 to 0.0027 inch
5.4L .... 0.0010 to 0.0025 inch
Connecting rod side clearance (end play)
Standard
4.6L .... 0.0006 to 0.0177 inch
5.4L .... 0.0049 to 0.0187 inch
Service limit.. 0.0197 inch

Main bearing journal

Diameter
4.6L.. 2.650 to 2.657 inches
5.4L.. 2.658 to 2.659 inches
Bearing oil clearance .... 0.0011 to 0.0027 inch

4.6L and 5.4L V8 engines (continued)

Pistons and rings

Piston diameter

Coded red 1	3.5500 to 3.5510 inches
Coded blue 2	3.5507 to 3.5515 inches
Coded yellow 3	3.5513 to 3.5521 inches

Piston diameter, 5.4L

Coded red 1	3.5488 to 3.5502 inches
Coded blue 2	3.5502 to 3.5506 inches
Coded yellow 3	3.5506 to 3.5510 inches

Piston-to-bore clearance limit

4.6L	0.0005 to 0.0010 inch
5.4L	0.0002 to 0.0010 inch

Piston ring end gap

4.6L

Compression rings	0.010 to 0.020 inch
Oil ring	0.006 to 0.026 inch

5.4L

Top compression ring	0.005 to 0.011 inch
Second compression ring	0.010 to 0.016 inch
Oil ring	0.006 to 0.026 inch

Piston ring side clearance

Compression ring (top)	0.0016 to 0.0031 inch
Compression ring (second)	0.0012 to 0.0031 inch
Service limit	0.006 inch maximum
Oil ring	Snug fit

Torque specifications*

Ft-lbs (unless otherwise indicated)

Main bearing cap bolts (tighten first)

First step	27 to 32
Second step	Rotate an additional 85 to 95-degrees

Main bearing cap - jack screws (REP engines only, tighten second)

First step	44 inch lbs
Second step	80 to 97 inch lbs

Main bearing cap - side bolts (tighten third)

REP engines

First step	89 in-lbs
Second step	14 to 17

WEP engines

First step	20 to 24
Second step	Rotate and additional 85 to 95-degrees

Connecting rod cap bolts

First step	29 to 33
Second step	Rotate an additional 90 to 120-degrees

* Note: *Refer to Chapter 2, Part D for additional torque specifications.*

6.8L V10 engines

General

Displacement	6.8 liters (415 cubic inches)
Bore and stroke	3.554 X 4.168 inches
Compression pressure minimum)	Lowest cylinder must be at least 15-percent of highest cylinder (100 psi
Oil pressure (at 1500 rpm, normal operating temperature)	40 to 70 psi

Engine block

Cylinder bore diameter

Grade 1	3.5540 inches
Grade 2	3.5544 inches
Grade 3	3.5548 inches

Out-of-round

Standard	0.0006 inch
Service limit	0.0008 inch
Taper	0.0002 inch maximum
Deck warpage limit	0.003 inch per 6 inch or 0.006 inch overall

Valves and related components

Intake valve

Seat angle	45 degrees

Seat width	
Models through 2004	0.0748 to 0.0827 inch
2005	0.0118 to 0.0591 inch
Seat runout limit	0.0010 inch maximum (total indicator reading)
Stem diameter (standard)	0.2748 to 0.2756 inch
Valve stem-to-guide clearance	0.0008 to 0.0027 inch
Valve face angle	45.5 degrees
Valve face runout limit	0.002 inch maximum
Exhaust valve	
Seat angle	45 degrees
Seat width	
Models through 2004	0.0748 to 0.0827 inch
2005	0.0118 to 0.0591 inch
Seat runout limit	0.0010 inch maximum (total indicator reading)
Stem diameter (standard)	0.2738 to 0.2746 inch
Valve stem-to-guide clearance	0.0018 to 0.0037 inch
Valve face angle	45.5 degrees
Valve face runout limit	0.002 inch maximum
Valve spring	
Free length	
Models through 2004	1.978 inches
2005	2.10 inches
Out-of-square limit	2.5 degrees maximum
Installed height	
Models through 2004	1.576 inches
2005	1.677 inches
Pressure, intake and exhaust	
Valve open	
Models through 2004	142 to 157 lbs at 1.104 inches
2005	not available
Valve closed	
Models through 2004	61 to 68 lbs at 1.576 inches
2005	68 lbs at 1.677 inches
Valve spring pressure service limit	10 percent pressure loss at 1.104 inches
Hydraulic lash adjuster (lifter)	
Diameter (standard)	0.6299 to 0.6304 inch
Lifter-to-bore clearance	
Standard	0.0007 to 0.0027 inch
Service limit	0.0006 inch maximum
Collapsed tappet gap - desired	0.0335 to 0.0177 inch
Rocker arm ratio (roller cam followers)	1.75:1

Crankshaft and connecting rods

Crankshaft	
Endplay	0.0029 to 0.0148 inch
Runout to rear face of block (standard)	0.002 inch
Connecting rods	
Connecting rod journal	
Diameter	2.0877 to 2.0883 inches
Bearing oil clearance	0.0010 to 0.0025 inch
Connecting rod side clearance (endplay)	
Standard	0.0006 to 0.0177 inch
Service limit	0.0197 inch
Main bearing journal	
Diameter	2.658 to 2.659 inches
Bearing oil clearance	0.0011 to 0.0027 inch

Pistons and rings

Piston diameter	3.5520 to 3.5540 inches
Piston-to-bore clearance limit	0.0002 to 0.0010 inch
Piston ring end gap	
Top compression ring	0.005 to 0.011 inch
Second compression ring	0.010 to 0.016 inch
Oil ring	0.006 to 0.026 inch
Piston ring side clearance	
Compression ring (top)	0.0016 to 0.0031 inch
Compression ring (second)	0.0012 to 0.0031 inch
Service limit	0.006 inch maximum
Oil ring	Snug fit

6.8L V10 engines (continued)

Torque specifications*

	Ft-lbs (unless otherwise indicated)
Main bearing cap bolts (tighten first)	
First step	27 to 32
Second step	Rotate an additional 85 to 95-degrees
Main bearing cap - side bolts (tighten second)	
First step	20 to 24
Second step	Rotate an additional 85 to 95-degrees
Connecting rod cap bolts	
First step	29 to 33
Second step	Rotate an additional 90 to 120-degrees

* **Note:** *Refer to Chapter 2, Part D for additional torque specifications.*

---

1   General information - engine overhaul

Included in this portion of Chapter 2 are the general overhaul procedures for the cylinder head and internal engine components.

The information ranges from advice concerning preparation for an overhaul and the purchase of replacement parts to detailed, step-by-step procedures covering removal and installation of internal engine components and the inspection of parts.

The following Sections have been written based on the assumption that the engine has been removed from the vehicle. For information concerning in-vehicle engine repair, as well as Removal and Installation of the external components necessary for the overhaul, see Chapter 2A (4.9L), 2B (4.2L), 2C (5.0L, 5.8L and 7.5L) or 2D (4.6L, 5.4L and 6.8L) and Section 8 of this Chapter.

The Specifications included in this Part are only those necessary for the inspection and overhaul procedures which follow.

It's not always easy to determine when, or if, an engine should be completely overhauled, as a number of factors must be considered.

High mileage is not necessarily an indication that an overhaul is needed, while low mileage doesn't preclude the need for an overhaul. Frequency of servicing is probably the most important consideration. An engine that's had regular and frequent oil and filter changes, as well as other required maintenance, will most likely give many thousands of miles of reliable service. Conversely, a neglected engine may require an overhaul very early in its life.

Excessive oil consumption is an indication that piston rings, valve seals and/or valve guides are in need of attention. Make sure that oil leaks aren't responsible before deciding that the rings and/or guides are bad. Perform a cylinder compression check to determine the extent of the work required (see Section 4). Also check the vacuum readings under various conditions (see Section 3).

Loss of power, rough running, knocking or metallic engine noises, excessive valve train noise and high fuel consumption rates may also point to the need for an overhaul, especially if they're all present at the same time. If a complete tune-up doesn't remedy the situation, major mechanical work is the only solution.

An engine overhaul involves restoring the internal parts to the specifications of a new engine. During an overhaul, the piston rings are replaced and the cylinder walls are reconditioned (re-bored and/or honed). If a re-bore is done by an automotive machine shop, new oversize pistons will also be installed. The main bearings, connecting rod bearings and camshaft bearings are generally replaced with new ones and, if necessary, the crankshaft may be reground to restore the journals. Generally, the valves are serviced as well, since they're usually in less-than-perfect condition at this point. While the engine is being overhauled, other components, such as the distributor, starter and alternator, can be rebuilt as well. The end result should be a like new engine that will give many trouble free miles. **Note:** *Critical cooling system components such as the hoses, drivebelts, thermostat and water pump should be replaced with new parts when an engine is overhauled. The radiator should be checked carefully to ensure that it isn't clogged or leaking (see Chapter 3). If you purchase a rebuilt engine or short block, some rebuilders will not warranty their engines unless the radiator has been professionally flushed. Also, we don't recommend overhauling the oil pump - always install a new one when an engine is rebuilt.*

Before beginning the engine overhaul, read through the entire procedure to familiarize yourself with the scope and requirements of the job. Overhauling an engine isn't difficult, but it is time-consuming. Plan on the vehicle being tied up for a minimum of two weeks, especially if parts must be taken to an automotive machine shop for repair or reconditioning. Check on availability of parts and make sure that any necessary special tools and equipment are obtained in advance. Most work can be done with typical hand tools, although a number of precision measuring tools are required for inspecting parts to determine if they must be replaced. Often an automotive machine shop will handle the inspection of

2.2a The oil pressure sending unit on the 4.2L engine is located on the left front of the block (arrow)

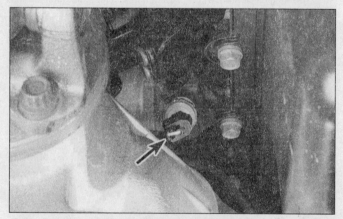

2.2b The oil pressure sending unit on the 4.6L and 5.4L engines is located on the lower left (driver's side) corner of the engine, near the oil filter

parts and offer advice concerning reconditioning and replacement. **Note:** *Always wait until the engine has been completely disassembled and all components, especially the engine block, have been inspected before deciding what service and repair operations must be performed by an automotive machine shop.* Since the block's condition will be the major factor to consider when determining whether to overhaul the original engine or buy a rebuilt one, never purchase parts or have machine work done on other components until the block has been thoroughly inspected. As a general rule, time is the primary cost of an overhaul, so it doesn't pay to install worn or substandard parts.

As a final note, to ensure maximum life and minimum trouble from a rebuilt engine, everything must be assembled with care in a spotlessly-clean environment.

2 Oil pressure check

Refer to illustrations 2.2a and 2.2b

1   Low engine oil pressure can be a sign of an engine in need of rebuilding. A "low oil pressure" indicator (often called an "idiot light") is not a test of the oiling system. Such indicators only come on when the oil pressure is dangerously low. Even a factory oil pressure gauge in the instrument panel is only a relative indication, although much better for driver information than a warning light. A better test is with a mechanical (not electrical) oil pressure gauge. When used in conjunction with an accurate tachometer, an engine's oil pressure performance can be compared to factory Specifications for that year and model.

2   Find the oil pressure indicator sending unit **(see illustrations)**. On most engines the sending unit is located near the oil filter, but on the 7.5L engine it's located at the upper rear of the engine block, behind the intake manifold.

3   Remove the oil pressure sending unit and install a fitting which will allow you to directly connect your hand-held, mechanical oil pressure gauge. Use Teflon tape or sealant on the threads of the adapter and the fitting on the end of your gauge's hose.

4   Connect an accurate tachometer to the engine, according to the tachometer manufacturer's instructions.

5   Check the oil pressure with the engine running (full operating temperature) at the specified engine speed, and compare it to this Chapter's Specifications. If it's extremely low, the bearings and/or oil pump are probably worn out.

3 Cylinder compression check

Refer to illustration 3.6

1   A compression check will tell you what mechanical condition the upper end (pistons, rings, valves, head gaskets) of the engine is in. Specifically, it can tell you if the compres-

sion is down due to leakage caused by worn piston rings, defective valves and seats or a blown head gasket. **Note:** *The engine must be at normal operating temperature and the battery must be fully charged for this check.*

2   Begin by cleaning the area around the spark plugs before you remove them. Compressed air should be used. The idea is to prevent dirt from getting into the cylinders as the compression check is being done.

3   Remove all of the spark plugs from the engine (see Chapter 1).

4   Block the throttle wide open.

5   Before beginning this procedure, be sure to disable the ignition system. On 1992 through 1996 models (TFI-IV ignition systems), disconnect the coil wire from the distributor cap and ground it to prevent damage to the coil (see Chapter 5). On distributorless ignition systems, disconnect the primary lead from the coil pack (DIS ignition systems) or the individual coil assemblies (COP ignition systems) at the spark plugs (see Chapter 5). The fuel pump circuit should also be disabled by removing the fuel pump relay (see Chapter 4).

6   Install the compression gauge in the number one spark plug hole **(see illustration)**.

7   Crank the engine over at least seven compression strokes and watch the gauge. The compression should build up quickly in a healthy engine. Low compression on the first stroke, followed by gradually increasing pressure on successive strokes, indicates worn piston rings. A low compression reading on the first stroke, which doesn't build up during successive strokes, indicates leaking valves or a blown head gasket (a cracked head could also be the cause). Deposits on the undersides of the valve heads can also cause low compression. Record the highest gauge reading obtained.

8   Repeat the procedure for the remaining cylinders, turning the engine over for the same length of time for each cylinder, and compare the results to this Chapter's Specifications.

9   If the readings are below normal, add some engine oil (about three squirts from a plunger-type oil can) to each cylinder, through the spark plug hole, and repeat the test.

10   If the compression increases after the oil is added, the piston rings are definitely worn. If the compression doesn't increase significantly, the leakage is occurring at the valves or head gasket. Leakage past the valves may be caused by burned valve seats and/or faces or warped, cracked or bent valves.

11   If two adjacent cylinders have equally low compression, there's a strong possibility the head gasket between them is blown. The appearance of coolant in the combustion chambers or the crankcase would verify this condition.

12   If the compression is unusually high, the combustion chambers are probably coated with carbon deposits. If that's the case, the cylinder heads should be removed and decarbonized.

13   If compression is way down or varies

3.6 A compression gauge with a threaded fitting for the spark plug hole is preferred over the type that requires hand pressure to maintain the seal during the compression check

greatly between cylinders, it would be a good idea to have a leak-down test performed by an automotive repair shop. This test will pinpoint exactly where the leakage is occurring and how severe it is.

14   Install the fuses and drive the vehicle to restore the "block learn" memory. Refer to Chapter 6 for additional information on the PCM.

4 Vacuum gauge diagnostic checks

Refer to illustration 4.6

1   A vacuum gauge provides valuable information about what is going on in the engine at a low cost. You can check for worn rings or cylinder walls, leaking head or intake manifold gaskets, incorrect carburetor adjustments, restricted exhaust, stuck or burned valves, weak valve springs, improper ignition or valve timing and ignition problems.

2   Unfortunately, vacuum gauge readings are easy to misinterpret, so they should be used in conjunction with other tests to confirm the diagnosis.

3   Both the gauge readings and the rate of needle movement are important for accurate interpretation. Most gauges measure vacuum in inches of mercury (in-Hg). As vacuum increases (or atmospheric pressure decreases), the reading will increase. Also, for every 1,000-foot increase in elevation above sea level, the gauge readings will decrease about one inch of mercury.

4   Connect the vacuum gauge directly to intake manifold vacuum, not to ported (before throttle plate) vacuum. Be sure no hoses are left disconnected during the test or false readings will result.

5   Before you begin the test, allow the engine to warm up completely. Block the wheels and set the parking brake. With the transmission in Park, start the engine and allow it to run at normal idle speed.

6   Read the vacuum gauge; an average, healthy engine should normally produce about 17 to 22 inches of vacuum with a fairly steady needle. Refer to the following vacuum gauge readings and what they indicate about the engine's condition (**see illustration**):

7   A low, steady reading usually indicates a leaking gasket between the intake manifold and carburetor or throttle body, a leaky vacuum hose, late ignition timing or incorrect camshaft timing. Eliminate all other possible causes, utilizing the tests provided in this Chapter before you remove the timing chain cover to check the timing marks.

8   If the reading is three to eight inches below normal and it fluctuates at that low reading, suspect an intake manifold gasket leak at an intake port.

9   If the needle has regular drops of about two to four inches at a steady rate, the valves are probably leaking. Perform a compression or leak-down test to confirm this.

10   An irregular drop or down-flick of the needle can be caused by a sticking valve or an ignition misfire. Perform a compression or leak-down test and read the spark plugs.

11   A rapid vibration of about four inches-Hg vibration at idle combined with exhaust smoke indicates worn valve guides. Perform a leak-down test to confirm this. If the rapid vibration occurs with an increase in engine speed, check for a leaking intake manifold gasket or head gasket, weak valve springs, burned valves or ignition misfire.

12   A slight fluctuation, say one inch up and down, may mean ignition problems. Check all the usual tune-up items and, if necessary, run the engine on an ignition analyzer.

13   If there is a large fluctuation, perform a compression or leak-down test to look for a weak or dead cylinder or a blown head gasket.

14   If the needle moves slowly through a wide range, check for a clogged PCV system, incorrect idle fuel mixture, throttle body or intake manifold gasket leaks.

15   Check for a slow return after revving the engine by quickly snapping the throttle open until the engine reaches about 2,500 rpm and let it shut. Normally the reading should drop to near zero, rise above normal idle reading (about 5 in-Hg over) and then return to the previous idle reading. If the vacuum returns slowly and doesn't peak when the throttle is snapped shut, the rings may be worn. If there is a long delay, look for a restricted exhaust system (often the muffler or catalytic converter). An easy way to check this is to temporarily disconnect the exhaust ahead of the suspected part and re-test.

5   Engine rebuilding alternatives

1   The do-it-yourselfer is faced with a number of options when performing an engine overhaul. The decision to replace the engine block, piston/connecting rod assemblies and crankshaft depends on a number of factors, with the number one consideration being the

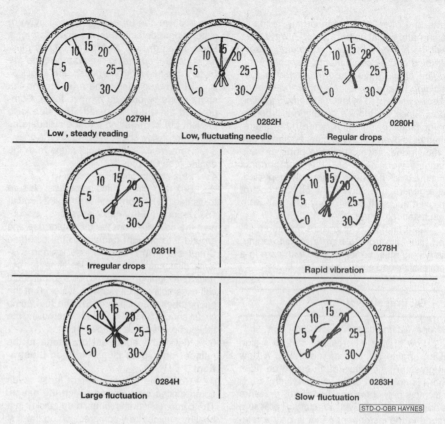

4.6 Typical vacuum gauge readings

condition of the block. Other considerations are cost, access to machine-shop facilities, parts availability, time required to complete the project and the extent of prior mechanical experience on the part of the do-it-yourselfer.

2   Some of the rebuilding alternatives include:

3   **Individual parts** - If the inspection procedures reveal that the engine block and most engine components are within specifications, purchasing individual parts may be the most economical alternative. The block, crankshaft and piston/connecting rod assemblies should all be inspected carefully. Even if the block shows little wear, the cylinder bores should be surface honed.

4   **Crankshaft kit** - This rebuild package consists of a reground crankshaft and a matched set of pistons and connecting rods. The pistons will already be installed on the connecting rods. Piston rings and the necessary bearings will be included in the kit. These kits are commonly available for standard cylinder bores, as well as for engine blocks which have been bored to a regular oversize.

5   **Short-block** - A short-block consists of an engine block with a crankshaft and piston/connecting rod assemblies already installed. All new bearings are incorporated and all clearances will be correct. The existing camshaft, valve train components, cylinder head and external parts can be bolted to the short block with little or no machine shop work necessary.

6   **Long-block** - A long-block consists of a short-block plus an oil pump, oil pan, cylinder head, valve cover, camshaft and valve train components, timing sprockets and chain and front cover. All components are installed with new bearings, seals and gaskets incorporated throughout. The installation of manifolds and external parts is all that is necessary.

7   Give careful thought to which alternative is best for you and discuss the situation with local automotive machine shops, auto parts dealers and experienced rebuilders before ordering or purchasing replacement parts.

6   Engine removal - methods and precautions

1   If it has been decided that an engine needs to be removed for overhaul or major repair work, certain preliminary steps should be taken.

2   Locating a suitable work area is of greatest importance. A shop is, of course, the most desirable place to work. Adequate work space along with storage space for the vehicle is very important. If a shop or garage is not available, at the very least a flat, level, clean work surface made of concrete or asphalt is required.

3   Cleaning of the engine compartment and engine prior to removal will help you keep tools clean and organized.

4   A hoist such as an engine A-frame will

also be necessary. Make sure that the equipment is rated in excess of the combined weight of the engine and its accessories. Safety is of primary importance, considering the potential hazards involved in lifting the engine out of the vehicle.

5   If the engine is being removed by a novice, a helper should be available. Advice and aid from someone more experienced would also be helpful. There are many instances when one person cannot simultaneously perform all of the operations which will be required when lifting the engine out of the vehicle.

6   Plan the operation ahead of time. Arrange for or obtain all of the tools and equipment you will need prior to beginning the job. Some of the equipment necessary to perform engine removal and installation safely and with relative ease are (in addition to an engine hoist) a heavy-duty floor jack, complete sets of wrenches and sockets as described in the front of this book, wooden blocks and plenty of rags and cleaning solvent for mopping up the inevitable spills. If the hoist is to be rented, make sure that you arrange for it in advance and perform all of the operations possible without it beforehand. This will save you money and time.

7   Always use extreme caution when removing and installing the engine; serious injury can result from careless actions. Plan ahead. Take your time and a job of this nature, although major, can be accomplished successfully.

7   Engine - removal and installation

Warning 1: *Gasoline is extremely flammable, so take extra precautions when you work on any part of the fuel system. Don't smoke or allow open flames or bare light bulbs near the work area, and don't work in a garage where a gas-type appliance (such as a water heater or clothes dryer) is present. Since gasoline is carcinogenic, wear latex gloves when there's a possibility of being exposed to fuel, and, if you spill any fuel on your skin, rinse it off immediately with soap and water. Mop up any spills immediately and do not store fuel-soaked rags where they could ignite. The fuel system on fuel-injected models is under constant pressure, so, if any fuel lines are to be disconnected, the fuel pressure in the system must be relieved first (see Chapter 4 for more information). When you perform any kind of work on the fuel system, wear safety glasses and have a Class B type fire extinguisher on hand.*

Warning 2: *The air-conditioning system is under high pressure. DO NOT loosen any hose or line fittings or remove any components until after the system has been discharged. Air conditioning refrigerant should be properly discharged into an EPA approved recovery/recycling unit at a dealer service department or an automotive air conditioning repair facility. Always wear eye protection when disconnecting air-conditioning system fittings.*

Warning 3: *Late models are equipped with airbags. Always disconnect the negative battery cable, then the positive cable and wait two minutes before working in the vicinity of the impact sensors, steering column or instrument panel to avoid the possibility of accidental deployment of the airbag, which could cause personal injury (see Chapter 12).*

Note: *The engine must be removed alone, with the transmission left in the vehicle or removed beforehand. Also, due to the wide range of vehicle models and engines covered by this manual, the following instructions are of a general nature and may cover some steps not applicable to your vehicle. If a step doesn't apply to your vehicle, move on to the next one.*

Removal

Refer to illustration 7.5

1   Refer to Chapter 4 and relieve the fuel system pressure.

2   Remove the engine cover.

3   Remove the air cleaner assembly.

4   Drain the cooling system (see Chapter 1).

5   Label the vacuum lines, emissions system hoses, wiring connectors, ground straps and fuel lines, to ensure correct reinstallation, then detach them. Pieces of masking tape with numbers or letters written on them work well **(see illustration)**. If there's any possibility of confusion, make a sketch of the engine compartment and clearly label the lines, hoses and wires. Plug or cap all open fittings or lines.

6   Label and detach all coolant hoses from the engine, including the hoses at the engine oil cooler, if equipped, then remove the oil cooler from the engine.

7   Remove the cooling fan, shroud and radiator (see Chapter 3). If the vehicle is equipped with air conditioning, remove the condenser also (see Chapter 3).

8   Remove the front bumper (see Chapter 11).

9   Remove the radiator grille and air deflector as one assembly.

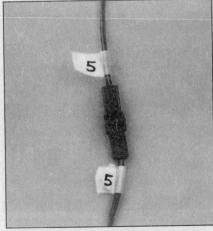

7.5 Label each wire before unplugging the connector

10   Remove the headlights and side marker lights (see Chapter 12).

11   Remove the hood latch from the radiator support and set aside (cable attached). Unclip the wiring harness from the radiator core support, then remove the fasteners and the upper and lower radiator supports from the body.

12   On engines equipped with distributors, remove the distributor and plug wires (see Chapter 5) and transmission fill tube. On all models, remove the intake manifold (see Chapters 2A, 2B, 2C or 2D).

13   On 7.5L engines, remove the oil fill tube, oil dipstick, rear engine-lifting eye and the fuel manifold with the injectors attached (see Chapter 4).

14   Remove the drivebelts (see Chapter 1).

15   Disconnect the throttle linkage or cable (and TV linkage/cruise control cable, if equipped) from the engine (see Chapter 4).

16   On power steering-equipped vehicles, unbolt the power steering pump (see Chapter 10). Leave the lines/hoses attached and make sure the pump is kept in an upright position in the engine compartment (use wire or rope to restrain it out of the way).

17   On air-conditioned models, unbolt the compressor (see Chapter 3) and set it aside. Do not disconnect the hoses.

18   Drain the engine oil (see Chapter 1) and remove the filter.

19   Remove the starter motor (see Chapter 5).

20   Remove the alternator (see Chapter 5).

21   Unbolt the exhaust system from the engine (see Chapter 4).

22   Refer to Chapter 7, and remove the driveplate-to-torque converter fasteners.

23   Support the transmission with a jack. Position a block of wood on the jack head to prevent damage to the transmission. Special transmission jacks with safety chains are available - use one if possible.

24   Attach an engine sling or a length of chain to the lifting brackets on the engine.

25   Roll the hoist into position and connect the sling to it. Take up the slack in the sling or chain, but don't lift the engine. **Warning:** *DO NOT place any part of your body under the engine when it's supported only by a hoist or other lifting device.*

26   Remove the transmission-to-engine-block bolts.

27   Remove the engine-mount-to-frame bolts.

28   Recheck to be sure nothing is still connecting the engine to the transmission or vehicle. Disconnect anything still remaining.

29   Raise the engine slightly. **Note:** *The engine is removed through the front of the vehicle.* Carefully work it forward to separate it from the transmission, making sure the torque-converter stays in the transmission (clamp a pair of vise-grips to the housing to keep the converter from sliding out). Slowly raise the engine out of the engine compartment. Check carefully to make sure nothing is hanging up.

30   Remove the driveplate and mount the engine on an engine stand.

Installation

31   Check the engine and transmission mounts. If they're worn or damaged, replace them.

32   Carefully lower the engine into the engine compartment - make sure the engine mounts line up.

33   Guide the nose of the converter into the crankshaft until the bellhousing is flush with the engine block.

34   Install the transmission-to-engine bolts and tighten them securely. **Caution:** *DO NOT use the bolts to force the transmission and engine together!*

35   Slide the torque-converter up to the driveplate and install the driveplate-to-torque converter bolts (see Chapter 7, Part B).

36   Reinstall the remaining components in the reverse order of removal.

37   Add coolant, oil, power steering and transmission fluid as needed (see Chapter 1).

38   Run the engine and check for leaks and proper operation of all accessories, then install the hood and test drive the vehicle.

39   Have the air-conditioning system recharged and leak tested. **Note:** *When the battery has been disconnected, some unusual driveability symptoms may be present until the vehicle is driven ten miles and the computer "relearns."*

8   Engine overhaul - disassembly sequence

Note: *When removing the external components from the engine, pay close attention to details that may be helpful or important during installation. Note the installed position of gaskets, seals, spacers, pins, washers, bolts and other small items.*

1   Before beginning the disassembly and overhaul procedures, make sure the following items are available:

Crankshaft vibration-damper puller
Common hand tools
Small cardboard boxes or plastic bags for storing parts
Gasket scraper
Ridge reamer
Vibration-damper installation tool
Micrometers
Telescoping gauges
Dial-indicator set
Valve-spring compressor
Cylinder surfacing hone
Piston-ring groove cleaning tool
Electric drill motor
Tap and die set
Wire brushes
Oil gallery brushes
Cleaning solvent

2   It's much easier to disassemble and work on the engine if it's mounted on a portable engine stand. These stands can often be rented quite cheaply from an equipment rental yard. Before the engine is mounted on a stand, the flywheel/driveplate should be removed from the crankshaft.

9.2 A small plastic bag, with an appropriate label, can be used to store the valve train components so they can be kept together and reinstalled in the correct guide

3   If a stand is not available, it's possible to disassemble the engine with it blocked up on a sturdy workbench or on the floor. Be extra careful not to tip or drop the engine when working without a stand.

4   Begin disassembly with the removal of external components as follows:

Alternator, if not already removed (see Chapter 5)
Accessory drivebelts and pulleys (if not previously removed, see Chapter 1)
Distributor and coil (see Chapter 5)
Upper intake manifold (see Chapters 2A, 2B, 2C and 2D) and fuel rail (see Chapter 4)
Oil dipstick and dipstick tube
Spark plugs (see Chapter 1)

5   With these components removed, the engine sub-assemblies can be removed in the following order:

Valve cover(s) and lifter cover (4.9L only) (see Chapter 2A)
Exhaust manifold(s)
Lower Intake manifold
Rocker arms and pushrods (OHV engines only)
Lifters (OHV engines only)

9.3a Use a valve spring compressor to compress the spring, then remove the keepers from the valve stem

Camshafts and balance shafts (if equipped) (OHC engines only)
Cylinder head assembly
Crankshaft vibration-damper assembly
Timing cover, timing chain/sprockets or gears. **Note:** *Perform timing chain/ gear wear check before removing components (see Section 9)*
Camshaft (OHV engines only)
Oil pan
Oil pump and pick-up assembly
Piston and rod assemblies (see Section 10)
Crankshaft and bearings (see Section 11)
Cylinder head disassembly (see Section 12)

9   Cylinder head - disassembly

Refer to illustrations 9.2, 9.3a and 9.3b

Note: *New and rebuilt cylinder heads are commonly available for most engines at dealerships and auto parts stores. Due to the fact that some specialized tools are necessary for the disassembly and inspection procedures, and replacement parts may not be readily available, it may be more practical and economical for the home mechanic to purchase a replacement head rather than taking the time to disassemble, inspect and recondition the original.*

1   Cylinder head disassembly involves removal of the intake and exhaust valves and related components. Remove the rocker arms and fulcrums from the cylinder heads (OHV engines). Label the parts and store them separately so they can be reinstalled in their original locations.

2   Before the valves are removed, arrange to label and store them, along with their related components, so they can be kept separate and reinstalled in the same valve guides they are removed from **(see illustration)**.

3   Compress the springs on the first valve with a spring compressor and remove the keepers **(see illustration)**. Carefully release the valve spring compressor and remove the

9.3b If the valve won't pull through the guide, deburr the edge of the stem end and the area around the keeper grooves with a file or whetstone

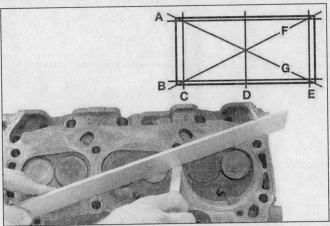

10.12 Check the cylinder head gasket surface for warpage by trying to slip a feeler gauge under the straightedge (see the Specifications for the maximum warpage allowed and use a feeler gauge of that thickness)

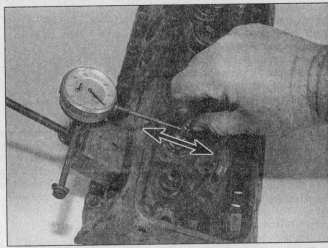

10.14 A dial-indicator can be used to determine the valve stem-to-guide clearance (move the valve stem as indicated by the arrows)

retainer, the valve spring, the valve spring damper, the valve stem seal and the valve. Store the components together and discard the seal. If the valve binds in the guide (won't pull through), push it back into the head and deburr the area around the keeper groove with a fine file or whetstone **(see illustration)**.

4   Repeat the above procedure for the remaining valves. Remember to keep all the parts for each valve together so they can be reinstalled in the same locations.

5   Once the valves and related components have been removed and stored in an organized manner, the head should be thoroughly cleaned and inspected. If a complete engine overhaul is being done, finish the engine disassembly procedures before beginning the cylinder head cleaning and inspection process.

10   Cylinder head - cleaning and inspection

Refer to illustrations 10.12, 10.14, 10.15, 10.16, 10.17, 10.18, 10.20a, 10.20b, 10.20c and 10.20d

Note: *Decarbonizing chemicals are available and may prove very useful when cleaning the cylinder head and valve train components. They are very caustic and should be used with caution. Be sure to follow the instructions on the container.*

1   Thorough cleaning of the cylinder head and related valve train components, followed by a detailed inspection, will enable you to decide how much valve service work must be done during the engine overhaul.

Cleaning

2   Scrape away all traces of old gasket material and sealing compound from the head, intake manifold and exhaust manifold sealing surfaces. Use a plastic scraper only, and be very careful not to gouge the cylinder head. Special gasket removal solvents, which soften gaskets and make removal much eas-

ier, are available at auto parts stores.

3   Remove any built up scale from the coolant passages.

4   Run a stiff wire brush through the various holes to remove any deposits that may have formed in them.

5   Run an appropriate-size tap into each of the threaded holes to remove any corrosion and thread sealant that may be present. If compressed air is available, use it to clear the holes of debris produced by this operation. **Warning:** *Wear eye protection!*

6   Clean the rocker arm bolt threads with a wire brush.

7   Clean the cylinder head with solvent and dry it thoroughly. Compressed air will speed the drying process and ensure that all holes and recessed areas are clean.

8   Clean the rocker arms, fulcrums and pushrods with solvent and dry them thoroughly (don't mix them up during cleaning). Compressed air will speed the drying process and can be used to clean out the oil passages

9   Clean all the valve springs, keepers and retainers with solvent and dry them thoroughly. Do the components from one valve at a time to avoid mixing up the parts.

10   Scrape off any heavy deposits that may have formed on the valves, then use a motorized wire brush to remove deposits from the valve heads and stems. Again, make sure the valves do not get mixed up.

Inspection

Cylinder head

11   Inspect the head very carefully for cracks, evidence of coolant leakage and other damage. If cracks are found, a new cylinder head should be obtained.

12   Using a straightedge and feeler gauge, check the head gasket mating surface for warpage **(see illustration)**. If the warpage exceeds the specified limit, the head can be resurfaced at an automotive machine shop.

13   Examine the valve seats in each of the combustion chambers. If they are pitted,

cracked or burned, the head will require valve service that is beyond the scope of the home mechanic.

14   Check the valve-stem-to-guide clearance by measuring the lateral movement of the valve stem with a dial indicator attached securely to the head **(see illustration)**. The valve must be in the guide and approximately 1/16-inch off the seat. The total valve stem movement indicated by the gauge needle must be divided by two to obtain the actual clearance. After this is done, if there is still some doubt regarding the condition of the valve guides they should be checked by an automotive machine shop (the cost should be minimal).

Valves

15   Carefully inspect each valve face for uneven wear, deformation, cracks, pits and burned spots **(see illustration)**. Check the valve stem for scuffing and galling and the neck for cracks. Rotate the valve and check

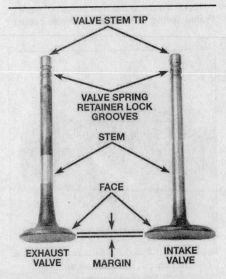

10.15 Check for valve wear at the points shown here

for any obvious indication that it's bent. Look for pits and excessive wear on the end of the stem. The presence of any of these conditions indicates the need for valve service by an automotive machine shop.

16   Measure the margin width on each valve (see illustration). Any valve with a margin narrower than 1/32-inch will have to be replaced with a new one.

Valve springs

17   Check each valve spring for wear (on the ends) and pits. Measure the free length and compare it to this Chapter's Specifications (see illustration). Any springs that are shorter than specified have sagged and should not be reused. The tension of all springs should be checked with a special fixture before deciding that they are suitable for use in a rebuilt engine (take the springs to an automotive machine shop for this check).

18   Stand each spring on a flat surface and check it for squareness (see illustration). If any of the springs are distorted or sagged, replace all of them with new parts.

19   Check the spring retainers and keepers for obvious wear and cracks. Any questionable parts should be replaced with new ones,

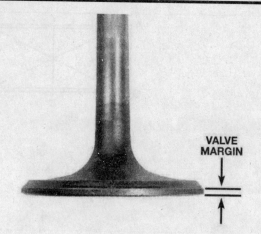

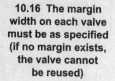

10.16 The margin width on each valve must be as specified (if no margin exists, the valve cannot be reused)

as extensive damage will occur if they fail during engine operation.

Rocker arms

20   Check the rocker arm faces (the areas that contact the pushrod ends and valve stems) for pits, wear, galling, score marks and rough spots. Check the rocker arm fulcrum contact areas and fulcrums as well (see illustrations). Look for cracks in each rocker arm.

21   Check the rocker arm bolts or studs for damaged threads.

22   Any damaged or excessively-worn parts must be replaced with new ones.

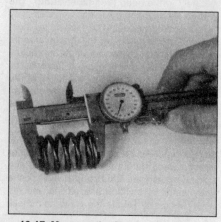

10.17 Measure the free length of each valve spring with a dial or vernier caliper

10.18 Check each valve spring for squareness

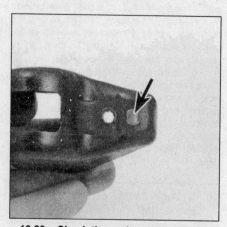

10.20a Check the rocker arm surfaces that contact the valve stem and pushrod (arrow) . . .

10.20b . . . the fulcrum seats in the rocker arm . . .

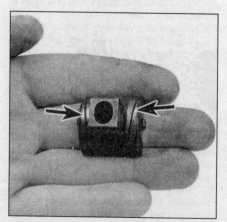

10.20c . . . and the fulcrums themselves for wear and galling

10.20d On 4.6L, 5.4L and 6.8L engines, check the rocker arms for wear (arrows) at the valve stem end, roller and the pocket that contacts the lash adjuster

11.3a If the lifters are pitted or rough, they shouldn't be re-used

11.3b The foot of each lifter should be slightly convex - the side of another lifter can be used as a straightedge to check it; if it appears flat, it is worn and must not be used

11.3c If the bottom of any lifter is worn concave, scratched or galled, replace the entire set with new lifters

General

23   If the inspection process indicates that the valve components are in generally poor condition and worn beyond the limits specified, which is usually the case in an engine that is being overhauled, reassemble the valves in the cylinder head and see Section 23 for valve servicing recommendations.
24   If the inspection turns up no excessively worn parts, and if the valve faces and seats are in good condition, the valve train components can be reinstalled in the cylinder head without major servicing. Refer to the appropriate Section for the cylinder head reassembly procedure.

11   Valve lifters and pushrods - inspection (OHV engines)

Refer to illustrations 11.3a, 11.3b, 11.3c, 11.3d and 11.5
Note: *These procedures apply only to six-cylinder and 1996 and earlier V8 engines.*

Lifters (non-roller)

1   Remove the lifters (refer to the appropriate engine Chapter).
2   Once the lifters have been removed,

clean them with solvent and dry them thoroughly without mixing them up. Remember that the lifters must be reinstalled in their original bores in the block.
3   Check each lifter wall, pushrod seat and foot for scuffing, score marks and uneven wear **(see illustrations)**. Each lifter foot (the surface that rides on the cam lobe) must be slightly convex, although this can be difficult to determine by eye. If the base of the lifter is concave, the lifters and camshaft must be replaced. If the lifter walls are damaged or worn, inspect the lifter bores in the engine block as well. If the pushrod seats are worn, check the pushrod ends.
4   If new lifters are being installed, a new camshaft must also be installed. If a new camshaft is installed, then use new lifters as well. Never install used lifters unless the original camshaft is used and the lifters can be installed in their original locations.

Roller lifters

5   Some late model engines are equipped with roller lifters. Check each lifter wall and pushrod seat for scuffing, score marks, and uneven wear. Check rollers for score marks,

ease of rotation and flat spots **(see illustration)**. If the lifters show signs of excessive wear, check the camshaft carefully. If the cam lobes aren't worn excessively, the camshaft can be re-used. If the lifter walls are damaged or worn (which is not very likely), inspect the lifter bores in the engine block as well. If the pushrod seats are worn, check the pushrod ends.
6   Used roller lifters can be installed with a new camshaft, provided they are in good condition. They must be installed in their original bores, however.

Pushrods

7   Inspect the pushrod ends for scuffing, cracks and excessive wear. Roll each pushrod on a flat surface, such as a piece of plate glass, to determine if it's bent. Replace any bent pushrods.
8   Check pushrod oil passage for possible blockage, clean as required.

12   Timing chain/sprockets or gears - wear checks (OHV engines)

Refer to illustrations 12.4
Note: *These procedures apply only to six-cylinder and 1996 and earlier V8 engines.*

Timing chain check - 5.0L, 5.8L and 7.5L engines

Note: *This procedure requires that the timing cover be removed.*
1   Turn the crankshaft in a counterclockwise direction (viewed from the front of the engine) to take up the slack on the left side of the chain.
2   At the approximate mid-point of the right-side chain run, force the chain out with your finger while holding a graduated scale against chain to establish initial measurement. The centerline of one link pin makes a good reference point.
3   Force the chain in the opposite direction and measure the amount of total deflection from the initial starting point.

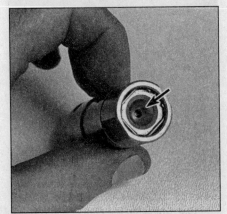

11.3d Check the pushrod seat (arrow) in the top of each lifter for wear

11.5 The roller on roller lifters must turn freely - check for wear and excessive play as well

12.4 With the timing chain cover removed, establish a reference point on the engine block and measure from that point to the chain

4   Compare the total deflection measurement **(see illustration)** to the figure listed in this Chapter's Specifications. If chain deflection is excessive, replace the chain and both sprockets with new ones. **Note:** *It is recommended to replace the timing chain and sprockets during a major overhaul regardless of condition since the investment is small in comparison to the time and effort required to replace them later.*

Endplay check - 4.9L, 5.0L, 5.8L and 7.5L engines

Note: *The following checking procedures require the use of a magnetic base dial indicator.*

5   Check the camshaft endplay by pushing the camshaft all the way to the rear of its travel in the block.
6   Install a dial indicator so the indicator stem is on the camshaft gear/sprocket retaining bolt. Zero the dial indicator in this position.
7   Using a large screwdriver between the camshaft gear/sprocket and the block, pull the camshaft forward and release it. The reading on the dial indicator will give you the endplay measurement. Compare it to the value listed in this Chapter's Specifications. If the endplay is excessive, check the spacer for correct installation. If the spacer is correctly installed, and the endplay is too great, the thrust plate must be replaced with a new one.

Timing gear check - 4.9L engine

8   Check the timing gear backlash by installing a dial indicator on the cylinder block and positioning the stem against the timing gear.
9   Zero the pointer on the dial indicator.
10   While holding the crankshaft still, move the camshaft timing gear until all slack is taken up.
11   Read the dial indicator to obtain the gear backlash.
12   Compare the results to the value listed in this Chapter's Specifications.

13   If the backlash is excessive, replace the timing gear and the crankshaft gear with new ones.
14   To check the timing gear runout, install a dial indicator on the engine block with the stem touching the face of the timing gear.
15   Hold the camshaft gear against the camshaft thrust plate and zero the indicator.
16   Rotate the crankshaft to turn the camshaft while holding the camshaft gear against the thrust plate.
17   Rotate the gear through one complete revolution of the camshaft. Observe the reading on the dial indicator during this revolution.
18   If the runout exceeds the Specifications, remove the camshaft gear and check for foreign objects or burrs between the camshaft and gear flanges. If this condition does not exist and the runout is excessive, the gears must be replaced with new ones.
19   Use a similar procedure to check the crankshaft gear runout. Make sure that the crankshaft is situated against one end of the thrust bearing (this will prevent you from obtaining a crankshaft endplay measurement as opposed to the actual runout of the crankshaft gear).

13   Piston/connecting rod assembly - removal

Refer to Illustrations 13.1, 13.3 and 13.5
Note: *Prior to removing the piston/connecting rod assemblies, remove the cylinder head, the oil pan and the oil pump by referring to the appropriate Sections in Chapter 2.*

1   Completely remove the ridge at the top of each cylinder with a ridge-reaming tool **(see illustration)**. Follow the manufacturer's instructions provided with the tool. Failure to remove the ridges before attempting to remove the piston/connecting rod assemblies will result in piston breakage.
2   After the cylinder ridges have been removed, turn the engine upside-down so the crankshaft is facing up.
3   Before the connecting rods are removed, check the endplay with feeler gauges. Slide them between the first connecting rod and the crankshaft throw until the play is removed **(see illustration)**. The endplay is equal to the thickness of the feeler gauge(s). If the endplay exceeds the service limit, new connecting rods will be required. If new rods (or a new crankshaft) are installed, the endplay may

13.1 A ridge reamer is required to remove the ridge from the top of the cylinder - do this *before* removing the pistons!

13.3 Checking the connecting rod endplay with a feeler gauge

13.5 To prevent damage to the crankshaft journals and cylinder walls, slip sections of hose over the rod bolts (if still in place) before removing the pistons

14.1 Checking crankshaft endplay with a dial indicator (4.6L engine shown)

fall under the specified minimum (if it does, the rods will have to be machined to restore it - consult an automotive machine shop for advice if necessary). Repeat the procedure for the remaining connecting rods.

4   Check the connecting rods and caps for identification marks. If they aren't plainly marked, use a small center-punch to make the appropriate number of indentations on each rod and cap (1, 2, 3 etc., depending on the cylinder they are associated with).

5   Loosen each of the connecting rod cap nuts or bolts 1/2-turn at a time until they can be removed by hand. Remove the number one connecting rod cap and bearing insert. Don't drop the bearing insert out of the cap. While supporting the connecting rod, slip a short length of plastic or rubber hose over each connecting rod cap bolt (if still in place) to protect the crankshaft journal and cylinder wall when the piston is removed (**see illustration**). Push the connecting rod/piston assembly out through the top of the engine. Use a wooden or plastic hammer handle to push on the upper bearing insert in the connecting rod. If resistance is felt, double-check to make

sure that all of the ridge was removed from the cylinder.

6   Repeat the procedure for the remaining cylinders. After removal, reassemble the connecting rod caps and bearing inserts in their respective connecting rods and install the cap nuts finger tight. Leaving the old bearing inserts in place until reassembly will help prevent the connecting rod bearing surfaces from being accidentally nicked or gouged.

14 Crankshaft - removal

Refer to illustrations 14.1, 14.3 and 14.4
Note: *The crankshaft can be removed only after the engine has been removed from the vehicle. It's assumed that the flywheel or driveplate, vibration damper, timing chain(s) or gears, oil pan, oil pump and piston/connecting rod assemblies have already been removed.*

1   Before the crankshaft removal procedure is started, check the endplay. Mount a dial indicator with the stem in line with the crankshaft and just touching the end of the crank-

shaft (**see illustration**).

2   Push the crankshaft all the way to the rear and zero the dial indicator. Next, pry the crankshaft to the front as far as possible and check the reading on the dial indicator. The distance that it moves is the endplay. If it's greater than limit listed in this Chapter's Specifications, check the crankshaft thrust surfaces for wear. If no wear is evident, new main bearings should correct the endplay.

3   If a dial indicator isn't available, feeler gauges can be used. Gently pry or push the crankshaft all the way to the front of the engine. Slip feeler gauges between the crankshaft and the front face of the thrust main bearing to determine the clearance (**see illustration**).

4   Check the main bearing caps to see if they're marked to indicate their locations (**see illustration**). They should be numbered consecutively from the front of the engine to the rear. If they aren't, mark them with number stamping dies or a center-punch. Main bearing caps generally have a cast-in arrow, which points to the front of the engine.

14.3 Checking crankshaft endplay with a feeler gauge

14.4 The main bearing caps are usually marked to indicate their locations (arrows). They should be numbered consecutively from the front of the engine to the rear

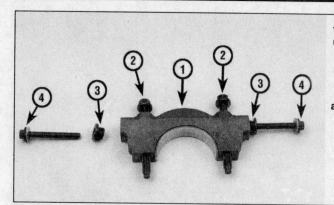

14.6 4.6L REP engines use main bearing caps that are fastened to the block through the use of a set of bolts, screws and specific adjustment procedures

1 *Main bearing cap*
2 *Main bearing bolts*
3 *Jack screws (left handed thread)*
4 *Side bolts*

14.7 Remove the side bolts - 1997 and later V8 and all V10 models

4.2L, 4.9L, 5.0L, 5.8L and 7.5L engines

Note: *The thrust bearing on these engines is the number three main bearing cap location (4.2L, 5.0L, 5.8L and 7.5L) or number five main bearing cap location (4.9L). They have an upper and lower thrust bearing shell.*

5   Loosen the main bearing cap bolts/studs 1/4-turn at a time each, until they can be removed by hand. Note if any stud bolts are used and make sure they're returned to their original locations when the crankshaft is reinstalled. **Note:** *On some 4.2L engines, there are two main cap support braces, each spanning two main caps, and attached with nuts to the main cap studs. Remove the braces.*

4.6L, 5.4L and 6.8L engines

Refer to illustrations 14.6, 14.7 and 14.8

6   These engines have a more complex crankshaft removal and assembly procedure than the other engines because of the number of bolts used to fasten the main caps to the cylinder block. On 4.6L REP models, there are two main cap bolts, two jack screws and two side bolts on each of the main caps. It is extremely important to follow the removal and the installation procedure to ensure correct assembly and operation. Loosen and remove the main cap side bolts, then back off the jack screws into the caps and away from the block **(see illustration)**.

7   On 5.4L and 6.8L engines, and WEP-design 4.6L engines, there are side bolts without the jacking screws, and the caps are securely positioned on the block with both bolts and dowel pins. Remove the side bolts **(see illustration)**.

8   Remove the main bearing cap bolts **(see illustration)**. On WEP 4.6L and 5.4L and 6.8L engines, also pull the dowel pins from the main caps. **Caution:** *The main bearing cap bolts are "torque-to-yield" bolts and are NOT reusable. A pre-determined stretch of the bolt, calculated by the manufacturer, gives the added rigidity required with this cylinder block. Once removed they must be replaced. The jack screws on REP engines are reusable.*

All engines

Refer to illustration 14.9

9   Gently tap the caps with a soft-face hammer, then separate them from the engine block. If necessary, use the bolts as levers to remove the caps. Try not to drop the bearing inserts if they come out with the caps. All main caps should have an arrow cast in to indicate the front of the engine, and a number to indicate which position they have on the block. On 4.6L engines, the number is stamped in on the left side of the cap **(see illustration)**.

10   Carefully lift the crankshaft out of the engine. It may be a good idea to have an assistant available, since the crankshaft is quite heavy. With the bearing inserts in place

in the engine block and main bearing caps, return the caps to their respective locations on the engine block and tighten the bolts finger tight.

15   Camshaft and bearings (OHV engines) - inspection

Refer to illustrations 15.2 and 15.4

Note: *This procedure applies only to six-cylinder and 1996 and earlier V8 engines.*

Inspection

1   After the camshaft has been removed from the engine, cleaned with solvent and dried, inspect the bearing journals for uneven wear, pitting and evidence of seizure. If the journals are damaged, the bearing inserts in the block are probably damaged as well. Both the camshaft and the bearings will have to be replaced.

2   If they're in good condition, measure the bearing journals with a micrometer **(see illustration)** to determine their size and whether or

14.8 Following the reverse order of the tightening sequence (see Section 23), remove the main bearing cap bolts, loosening them 1/4 turn at a time until they can be removed by hand

14.9 Main caps should be numbered (arrow) and have an indicator (circle) of the direction facing the front of the engine

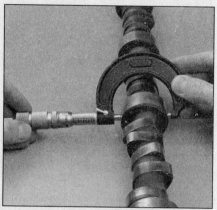

15.2 Check the diameter of each camshaft bearing journal to pinpoint excessive wear and out-of-round conditions

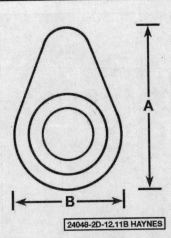

24048-2D-12.11B HAYNES

15.4 To verify camshaft lobe lift, measure the major (A) and minor (B) diameters of each lobe with a micrometer - subtract each minor diameter from the major diameter to arrive at the lobe lift

16.1a A hammer and large punch can be used to knock the core plugs sideways in their bores

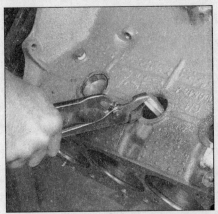

16.1b Pull the core plugs from the block with pliers

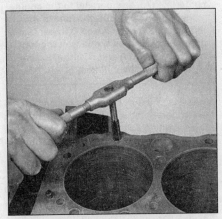

16.8 All bolt holes in the block - particularly the main bearing cap and head bolt holes - should be cleaned and restored with a tap (be sure to remove debris from the holes after this is done)

16.10 A large socket on an extension can be used to drive the new core plugs into the block

not they're out-of-round. The inside diameter of each bearing can be measured with a telescoping gauge and micrometer. Subtract each cam journal diameter from the corresponding bearing inside diameter to obtain the bearing oil clearance. Compare the clearance for each bearing to the Specifications. If it's excessive for any of the bearings, have new bearings installed by an automotive machine shop.

3   Check the camshaft lobes for heat discoloration, score marks, chipped areas, pitting and uneven wear. If the lobes are in good condition and the lobe lift measurements are within the specified limits, the camshaft can be reinstalled (assuming that the bearing journals are in acceptable condition).

4   Camshaft lobe lift can be checked with the camshaft installed in the engine or after it has been removed using the following procedure. Measure the major (A) and minor (B) diameters of each lobe with a micrometer and record the results **(see illustration)**. The difference between the two is the lobe lift. If the measured lift for any lobe is less than specified, replace the camshaft.

Bearing replacement

5   Camshaft bearing replacement requires special tools and expertise that place it outside the scope of the home mechanic. Take the block to an automotive machine shop to ensure that the job is done correctly.

16 Engine block - cleaning

Refer to illustrations 16.1a, 16.1b, 16.8 and 16.10

1   Using a hammer and punch, tap the core plug on one side to rotate it within its bore, then remove it from the block with pliers **(see illustrations). Caution:** *The core plugs may be difficult or impossible to remove if driven into the cooling passages.*

2   Using a gasket scraper, remove all traces of gasket material from the engine block. Be very careful not to nick or gouge the gasket sealing surfaces.

3   Remove the main bearing caps and separate the bearing inserts from the caps and the engine block. Tag the bearings, indicating which cylinder they were removed from and whether they were in the cap or the block, then set them aside.

4   Remove all of the threaded oil-gallery plugs from the block. Discard the plugs and use new ones when the engine is reassembled.

5   If the engine is extremely dirty it should be taken to an automotive machine shop for cleaning.

6   After the block is returned, clean all oil holes and oil galleries one more time. Brushes specifically designed for this purpose are available at most auto parts stores. Flush the passages with warm water until the water runs clear, dry the block thoroughly and wipe all machined surfaces with a light, rust preventive oil. If you have access to compressed air, use it to speed the drying process and to

blow out all the oil holes and galleries. **Warning:** *Wear eye protection!*

7   If the block isn't extremely dirty or sludged up, you can do an adequate cleaning job with warm soapy water and a stiff brush. Take plenty of time and do a thorough job. Regardless of the cleaning method used, be sure to clean all oil holes and galleries very thoroughly, dry the block completely and coat all machined surfaces with light oil.

8   The threaded holes in the block must be clean to ensure accurate torque readings during reassembly. Run the proper size tap into each of the holes to remove any rust, corrosion, thread sealant or sludge and to restore any damaged threads **(see illustration)**. If possible, use compressed air to clear the holes of debris produced by this operation. **Warning:** *Wear eye protection!* Now is a good time to clean the threads on the head bolts and the main bearing cap bolts as well.

9   Reinstall the main bearing caps and tighten the bolts finger tight.

10   After coating the sealing surfaces of the new core plugs with core plug sealant, install them in the engine block **(see illustration)**. Make sure they are driven in straight and seated properly or leakage could result. Special tools are available for this purpose, but a

large socket, with an outside diameter that will just slip into the core plug, and a hammer will work just as well.

11   Apply non-hardening sealant (such as Permatex number 2 or Teflon tape) to the new oil gallery plugs and thread them into the holes in the block. Make sure they're tightened securely.

12   If the engine isn't going to be reassembled right away, cover it with a large plastic trash bag to keep it clean.

17   Engine block - inspection

Refer to illustrations 17.4a, 17.4b and 17.4c

1   Before the block is inspected, it should be cleaned as described in Section 16. Double-check to make sure that the ridge at the top of each cylinder has been completely removed.

2   Visually check the block for cracks, rust and corrosion. Look for stripped threads in the threaded holes. It's also a good idea to have the block checked for hidden cracks by an automotive machine shop that has the special equipment to do this type of work. If defects are found, have the block repaired, if possible, or replaced.

3   Check the cylinder bores for scuffing and scoring.

4   Measure the diameter of each cylinder at the top (just under the ridge area), center and bottom of the cylinder bore, parallel to the crankshaft axis **(see illustrations)**. **Note:** *These measurements should not be made with the bare block mounted on an engine stand - the cylinders will be distorted and the measurements will be inaccurate.*

5   Next, measure each cylinder's diameter at the same three locations across the crankshaft axis. To calculate an out-of-round condition, subtract each measurement (A, B and C) taken parallel to the crankshaft axis from the ones taken across the crankshaft axis. The difference is the out-of-round reading. To determine cylinder taper, subtract measurement C from measurement A. Compare your results to this Chapter's Specifications.

6   If the required precision measuring tools aren't available, the piston-to-cylinder clearances can be obtained, though not quite as accurately, using feeler gauge stock. Feeler gauge stock comes in 12-inch lengths and various thicknesses and is generally available at auto parts stores.

7   To check the clearance, select a feeler gauge and slip it into the cylinder along with the matching piston. The piston must be positioned exactly as it normally would be. The feeler gauge must be between the piston and cylinder on one of the thrust faces (90-degrees to the piston pin bore).

8   The piston should slip through the cylinder (with the feeler gauge in place) with moderate pressure.

9   If it falls through or slides through easily, the clearance is excessive and a new piston will be required. If the piston binds at the

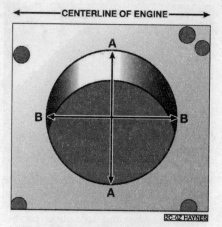

17.4a Measure the diameter of each cylinder at a right angle to the engine centerline (A), and parallel to the engine centerline (B) - out-of-round is the difference between A and B; taper is the difference between A and B at the top of the cylinder and A and B at the bottom of the cylinder

lower end of the cylinder and is loose toward the top, the cylinder is tapered. If tight spots are encountered as the piston/feeler gauge is rotated in the cylinder, the cylinder is out-of-round.

10   Repeat the procedure for the remaining pistons and cylinders.

11   If the cylinder walls are badly scuffed or scored, or if they're out-of-round or tapered beyond the limits given in this Chapter's Specifications, have the engine block rebored and honed at an automotive machine shop. If a rebore is done, oversize pistons and rings will be required.

12   If the cylinders are in reasonably good condition and not worn to the outside of the limits, and if the piston-to-cylinder clearances can be maintained properly, they don't have to be rebored. Honing is all that's necessary (see Section 25).

18   Piston/connecting rod assembly - inspection

Refer to illustrations 18.4a, 18.4b, 18.10 and 18.11

1   Before the inspection process can be carried out, the piston/connecting rod assemblies must be cleaned and the original piston rings removed from the pistons. **Note:** *Always use new piston rings when the engine is reassembled.*

2   Using a piston-ring expander, carefully remove the rings from the pistons. Be careful not to nick or gouge the pistons in the process.

3   Scrape all traces of carbon from the crown (top) of the piston. A hand-held wire brush or a piece of fine emery cloth can be used once the majority of the deposits have been scraped away. Do not, under any cir-

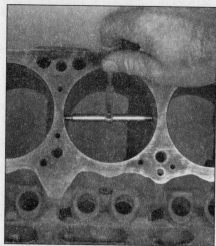

17.4b The ability to "feel" when the telescoping gauge is at the correct point will be developed over time, so work slowly and repeat the check until you are satisfied that the bore measurement is accurate

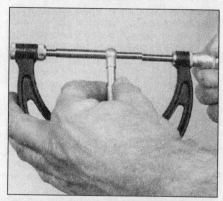

17.4c The gauge is then measured with a micrometer to determine the bore size

cumstances, use a wire brush mounted in a drill motor to remove deposits from the pistons. The piston material is soft and will be eroded away by the wire brush.

4   Use a piston ring groove-cleaning tool to remove carbon deposits from the ring grooves **(see illustration)**. If a ring groove cleaning tool isn't available, use a broken piece from one of the old rings **(see illustration)**. Be very careful to remove only the carbon deposits-don't remove any metal and do not nick or scratch the sides of the ring grooves.

5   Once the deposits have been removed, clean the piston/rod assemblies with solvent and dry them with compressed air (if available). Make sure that the oil return holes in the back sides of the ring grooves are clear.

6   If the pistons aren't damaged or worn excessively, and if the engine block isn't rebored, new pistons won't be necessary. Normal piston wear appears as even vertical wear on the piston thrust surfaces and slight looseness of the top ring in its groove. New piston rings, on the other hand, should always be used when an engine is rebuilt.

18.4a The piston ring grooves can be cleaned with a special tool, as shown here . . .

18.4b . . . or a section of a broken ring

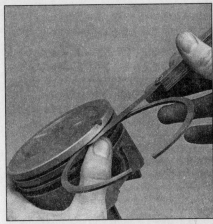

18.10 Check the ring side clearance with a feeler gauge at several points around the groove

7 Carefully inspect each piston for cracks around the skirt, at the pin bosses and at the ring lands.
8 Look for scoring and scuffing on the thrust faces of the skirt, holes in the piston crown and burned areas at the edge of the crown. If the skirt is scored or scuffed, the engine may have been suffering from overheating and/or abnormal combustion, which caused excessively high operating temperatures. The cooling and lubrication systems should be checked thoroughly. A hole in the piston crown is an indication that abnormal combustion (preignition) was occurring. Burned areas at the edge of the piston crown are usually evidence of spark knock (detonation). If any of the above conditions are noted, the causes must be corrected or the damage will occur again.
9 Corrosion of the piston, in the form of small pits, indicates that coolant is leaking into the combustion chamber and/or the crankcase. Again, the cause must be corrected or the problem may persist in the rebuilt engine.
10 Measure the piston ring side clearance by laying a new piston ring in each ring groove

and slipping a feeler gauge in beside it **(see illustration)**. Check the clearance at three or four locations around each groove. Be sure to use the correct ring for each groove - they are different. If the side clearance is greater than specified, new pistons will have to be used.
11 Check the piston-to-bore clearance by measuring the bore (see Section 17) and the piston diameter. Make sure that the pistons and bores are correctly matched. Measure the piston across the skirt, at a 90-degree angle to and in line with the piston pin **(see illustration)**. Subtract the piston diameter from the bore diameter to obtain the clearance. If it's greater than specified, the block will have to be rebored and new pistons and rings installed.
12 Check the piston-to-rod clearance by twisting the piston and rod in opposite directions. Any noticeable play indicates that there is excessive wear, which must be corrected. The piston/connecting rod assemblies should be taken to an automotive machine shop to have the pistons and rods rebored and new pins installed.
13 If the pistons must be removed from the

connecting rods for any reason, they should be taken to an automotive machine shop. While they are there, have the connecting rods checked for bend and twist, since automotive machine shops have special equipment for this purpose. **Note:** *Unless new pistons and/or connecting rods must be installed, do not disassemble the pistons from the connecting rods.*
14 Check the connecting rods for cracks and other damage. Temporarily remove the rod caps, lift out the old bearing inserts, wipe the rod and cap bearing surfaces clean and inspect them for nicks, gouges and scratches. After checking the rods, replace the old bearings, slip the caps into place and tighten the nuts finger tight.

19 Crankshaft - inspection

Refer to illustrations 19.1, 19.2, 19.4, 19.6 and 19.8
1 Remove all burrs from the crankshaft oil holes with a stone, file or scraper **(see illustration)**.

18.11 Measure the piston diameter at a 90-degree angle to the piston pin, at the centerline of the piston pin hole

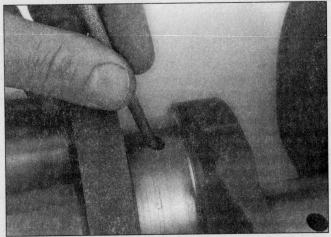

19.1 The oil holes should be chamfered so sharp edges don't gouge or scratch the new bearings

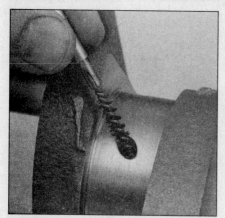

19.2 Use a wire or stiff plastic bristle brush to clean the oil passages in the crankshaft

19.4 Rubbing a penny lengthwise on each journal will reveal its condition - if copper rubs off and is embedded in the crankshaft, the journals should be reground

19.6 Measure the diameter of each crankshaft journal at several points to detect taper and out-of-round conditions

2   Clean the crankshaft with solvent and dry it with compressed air (if available). Be sure to clean the oil holes with a stiff brush and flush them with solvent **(see illustration)**.

3   Check the main and connecting rod bearing journals for uneven wear, scoring, pits and cracks.

4   Rub a penny across each journal several times **(see illustration)**. If a journal picks up copper from the penny, it's too rough and must be reground.

5   Check the rest of the crankshaft for cracks and other damage. It should be magnafluxed to reveal hidden cracks - an automotive machine shop will handle the procedure.

6   Using a micrometer, measure the diameter of the main and connecting rod journals and compare the results to the Specifications **(see illustration)**. By measuring the diameter at a number of points around each journal's circumference, you'll be able to determine whether or not the journal is out-of-round. Take the measurement at each end of the journal, near the crank throws, to determine if the journal is tapered. Crankshaft runout should be checked also, but large V-blocks and a dial indicator are needed to do it correctly. If you don't have the equipment, have a

machine shop check the runout.

7   If the crankshaft journals are damaged, tapered, out-of-round or worn beyond the limits given in the Specifications, have the crankshaft reground by an automotive machine shop. Be sure to use the correct-size bearing inserts if the crankshaft is reconditioned.

8   Check the oil seal journals at each end of the crankshaft for wear and damage **(see illustration)**. If the seal has worn a groove in the journal, or if it's nicked or scratched, the new seal may leak when the engine is reassembled. In some cases, an automotive machine shop may be able to repair the journal by pressing on a thin sleeve. If repair isn't

feasible, a new or different crankshaft should be installed.

9   Examine the main and rod bearing inserts (see Section 20).

20 Main and connecting rod bearings - inspection

Refer to illustration 20.1

1   Even though the main and connecting rod bearings should be replaced with new ones during the engine overhaul, the old bearings should be retained for close examination, as they may reveal valuable information about the condition of the engine **(see illustration)**.

19.8 If the seals have worn grooves in the crankshaft journals, or if the seal contact surfaces are nicked or scratched, the new seals will leak

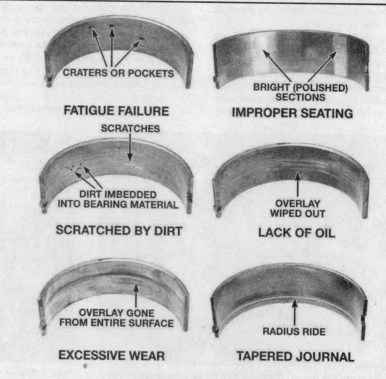

20.1 Typical bearing failures

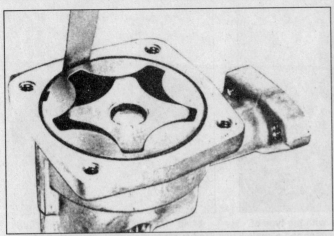

21.6 Measuring the oil pump outer race-to-housing clearance with a feeler gauge

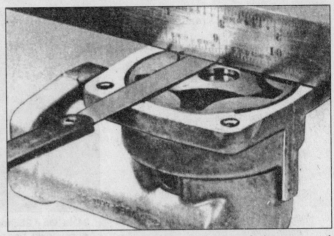

21.7 Checking the oil pump rotor endplay with a feeler gauge and straightedge

2   Bearing failure occurs because of lack of lubrication, the presence of dirt or other foreign particles, overloading the engine and corrosion. Regardless of the cause of bearing failure, it must be corrected before the engine is reassembled to prevent it from happening again.

3   When examining the bearings, remove them from the engine block, the main bearing caps, the connecting rods and the rod caps and lay them out on a clean surface in the same general position as their location in the engine. This will enable you to match any bearing problems with the corresponding crankshaft journal.

4   Dirt and other foreign particles get into the engine in a variety of ways. It may be left in the engine during assembly, or it may pass through filters or the PCV system. It may get into the oil, and from there into the bearings. Metal chips from machining operations and normal engine wear are often present. Abrasives are sometimes left in engine components after reconditioning, especially when parts are not thoroughly cleaned using the proper cleaning methods. Whatever the source, these foreign objects often end up embedded in the soft bearing material and are easily recognized. Large particles will not embed in the bearing and will score or gouge the bearing and journal. The best prevention for this cause of bearing failure is to clean all parts thoroughly and keep everything spotlessly clean during engine assembly. Frequent and regular engine oil and filter changes are also recommended.

5   Lack of lubrication (or lubrication breakdown) has a number of interrelated causes. Excessive heat (which thins the oil), overloading (which squeezes the oil from the bearing face) and oil leakage or throw off (from excessive bearing clearances, worn oil pump or high engine speeds) all contribute to lubrication breakdown. Blocked oil passages, which usually are the result of misaligned oil holes in a bearing shell, will also oil starve a bearing and destroy it. When lack of lubrication is the cause of bearing failure, the bearing

material is wiped or extruded from the steel backing of the bearing. Temperatures may increase to the point where the steel backing turns blue from overheating.

6   Driving habits can have a definite effect on bearing life. Lugging the engine (using too high a gear for the speed and engine rpm) puts very high loads on bearings, which tends to squeeze out the oil film. These loads cause the bearings to flex, which produces fine cracks in the bearing face (fatigue failure). Eventually the bearing material will loosen in pieces and tear away from the steel backing. Short trip driving leads to corrosion of bearings because insufficient engine heat is produced to drive off the condensed water and corrosive gases. These products collect in the engine oil, forming acid and sludge. As the oil is carried to the engine bearings, the acid attacks and corrodes the bearing material.

7   Incorrect bearing installation during engine assembly will lead to bearing failure as well. Tight fitting bearings leave insufficient bearing oil clearance and will result in oil starvation. Dirt or foreign particles trapped behind a bearing insert result in high spots on the bearing which lead to failure.

21   Oil pump - inspection

Refer to illustrations 21.6 and 21.7
Note: *This procedure covers only the oil pumps installed in the 4.9L, 5.0L, 5.8L and 7.5L engines. Refer to Chapter 2B for the oil pump removal and inspection procedure for the 4.2L engine. The oil pumps equipped in the 4.6L, 5.4L and 6.8L engines are replaced as a unit (see Chapter 2D). The oil pump must be removed from the engine prior to this inspection procedure (see Chapter 2A or 2C).*

1   Remove the two bolts securing the pick-up tube to the oil pump, then remove the pick-up.

2   Clean the oil pump with solvent and dry it thoroughly with compressed air. **Warning:** *Wear eye protection.*

3   Remove the oil pump housing cover. It is

retained by four bolts.

4   Use solvent and a brush to clean the inside of the pump housing and the pressure relief valve chamber. Make sure that the interior of the oil pump is clean.

5   Visually check the inside of the pump housing and the outer race and rotor for excessive wear, scoring or damage. Check the mating surface of the pump cover for wear, grooves or damage. If any of these conditions exist, replace the pump with a new one.

6   Measure the outer race-to-housing clearance with a feeler gauge and compare the results with the Specifications **(see illustration)**.

7   Using a straightedge and feeler gauge, measure the end-plate-to-rotor-assembly clearance and compare the results with this Chapter's Specifications **(see illustration)**.

8   Check the driveshaft-to-housing bearing clearance by measuring the inside diameter of the housing bearing and subtracting that figure from the outside diameter of the driveshaft. Compare the results with this Chapter's Specifications.

9   If any components fail the checks mentioned, replace the entire oil pump, as the components are not serviced as separate parts.

10   Inspect the relief valve spring for wear or a collapsed condition.

11   Check the relief valve piston for scoring, damage and free operation within its bore.

12   If the relief valve fails any of the above tests, replace the entire relief valve assembly with a new one.

13   Install the rotor, outer housing and race in the oil pump. Pack the pump cavities with petroleum jelly (this will prime the pump and ensure good suction when the engine is started).

14   Install the cover and the four retaining bolts and tighten them to the torque listed in this Chapter's Specifications.

15   Attach the pick-up tube to the oil pump body using a new gasket. Tighten the bolts to the torque listed in the appropriate chapter's Specifications.

22 Engine overhaul - reassembly sequence

1   Before beginning engine reassembly, make sure you have all the necessary new parts, gaskets and seals as well as the following items on hand:

> Common hand tools
> Crankshaft damper removal/installation tool
> 1/2-inch-drive torque wrench
> Piston-ring installation tool
> Piston-ring compressor
> Short lengths of rubber or plastic hose to fit over connecting rod bolts
> Plastigage
> Feeler gauges
> A fine-tooth file
> New engine oil
> Engine assembly lube or moly-base grease
> RTV gasket sealant
> Thread-locking compound

2   In order to save time and avoid problems, engine tolerance checks and reassembly should be done in the suggested order:

> If necessary, have the cylinder head and valves serviced (see Section 23)
> If necessary, reassemble cylinder head (see Section 24)
> Hone the cylinder walls in block (see Section 25)
> Crankshaft and main bearings (see Section 26)
> Piston/connecting rod assemblies (see Sections 27 and 28)
> Camshaft in cylinder head (OHC engine) (see Chapter 2D)
> Timing chain and sprockets
> Timing chain cover
> Cylinder head(s)
> Oil pump
> Rear main oil seal
> Oil pan
> Camshaft in engine block (OHV engine) (see Chapters 2A, 2B or 2C)
> Valve lifters (see Chapter 2A, 2B or 2C)
> Rocker arms and pushrods (see Chapter 2A, 2B and 2C)
> Intake manifold (upper and lower)
> Exhaust manifolds
> Check, and if necessary, adjust the valve clearances (see Section 29)
> Valve cover(s) and (on the 4.9L engine) pushrod cover
> Front pulley and vibration-damper assembly

3   Remaining engine build operations are reverse of removal operations.

4   Prior to engine start-up, perform engine initial start-up checks (see Section 30).

23 Valves - servicing

1   Because of the complex nature of the job and the special tools and equipment needed, servicing of the valves, the valve seats and

24.4a   On 4.2L models with the type of seal shown, use a hammer and a seal installer (or a deep socket, as shown here) to drive the seal onto the valve guide/head casting boss (make sure the valve spring seat is in place first)

the valve guides, commonly known as a valve job, is best left to a professional.

2   The home mechanic can remove and disassemble the head, do the initial cleaning and inspection, then reassemble and deliver the head to a dealer service department or an automotive machine shop for the actual valve servicing.

3   The dealer service department, or automotive machine shop, will remove the valves and springs, recondition or replace the valves and valve seats, recondition or replace the valve guides, check and replace the valve springs, spring retainers and keepers as required, replace the valve seals with new ones, reassemble the valve components and make sure the installed spring height is correct. The cylinder head gasket surface will also be resurfaced if it's warped.

4   After the valve job has been performed by a professional, the head will be in like new condition. When the head is returned, be sure to clean it again before installation on the engine to remove any metal particles and abrasive grit that may still be present from the valve service or head resurfacing operations. Use compressed air, if available, to blow out all the oil holes and passages. **Warning:** Wear eye protection.

24 Cylinder head - reassembly

Refer to illustrations 24.4a, 24.4b, 24.4c, 24.6 and 24.8

1   Regardless of whether or not the head was sent to an automotive repair shop for valve servicing, make sure it's clean before beginning reassembly.

2   If the head was sent out for valve servicing, the valves and related components will already be in place. Refer to Step 8.

3   Beginning at one end of the head, lubricate and install the first valve. Apply moly-base grease or clean engine oil to the valve stem.

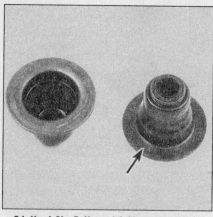

24.4b   4.6L, 5.4L and 6.8L engines use valve stem seals that are a valve spring seat and seal combined into one part - make sure replacement parts are the same as the ones removed earlier

24.4c   Installing a valve stem seal on an OHC engine - the socket must contact the flange (spring seat) of the seal

4   Slide a new valve stem seal over the valve and seat it on the guide with a deep socket and hammer. Gently tap the seal until it's completely seated on the guide **(see illustration)**. Be very careful not to deform or cock the seal during installation. **Note:** On 4.2L engines, the spring seat must be in

24.6   Apply a small dab of grease to each keeper as shown here before installation - it will hold them in place on the valve stem as the spring is released

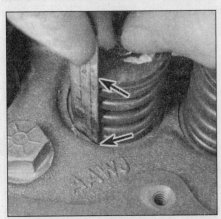

24.8 Be sure to check the valve spring installed height (the distance from the bottom of the spring/shield to the underside of the retainer)

25.3a A "bottle brush" hone will produce better results if you've never done cylinder honing before

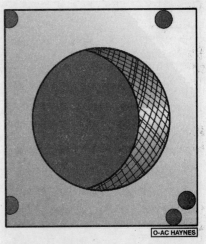

25.3b The cylinder hone should leave a smooth, cross-hatch pattern with the lines intersecting at approximately a 60-degree angle

place before installing the seal. On 4.6L, 5.4L and 6.8L engines, the seal and spring seal are one piece (see illustrations).

5   Install the valve spring seats or shims if any, then set the valve spring, damper and retainer in place.

6   Compress the springs with a valve spring compressor. Position the keepers in the valve stem grooves, then slowly release the compressor and make sure the keepers seat properly. Apply a small dab of grease to each keeper to hold it in place if necessary **(see illustration)**.

7   Repeat the same procedure for each valve. Be sure to return the components to their original locations - don't mix them up!

8   Check the installed valve spring height with a ruler graduated in 1/64-inch increments or a dial caliper. If the head was sent out for service work, the installed height should be correct (but don't automatically assume that it is). The measurement is taken from the underside of the spring damper to the underside of the spring retainer **(see illustration)**. If the height is greater than specified, shims can be added under the springs to correct it. **Caution:** *Do not, under any circumstances, shim the springs to the point where the installed height is less than specified.*

25   Cylinder honing

Refer to illustrations 25.3a and 25.3b
Note: *If you don't have the tools or don't want to tackle the honing operation, most automotive machine shops will do it for a reasonable fee.*

1   Prior to engine reassembly, the cylinder bores must be honed so the new piston rings will seat correctly and provide the best possible combustion-chamber seal.

2   Before honing the cylinders. install the main bearing caps and tighten the bolts to the torque listed in this Chapter's Specifications.

3   Two types of cylinder hones are com-

monly available - the flex-hone or "bottle brush" type and the more traditional surfacing hone with spring-loaded stones. Both will do the job, but for the less experienced mechanic the "bottle brush" hone will probably be easier to use. You'll also need plenty of light oil or honing oil, some rags and an electric drill motor. Proceed as follows:

a)   *Mount the hone in the drill motor, compress the stones and slip it into the first cylinder (see illustration).*

b)   *Lubricate the cylinder with plenty of oil, turn on the drill and move the hone up-and-down in the cylinder at a pace which will produce a fine crosshatch pattern on the cylinder walls. Ideally, the crosshatch lines should intersect at approximately a 60° angle (see illustration). Be sure to use plenty of lubricant and don't take off any more material than is absolutely necessary to produce the desired finish.* **Note:** *Piston ring manufacturers may specify a smaller crosshatch angle than the traditional 60-degrees - read and follow any instructions printed on the piston ring packages.*

c)   *Don't withdraw the hone from the cylinder while it's running. Instead, shut off the drill and continue moving the hone up-and-down in the cylinder until it comes to a complete stop, then compress the stones and withdraw the hone. If you're using a "bottle brush" type hone, stop the drill motor, then turn the chuck in the normal direction of rotation while withdrawing the hone from the cylinder.*

d)   *Wipe the oil out of the cylinder and repeat the procedure for the remaining cylinders.*

4   After the honing job is complete, chamfer the top edges of the cylinder bores with a small file so the rings won't catch when the pistons are installed. Be very careful not to nick the cylinder walls with the end of the file.

5   The entire engine block must be washed again very thoroughly with warm, soapy

water and a brush to remove all traces of the abrasive grit produced during the honing operation. **Note:** *The bores can be considered clean when a white cloth-dampened with clean engine oil-used to wipe down the bores doesn't pick-up any more honing residue, which will show up as gray areas on the cloth. Be sure to run a brush through all oil holes and galleries and flush them with running water.*

6   After rinsing, dry the block and apply a coat of light rust preventive oil to all machined surfaces. Wrap the block in a plastic trash bag to keep it clean and set it aside until reassembly.

26   Crankshaft - installation and main bearing oil clearance check

1   Crankshaft installation is the first step in engine reassembly. It's assumed at this point that the engine block and crankshaft have been cleaned, inspected and repaired or reconditioned.

2   Position the engine on the stand with the bottom facing up.

3   Remove the main bearing cap bolts and lift off the caps. Lay them out in the proper order to ensure that they are reinstalled correctly.

4   If they're still in place, remove the old bearing inserts from the block and the main bearing caps. Wipe the main bearing surfaces of the block and caps with a clean, lint free cloth. They must be kept spotlessly clean.

Main bearing oil clearance check

Refer to illustrations 26.10 and 26.14
5   Clean the back sides of the new main bearing inserts and lay one bearing half in each main bearing saddle in the block. Lay

26.10 Lay the Plastigage strips (arrow) on the main bearing journals, parallel to the crankshaft centerline

26.14 Compare the width of the crushed Plastigage to the scale on the container to determine the main bearing oil clearance (always take the measurement at the widest point of the Plastigage); be sure to use the correct scale - standard and metric scales are included

the other bearing half from each bearing set in the corresponding main bearing cap. Make sure the tab on the bearing insert fits into the recess in the block or cap. **Caution:** *The oil holes in the block must line up with the oil holes in the bearing insert. Do not hammer the bearing into place and don't nick or gouge the bearing faces. No lubrication should be used at this time.*

6   The thrust bearing must be installed in the appropriate bearing saddle. Refer to Section 14 for additional information.

7   Clean the faces of the bearings in the block and the crankshaft main bearing journals with a clean, lint free cloth. Check or clean the oil holes in the crankshaft, as any dirt here can only go one way - straight through the new bearings!

8   Once you're certain that the crankshaft is clean, carefully lay it in position (an assistant would be very helpful here) in the main bearings.

9   Before the crankshaft can be permanently installed, the main bearing oil clearance must be checked.

10   Trim several pieces of the appropriate size Plastigage - they must be slightly shorter than the width of the main bearings - and place one piece on each crankshaft main bearing journal, parallel with the journal axis **(see illustration)**.

11   Clean the faces of the bearings in the caps and install the caps in their respective positions-don't mix them up with the arrows pointing toward the front of the engine. Do not disturb the Plastigage! . **Note:** *On 4.6L, 5.4L and 7.5L engines, the caps should be seated with a brass hammer or a dead-blow plastic mallet before installing any main cap bolts **(see illustration)**. On models with jacking screws, make sure the screws are well into the caps and clear of the block.*

12   Starting with the center main and working out toward the ends, tighten the main bearing cap bolts, in three steps, to the

specified torque. DO NOT rotate the crankshaft at any time during this operation! **Note:** *On 4.6L, 5.4L and 6.8L engines, it is not necessary to tighten the jack screws or install the side bolts for Plastigage measurement purposes. Don't rotate the crankshaft at any time during this operation.*

13   Remove the bolts and carefully lift off the main bearing caps. Keep them in order. Don't disturb the Plastigage or rotate the crankshaft. If any of the main bearing caps are difficult to remove, tap them gently from side-to-side with a soft-face hammer to loosen them.

14   Compare the width of the crushed Plastigage on each journal to the scale printed on the Plastigage container to obtain the main bearing oil clearance **(see illustration)**. Check the Specifications to make sure it's correct.

15   If the clearance is not as specified, the bearing inserts may be the wrong size (which means different ones will be required). Before deciding that different inserts are needed, make sure that no dirt or oil was between the bearing inserts and the caps or block when the clearance was measured. If the Plastigage was wider at one end than the other, the journal may be tapered.

16   Carefully scrape all traces of the Plastigage material off the main bearing journals and/or the bearing faces. Don't nick or scratch the bearing faces.

Final crankshaft installation

17   Carefully lift the crankshaft out of the engine. Clean the bearing faces in the block, then apply a thin, uniform layer of clean moly-base grease or engine-assembly lube to each of the bearing surfaces. Be sure to coat the thrust faces as well as the journal face of the center bearing. On engines equipped with a two-piece rear main oil seal, install the upper half of the rear main seal.

18   Make sure the crankshaft journals are

clean, then lay the crankshaft back in place in the block. Clean the faces of the bearings in the caps, then apply lubricant to them.

4.2L, 4.9L, 5.0L, 5.8L and 7.5L engines

19   Install the caps in their respective positions with the arrows pointing toward the front of the engine and tighten bolts finger tight. On engines equipped with a two-piece rear main oil seal, install the lower half of the rear main oil seal prior to installing the rear bearing cap. **Note:** *On 4.2L engines, apply a thin bead of RTV sealant at the side joints between the rear main cap and the block. Install the cap and tighten the bolts (see Steps 23 and 24 below) within four minutes of applying the sealant.*

20   Tighten all except the thrust bearing cap bolts to the torque listed in this Chapter's Specifications (work from the center out and approach the final torque in three steps). Pry the crankshaft forward against the thrust surface of the bearing. Hold the crankshaft in this position, then pry the thrust bearing cap to the rear. Maintain the forward pressure on the crankshaft and tighten the thrust bearing cap bolts to the specified torque. Recheck the torque on all of the cap bolts.

21   Rotate the crankshaft a number of times by hand to check for any obvious binding. The effort required to turn the crankshaft should not be excessive.

22   The final step is to check the crankshaft endplay with a feeler gauge or a dial indicator as described in Section 14. The endplay should be correct if the crankshaft thrust faces are not worn or damaged and new bearings have been installed.

23   Install a new one-piece rear main oil seal, if equipped. If it was removed, install the Woodruff key in the front of the crankshaft. Fill the keyway chamfer cavity with Loctite 518 or equivalent, up to where the front face of the sprocket will fall.

26.25 "Roll" the lubricated crankshaft thrust washer (arrow) into place in front of the last crankshaft journal on 1997 and later V8 and all V10 engines - the grooved side of the thrust washer must face the crankshaft (away from the main bearing saddle)

4.6L, 5.4L and 6.8L engines

Refer to illustrations 26.25, 26.27a, 26.27b, 26.30, 26.31a and 26.31b

Caution: *The main bearing cap bolts on the 4.6L, 5.4L and 6.8L engines are all "torque-to-yield" bolts and are NOT reusable. A pre-determined stretch of the bolt, calculated by the manufacturer, gives the added rigidity required with this cylinder block. Once removed they must be replaced with new bolts. The main cap side bolts and jack screws (REP engines) are reusable. During clearance checks using Plastigage, use the old bolts and torque to Specifications, but use only new bolts for final assembly.*

24   On 4.6L REP engines, install the jack screws (if removed earlier) into the main caps and bottom them lightly against the caps, this must be done before the caps are placed into the block.

25   Lubricate the upper thrust washer with moly-base grease and rotate it into the block while prying rearward on the crankshaft **(see illustration)**. The side of the washer with the oil grooves must face the crankshaft. REP 4.6L engines use one thrust washer at the back of the last crank journal, while 4.6L WEP and 5.4L and 6.8L engines use two thrust washers, one behind the last journal and one ahead of the last journal. When installing the rearward thrust washer, the crankshaft should be pried rearward. After installing the rearward thrust washer, pry the crankshaft forward on 4.6L WEP and 5.4L engines and install the lubricated front thrust washer by rotating it into place.

26   Place the main caps on their correct journals and tap the caps into place with a brass or soft-face hammer. **Caution:** *All main bearing caps MUST be tapped into position prior to tightening. Failure to do so may result in*

improper torque.

27   Install the NEW main cap bolts and tighten them to 10-to-12 ft-lbs in the recommended sequence **(see illustrations)**. On 4.6L WEP engines, 5.4L and 6.8L engines, install the dowel pins in the outboard holes of the caps with their flat sides toward the center of the engine.

28   Push the crankshaft forward using a screwdriver or prybar to seat the thrust bearing. **Caution:** *Once the crankshaft is pushed fully forward, to seat the thrust bearing, leave the screwdriver in position so that pressure stays placed on the crankshaft until after all main bearing cap bolts have been tightened.*

29   Tighten the main bearing cap bolts in two steps in the sequence shown **(see illustrations 26.27a and 26.27b)** and to the torque and angle indicated in the Specifications listed at the beginning of this Chapter.

30   On REP 4.6L engines, tighten all jack

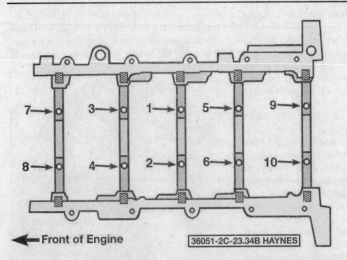

◀ Front of Engine   36051-2C-23.34B HAYNES

26.27a Main cap bolt tightening sequence - 4.6L and 5.4L engines

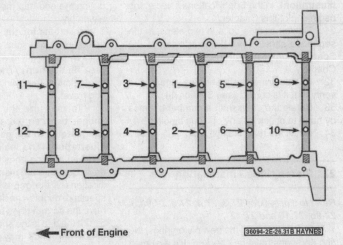

◀ Front of Engine   36094-2E-26.31B HAYNES

26.27b Main cap bolt tightening sequence - 6.8L engines

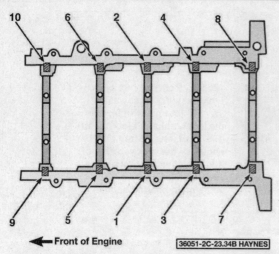

26.30 On REP 4.6L engines, tighten the ten jacking
screws in this sequence

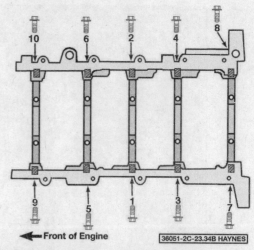

26.31a On all 4.6L and 5.4L engines tighten the
side bolts in this sequence in two steps

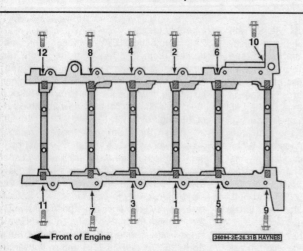

26.31b 6.8L side bolt tightening sequence

27.3 When checking the piston ring end gap, the ring must be
square in the cylinder bore. This is done by pushing the ring
down with the top of the piston as shown.

screws against the block (left-hand threads) in two steps, in the sequence shown **(see illustration)**, to the Specifications listed at the beginning of this Chapter.

31   Tighten all side bolts in two steps, in the sequence shown **(see illustrations)**, to the Specifications listed at the beginning of this Chapter.

32   Check crankshaft endplay again and verify that it is correct (see Section 14).

33   Rotate the crankshaft a number of times by hand to check for any obvious binding.

34   Install the rear main oil seal.

27   Piston rings - installation

Refer to illustrations 27.3, 27.4, 27.5, 27.9a, 27.9b, 27.10 and 27.12

1   Before installing the new piston rings, the ring end gaps must be checked. It's assumed that the piston ring side clearance has been checked and verified correct (see Section 18).

2   Lay out the piston/connecting rod assem-

blies and the new rings so the ring sets will be matched with the same piston and cylinder during the end gap measurement and engine assembly.

3   Insert the top (number one) ring into the first cylinder and square it up with the cylinder walls by pushing it in with the top of the piston **(see illustration)**. The ring should be near the bottom of the cylinder, at the lower limit of ring travel.

4   To measure the end gap, slip feeler gauges between the ends of the ring until a gauge equal to the gap width is found **(see illustration)**. The feeler gauge should slide between the ring ends with a slight amount of drag. Compare the measurement to the Specifications. If the gap is larger or smaller than specified, double-check to make sure that you have the correct rings before proceeding.

5   If the gap is too small, it must be enlarged or the ring ends may come in contact with each other during engine operation, which can cause serious damage. The end gap can be increased by filing the ring ends very carefully with a fine file. Mount the file in a vise

equipped with soft jaws, slip the ring over the file with the ends contacting the file face and slowly move the ring to remove material from the ends - file only from the outside in **(see illustration)**. After achieving the proper gap, use a fine file to slightly chamfer the edges of

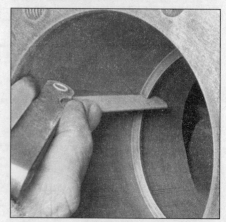

27.4 With the ring square in the cylinder,
measure the end gap with a feeler gauge

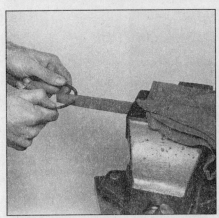

27.5 If the end gap is too small, clamp a file in a vise and file the ring ends (from the outside in only) to enlarge the gap slightly

27.9a Installing the spacer/expander in the oil control ring groove

27.9b DO NOT use a piston ring installation tool when installing the oil ring side rails

the rings where they were filed, to remove any tiny burrs.

6   End gap should not exceed the value listed in this Chapter's Specifications.

7   Repeat the procedure for each ring that will be installed in the first cylinder and for each ring in the remaining cylinders. Remember to keep rings, pistons and cylinders matched up.

8   Once the ring end gaps have been checked/corrected, the rings can be installed on the pistons.

9   The oil control ring (lowest one on the piston) is installed first. It's composed of three separate components. Slip the spacer/expander into the groove **(see illustration)**. Next, install the lower side rail. Don't use a piston ring installation tool on the oil ring side rails, as they may be damaged. Instead, place one end of the side rail into the groove between the spacer/expander and the ring land, hold it firmly in place and slide a finger around the piston while pushing the rail into the groove **(see illustration)**. Install the upper side rail in the same manner.

10   After the three oil ring components have been installed, check to make sure that both the upper and lower side rails can be turned smoothly in the ring groove and stagger the gaps **(see illustration)**.

11   The number two (middle) ring is installed next. It's stamped with a mark which must face up, toward the top of the piston. **Note:** *Always follow the instructions printed on the ring package or box - different manufacturers may require different approaches. Don 't mix up the top and middle rings, as they have different cross sections.*

12   Use a piston ring installation tool and make sure that the identification mark is facing the top of the piston, then slip the ring into the middle groove on the piston **(see illustration)**. Don't expand the ring any more than necessary to slide it over the piston.

13   Install the number one (top) ring in the same manner. Make sure the mark is facing up. Be careful not to confuse the number one and number two rings.

14   Repeat the procedure for the remaining pistons and rings.

28   Piston/connecting rod assembly - installation and rod bearing oil clearance check

Refer to illustrations 28.9, 28.11 and 28.13

1   Before installing the piston/connecting rod assemblies, the cylinder walls must be perfectly clean, the top edge of each cylinder must be chamfered (to remove the sharp edge) and the crankshaft must be in place.

2   Remove the connecting rod cap from the end of the number one connecting rod. Remove the old bearing inserts and wipe the bearing surfaces of the connecting rod and cap with a clean, lint free cloth. They must be kept spotlessly clean.

3   Clean the back side of the new upper bearing half, then lay it in place in the connecting rod. Make sure that the tang on the bearing fits into the appropriate slot in the rod. Do not hammer the bearing insert into place and be very careful not to nick or gouge the bearing face. Do not lubricate the bearing at this time.

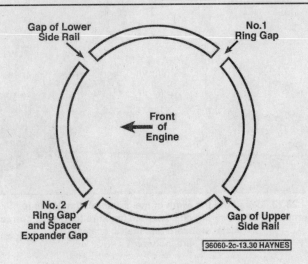

27.10 Correct piston ring spacing on piston

27.12 Installing the compression rings with a ring expander - the mark (arrow) must face up

4   Clean the back side of the other bearing insert and install it in the rod cap. Again, make sure the tang on the bearing fits into the slot in the cap, and do not apply any lubricant. It is critically important that the mating surfaces of the bearing and connecting rod are perfectly clean and oil free when they are assembled for checking oil clearances.

5   Position the piston ring gaps at intervals around the piston (see illustration 27.10), then slip a section of plastic or rubber hose over each connecting rod cap bolt.

6   Lubricate the piston and rings with clean engine oil and attach a piston ring compressor to the piston. Leave the skirt protruding about 1/4-inch to guide the piston into the cylinder. The rings must be compressed until they are flush with the piston.

7   Rotate the crankshaft until the number one connecting rod journal is at BDC (bottom dead center) and apply a coat of engine oil to the cylinder walls.

8   With the notch on top of the piston facing the front of the engine, gently insert the piston/connecting rod assembly into the number one cylinder bore and rest the bottom edge of the ring compressor on the engine block. Tap the top edge of the ring compressor to make sure it's contacting the block around its entire circumference.

9   Carefully tap on the top of the piston with the end of a wooden or plastic hammer handle (see illustration) while guiding the end of the connecting rod into place on the crankshaft journal. The piston rings may try to pop out of the ring compressor just before entering the cylinder bore, so keep some down pressure on the ring compressor. Work slowly, and if any resistance is felt as the piston enters the cylinder, stop immediately! Find out what's hanging up and fix it before proceeding. DO NOT, for any reason, force the piston into the cylinder - you'll break a ring and/or the piston!

10   Once the piston/connecting rod assem-

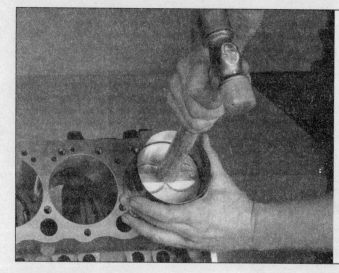

28.9 The piston can be driven (gently) into the cylinder bore with the end of a wooden or plastic hammer handle

bly is installed, the connecting rod bearing oil clearance must be checked before the rod cap is permanently bolted in place.

11   Cut a piece of the appropriate-size Plastigage slightly shorter than the width of connecting rod bearing and lay it in place on the number one connecting rod journal, parallel with the journal axis (see illustration).

12   Clean the connecting rod cap bearing face. remove the protective hoses from the connecting rod bolts and install the rod cap. Make sure the mating mark on the cap is on the same side as the mark on the connecting rod. Install the nuts and tighten them to the specified torque, working up to it in three steps. **Note:** *Use a thin-wall socket to avoid erroneous torque readings that can result if the socket becomes wedged between the rod cap and nut. Do not rotate the crankshaft at any time during this operation.*

13   Remove the rod cap, being very careful not to disturb the Plastigage. Compare the

width of the crushed Plastigage to the scale printed on the Plastigage container to obtain the oil clearance (see illustration). Compare it to the value listed in this Chapter's Specifications to make sure the clearance is correct. If the clearance is not as specified, the bearing inserts may be the wrong size (which means different ones will be required). Before deciding that different inserts are needed, make sure that no dirt or oil was between the bearing inserts and the connecting rod or cap when the clearance was measured. Also, recheck the journal diameter. If the Plastigage was wider at one end than the other, the journal may be tapered.

14   Carefully scrape all traces of the Plastigage material off the rod journal and/or bearing face. Be very careful not to scratch the bearing - use your fingernail or a piece of hardwood. Make sure the bearing faces are perfectly clean, then apply a uniform layer of clean moly-base grease or engine assembly

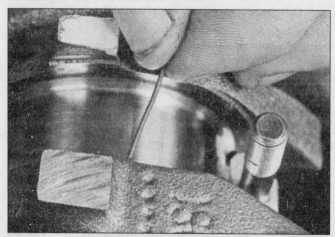

28.11 Lay the Plastigage strips on each rod bearing journal, parallel to the crankshaft centerline

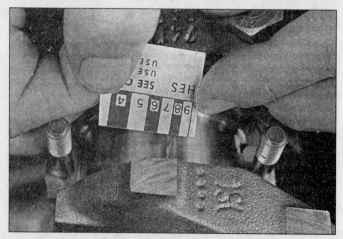

28.13 Measuring the width of the crushed Plastigage to determine the rod bearing oil clearance (be sure to use the correct scale- standard and metric scales are included)

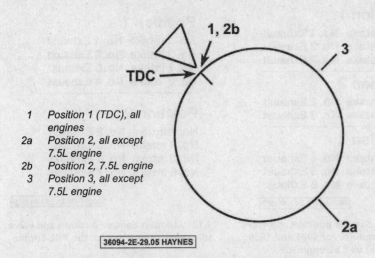

1   Position 1 (TDC), all
    engines
2a Position 2, all except
    7.5L engine
2b Position 2, 7.5L engine
3   Position 3, all except
    7.5L engine

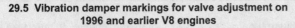

**29.5 Vibration damper markings for valve adjustment on
1996 and earlier V8 engines**

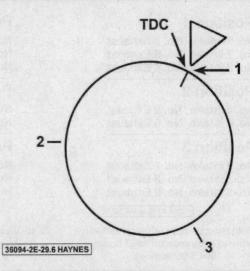

**29.6 Vibration-damper markings for valve adjustment
on the inline six-cylinder (4.9L) engine**

lube to both of them. You'll have to push the piston into the cylinder to expose the face of the bearing insert in the connecting rod - be sure to slip the protective hoses over the rod bolts first.

15 Slide the connecting rod back into place on the journal, remove the protective hoses from the rod cap bolts, install the rod cap and tighten the nuts to the torque listed in this Chapter's Specifications. Again, work up to the final torque in three steps.

16 Repeat the above procedure for each of the remaining piston/connecting rod assemblies. Keep the back sides of the bearing inserts and the inside of each connecting rod and cap perfectly clean during reassembly. Make sure that you have the correct piston for each cylinder and the notch on the piston faces the front (timing chain end) of the engine when the piston is installed. Remember, use plenty of oil to lubricate the piston and rings before installing the ring compressor. Also, when installing the rod caps for the final time, be sure to lubricate the bearing faces adequately.

17 After all the piston/connecting rod assemblies have been properly installed, rotate the crankshaft a number of times by hand to check for any obvious binding.

18 As a final step, the connecting rod endplay must be checked. See Section 9 for this procedure. Compare the measured endplay to the Specifications to make sure it's correct. If it was correct before disassembly and the original crankshaft and rods were reinstalled, it should still be right. If new rods or a new crankshaft were installed, the endplay may be too small. If so, the rods will have to be removed and taken to an automotive machine shop for machining.

29 Valve adjustment (4.9L, 5.0L, 5.8L and 7.5L engines only)

Refer to illustrations 29.5, 29.6, 29.8, 29.12, 29.15 and 29.18.

Note: *This valve adjustment procedure applies only to 4.9L, 5.0L, 5.8L and 7.5L engines. The 1997 and later 4.6L, 5.4L and 6.8L engines are equipped with hydraulic lash adjusters installed into the cylinder head near the camshaft. Engines equipped with hydraulic lifters do not normally require a valve adjustment. However, after engine machining, it is generally necessary to check the clearances. No clearance specifications are provided for 4.2L engines, so checking is not normally necessary.*

1 On 5.0L, 5.8L and 7.5L engines, the valve arrangement on the left bank is E-I-E-I-E-I-E-I and on the right bank is I-E-I-E-I-E-I-E. For the inline six-cylinder engine, the valve arrangement is E-I-E-I-E-I-E-I-E-I-E-I.

2 Normally these engines do not need any valve adjustments because the lash is accounted for by the hydraulic lifter. If you have a running engine that has symptoms of valve clearance problems (such as excessive noise from a lifter), check for a defective part. Normally an engine will not reach a point at which it needs a valve adjustment unless a component malfunction has occurred. Hydraulic lifter failure and excessive rocker arm wear are two examples of likely component failure. Also, if major engine work is done, such as a valve job, which alters the relationship among valve train components, a means of compensating for the dimensional changes must be provided. Shorter and longer pushrods are available for this purpose. To determine whether a shorter or longer pushrod is necessary, proceed as follows.

3 Connect an auxiliary starter switch to the starter solenoid. If this is not used, the crankshaft will have to be rotated with a socket and breaker bar.

4 Position the piston in the number one cylinder at top dead center (TDC) on the compression stroke. Refer to the appropriate chapter.

5 On 5.0L, 5.8L and 7.5L engines with the crankshaft in the TDC position, make a mark at 0-degrees TDC. On 5.0L and 5.8L engines, mark a line from the zero mark across the pulley (at 180-degrees), and mark another line 90-degrees from the timing mark **(see illustration)**.

6 On 4.9L engines, mark the pulley with two chalk marks spaced 120-degrees on either side of the zero timing mark **(see illustration)**.

7 Remove the valve cover(s) (see the appropriate Chapter for your engine).

8 Make sure the lifters are compressed (not pumped up with oil). This is accomplished during engine assembly by installing new lifters, or by compressing the lifters and relieving them of all internal oil pressure if they have been in service. A special tool is available for this procedure.

9 With the number one piston at TDC, position the lifter compressor tool on the number one intake rocker arm and slowly apply pressure to bleed down the lifter until the plunger is completely bottomed. Hold the lifter in this position and check the clearance between the rocker arm and the valve stem tip with a feeler gauge. Compare the measurements to the value listed in this Chapter's Specifications. If the clearance is greater than specified, install a longer pushrod. If the clearance is less than specified, install a shorter pushrod. Repeat the procedure on the number one exhaust valve.

Position 1

No. 1 intake No. 1 Exhaust
No. 7 intake No. 5 Exhaust
No. 8 intake No. 4 Exhaust

Position 2

No. 5 intake No. 2 Exhaust
No. 4 intake No. 6 Exhaust

Position 3

No. 2 intake No. 7 Exhaust
No. 3 intake No. 3 Exhaust
No. 6 intake No. 8 Exhaust

36054-2c-5.2c HAYNES

29.12 Vibration damper position and valve adjustment sequence for 1992 through 1994 5.0L engines

Position 1

No. 1 intake No. 1 Exhaust
No. 4 intake No. 3 Exhaust
No. 8 intake No. 7 Exhaust

Position 2

No. 3 intake No. 2 Exhaust
No. 7 intake No. 6 Exhaust

Position 3

No. 2 intake No. 4 Exhaust
No. 5 intake No. 5 Exhaust
No. 6 intake No. 8 Exhaust

36054-2c-5.2d HAYNES

29.15 Vibration damper position and valve adjustment sequence for 1995 and 1996 5.0L and all 5.8L engines

Position 1

No. 1 intake No. 1 Exhaust
No. 3 intake No. 8 Exhaust
No. 7 intake No. 5 Exhaust
No. 8 intake No. 4 Exhaust

Position 2

No. 2 intake No. 2 Exhaust
No. 4 intake No. 3 Exhaust
No. 5 intake No. 6 Exhaust
No. 6 intake No. 7 Exhaust

36058-2D-29.20 HAYNES

29.18 Vibration damper position and valve adjustment sequence for the 7.5L engine

10   Employing the lifter bleed-down and measuring procedures stated in Step 9, complete the valve clearance check as follows:

4.9L engines

11   Rotate the crankshaft with the auxiliary starter, one-third revolution at a time (120 degrees), and adjust both intake and exhaust valves at each position in the remaining firing order sequence (1-5-3-6-2-4).

1992 through 1994 5.0L V8 engines

12   After checking the clearances on both number one cylinder valves, check the remaining valves as shown **(see illustration)**.
13   Rotate the engine 180-degrees with the auxiliary starter switch to Position 2 and check the valves as indicated.
14   Rotate the engine 270-degrees to Position 3 and check the remaining valves as indicated.

1995 and 1996 5.0L and all 5.8L engines

15   After checking the clearances on both number one cylinder valves, check the remaining valves as shown **(see illustration)**.
16   Rotate the engine 180-degrees with the auxiliary starter switch to Position 2 and check the valves as indicated.
17   Rotate the engine 270-degrees to Position 3 and check the remaining valves as indicated.

7.5L engine

18   After checking the clearances on both number one cylinder valves, check the remain-

ing valves as shown **(see illustration)**.
19   Rotate the crankshaft 360-degrees with the auxiliary starter switch to Position 2 and check the remaining valves as indicated.

All engines

20   After completion of the entire valve clearance checking/adjustment procedure, install the remaining engine components and run the engine. It may be necessary for an engine to run several minutes for the clearance in the valve train to be taken up completely by the hydraulic lifter(s), particularly if new lifters were installed, so expect initial operation to be noisier than normal.
21   If the components are all in good shape and a valve lash problem is indicated by excessive noise or rough engine idling, use the special service tool to compress the lifter to recheck the valve clearance.

30   Initial start-up and break-in after overhaul

Warning: *Have a fire extinguisher handy when starting the engine for the first time.*
1   Once the engine has been installed in the vehicle, double-check the engine oil and coolant levels.
2   With the spark plugs out of the engine and the primary wires disconnected from the ignition coil, crank the engine until oil pressure registers on the gauge or until the oil light goes out.
3   Install the spark plugs, hook up the plug wires and reconnect the primary wires to the coil.

4   Start the engine. It may take a few moments for the gasoline to reach the carburetor or fuel-injectors, but the engine should start without a great deal of effort. **Note:** *If the engine keeps backfiring, recheck the ignition timing and spark plug wire routing.*
5   After the engine starts, it should be allowed to warm up to normal operating temperature. Try to keep the engine speed at approximately 2000 rpm. While the engine is warming up, make a thorough check for oil and coolant leaks.
6   Return the engine to idle, then shut the engine off ,and recheck the engine oil and coolant levels. **Note:** *When the battery has been disconnected, some unusual driveability symptoms may be present until the vehicle is driven ten miles and the computer "relearns."*
7   Drive the vehicle to an area with minimum traffic, accelerate from 30 to 50 mph, then allow the vehicle to slow to 30 mph with the throttle closed. Repeat the procedure 10 or 12 times. This will load the piston rings and cause them to seat properly against the cylinder walls. Check again for oil and coolant leaks.
8   Drive the vehicle gently for the first 500 miles (no sustained high speeds) and keep a constant check on the oil level. It's not unusual for an engine to use oil during the break-in period.
9   At approximately 500 to 600 miles, change the oil and filter.
10   For the next few hundred miles, drive the vehicle normally. Don't pamper it or abuse it.
11   After 2000 miles, change the oil and filter again and consider the engine fully broken-in.

Chapter 3
Cooling, heating and air conditioning systems

Contents

Specifications

Refrigerant type
1992 and 1993	R-12
1994 on	R-134a

Torque specifications
Ft-lbs (unless otherwise indicated)

Engine oil cooler insert fastener (5.4L and 6.8L engines)	41 to 44
Fan clutch-to-water pump	
5.0L, 5.8L, 7.5L engines	12 to 18
4.9L engine	40 to 53
4.2L, 4.6L and 5.4L engines	not available
6.8L engine	83 to 117
Fan-to-clutch bolts	12 to 18
Oil cooler adapter bolt (7.5L)	40 to 65
Thermostat housing bolts	
4.9L, 5.0L and 5.8L engines	12 to 18
7.5L engines	23 to 38
4.2L	71 to 103 in-lbs
4.6L, 5.4L and 6.8L engines	15 to 22
Water pump bolts	
4.9L, 5.0L, 5.8L and 7.5L engines	12 to 18
4.2L, 4.6L, 5.4L and 6.8L engines	15 to 22

1   General information

Engine cooling system

The cooling system consists of a radiator and coolant reserve system (1992 through 1996 models) or expansion tank (1997 and later models), a pressure cap (radiator or expansion tank), a thermostat, a cooling fan, and a pulley/belt-driven water pump.

The radiator cooling fan is mounted on the front of the water pump. The fan incorporates a fluid-drive fan clutch, which saves horsepower and reduces noise. When the engine is cold, the fluid in the clutch offers little resistance and allows the fan to freewheel. As the engine heats up and reaches a predetermined temperature, the fluid in the clutch thickens and drives the fan.

1992 through 1996 models are equipped with a coolant recovery system similar to a conventional early model design. The cooling system is sealed by a pressure type radiator cap, which raises the boiling point of the coolant and increases the cooling efficiency of the radiator. If the system pressure exceeds the cap pressure relief valve, the excess pressure in the system forces the spring loaded valve inside the cap off its seat and allows the coolant to escape through the overflow tube into a coolant reservoir. When the system cools the excess coolant is automatically drawn from the reservoir back into the radiator. The coolant reservoir serves as both the point at which fresh coolant is added to the cooling system to maintain the proper fluid level and as a holding tank for overheated coolant. This type of cooling system is known as a closed design because coolant that escapes past the pressure cap is saved and reused.

1997 and later models are equipped with a different coolant recovery system. The recovery tank is called a de-gas bottle (expansion tank), and it functions somewhat differently than traditional recovery tanks. Designed to separate any trapped air in the coolant, it is pressurized by the radiator and has a pressure cap on top. The radiator on these models does not incorporate a radiator cap. When the engine's thermostat is closed, no coolant flows in the de-gas bottle (expansion tank), but when the engine is fully warmed up, coolant flows from the top of the radiator through a small hose that enters the top of the de-gas bottle. There, air separates and coolant falls to the approximately one quart coolant reserve in the bottle, which is fed to the cooling system through a larger hose connected to the lower radiator hose. Unlike traditional coolant recovery tanks, the cap on the expansion tank should never be opened when the engine is running, since there is a danger of injury from steam or scalding coolant (see the **Warning** in Section 5).

Coolant in the left side of the radiator circulates through the lower radiator hose to the water pump, where it is forced through the water passages in the cylinder block. The coolant then travels up into the cylinder head, circulates around the combustion chambers and valve seats, travels out of the cylinder head past the open thermostat into the upper radiator hose and back into the radiator.

When the engine is cold, the thermostat restricts the circulation of coolant to the engine. When the minimum operating temperature is reached, the thermostat begins to open, allowing coolant to return to the radiator.

Transmission cooling system

Automatic transmission-equipped models have a cooler element incorporated into the radiator to cool the transmission fluid.

Oil cooling system

On some models, in addition to conventional engine cooling and transmission cooling as described above, engine heat is also dissipated through the lubrication system. Oil coolers on vehicles equipped with 5.4L and 7.5L V8 and 6.8L V10 engines help keep engine and oil temperatures within design limits under extreme load conditions. The oil cooler on the 7.5L engine is an integral component of the oil filter adapter and assembly. The oil cooler on the 5.4L and 6.8L engine incorporates an adapter mounted to the oil filter that disperses oil through metal lines to the radiator much like a transmission cooling system.

Heating system

The heating system consists of a passenger compartment mounted heater blower assembly (which houses the blower motor, blower resistor, heater core and air conditioning evaporator), the cab mounted heater plenum assembly, the hoses connecting the heater core to the engine cooling system and the heater/air conditioning control assembly on the dashboard. Hot engine coolant is circulated through the heater core. When the heater mode is activated, a flap door opens to expose the heater box to the passenger compartment. A fan switch on the control assembly activates the blower motor, which forces air through the core, heating the air.

Air conditioning system

The air conditioning system consists of a condenser mounted in front of the radiator, a passenger compartment mounted evaporator case assembly, a compressor mounted on the engine, and the plumbing connecting all of the above components. The evaporator case replaces the heater blower assembly normally found in non-air conditioned models.

A blower fan forces the warmer air of the passenger compartment through the evaporator core (sort of a radiator-in-reverse), transferring the heat from the air to the refrigerant. The liquid refrigerant boils off into low pressure vapor, taking the heat with it when it leaves the evaporator.

An optional auxiliary heating and air conditioning system is available for these models. The rear mounted system is located on the left side of the vehicle between the side windows and the floorpan, behind the rear wheelwell. Some auxiliary systems are equipped with a separate blower motor switch mounted in the rear of the vehicle. The auxiliary heating and air conditioning system incorporates a blower motor, heater core and evaporator core for complete control of the climate in the rear of the vehicle.

2   Antifreeze - general information

Refer to illustration 2.5

Warning: *Do not allow antifreeze to come in contact with your skin or painted surfaces of the vehicle. Rinse off spills immediately with plenty of water. Antifreeze is highly toxic if ingested. Never leave antifreeze lying around in an open container or in puddles on the floor; children and pets are attracted by it's sweet smell and may drink it. Check with local authorities about disposing of used antifreeze. Many communities have collection centers which will see that antifreeze is disposed of safely. Never dump used antifreeze on the ground or pour it into drains.*

Caution: *Beginning in 2001, some models are equipped with red-colored, long life coolant. Do not mix green-colored ethylene glycol coolant and red-colored coolant because doing so will cause cooling system damage. Read the warning label in the engine compartment for additional information.*

Note: *Non-toxic antifreeze is now manufactured and available at local auto parts stores, but even this type should be disposed of properly.*

The cooling system should be filled with a water/ethylene glycol based antifreeze solution, which will prevent freezing down to at least -20-degrees F (even lower in cold climates). It also provides protection against corrosion and increases the coolant boiling point. The engines in these vehicles have either cast iron heads (1992 through 1996) or aluminum heads (1997 and later). The manufacturer recommends that only the proper type of coolant be used. Refer to Chapter 1 specifications.

The cooling system should be drained, flushed and refilled at least every other year (see Chapter 1). The use of antifreeze solutions for periods of longer than two years is likely to cause damage and encourage the formation of rust and scale in the system.

Before adding antifreeze to the system, check all hose connections. Antifreeze can leak through very minute openings.

Starting in 2001, models produced for Oregon and Canada are equipped with a special coolant designed for long-life and environmental recycling programs. Do not mix green-colored ethylene glycol anti-freeze with red-colored anti-freeze because doing so will destroy the cooling system. Consult a dealer parts department for additional information concerning cooling system servicing.

The exact mixture of antifreeze to water, which you should use, depends on the rela-

2.5 An inexpensive hydrometer can be used to test the condition of your coolant

tive weather conditions. The mixture should contain at least 50-percent antifreeze, but should never contain more than 70-percent anti-freeze. Consult the mixture ratio chart on the container before adding coolant. Hydrometers are available at most auto parts stores to test the coolant **(see illustration)**. Use antifreeze that meets manufacturer specifications for engines with aluminum heads.

3   Thermostat - check and replacement

Warning: *The engine must be completely cool when this procedure is performed.*
Note: *Don't drive the vehicle without a thermostat! The computer may stay in open loop and emissions and fuel economy will suffer.*

Check

1   Before condemning the thermostat, check the coolant level, drivebelt tension and temperature gauge (or light) operation.
2   If the engine takes a long time to warm up, the thermostat is probably stuck open. Replace the thermostat.

3   If the engine runs hot, check the temperature of the upper radiator hose. If the hose isn't hot, the thermostat is probably stuck shut. Replace the thermostat.
4   If the upper radiator hose is hot, it means the coolant is circulating and the thermostat is open. Refer to the *Troubleshooting* Section at the front of this manual for the cause of overheating.
5   If an engine has been overheated, you may find damage such as leaking head gaskets, scuffed pistons and warped or cracked cylinder heads.

Removal

6   Drain the radiator so that the coolant level is below the thermostat.

4.9L engine

7   Remove the coolant outlet elbow attaching bolts, then pull the elbow away from the cylinder head sufficiently to provide access to the thermostat.
8   Remove the thermostat and gasket, noting the top and bottom to assure proper installation.

5.0L, 5.8L and 7.5L engines

9   Disconnect the bypass hoses at the water pump and intake manifold.
10   Remove the bypass tube, then remove the water outlet housing attaching bolts.
11   Bend the radiator upper hose up and remove the thermostat and gasket, taking note of the top and bottom to assure proper installation.

4.2L, 4.6L, 5.4L and 6.8L engines

Refer to illustrations 3.13a, 3.13b and 3.15

12   Disconnect the upper radiator hose from the thermostat housing. On later models, remove the air cleaner housing.
13   Remove the bolts and lift the cover off **(see illustrations)**. Remove the O-ring seal. On 4.6L, 5.4L and 6.8L models, loosen the bolts on the power steering reservoir bracket enough to allow the thermostat housing to be withdrawn (one bracket bolt threads into the

top of the thermostat housing).
14   Note how it's installed, then remove the thermostat. Be sure to use a replacement thermostat with the correct opening temperature (see this Chapter's Specifications).
15   On thermostat housings that use gaskets instead of rubber seals, use a scraper or putty knife to remove all traces of old gasket material and sealant from the mating surfaces. Later models have an O-ring **(see illustration)**. Make sure no gasket material falls into the coolant passages; it is a good idea to stuff a rag in the passage. Wipe the mating surfaces with a rag saturated with lacquer thinner or acetone.

Installation

4.9L engine

16   After cleaning the coolant outlet elbow and cylinder head gasket surfaces, coat a new gasket with water-resistant sealer and position the gasket on the cylinder head opening. **Note:** *The gasket must be positioned on the cylinder head before the thermostat is installed.*
17   The coolant elbow contains a locking recess into which the thermostat is turned and locked. Install the thermostat with the bridge section in the outlet elbow.
18   Turn the thermostat clockwise to lock it in position on the flats cast into the elbow.
19   Position the elbow against the cylinder head and tighten the attaching bolts to the torque listed in this Chapter's Specifications.

5.0L, 5.8L and 7.5L engines

20   After cleaning the water outlet gasket surfaces, coat a new water outlet gasket with water-resistant sealer.
21   Position the gasket on the intake manifold opening.
22   Install the thermostat in the intake manifold with the copper element toward the engine and the thermostat flange positioned in the recess.
23   Position the water outlet housing against the intake manifold and install and tighten

3.13a Thermostat location for the 4.2L engine - arrows indicate the location of the two bolts

3.13b On 4.6L, 5.4L and 6.8L engines, remove the upper bolt (upper arrow) and loosen the power steering reservoir bolts, then remove the two thermostat housing bolts (lower bolts)

3.15 When installing the thermostat, pay special attention to the direction in which it's placed in the engine; the spring side will go into the intake manifold (4.2L shown) - arrow indicates the new O-ring

4.7 Hold the water pump pulley with a large wrench and turn the fan clutch nut with the small wrench counterclockwise to remove

4.12 On some engines the fan clutch is bolted to the water pump hub with four bolts

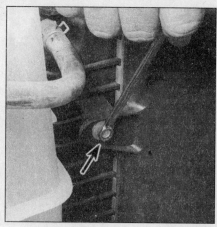

4.20 Remove the two fan shroud screws (arrow indicates the one on the left side) and pull the shroud out with the fan assembly

the attaching bolts to the torque listed in this Chapter's Specifications.

24   Install the water bypass line and tighten the hose connections.

4.2L, 4.6L, 5.4L and 6.8L engines

25   Install the thermostat and make sure the correct end faces out - the spring end is directed toward the engine. **Note:** *On some models, the thermostat housing has a notch that a tab on the thermostat fits into, which automatically locates the thermostat correctly.*

26   On models that use a conventional paper gasket, apply a thin coat of RTV sealant to both sides of the new gasket and position it on the engine side, over the thermostat, and make sure the gasket holes line up with the bolt holes in the housing. **Note:** *No RTV sealant should be used on the O-ring seal.*

27   On models that use an O-ring seal, install the new O-ring into the intake manifold or onto the thermostat housing.

28   Carefully position the cover and install the bolts. Tighten them to the torque listed in this Chapter's Specifications - do not overtighten them or the cover may be cracked or distorted.

29   Reattach the radiator hose to the cover and tighten the clamp - now may be a good time to check and replace the hoses and clamps (see Chapter 1).

All engines

30   Fill the cooling system with the proper amount and type of coolant (see Chapter 1).

31   Start and run the engine until it reaches normal operating temperature, then check the coolant level and look for leaks.

---

4   Cooling fan and clutch - check, removal and installation

Warning 1: *The late models covered by this manual are equipped with Supplemental Restraint Systems (SRS), more commonly*

known as airbags. Always disconnect the negative battery cable, then the positive battery cable and wait two minutes before working in the vicinity of the impact sensors, steering column or instrument panel to avoid the possibility of accidental deployment of the airbag, which could cause personal injury (see Chapter 12). Do not use any electrical test equipment on any of the airbag system wires or tamper with them in any way.

Warning 2: *Keep hands, tools and clothing away from the fan when the engine is running. To avoid injury or damage DO NOT operate the engine with a damaged fan. Do not attempt to repair fan blades - replace a damaged fan with a new one.*

Check

Warning: *In order to check the fan clutch, the engine will need to be at operating temperature, so while going through checks prior to Step 6 be careful that the engine is NOT started while the checks are being completed. Severe personal injury can result!*

1   Symptoms of failure of the fan clutch are continuous noisy operation, looseness, vibration and evidence of silicone fluid leaks.

2   Rock the fan back and forth by hand to check for excessive bearing play.

3   With the engine cold, turn the blades by hand. The fan should turn freely.

4   Visually inspect for substantial fluid leakage from the fan clutch assembly, a deformed bi-metal spring or grease leakage from the cooling fan bearing. If any of these conditions exist, replace the fan clutch.

5   When the engine is warmed up, turn off the ignition switch. Turn the fan by hand. Some resistance should be felt. If the fan turns easily, replace the fan clutch.

Fan clutch removal and installation

4.9L engine
Refer to illustration 4.7

6   Remove the radiator shroud.

7   Using special tools designed for fan clutch removal (fan clutch nut wrench and fan drive hub nut wrench) **(see illustration)**, hold the pulley while turning the large clutch nut counterclockwise to remove clutch.

8   Remove the clutch and fan assembly from the vehicle.

9   If necessary, remove the four bolts and separate the clutch from the fan.

10   Installation is the reverse of removal.

5.0L, 5.8L and 7.5L engines
Refer to illustration 4.12

11   Remove the radiator shroud and radiator, if necessary.

12   Remove the four bolts retaining the clutch hub to the water pump and remove the fan assembly **(see illustration)**.

13   If necessary, remove the four bolts and separate the clutch from the fan.

14   Installation is the reverse of removal.

4.2L, 4.6L, 5.4L and 6.8L engines
Refer to illustrations 4.20 and 4.21

15   Disconnect the battery cable at the negative battery terminal.

16   Remove the air cleaner assembly (see Chapter 4).

17   Drain the cooling system (see Chapter 1).

18   Remove the upper radiator hose.

19   A special two-part fan wrench set, obtainable at most auto parts stores, is required to remove the cooling fan assembly. The clutch attaches to the drive hub with a large nut. Hold the water pump pulley with the holding tool and a breaker bar, while turning the clutch nut with the longer tool **(see illustration 4.7)**. **Note:** *On most models, the fan clutch hub nut is right-hand thread (turn counterclockwise to loosen). Refer to the belt routing label on the fan shroud; if the hub nut is left-hand thread it should be stated as such on the label.*

20   Unbolt the fan shroud **(see illustration)** and lift the fan assembly and shroud up and out of the engine compartment together.

4.21 Remove the four bolts (arrows) and separate the fan from the fan clutch

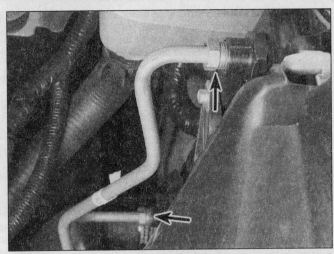

5.7 Use a flare-nut wrench on the line fittings (arrows) and a back-up wrench on the radiator fittings to prevent damage to the transmission cooler lines or radiator when disconnecting them from the radiator (1997 and later models)

Note: *Two people are required for this procedure. Have an assistant below the engine compartment to hold the fan pulley using one of the special tools. Access the clutch nut from above at the 12 o'clock position using the other wrench. After the clutch nut has been loosened, rotate the fan and fan clutch until it separates from the water pump shaft.*

21   The fan clutch can be unbolted from the fan blade assembly for replacement **(see illustration). Caution:** *To prevent silicone fluid from draining from the clutch assembly into the fan drive bearing and ruining the lubricant, DON'T place the drive unit in a position with the rear of the shaft pointing down. Store the fan in its upright position.*

22   Installation is the reverse of removal.

5   Radiator - removal and installation

Refer to illustrations 5.7 and 5.10

Warning 1: *The engine must be completely cool when this procedure is performed.*

Warning 2: *Late models covered by this manual are equipped with Supplemental Restraint Systems (SRS), more commonly known as airbags. Always disconnect the negative battery cable, then the positive battery cable and wait two minutes before working in the vicinity of the impact sensors, steering column or instrument panel to avoid the possibility of accidental deployment of the airbag, which could cause personal injury (see Chapter 12). Do not use any electrical test equipment on any of the airbag system wires or tamper with them in any way.*

1   Disconnect the cable from the negative battery terminal.

2   Drain the cooling system (see Chapter 1).

3   Remove the air cleaner assembly (see Chapter 4).

4   On 1997 and later models, remove the plastic rivet retainers and the front air deflector from the radiator support.

5   Disconnect the overflow hose from the coolant reservoir (1992 through 1996 models) or expansion tank (1997 and later models) at the radiator.

6   Refer to Section 4 and remove the cooling fan and shroud assembly.

7   Detach the transmission cooler lines from the radiator **(see illustration)** - be careful not to damage the lines or fittings. Plug the ends of the disconnected lines to prevent leakage and stop dirt from entering the system. Have a drip pan ready to catch any spills.

8   Disconnect the upper and lower radiator hoses.

9   Remove the engine protection shield from under the front body, if equipped.

10   Remove the mounting bolts from the sides of the radiator (1992 through 1996 models) or from the two upper radiator mounts (1997 and later models) **(see illustration)**. Carefully lift the radiator out of the vehicle.

11   Prior to installation of the radiator,

5.10 Remove the two bolts (arrow indicates right side mount) and mounts holding the top of the radiator

replace any damaged hose clamps and radiator hoses.

12   Radiator installation is the reverse of removal. When installing the radiator, make sure it seats properly in the lower saddles and that the rubber mounts (1997 and later models) are intact.

13   After installation, fill the system with the proper mixture of antifreeze, and also check the automatic transmission fluid level.

14   Start the engine and allow it to reach normal operating temperature, then check for leaks.

6   Water pump - check

Refer to illustrations 6.2a and 6.2b

Warning: *Late models covered by this manual are equipped with Supplemental Restraint Systems (SRS), more commonly known as airbags. Always disconnect the negative battery cable, then the positive battery cable and wait two minutes before working in the vicinity of the impact sensors, steering column or instrument panel to avoid the possibility of accidental deployment of the airbag, which could cause personal injury (see Chapter 12). Do not use any electrical test equipment on any of the airbag system wires or tamper with them in any way.*

1   Water pump failure can cause overheating and serious damage to the engine. There are three ways to check the operation of the water pump while it's installed on the engine. If any one of the following quick checks indicates water pump problems, it should be replaced immediately.

2   A seal protects the water pump impeller shaft bearing from contamination by engine coolant. If this seal fails, a weep hole in the water pump snout will leak coolant (an inspection mirror can be used to look at the underside of the pump if the hole isn't on top). If the weep hole is leaking, shaft bearing failure will

follow **(see illustrations)**. Replace the water pump immediately. **Note:** *A small amount of gray discoloration is normal. A wet area or heavy brown deposits indicate the pump seal has failed.*

3   Besides contamination by coolant after a seal failure, the water pump impeller shaft bearing can also prematurely wear out. If a noise is coming from the water pump during engine operation, the shaft bearing has failed - replace the water pump immediately. **Note:** *Do not confuse drivebelt noise with bearing noise. Loose or glazed drivebelts may emit a high-pitched squealing noise.*

4   To identify excessive bearing wear before the bearing actually fails, grasp the water pump pulley (with the drivebelt removed) and try to force it up-and-down or from side-to-side. If the pulley can be moved either horizontally or vertically, the bearing is nearing the end of its service life. Replace the water pump.

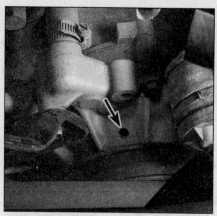

6.2a Check for leakage at the water pump drain hole (arrow) (1992 through 1996 models)

6.2b Location of the water pump weep hole on 1997 and later models

---

7   Water pump - removal and installation

Warning 1: *Late models covered by this manual are equipped with Supplemental Restraint Systems (SRS), more commonly known as airbags. Always disconnect the negative battery cable, then the positive battery cable and wait two minutes before working in the vicinity of the impact sensors, steering column or instrument panel to avoid the possibility of accidental deployment of the airbag, which could cause personal injury (see Chapter 12). Do not use any electrical test equipment on any of the airbag system wires or tamper with them in any way.*
Warning 2: *Wait until the engine is completely cold before beginning this procedure.*

1   Disconnect the cable from the negative battery terminal.

2   With the engine cold, drain the cooling system (see Chapter 1).

Removal

4.2L, 4.9L, 5.0L, 5.8L and 7.5L engines

Refer to illustrations 7.8 and 7.9

3   Remove the fan or fan clutch assembly (see Section 4).

4   Release the accessory drivebelt from the water pump pulley. On 7.5L engines, release tension on both accessory belts (refer to Chapter 1).

5   On 5.0L, 5.8L and 7.5L engines, remove the bolts retaining the air conditioning compressor/power steering pump bracket to the front of the engine (see Section 15). Move the bracket and attached accessories off of the water pump studs and away from the water pump enough to gain access to the water pump attaching bolts.

6   On 7.5L engines, remove the bolt securing the alternator adjusting bracket to the water pump, then remove the bolts retaining the air pump/alternator bracket to the front of the engine. Move the bracket and attached

accessories away from the water pump enough to gain access to the water pump attaching bolts.

7   Disconnect the lower radiator hose from the water pump inlet.

8   Disconnect the heater and bypass hoses from the water pump **(see illustra-tion)**.

9   Remove the water pump retaining bolts **(see illustration)** and remove the water pump from the front cover or the engine block (depending on engine type). **Note:** *Take note of the installed positions of the various-sized bolts and studs.*

10   Remove the gaskets from the mating faces of the water pump and from the front cover or cylinder block.

11   Before installing, remove and clean all gasket material from the water pump, front cover, separator plate mating surfaces and/or cylinder block as applicable.

12   If necessary, transfer hose ports and/or fittings from the old pump if you are replacing it with a new pump. Use sealer on the threads of the fittings.

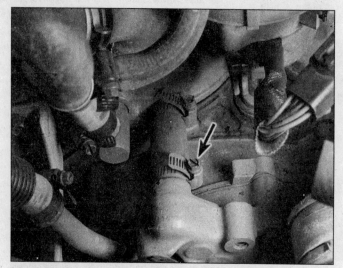

7.8 Remove the heater and by-pass hose clamps and hoses from the water pump (arrow)

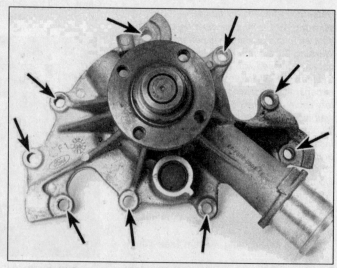

7.9 Water pump bolt locations on the 4.2L engine

7.14 While the drivebelt is still in place, remove the four bolts (arrows) holding the water pump pulley

7.15 Water pump bolt locations on the 4.6L, 5.4L and 6.8L engines

4.6L, 5.4L and 6.8L engines

Refer to illustrations 7.14 and 7.15

Warning: *Wait until the engine is completely cool before starting this procedure.*

13   Remove the fan shroud and the fan assembly (see Section 4).

14   Remove the drivebelt(s) (see Chapter 1) and remove the water pump pulley **(see illustration)**. **Note:** *It's helpful to loosen the pulley bolts/nuts while the belt is still in place. It helps hold the pulley from turning.*

15   Remove the water pump retaining bolts and remove the water pump **(see illustration)**. Take note of the installed positions of the various length bolts and studs. **Note:** *If the water pump sticks, dislodge it with a soft-face hammer or a hammer and a block of wood.*

Installation

4.2L, 4.9L, 5.0L, 5.8L and 7.5L engines

16   Apply a thin film of RTV sealant to both sides of the new water pump gaskets, then position new gaskets onto the water pump.

17   Carefully install the water pump.

18   Install the retaining bolts finger-tight and make sure that all gaskets are in place and that the hoses line up in the correct position.

19   Tighten the water pump retaining bolts to the torque listed in this Chapter's Specifications.

20   Connect the radiator lower hose and clamp.

21   Connect the heater return hose and clamp.

22   Connect the bypass hose to the water pump.

23   Attach the remaining components to the water pump and engine in the reverse order of removal.

24   Install all of the accessory drivebelts and adjust, if required (see Chapter 1).

25   Fill the cooling system with the proper coolant mixture (see Chapter 1).

26   Start the engine and make sure there are no leaks. Check the level frequently during the first few weeks of operation.

4.6L, 5.4L and 6.8L engines

Refer to illustrations 7.28 and 7.29

27   Before installation, remove and clean all gasket or sealant material from the water pump and cylinder block.

28   Inspect the O-ring and sealing surface of water pump housing in the block for dirt and/or debris **(see illustration)**. Clean them thoroughly before reassembly.

29   Lubricate a new O-ring seal with clean antifreeze and install it to the water pump **(see illustration)**.

30   Install the water pump and tighten the bolts to the torque listed in this Chapter's Specifications.

31   The remainder of the installation is the reverse of the disassembly sequence.

32   Fill the cooling system with the proper coolant mixture (see Chapter 1).

33   Start the engine and make sure there are no leaks. Check the level frequently during the first few weeks of operation to ensure there are no leaks and that the level in the system is stable.

7.28 Inspect the sealing surface (arrow) in the pump cavity for dirt or signs of pitting

7.29 Install a new O-ring seal on the water pump

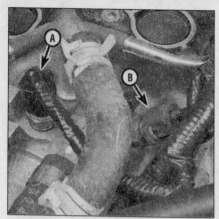

8.1a The coolant temperature sending unit (A) on 4.2L models is on the intake manifold - (B) indicates the coolant temperature sensor for the computer

8.1b On 4.6L, 5.0L 5.4L, 5.8L and 6.8L engines, the coolant temperature sending unit (arrow) is at the left front of the intake manifold

9.8 The thermal limiter (arrow) protects the components from excessive heat - check the thermal limiter for damage

8   Coolant temperature sending unit - check and replacement

Refer to illustrations 8.1 and 8.1b

Check

1   The coolant temperature indicator system is composed of a temperature gauge mounted in the dash and a coolant temperature sending unit mounted on the engine **(see illustrations)**. Some vehicles have more than one sending unit, but only one is used for the indicator system and the other is used to send engine temperature information to the computer. **Note:** *On 2001 through 2003 models, there is both a coolant temperature sensor and a cylinder head temperature sensor, while 2004 and later models have only a cylinder head temperature sensor.*

2   If an overheating indication occurs, check the coolant level in the system. Make sure the wiring between the gauge and the sending unit is secure and all fuses are intact.

3   To test the temperature sender, check that it reads in the cold range when the engine is cold. Disconnect the electrical connector from the sender and attach a jumper wire between the two pins of the connector. With the key ON, the gauge should now swing to full hot. If it doesn't, the problem is in the circuit from the sender to the instrument panel. If the gauge does swing to full hot when testing, but doesn't when the connector is in place and the engine is hot, replace the coolant temperature sending unit.

Replacement

Warning: *Wait until the engine is completely cool before beginning this procedure.*

4   Prepare the new sending unit by wrapping its threads with Teflon tape or applying sealer. Remove the pressure cap from the expansion tank (de-gas bottle) to release any pressure that may remain in the system, then reinstall it.

5   Disconnect the electrical connector and unscrew the sensor from the engine. Install the replacement as quickly as possible to minimize coolant loss. There will be some coolant loss as the unit is removed, so be prepared to catch it. **Caution:** *The sending unit is made of metal and plastic and is fragile. Use care not to crack the unit when removing it.*

6   Check the coolant level after the replacement unit has been installed (see Chapter 1).

9   Heater and air conditioning blower motor and circuit - check

Refer to illustrations 9.8 and 9.10

Warning: *Late models covered by this manual are equipped with Supplemental Restraint Systems (SRS), more commonly known as airbags. Always disconnect the negative battery cable, then the positive battery cable and wait two minutes before working in the vicinity of the impact sensors, steering column or instrument panel to avoid the possibility of accidental deployment of the airbag, which could cause personal injury (see Chapter 12). Do not use any electrical test equipment on any of the airbag system wires or tamper with them in any way.*

Note: *The blower motor is switched on the ground-side of the circuit.*

1   Check the fuse and all connections in the circuit for looseness and corrosion. Make sure the battery is fully charged. **Note:** *The blower motor fuse and relay is located in the engine compartment fuse panel.*

2   With the transmission in Park, the parking brake securely set, turn the ignition switch to the On position. It isn't necessary to start the vehicle.

3   Switch the heater controls to FLOOR and the blower speed to HIGH. Listen at the ducts to hear if the blower is operating. If it is, then switch the blower speed to LOW and listen again. Try all the speeds.

4   Backprobe the blower motor electrical connector and connect a voltmeter to the blower motor and ground.

5   Move the blower motor switch through each of its positions and note the voltage readings. Changes in voltage indicate that the motor speeds will also vary as the switch is moved to the different positions.

6   If there is voltage present, but the blower motor does not operate, the blower motor is probably faulty. Disconnect the blower motor connector, then hook one side of the blower motor terminals to a chassis ground and the other to a fused source of battery voltage. If the blower doesn't operate, it is faulty.

7   If there was no voltage present at the blower motor, and the motor itself tested OK, follow the blower motor ground wire from the motor to the chassis and check the ground terminal for continuity to ground against the chassis metal. If no continuity exists, repair the ground circuit as necessary.

8   If the ground was OK, disconnect the harness connector from the blower motor resistor. With the ignition ON (engine not running), check for voltage at the resistor connector as the blower speed switch is moved to the different positions. If the voltmeter responds correctly to the switch and the blower is known to be good then the resistor is probably faulty. If there is no voltage present from the switch, then the blower motor switch or related wiring circuit is faulty. Refer to the wiring diagrams at the end of Chapter 12. **Note:** *The blower motor resistor assembly is located on the blower motor housing in the engine compartment. There are three resistor elements mounted on the resistor board to provide medium low, medium high and high blower speeds (LOW bypasses the resistor). The blower operates continuously, anytime the ignition switch is On and the mode switch is in any position other than Off. A thermal limiter resistor is integrated into the resistor assembly* **(see illustration)**, *near the motor, to prevent heat damage to the components. If the thermal limiter circuit has been opened as a result of excessive heat, it should be replaced only with the identical replacement part. Do not replace your blower resistor with a resistor that does not incorporate the thermal limiter.*

9.10 Check the blower speed switch for continuity

10.6 Location of the blower motor screws (arrows)

9   To check the blower motor resistor, use an ohmmeter to test for continuity between the blower motor power terminal (orange/black wire) and the remaining terminals on the blower motor resistor. There should be continuity at all four terminals with varied resistance between them.
10   If the blower operates, but not at all speeds and you have already checked the blower resistor, refer to Section 12 and remove the heater/air conditioning control panel. Disconnect the electrical connector from the back of the blower speed switch and test the terminals for continuity (see illustration). In the LOW position, there should be no continuity between any terminals; in Medium Low position, there should be continuity between terminals 2 and 3; in Medium Hi position there should be continuity between terminals 2 and 4, and in HI position, there should be continuity between terminals 2 and 1. If the continuity is not as described, replace the blower speed switch.
11   Locate the blower motor relay, in the relay box in the engine compartment (see Chapter 12). Test the relay (see Chapter 12). If the relay fails any of the tests, replace the relay.
12   With the blower motor relay removed, check for battery voltage to the relay. Refer to the wiring diagrams at the end of Chapter 12. Replace the fuse or repair the circuit to the battery if power is not available.

10   Heater and air conditioning blower motor and resistor - removal and installation

Warning: *Late models covered by this manual are equipped with Supplemental Restraint Systems (SRS), more commonly known as airbags. Always disconnect the negative battery cable, then the positive battery cable and wait two minutes before working in the vicinity of the impact sensors, steering column or instrument panel to avoid the possibility of accidental deployment of the airbag, which could cause personal injury (see Chapter 12).*

Do not use any electrical test equipment on any of the airbag system wires or tamper with them in any way.

Blower motor
Refer to illustrations 10.6 and 10.7
1   Disconnect the cable from the negative battery terminal.
2   Remove the battery and battery tray (see Chapter 5) from the engine compartment.
3   On A/C equipped vehicles, remove the mounting bolts from the air conditioning accumulator and separate the assembly from the firewall. Move the assembly to the side without disconnecting the A/C lines.
4   Working in the engine compartment, disconnect the blower motor electrical connector from the motor.
5   Remove the blower motor housing tube.
6   Remove the blower motor cover screws (see illustration) and retaining clip. On A/C equipped vehicles, rotate the blower motor mounting plate until the flat spot on the metal plate aligns with the accumulator to allow easy removal.
7   Separate the blower fan from the motor.
 a) On 1992 through 1996 models, the blower fan is attached to the blower motor shaft with a hub clamp and washer. Loosen the clamp and slide it off the shaft.
 b) On 1997 and later models, the blower fan is attached to the blower motor shaft with a push nut. Grasp the nut with pliers and pull it off or pry it off with a small screwdriver, being careful not to crack the push nut or the fan (see illustration). To reinstall the nut, simply push it on to the shaft.
8   Installation is the reverse of removal.

Resistor
9   In the engine compartment, locate the resistor on the blower housing near the blower motor.
10   Disconnect the negative cable from the battery.
11   Disconnect the resistor electrical connector.

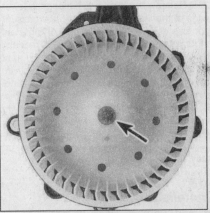

10.7 Pry off the retaining clip (arrow) from the blower fan motor shaft (arrow) (1997 and later models)

12   Remove the resistor screws and remove the resistor from the housing.
13   Installation is the reverse of removal.

11   Heater core - removal and installation

Refer to illustration 11.1
Warning: *Late models covered by this manual are equipped with Supplemental Restraint Systems (SRS), more commonly known as airbags. Always disconnect the negative battery cable, then the positive battery cable and wait two minutes before working in the vicinity of the impact sensors, steering column or instrument panel to avoid the possibility of accidental deployment of the airbag, which could cause personal injury (see Chapter 12). Do not use any electrical test equipment on any of the airbag system wires or tamper with them in any way.*

Removal
1   Working in the engine compartment, remove and plug the heater inlet and outlet hoses from the heater core. **Note:** *Some models use quick disconnect couplings on the*

11.1 Remove the heater hoses from the heater inlet and outlet tubes (arrows)

heater hoses and require coupling tools **(see illustration)**.

2   Remove the hush panel along the lower edge of the instrument panel on the passenger side of the vehicle by gently prying it out of its retainers. On 2004 and 2005 models, remove the bolts securing the instrument panel reinforcement, just behind the trim panel, then remove the reinforcement panel mounting bracket.

3   Remove the heater core cover screws from both sides of the heater case.

4   Remove the heater core cover, being careful not to tear any sealing material that may be in place.

5   Remove the heater core.

Installation

6   Installation is reverse of removal noting for the following:

a) *Fill the radiator with the proper type and amount of coolant (see Chapter 1).*

b) *Start the engine and check for leaks.*

---

12   Heater and air conditioning control assembly - removal and installation

Refer to illustrations 12.3 and 12.5

Warning 1: *Late models covered by this man-ual are equipped with Supplemental Restraint Systems (SRS), more commonly known as airbags. Always disconnect the negative battery cable, then the positive battery cable and wait two minutes before working in the vicinity of the impact sensors, steering column or instrument panel to avoid the possibility of accidental deployment of the airbag, which could cause personal injury (see Chapter 12). Do not use any electrical test equipment on any of the airbag system wires or tamper with them in any way.*

Warning 2: *The air conditioning system is under high pressure. DO NOT loosen any fittings or remove any components until after the system has been discharged. Air conditioning refrigerant should be properly discharged into an EPA-approved container at a dealer service department or an automotive air conditioning repair facility. Always wear eye protection when disconnecting air conditioning system fittings.*

Removal

1   Disconnect the cable from the negative battery terminal.

2   Remove the instrument cluster trim panel (see Chapter 12).

3   Remove the control assembly retaining screws **(see illustration)**.

4   Pull the control assembly out far enough through the opening in the panel to allow dis-

engagement of the electrical connectors for the blower switch, vacuum selector valve and illumination lamp.

5   Disconnect electrical connectors **(see illustration)**.

6   Remove the vacuum harness connector retaining clips and disconnect the vacuum harness.

7   Remove the control assembly.

Installation

8   Installation is the reverse of removal.

9   Check for proper operation of all the control assembly functions.

---

13   Air conditioning system - check and maintenance

Warning 1: *Late models covered by this manual are equipped with Supplemental Restraint Systems (SRS), more commonly known as airbags. Always disconnect the negative battery cable, then the positive battery cable and wait two minutes before working in the vicinity of the impact sensors, steering column or instrument panel to avoid the possibility of accidental deployment of the airbag, which could cause personal injury (see Chapter 12). Do not use any electrical test equipment on any of the airbag system wires or tamper with them in any way.*

Warning 2: *The air conditioning system is under high pressure. DO NOT loosen any fittings or remove any components until after the system has been discharged. Air conditioning refrigerant should be properly discharged into an EPA-approved container at a dealer service department or an automotive air conditioning repair facility. Always wear eye protection when disconnecting air conditioning system fittings.*

Caution 1: *1992 and 1993 vehicles use R-12 refrigerant, later models use R134a refrigerant. This refrigerant (and its appropriate refrigerant oils) are not compatible with R-12 refrigerant system components and must never be mixed or the components will be damaged.*

Caution 2: *When replacing entire compo-*

12.3 Remove the heater/air conditioning control assembly retaining screws (arrows) (1992 through 1996 models)

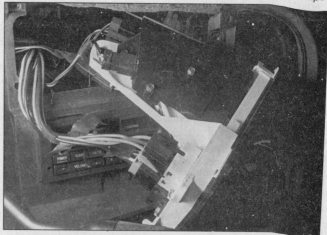

12.5 Disconnect the electrical connectors and vacuum harness from the heater/air conditioning control assembly

13.9 Place an accurate thermometer in the center dash vent, turn the air conditioning on and check the output temperature

nents, additional refrigerant oil should be added equal to the amount that is removed with the component being replaced. Be sure to read the can before adding any oil to the system, to make sure it is compatible with the R-134a system.

Note: Kits are available at auto parts stores to convert older R-12 systems to utilize R-134A refrigerant. The kits typically include a new receiver/drier or accumulator, new fittings and O-rings.

Air conditioning system

1   The following maintenance checks should be performed on a regular basis to ensure that the air conditioning continues to operate at peak efficiency.

  a) Inspect the condition of the compressor drivebelt. If it is worn or deteriorated, replace it (see Chapter 1).
  b) Check the drivebelt tension and, if necessary, adjust it (see Chapter 1).
  c) Inspect the system hoses. Look for cracks, bubbles, hardening and deterioration. Inspect the hoses and all fittings for oil bubbles or seepage. If there is any evidence of wear, damage or leakage, replace the hose(s).
  d) Inspect the condenser fins for leaves, bugs and any other foreign material that may have embedded itself in the fins. Use a "fin comb" or compressed air to remove debris from the condenser.
  e) Make sure the system has the correct refrigerant charge.
  f) If you hear water sloshing around in the dash area or have water dripping on the carpet, check the evaporator housing drain tube and insert a piece of wire into the opening to check for blockage.

2   It's a good idea to operate the system for about ten minutes at least once a month. This is particularly important during the winter months because long term non-use can cause hardening, and subsequent failure, of the seals. Note that using the Defrost function operates the compressor.

3   If the air conditioning system is not working properly, proceed to Step 6 and perform the general checks outlined below.

4   Because of the complexity of the air conditioning system and the special equipment necessary to service it, in-depth troubleshooting and repairs beyond checking the refrigerant charge and the compressor clutch operation are not included in this manual. However, simple checks and component replacement procedures are provided in this Chapter. For more complete information on the air conditioning system, refer to the Haynes Automotive Heating and Air Conditioning Manual.

5   The most common cause of poor cooling is simply a low system refrigerant charge. If a noticeable drop in system cooling ability occurs, one of the following quick checks will help you determine whether the refrigerant level is low. Should the system lose its cooling ability, the following procedure will help you pinpoint the cause.

Check
Refer to illustration 13.9

6   Warm the engine up to normal operating temperature.

7   Place the air conditioning temperature selector at the coldest setting and put the blower at the highest setting. Open the doors (to make sure the air conditioning system doesn't cycle off as soon as it cools the passenger compartment).

8   After the system reaches operating temperature, feel the two pipes connected to the evaporator at the firewall.

9   The pipe (thinner tubing) leading from the expansion (orifice) tube (see Section 17) to the evaporator should be cold, and the evaporator outlet line (the thicker tubing that leads back to the compressor) should be slightly warmer (about 3 to 10 degrees F warmer). If the evaporator outlet is considerably warmer than the inlet, or if the evaporator inlet isn't cold, the system needs a charge. Insert a thermometer in the center air distribution duct **(see illustration)** while operating the air conditioning system at its maximum setting - the temperature of the output air should be 35 to 40 degrees F below the ambient air temperature (down to approximately 40 degrees F). If the ambient (outside) air temperature is very high, say 110 degrees F, the duct air temperature may be as high as 60 degrees F,

but generally the air conditioning is 35 to 40 degrees F cooler than the ambient air.

10   If the air isn't as cold as it used to be, the system probably needs a charge.

11   If the air warm and the system doesn't seem to be operating properly check the operation of the compressor clutch.

12   Have an assistant switch the air conditioning On while you observe the front of the compressor. The clutch will make an audible click and the center of the clutch should rotate. If it doesn't, shut the engine off and disconnect the air conditioning system pressure switch. Bridge the terminals of the connector with a jumper wire and turn the air conditioning On again. If it works now, the system pressure is too high or too low. Have your system tested by a dealer service department or air conditioning shop.

13   If the clutch still didn't operate, check the appropriate fuses. Inspect the fuses in the interior fuse panel.

14   Remove the compressor clutch (A/C) relay from the relay panel and test it (see Chapter 12). With the relay out and the ignition On, check for battery power at two of the relay terminals (refer to the wiring diagrams for wire color designations to determine which terminals to check). There should be battery power with the key On, at the terminals for the relay control and power circuits.

15   Using a jumper wire, connect the terminals in the relay box from the relay power circuit to the terminal that leads to the compressor clutch (refer to the wiring diagrams for wire color designations to determine which terminals to connect). Listen for the clutch to click as you make the connection. If the clutch doesn't respond, disconnect the clutch connector at the compressor and check for battery voltage at the compressor clutch connector. Check for continuity to ground on the black wire terminal of the compressor clutch connector. If power and ground are available and the clutch doesn't operate when connected, the compressor clutch is defective.

16   If the compressor clutch, relay and related circuits are good and the system is fully charged with refrigerant and the compressor does not operate under normal conditions, have the computer and related circuits checked by a dealer service department or other properly equipped repair facility.

17   Further inspection or testing of the system is beyond the scope of the home mechanic and should be left to a professional.

Adding refrigerant
Refer to illustration 13.18

Caution: Make sure any refrigerant, refrigerant oil or replacement component you purchase is designated as compatible with the system (R-12 or R-134a) equipped on your vehicle.

18   Only R-134a systems can be recharged by the home mechanic. R-12 systems must be recharged by a qualified A/C technician using specialized equipment. If your system is R-134a compatible, then purchase an R-134a automotive charging kit at an auto

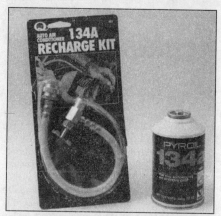

13.18 A basic charging kit for R-134a systems is available at most auto parts stores - it must say R-134a (not R-12) and so must the can of refrigerant

parts store **(see illustration)**. A charging kit includes a 12-ounce can of refrigerant, a tap valve and a short section of hose that can be attached between the tap valve and the system low side service valve. Because one can of refrigerant may not be sufficient to bring the system charge up to the proper level, it's a good idea to buy an additional can. **Warning:** *Never add more than two cans of refrigerant to the system.*

19   Hook up the charging kit by following the manufacturer's instructions. **Warning:** *DO NOT hook the charging kit hose to the system high side!* The fittings on the charging kit are designed to fit **only** on the low side of the system.

20   Back off the valve handle on the charging kit and screw the kit onto the refrigerant can, making sure first that the O-ring or rubber seal inside the threaded portion of the kit is in place. **Warning:** *Wear protective eyewear when dealing with pressurized refrigerant cans.*

21   Remove the dust cap from the low-side charging port and attach the quick-connect fitting on the kit hose.

22   Warm up the engine and turn on the air conditioning. Keep the charging kit hose away from the fan and other moving parts. **Note 1:** *The charging process requires the compressor to be running. If the clutch cycles off, you can put the air conditioning switch on High and leave the car doors open to keep the clutch on and the compressor working.* **Note 2:** *The compressor can be kept on during the charging by removing the connector from the pressure cycling switch (located on the accumulator - refer to Sections 14 and 18) and bridging it with a paper clip or jumper wire during the procedure.*

23   Turn the valve handle on the kit until the stem pierces the can, then back the handle out to release the refrigerant. You should be able to hear the rush of gas. Add refrigerant to the low side of the system, keeping the can upright at all times, but shaking it occasionally. Allow stabilization time between each addition. **Note:** *The charging process will go*

faster if you wrap the can with a hot-water-soaked shop rag to keep the can from freezing up.

24   If you have an accurate thermometer, you can place it in the center air conditioning duct inside the vehicle and keep track of the output air temperature **(see illustration 13.9)**. A charged system that is working properly should cool down to approximately 40-degrees F. If the ambient (outside) air temperature is very high, say 110 degrees F, the duct air temperature may be as high as 60 degrees F, but generally the air conditioning is 30-40 degrees F cooler than the ambient air.

25   When the can is empty, turn the valve handle to the closed position and release the connection from the low-side port. Replace the dust cap.

26   Remove the charging kit from the can and store the kit for future use with the piercing valve in the UP position, to prevent inadvertently piercing the can on the next use.

Heating systems

27   If the carpet under the heater core is damp, or if antifreeze vapor or steam is coming through the vents, the heater core is leaking. Remove it (see Section 11) and install a new unit (most radiator shops will not repair a leaking heater core).

28   If the air coming out of the heater vents isn't hot, the problem could stem from any of the following causes:

a)   *The thermostat is stuck open, preventing the engine coolant from warming up enough to carry heat to the heater core. Replace the thermostat (see Section 3).*

b)   *There is a blockage in the system, preventing the flow of coolant through the heater core. Feel both heater hoses at the firewall. They should be hot. If one of them is cold, there is an obstruction in one of the hoses or in the heater core, or the heater control valve is shut. Detach the hoses and back flush the heater core with a water hose. If the heater core is clear but circulation is impeded, remove the two hoses and flush them out with a water hose.*

c)   *If flushing fails to remove the blockage from the heater core, the core must be replaced (see Section 11).*

Eliminating air conditioning odors

29   Unpleasant odors that often develop in air conditioning systems are caused by the growth of a fungus, usually on the surface of the evaporator core. The warm, humid environment there is a perfect breeding ground for mildew to develop.

30   The evaporator core on most vehicles is difficult to access, and factory dealerships have a lengthy, expensive process for eliminating the fungus by opening up the evaporator case and using a powerful disinfectant and rinse on the core until the fungus is gone. You can service your own system at home, but it takes something much stronger than basic

household germ-killers or deodorizers.

31   Aerosol disinfectants for automotive air conditioning systems are available in most auto parts stores, but remember when shopping for them that the most effective treatments are also the most expensive. The basic procedure for using these sprays is to start by running the system in the RECIRC mode for ten minutes with the blower on its highest speed. Use the highest heat mode to dry out the system and keep the compressor from engaging by disconnecting the wiring connector at the compressor (see Section 14).

32   The disinfectant can usually comes with a long spray hose. If equipped, remove the passenger compartment air filter, point the nozzle inside the hole and to the left towards the evaporator core, and spray according to the manufacturer's recommendations. On models without a cabin air filter, remove the blower motor resistor (or air discharge temperature sensor, if equipped) and aim the disinfectant nozzle through the hole. Try to cover the whole surface of the evaporator core, by aiming the spray up, down and sideways. Follow the manufacturer's recommendations for the length of spray and waiting time between applications.

33   Once the evaporator has been cleaned, the best way to prevent the mildew from coming back again is to make sure your evaporator housing drain tube is clear.

14   Air conditioning accumulator - removal and installation

Warning: *The air conditioning system is under high pressure. DO NOT loosen any fittings or remove any components until after the system has been discharged. Air conditioning refrigerant should be properly discharged into an EPA-approved container at a dealer service department or an automotive air conditioning repair facility. Always wear eye protection when disconnecting air conditioning system fittings.*
Caution: *Whenever disconnecting air conditioning fittings, replace the O-rings and lubricate them only with manufacturer "refrigerant compressor oil," but when system components are replaced, use only PAG compressor to replenish system lubrication (i.e. do not use PAG oil on the O-rings).*

Removal

1   Have the air conditioning system discharged (see **Warning** above).

2   Disconnect the cable from the negative battery terminal.

3   Remove the battery and battery tray (see Chapter 5) from the engine compartment.

4   Disconnect the evaporator discharge line. Use caution and install a back-up wrench to prevent the line from twisting.

5   If equipped with an auxiliary air conditioning system, disconnect the auxiliary evaporator line using a special spring lock disconnect tool. Refer to Chapter 4 for additional information on spring lock disconnect tools.

6   Unplug the electrical connector from the pressure switch near the top of the accumulator and remove the switch.
7   Disconnect the refrigerant lines from the accumulator using two wrenches to prevent component damage or the appropriate quick disconnect tool. Cap the lines to prevent contamination.
8   Remove the vacuum reservoir.
9   Remove the accumulator mounting bolts and remove the accumulator.

Installation

10   Installation is the reverse of removal. Replace all O-rings with new ones specifically designed for air conditioning systems. Use and lubricate them with refrigerant oil of the correct type (R-12 or R-134a).
11   Take the vehicle to the shop that discharged it and have the system evacuated and recharged.

15   Air conditioning compressor - removal and installation

Warning: *The air conditioning system is under high pressure. DO NOT loosen any fittings or remove any components until after the system has been discharged. Air conditioning refrigerant should be properly discharged into an EPA-approved container at a dealer service department or an automotive air conditioning repair facility. Always wear eye protection when disconnecting air conditioning system fittings.*
Caution: *Whenever disconnecting air conditioning fittings, replace the O-rings and lubricate them only with manufacturer "refrigerant compressor oil," but when system components are replaced, use only PAG compressor to replenish system lubrication (i.e. do not use PAG oil on the O-rings).*
Note: *The accumulator and evaporator core orifice should be replaced whenever the compressor is replaced.*

Removal

1   Have the air conditioning system discharged (see **Warning** above).
2   Drain the cooling system (see Chapter 1).
3   Remove the air cleaner housing and air intake duct (see Chapter 4).

1992 through 1996 models

4   Remove the fan clutch assembly and set it inside the fan shroud temporarily (see Section 4).
5   Remove the fan shroud bolts, then remove the shroud and fan clutch.
6   Remove the drivebelt (see Chapter 1)
7   Disconnect the refrigerant lines from the compressor and cover the open fittings to prevent contamination.
8   Unbolt the compressor from the mounting brackets and lift it out of the vehicle.

1997 and later 4.6L, 5.4L and 6.8L models

Note: *The compressor on 1997 and later 4.2L models equipped with the SC115 or the FS10 model compressor, is mounted to the bracket with three large bolts that are easily accessible from the top of the compressor.*
9   Remove the drivebelt (see Chapter 10).
10   Raise the vehicle and secure it on jackstands.
11   Working under the vehicle, remove the bolt that retains the manifold tube.
  a) *On models equipped with the SC115 compressor, reach under the right, front fenderwell between the frame and body, remove the bolt and separate the manifold tube from the compressor.*
  b) *On models equipped with the FS10 compressor, loosen the bolt to the manifold tube, slide the compressor forward and separate the tube from the compressor.*
  Warning: *Be sure to support the compressor using a floor jack to avoid damaging the compressor or personal injury.*
12   Remove the engine splash shield from under the vehicle.
13   Remove the harness connector from the crankshaft sensor and position it off to the side (see Chapter 6).
14   Unclip the bracket and separate the wiring harness from the compressor.
15   Disconnect the compressor clutch harness connector.
16   Access the compressor mounting bolts from the frame access hole(s), remove the bolts and separate the compressor from the engine. **Note:** *The compressor bolts and their accessibility vary slightly with the different model compressors but use the access holes in the frame to ease removal.*

Installation

17   If a new compressor is being installed, follow the directions with the compressor regarding the draining of excess oil prior to installation.
18   The clutch may have to be transferred from the original to the new compressor.
19   Installation is the reverse of removal. Replace all O-rings with new ones specifically designed for air conditioning system use and lubricate them with refrigerant oil of the correct type (R-12 or R-134a). Position the O-rings in the manifold.
20   Have the system evacuated, recharged and leak tested by the shop that discharged it.

16   Air conditioning condenser - removal and installation

Warning: *The air conditioning system is under high pressure. DO NOT loosen any fittings or remove any components until after the system has been discharged. Air conditioning refrigerant should be properly discharged into an EPA-approved container at a dealer service*

department or an automotive air conditioning repair facility. Always wear eye protection when disconnecting air conditioning system fittings.

Removal

1   Have the air conditioning system discharged (see **Warning** above).
2   Drain the cooling system (see Chapter 1).
3   Remove the air deflector from the radiator support.
4   Remove the upper radiator hose.
5   Disconnect the refrigerant lines from the condenser. Some models may use threaded type fittings and others may use a quick-connect spring lock coupling. On threaded fittings, use a back-up wrench to prevent twisting of the hard lines. A spring lock coupling tool will be required on quick connect type fittings. Plug the lines to keep dirt and moisture out.
6   Remove the two lower bolts attaching the condenser to the front radiator supports. On 2001 and later models, the condenser is retained only by the upper mounting brackets.
7   Remove the radiator mounting bolts (see Section 5) and tilt the top of the radiator rearwards to gain access to the two top condenser attaching bolts.
8   If equipped with condenser seals, remove the retaining pins from the seal strip and separate the rubber seal from the condenser.
9   Remove the attaching bolts and lift the condenser out of the vehicle.

Installation

10   If the original condenser will be reinstalled, store it with the line fittings on top to prevent oil from draining out.
11   If a new condenser is being installed, pour one ounce of refrigerant oil of the correct type (R-12 or R-134a) into it prior to installation.
12   Reinstall the components in the reverse order of removal.
13   Have the system evacuated, recharged and leak tested by the shop that discharged it.

17   Air conditioning evaporator orifice - removal and installation

Refer to illustration 17.4
Warning: *The air conditioning system is under high pressure. DO NOT loosen any fittings or remove any components until after the system has been discharged. Air conditioning refrigerant should be properly discharged into an EPA-approved container at a dealer service department or an automotive air conditioning repair facility. Always wear eye protection when disconnecting air conditioning system fittings.*
Caution: *Whenever disconnecting air conditioning fittings, replace the O-rings and lubricate them with manufacturer "refrigerant*

compressor oil," but when system components are replaced, use only PAG compressor to replenish system lubrication (i.e. do not use PAG oil on the O-rings).

Removal

1   Disconnect the condenser to evaporator core refrigerant line. If equipped with threaded fittings, use a back-up wrench to prevent twisting of the hard lines. A spring lock coupling tool will be required on quick connect type fittings. Plug the lines to keep dirt and moisture out.

2   Using the orifice tube removal tool engage the notches of the tool with the tabs on the orifice by gently rotating the tool. **Caution:** *Do not twist the orifice, it can break off inside the evaporator or damage the evaporator inlet tube.*

3   Remove the orifice tube by gently tightening the collar of the tool while maintaining a steady pull on the tee handle of the tool.

4   Inspect the evaporator inlet for debris and clean as necessary **(see illustration)**.

Installation

5   Lubricate the inside of the evaporator inlet tube and the O-rings of the orifice with clean air conditioning refrigerant oil of the correct type (R-12 or R-134a). See the **Caution** at the beginning of this Section.

6   Set the orifice in the orifice tool and push the orifice into the evaporator inlet tube until you feel it stop. Remove the tool.

7   Reattach the condenser to evaporator refrigerant line.

8   Have the system evacuated, recharged and leak tested by the shop that discharged it.

18   Air conditioning pressure cycling switch - replacement

Note: *A Schrader valve in the accumulator prevents refrigerant loss during pressure cycling switch replacement.*

1   Unplug the electrical connector from the pressure cycling switch.

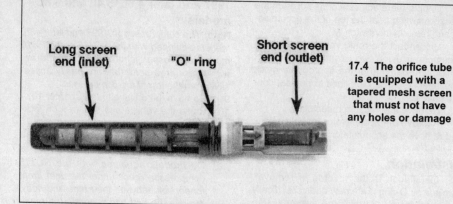

Long screen end (inlet)   "O" ring   Short screen end (outlet)

17.4 The orifice tube is equipped with a tapered mesh screen that must not have any holes or damage

2   Unscrew the pressure cycling switch from the accumulator.

3   Lubricate the switch O-ring with clean refrigerant oil of the correct type (R-12 or R-134a).

4   Screw the new switch onto the accumulator threads until tight. Do not overtighten.

5   Reattach the electrical connector.

19   Oil cooler (7.5L engine) - removal and installation

Warning: *Wait until the engine is completely cool before beginning this procedure.*
Note: *The oil cooler on the 7.5L engine is an integral component of the oil filter adapter and assembly. The oil cooler on the 5.4L and 6.8L engine incorporates an adapter mounted to the oil filter that disperses oil through metal lines to the radiator much like a transmission cooling system.*

Removal

1   Drain the radiator of coolant.

2   Remove the lower radiator to oil cooler hose.

3   Disconnect the oil cooler to water pump hose.

4   Remove the oil cooler adapter to engine block bolt and remove the oil cooler assembly.
Note: *Some loss of oil will result from residual oil in the filter and cooler.*

Installation

5   Prior to reinstallation, verify that the oil cooler-to-engine block seal is present and in good condition.

6   To install, push the oil cooler onto the water pump hose and align the arrow on the hose with the ridge on the inlet of the oil cooler.

7   Place the oil cooler assembly against the engine block and center it over the threaded insert in the block.

8   Install the oil cooler adapter bolt into the block and tighten it only hand tight at this time. **Warning:** *This is a special hollow bolt which allows oil to flow - do not replace it with a standard fastener.*

9   Rotate the oil cooler assembly until the adapter housing flange rests against the machined boss on the engine block.

10   Tighten the oil filter adapter-to-engine block bolt to the torque listed in this Chapter's Specifications.

11   Install the lower radiator hose to the oil cooler and tighten all hose clamps securely.

12   Install a new oil filter and add approximately 1/2-quart of engine oil to the crankcase.

13   Refill the radiator and check for leaks. Check the engine oil level and coolant level and fill as required (see Chapter 1).

Chapter 4
Fuel and exhaust systems

Contents

Specifications

Fuel pressure

Fuel system pressure (at idle)	
4.9L engines	
Vacuum hose attached	45 to 60 psi
Vacuum hose detached	50 to 65 psi
All other engines	
Vacuum hose attached	30 to 45 psi
Vacuum hose detached	40 to 50 psi
Fuel system hold pressure (after 5 minutes)	30 to 40 psi
Fuel pump pressure (maximum)	65 psi

Injector resistance

4.9L, 5.0L, 5.8L and 7.5L engines	11 to 18 ohms
4.2L engines	9 to 16 ohms
4.6L, 5.4L and 6.8L engines	11 to 18 ohms

Torque specifications

	Ft-lbs (unless otherwise indicated)
Throttle body mounting nuts	
4.2L engine	70 to 106 in-lbs
4.9L, 5.0L, 5.8L and 7.5L engines	12 to 18
4.6L, 5.4L and 6.8L engines	
Models through 2003	71 to 89 in-lbs
2004 and later	
Step 1	80 in-lbs
Step 2	Rotate an additional 90 degrees
EGR valve-to-intake manifold	
Models through 2000	12 to 18
2001 and later	
4.2L	89 in-lbs
4.6L, 5.4L and 6.8L	
Step 1	15
Step 2	Rotate and additional 90 degrees
Fuel pressure regulator mounting bolts	27 to 44 in-lbs
Fuel rail mounting bolts	
4.2L, 4.9L, 5.0L, 5.8L and 7.5L engines	70 to 106 in-lbs
4.6L, 5.4L and 6.8L engines	71 to 97 in-lbs
Exhaust pipe-to-exhaust manifold bolts	25 to 35

2.3 This aftermarket fuel pressure testing kit contains all the necessary fittings and adapters, along with the fuel pressure gauge, to test most automotive fuel systems

2.7a Separate the passenger's side kick panel from the beam

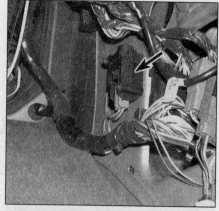

2.7b The inertia switch (arrow) is located behind the passenger side kick panel. Disconnect the electrical connector to disable the fuel pump

1   General information

The fuel system consists of a fuel tank, an electric fuel pump (located in the fuel tank), a fuel pump relay, the fuel rail and fuel injectors, an air cleaner assembly and a throttle body unit. All models are equipped with an Electronic Fuel Injection (EFI) system.

Electronic Fuel Injection (EFI) system

Electronic Fuel Injection uses timed impulses to inject the fuel directly into the intake port of each cylinder according to its firing order. The injectors are controlled by the Powertrain Control Module (PCM) or On-Board computer. The PCM monitors various engine parameters and delivers the exact amount of fuel required into the intake ports. The throttle body serves only to control the amount of air passing into the system. Because each cylinder is equipped with its own injector, much better control of the fuel/air mixture ratio is possible.

Fuel pump and lines

Fuel is circulated from the fuel tank to the fuel injection system, and back to the fuel tank, through a pair of metal lines running along the underside of the vehicle. An electric fuel pump and fuel level sending unit is located inside the fuel tank. A vapor return system routes all vapors back to the fuel tank through a separate return line.

The fuel pump relay is equipped with a primary and secondary voltage circuit. The primary circuit is controlled by the PCM and the secondary circuit is linked directly to battery voltage from the ignition switch. With the ignition switch ON (engine not running), the PCM will ground the relay for one second. During cranking, the PCM grounds the fuel pump relay as long as the ignition signal is present (see Chapter 5). If there are no reference pulses from the ignition system, the fuel

pump will shut off after two or three seconds.

The inertia switch (located behind passenger side kick panel) will disable the fuel pump circuit in the event of collision. The inertia switch is a cylindrical magnet with a steel ball that will release (breakaway) and trip a shutdown lever when the vehicle inertia reaches a certain peak value.

Exhaust system

The exhaust system includes an exhaust manifold, diverter pipes fitted with upstream (before catalytic converter) and downstream (after catalytic converter) oxygen sensors, a catalytic converter and a muffler.

The catalytic converter is an emission control device added to the exhaust system to reduce pollutants. A single-bed converter is used in combination with a three-way (reduction) catalyst. Refer to Chapter 6 for more information regarding the catalytic converter.

2   Fuel pressure relief procedure

Warning: *Gasoline is extremely flammable, so take extra precautions when you work on any part of the fuel system. Don't smoke or allow open flames or bare light bulbs near the work area, and don't work in a garage where a gas-type appliance (such as a water heater or a clothes dryer) is present. Since gasoline is carcinogenic, wear fuel-resistant gloves when there's a possibility of being exposed to fuel, and, if you spill any fuel on your skin, rinse it off immediately with soap and water. Mop up any spills immediately and do not store fuel-soaked rags where they could ignite. The fuel system is under constant pressure, so, if any fuel lines are to be disconnected, the fuel pressure in the system must be relieved first. When you perform any kind of work on the fuel system, wear safety glasses and have a Class B type fire extinguisher on hand.*
Note: *After the fuel pressure has been relieved, it's a good idea to lay a shop towel*

over any fuel connection to be disassembled, to absorb the residual fuel that may leak out when servicing the fuel system.

1   There are two methods for relieving the fuel system pressure; the easiest and most accessible is using a special fuel pressure gauge with a bleed-off valve. This special tool can be purchased at an automotive parts or tool company. In the event the tool is not available, locate the inertia switch and disable the fuel pump.

Fuel pressure gauge bleeding method

Refer to illustration 2.3

2   Locate the fuel pressure test port on the fuel rail and install the fuel pressure gauge onto the Schrader valve.
3   Direct the bleed-off hose into a metal cup or suitable container for gasoline storage **(see illustration)**.
4   Turn the valve and allow the excess fuel to bleed into the container.
5   Close the valve, remove the fuel pressure gauge and cap the test port.

Inertia switch method

Refer to illustrations 2.7a and 2.7b

6   The fuel pump switch - sometimes called the "inertia switch" - which shuts off fuel to the engine in the event of a collision, affords a simple and convenient means by which fuel pressure can be relieved before servicing fuel injection components. The switch is located behind the passenger's side kick panel.
7   Unplug the inertia switch electrical connector **(see illustrations)**.
8   Start the engine and allow it to run until it stops. This should take only a few seconds.
9   The fuel system pressure is now relieved. When you're finished working on the fuel system, simply plug the electrical connector back into the switch. If the inertia switch was "popped" (activated) during this procedure, push the reset button on the top of the switch.

3   Fuel pump/fuel pressure - check

Warning: *Gasoline is extremely flammable, so take extra precautions when you work on any part of the fuel system. See the* **Warning** *in Section 2.*

Note 1: *To perform the fuel pressure test, you will need to obtain a fuel pressure gauge and adapter set (fuel line fittings).*

Note 2: *The fuel pump will operate as long as the engine is cranking or running and the PCM is receiving ignition reference pulses from the electronic ignition system. If there are no reference pulses, the fuel pump will shut off after two or three seconds.*

Note 3: *After the fuel pressure has been relieved, it's a good idea to lay a shop towel over any fuel connection to be disassembled, to absorb the residual fuel that may leak out when servicing the fuel system.*

Preliminary check

Refer to illustration 3.2

1   Should the fuel system fail to deliver the proper amount of fuel, or any fuel at all, inspect it as follows. Remove the fuel filler cap. Have an assistant turn the ignition key to the On position (engine not running) while you listen at the fuel filler opening. You should hear a whirring sound that lasts for a couple of seconds.

2   If you don't hear anything, check the fuel pump fuse (see Chapter 12). If the fuse is blown, replace it and see if it blows again **(see illustration)**. If it does, trace the fuel pump circuit for a short. Refer to the wiring diagrams at the end of Chapter 12.

3   Check for battery voltage to the fuel pump relay connector and the PCM relay connector. If there is battery voltage present, have the relay(s) tested at a dealer service department or other qualified automotive repair shop. **Note 1:** *The inertia switch is an electrical device wired into the fuel pump circuit that will shut down power to the fuel pump in an accident. Be sure to check that the inertia switch is activated and in working order if the fuel pump is not receiving the proper voltage (see Section 2).* **Note 2:** *The fuel pump relay is equipped with a primary and secondary voltage circuit. The primary circuit is controlled by the PCM and the secondary circuit is linked directly to battery voltage from the ignition switch. With the ignition switch ON (engine not running), the PCM will ground the relay for one second. During cranking, the PCM grounds the fuel pump relay as long as the reference signal from the ignition system is received (see Chapter 5). If there are no reference pulses, the fuel pump will shut off after two or three seconds. Refer to the wiring schematics at the end of Chapter 12 for additional information on the wiring color designations for the fuel pump relay.*

4   If there is no voltage present, check the fuse(s) and the wiring circuit for the fuel pump relay and/or PCM power relay (see Chapter 12). If voltage is present, check for battery

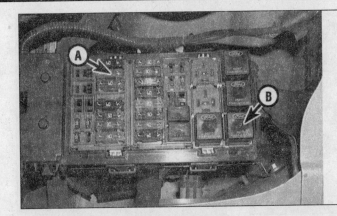

3.2 Remove the fuel pump fuse and make sure it is not blown (2001 model shown)

A   Fuel pump fuse
B   Fuel pump relay

voltage at the fuel pump harness connector located near the fuel tank. If voltage is reaching the fuel pump, remove the fuel pump and have it checked by a dealer service department or other qualified automotive repair facility.

Pressure check

Refer to illustrations 3.7, 3.13 and 3.15

Note: *In order to perform the fuel pressure test, you will need a fuel pressure gauge capable of measuring high fuel pressure. The fuel gauge must be equipped with the proper fitting required to attach it to the test port. To test the fuel pressure regulator, a fuel shut off valve must be installed in the fuel return line with the necessary adapters.*

5   Relieve the fuel system pressure (see Section 2).

6   Detach the cable from the negative battery terminal.

7   Remove the cap from the fuel pressure test port and attach a fuel pressure gauge **(see illustration)**. If you don't have the correct adapter for the test port, remove the Schrader valve and connect the gauge hose to the fitting, using a hose clamp.

8   Attach the cable to the negative battery terminal.

9   Start the engine.

10   Check the fuel pressure at idle. Com-

pare your readings with the values listed in this Chapter's Specifications. Disconnect the vacuum hose from the fuel pressure regulator and watch the fuel pressure gauge - the fuel pressure should increase considerably as soon as the hose is disconnected. If it doesn't, check for a vacuum signal to the fuel pressure regulator (see Step 15).

11   If the fuel pressure is low, pinch the fuel return line shut and watch the gauge. If the pressure doesn't rise, the fuel pump is defective or there is a restriction in the fuel feed line. If the pressure rises sharply, replace the pressure regulator. **Note:** *If the vehicle is equipped with a nylon fuel return line (or fuel lines made up of steel or other rigid material), it will be necessary to install a special fuel testing harness between the fuel rail and the return line. These tools are available at automotive tool suppliers and some auto parts retailers.*

12   If the fuel pressure is too high, turn the engine off. Disconnect the fuel return line and blow through it to check for a blockage. If there is no blockage, replace the fuel pressure regulator.

13   Hook up a hand-held vacuum pump to the port on the fuel pressure regulator **(see illustration)**.

14   Read the fuel pressure gauge with vacuum applied to the fuel pressure regulator and also with no vacuum applied. The fuel pres-

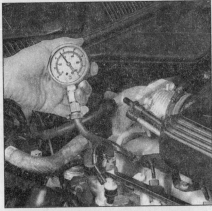

3.7 If you don't have the correct adapter, it is possible to remove the Schrader valve from the fitting and install a standard fuel pressure gauge, using a hose clamp (typical)

3.13 Connect a hand-held vacuum pump to the fuel pressure regulator and read fuel pressure with vacuum applied. Pressure should decrease as vacuum is increased

3.15 Detach the vacuum line from the fuel pressure regulator and verify vacuum is present when the engine is running

4.5 A hairpin clip type push-connect fitting

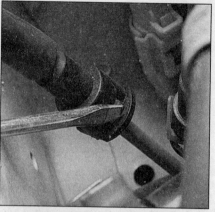

4.10 A push-connect fitting with a duck bill clip

4.13 Remove the safety clamp

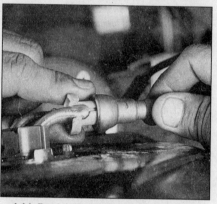

4.14 Duck bill clip fitting disassembly using the special tool

sure should decrease as vacuum increases (and increase as vacuum decreases).

15   Connect a vacuum gauge to the pressure regulator vacuum hose. Start the engine and check for vacuum **(see illustration)**. If there isn't vacuum present, check for a clogged hose or vacuum port. If the amount of vacuum is adequate, replace the fuel pressure regulator.

16   Turn the engine off and monitor the fuel pressure for five minutes. The fuel pressure should not drop more than 5 psi within five minutes. If it does, there is a leak in the fuel line, a fuel injector is leaking or the fuel pump module check valve is defective. To determine if the fuel injectors are leaking, cycle the ignition key On and Off several times to obtain the highest fuel pressure reading, then immediately shut off both the fuel supply and return lines. If the pressure drops below 5 psi within five minutes, a fuel injector (or injectors) is leaking (or the fuel line or fuel rail may be leaking, but such a leak would be very apparent). If the fuel injectors hold pressure, the main fuel line is leaking or the fuel pump is defective.

---

4   Fuel lines and fittings - general information

Warning: *Gasoline is extremely flammable, so take extra precautions when you work on any part of the fuel system. See the* **Warning** *in Section 2.*

Push-connect fittings - disassembly and reassembly

1   The manufacturer uses two different push-connect fitting designs. Fittings used with 3/8 and 5/16-inch diameter lines have a "hairpin" type clip; fittings used with 1/4-inch diameter lines have a "duck bill" type clip. The procedure used for releasing each type of fitting is different. The clips should be replaced whenever a connector is disassembled.

2   Disconnect all push-connect fittings from fuel system components such as the fuel fil-

ter, the fuel charging assembly, the fuel tank, etc. before removing the assembly.

3/8 and 5/16-inch fittings (hairpin clip)

Refer to illustration 4.5

3   Inspect the internal portion of the fitting for accumulations of dirt. If more than a light coating of dust is present, clean the fitting before disassembly.

4   Some adhesion between the seals in the fitting and the line will occur over a period of time. Twist the fitting on the line, then push and pull the fitting until it moves freely.

5   Remove the hairpin clip from the fitting by bending the shipping tab down until it clears the body. Then, using nothing but your hands, spread each leg about 1/8-inch to disengage the body and push the legs through the fitting. Remember, don't use any tools to perform this part of the procedure. Finally, pull lightly on the triangular end of the clip and work it clear of the line and fitting **(see illustration)**.

6   Grasp the fitting and hose and pull it straight off the line.

7   Do not reuse the original clip in the fitting. A new clip must be used.

8   Before reinstalling the fitting on the line, wipe the line end with a clean cloth. Inspect the inside of the fitting to ensure that it's free of dirt and/or obstructions.

9   To reinstall the fitting on the line, align

them and push the fitting into place. When the fitting is engaged, a definite click will be heard. Pull on the fitting to ensure that it's completely engaged. To install the new clip, insert it into any two adjacent openings in the fitting with the triangular portion of the clip pointing away from the fitting opening. Using your index finger, push the clip in until the legs are locked on the outside of the fitting.

1/4-inch fittings (duck bill clip)

Refer to illustrations 4.10, 4.13 and 4.14

10   The duck bill clip type fitting consists of a body, spacers, O-rings and the retaining clip **(see illustration)**. The clip holds the fitting securely in place on the line. One of the two following methods must be used to disconnect this type of fitting.

11   Before attempting to disconnect the fitting, check the visible internal portion of the fitting for accumulations of dirt. If more than a light coating of dust is evident, clean the fitting before disassembly.

12   Some adhesion between the seals in the fitting and line will occur over a period of time. Twist the fitting on the line, then push and pull the fitting until it moves freely.

13   Remove the safety clamp from the fuel line **(see illustration)**.

14   The preferred method used to disconnect the fitting requires a special tool. To disengage the line from the fitting, align the slot in

4.26a If the spring lock couplings are equipped with safety clips, pry them off with a small screwdriver

the push-connect disassembly tool, available at most auto parts stores, with either tab on the clip (90-degrees from the slots on the side of the fitting) and insert the tool **(see illustration)**. This disengages the duck bill from the line. **Note:** *Some fuel lines have a secondary bead which aligns with the outer surface of the clip. The bead can make tool insertion difficult. If necessary, use the alternative disassembly method described in Step 16.* Holding the tool and the line with one hand, pull the fitting off. **Note:** *Only moderate effort is necessary if the clip is properly disengaged. The use of anything other than your hands should not be required.*

15   After disassembly, inspect and clean the line sealing surface. Also inspect the inside of the fitting and the line for any internal parts that may have been dislodged from the fitting. Any loose internal parts should be immediately reinstalled (use the line to insert the parts).

16   The alternative disassembly procedure requires a pair of small adjustable pliers. The pliers must have a jaw width of 3/16-inch or less.

17   Align the jaws of the pliers with the openings in the side of the fitting and compress the portion of the retaining clip that engages the body. This disengages the retaining clip from the body (often one side of the clip will disengage before the other - both sides must be disengaged).

18   Pull the fitting off the line. **Note:** *Only moderate effort is required if the retaining clip has been properly disengaged. Do not use any tools for this procedure.*

19   Once the fitting is removed from the line end, check the fitting and line for any internal parts that may have been dislodged from the fitting. Any loose internal parts should be immediately reinstalled (use the line to insert the parts).

20   The retaining clip will remain on the line. Disengage the clip from the line bead to remove it. Do not reuse the retaining clip - install a new one!

21   Before reinstalling the fitting, wipe the line end with a clean cloth. Check the inside of the fitting to make sure that it's free of dirt and/or obstructions.

22   To reinstall the fitting, align it with the line and push it into place. When the fitting is engaged, a definite click will be heard. Pull on the fitting to ensure that it's fully engaged.

23   Install the new replacement clip by inserting one of the serrated edges on the duck bill portion into one of the openings. Push on the other side until the clip snaps into place.

Spring lock couplings - disassembly and reassembly

Refer to illustrations 4.26a, 4.26b and 4.26c

24   The fuel supply and return lines used on EFI engines utilize spring lock couplings at the engine fuel rail end instead of plastic push-connect fittings. The male end of the spring lock coupling, which is girded by two O-rings, is inserted into a female flared end engine fitting. The coupling is secured by a garter spring which prevents disengagement by gripping the flared end of the female fitting.

A cup-tether assembly provides additional security.

25   To disconnect the 1/2-inch spring lock coupling supply fitting, you will need to obtain a spring lock coupling tool, available at most auto parts sales stores. Be aware that 1/2-inch and 3/8-inch fittings require different tools.

26   Study the accompanying illustrations carefully before detaching either spring lock coupling fitting **(see illustrations)**.

5   Fuel tank - removal and installation

Refer to illustration 5.7

Warning: *Gasoline is extremely flammable, so take extra precautions when you work on any part of the fuel system. See the* **Warning** *in Section 2.*

Note 1: *Don't begin this procedure until the gauge indicates that the tank is empty or nearly empty. If the tank must be removed when it's full (for example, if the fuel pump malfunctions), siphon any remaining fuel from the tank prior to removal.*

Note 2: *Some models have the fuel tank mounted to the left frame rail near the middle of the vehicle, while on others the tank is mounted between the frame rails behind the rear axle. Tank removal procedures are similar.*

1   Relieve the fuel pressure (see Section 2).

2   Detach the cable from the negative terminal of the battery.

3   Unless the vehicle has been driven far enough to completely empty the tank, it's a good idea to siphon the residual fuel out before removing the tank from the vehicle. **Warning:** *DO NOT start the siphoning action by mouth! Use a siphoning kit (available at most auto parts stores).*

4   Raise the vehicle and support it securely on jackstands.

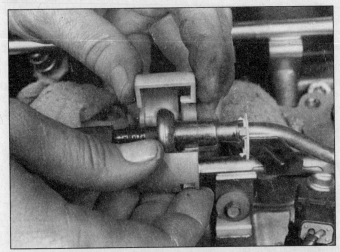

4.26b Open the spring-loaded halves of the spring lock coupling tool and place it in position around the coupling, then close it

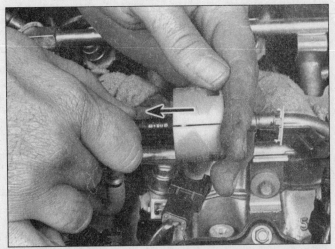

4.26c To disconnect the coupling, push the tool into the cage opening to expand the garter spring and release the female fitting, then pull the male and female fittings apart

5.7 Loosen the hose clamps and remove the hoses from the fuel filler and overflow pipes

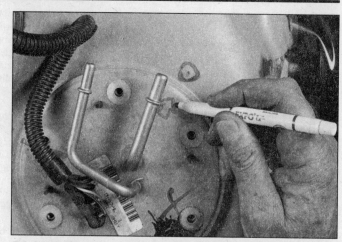

7.6 Using paint or a marker, highlight the alignment marks on the fuel pump assembly (late model shown)

5   Determine the location of the fuel tank. Depending on the model and optional equipment, the fuel tank may be located either forward of the rear axle or behind the rear axle.

6   If equipped, remove the fuel tank skid plate mounting bolts and lower the assembly.

7   Remove the fuel tank filler hose and vapor hose from the fuel filler neck and the fuel tank **(see illustration)** and slide the assembly from the vehicle.

8   Place a floor jack under the tank and position a block of wood between the jack pad and the tank. Raise the jack until it's supporting the tank.

9   Disconnect the fuel lines (see Section 4) and EVAP vapor lines. **Note:** *Disconnect the fuel tank pressure sensor, if equipped (1997 and later models).*

10   Disconnect the electric fuel pump and sending unit electrical connector. It may be necessary to lower the fuel tank slightly to access the components located directly on top of the fuel tank (see Step 11).

11   Remove the bolts that retain the fuel tank mounting straps. The straps are hinged at the other end so you can swing them out of the way. **Note:** *On some late model fuel tanks, it will be necessary to remove the bolts from one side of the fuel tank and the nuts from the other side of the tank and drop the fuel tank and the tank straps as a complete assembly.*

12   Lower the tank far enough to unplug any vapor lines or wire harness brackets that may be difficult to reach when the fuel tank is in the vehicle.

13   Slowly lower the jack while steadying the tank. Remove the tank from the vehicle.

14   If you're replacing the tank, or having it cleaned or repaired, refer to Section 6.

15   Refer to Section 7 to remove and install the fuel pump or Section 8 to replace the sending unit.

16   Installation is the reverse of removal. Clean engine oil can be used as an assembly aid when pushing the fuel filler neck back into the tank.

17   Make sure the fuel tank heat shields are assembled correctly onto the fuel tank before reinstalling the tank in the vehicle.

18   Carefully angle the fuel tank filler neck into the filler pipe assembly and lift the tank into place.

---

6   Fuel tank - cleaning and repair

1   Fuel tanks may be steam-cleaned to remove sediment or rust in the bottom of the tank. Remove the fuel tank sending unit/fuel pump and vapor valve prior to cleaning. Allow plenty of time for the tank to air dry before returning it to service.

2   Repairs to the steel fuel tank or filler pipe should be performed by a professional with the proper training to carry out this critical and potentially dangerous job. Even after cleaning and flushing, explosive fumes can remain and could explode during repair of the tank.

3   The polyethylene fuel tank cannot be repaired. No reliable repair procedures are available to correct leaks or damage. Fuel tank replacement is the only approved service.

4   If the fuel tank is removed from the vehicle, it should not be placed in an area where sparks or open flames could ignite the fumes coming out of the tank. Be especially careful inside garages where a gas-type appliance is located, because the appliance could cause an explosion.

5   Whenever the fuel tank is steam-cleaned or otherwise serviced, the vapor valve assembly should be replaced. All grommets and seals must be replaced to prevent possible leakage.

---

7   Fuel pump - removal and installation

Refer to illustrations 7.6, 7.7, 7.8, 7.10, 7.11 and 7.12

Warning: *Gasoline is extremely flammable, so take extra precautions when you work on any part of the fuel system. See the* **Warning** *in Section 2.*

1   Relieve the fuel pressure (refer to Section 2).

2   Detach the cable from the negative terminal of the battery.

3   Unless the vehicle has been driven far enough to completely empty the tank, it's a good idea to siphon out the residual fuel before removing the fuel pump from the vehicle. **Warning:** *DO NOT start the siphoning action by mouth! Use a siphoning kit (available at most auto parts stores).*

4   Raise the vehicle and support it securely on jackstands.

5   Remove the fuel tank from the vehicle (see Section 5). **Note:** *A special fuel pump line removal tool, available at most auto parts stores, may be required to disconnect the fuel lines from the fuel pump (see Section 4).*

6   Use paint or a marking pen to highlight the alignment marks that are scribed into the fuel pump assembly and the fuel tank **(see illustration).**

7   Remove the fuel pump assembly from the fuel tank.

a)   On 1992 through 1996 models, turn the lock ring counterclockwise, until it's loose, using a special tool designed for fuel pump removal. Remove the lock ring. **Note:** The special fuel pump lock ring tool is available at automotive tool suppliers and some auto parts retailers. If the special tool is not available, use a hammer and a brass punch to turn the lock ring.

b)   On 1997 and later models, remove the mounting bolts **(see illustration)** from the fuel pump assembly.

8   Carefully pull the fuel pump assembly from the tank **(see illustration).**

9   Remove the old seal ring and discard it.

10   If you're planning to reinstall the original fuel pump unit, remove the strainer **(see illustration)** by prying it off with a screwdriver, wash it in clean solvent, then push it back into place on the pump. If you're installing a new fuel pump/sending unit, the assembly will include a new strainer.

11   To separate the fuel pump from the

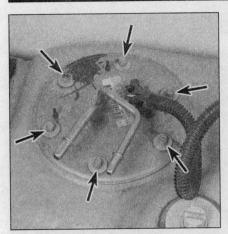

7.7 Remove the mounting bolts (arrows) from the fuel pump assembly

7.8 Carefully angle the fuel pump out of the fuel tank without damaging the fuel strainer

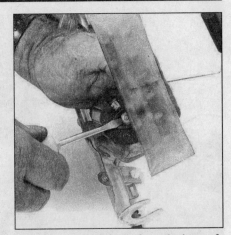

7.10 Remove the C-clip from the base of the fuel pump then separate the strainer from the fuel pump

assembly, remove the clamp and disconnect the electrical connector from the fuel pump **(see illustration)**.

12 Remove the fuel pump mounting clamp bolt **(see illustration)**.

13 Clean the fuel pump mounting flange and the tank mounting surface and seal ring groove.

14 Installation is the reverse of removal. Apply a thin coat of heavy grease to the new seal ring to hold it in place during assembly.

8 Fuel level sending unit - check and replacement

Check
Refer to illustration 8.5

1 Remove the fuel tank and the fuel pump/fuel level sending unit assembly (see Sections 5 and 7).

2 Connect the probes of an ohmmeter to the fuel level sensor terminals of the fuel pump electrical connector. Refer to the wiring diagrams at the end of Chapter 12 for the appropriate terminals.

3 Position the float in the down (empty)

position and note the reading on the ohmmeter.

4 Move the float up to the full position while watching the meter.

5 If the fuel level sending unit resistance does not change smoothly as the float travels from empty to full **(see illustration)**, replace the fuel level sending unit assembly.

Replacement
Refer to illustration 8.9

6 Remove the fuel tank (see Section 5).

7 Remove the fuel pump assembly mounting screws (1997 and later) or threaded retainer (1992 through 1996) (see Section 7).

8 Carefully angle the fuel pump/fuel level sending unit out of the opening without damaging the fuel level float located at the bottom of the assembly.

9 Remove the mounting bolt **(see illustration)** and harness connectors.

10 Installation is the reverse of removal.

11 Be sure to install a new rubber gasket.

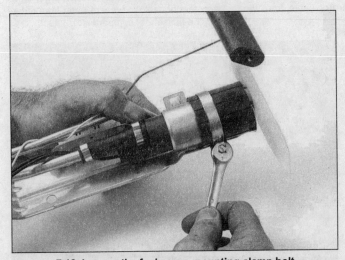

7.11 Disconnect the fuel pump electrical connector from the fuel pump

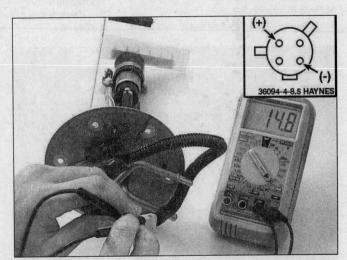

7.12 Loosen the fuel pump mounting clamp bolt

36094-4-8.5 HAYNES

8.5 Connect the ohmmeter probes to the connector and check the resistance of the sending unit with the float positioned on "empty" and "full". Check for a smooth change in resistance as the float is moved between the positions

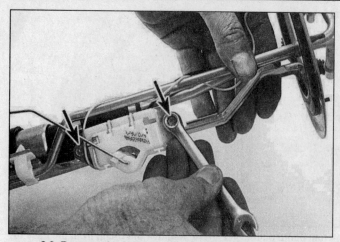

8.9 Remove the fuel level sending unit bolts (arrows) from the fuel pump assembly frame

9.9 Remove the bolts (arrows) from the air cleaner housing

9   Air cleaner housing - removal and installation

1   Detach the cable from the negative terminal of the battery.
2   Disconnect the IAT sensor, the MAF sensor, the PCV hose and the IAC inlet hose. **Note:** *Depending on the engine size and model year, the location and the types of electrical connectors will vary slightly.*
3   Refer to Chapter 1 and remove the air filter.

1992 through 1996 models
4   Remove the air cleaner inlet and outlet ducts from the air cleaner assembly.
5   Remove the air cleaner cover from the assembly and remove the air cleaner element (see Chapter 1).
6   Remove the air cleaner mounting bolts and lift the air cleaner housing assembly.
7   Installation is the reverse of removal.

1997 and later models
Refer to illustration 9.9
8   Remove the air cleaner outlet duct at the throttle body and the air cleaner assembly.
9   Remove the mounting bolts from the air cleaner assembly **(see illustration)** and lift the air cleaner housing from the engine compartment.
10   Installation is the reverse of removal.

10   Accelerator cable - removal, installation and adjustment

Note: *On 2005 models, the throttle body does not have an accelerator cable. The electronic throttle body has a large electrical connector - to disconnect it, pull out the red clip first.*

Removal
Refer to illustrations 10.4a, 10.4b, 10.5 and 10.6
1   Remove the accelerator control protection shield.
2   Detach the cruise control cable end from the throttle lever.
3   Detach the accelerator cable from the throttle lever.

4   Separate the accelerator cable from the cable bracket.
    a)   *On 1992 through 1996 models, pry the cable end off the throttle body ball stud* **(see illustration).**
    b)   *On 1997 and later models, pinch the retaining tabs and push the cable through the bracket opening* **(see illustration).**
5   Disconnect the accelerator cable from the pedal **(see illustration).**
6   Pull the cable end out from the accelerator pedal recess in the driver's compartment **(see illustration).**
7   Disconnect any cable clips or brackets securing the accelerator cable.
8   Remove the cable through the firewall from the engine compartment.

Installation
9   Installation is the reverse of removal. Be sure the cable is routed correctly and the grommet seats completely in the firewall.
10   If necessary, at the engine compartment side of the firewall, apply sealant around the accelerator cable to prevent water from entering the passenger compartment.

10.4a Using a screwdriver, gently pry the cable end off of the throttle body ball stud (arrow) and disconnect the cable from the bracket

10.4b First, remove the cruise control cable (A) then the accelerator cable (B)

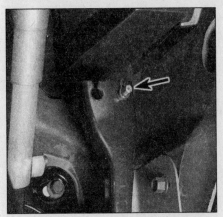

10.5 Disconnect the cable end from the accelerator pedal assembly (arrow)

10.6 Depress the cable housing retaining clips (arrow) and push the cable through the bulkhead

Adjustment

11   Measure the freeplay by firmly gripping the cable and pressing it down from the cable housing. There should be a slight amount of cable freeplay.

12   If there is no cable freeplay or the cable is binding and not allowing the throttle lever to completely close, replace the cable.

11   Fuel injection system - general information

Electronic Fuel Injection (EFI) system (1992 through 1996 models)

The Electronic Fuel Injection (EFI) system is a multi-point fuel injection system. On the EFI system, fuel is metered into each intake port, pulsed in groups, in accordance with engine demand through injectors mounted on an intake manifold. For example, on the 4.9L inline six cylinder engine, the injectors are energized in two sets of three injectors, 1, 3, 5 in one group and 2, 4, 6 in the other group. Each group is energized every crankshaft rotation. V8 engines are typically grouped in banks. Right bank is 1, 2, 3, 4 and the left bank is 5, 6, 7, 8. The intake manifold incorporates an upper intake manifold to aid in air flow and distribution. Each engine uses a slightly different upper intake manifold design and fuel rail arrangement. The throttle body is mounted to the upper intake manifold.

Sequential Electronic Fuel Injection (SEFI) system (1997 and later models)

The Sequential Electronic Fuel Injection (SEFI) system is a multi-point fuel injection system. On the SEFI system, fuel is metered into each intake port in sequence with the engine firing order in accordance with engine demand through one injector per cylinder mounted on a tuned intake manifold. The intake manifold incorporates an air intake plenum to aid in air flow and distribution. Each

engine uses a slightly different plenum design and fuel rail arrangement. The 4.2L engine uses a one-piece plenum mounted with twelve bolts. The air intake plenum bolts to the top of the intake manifold which sits directly in the middle of the engine block. The 4.6L, 5.4L and 6.8L engines incorporate an upper intake manifold with the Intake Manifold Tuning (IMT) system mounted to the lower section. The throttle body is mounted to the upper intake manifold but the IMT valve and assembly is mounted below onto the lower section (see Chapter 2D for additional information).

The 4.2L engine is equipped with the Intake Manifold Runner Control (IMRC) system. The IMRC system controls the air intake charge by opening or closing the butterfly valve on the secondary intake valve directly at the intake manifold. By closing the butterfly to the secondary intake valves under 3,000 rpm, low end driveability is improved. Above 3,000 rpm the butterfly valves open to increase high-end performance. The butterfly valves are controlled by the IMRC actuator and cable assembly.

4.6L, 5.4L and 6.8L engines are equipped with the Intake Manifold Tuning (IMT) system. The IMT system controls the air intake charge by opening or closing the Intake Manifold Tuning Valve located in the center of the air intake manifold, directly below the air intake plenum. By closing the IMTV, the dual plenum design sends the air intake charge through a single corridor into the intake system of the engine. Above 3,000 rpm, the IMTV is opened, allowing the intake pulses to blend together at the intake manifold thereby creating a more efficient air/fuel intake charge for the additional rpm and engine load.

The Sequential Electronic Fuel Injection system incorporates an on-board Electronic Engine Control (EEC-V) computer that accepts inputs from various engine sensors to compute the required fuel flow rate necessary to maintain a prescribed air/fuel ratio throughout the entire engine operational range. The computer then outputs a command to the fuel injectors to meter the approximate quantity of

fuel. The system automatically senses and compensates for changes in altitude, load and speed. **Note:** *The computer terminology has changed from Electronic Control Module (ECM) to the Powertrain Control Module (PCM) due to standardization of the Self Diagnosis system within the automotive industry.*

Fuel delivery system

The fuel delivery systems include an electric in-tank fuel pump which forces pressurized fuel through a series of metal and plastic lines and an inline fuel filter/reservoir to the fuel charging manifold assembly. The SEFI system uses a single high-pressure pump mounted inside the tank.

The fuel rail assembly incorporates an electrically actuated fuel injector directly above each intake port. When energized, the injectors spray a metered quantity of fuel into the intake air stream.

A constant fuel pressure drop is maintained across the injector nozzles by a pressure regulator. The regulator is positioned downstream from the fuel injectors. Excess fuel passes through the regulator and returns to the fuel tank through a fuel return line.

On the SEFI system, each injector is energized once every other crankshaft revolution in sequence with engine firing order. The period of time that the injectors are energized (known as "on time" or "pulse width") is controlled by the PCM. Air entering the engine is sensed by speed, pressure and temperature sensors. The outputs of these sensors are processed by the PCM. The computer determines the needed injector pulse width and outputs a command to the injector to meter the exact quantity of fuel.

12   Fuel injection system - check

Warning: *Gasoline is extremely flammable, so take extra precautions when you work on any part of the fuel system. See the* **Warning** *in Section 2.*
Note: *The following procedure is based on the assumption that the fuel pump is working and the fuel pressure is adequate (see Section 3).*

Preliminary checks

1   Check all electrical connectors that are related to the system. Loose electrical connectors and poor grounds can cause many problems that resemble more serious malfunctions.

2   Check to see that the battery is fully charged, as the control unit and sensors depend on an accurate supply voltage in order to properly meter the fuel.

3   Check the air filter element - a dirty or partially blocked filter will severely impede performance and economy (see Chapter 1).

4   Check the related fuses. If a blown fuse is found, replace it and see if it blows again. If it does, search for a grounded wire in the harness to the fuel pump (see Chapter 12).

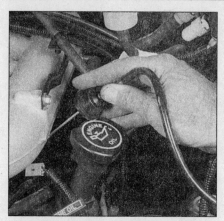

12.7 Use a stethoscope or screwdriver to determine if the injectors are working properly - they should make a steady clicking sound that rises   and falls as engine speed changes

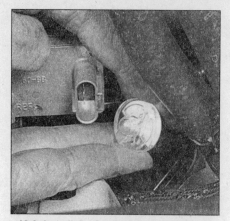

12.8 Install the fuel injector test light or "noid light" into the fuel injector electrical connector and confirm that it blinks when the engine is cranked or running

12.9 Measure the resistance of each injector. It should be within Specifications

System checks

Refer to illustrations 12.7, 12.8 and 12.9

5   Check the condition of the vacuum hoses connected to the intake manifold.

6   Remove the air intake duct from the throttle body and check for dirt, carbon or other residue build-up in the throttle body, particularly around the throttle plate. **Caution:** *The throttle body on late models is coated with a sludge-resistant material designed to protect the bore and throttle plate. Do not attempt to clean the interior of the throttle body with carburetor or other spray cleaners. This throttle body is designed to resist sludge accumulation and cleaning may impair the performance of the engine. Consult with a dealer parts department for additional information.*

7   With the engine running, place an automotive stethoscope against each injector, one at a time, and listen for a clicking sound, indicating operation **(see illustration)**. If you don't have a stethoscope, you can place the tip of a long screwdriver against the injector and listen through the handle.

8   If an injector isn't functioning (not clicking), purchase a special injector test light (sometimes called a "noid" light) and install it into the injector electrical connector **(see**

illustration). Start the engine and check to see if the noid light flashes. If it does, the injector is receiving proper voltage. If it doesn't flash, further diagnosis should be performed by a dealer service department or other properly equipped repair facility.

9   With the engine OFF and the fuel injector electrical connectors disconnected, measure the resistance of each injector **(see illustration)**. Check the Specifications listed in this Chapter for the correct injector resistance.

10   The remainder of the system checks can be found in Section 13, 14 and 15 and Chapter 6.

13   Throttle body - removal and installation

Caution: *The throttle body on late models is coated with a sludge-resistant material designed to protect the bore and throttle plate. Do not attempt to clean the interior of the throttle body. The throttle body is designed to resist sludge accumulation and cleaning may impair the performance of the engine. Consult with a dealer parts department for additional information.*

Removal

Refer to illustration 13.5

1   Detach the cable from the negative terminal of the battery.

2   Remove the air cleaner housing (see Section 9). On 2004 and later 5.4L models, drain the cooling system (see Chapter 1) and disconnect the two coolant hoses from the throttle body.

3   Detach the throttle position sensor (TPS) and Idle Air Control (IAC) valve electrical connectors.

4   Disconnect the accelerator cable (see Section 10) and the Throttle Valve (TV) cable from the throttle body. On 2005 models, the throttle body does not have an accelerator cable. The electronic throttle body has a large

electrical connector - to disconnect it, pull out the red clip first.

5   Remove the throttle body mounting nuts **(see illustration)**.

6   Remove and discard the throttle body gasket.

Installation

7   Clean the gasket mating surfaces. If scraping is necessary, be careful not to damage the gasket surfaces or allow material to drop into the manifold. Installation is the reverse of removal. Be sure to tighten the throttle body mounting nuts to the torque listed in this Chapter's Specifications.

14   Fuel pressure regulator - removal and installation

Warning: *Gasoline is extremely flammable, so take extra precautions when you work on any part of the fuel system. See the* **Warning** *in Section 2.*

Check

Note: *This procedure assumes the fuel filter is in good condition and there are no leaks within the entire fuel rail and hoses network from the engine to the fuel tank.*

1   Refer to the fuel system pressure checks in Section 3.

Replacement

2   Relieve the fuel pressure from the system (see Section 2).

3   Disconnect the cable from the negative terminal of the battery.

4   Remove the air cleaner housing (see Section 9).

5   Clean any dirt from around the fuel pressure regulator.

6   Detach the vacuum hose from the fuel pressure regulator.

7   Remove the fuel pressure regulator:

a) *On 1992 through 1999 models, remove the two bolts retaining the fuel pressure regulator and detach the regulator from the fuel rail.*

13.5 Typical throttle body and mounting bolt locations (arrows)

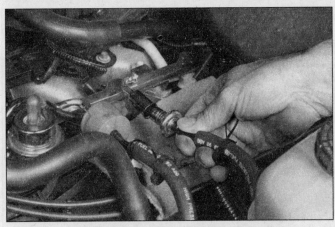

15.4 Detach the fuel line from the fuel rail

15.9a Fuel rail mounting bolt locations (arrows) - 4.2L engine

b) On 2000 and later models, remove the retaining clip from the circumference of the outer body of the fuel pressure regulator and wiggle the regulator from the fuel rail.

8   Install new O-rings on the pressure regulator and lubricate them with a light coat of oil.
9   Installation is the reverse of removal. Tighten the pressure regulator mounting bolts securely.

15 Fuel rail and injectors - removal and installation

Warning: *Gasoline is extremely flammable, so take extra precautions when you work on any part of the fuel system. See the* **Warning** *in Section 2.*

Removal
Refer to illustrations 15.4, 15.9a, 15.9b and 15.11

1   Relieve the fuel pressure (see Section 2).
2   Detach the cable from the negative terminal of the battery.
3   Remove the air cleaner housing (see Section 9).
4   Using the special spring lock coupling

tool, disconnect the fuel feed and return lines from the fuel rail assembly **(see illustration)**. **Note:** *Refer to Section 4 for additional information on disconnecting fuel lines.*
5   Disconnect the fuel injector connectors.
6   Remove the upper intake manifold, if necessary:

a) On 4.9L, 5.0L, 5.8L and 7.5L engines, remove the upper intake manifold (see Chapters 2A and 2C)
b) On 4.2L engines, remove the upper intake manifold (see Chapter 2B).
c) On 4.6L, 5.4L and 6.8L engines, it will not be necessary to remove the intake manifold.

7   Remove the EGR tube from the intake manifold and the exhaust manifold (see Chapter 6). **Note:** *There are a variety of different types of EGR systems and EGR tubes for the various engines. Refer to Chapter 6 for additional information.*
8   Disconnect the PCV hose from the engine (see Chapter 6).
9   Remove the fuel rail mounting bolts **(see illustrations)**.
10   Carefully remove the fuel rail with the fuel injectors attached as an assembly.
11   Use a rocking, side-to-side motion while lifting to remove the injectors from the fuel rail **(see illustration)**.

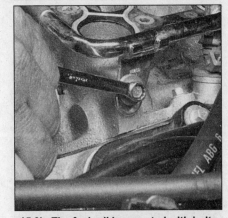

15.9b The fuel rail is mounted with bolts on each side of the air intake plenum - 4.2L engine

Installation
Refer to illustrations 15.12a and 15.12b

12   Inspect the injector O-rings (two per injector) for signs of deterioration **(see illustrations)**. Replace as required. **Note:** *As long as you have the fuel rail off, it's a good idea to replace all of the O-rings.*
13   Inspect the injector plastic "hat" (covering the injector pintle) and washer for signs of

15.11 A firm pull will disengage the fuel injector from the fuel rail

15.12a Remove the O-ring from the top of the fuel injector . . .

15.12b . . . then remove the lower O-ring from the injector

deterioration. Replace as required. If the hat is missing, look for it in the intake manifold.

14   Ensure that the injector caps are clean and free of contamination.

15   Place the fuel rail over each of the injectors and seat the injectors into the fuel rail. Ensure that the injectors are well seated in the fuel rail assembly. **Note:** *It may be easier to seat the injectors in the fuel rail and then seat the entire assembly in the lower intake manifold.*

16   Secure the fuel rail assembly with the retaining bolts and tighten them to the torque listed in this Chapter's Specifications.

17   The remainder of installation is the reverse of removal.

16   Intake Air Systems

Intake Manifold Runner Control (IMRC) system (4.2L models)

General information

1   The IMRC system controls the air intake charge by opening or closing the butterfly valve on the secondary intake valve directly at the intake manifold. By closing the butterfly to the secondary intake valves under 3,000 rpm, low end driveability is improved. Yet above 3,000 rpm the butterfly valves open to increase high-end performance. The butterfly valves are controlled by the IMRC actuator and cable assembly.

2   The IMRC system is difficult to check and requires a special SCAN tool to access the PCM for information and operating conditions. Have the system diagnosed by a dealer service department or a qualified repair shop.

Replacement

Refer to illustrations 16.4

3   Remove the upper intake manifold (see Chapter 2B).

4   Remove the bolts that retain the IMRC actuator assembly to the cylinder head/intake manifold area **(see illustration)**.

5   Disconnect the actuator cable from the lever on the intake manifold runner.

6   Installation is the reverse of removal.

Intake Manifold Tuning (IMT) system (4.6L, 5.4L and 6.8L models)

General information

7   The IMT system controls the air intake charge by opening or closing the Intake Manifold Tuning Valve located in the center of the air intake manifold, directly below the air intake plenum. By closing the IMTV, the dual

16.4 Remove the IMRC actuator mounting bolts (arrows)

plenum design sends the air intake charge through a single corridor into the intake system of the engine. Above 3,000 rpm, the IMTV is opened, allowing the intake pulses to blend together at the intake manifold thereby creating a more efficient air/fuel intake charge for the additional rpm and engine load.

8   The IMT system is difficult to check and requires a special SCAN tool to access the PCM for information and operating conditions. Have the system diagnosed by a dealer service department or other qualified repair shop.

Replacement

9   Remove the intake manifold from the engine (see Chapter 2D) and then remove the lower section from the intake manifold.

10   Remove the bolts that retain the IMT valve to the lower air intake plenum.

11   Installation is the reverse of removal.

17   Exhaust system servicing - general information

Warning: *Inspection and repair of exhaust system components should be done only after enough time has elapsed after driving the vehicle to allow the system components to cool completely. Also, when working under the vehicle, make sure it is securely supported on jackstands.*

1   The exhaust system consists of the exhaust manifold(s), the catalytic converter, the muffler, the tailpipe and all connecting pipes, brackets, hangers and clamps. The exhaust system is attached to the body with mounting brackets and rubber hangers. If any of the parts are improperly installed, excessive noise and vibration will be transmitted to the body.

2   Conduct regular inspections of the exhaust system to keep it safe and quiet. Look for any

damaged or bent parts, open seams, holes, loose connections, excessive corrosion or other defects which could allow exhaust fumes to enter the vehicle. Deteriorated exhaust system components should not be repaired; they should be replaced with new parts.

3   If the exhaust system components are extremely corroded or rusted together, welding equipment will probably be required to remove them. The convenient way to accomplish this is to have a muffler repair shop remove the corroded sections with a cutting torch. If, however, you want to save money by doing it yourself (and you don't have a welding outfit with a cutting torch), simply cut off the old components with a hacksaw. If you have compressed air, special pneumatic cutting chisels can also be used. If you do decide to tackle the job at home, be sure to wear safety goggles to protect your eyes from metal chips and work gloves to protect your hands.

4   Here are some simple guidelines to follow when repairing the exhaust system:

a) *Work from the back to the front when removing exhaust system components.*

b) *Apply penetrating oil to the exhaust system component fasteners to make them easier to remove.*

c) *Use new gaskets, hangers and clamps when installing exhaust systems components.*

d) *Apply anti-seize compound to the threads of all exhaust system fasteners during reassembly.*

e) *Be sure to allow sufficient clearance between newly installed parts and all points on the underbody to avoid overheating the floor pan and possibly damaging the interior carpet and insulation. Pay particularly close attention to the catalytic converter and heat shield.*

Chapter 5
Engine electrical systems

Contents

Specifications

Battery voltage
Engine off	12-volts
Engine running	14-to-15 volts

Firing order
	See Chapter 2

Ignition coil-to-distributor cap wire resistance
	5,000 ohms per foot

Ignition coil resistance
Thick Film Integrated (TFI-IV) systems
Primary resistance	0.8 to 1.6 ohms
Secondary resistance	8.0 to 11.5 K-ohms

Electronic Integrated Ignition (EI) Systems
Primary resistance	0.3 to 1.0 ohms
Secondary resistance	6.5 to 11.5 K-ohms

EI systems with Coil Over Plug (COP)
Primary resistance	0.55 ohms
Secondary resistance	5,500 ohms

Ignition timing
1992 through 1996	10-degrees BTDC at idle with SPOUT disconnected
1997 and later	10-degrees BTDC (base timing - not adjustable)

Alternator brush length
New	1/2 inch
Minimum	1/4 inch

1 General information

The engine electrical systems include all ignition, charging and starting components. Because of their engine-related functions, these components are discussed separately from body electrical devices such as the lights, the instruments, etc. (which are included in Chapter 12).

Precautions

Always observe the following precautions when working on the electrical system:

a) *Be extremely careful when servicing engine electrical components. They are easily damaged if checked, connected or handled improperly.*
b) *Never leave the ignition switched on for long periods of time when the engine is not running.*
c) *Never disconnect the battery cables while the engine is running.*
d) *Maintain correct polarity when connecting battery cables from another vehicle during jump starting - see the "Booster battery (jump) starting" section at the front of this manual.*
e) *Always disconnect the negative battery cable before working on the electrical system.*

It's also a good idea to review the safety-related information regarding the engine electrical systems located in the *"Safety first!"* section at the front of this manual, before beginning any operation included in this Chapter.

Battery disconnection

Several systems on the vehicle require battery power to be available at all times, either to ensure their continued operation (such as the clock) or to maintain control unit memories (such as that in the engine management system's computer [ECM/PCM]) which would be wiped out if the battery were to be disconnected. Therefore, whenever the battery is to be disconnected, first note the fol-

lowing to ensure that there are no unforeseen consequences of this action:

a) *First, on any vehicle with power door locks, it is a wise precaution to remove the key from the ignition and to keep it with you, so that it does not get locked inside if the power door locks should engage accidentally when the battery is reconnected!*
b) *The engine management system's ECM/PCM will lose the information stored in its memory when the battery is disconnected. This includes idling and operating values, and any fault codes detected (see Chapter 6). Whenever the battery is disconnected, the information relating to idle speed control and other operating values will have to be re-programmed into the unit's memory. The ECM/PCM does this by itself, but until then, there may be surging, hesitation, erratic idle and a generally inferior level of performance. To allow the ECM/PCM to relearn these values, start the engine and run it as close to idle speed as possible until it reaches its normal operating temperature, then run it for approximately two minutes at 1200 rpm. Next, drive the vehicle as far as necessary - approximately 5 miles of varied driving conditions is usually sufficient - to complete the relearning process.*

Devices known as "memory-savers" can be used to avoid some of the above problems. Precise details vary according to the device used. Typically, it is plugged into the cigarette lighter, and is connected by its own wires to a spare battery; the vehicle's own battery is then disconnected from the electrical system, leaving the "memory-saver" to pass sufficient current to maintain audio unit security codes and ECM/PCM memory values, and also to run permanently live circuits such as the clock, all the while isolating the battery in the event of a short-circuit occurring while work is carried out. **Warning:** *Some of these devices allow a*

considerable amount of current to pass, which can mean that many of the vehicle's systems are still operational when the main battery is disconnected. If a "memory-saver" is used, ensure that the circuit concerned is actually "dead" before carrying out any work on it!

2 Battery - emergency jump starting

Refer to the *Booster battery (jump) starting* procedure at the front of this manual.

3 Battery – check and replacement

Warning: *Hydrogen gas is produced by the battery, so keep open flames and lighted cigarettes away from it at all times. Always wear eye protection when working around a battery. Rinse off spilled electrolyte immediately with large amounts of water.*

Check

Refer to illustrations 3.2 and 3.3

1   The battery's surface charge must be removed before accurate voltage measurements can be made. Turn On the high beams for ten seconds, then turn them Off, let the vehicle stand for two minutes. Remove the battery from the vehicle (see Steps 4 through 10).

2   Check the battery state of charge. Visually inspect the indicator eye on the top of the battery; if the indicator eye is clear, charge the battery as described in Chapter 1. Next perform an open voltage circuit test using a digital voltmeter **(see illustration)**. With the engine and all accessories Off, connect the negative probe of the voltmeter to the negative terminal of the battery and the positive probe to the positive terminal of the battery. The battery voltage should be 12.4 volts or more. If the battery is less than the specified voltage, charge the battery before proceeding to the next test. Do not proceed with the battery load test unless the battery charge is correct.

3   Perform a battery load test. An accurate check of the battery condition can only be performed with a load tester (available at most auto parts stores). This test evaluates the ability of the battery to operate the starter and other accessories during periods of heavy amperage draw (load). Install a special battery load testing tool onto the terminals **(see illustration)**. Load test the battery according to the tool manufacturer's instructions. This tool utilizes a carbon pile to increase the load demand (amperage draw) on the battery. Maintain the load on the battery for 15 seconds or less and observe that the battery voltage does not drop below 9.6 volts. If the battery condition is weak or defective, the tool will indicate this condition immediately. **Note:** *Cold temperatures will cause the minimum voltage requirements to drop slightly. Follow*

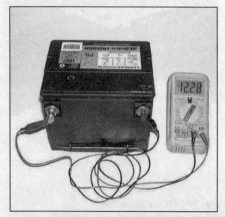

3.2 To test the open circuit voltage of the battery, connect a voltmeter to the battery - a fully charged battery should measure at least 12.4 volts (depending on outside air temperature)

3.3 Connect a battery load tester to the battery and check the battery condition under load following the tool manufacturers instructions

3.6 Remove the bolt and the wedge that holds the base of the battery to the battery tray

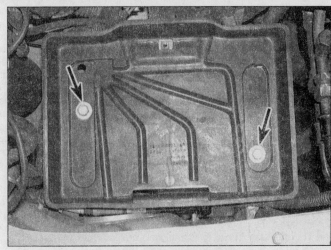

3.8 Remove the mounting bolts for the battery tray - some later models have four mounting bolts

the chart given in the tool manufacturer's instructions to compensate for cold climates. Minimum load voltage for freezing temperatures (32 degrees F) should be approximately 9.1 volts.

Replacement

Refer to illustrations 3.6 and 3.8

4   Disconnect the cable from the negative battery terminal.

5   Disconnect the positive battery cable.

6   Remove the battery retainer bolt and retainer **(see illustration)**.

7   Remove the battery and place it on a workbench. Remove the battery insulator. **Note:** *Battery handling tools are available at most auto parts stores for a reasonable price. They make it easier to remove and carry the battery.*

8   While the battery is removed, inspect the tray, retainer brackets and related fasteners for corrosion or damage **(see illustration)**.

9   If corrosion is evident, remove the battery tray and use a baking soda/water solution to clean the corroded area to prevent further

oxidation. Repaint the area as necessary using rust resistant paint.

10   Clean and service the battery and cables (see Chapter 1).

11   If you are replacing the battery, make sure you purchase one that is identical to yours, with the same dimensions, amperage rating, cold cranking amps rating, etc. Make sure it is fully charged prior to installation in the vehicle.

12   Installation is the reverse of removal. Connect the positive cable first and the negative cable last.

13   After connecting the cables to the battery, apply a light coating of petroleum jelly or grease to the connections to help prevent corrosion.

4   Battery cables - check and replacement

Refer to illustration 4.4

1   Periodically inspect the entire length of each battery cable for damage, cracked or burned insulation and corrosion. Poor battery cable connections can cause starting problems and decreased engine performance.

2   Check the cable-to-terminal connections at the ends of the cables for cracks, loose wire strands and corrosion. The presence of white, fluffy deposits under the insulation at the cable terminal connection is a sign that the cable is corroded and should be replaced. Check the terminals for distortion, missing mounting bolts and corrosion.

3   When removing the cables, always disconnect the negative cable first and hook it up last or the battery may be shorted by the tool used to loosen the cable clamps. Even if only the positive cable is being replaced, be sure to disconnect the negative cable from the battery first.

4   Remove the battery tray (see Section 3) and remove the negative battery cable ground nut **(see illustration)**.

5   Remove the starter B+ terminal connection and the ignition enable connection from the starter relay switch.

6   Remove the battery cable, the solenoid connection and the ground connection from the starter motor.

7   Remove the shield from below the engine compartment, remove the transmission cooler line bracket at the front of the engine block and pull the battery cable through the engine support crossmember.

8   Remove the battery cable(s) from the engine compartment.

9   Clean the threads of the relay or ground connection with a wire brush to remove rust and corrosion. Apply a light coat of petroleum jelly to the threads to prevent future corrosion.

10   Attach the cable to the relay or ground connection and tighten the mounting nut/bolt securely.

11   Before connecting the new cable to the battery, make sure that it reaches the battery post without having to be stretched. Clean the battery posts thoroughly and apply a light coat of petroleum jelly to prevent corrosion (see Chapter 1).

12   Connect the positive cable first, followed by the negative cable.

5   Ignition system - general information

The ignition system consists of the ignition switch, the battery, the coil, the primary (low tension) and secondary (high tension) circuits, the distributor and the spark plugs.

1992 through 1996 models use the Thick Film Integrated IV (TFI-IV) system. 1997 and later models use the Distributorless Ignition System (DIS). Late models are equipped with the Coil Over Plug (COP) version of DIS. Each cylinder on the COP ignition system is equipped with a coil/spark plug assembly over each cylinder along with an ignition module.

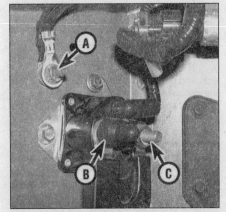

4.4 Battery cable details

A   Negative cable ground nut
B   B+ terminal
C   Ignition enable terminal

Thick Film Integrated IV (TFI-IV) ignition system

TFI-IV systems are equipped with a module housed in a thermoplastic box mounted in the left corner of the engine compartment. "Thick Film" refers to the type of manufactured solid state trigger and power units within the module. TFI-IV modules are controlled by the EEC-IV computer. The computer uses information from the Profile Ignition Pick-up (PIP) and Cylinder Identification (CID) sensor to determine the proper point to fire the coil. The ignition control module sends the Spark Output (SPOUT) signal to the TFI module to turn the coil ON and OFF. The TFI module also generates an Ignition Diagnostic Monitor signal so the EEC-IV module can check the TFI operation. These ignition signals are important in diagnosing problems with the ignition system. The TFI distributor system uses a distributor containing a Hall Effect sensor and a module mounted externally to the distributor.

Electronic Integrated (EI) Ignition system

The Electronic Integrated (EI) Ignition system is a complete electronically controlled ignition system that does not incorporate a distributor or rotor and cap. The EI system consists of a crankshaft timing sensor (variable reluctance sensor), camshaft sensor, ignition coil packs, an EEC-V module (PCM), the spark plug wires and the spark plugs. This engine is equipped with an ignition coil for each pair of spark plugs. The EI system features a waste-spark method of spark distribution. Each cylinder is paired with its companion cylinder in the firing order (1-5, 2-6, 3-4 [4.2L engine]) or (1-6, 5-3, 4-7, 2-8 [4.6L engine]) so one cylinder under compression fires simultaneously with its opposing cylinder, where the piston is on the exhaust stroke. Since the cylinder on the exhaust stroke requires very little of the available voltage to fire its plug, most of the voltage is used to fire the plug under compression. **Note:** *The EI system is not equipped with an ignition module. Here the PCM functions as the overall controller of the ignition system by receiving engine speed, camshaft and crankshaft position signals and determining the correct ignition timing and injector ON-TIME (rich/lean) but also functions as the controller of the ignition coil(s) primary circuit which was basically the job of the ignition module in earlier distributorless ignition systems.* **Note:** *The camshaft sensor on 4.2L engines is a Hall-Effect switching device mounted in a distributor-like housing on the intake manifold. The camshaft sensor on 4.6L engines is a variable reluctance device mounted on the front cover near the camshaft sprocket. Refer to Chapter 6 for additional information.*

This ignition system does not have any moving parts (no distributor) and all engine timing and spark distribution is handled electronically. This system has fewer parts that require replacement and provides more accurate spark timing. During engine operation, the EI ignition module (PCM) calculates spark angle and determines the turn-on and firing time of the ignition coil.

The crankshaft timing sensor is a variable reluctance sensor mounted above the front pulley timing gear. This electromagnetic device senses movement of the teeth on the pulley timing gear and generates an A/C voltage signal which increases with engine rpm. This sensor provides engine speed and crankshaft position signals to the PCM. The main function of the EI module is to synchronize the ignition coils so they are turned ON an OFF in the proper sequence for accurate spark control. Refer to Chapter 6 for additional information and testing procedures on the crankshaft sensor.

EI ignition Coil Over Plug (COP) system

4.6L, 5.4L and 6.8L models are equipped with a Coil Over Plug (COP) distributorless ignition system. This system works basically the same as the EI system on the other models except each cylinder is equipped with its own coil and there are no ignition wires to the spark plugs. Each cylinder is fired sequentially on its compression stroke, thus eliminating the waste spark method. COP ignition systems operate in three different modes; **engine crank, engine running** and **CMP Failure Mode Effects Management (FMEM).** Although the system operates sequentially in engine running mode, the PCM fires two cylinders simultaneously (companion cylinders) like the waste spark systems previously described. This is only to enhance driveability during warm-up or limp home modes of operation.

The COP ignition system uses the camshaft position sensor to identify the TDC of the compression stroke to fire the individual coils.

---

6   Ignition system - check

Warning 1: *Because of the high voltage generated by the ignition system, extreme care should be taken whenever an operation is performed involving ignition components. This not only includes the ignition coil, but related components and test equipment.*
Warning 2: *The following procedure requires the engine to be cranked during testing. Make sure the meter leads, loose clothing, long hair, etc. are away from the moving parts of the engine (drivebelt, cooling fan, etc.) before cranking the engine.*
Note: *Beginning in 1994, the manufacturer began to produce a second generation self diagnosis system specified by EPA regulations called On Board Diagnosis (OBD) II. This system incorporates a series of diagnostic monitors that detect and identify emissions*

6.2 To use a calibrated ignition tester, simply disconnect a spark plug wire, clip the tester to a convenient ground (like a valve cover bolt) and operate the starter - if there is enough power to fire the plug, sparks will be visible between the electrode tip and the tester body

systems faults and store the information in the computer memory. This updated system also tests sensors and output actuators, diagnoses drive cycles, freezes data and clears codes. This powerful diagnostic computer must be accessed using an OBD II SCAN tool and 16 pin Data Link Connector (DTC) located under the driver's dash area. All engines and power-train combinations 1997 and later, described in this manual, are equipped with the On Board Diagnosis II (OBD-II) system. Refer to Chapter 6 for additional information on the OBD II system and its diagnostic capabilities.

TFI-IV ignition system
Refer to illustrations 6.2 and 6.4

1   If the engine turns over but won't start, disconnect the spark plug lead from any spark plug and attach it to a calibrated ignition tester (available at most auto parts stores).
2   Connect the clip on the tester to a bolt or metal bracket on the engine **(see illustration)**, crank the engine and watch the end of the tester to see if bright blue, well-defined sparks occur.
3   If sparks occur, sufficient voltage is reaching the plug to fire it (repeat the check at the remaining plug wires to verify that the distributor cap and rotor are OK). However, the plugs themselves may be fouled, so remove and check them as described in Chapter 1 or install new ones.
4   If no sparks occur, check the primary wire connections at the coil to make sure they are clean and tight. Check for voltage to the ignition coil **(see illustration)**.
5   If there is still no spark, the ignition coil, module or other internal components may be defective (see Sections 7 and 10).

6.4 Disconnect the electrical connector from the ignition coil and check for battery voltage to the coil with the ignition key on (TFI-IV ignition system)

6.7 Disconnect the electrical connector from the ignition coil and check for battery voltage to the coil with the ignition key on (El ignition system)

EI Ignition system

General checks

Refer to illustration 6.7 and 6.10

6   If no sparks or intermittent sparks occur, check for a bad spark plug wire by swapping wires.

7   If the problem isn't caused by the spark plug wire, check for battery voltage to the ignition coil with the ignition key ON (engine not running). Attach a 12 volt test light to the battery negative (-) terminal. Disconnect the coil electrical connector and check for power at the positive (+) terminal **(see illustration)**. Battery voltage should be available. If there is no battery voltage, check the 30 amp fuse that protects the ignition circuit (see Chapter 12 for additional information on the fuses and the wiring schematics).

8   Be sure to check the primary and secondary resistances of the ignition coils (see Section 7).

9   Check the ignition coil electrical connectors for dirt, corrosion and damage.

10   If battery voltage is available to the ignition coils, attach an LED test light to the battery posi-

tive (+) terminal and each negative (-) terminal to the coil (on the vehicle harness side) **(see illustration)**, then crank the engine (be sure to check each negative terminal). Confirm that the test light flashes. This test checks for the trigger signal (ground) from the computer. **Caution:** *Use only an LED test light to avoid damaging the PCM.*

11   If the test light does not flash, check the crankshaft position sensor (see Chapter 6). If the crankshaft sensor checks out OK, have the PCM checked by a dealer service department or other qualified automotive repair facility.

Sensor checks

12   These models are equipped with a camshaft sensor as well as a crankshaft sensor. The camshaft sensor signals the PCM to begin sequential pulsation of the fuel injectors. This camshaft sensor on 4.2L engines is a Hall Effect switching device activated by a single vane. This camshaft sensor is mounted on the top of the engine in the normal location of the distributor. The camshaft sensor in the 4.6L, 5.4L and 6.8L engines is a variable reluctance device which is triggered by

the high point mark on the camshaft sprocket. This sensor is mounted in the timing cover on the left cylinder head near the camshaft sprocket. This type of camshaft sensor can be checked on the bench using an A/C voltmeter.

13   The crankshaft sensor is located near the crankshaft front pulley mounted in a bracket. These sensors are difficult to reach for testing purposes but it is of major importance that they be checked when dealing with ignition system diagnostics. In the event the crankshaft sensor or camshaft sensor is defective (or both), replace them with new parts and continue checking the ignition system to verify the working condition of all ignition system components. Refer to Chapter 6 for all the locations, checking and replacement procedures on the crankshaft and camshafts sensors.

EI ignition with Coil Over Plug (COP) system

Refer to illustration 6.14 and 6.17

14   If no sparks or intermittent sparks occur, check for battery voltage to the igni-

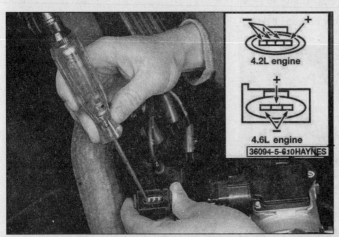

6.10 Connect an LED test light to the positive battery terminal and the coil negative (-) terminals on the ignition coil harness connectors and watch for a blinking light when the engine is cranked

6.14 Disconnect the electrical connectors from each individual coil assembly and check for battery voltage to the coil with the ignition switch ON (engine not running)

6.17 Connect an LED test light to the battery positive (+) terminal and check for a trigger signal on each of the COP harness connector negative terminals (-) while an assistant cranks the engine

7.2 Disconnect the electrical connector and check the primary resistance across the two small primary terminals

7.3 Check the secondary resistance between the coil wire terminal and the negative primary terminal

tion coil **(see illustration)** with the ignition key ON (engine not running). Attach a 12 volt test light to the battery negative (-) terminal. Disconnect the coil harness connector and check for power to the positive (+) terminal. Battery voltage should be available with the ignition key ON (engine not running). If there is no battery voltage, check the 30 amp fuse that governs the ignition circuit (see Chapter 12 for additional information on the fuses and the wiring diagrams).

15   Check the individual ignition coils (see Section 7).

16   Unplug the ignition coil wiring harness connectors and inspect them for dirt, corrosion and damage.

17   If battery voltage is available to the ignition coils, attach an LED test light to the battery positive (+) terminal and to each coil negative (-) terminal, one at a time **(see illustration)** and crank the engine. **Note:** *It will be necessary to disconnect all of the COP electrical connectors while testing to prevent the engine from starting.* This test checks for the trigger

signal (ground) from the computer.

18   The test light should flash as the engine is cranked over. If the test light does not flash, check the crankshaft position sensor (see Chapter 6). If the crankshaft sensor checks out OK, have the PCM checked by a dealer service department or other qualified automotive repair facility.

7   Ignition coil - check and replacement

Check

TFI-IV ignition system

Refer to illustrations 7.2 and 7.3

1   With the ignition off, disconnect the electrical connector from the coil and remove the distributor cap-to-coil wire from the coil terminal.

2   Connect an ohmmeter across the coil primary terminals **(see illustration)**. The primary resistance should be as listed in this Chapter's Specifications. If not, replace the coil.

3   Connect an ohmmeter between the neg-

ative primary terminal and the secondary terminal (the coil wire tower) **(see illustration)**. The secondary resistance should be as listed in this Chapter's Specifications. If not, replace the coil.

Electronic Integrated (EI) ignition system (models through 2000)

Refer to illustrations 7.4 and 7.5

4   With the ignition off, disconnect the primary electrical connector(s) from the coil. Connect an ohmmeter across the coil positive (+) terminal and each negative (-) terminal **(see illustration)**. The resistance should be as listed in this Chapter's Specifications. If not, replace the coil.

5   Connect an ohmmeter between the secondary terminals **(see illustration)** of each coil pack. The resistance should be as listed in this Chapter's Specifications. If not, replace the coil. **Note:** *Each coil pack is paired according to the companion cylinders. Be sure to check resistance with these designated terminals only:*

4.2L engines	1/5, 2/6, 3/4
4.6L engines	7/4, 8/2, 1/6 and 3/5
	1/6, 5/3, 4/7 and 2/8

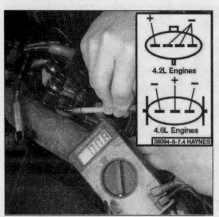

7.4 To check the primary resistance of the EI coil, connect the probes to the positive (+) terminal and each negative (-) terminal of the coil. The resistance should be the same for each check

7.5 Check the coil secondary resistance by probing the paired companion cylinders

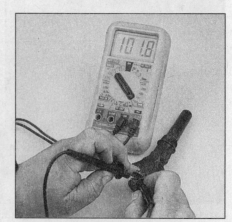

7.6 Check the COP assembly primary resistance

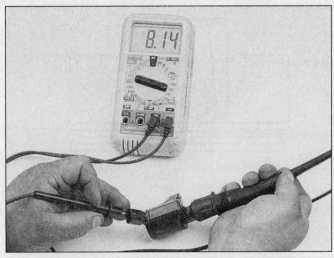

7.7 Check the COP assembly secondary resistance

7.14 Remove the coil pack mounting screws (arrows) and lift it from the engine

El ignition with Coil Over Plug (COP) ignition system

Refer to illustrations 7.6 and 7.7

6   With the ignition off, disconnect the electrical connector(s) from each coil assembly. Connect an ohmmeter across the coil primary terminal (+) and the negative terminal (-) **(see illustration)**. The resistance should be as listed in this Chapter's Specifications. If not, replace the coil.

7   Remove the COP assembly from the cylinder head. Connect an ohmmeter between the secondary terminals **(see illustration)** (the one that fits over the spark plug). The resistance should be as listed in this Chapter's Specifications.

Replacement

TFI-IV ignition systems

8   If not already done, remove the electrical connector and coil wire from the coil.

9   Remove the coil bracket bolts and remove the coil.

10   Installation is the reverse of removal.

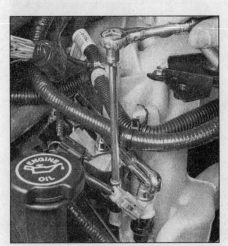

7.18 Remove the COP mounting bolt and lift the assembly from the cylinder head

Electronic Integrated (El) ignition system

Refer to illustration 7.14

11   Disconnect the negative cable from the battery.

12   Disconnect the ignition coil electrical connector(s) from each individual coil pack.

13   Disconnect the spark plug wires by squeezing the locking tabs and twisting while pulling. DO NOT just pull on the wires to disconnect them. Disconnect all of the spark plug wires.

14   Remove the bolts securing the ignition coil to the mounting bracket on the engine **(see illustration)**.

15   Installation is the reverse of the removal procedure with the following additions:

a)   *Prior to installing the spark plug wire into the ignition coil, coat the entire interior of the rubber boot with silicone dielectric compound.*

b)   *Insert each spark plug wire into the proper terminal of the ignition coil. Push the wire into the terminal and make sure the boots are fully seated and both locking tabs are engaged properly.*

El ignition with Coil Over Plug (COP) ignition system

Refer to illustration 7.18

16   Disconnect the negative cable from the battery.

17   Disconnect the ignition coil electrical connector(s) from each individual coil. Mark each electrical connector with tape to prevent mix-ups during reassembly.

18   Remove the bolt securing the ignition coil **(see illustration)**, then pull the coil from the cylinder head.

19   Installation is the reverse of the removal procedure with the following additions:

a)   *Prior to installing the coil over plug (COP) assembly into the cylinder head, coat the entire interior of the assembly with silicone dielectric compound.*

b)   *Connect each COP electrical connector to its correct coil and make sure they are tight and secure.*

---

8   Ignition timing - check

Refer to illustrations 8.3 and 8.5

Note 1: *This ignition timing procedure only checks the base timing setting specified by the factory. Timing cannot be adjusted, therefore the purpose of this check is to verify that the computer is controlling the ignition timing and that the base setting is correct. In most cases, the ignition system can be checked (see Section 6) but if the base setting remains incorrect, the PCM (computer) is defective. Take the vehicle to the dealer service department to verify and repair the ignition system problem(s).*

Note 2: *1992 through 1996 models are equipped with a "shorting bar" inserted into the SPOUT (spark output) connector. This harness disconnect is used to remove the computer from the ignition timing control functions. Removal of the bar from the connector will retard the timing 2 to 3 degrees. The SPOUT connector is located in the left rear corner of the engine compartment. Do not remove the shorting bar except for checking ignition base timing.*

1   Apply the parking brake and block the wheels. Turn off all accessories (heater, air conditioner, etc.).

2   Start the engine and warm it up. Once it has reached operating temperature, turn it off.

3   On 1992 through 1996 models, unplug the shorting bar from the SPOUT (Spark Output) connector. The SPOUT connector is located in the left rear corner of the engine compartment where it goes into the TFI/ICM module harness connector **(see illustration)**.

Note: *This operation disconnects the PCM SPOUT signal to the number 5 terminal on the module. When no signal is received, the TFI-IV or ICM module reverts to an internal back-up timing mode. Accurate timing mea-*

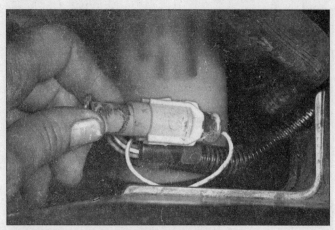

8.3 Remove the shorting bar from the SPOUT connector to check base timing (1992 through 1996 models)

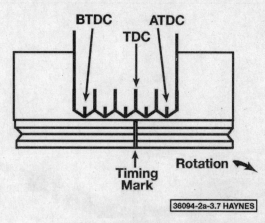

8.5 Typical ignition timing marks

surements can only be made in this mode.

4   Connect an inductive timing light and a tachometer in accordance with the manufacturer's instructions. **Caution:** *Make sure that the timing light and tachometer wires don't hang anywhere near the cooling fan or they may become entangled.*

5   Locate the timing marks on the crankshaft vibration damper and timing chain cover **(see illustration)**. Clean the marks of dirt or grease if necessary for easy identification.

6   Start the engine again. Place the transmission in DRIVE (parking brake applied).

7   Point the timing light at the pulley timing marks and note whether the specified timing mark is aligned with the timing pointer on the front of the timing chain cover. Refer to the Specifications listed in this Chapter.

8   If the proper mark isn't aligned with the stationary pointer, have the on-board computer (ECM/PCM) checked by a dealer service department or other qualified repair shop.

9   Turn off the engine.

10   Insert the shorting bar into the SPOUT connector (1992 through 1996 models).

11   Remove the timing light and tachometer from the engine compartment.

---

9   Distributor - removal and installation

Refer to illustration 9.4a and 9.4b

Removal

1   Detach the cable from the negative terminal of the battery.

2   Detach the coil secondary lead from the coil and the wires from the plugs, then remove the distributor cap from the distributor.

3   Unplug the module electrical connector.

4   Make a mark on the edge of the distributor housing directly below the rotor tip and in line with it. Also, mark the base of the distributor to the engine block or intake manifold to ensure that the distributor is positioned correctly upon re-installation **(see illustrations)**.

5   Remove the distributor bolt and clamp, then pull the distributor straight up to remove

it. Be careful not to disturb the intermediate driveshaft. **Caution:** *If the crankshaft is turned while the distributor is removed, or if a new distributor is required, the alignment marks will be useless.*

Installation

Crankshaft not turned after distributor removal

6   Insert the distributor into the engine so its mark lines up with the corresponding engine block or intake manifold mark. Due to the helical gears involved, upon initial insertion it will be necessary to position the rotor in such a way that it leads its alignment mark on the distributor housing slightly. The distributor shaft will rotate as the gears mesh, bringing the rotor and housing marks into alignment. This process may take several attempts until the correct "lead" is found.

7   If the distributor doesn't seat completely, the hex shaped recess in the lower end of the distributor shaft is not mating properly with the oil pump shaft. If this is the case, remove

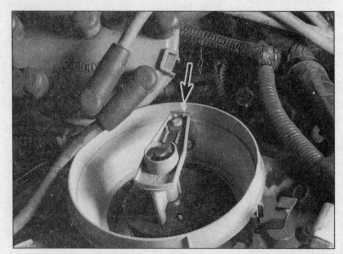

9.4a Mark the position of the rotor on the edge of the distributor housing (arrow) . . .

9.4b . . . and make a second mark between the distributor base and engine block or intake manifold (arrow) to ensure proper re-installation of the distributor

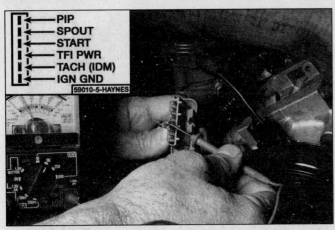

10.1 Checking for battery voltage on terminal number 4 (TFI PWR) with the ignition key ON (engine not running). If the probes of the voltmeter do not penetrate the electrical connector, install a pin into the terminal and place the probe onto the pin

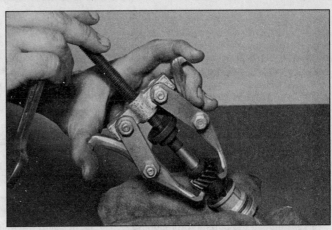

10.13 After removing the roll pin, use a small gear puller to remove the gear from the shaft

the distributor and rotate the oil pump shaft. It shouldn't take much. Repeat step 6 until the distributor seats properly and both distributor to engine and rotor to distributor marks are correctly aligned. Proceed to Step 12.

Crankshaft turned after distributor removal, or new distributor

8   See Chapter 2A, 2B or 2C and position the number one piston at TDC on the compression stroke.

9   Temporarily install the cap onto distributor and note the location of the number one spark plug wire (trace the correct wire back from the number one spark plug if necessary). Make a mark on the side of the distributor directly under the number one wire and as close to the cap as possible. Remove the cap.

10   If a new distributor is being installed, use the old distributor base mark as a reference and create a new mark in approximately the same location on the new distributor.

11   Perform Steps 6 and 7 using the new reference mark(s).

Final installation

12   With the distributor marks aligned, the

10.15 After removing the shaft, note the position of the spacer washer and remove the washer

rotor should be pointing at the alignment mark you made on the distributor housing, and the distributor base-to-engine block or manifold marks should be in alignment as they were before removal.

13   Place the clamp in position and loosely install the bolt.

14   Install the distributor cap and tighten the cap screws securely.

15   Plug in the module electrical connector.

16   Reattach any vacuum hoses.

17   Connect the cable to the negative terminal of the battery.

18   Start the engine, check the ignition timing (see Section 11), then tighten the distributor clamp bolt securely.

10   Ignition module and stator assembly (TFI-IV ignition system) - check and replacement

Caution: *The ignition module is a delicate and relatively expensive electronic component. Failure to follow the step-by-step procedures could result in damage to the module and/or other electronic devices, including the on-board computer (microprocessor) itself. Additionally, all devices under computer control are protected by a Federally mandated extended warranty. Check with your dealer concerning this warranty before attempting to diagnose and replace the module yourself.*

Ignition module checks

Refer to illustration 10.1

1   Check for power to the ignition module. Using a voltmeter, probe terminal number 4 (TFI PWR) from the module **(see illustration)**. With the ignition ON (engine not running), there should be battery voltage.

2   If no voltage is available, check the 30 amp ignition fuse.

3   Check the PIP signal at the distributor. Probe the PIP signal at the distributor connector (GY/O wire) with the LED test light and

crank the engine. The light should blink if the PIP signal is present. If not, check the wiring harness and replace the stator if necessary. Refer to the wiring schematics at the end of Chapter 12.

4   Check the SPOUT signal at the shorting bar (see Section 8). Backprobe either terminal on the SPOUT connector with an LED test light and crank the engine. The light should blink if the SPOUT signal is present. If not, check the wiring and replace the ignition module if necessary. Refer to the wiring schematics at the end of Chapter 12.

Replacement

Ignition module

5   Disconnect the negative battery cable.

6   Disconnect the harness electrical connector from the ignition control module.

7   Working in the left corner of the engine compartment, remove the two module mounting screws. Remove the module.

8   Remove the two screws retaining the module to the heat sink. Coat the new module baseplate with silicon dielectric grease before installing it back onto the heat sink.

9   Installation is the reverse of removal.

Stator

Refer to illustrations 10.13, 10.15, 10.16 and 10.18

10   Detach the cable from the negative terminal of the battery. Remove the distributor (see Section 9).

11   Remove the rotor from the distributor.

12   Using the appropriate size pin-punch, remove the roll pin from the gear and shaft assembly.

13   Using a small gear puller, remove the gear from the shaft **(see illustration)**. Be very careful not to chip or break the gear teeth when removing the gear.

14   Remove the shaft assembly from the housing.

15   Note the position of the spacer washer for reassembly and remove the washer **(see illustration)**.

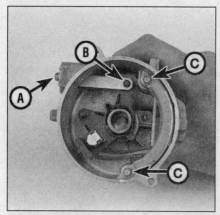

10.16 Remove the octane rod retaining screw (A) and lift the end of the rod off the post (B) - remove the stator retaining screws (C) and remove the stator from the housing

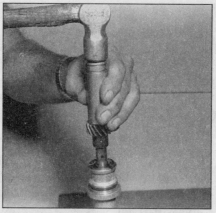

10.18 Align the holes and carefully drive the gear on the shaft - if the holes do not align perfectly, remove the gear and reposition it before installing the roll pin

12.2 To measure charging voltage, attach the voltmeter leads to the battery terminals, start the engine and record the voltage reading

16   Remove the octane rod and the stator from the distributor **(see illustration)**.
17   Reassemble the distributor in the reverse order of disassembly. Apply a light coat of engine oil to the distributor shaft before installing it in the housing.
18   Using a deep socket and a hammer, lightly tap the gear onto the shaft. Make sure the hole in the gear and the hole in the shaft are perfectly aligned and the roll pin cannot be installed **(see illustration)**.
19   Replace the O-ring at the base of the distributor and install the distributor in the engine (see Section 9).

11   Charging system - general information and precautions

The charging system includes the alternator, a voltage regulator (mounted on the backside of the alternator), a charge indicator or warning light, the battery, a large fuse (called a mega fuse) and the wiring between all the components. The charging system supplies electrical power for the ignition system, the lights, the radio, etc. The alternator is driven by a drivebelt at the front of the engine.

The purpose of the voltage regulator is to limit the alternator's voltage to a preset value. This prevents power surges, circuit overloads, etc., during peak voltage output. On integral voltage regulator systems, a solid state regulator is housed inside a plastic module mounted on the alternator itself.

These models are equipped with either a Motorcraft 95 amp or a 130 amp output rated alternator. The voltage regulator can be removed from the backside of the alternator but the alternator must be removed from the engine first.

The charging system is protected by a series of large fusible links. In the event of charging system problems, check these fusible links for damage or broken contacts.

The charging system doesn't ordinarily require periodic maintenance. However, the drivebelt, battery and wires and connections should be inspected at the intervals outlined in Chapter 1.

Be very careful when making electrical circuit connections to a vehicle equipped with an alternator and note the following:

a) *When reconnecting wires to the alternator from the battery, be sure to note the polarity.*
b) *Before using arc welding equipment to repair any part of the vehicle, disconnect the wires from the alternator and the battery terminals.*
c) *Never start the engine with a battery charger connected.*
d) *Always disconnect both battery cables before using a battery charger (negative cable first, positive cable last).*

12   Charging system - check

General checks
Refer to illustration 12.2
1   If a malfunction occurs in the charging circuit, do not immediately assume that the alternator is causing the problem. First, check the following items:

a) *The battery cables where they connect to the battery. Make sure the connections are clean and tight.*
b) *The battery electrolyte specific gravity. If it is low, charge the battery.*
c) *Check the external alternator wiring and connections.*
d) *Check the drivebelt condition and tension (see Chapter 1).*
e) *Check the alternator mounting bolts for tightness.*
f) *Run the engine and check the alternator for abnormal noise.*

2   Using a voltmeter, check the battery voltage with the engine off. It should be approxi-

mately 12-volts **(see illustration)**.
3   Start the engine and check the battery voltage again. It should now be approximately 14 to 15-volts.
4   If the indicated voltage reading is less or more than the specified charging voltage, replace the voltage regulator (see Section 14). If replacing the regulator fails to restore the voltage to the specified range, the problem may be within the alternator. **Note:** *The following checks are intended to direct the home mechanic to circuit problems that may be interfering with the charging system's ability to function properly. Many times a charging system problem results from corroded, damaged or broken terminals or harness connectors that operate within the charging system. Due to the special equipment necessary to test or service the alternator, it is recommended that if a fault is suspected the vehicle be taken to a dealer or a shop with the proper equipment.*

Overcharging condition
Refer to illustration 12.5a and 12.5b
5   Most models are equipped with a voltmeter on the instrument panel that indicates battery voltage with the ignition key ON (engine not running), and alternator output when the engine is running. Observe the voltmeter at idle and high rpm. If the gauge reads high (15 volts and over), check for an overcharging condition. Measure the voltage drop between the voltage regulator test point A and the battery positive post **(see illustration)**. The voltage drop should be 0.25 volts or less. If the voltage drop exceeds this value, check and repair the circuit to the fusible link(s) and check the fusible links for damage. Refer to the wiring diagrams at the end of Chapter 12. **Note:** *If the alternator is not equipped with test ports on the voltage regulator, disconnect the alternator harness connector and test between terminal A and the battery* **(see illustration)**.
6   Next, check the field circuit drain for a

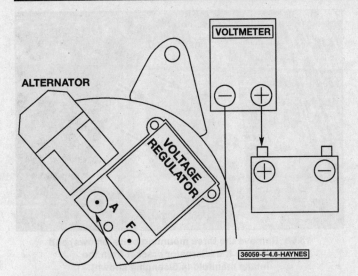

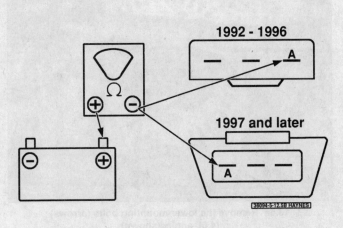

12.5a   Check for a voltage drop between terminal A on the voltage regulator and the battery positive terminal (+). The voltage drop, from battery voltage, should be 0.25 volts or less

12.5b   Measure the voltage drop from the voltage regulator harness connector to the B+ terminal on the battery

possible internal problem that could cause overcharging. With the ignition key OFF, measure the voltage between the voltage regulator test point F and the chassis ground **(see illustration 12.5a)**. If battery voltage is available, replace the voltage regulator (internal short). If there is no voltage, have the alternator tested by a dealer service department or automotive electrical repair facility.

7   Another possible cause of overcharging is excessive resistance in the ground connections between the voltage regulator and the alternator. Disconnect the negative and positive battery cables and repair any damaged ground connection terminals.

Charge light remains ON

8   The charge light on the instrument panel illuminates with the key ON and engine not running, and should go out when the engine runs. If the light remains ON, with the ignition key OFF, measure the voltage between the voltage regulator test point A and chassis ground **(see illustration 12.5a)**. There should be battery voltage. If there is no voltage available, repair the circuit. Refer to the wiring diagrams at the end of Chapter 12.

9   Check for a defective one-way circuit. Remove the alternator one-way terminal (light green/red), install a jumper wire from the battery positive terminal (+) and check that the light illuminates. Because the light is canceled (OFF) when the harness is disconnected from the battery and the light illuminates when battery voltage is applied, the circuit from the alternator to the light and the light bulb in the dash is correct. If the charge light remains ON when the engine is running, check the voltage regulator and electrical connections (see Section 12).

10   Also, check the fusible link(s). They should be intact and making positive connections. Replace any broken fusible links.

Charge light flickers intermittently (slight undercharge)

Refer to illustration 12.12

11   If the charge light on the dash flickers intermittently, check the voltage regulator connections, the alternator one-way connection, the alternator B+ eyelet connection and the battery cables. They should be clean and tight.

12   With the ignition key OFF, measure the resistance between the voltage regulator test point F and test point A **(see illustration)**. The ohmmeter should indicate less than 5 ohms. If the resistance is correct, the alternator is most likely defective. If the resistance is excessive, remove the voltage regulator brushes and check the brush holder screws for tightness.

13   With the ignition key ON (engine not running), connect a wire to the alternator test point A and the positive battery post. If the charge light flickers, the voltage regulator is

defective. Have the alternator checked by a dealer service department or other qualified automobile electric repair facility. If the charge light does not flicker, repair the alternator harness. Refer to the wiring diagrams at the end of Chapter 12.

13   Alternator - removal and installation

Refer to illustrations 13.6a, 13.6b and 13.6c

1   Detach the cable from the negative terminal of the battery.

2   Remove the air intake ducts and the air cleaner assembly (see Chapter 4).

3   Unplug the electrical connectors from the alternator.

4   Remove the drivebelt (see Chapter 1).

5   On 4.6L models through 2000, remove the ignition wire assembly from the intake manifold area (see Chapter 1).

12.12   Connect an ohmmeter between the A and F terminal screws

13.6a Remove the lower mounting bolts (arrows) (4.6L engine shown)

13.6b Remove the three mounting bolts (arrows) and separate the alternator bracket from the intake manifold (4.6L engine shown)

6   On 2001 and later 5.4L and 6.8L engines, remove the alternator bracket bolts from the upper intake manifold. Remove the bolts and separate the alternator from the engine (see illustrations).

7   Installation is the reverse of removal.

8   After the alternator is installed, install the drivebelt and reconnect the cable to the negative terminal of the battery.

14   Alternator components - replacement

Refer to illustrations 14.3, 14.4, 14.5, 14.9a and 14.9b

1   Remove the alternator (see Section 13).

2   Set the alternator on a clean workbench.

3   Remove the four voltage regulator mounting screws (see illustration).

4   Detach the voltage regulator (see illustration).

5   Detach the rubber plugs and remove the brush lead retaining screws and nuts to separate the brush leads from the holder (see illustration). Note that the screws have Torx

13.6c Alternator mounting bolts - 4.2L engine

heads and require a special screwdriver.

6   After noting the relationship of the brushes to the brush holder assembly, remove both brushes. Don't lose the springs.

7   If you're installing a new voltage regulator, insert the old brushes into the brush holder of the new regulator. If you're installing new

14.3 To detach the voltage regulator/ brush holder assembly, remove the four screws

brushes, insert them into the brush holder of the old regulator. Make sure the springs are properly compressed and the brushes are properly inserted into the recesses in the brush holder.

14.4 Lift the assembly from the alternator

14.5 To remove the brushes from the voltage regulator/brush holder assembly, detach the rubber plugs from the two brush lead screws and remove both screws (arrows)

14.9a Before installing the voltage regulator/brush holder assembly, insert a paper clip as shown to hold the brushes in place during installation - after installation, simply pull the paper clip out

14.9b Be sure the paper clip is properly positioned to retain the brushes

8   Install the brush lead retaining screws and nuts.
9   Insert a short section of wire, like a paper clip, through the hole in the voltage regulator **(see illustrations)** to hold the brushes in the retracted position during regulator installation.
10   Carefully install the regulator. Make sure the brushes don't hang up on the rotor.
11   Install the voltage regulator screws and tighten them securely.
12   Remove the wire or paper clip.
13   Install the alternator (see Section 13).

15 Starting system - general information and precautions

1   The starting system is composed of the starter motor, starter relay, battery, switch and connecting wires.
2   Turning the ignition key to the Start position actuates the starter relay through the starter control circuit. The starter relay then connects the battery to the starter solenoid.
3   These models are equipped with a starter/solenoid assembly that is mounted to the transmission bellhousing.
4   Vehicles equipped with an automatic transmission are equipped with a Transmission Range sensor in the starter control circuit, which prevents operation of the starter unless the shift lever is in Neutral or Park. Refer to the wiring diagrams at the end of Chapter 12.
5   The starter circuit is equipped with a starter relay. This relay is located on the firewall in the right side of the engine compartment near the battery.
6   Never operate the starter motor for more than 15 seconds at a time without pausing to allow it to cool for at least two minutes. Excessive cranking can cause overheating, which can seriously damage the starter.

16 Starter motor and circuit - in-vehicle check

Refer to illustration 16.6
Note: *Before diagnosing starter problems, make sure the battery is fully charged.*
1   If the starter motor doesn't turn at all when the switch is operated, make sure the shift lever is in Neutral or Park.
2   Make sure the battery is charged and that all cables at the battery and starter solenoid terminals are secure.

3   If the starter motor spins but the engine doesn't turn over, then the drive assembly in the starter motor is slipping and the starter motor must be replaced (see Section 15).
4   If, when the switch is actuated, the starter motor doesn't operate at all but the starter solenoid operates (clicks), then the problem lies with either the battery, the starter solenoid contacts or the starter motor connections.
5   If the starter solenoid doesn't click when the ignition switch is actuated, either the starter solenoid is defective, the starter relay is bad, the ignition switch is faulty, the Transmission Range sensor (automatic) or clutch switch (manual) is bad, or there is a problem in the wiring between the components. Check the starter circuit.
6   To check the starter circuit, remove the push-on connector from the relay - this is the signal wire from the ignition switch **(see illustration)**. Make sure that the connection is clean and secure. If the connections are good, check the operation of the relay with a jumper wire. To do this, place the transmission in Park. Remove the push-on connector from the relay. Connect a jumper wire between the battery positive terminal and the exposed terminal on the relay. If the starter motor now operates, the starter relay is okay. The problem is in the ignition switch, Transmission Range sensor or in the wiring between these components (look for open or loose connections).
7   If the starter motor still doesn't operate, bridge the two large terminals on the relay with a screwdriver. If the starter now works, replace the relay. If it doesn't operate, check for voltage to the relay (it should be available on one of the large terminals). If voltage isn't present, check the two main battery fuses (adjacent to the relay, under the plastic covers) and the cable to the relay.
8   If voltage is present, check for voltage to the starter motor while the ignition key is turned to Start. If voltage is present, replace the starter assembly. If voltage is not present

16.6 The starter relay is mounted on the firewall, near the battery

A   *Signal wire from ignition switch*
B   *B+ terminal*
C   *Ignition enable terminal*

and the relay checked out OK, trace the wiring between the relay and the starter for an open circuit condition.

9   If the starter motor cranks the engine at an abnormally slow speed, first make sure the battery is fully charged and all terminal connections are clean and tight. Also check the connections at the starter solenoid and battery ground. Eyelet terminals should not be easily rotated by hand. If the engine is partially seized, or has the wrong viscosity oil in it, it will crank slowly.

17   Starter motor - removal and installation

Refer to illustration 17.4

1   Detach the cable from the negative terminal of the battery.

2   Raise the vehicle and support it securely on jackstands.

3   Pull back the rubber cover and disconnect the large cable from the terminal on the starter motor and the solenoid terminal connections.

Disconnect the large cable from the terminal on the starter motor and the solenoid terminal connections.

4   Remove the starter motor mounting bolt and nut **(see illustration)** and detach the starter from the engine. Later models have a stud and two bolts.

5   Installation is the reverse of removal.

18   Starter solenoid - replacement

Refer to illustrations 18.3a and 18.3b

1   Remove the starter assembly from the engine compartment (see Section 17).

2   Remove the electrical connector from the solenoid M terminal.

3   Remove the solenoid mounting bolts and separate the solenoid from the starter body **(see illustrations)**.

4   Installation is the reverse of removal.

17.4 Remove the starter mounting bolt and nut (arrows) and separate the assembly from the transmission bellhousing

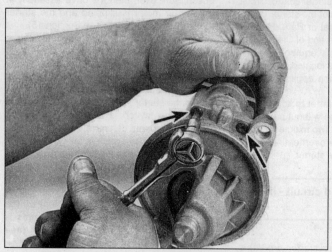

18.3a Remove the solenoid mounting bolts (arrows)

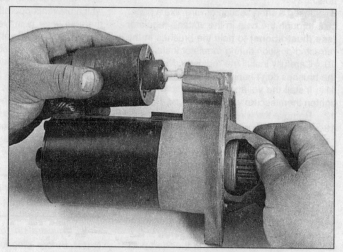

18.3b Separate the solenoid from the starter

Chapter 6
Emissions and engine control systems

Contents

1 General information

Refer to illustration 1.6

To prevent pollution of the atmosphere from incompletely-burned and evaporating gases, and to maintain good driveability and fuel economy, a number of emission control systems are incorporated. They include the:

Electronic Engine Control (EEC) system
Evaporative Emission Control (EECS) system
Positive Crankcase Ventilation (PCV) system
Exhaust Gas Recirculation (EGR) system
Catalytic converter

All of these systems are linked, directly or indirectly, to the emission control system.

The Sections in this Chapter include general descriptions, checking procedures within the scope of the home mechanic and component replacement procedures (when possible) for each of the systems listed above.

Before assuming that an emissions control system is malfunctioning, check the fuel and ignition systems carefully. The diagnosis of some emission-control devices requires specialized tools, equipment and training. If checking and servicing become too difficult or if a procedure is beyond your ability, consult a dealer service department. Remember, the most frequent cause of emissions problems is simply a loose or broken vacuum hose or wire, so always check the hose and wiring connections first.

This doesn't mean, however, that emission control systems are particularly difficult to maintain and repair. You can quickly and easily perform many checks and do most of the regular maintenance at home with common tune-up and hand tools. **Note:** *Because of a Federally-mandated extended warranty which covers the emission control system components, check with your dealer about warranty coverage before working on any emissions-related systems. Once the warranty has expired, you may wish to perform some of the component checks and/or replacement procedures in this Chapter to save money.*

Pay close attention to any special precautions outlined in this Chapter. It should be noted that the illustrations of the various systems may not exactly match the system installed on the vehicle you're working on because of changes made by the manufacturer during production or from year-to-year.

A Vehicle Emissions Control Information (VECI) label is located in the engine compartment **(see illustration)**. This label contains important emissions specifications and adjustment information, as well as a vacuum hose schematic with emissions components identified. When servicing the engine or emissions systems, the VECI label in your particular vehicle should always be checked for up-to-date information.

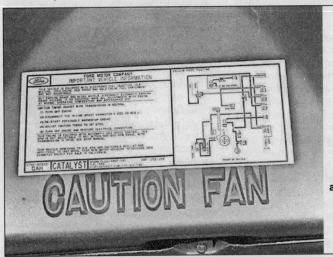

1.6 The Vehicle Emission Control Information label contains essential emission control and adjustment information, as well as a vacuum diagram

2   Electronic Engine Control (EEC) system and trouble codes

General description

Refer to illustrations 2.15 and 2.19

1   All models use the Electronic Engine Control (EEC-IV [1992 through 1995] or EEC-V [1996 and later]) system. The EEC system consists of an onboard computer, known as the Powertrain Control Module (PCM), and information sensors, which monitor various functions of the engine and send data to the PCM. Based on the data and the information programmed into the computer's memory, the PCM generates output signals to control various engine functions via control relays, solenoids and other output actuators.

2   The PCM, located under the instrument panel, is the "brain" of the EEC-IV system. It receives data from a number of sensors and other electronic components (switches, relays, etc.). Based on the information it receives, the PCM generates output signals to control various relays, solenoids and other actuators. The PCM is specifically calibrated to optimize the emissions, fuel economy and driveability of the vehicle.

3   Because of a Federally-mandated extended warranty which covers the EEC-IV system components and because any owner-induced damage to the PCM, the sensors and/or the control devices may void the warranty, it isn't a good idea to attempt diagnosis or replacement of the PCM at home while the vehicle is under warranty. Take the vehicle to a dealer service department if the PCM or a system component malfunctions.

Information sensors

4   When battery voltage is applied to the air conditioning compressor clutch, a signal is sent to the PCM, which interprets the signal as an added load created by the compressor and increases engine idle speed accordingly to compensate.

5   The Intake Air Temperature sensor (IAT), threaded into a runner of the intake manifold, provides the PCM with fuel/air mixture temperature information. The PCM uses this information to control fuel flow, ignition timing and EGR system operation.

6   The Engine Coolant Temperature (ECT) sensor, which is threaded into a coolant passage in the intake manifold, monitors engine coolant temperature. The ECT sends the PCM a constantly varying voltage signal which influences PCM control of the fuel mixture, ignition timing and EGR operation.

7   The Heated Exhaust Gas Oxygen sensors (HEGO), which are threaded into the exhaust manifolds, constantly monitor the oxygen content of the exhaust gases. A voltage signal which varies in accordance with the difference between the oxygen content of the exhaust gases and the surrounding atmosphere is sent to the PCM. The PCM converts this exhaust gas oxygen content signal to the

fuel/air ratio, compares it to the ideal ratio for current engine operating conditions and alters the signal to the injectors accordingly.

8   The Throttle Position Sensor (TPS), which is mounted on the side of the throttle body (see Section 4) and connected directly to the throttle shaft, senses throttle movement and position, then transmits an electrical signal to the PCM. This signal enables the PCM to determine when the throttle is closed, in its normal cruise condition or wide open.

9   The Mass Air Flow (MAF) sensor, which is mounted in the air cleaner intake passage, measures the mass of the air entering the engine (see Section 4). Because air mass varies with air temperature (cold air is denser than warm air), measuring air mass provides the PCM with a very accurate way of determining the correct amount of fuel to obtain the ideal fuel/air mixture.

Output devices

10   The EEC power relay, which is activated by the ignition switch, supplies battery voltage to the EEC-IV system components when the switch is the Start or Run position.

11   The canister purge solenoid (CANP) switches manifold vacuum to operate the canister purge valve when a signal is received from the PCM. Vacuum opens the purge valve when the solenoid is energized allowing fuel vapor to flow from the canister to the intake manifold.

12   The solenoid-operated fuel injectors are located above the intake ports (see Chapter 4). The PCM controls the length of time the injector is open. The "open" time of the injector determines the amount of fuel delivered. For information regarding injector replacement, refer to Chapter 4.

13   The fuel pump relay is activated by the PCM with the ignition switch in the On position. When the ignition switch is turned to the On position, the relay is activated to supply initial line pressure to the system. For information regarding fuel pump check and replacement, refer to Chapter 4.

14   The PCM uses a signal from the Profile Ignition Pick-Up (PIP) to determine crankshaft position. Ignition timing is determined by the PCM, which then signals the module to fire the coil.

Obtaining codes - 1995 and earlier models

15   The diagnostic codes for the EEC-IV systems are arranged in such a way that a series of tests must be completed in order to extract ALL the codes from the system. If one portion of the test is performed without the others, there may be a chance the trouble code that will pinpoint a problem in your particular vehicle will remain stored in the PCM without detection. The tests start first with a Key On, Engine Off (KOEO) test followed by a computed timing test then finally a Engine Running (ER) test. Here is a brief overview of

the code-extracting procedures of the EEC-IV system followed by the actual test:

Note: *Before attempting to repair or replace a component, always check vacuum lines and electrical connectors first, as a majority of problems are simple connections and leaking vacuum lines.*

Quick Test - Key On Engine Off (KOEO)

16   The following tests are all included with the key on, engine not running:

   Self test codes - These codes are accessed on the test connector by using a jumper wire and an analog voltmeter or the factory diagnostic tool called the Star tester. These codes are also called *Hard Codes*.

   Separator pulse codes - After the initial Hard Codes, the system will flash a code 11 or 111 and then will flash a series of Soft Codes.

   Continuous Memory Codes - These codes indicate a fault that may or may not be present at the time of testing. These codes usually indicate an intermittent failure. Continuous Memory codes are stored in the system and they will flash after the normal Hard Codes. These codes are three digit codes. These codes can indicate chronic or intermittent problems. Also called Soft Codes.

   Fast codes - These codes are transmitted 100 times faster than normal codes and can only be read by a Star Tester from the manufacturer or an equivalent SCAN tool.

Engine running codes (KOER) or (ER)

17   **Running tests** - These tests make it possible for the PCM to pick-up a diagnostic trouble code that cannot be set while the engine is in KOEO. These problems usually occur during driving conditions. Some codes are detected by cold or warm running conditions, some are detected at low rpm or high rpm and some are detected at closed throttle or WOT.

   I.D. Pulse codes - These codes indicate the type of engine (4, 6 or 8 cylinder) or the correct module and Self Test mode access.

   Computed engine timing test - This engine running test determines base timing for the engine and starts the process of allowing the engine to store running codes.

   Wiggle test - This engine running test checks the wiring system to the sensors and output actuators as the engine performs.

   Cylinder balance test - This engine running test determines injector balance as well as cylinder compression balance. **Note:** *This test should be performed by a dealer service department.*

Beginning the test

18   Apply the parking brake. Position the shift lever in PARK and block the drive wheels. Turn off all electrical loads - air conditioning, radio, heater fan blower etc. Make sure the engine is warmed to operating temperatures (if possible).

19   Perform the KOEO tests:

a)   *Turn the ignition key off for at least 10 seconds*

b)   *Locate the Diagnostic Test connector inside the engine compartment. Install the positive voltmeter lead onto the positive battery terminal and the negative voltmeter lead onto pin number 4 (STO) of the test connector* (see illustration). *Install a jumper wire from the test terminal (STI) to pin number 2 of the Diagnostic Test terminal.*

c)   *Turn the ignition key ON (engine not running) and observe the needle sweeps on the voltmeter. For example code 23, the voltmeter will sweep once, pause 1/2 second and sweep again. There will be a two second pause between digits and then there will be three distinct sweeps of the needle to indicate the second digit of the code number. On three digit codes, the sequence is the same except there will be an additional sequence of numbers (sweeps) to indicate the third digit in the code. Additional codes will be separated by a four second pause and then the indicated sweeps on the voltmeter. Be aware that the code sequence may continue into the continuous memory codes (read further).* **Note:** *Later models will flash the CHECK ENGINE light on the dash in place of the voltmeter.*

20   Interpreting the continuous memory codes:

a)   *After the KOEO codes are reported, there will be a short pause and any stored Continuous Memory codes will appear in order. Remember that the "Separator" code is 11 or 111. The computer will not enter the Continuous Memory mode without flashing the separator pulse code. The Continuous Memory codes are read the same as the initial codes or "Hard Codes." Record these codes onto a piece of paper and continue the test.*

21   Perform the Engine Running (ER) tests.

a)   *Remove the jumper wires from the Diagnostic Test connector to start the test.*

b)   *Run engine until it reaches normal operating temperature.*

c)   *Turn the engine OFF for at least 10 seconds.*

d)   *Install the jumper wire onto Diagnostic Test connector* (see illustration 2.19) *and start the engine.*

e)   *Observe that the voltmeter or CHECK ENGINE light will flash the engine identification code. This code indicates 1/2 the number of cylinders of the engine. For example, 4 flashes represent an 8 cylinder engine, or 3 flashes represent a six-cylinder engine.*

f)   *Within 1 to 2 seconds of the I.D. code, turn the steering wheel at least 1/2 turn and release. This will store any power steering pressure switch trouble codes.*

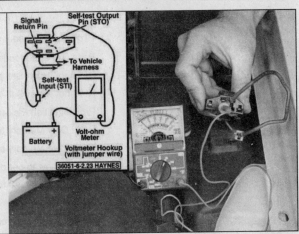

2.19 To read any stored trouble codes, connect a voltmeter to the Diagnostic Test connector as shown, then connect a jumper wire between the self-test input and pin number 2 on the larger connector - turn the key ON (engine not running) and watch the voltmeter or CHECK ENGINE light on later models - the test connector on all OBD II models is at the instrument panel

g)   *Depress the brake pedal and release.* **Note:** *Perform the steering wheel and brake pedal procedure in succession immediately (1 to 2 seconds) after the I.D. codes are flashed.*

h)   *Observe all the codes and record them on a piece of paper. Be sure to count the sweeps or flashes very carefully as you jot them down.*

22   On some models the PCM will request a Dynamic Response check. This test quickly checks the operation of the TPS, MAF or MAP sensors in action. This will be indicated by a code 1 or a single sweep of the voltmeter needle (one flash on CHECK ENGINE light). This test will require the operator to simply full throttle ("goose") the accelerator pedal for one second. DO NOT throttle the accelerator pedal unless it is requested.

23   The next part of this test makes sure the system can advance the timing. This is called the Computed Timing test. After the last ER code has been displayed, the PCM will advance the ignition timing a fixed amount and hold it there for approximately 2 minutes. Use a timing light to check the amount of advance. The computed timing should equal the base timing plus 20 BTDC. The total advance should equal 27 to 33 degrees advance. If the timing is out of specification, have the system checked at a dealer service department. **Note:** *If it's necessary to adjust the base timing, remember to remove the SPOUT from the connector as described in the ignition timing procedure in Chapter 5. This will remove the computer from the loop and give base timing.*

24   Finally, perform the Wiggle Test. This test can be used to recreate a possible intermittent fault in the harness wiring system:

a)   *Use a jumper wire to ground the STI lead on the Diagnostic Test connector* (see illustration 2.19).

b)   *Turn the ignition key ON (engine not running).*

c)   *Now deactivate the self-test mode (remove the jumper wire) and then immediately reactivate self test mode. Now the system has entered Continuous Monitor Test Mode.*

d)   *Carefully wiggle, tap or remove any suspect wiring to a sensor or output actuator. If a problem exists, a trouble code will be stored that indicates a problem with the circuit that governs the particular component. Record the codes that are indicated.*

e)   *Next, enter Engine Running Continuous Monitor Test Mode to check for wiring problems only when the engine is running. Start first by deactivating the Diagnostic Test connector and turning the ignition key OFF. Now start the engine and allow it to idle.*

f)   *Use a jumper wire to ground the STI lead on the Diagnostic Test connector* (see illustration 2.19). *Wait ten seconds and then deactivate the test mode and reactivate it again (install jumper wire). This will enter Engine Running Continuous Monitor Test Mode.*

g)   *Carefully wiggle, tap or remove any suspect wiring to a sensor or output actuator. If a problem exists, a trouble code will be stored that indicates a problem with the circuit that governs the particular component. Record the codes that are indicated.*

25   If necessary, perform the Cylinder Balance Test. This test must be performed by a dealer service department or other qualified auto repair facility.

Clearing codes (OBD-I models)

26   To clear the codes from the PCM memory, start the KOEO self test diagnostic procedure (see illustration 2.19) and install the jumper wire into the Diagnostic Test connector. When the codes start to display themselves on the voltmeter or CHECK ENGINE light, remove the jumper wire from the Diagnostic Test connector. This will erase any stored codes within the system. **Caution:** *Do not disconnect the battery from the vehicle to clear the codes. This will erase stored operating parameters from the KAM (Keep Alive Memory) and cause the engine to run rough for a period of time while the computer relearns the information.*

2 Digit Trouble Codes

Code	Test Condition*	Probable Cause
11	O,C,R	Pass (separator code)
12	R	RPM not within Self-test upper limit
13	R	RPM not within Self-test lower limit
14	C	Profile Ignition Pick-up circuit fault
15	O	Read Only Memory test failed
15	C	Keep Alive Memory test failed
16	R	RPM too low to perform Oxygen Sensor/fuel test
18	C	Loss of TACH input to PCM; SPOUT circuit grounded
18	R	SPOUT circuit open
19	O	Failure in EEC reference voltage
21	O,R	Coolant Temperature Sensor out of range
22	O,C	Manifold Absolute/Baro Pressure Sensor out of range
23	O,R	Throttle Position Sensor out of range
24	O,R	Intake Air Temperature sensor out of range
26	O,R	Mass Air Flow Sensor out of range
29	C	No input from Vehicle Speed Sensor
31	O,C,R	EGR Valve Position Sensor out of range (low)
32	O,C,R	EGR valve not seated; closed voltage low
33	C,R	EGR valve not opening; Insufficient flow detected
33	C	Throttle Position erratic output
34	O,C,R	EGR Valve Pressure Transducer/Position Sensor sonic voltage above closed limit
35	O,C,R	EGR Valve Pressure Transducer/Position Sensor voltage out of range (high)
41	R	Heated Oxygen Sensor circuit indicates system lean, right side
41	C	No Heated Oxygen Sensor switch detected, right side
42	R	Heated Oxygen Sensor circuit indicates system rich, right side
43	C	Throttle Position sensor out of range (low)
44	R	Thermactor Air system inoperative, right side
45	R	Thermactor Air upstream during Self-test (5.0L only)
46	R	Thermactor Air not by-passed during Self-test (5.0L only)
51	O,C	Coolant Temperature sensor circuit open
53	O,C	Throttle Position sensor out of range (high)
54	O,C	Intake Air Temperature sensor circuit open
56	O,C	Mass Air Flow sensor out of range (high)
61	O,C	Coolant Temperature sensor circuit grounded
63	O,C	Throttle Position sensor circuit out of range (low)
64	O,C	Intake Air Temperature sensor circuit grounded
66	C	Mass Air Flow sensor circuit out-of-range (low)
67	O	Neutral Drive Switch circuit open
72	R	Insufficient Mass Air Flow change during Dynamic Response Test
73	R	Insufficient Throttle Position output during Dynamic Response Test
74	R	Brake On/Off switch failure
75	R	Brake On/Off circuit failure
77	R	Wide Open Throttle not sensed during Self-test
79	O	Air conditioning on during self-test
81	O	Air Management 2 circuit failure (5.0L only)

* *O = Key On, Engine Off; C = Continuous Memory; R = Engine Running*

2 Digit Trouble Codes (continued)

Code	Test Condition*	Probable Cause
82	O	Air Management 1 circuit failure (5.0L only)
84	O	EGR Vacuum Regulator circuit failure
85	O	Canister Purge circuit failure
87	O,C	Primary Fuel Pump circuit failure
91	R	Heated oxygen sensor indicates system lean, left side
91	C	No heated oxygen sensor switching indicated, left side
92	R	Heated oxygen sensor indicates system rich, left side
94	R	Thermactor Air system inoperative, left side (5.0L only)
95	O,C	Fuel Pump circuit open, PCM to motor
96	O,C	Fuel Pump circuit open, Battery to PCM
98	R	Hard Fault present

* O = Key On, Engine Off; C = Continuous Memory; R = Engine Running

3 and 4 Digit Trouble Codes

Code	Test Condition*	Probable Cause
102	O,C,R	MAF sensor circuits open or sensor defective
103	O,C,R	MAF sensor screen blocked or sensor defective
106	O,C,R	BARO sensor slow responding
107	O,C,R	BARO sensor low voltage, open sensor circuits or defective sensor.
108	O,C,R	BARO sensor high voltage detected. BARO circuit shorted to power or defective sensor.
109	O,C,R	BARO sensor intermittent. Check for loose connections.
111	O,C,R	Pass
112	O,R	Intake Air Temperature sensor circuit indicates circuit grounded/above 245 degrees F
113	O,R	Intake Air Temperature sensor circuit indicates open circuit/below -40 degrees F
114	O,R	Intake Air Temperature sensor out of self-test range
116	O,R	Coolant Temperature sensor out of self-test range
117	O,C	Coolant Temperature circuit below minimum voltage or indicates above 245 degrees F
118	O,C	Coolant Temperature sensor circuit above maximum voltage or indicates below -40 degrees F
121	O,C,R	Throttle Position sensor out of self-test range
122	O,C	Throttle Position sensor below minimum voltage
123	O,C	Throttle Position sensor above maximum voltage
124	C	Throttle Position Sensor voltage higher than expected
125	C	Throttle Position Sensor voltage lower than expected
125	O,C,R	Coolant Temp sensor slow response. Check coolant level
126	O,C,R	MAP/BARO sensor higher than expected
128	C	MAP sensor vacuum hose damaged or disconnected
129	R	Insufficient Manifold Absolute Pressure/Mass Air Flow change during Dynamic Response Check
131	O,C,R	Heated oxygen sensor out of range
133	O,C,R	Heated oxygen sensor slow response
135	O,C,R	Heated oxygen sensor circuits open, shorted or grounded
136	O,C,R	Heated oxygen sensor circuits open, shorted or have corroded connections
136	R	Heated oxygen sensor indicates lean condition, left side
137	R	Heated oxygen sensor indicates rich condition, left side
139	C	No heated oxygen sensor switching detected, left side
141	O,C,R	Heated oxygen sensor circuits open shorted or grounded
144	C	No heated oxygen sensor switching detected, right side

* O = Key On, Engine Off; C = Continuous Memory; R = Engine Running

3 and 4 Digit Trouble Codes (continued)

Code	Test Condition*	Probable Cause
151	O,C,R	Heated oxygen sensor out of range
153	O,C,R	Heated oxygen sensor slow response
155	O,C,R	Heated oxygen sensor circuits open, shorted or grounded
156	O,C,R	Heated oxygen sensor circuits open, shorted or have corroded connections
157	R,C	Mass Air Flow Sensor below minimum voltage
158	O,R,C	Mass Air Flow Sensor above maximum voltage
159	O,R	Mass Air Flow Sensor out of self-test range
161	O,C,R	Heated oxygen sensor circuits open shorted or grounded
167	R	Insufficient Throttle Position Sensor change during Dynamic Response Check
171	C	Heated oxygen sensor unable to switch, right side
171	R	Heated oxygen sensor indicates lean condition, left side
172	R,C	Heated oxygen sensor indicates lean condition, right side
172	R	Heated oxygen sensor indicates rich condition, left side
173	R,C	Heated oxygen sensor indicates rich condition, right side
174	C	Heated oxygen sensor switching slow, right side
174	R	Heated oxygen sensor indicates lean condition, right side
175	C	Heated oxygen sensor unable to switch, left side
175	R	Heated oxygen sensor indicates rich condition, right side
176	C	Heated oxygen sensor indicates lean condition, left side
176	O,C,R	Flexible fuel sensor malfunction
177	C	Heated oxygen sensor indicates rich condition, left side
178	C	Heated oxygen sensor switching slow, left side
179	C	Adaptive Fuel lean limit reached at part throttle, system rich, right side
180	O,C,R	Engine fuel temperature sensor circuit open, shorted or grounded
181	C	Adaptive Fuel rich limit reached at part throttle, right side
181	O,C,R	Engine fuel temperature sensor circuit open, shorted or grounded
182	O,C,R	Engine fuel temperature sensor circuit open, shorted or grounded
182	C	Adaptive Fuel lean limit reached at idle, right side
183	C	Adaptive Fuel rich limit reached at idle, right side
183	O,C,R	Engine fuel temperature sensor circuit open, shorted or grounded
184	C	Mass Air Flow higher than expected
185	C	Mass Air Flow lower than expected
186	C	Injector Pulse-width higher than expected
186	O,C,R	Engine fuel temperature sensor circuit open, shorted or grounded
187	C	Injector Pulse-width lower than expected
187	O,C,R	Engine fuel temperature sensor circuit open, shorted or grounded
188	C	Adaptive Fuel lean limit reached, left side
188	O,C,R	Engine fuel temperature sensor circuit open, shorted or grounded
189	C	Adaptive Fuel rich limit reached, left side
190	O,C,R	Fuel rail pressure sensor circuit open
191	C	Adaptive Fuel lean limit reached at idle, left side
191	O,C,R	Fuel rail pressure sensor circuit performance
192	C	Adaptive Fuel rich limit reached at idle, left side
192	O,C,R	Fuel rail pressure sensor circuit low input
193	O,C,R	Fuel rail pressure sensor circuit high input

* O = Key On, Engine Off; C = Continuous Memory; R = Engine Running

Code	Test Condition*	Probable Cause
211	C	Profile Ignition Pick-up circuit fault
212	C	Ignition module circuit failure/SPOUT circuit grounded
213	R	SPOUT circuit open
214	C	Cylinder identification (CID) circuit failure
215	C	PCM detected coil 1 primary circuit failure
216	C	PCM detected coil 2 primary circuit failure
217	C	PCM detected coil 3 primary circuit failure
219	C	Spark timing defaulted to 10 degrees SPOUT circuit open (EI)
221	C	Spark timing error (1993 and 1994 only)
225	C	Knock sensor not detected during dynamic response test KOER
226	O	Ignition Diagnostic Module (IDM) signal not received (EI)
230	O,R	Fuel pump primary circuit malfunction. Check fuel pump relay and for open, shorted or grounded wiring
231	O,R	Fuel pump primary circuit low. Check fuel pump relay and for open, shorted or grounded wiring
232	O,R	Fuel pump primary circuit high. Check fuel pump relay and for open, shorted or grounded wiring. Also, inertia switch may be open
232	C	PCM detected coil 1,2,3,4 primary circuit failure (EI)
298	O,R	Engine oil overheat. Check oil level
300	O,C,R	Random misfire. Check ignition and fuel system
301 - 308	O,C,R	Misfire in the corresponding cylinder. Check ignition and fuel system
311	R	Thermactor Air System inoperative, right side
313	R	Thermactor Air not by-passed
314	R	Thermactor Air inoperative, left side
320	O,C,R	Engine ignition speed input circuit malfunction
325	O,C,R	knock sensor circuit bank 1
326	C,R	EGR circuit voltage lower than expected
326	O,C,R	Knock sensor circuit bank 1
327	O,C,R	EGR Valve Pressure Transducer/Position Sensor circuit below minimum voltage
328	O,C,R	EGR Valve Position Sensor voltage below closed limit
330	O,C,R	Knock sensor circuit bank 2
331	O,C,R	Knock sensor circuit bank 2
332	C,R	EGR valve opening not detected
334	O,C,R	EGR valve position sensor voltage above closed limit
335	O	EGR Sensor voltage out-of-range
336	R	EGR circuit higher than expected
337	O,C,R	EGR Valve Pressure Transducer/Position Sensor circuit above maximum voltage
340	O,C,R	Camshaft position sensor circuit. Check wiring for opens, shorts and grounds
341	O	Octane adjust service pin open
350	O,C,R	Ignition coil primary circuit malfunction. Check each coil primary circuit
351-358	O,C,R	Ignition coil primary circuit malfunction. Check the corresponding coil primary circuit
401	O,C,R	EGR low flow. Check vacuum supply and valve operation
402	O,C,R	EGR flow at idle. Check for a stuck-open valve
411	R	Unable to control RPM during Low RPM Self-test
411	O,C,R	Secondary Air System no or low flow
412	R	Unable to control RPM during High RPM Self-test
412	O,C,R	Secondary Air System circuit open
415	R	Idle Air Control (IAC) system at maximum adaptive lower limit
416	C	Idle Air Control (IAC) system at upper adaptive learning limit

* *O = Key On, Engine Off; C = Continuous Memory; R = Engine Running*

3 and 4 Digit Trouble Codes (continued)

Code	Test Condition*	Probable Cause
420	O,C,R	Catalyst system low efficiency, left bank
430	O,C,R	Catalyst system low efficiency, right bank
442	O,C,R	Evaporative control system - small leak detected
443	O,C,R	Evaporative control system canister purge valve circuit malfunction
452	C	No input from Vehicle Speed Sensor
452	O,C,R	FTP sensor circuit
453	O,C,R	FTP sensor circuit high voltage
455	O,C,R	Evaporative control system large leak detected
460	O,C,R	Fuel level sensor circuit
500	O,C,R	Vehicle speed sensor. Check for opens, shorts and grounds in the VSS circuits
501	O,C,R	Vehicle speed sensor. Check for opens, shorts and grounds in the VSS circuits
503	O,C,R	Vehicle speed sensor signal intermittent. Check for opens, shorts and grounds in the VSS circuits
505	O	Idle air control fail during self test
511	O	Read Only Memory test failed - replace PCM
512	C	Keep Alive Memory test failed
513	O	Internal voltage failure in PCM
519	O	Power steering pressure switch (PSP) circuit open
521	R	Power steering pressure switch (PSP) circuit did not change states
522	O	Manual Lever Position (MLP) sensor circuit open/vehicle in gear
525	O	Indicates vehicle in gear, air conditioning on
527	O	Manual Lever Position (MLP) sensor circuit open, air conditioning on during KOEO
529	C	Data Communication link (DCL) or PCM circuit failure (1993 and 1994 only)
532	C	Cluster Control Assembly (CCA) circuit failure
533	C	Data Communications Link (DCL) or Electronic Instrument Cluster (EIC) circuit failure
536	C,R	Brake ON/Off (BOO) circuit failure/not activated during the KOER
538	R	Insufficient change in RPM/operator error in Dynamic Response Check
539	O	Air conditioning on during Self-test
542	O,C	Fuel Pump circuit open; PCM to motor
543	O,C	Fuel Pump circuit open; Battery to PCM
551	O	Idle Air Control (IAC) circuit failure KOEO
552	O	Air Management 1 circuit failure
552	O,C,R	Power steering pressure sensor open or shorted to ground
552	O	Secondary Air Injection Bypass (AIRB) circuit failure
553	O	Secondary Air Injection Diverter (AIRB) circuit failure
553	O,C,R	Power steering pressure sensor shorted to power
554	O	Fuel Pressure Regulator Control (FPRC) circuit failure
556	O,C	Primary Fuel Pump circuit failure
557	O,C	Low speed fuel pump primary circuit failure
558	O	EGR Vacuum Regulator circuit failure
559	O	Air Conditioning On (ACON) relay circuit failure
563	O	High fan control (HFC) circuit failure
564	O	Fan control (FC) circuit failure
565	O	Canister Purge circuit failure
569	O	Auxiliary Canister Purge (CANP2) circuit failure KOEO
571	O	EGRA solenoid circuit failure KOEO

* O = Key On, Engine Off; C = Continuous Memory; R = Engine Running

Code	Test Condition*	Probable Cause
572	O	EGRV solenoid circuit failure KOEO
578	C	A/C pressure sensor circuit shorted
579	C	Insufficient AIR CONDITIONING pressure change
581	C	Power to Fan circuit over current
582	O	Fan circuit open
583	C	Power to Fuel pump over current
584	C	VCRM Power ground circuit open (VCRM Pin 1)
585	C	Power to A/C clutch over current
586	C	A/C clutch circuit open
587	O,C	Variable Control Relay Module (VCRM) communication failure
602	O,C,R	Control module programming error
603	O,C,R	Powertrain control module test error
617	C	1-2 shift error
618	C	2-3 shift error
619	C	3-4 shift error
621	O,C	Shift Solenoid 1 (SS 1) circuit failure KOEO
622	O	Shift Solenoid 2 (SS2) circuit failure KOEO
623	O	Transmission Control Indicator Light (TCIL) circuit failure
624	O,C	Electronic Pressure Control (EPC) circuit failure
625	O,C	Electronic Pressure Control (EPC) driver open in PCM
626	O	Coast Clutch Solenoid (CCS) circuit failure KOEO
627	O	Torque Converter Clutch (TCC) solenoid circuit failure
628	C	Excessive converter clutch slippage
629	O,C	Torque Converter Clutch (TCC) solenoid circuit failure
631	O	Transmission Control Indicator Lamp (TCIL) circuit failure KOEO
632	R	Transmission Control Switch (TCS) circuit did not change states during KOER
634	O,C,R	Manual Lever Position (MLP) sensor voltage higher or lower than expected
636	O,R	Transmission Fluid Temp (TFT) higher or lower than expected
637	O,C	Transmission Fluid Temp (TFT) sensor circuit above maximum voltage/ -40°F (-40°C) indicated / circuit open
638	O,C	Transmission Fluid Temp (TFT) sensor circuit below minimum voltage/ 290°F (143°C) indicated / circuit shorted
639	R,C	Insufficient input from Transmission Speed Sensor (TSS)
641	O,C	Shift Solenoid 3 (SS3) circuit failure
643	O,C	Torque Converter Clutch (TCC) circuit failure
645	C	Incorrect gear ratio obtained for first gear
646	C	Incorrect gear ratio obtained for second gear
647	C	Incorrect gear ratio obtained for third gear
648	C	Incorrect gear ratio obtained for fourth gear
649	C	Electronic Pressure Control (EPC) higher or lower than expected
651	C	Electronic Pressure Control (EPC) circuit failure
652	O	Torque Converter Clutch (TCC) solenoid circuit failure
653	R	Transmission Control Switch (TCS) did not change states during KOER
654	O	Transmission Range (TR) sensor not indicating PARK during KOEO
656	C	Torque Converter Clutch continuous slip error
657	C	Transmission over temperature condition occurred

* O = Key On, Engine Off; C = Continuous Memory; R = Engine Running

3 and 4 Digit Trouble Codes (continued)

Code	Test Condition*	Probable Cause
659	C	High vehicle speed in park indicated
667	C	Transmission Range sensor circuit voltage below minimum
668	C	Transmission Range circuit voltage above maximum
675	C	Transmission Range sensor circuit voltage out of range
703	O,C,R	Brake switch input, check for open switch
704	O,C,R	Clutch pedal position switch, check for opens, shorts and grounds
720	O,C,R	Insufficient input from output shaft speed sensor
721	O,C,R	Noise interference on output shaft speed sensor signal
722	O,C,R	No signal from output shaft speed sensor
723	O,C,R	Output shaft speed sensor circuit intermittent signal
812	O,C,R	Reverse switch input circuit
998	O	Hard fault present
1000	O,C,R	Monitor testing not complete
1001	O,C,R	KOER not able to complete
1100	O,C,R	MAF sensor intermittent
1101	O,C,R	MAF sensor out of self test range
1109	O,C,R	IAT sensor intermittent signal
1112	O,C,R	IAT sensor intermittent signal
1114	O,C,R	IAT sensor low input
1115	O,C,R	IAT sensor high input
1116	O,C,R	ECT sensor out of range
1117	O,C,R	ECT sensor out intermittent
1120	O,C,R	TPS out of range
1121	O,C,R	TPS sensor
1124	O,C,R	TPS sensor out of self test range
1125	O,C,R	TPS sensor intermittent
1127	O,C,R	Exhaust not warm enough to test sensor
1128	O,C,R	Oxygen sensors swapped from bank to bank, check O2 sensor for correct connection
1129	O,C,R	Oxygen sensors swapped from bank to bank, check O2 sensor for correct connection
1130	O,C,R	Lack of O2 sensor switch, left bank sensor 1(1/1)
1131	O,C,R	Lack of O2 sensor switch, lean(1/1)
1132	O,C,R	Lack of O2 sensor switch, rich 91/1)
1137	O,C,R	Lack of O2 sensor switch, lean, left bank sensor 2(1/2)
1138	O,C,R	Lack of O2 sensor switch, rich, left bank sensor 2(1/2)
1150	O,C,R	Lack of O2 sensor switch, right bank sensor 1 (2/1)
1151	O,C,R	Lack of O2 sensor switch, right bank sensor 1 (2/1) lean
1152	O,C,R	Lack of O2 sensor switch, right bank sensor 1 (2/1) rich
1157	O,C,R	Lack of O2 sensor switch, right bank sensor 1 (2/2) lean
1158	O,C,R	Lack of O2 sensor switch, right bank sensor 1 (2/2) rich
1168	O,C,R	Fuel rail pressure sensor, low pressure indicated
1169	O,C,R	Fuel rail pressure sensor, high pressure indicated
1180	O,C,R	Fuel delivery system low, check fuel filter
1181	O,C,R	Fuel delivery system high
1183	O,C,R	Engine oil temperature sensor circuit
1184	O,C,R	Engine oil temperature sensor self test fail

* O = Key On, Engine Off; C = Continuous Memory; R = Engine Running

Code	Test Condition*	Probable Cause
1233	O,C,R	Fuel system disabled, check inertia switch
1234	O,C,R	Fuel system disabled, check inertia switch
1235	O,C,R	Fuel pump control out of range
1236	O,C,R	Fuel pump control out of range
1237	O,C,R	Fuel pump secondary circuit malfunction
1238	O,C,R	Fuel pump secondary circuit malfunction
1244	O,C,R	Generator load input low, check charging system
1245	O,C,R	Generator load input high, check charging system
1246	O,C,R	Generator load input failed, check charging system
1260	O,C,R	Theft detected vehicle immobilized
1270	O,C,R	Engine RPM vehicle speed limiter
1285	O,C,R	Cylinder head over temperature sensed
1288	O,C,R	Cylinder head temperature sensor circuit out of self test range
1289	O,C,R	Cylinder head temperature sensor circuit high input
1290	O,C,R	Cylinder head temperature sensor circuit low input
1299	O,C,R	Cylinder head over temperature protection active
1309	O,C,R	Misfire monitor disabled
1400	O,C,R	DPF-EGR sensor circuit low voltage, check EGR circuits for shorts, opens and grounds
1401	O,C,R	DPF-EGR sensor circuit high voltage, check EGR circuits for shorts, opens and grounds
1405	O,C,R	DPF-EGR sensor upstream hose off or plugged
1406	O,C,R	DPF-EGR sensor downstream hose off or plugged
1408	O,C,R	EGR flow out of self test range
1409	O,C,R	EGR vacuum regulator solenoid circuit malfunction
1411	O,C,R	Secondary Air Injection system downstream flow
1413	O,C,R	Secondary Air Injection system monitor circuit high
1414	O,C,R	Secondary Air Injection system monitor circuit low
1443	O,C,R	EVAP control system canister purge valve malfunction
1450	O,C,R	Unable to bleed up fuel tank vacuum
1451	O,C,R	EVAP control system canister vent solenoid circuit malfunction
1460	O,C,R	Wide Open Throttle A/C cutout primary circuit malfunction
1461	O,C,R	Air Conditioning pressure sensor (ACP) high voltage
1462	O,C,R	Air Conditioning pressure sensor (ACP) low voltage
1463	O,C,R	Air Conditioning pressure sensor (ACP) insufficient pressure change
1464	O,C,R	A/C demand out of self test range
1469	O,C,R	Low A/C cycling period
1500	O,C,R	Vehicle speed sensor intermittent (VSS)
1501	O,C,R	Vehicle speed sensor (VSS) out of self test range
1502	O,C,R	Vehicle speed sensor intermittent (VSS)
1504	O,C,R	Idle Air Control (IAC) circuit malfunction
1506	O,C,R	Idle Air Control (IAC) overspeed error
1507	O,C,R	Idle Air Control (IAC) underspeed error
1550	O,C,R	Power steering pressure (PSP) sensor malfunction
1605	O,C,R	Keep Alive Memory test failure
1633	O,C,R	Keep Alive power voltage too low
1635	O,C,R	Tire/Axle ratio out of acceptable range

* *O = Key On, Engine Off; C = Continuous Memory; R = Engine Running*

2.30a Scan tools like these from Actron and AutoXray are powerful and relatively inexpensive. They have a lot of features that were once found only on expensive professional scanners

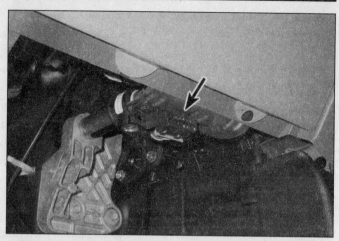

2.30b The 16-pin Data Link Connector (DLC) is located under the left side of the dash

Obtaining codes - 1996 and later models

OBD-II Diagnostic Trouble Codes (DTCs) and the Malfunction Indicator Light (MIL)

27   To test the critical emission control components, circuit and systems on an OBD-II vehicle, the PCM runs a series of *monitors* during each vehicle *trip*. The monitors are a series of testing protocols used by the PCM to determine whether each monitored component, circuit or system is functioning satisfactorily. The monitors must be run in a certain order. For example, the oxygen sensor monitor cannot run until the engine, the catalytic converter and the oxygen sensors are all warmed up. Another example, the misfire monitor cannot run until the engine is in closed-loop operation. (For a good overview of the OBD-II monitors, see the Haynes *OBD-II and Electronic Engine Management Systems* Techbook). An OBD-II *trip* consists of operating the vehicle (after an engine-off period) and driving it in such a manner that the PCM's monitors test all of the monitored components, circuits and systems at least once.

28   If the PCM recognizes a fault in some component, circuit or system while it's running the monitors, it stores a Diagnostic Trouble

Code (DTC) and turns on the Malfunction Indicator Light (MIL) on the instrument cluster. A DTC can self-erase, but only after the MIL has been extinguished. For example, the MIL might be extinguished for a misfire or fuel system malfunction if the fault doesn't recur when monitored during the next three subsequent sequential driving cycles in which the conditions are similar to those under which the malfunction was first identified. (For other types of malfunctions, the criteria for extinguishing the MIL can vary.)

29   Once the MIL has been extinguished, the PCM must pass the diagnostic test for the most recent DTC for 40 *warm-up cycles* (80 warm-up cycles for the fuel system monitor and the misfire monitor). A warm-up cycle consists of the following components:

The engine has been started and is running
The engine temperature rises by at least 40-degrees above its temperature when it was started
The engine coolant temperature crosses the 160-degree F mark
The engine is turned off after meeting the above criteria

Obtaining DTCs

Refer to illustrations 2.30a and 2.30b
30   Of course, if the MIL does NOT go out

after several driving cycles, it's probably an indication that something must be repaired or replaced before the DTC can be erased and the MIL extinguished. This means that you will need to extract the DTC(s) from the PCM, make the necessary repair or replace a component, then erase the DTC yourself. You can extract the DTCs from the PCM by plugging a generic OBD-II scan tool **(see illustration)** into the PCM's data link connector **(see illustration)**, which is located under the left side of the dash. Plug the scan tool into the 16-pin data link connector (DLC), then follow the instructions included with the scan tool to extract all the diagnostic codes.

Erase the DTC(s), turn off the MIL and verify the repair

31   Once you've completed the repair or replaced the component, use your code reader or scan tool to erase the DTC(s) and turn off the MIL. On most tools, you simply press a button to erase DTCs and turn off the MIL, but on some tools you'll have to locate this function by using the menu on the tool's display. If it isn't obvious, follow the instructions that come with your tool.

OBD-II trouble codes

Note: *Not all trouble codes apply to all models.*

Code	Probable cause
P0010	Intake camshaft position actuator circuit, open/short in Variable Cam Timing (VCT) circuit or solenoid (Bank 1)
P0011	Intake camshaft position timing over-advanced (Bank 1)
P0012	Variable cam timing over-retarded (Bank 1)
P0013	Exhaust cam position actuator circuit, open/short in VCT circuit or solenoid or open in VPWR circuit (Bank 1)
P0020	Intake camshaft position actuator circuit, open circuit (Bank 2)
P0021	Intake camshaft position timing over-advanced (Bank 2)
P0022	Intake camshaft position timing over-retarded (Bank 2)

Code	Probable cause
P0040	Upstream oxygen sensors swapped from bank to bank (crossed wiring harnesses)
P0041	Downstream oxygen sensors swapped from bank to bank (crossed wiring harnesses)
P0053	Upstream oxygen sensor heater resistance, heater current requirements too low or too high (Bank 1)
P0054	Downstream oxygen sensor heater resistance, heater current requirements too low or too high (Bank 1)
P0055	Second downstream oxygen sensor heater resistance, heater current requirements too low or too high (Bank 1)
P0059	Upstream oxygen sensor heater resistance, heater current requirements too low or too high (Bank 2)
P0060	Downstream oxygen sensor heater resistance, heater current requirements too or too high (Bank 2)
P0061	Second downstream oxygen sensor heater resistance, heater current requirements too low or too high (Bank 2)
P0068	Throttle Position (TP) sensor inconsistent with Mass Air Flow sensor
P0102	Mass Air Flow (MAF) sensor circuit, low input
P0103	Mass Air Flow (MAF) sensor circuit, high input
P0104	Mass Air Flow (MAF) sensor circuit, intermittent or erratic
P0106	Barometric (BARO) pressure sensor circuit, performance problem
P0107	Barometric (BARO) pressure sensor/MAP sensor circuit, low voltage
P0108	Barometric (BARO) pressure sensor/MAP sensor circuit, high voltage
P0109	BARO sensor circuit intermittent
P0112	Intake Air Temperature (IAT) sensor circuit, low input
P0113	Intake Air Temperature (IAT) sensor circuit, high input
P0114	Intake Air Temperature (IAT) sensor circuit, intermittent or erratic
P0116	Engine Coolant Temperature (ECT) circuit range or performance problem
P0117	Engine Coolant Temperature (ECT) sensor circuit, low input
P0118	Engine Coolant Temperature (ECT) sensor circuit, high input
P0119	Engine Coolant Temperature (ECT) sensor circuit, intermittent or erratic
P0121	ETC Throttle Position (TP) circuit, performance problem
P0121	Throttle Position (TP) circuit, performance problem
P0122	ETC Throttle Position (TP) sensor circuit, low input
P0122	Throttle Position (TP) sensor circuit, low input
P0123	ETC Throttle Position (TP) sensor circuit, high input
P0123	Throttle Position (TP) sensor circuit, high input
P0125	Insufficient coolant temperature for closed loop fuel control
P0127	Intake air temperature too high
P0128	Coolant temperature below thermostat regulated temperature
P0131	Upstream heated O2 sensor circuit low voltage (Bank 1)
P0133	Upstream heated O2 sensor circuit slow response (Bank 1)
P0135	Upstream heated O2 sensor heater circuit fault (Bank 1)
P0136	Downstream heated O2 sensor fault (Bank 1)
P0141	Downstream heated O2 sensor heater circuit fault (Bank 1)
P0148	Fuel delivery error
P0151	Upstream heated O2 sensor circuit low voltage (Bank 2)
P0153	Upstream heated O2 sensor circuit slow response (Bank 2)
P0155	Upstream heated O2 sensor heater circuit fault (Bank 2)
P0156	Downstream heated O2 sensor fault (Bank 2)
P0161	Downstream heated O2 sensor heater circuit fault (Bank 2)
P0171	System too lean (Bank 1)
P0172	System too rich (Bank 1)
P0174	System too lean (Bank 2)
P0175	System too rich (Bank 2)
P0180	Engine Fuel Temperature (EFT) sensor A circuit, low input

OBD-II trouble codes (continued)

Note: *Not all trouble codes apply to all models.*

Code	Probable cause
P0181	Engine Fuel Temperature (EFT) sensor A circuit, range/performance problem
P0182	Engine Fuel Temperature (EFT) sensor A circuit, low input
P0183	Engine Fuel Temperature (EFT) sensor A circuit, high input
P0186	Engine Fuel Temperature (EFT) sensor B circuit, range/performance problem
P0187	Engine Fuel Temperature (EFT) sensor B circuit, low input
P0188	Engine Fuel Temperature (EFT) sensor B circuit, high input
P0190	Fuel Rail Pressure (FRP) sensor circuit malfunction
P0191	Fuel Rail Pressure (FRP) sensor circuit performance
P0192	Fuel Rail Pressure (FRP) sensor circuit, low input
P0193	Fuel Rail Pressure (FRP) sensor circuit, high input
P0196	Engine Oil Temperature (EOT) sensor circuit, range/performance problem
P0197	Engine Oil Temperature (EOT) sensor circuit, low input
P0198	Engine Oil Temperature (EOT) sensor circuit, high input
P0201	Injector No. 1 circuit malfunction
P0202	Injector No. 2 circuit malfunction
P0203	Injector No. 3 circuit malfunction
P0204	Injector No. 4 circuit malfunction
P0205	Injector No. 5 circuit malfunction
P0206	Injector No. 6 circuit malfunction
P0207	Injector No. 7, circuit malfunction
P0208	Injector No. 8, circuit malfunction
P0217	Engine coolant over-temperature condition
P0218	Transmission Fluid Temperature (TFT), overheating condition
P0219	Engine over speed condition
P0221	Throttle Position (TP) sensor 2 circuit, range/performance problem
P0222	Throttle Position (TP) sensor 2 circuit, low input
P0223	Throttle Position (TP) sensor 2 circuit, high input
P0230	Fuel pump primary circuit malfunction
P0231	Fuel pump secondary circuit, low voltage
P0232	Fuel pump secondary circuit, high voltage
P0234	Supercharger overboost condition
P0243	Supercharger boost bypass solenoid, circuit malfunction
P0297	Vehicle over speed condition
P0298	Engine oil high-temperature condition
P0300	Random misfire detected
P0301	Cylinder No. 1, misfire detected
P0302	Cylinder No. 2, misfire detected
P0303	Cylinder No. 3, misfire detected
P0304	Cylinder No. 4, misfire detected
P0305	Cylinder No. 5, misfire detected
P0306	Cylinder No. 6, misfire detected
P0307	Cylinder No. 7, misfire detected
P0308	Cylinder No. 8, misfire detected
P0310	Misfire detection monitor
P0315	PCM unable to learn crankshaft pulse wheel tooth spacing (exceeds allowable correction tolerances)
P0316	Misfire occurred during first 1000 engine revolutions

Code	Probable cause
P0320	Ignition engine speed input, circuit malfunction
P0325	Knock sensor No. 1, circuit malfunction (Bank 1)
P0326	Knock sensor No. 1, circuit range or performance problem (Bank 1)
P0330	Knock sensor No. 2, circuit malfunction (Bank 2)
P0331	Knock sensor No. 2, circuit range or performance problem (Bank 2)
P0340	Camshaft Position (CMP) sensor, circuit malfunction (Bank 1)
P0345	Camshaft Position (CMP) sensor, circuit malfunction (Bank 2)
P0350	Ignition coil (undetermined), primary or secondary circuit malfunction
P0351	Ignition coil A, primary or secondary circuit malfunction
P0352	Ignition coil B, primary or secondary circuit malfunction
P0353	Ignition coil C, primary or secondary circuit malfunction
P0354	Ignition coil D, primary or secondary circuit malfunction
P0355	Ignition coil E, primary or secondary circuit malfunction
P0356	Ignition coil F, primary or secondary circuit malfunction
P0357	Ignition coil G, primary or secondary circuit malfunction
P0358	Ignition coil H, primary or secondary circuit malfunction
P0400	EGR flow failure (outside the minimum or maximum limits)
P0401	Exhaust Gas Recirculation (EGR) valve, insufficient flow detected
P0402	Exhaust Gas Recirculation (EGR) valve, excessive flow detected
P0403	EGR vacuum regulator solenoid, circuit malfunction (vehicles without electric EGR)
P0405	Differential Pressure Feedback (DPF) EGR sensor circuit, low voltage detected
P0406	Differential Pressure Feedback (DPF) EGR sensor circuit, high voltage detected
P0411	Secondary Air Injection (AIR) system, upstream flow
P0412	Secondary Air Injection (AIR) system, circuit malfunction
P0420	Catalyst system efficiency below threshold (Bank 1)
P0421	Catalyst system efficiency below threshold (Bank 1)
P0430	Catalyst system efficiency below threshold (Bank 2)
P0431	Catalyst system efficiency below threshold (Bank 2)
P0442	EVAP control system, small leak detected
P0443	EVAP control system, canister purge valve, circuit malfunction
P0446	EVAP control system canister vent solenoid, circuit malfunction
P0451	EVAP system Fuel Tank Pressure (FTP) sensor, circuit out of range or performance problem
P0452	Fuel Tank Pressure (FTP) sensor circuit, low voltage detected
P0453	Fuel Tank Pressure (FTP) sensor circuit, high voltage detected
P0454	Fuel Tank Pressure (FTP) sensor, noisy circuit
P0455	EVAP control system, leak detected (no purge flow or large leak)
P0456	EVAP control system, very small leak detected
P0457	EVAP control system, leak detected (fuel filler neck cap loose or off)
P0460	Fuel level sensor, circuit malfunction
P0461	Fuel level sensor circuit, range or performance problem
P0462	Fuel level sensor circuit, low input
P0463	Fuel level sensor circuit, high input
P0480	Cooling fan electrical malfunction
P0480	Low Fan Control (LFC)/Fan Control No. 1 (FC1) primary circuit malfunction
P0481	High Fan Control (HFC)/Fan Control No. 3 (FC3) primary circuit malfunction
P0482	Medium Fan Control (MFC), primary circuit failure
P0500	Vehicle Speed Sensor (VSS) malfunction
P0501	Vehicle Speed Sensor (VSS), range or performance problem

OBD-II trouble codes (continued)

Note: *Not all trouble codes apply to all models.*

Code	Probable cause
P0503	Vehicle Speed Sensor (VSS), intermittent malfunction
P0505	Idle Air Control (IAC) system malfunction
P0506	Idle Air Control (IAC) system, rpm lower than expected
P0507	Idle Air Control (IAC) system, rpm higher than expected
P0511	Idle Air Control (IAC) system, circuit malfunction
P0532	Air Conditioning Pressure (ACP) sensor, high voltage detected
P0533	Air Conditioning Pressure (ACP) sensor, low voltage detected
P0534	Low air conditioning cycling period (frequent A/C compressor clutch cycling)
P0537	Air Conditioning Evaporator Temperature (ACET) circuit, low input
P0538	Air Conditioning Evaporator Temperature (ACET) circuit, high input
P0552	Power Steering Pressure (PSP) sensor circuit, low input
P0553	Power Steering Pressure (PSP) sensor circuit, high input
P0602	Control module programming error
P0603	Powertrain Control Module (PCM) Keep-Alive-Memory (KAM) error
P0605	Powertrain Control Module (PCM) Read-Only-Memory (ROM) error
P0606	Powertrain Control Module (PCM) internal communication error
P0620	Alternator control circuit failure
P0622	Alternator field terminal circuit failure
P0645	Open or shorted Wide-Open Throttle A/C cutoff (WAC) circuit shorted or open or damaged WAC relay
P0660	Intake Manifold Tuning Valve (IMTV) control circuit open (Bank 1)
P0663	Intake Manifold Tuning Valve (IMTV) control circuit open (Bank 2)
P0703	Brake switch circuit input malfunction
P0704	Clutch pedal position switch malfunction
P0720	Insufficient input from Output Shaft Speed (OSS) sensor
P0721	Noise interference on Output Shaft Speed (OSS) sensor signal
P0722	No signal from Output Shaft Speed (OSS) sensor
P0723	Output Shaft Speed (OSS) sensor circuit, intermittent failure

3 Powertrain Control Module (PCM)

Refer to illustration 3.1

1   Disconnect the negative battery cable.
2   The Powertrain Control Module (PCM) is located on the drivers side of the engine compartment, above and to the right of the steering column **(see illustration)**. The PCM is easily distinguished by the aluminum casing surrounding the module.
3   Remove the air cleaner assembly and the air ducts (see Chapter 4).
4   Disconnect the PCM wiring harness. On some models there is a large connector retained by a bolt, on some later models there are several pull-out connectors.
5   Remove the retainers securing the PCM and bracket to the firewall and remove the PCM. **Note:** *Avoid any static electricity damage to the computer by using gloves and a special anti-static pad to store the PCM on once it is removed.*
6   Installation is reversal of removal. **Note:**

The vehicle may have to be driven up to ten miles after PCM replacement to allow the PCM to relearn its adaptive strategy.

4 Information sensors

Engine coolant temperature sensor

Refer to illustrations 4.2, 4.3 and 4.4
Note: *Later models have both a coolant temperature sensor and a cylinder head temperature sensor. The following checks apply only to coolant temperature sensors. 2005 models have only a cylinder head temperature sensor.*

General description

1   The coolant sensor is a thermistor (a resistor which varies the value of its voltage output in accordance with temperature changes). The change in the resistance values will directly affect the voltage signal

3.2 Typical PCM location (arrow)

from the coolant sensor. As the sensor temperature DECREASES, the resistance values will INCREASE. As the sensor temperature INCREASES, the resistance values will DECREASE. A failure in the coolant sensor

4.2 Check the resistance of the coolant temperature sensor with the engine completely cold and then with the engine at operating temperature. Resistance should decrease as temperature increases (4.6L engine shown)

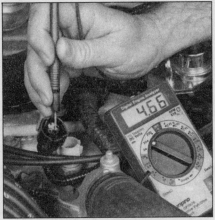

4.3 Working on the harness side, check the voltage from the PCM to the coolant temperature sensor with the ignition key ON and the engine not running. It should be approximately 5.0 volts (4.6L model shown)

4.4 To prevent leakage, wrap the threads of the coolant temperature sensor with Teflon tape before installing it

circuit should set a Code 21, 51 or 61 for the two-digit code system or 116, 117 or 118 for the three digit code system. These codes indicate a failure in the coolant temperature circuit, so in most cases the appropriate solution to the problem will be either repair of a wire or replacement of the sensor.

Check

2   Check the resistance value of the coolant temperature sensor while it is completely cold (50 to 65-degrees F). The resistance should be approximately 58,750 to 40,500 ohms (**see illustration**). Next, start the engine and warm it up until it reaches operating temperature (180 to 220-degrees F). The resistance should be lower, approximately 3,600 to 1,840 ohms. **Note:** *Access to the coolant temperature sensor makes it difficult to position electrical probes on the terminals. If necessary, remove the sensor and perform the tests in a pan of heated water to simulate the conditions.*

3   If the resistance values on the sensor are correct, check the signal voltage to the sensor from the PCM (**see illustration**). It should be approximately 5.0 volts.

Replacement

Warning: *The engine must be completely cool before beginning this procedure.*

4   Before installing the new sensor, wrap the threads with Teflon sealing tape to prevent leakage and thread corrosion (**see illustration**).

5   To remove the sensor, unplug the electrical connector, then carefully unscrew it. **Caution:** *Handle the coolant sensor with care. Damage to this sensor will affect the operation of the entire fuel injection system.* Install the sensor and tighten it securely.

Manifold Absolute Pressure (MAP) sensor

Refer to illustration 4.9

Note: *Later models do not have a MAP sensor.*

General description

6   The Manifold Absolute Pressure (MAP) sensor monitors the intake manifold pressure changes resulting from changes in engine load and speed and converts the information into a voltage output. The PCM uses the MAP sensor to control fuel delivery and ignition timing. The PCM will receive information as a frequency-generated voltage signal. This signal can be detected using a tachometer. The frequency will vary from 310 "rpm" at closed throttle (high vacuum) to 200 "rpm" at wide open throttle (low vacuum).

7   A failure in the MAP sensor circuit should set a Code 22 or 72 for the two digit code system or 126, 128 or 129 for the three digit code system.

Check

8   Disconnect the electrical connector from the MAP sensor. Using a voltmeter, check for reference voltage to the MAP sensor on the VREF wire. With the ignition key ON (engine not running), the reference voltage should be approximately 4.0 to 6.0 volts.

9   Connect the electrical connector to the MAP sensor and backprobe the harness with a tachometer. With the ignition key ON (engine not running) check the signal from the MAP/BP Signal wire (middle terminal) to the

signal return wire (ground) (**see illustration**). Connect a tachometer to the signal wire and set the meter to the six-cylinder scale.

10   Use a hand-held vacuum pump and apply 10 in-Hg of vacuum to the MAP sensor and observe the tachometer readings. Without vacuum, the tachometer should read approximately 310 rpm. With 20 in-Hg of vacuum applied, the tachometer should read about 200 rpm. Look for a smooth transition between these two readings.

11   If the test results are incorrect, replace the MAP sensor.

Oxygen sensor

Refer to illustrations 4.14, 4.16 and 4.23

General description and check

12   The heated oxygen sensors (HEGO), which are located in the exhaust manifolds, monitor the oxygen content of the exhaust gas stream. The oxygen content in the exhaust reacts with the oxygen sensor to produce a voltage output which varies from 0.1-volt (high oxygen, lean mixture) to 0.9-volts (low oxygen, rich mixture). The PCM constantly monitors this variable voltage output to determine the ratio of oxygen to fuel in the mixture. The PCM alters the air/fuel mixture ratio by controlling the pulse width (open time) of the fuel injectors. A mixture ratio of 14.7 parts air to 1 part fuel is the ideal mixture ratio for minimizing exhaust

---

4.9 Using a tachometer set on the 6-cylinder scale, probe the backside of the MAP electrical sensor MAP/BP Signal wire and SIGNAL RETURN (ground wire) and check for a frequency voltage. It should be between 300 and 320 rpm with no vacuum, depending on the altitude. It is possible to place the negative probe of the voltmeter onto another more convenient ground (valve cover bolt). Now apply a vacuum of 20 in-Hg. and conform that the reading decreases to 200 to 230 rpm. There should be a smooth transition between the readings

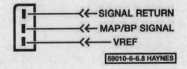

◄◄ SIGNAL RETURN
◄◄ MAP/BP SIGNAL
◄◄ VREF

59010-6-6.8 HAYNES

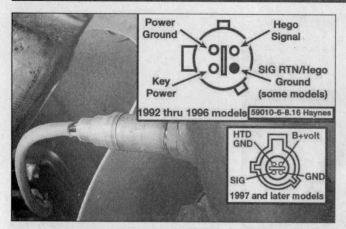

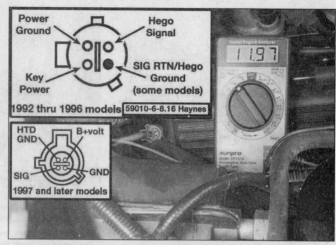

4.14 Using pins or paper clips, backprobe SIG (signal) and GND (ground) and check for a varying millivolt signal as the system adjusts the air/fuel ratio. Voltage should remain steady as the engine warms-up (open loop) and then vary from 0.10 volts (100 millivolts) to 0.9 volts (900 millivolts) if the system is operating properly (closed loop)

4.16 Working on the harness side, probe the electrical connector (Key Power) and check for battery voltage with the ignition key On and the engine not running

emissions, thus allowing the catalytic converter to operate at maximum efficiency. It is this ratio of 14.7 to 1 which the PCM and the oxygen sensor attempt to maintain at all times.

13   The oxygen sensor produces no voltage when it is below its normal operating temperature of about 600-degrees F. During this initial period before warm-up, the PCM operates in open loop mode.

14   Allow the engine to reach normal operating temperature and check that the oxygen sensor is producing a steady signal voltage between 0.35 and 0.55-volts **(see illustration)**.

15   A delay of two minutes or more between engine start-up and normal operation of the sensor, followed by a low or a high voltage signal or a short in the sensor circuit, will cause the PCM to also set a code. Codes that indicate problems in the oxygen sensor system are 41 and 42 for the two digit code system and 136, 137, 144 and 171 through 183 for the three digit code system.

16   Also check to make sure the oxygen sensor heater(s) is supplied with battery voltage **(see illustration)**.

17   When any of the above codes occur, the PCM operates in the open loop mode - that is, it controls fuel delivery in accordance with a programmed default value instead of feedback information from the oxygen sensor.

18   The proper operation of the oxygen sensor depends on four conditions:

a) *Electrical* - The low voltages generated by the sensor depend upon good, clean connections which should be checked whenever a malfunction of the sensor is suspected or indicated.

b) *Outside air supply* - The sensor is designed to allow air circulation to the internal portion of the sensor. Whenever the sensor is removed and installed or replaced, make sure the air passages are not restricted.

c) *Proper operating temperature* - The PCM will not react to the sensor signal until the sensor reaches approximately 600-degrees F. This factor must be taken into consideration when evaluating the performance of the sensor.

d) *Unleaded fuel* - The use of unleaded fuel is essential for proper operation of the sensor. Make sure the fuel you are using is of this type.

19   In addition to observing the above conditions, special care must be taken whenever the sensor is serviced:

a) The oxygen sensor has a permanently-attached pigtail and electrical connector which should not be removed from the sensor. Damage or removal of the pigtail or electrical connector can adversely affect operation of the sensor.

b) Grease, dirt and other contaminants should be kept away from the electrical connector and the louvered end of the sensor.

c) Do not use cleaning solvents of any kind on the oxygen sensor.

d) Do not drop or roughly handle the sensor.

e) The silicone boot must be installed in the correct position to prevent the boot from being melted and to allow the sensor to operate properly.

Replacement

Note: *Because it is installed in the exhaust manifold or pipe, which contracts when cool, the oxygen sensor may be very difficult to loosen when the engine is cold. Rather than risk damage to the sensor (assuming you are planning to reuse it in another manifold or pipe), start and run the engine for a minute or two, then shut it off. Be careful not to burn yourself during the following procedure.*

20   Disconnect the cable from the negative terminal of the battery.

21   Raise the vehicle and place it securely on jackstands.

22   Carefully disconnect the electrical connector from the sensor.

23   Carefully unscrew the sensor from the exhaust manifold **(see illustration)**.

24   Anti-seize compound must be used on the threads of the sensor to facilitate future removal. The threads of new sensors will already be coated with this compound, but if an old sensor is removed and reinstalled, recoat the threads.

25   Install the sensor and tighten it securely.

26   Reconnect the electrical connector of the pigtail lead to the main engine wiring harness.

27   Lower the vehicle and reconnect the cable to the negative terminal of the battery.

Throttle Position Sensor (TPS)

General description

28   The Throttle Position Sensor (TPS) is located on the end of the throttle shaft on the throttle body. By monitoring the output voltage from the TPS, the PCM can determine fuel delivery based on throttle valve angle (driver demand). A broken or loose TPS can cause intermittent bursts of fuel from the injector and an unstable idle because the PCM thinks the throttle is moving. Any problems in the TPS or circuit will set a code 23 or 53 for the two digit code system or 122 through 125 for the three digit code system.

Check

Refer to illustrations 4.29 and 4.32

29   To check the TPS, turn the ignition switch to ON (engine not running) and install the probes of the voltmeter into the ground wire and signal wire on the backside of the electrical connector **(see illustration)**. This test checks for the proper signal voltage from the TPS. **Note:** *Be careful when backprobing the electrical connector. Do not damage the wiring harness or pull on any connectors to make clean contact. Be sure the probes are placed*

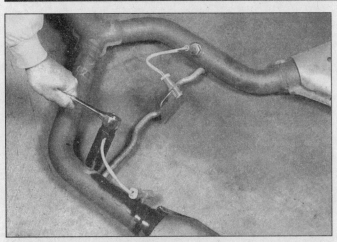

4.23 Removing an oxygen sensor using a special socket (exhaust system removed for clarity)

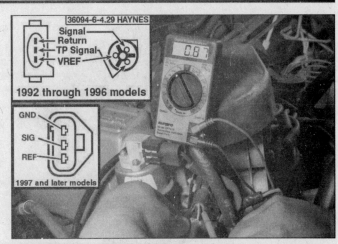

4.29 Check the signal voltage from the TPS with a voltmeter. Backprobe terminal SIG (signal) with the positive (+) probe of the voltmeter and SIG RTN (ground) with the negative probe (-) of the voltmeter. With the throttle closed, the voltage should read 0.5 to 1.0 volts

in the correct position by referring to the illustration.

30   The sensor should read 0.50 to 1.0-volt at idle. Have an assistant depress the accelerator pedal to simulate full throttle and the sensor should increase voltage to 4.0 to 5.0-volts. If the TPS voltage readings are incorrect, replace it with a new unit.

31   Also, check the TPS reference voltage. With the ignition key ON (engine not running), install the positive (+) probe of the voltmeter onto the voltage reference wire (REF). There should be approximately 5.0 volts sent from the PCM to the TPS.

32   Also, check the resistance of the potentiometer within the TPS. Disconnect the TPS electrical connector and, working on the sensor side, connect the probes of the ohmmeter onto the ground wire and the TPS signal wire. With the throttle valve fully closed, read the resistance in K-ohms **(see illustration).**

33   Now open the throttle with one hand and check the resistance again. Slowly advance the throttle until fully open. The resistance should be approximately 350 ohms. The potentiometer should exhibit a smooth change in resistance as it travels from fully closed to wide open throttle. Any deviations indicate a possible worn or damaged TPS. **Note:** *Resistance specifications vary according to year, engine and model. Be sure to observe fluctuations in the resistance readings as the throttle goes from closed to wide open.*

Replacement

34   The TPS is a non-adjustable unit. Remove the throttle body (see Chapter 4) and working on a bench, remove the two retaining screws and separate the TPS from the throttle body. **Note:** *On 1997 and later models, it will not be necessary to remove the throttle body to access the TPS mounting bolts.*

35   Installation is the reverse of removal. Be sure to use a new throttle body gasket between the upper intake manifold and the throttle body.

Mass Airflow Sensor (MAF)

General Information

36   The Mass Airflow Sensor (MAF) is located on the air intake duct. This sensor uses a hot wire sensing element to measure the amount of air entering the engine. The air passing over the hot wire causes it to cool. Consequently this change in temperature can be converted into an analog voltage signal to the PCM which in turn calculates the required fuel-injector pulse width. The MAF sensor on 1993 through 1996 models is located on top of the air cleaner housing. The MAF sensor on 1997 and later models is located inside the air cleaner housing.

Check

Refer to illustration 4.37

37   Check for power to the MAF sensor. Disconnect the MAF sensor electrical connector, work on the harness side and probe the connector to check for battery voltage **(see illustration).** Use the VPWR terminal.

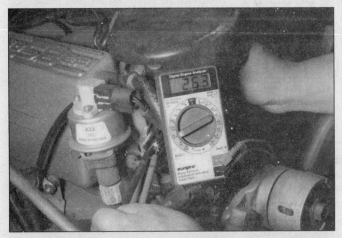

4.32 With the TPS electrical connector disconnected, check the resistance of the TPS with the throttle completely closed

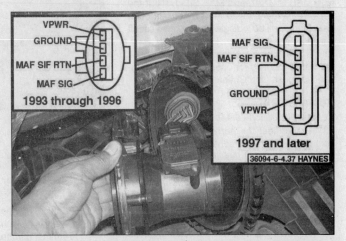

4.37 Probe the VPWR terminal on the harness side of the MAF sensor and check for battery voltage to the MAF sensor (2001 model shown)

4.44a Remove the four bolts (arrows) and separate the MAF sensor from the air cleaner housing (1994 model shown)

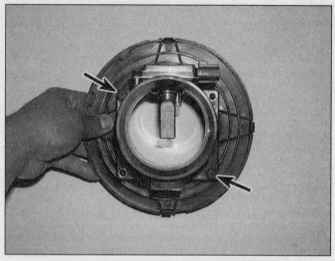

4.44b Remove the MAF sensor mounting bolts (arrows)

38   Reconnect the harness electrical connector and backprobe the MAF SIGNAL and MAF SIG RTN **(see illustration 4.37)** with the voltmeter and check for the voltage. The voltage should be 0.2 to 1.5 volts at idle. **Note:** *This test will not apply to 1997 and later models. The MAF sensor harness connector is not accessible for backprobing while the engine is running. Have the MAF sensor tested by a dealer service department or other qualified auto repair facility.*

39   Raise the engine rpm with the vehicle transmission in Park. The signal voltage from the MAF sensor should increase to about 2.0 volts at 60 mph. It is impossible to simulate these conditions in the driveway at home but it is necessary to observe the voltmeter for a fluctuation in voltage as the engine speed is raised. The vehicle will not be under load conditions in the driveway but it should manage to vary slightly.

40   Disconnect the MAF harness connector and use an ohmmeter and probe the terminals MAF SIGNAL and MAF SIG RTN. If the hot wire element inside the sensor has been damaged it will be indicated by an open circuit (infinite resistance).

41   If the voltage readings are correct, check the wiring harness for open circuits or a damaged harness (see Chapter 12).

Replacement

Refer to illustrations 4.44a and 4.44b

42   Disconnect the harness electrical connector from the MAF sensor. **Note:** *On 1997 and later models, it will be necessary to remove the air cleaner assembly from the engine (see Chapter 4) to access the MAF sensor.*

43   Remove the air cleaner outlet tube assembly (see Chapter 4).

44   Remove the MAF sensor retaining bolts **(see illustrations)**.

45   Installation is the reverse of removal.

Transmission Range (TR) sensor

Refer to illustration 4.48

General description

Note: *Most transmissions on 1992 through 1995 models are equipped with a manual lever position (MLP) sensor. The MLP sensor functions as a switching device for the starting system. The MLP sensor information is not processed by the PCM. The transmission range sensor, on 1996 and later models, relays information to the PCM for starting, TCC engagement and other driveability features of the EEC-IV and EEC-V systems. However, there are some earlier models with the 5.0L SFI and 4R70W transmissions that also are equipped with a range sensor. This sensor is powered by the PCM and cannot be*

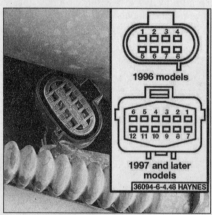

4.48 Check for battery voltage to the TR sensor on:

Terminal number 2 on 1996 4R70W transmissions
Terminal number 7 on 1996 E4OD transmissions
Terminal number 9 on all 1997 and later transmissions

tested. Have the range sensor checked by a dealer service department or other qualified auto repair facility.

46   The range sensor located on the transmission indicates to the PCM when the transmission is in Park, Neutral, Drive or Reverse. This information is used for starting, Transmission Converter Clutch (TCC), Exhaust Gas Recirculation (EGR) and Idle Speed Control (ISC) valve operation. For example, if the signal wire(s) become grounded, it may be difficult to start the engine in Park or Neutral.

47   In the event there is a problem with the range sensor, first check the terminal connectors for proper attachment.

48   Use a voltmeter and with the ignition key ON (engine not running), check for power from the fused RUN circuit **(see illustration)** of the switch. There should be voltage present.

49   Check the adjustment of the switch (see Chapter 7). If the switch is out of adjustment, perform the procedure and clear the codes. Recheck the system for any other problems.

50   Any further diagnostics of the range sensor must be performed by a dealer service department or other repair shop because this system requires a special SCAN tool to access the working parameters from the PCM.

Adjustment

51   To adjust the range sensor or to replace the sensor, refer to Chapter 7.

Air conditioning control

Air conditioning clutch control

Note: *Refer to Chapters 4 and 12 for additional information on the location of the relays.*

52   During air conditioning operation, the PCM controls the application of the air conditioning compressor clutch. The PCM controls the air conditioning clutch control relay to delay clutch engagement after the air condi-

4.57 Disconnect the VSS harness connector and check for voltage at the connector

4.58 Remove the VSS and check for a pulsing AC voltage signal as the VSS gear is slowly turned

4.66 The power steering pressure switch (arrow) is located under the power steering pump

tioning is turned ON to allow the idle air control valve to adjust the idle speed of the engine to compensate for the additional load. 53 The PCM also controls the relay to disengage the clutch in the event of an excessively high or low pressure within the system or an overheating problem.

54 In most cases, if the air conditioning does not function, the problem is probably related to the air conditioning system relays and switches and not the PCM.

55 If the air conditioning is operating properly and idle is too low when the air conditioning compressor turns on or is too high when the air conditioning compressor turns off, check for an open circuit between the air conditioning control relay and the PCM.

Vehicle Speed Sensor (VSS)

General description

56 The Vehicle Speed Sensor (VSS) is located near the rear section of the transmission. This sensor is a magnetic variable-reluctance sensor that produces a pulsing voltage whenever vehicle speed is over 3 mph. These pulses are translated by the PCM and provided for other systems for fuel and transmission shift control. The VSS is part of the Transmission Converter Clutch (TCC) system. Any problems with the VSS will usually set a Code 452.

Check

Refer to illustrations 4.57 and 4.58

57 To check the vehicle speed sensor, remove the electrical connector in the wiring harness near the sensor. Using a voltmeter, check for voltage to the sensor with the ignition key on (engine not running) **(see illustration)**. The circuit should have 10 volts or more available. If there is no voltage available, have the PCM diagnosed by a dealer service department or other qualified repair shop.

58 Place the VSS on a bench and check for a pulsing voltage signal. Observe that the voltage signal pulses from 0 to 0.5 volts. Use the AC scale on the voltmeter **(see illustra-**

tion). Replace the sensor if there are no voltage pulses produced.

Replacement

59 To replace the VSS, disconnect the electrical connector from the VSS. Remove the retaining bolt and lift the VSS from the transmission.

60 Installation is the reverse of removal.

Intake Air Temperature (IAT) Sensor

Note: *2001 and later models are not equipped with an IAT sensor.*

General description

61 The Intake Air Temperature (IAT) sensor is located inside the air intake duct. This sensor acts as a resistor which changes value according to the temperature of the air entering the engine. Low temperatures produce a high resistance value (for example on OBD-I models, at 68 degrees F the resistance is 27.3 K-ohms) while high temperatures produce low resistance values (at 212-degrees F the resistance is 2.07 K-ohms. The PCM supplies approximately 5-volts (reference voltage) to the IAT sensor. The signal voltage back to the PCM will vary according to the temperature of the incoming air. The voltage will be high when the air temperature is cold and low when the air temperature is warm. Any problems with the IAT sensor will usually set a code 54 or 64 on the two digit code system or 112, 113 or 114 on the three digit code system.

Check

62 To check the IAT sensor, disconnect the two-prong electrical connector and turn the ignition key ON but do not start the engine.

63 Measure the voltage (reference voltage). The VOM should read approximately 5-volts.

64 If the voltage signal is not correct, have the PCM diagnosed by a dealer service department or other repair shop.

65 Measure the resistance across the sensor terminals. The resistance should be HIGH

when the air temperature is LOW. Next, start the engine and let it idle (cold). Wait awhile and let the engine reach operating temperature. Turn the ignition OFF, disconnect the IAT sensor and measure the resistance across the terminals. The resistance should be LOW when the air temperature is HIGH. If the sensor does not exhibit this change in resistance, replace it with a new part.

Power steering pressure switch

Refer to illustration 4.66

66 Turning the steering wheel increases power steering fluid pressure and engine load. The pressure switch **(see illustration)** will close before the load can cause an idle problem. A problem in the power steering pressure switch circuit will set a code 519 or 521 (three digit code system only).

67 A pressure switch that will not open or an open circuit from the PCM will cause timing to retard at idle and this will affect idle quality.

68 A pressure switch that will not close or an open circuit may cause the engine to die when the power steering system is used heavily.

69 Any problems with the power steering pressure switch or circuit should be repaired by a dealer service department or other qualified repair shop.

Brake On/Off (BOO) switch

General Information

70 The brake On/Off switch (BOO) tells the PCM when the brakes are being applied. The switch closes when brakes are applied and opens when the brakes are released. The BOO switch is located on the brake pedal assembly.

71 The brake light circuit and bulbs are wired into the BOO circuit so it is important in diagnosing any driveability problems to make sure all the brake light bulbs are working properly (not burned out) or the driver may experience poor idle quality.

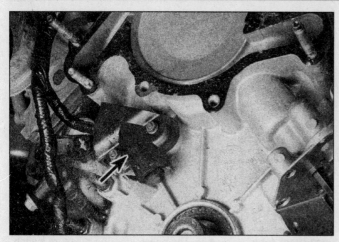

4.75 Location of the crankshaft sensor (arrow) on the V6 engine

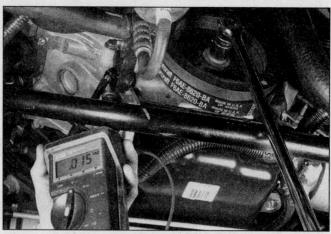

4.77 With the voltmeter set on the AC scale, check for a pulsing voltage signal between 0 and 0.05 volts as the engine is slowly rotated

Check

72   Disconnect the electrical connector from the BOO switch and using a 12 volt test light, check for battery voltage to the BOO switch.

73   Also, check continuity from the BOO switch to the brake light bulbs. Change any burned out bulbs or damaged wire looms.

Replacement

74   Refer to Chapter 9 for the replacement procedure.

Crankshaft position sensor (CKP)

General information

Refer to illustrations 4.75

75   Later models are equipped with a crankshaft position sensor. The crankshaft position sensor **(see illustration)** is mounted adjacent to a pulse wheel located on the crankshaft. The crankshaft sensor monitors the pulse wheel as the teeth pass under the magnetic field created by the sensor. The pulse wheel has 35 teeth and a spot where one tooth is missing. By monitoring the lost tooth, the crankshaft sensor determines the piston travel, crankshaft position and speed information and sends the information to the PCM. The OBD-II system can detect a variety of different CKP sensor problems and set codes to indicate the specific trouble area. Trouble code 385 is a designated CKP circuit code. If an OBD-II SCAN tool or code reader is not available, have the codes extracted from the PCM by a dealer service department or other qualified automotive repair facility. **Note:** *The crankshaft sensor is also used to detect misfire in any one of the 8 or 10 cylinders. This special misfire detection system will record a trouble code to indicate which cylinder is misfiring. Trouble codes 301 through 310 are all misfire detection trouble codes,*

Check

Refer to illustration 4.77

76   Disconnect the CKP sensor electrical connector and with the ignition key ON (engine not running), check for battery voltage to the CKP sensor.

77   Connect a voltmeter to the crankshaft sensor and using the AC scale, check the voltage pulses as the gear is slowly rotated **(see illustration)**. Use a large socket and breaker bar to rotate the crankshaft pulley.

78   If no pulsing voltage signal is produced, replace the crankshaft sensor.

Replacement

79   Remove the electrical connector and the retaining bolt and lift the assembly from the engine block. **Note:** *On 2001 through 2003 4.6L, 5.4L and 6.8L engines, unbolt and set aside the AC compressor without disconnecting the refrigerant lines. On 2004 and later models, it is only necessary to remove the drivebelt for access to the CKP.*

80   Installation is the reverse of removal.

Camshaft position sensor

General information

Refer to illustration 4.81

81   OBD-II models are equipped with a camshaft sensor as well as a crankshaft sensor. The camshaft sensor signals the PCM to begin sequential pulsation of the fuel injectors. This camshaft sensor on 4.2L V6 models is a Hall Effect switching device activated by a single vane. This camshaft sensor is mounted on the top of the engine in the normal location of the distributor **(see illustration)**. The camshaft sensor in the 4.6L, 5.4L and 6.8L models is a variable reluctance device which is triggered by the high point mark on the camshaft. The sensor is mounted on the front of the cylinder head near the camshaft sprocket. **Note:** *On 1992 through 1996 models, the camshaft position sensor, also called the PIP sensor, is located in the distributor. It consists of the distributor hall-effect switch and a rotary-vane cup. The passing of the open and closed portion of the vane past the hall switch results in a high/low voltage change that is seen by the PCM. The PCM then determines when to trigger the ignition module. Have the vehicle diagnosed by a dealer service department or other qualified auto repair facility.*

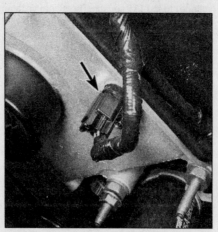

4.81 Location of the camshaft position sensor on the 4.2L engine

4.85 Location of the camshaft position sensor on a 4.6L engine

4.86 Working on the bench, carefully pass a metal object close to the tip of the camshaft sensor and see if the AC voltage fluctuates - if the camshaft sensor does not exhibit any reaction as the magnetic field is broken, the sensor must be replaced

Check

V6 models

82   With the ignition key ON (engine not running), check the signal voltage. Backprobe the signal wire (+) (dark green) from the computer and the ground wire (-) (black/white) and while slowly rotating the engine, observe that the voltage pulses from 0 to 5.0 volts. **Note:** *Do not crank the engine over using the starter but instead install a breaker bar and socket onto the front crankshaft pulley bolt and rotate the engine slowly by hand.*

83   If there is no pulsing signal voltage but instead a steady 5.0 volt signal, then most likely the camshaft sensor is defective. If there is no voltage available, then the PCM is not supplying voltage to the camshaft sensor. In the former case, replace the camshaft sensor. In the latter case, have the PCM checked by a dealer service department or other qualified automotive repair facility.

V8 models

Refer to illustrations 4.85 and 4.86

84   Check for battery voltage to the camshaft position sensor with the ignition key ON (engine not running).

85   Remove the camshaft sensor from the engine and place it on a clean workbench **(see illustration)**.

86   Check the AC voltage output. Connect the probes of a voltmeter set on the AC scale onto the camshaft sensor and observe that it produces a voltage pulse as a metal object is passed over the tip of the sensor **(see illustration)**.

87   If no pulsing voltage signal is produced, replace the camshaft sensor.

Replacement

V6 models

Refer to illustrations 4.94 and 4.98

Note: *The camshaft position sensor on 4.2L models so equipped is mounted on a synchronizer assembly, which is essentially a drive*

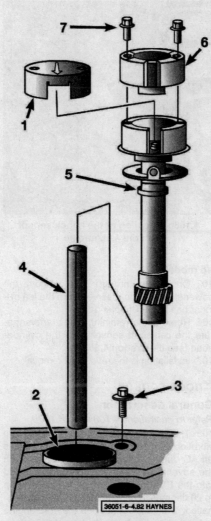

4.94 Exploded view of the camshaft position sensor and synchronizer assembly - 4.2L engine

1   *Synchro positioning tool*
2   *Timing chain cover*
3   *Clamp*
4   *Oil pump intermediate shaft*
5   *Synchronizer*
6   *Camshaft Position sensor*
7   *Bolt*

unit for the sensor. If you are simply replacing the cam position sensor, it is not necessary to remove the synchronizer assembly from the engine - just remove the screws from the sensor, detach it from the synchronizer and install the new sensor. However, many engine repair procedures require removal of the synchronizer assembly, in which case it will be necessary to perform the following procedure to time the synchronizer. This procedure requires the use of a special tool to properly align the sensor; read through the entire procedure and obtain the necessary tool before beginning.

88   Position the number 1 piston at TDC. Refer to Chapter 2B for the procedure.

89   Disconnect the cable from the negative battery terminal.

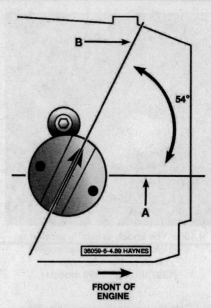

FRONT OF ENGINE

4.98 With the cam synchronizer installed and fully seated in the timing cover, the arrow on the tool (B) should point 54 degrees from the centerline of the engine (A)

90   Mark the relative position of the camshaft position sensor electrical connector so the assembly can be oriented properly upon installation (this is only necessary if the synchronizer assembly will be removed). Disconnect the electrical connector from the camshaft position sensor. Remove the screws and detach the sensor from the synchronizer assembly.

91   Partially drain the cooling system (see Chapter 1).

92   Remove the EGR valve and EGR tube (see Section 6).

93   Disconnect the heater hose outlet line (see Chapter 3).

94   Remove the sensor mounting screws **(see illustration)** and lift the sensor from the housing.

95   If you will be removing the synchronizer assembly, remove the bolt and withdraw the synchronizer from the engine. **Note:** *Remove the oil pump intermediate shaft along with the camshaft position sensor synchronizer assembly.*

96   Place the special alignment tool onto the synchronizer assembly. Align the vane of the synchronizer with the radial slot in the special tool.

97   Turn the tool on the synchronizer until the boss on the tool is engaged with the notch on the synchronizer.

98   Transfer the oil pump intermediate shaft onto the synchronizer assembly. Lubricate the gear, thrust washer and lower bearing of the synchronizer assembly with clean engine oil. Insert the assembly into the engine, with the arrow on the tool pointing 54-degrees clockwise from the engine's centerline **(see illustration)**.

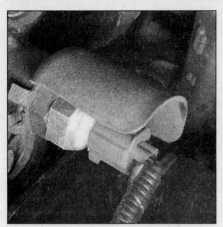

4.108a The knock sensor is located on the right side of the lower engine block on the 4.2L engine (1997 through 1999 models)

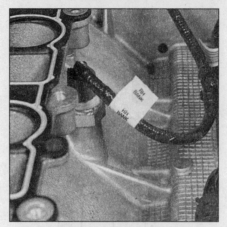

4.108b Location of the knock sensor on the 4.6L engine

99 Turn the tool clockwise a little so the synchronizer engages with the oil pump intermediate shaft. Push down on the synchronizer, turning the tool gently until the gear on the synchronizer engages with the gear on the camshaft.

100 Install the hold-down bolt and tighten it securely. Remove the positioning tool.

101 Install the EGR assembly.

102 Reconnect the heater hose outlet to the engine block.

103 Install the camshaft position sensor and tighten the screws securely. **Caution:** *Check the position of the electrical connector on the sensor to make sure it is aligned with the mark you made in Step 90. If it isn't oriented correctly, DO NOT rotate the synchronizer to reposition it - doing so will result in the fuel system being out of time with the engine, possibly damaging the engine (and at the very least cause driveability problems). If the connector is not oriented properly, repeat the synchronizer installation procedure.*

104 Plug in the electrical connector to the sensor and reconnect the cable to the negative terminal of the battery.

V8 models

105 On models through 2000, remove the power steering fluid reservoir from the left cylinder head (see Chapter 10).

106 Remove the retaining screw and separate the camshaft sensor from the cylinder head **(see illustration 4.85)**.

107 Installation is the reverse of removal.

Knock sensor

General description

Refer to illustrations 4.108a and 4.108b

108 The knock sensor detects abnormal vibration in the engine. The sensor produces an AC output voltage which increases with the severity of the knock. The signal is fed into the PCM and the timing is retarded up to 20 degrees to compensate for severe detonation. The knock sensor on the 4.9L engine is located on the lower section of the intake manifold. The knock sensor on 1997 through 1999 4.2L models is located on the right side of the engine block under the exhaust manifold **(see illustration)** or on the back of the cylinder head on 2000 and later 4.2L models. The knock sensor is located in the lifter valley under the intake manifold on 4.6L, 5.4L and 6.8L models **(see illustration)**.

Check

109 Problems with the knock sensor can be monitored using a scan tool, have a dealer service department check the system for correct operation.

Cylinder Head Temperature (CHT) sensor (4.6L, 5.4L and 6.8L engines)

General description

Refer to illustration 4.110

110 The cylinder head temperature sensor is a major component of the Fail Safe Cooling system. This sensor varies the value of its voltage output in accordance with temperature changes **(see illustration)**. The change in the resistance values will directly affect the voltage signal from the CHT sensor. As the sensor temperature DECREASES, the resistance values will INCREASE (voltage increases). If the cylinder head temperature exceeds 265-degrees F, the PCM disables four (V8) or 5 (V10) fuel injectors at a time. The cylinders that do not receive fuel act as cooling air pumps for the other cylinders. If the temperature exceeds 330-degrees F, the PCM disables all the fuel injectors.

Check

111 Check the resistance value of the CHT sensor while it is completely cold (50 to 65-degrees F = 37,000 to 59,000 ohms). Next, start the engine and warm it up until it reaches operating temperature. The resistance should be lower (185 to 195-degrees F = 2,750 to 3,200 ohms). **Note:** *Access to the CHT sensor makes it difficult to position electrical probes on the terminals. If necessary, remove the sensor and perform the tests in a pan of heated water to simulate the conditions.*

112 If the resistance values on the sensor are correct, check the reference voltage from the PCM to the sensor. The reference voltage should be approximately 5.0 volts.

Replacement

113 To remove the sensor, the alternator must be removed from the engine (see Chap-

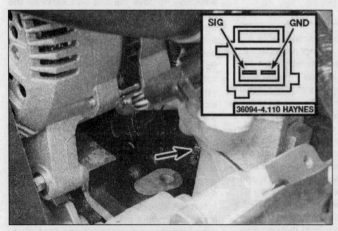

4.110 Location of the cylinder head temperature sensor on the 5.4L engine

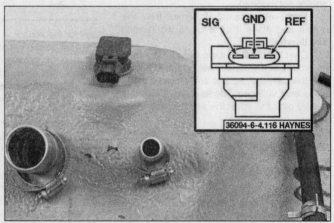

4.116 The fuel tank pressure sensor is located on the top of the fuel tank

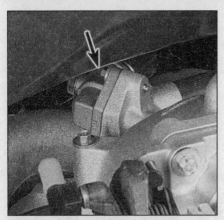

5.2 Location of the IAC valve (arrow) on the 4.6L engine

ter 5). **Note:** *On 2001 and later 4.6L, 5.4L and 6.8L engines, disconnect the intake manifold tuning valve connector. On 2004 and later models, the intake manifold must be removed to replace the CHT sensor.*

114 Unplug the electrical connector, then carefully unscrew the CHT sensor. **Caution:** *Handle the CHT sensor with care. Damage to this sensor will affect the operation of the entire fuel injection system.* Install the sensor and tighten it securely.

Fuel tank pressure (FTP) sensor

General information

115 The fuel tank pressure (FTP) sensor is used to monitor the fuel tank pressure or vacuum during the OBD-II test portion for emissions integrity. This test scans various sensors and output actuators to detect abnormal amounts of fuel vapors that may not be purging into the canister and/or the intake system for recycling. The FTP sensor helps the PCM monitor this pressure differential (pressure vs. vacuum) inside the fuel tank.

Check

Refer to illustration 4.116

116 With the ignition key ON (engine not running), check for REF voltage to the fuel tank pressure sensor **(see illustration)**. Voltage should be available. It may be difficult to access the harness with the fuel tank in place. Find a location in the harness near the tank to check for voltage without removing the FTP sensor and fuel tank from the vehicle.

117 If voltage is available, the remaining checks must be performed with a specialized scan tool. Have the FTP sensor and EVAP system checked by a dealer service department or other qualified repair facility.

5 Idle Air Control (IAC) valve - check, removal and adjustment

Caution: *The throttle body on these models is coated with a sludge resistant material*

designed to protect the bore and throttle plate. Do not attempt to clean the interior of the throttle body. The throttle body is designed to resist sludge accumulation and cleaning may impair the performance of the engine.

Note: *The minimum idle speed is pre-set at the factory and is not adjustable under normal circumstances. If the idle fluctuates, stalls, idles high or speeds out of control, follow these quick checks to determine if the IAC valve is damaged. Because idle problems involve possible air leaks, fuel injector problems, malfunctioning TPS, PCM problems, etc. have the IAC valve and system diagnosed by a dealer service department or other qualified repair facility.*

Note: *1992 through 1996 models are equipped with a Bypass Air-Idle Speed Control (BPA-ISC) valve. This valve is designed differently than the later IAC valves but functions the same. Follow the procedure below to check the idle speed control system.*

Check

Refer to illustration 5.2

1 The Idle Air Control (IAC) valve controls the amount of air that bypasses the throttle valve, which controls the engine idle speed. This output actuator is mounted on the throttle body and is controlled by voltage pulses sent from the PCM (computer). The IAC valve within the body moves in or out, allowing more or less intake air into the system. To increase idle speed, the PCM extends the IAC valve from the seat and allows more air to bypass the throttle bore. To decrease idle speed, the PCM retracts the IAC valve towards the seat, reducing the air flow.

2 To check the system, first check for the voltage signal from the PCM. Turn the ignition key On (engine not running) and with a voltmeter, probe the wires of the IAC valve electrical connector (harness side). It should be approximately 10.5 to 12.5 volts **(see illustration)**. This indicates that the IAC valve is receiving the proper signal from the PCM.

3 Next, remove the valve (see Step 6) and check the pintle for excessive carbon deposits. If necessary, clean it with carburetor cleaner spray. Also, clean the valve housing to remove any deposits.

4 Any further testing of the PCM must be performed by a dealer service department or other qualified auto repair facility.

Adjustment

5 The idle speed is not adjustable. This procedure requires a special scan tool to extract working parameters from the Electronic Engine Control (EEC) system while it is running. Have the procedure performed by a dealer service department or other qualified repair shop.

Removal

6 Unplug the electrical connector from the IAC valve.

7 Remove the two valve attaching screws and withdraw the valve assembly from the throttle body.

8 Check the condition of the O-ring. If it's hardened or deteriorated, replace it.

9 Clean the sealing surface and the bore of the throttle body assembly with a shop rag or soft cloth to ensure a good seal. **Caution:** *The IAC valve itself is an electrical component and must not be soaked in any liquid cleaner, as damage may result.*

Installation

10 Position the new O-ring on the IAC valve. Lubricate the O-ring with a light film of engine oil. **Note:** *On BPA-ISC valves, replace the gasket.*

11 Install the IAC valve and tighten the screws securely.

12 Plug in the electrical connector at the IAC valve assembly.

6 Exhaust Gas Recirculation (EGR) system

General description

1 The EGR system is used to lower NOx (oxides of nitrogen) emission levels caused by high combustion temperatures. The EGR recirculates a small amount of exhaust gases into the intake manifold. The additional mixture lowers the temperature of combustion thereby reducing the formation of NOx compounds.

2 All engines are equipped with the Electronic Exhaust Gas Recirculation (EEGR) system. This system relies upon the PCM for EGR control. There are two different types of EGR systems on these models:

a) *On 1992 through 1996 models, the control module (PCM) calculates the desired flow of exhaust gases into the combustion chamber and subsequently controls the EGR valve position with the EGR vacuum regulator. The EGR Valve Position (EVP) sensor detects the exact position of the EGR valve pintle and relays the information to the PCM. The PCM in turn, uses this information to regulate the duty cycle (On/Off time) of the EGR vacuum regulator. A duty cycle of 50-percent would hold the EGR valve half way open. The EEGR system uses "electronic" components to control the EGR valve.*

b) *On 1997 and later models, the EGR flow rate is determined by monitoring the pressure across a fixed metering orifice as exhaust gasses pass through it. This system is called the Differential Pressure Feedback (DPFE) system. The pressure sensor monitors upstream (before) and downstream (after) exhaust backpressure. This backpressure coefficient is relayed to the PCM and the correct amount of EGR (duty cycle) is applied to the EGR vacuum regulator control (EVR). By calculating the difference between the two pressures, the PCM determines exactly the EGR flow rate at all driving conditions. The DPFE is more accurate than early systems in that the computer does not have to guess at the upstream pressure coefficient to determine EGR flow rate as the engine drives through various road conditions such as hard acceleration, downshifting, engine misfire, poor fuel combustion, etc. All these conditions will cause the exhaust backpressure to vary and requires more strict and responsive EGR control to limit NOx emission levels.*

Check

3   Too much EGR flow tends to weaken combustion, causing the engine to run rough or stop. When EGR flow is excessive, the engine can stop after a cold start or at idle after deceleration, the vehicle can surge at cruising speeds or the idle may be rough. If the EGR valve remains constantly open, the engine may not idle at all.

4   Too little or no EGR flow allows combustion temperatures to get too high during acceleration and load conditions. This can cause spark knock (detonation), engine overheating or emission test failure.

5   The following checks will help you pinpoint problems in the EGR system. **Warning**: *Where the procedure says to lift up on the EGR valve diaphragm, it's a good idea to wear a heat-resistant glove to prevent burns.*

EGR valve

6   The EGR valve is controlled by a normally-open EGR vacuum regulator (EVR), which allows vacuum to pass when energized. The PCM energizes the EVR to turn on the EGR. The PCM controls the EGR when three conditions are present: engine coolant is above 113-degrees F, the TPS is at part throttle and the MAF sensor (if equipped) is in its mid-range.

7   Make sure the vacuum hoses are in good condition and hooked up correctly.

6.14 Working on the harness side of the Electronic Vacuum Regulator (arrow) electrical connector, check for battery voltage (4.6L engine)

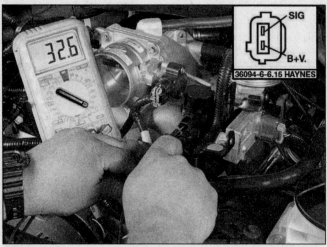

6.15 Check the resistance of the EGR vacuum regulator. It should be 30 to 70 ohms (4.6L engine)

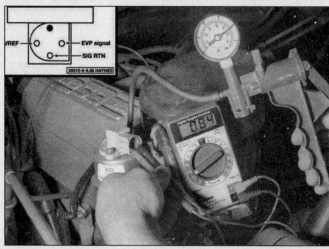

6.16 Check the resistance across terminals EVP and VREF on the sensor - without vacuum it should be about 5,500 ohms and with 20 in-Hg of vacuum about 100 ohms (watch for a smooth transition between the two resistance values as vacuum is applied)

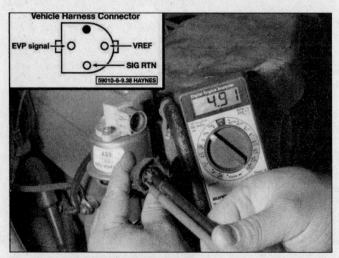

6.17 With the ignition key On (engine not running), probe terminals VREF and SIG-RTN with a voltmeter and check for reference voltage from the PCM - it should be about 5.0 volts

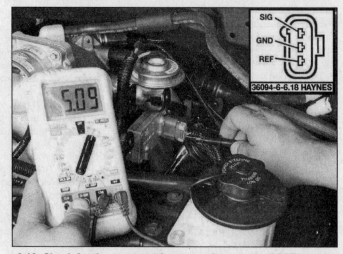

6.18 Check for the correct reference voltage to the DPFE sensor with the ignition key ON (engine not running)

8   To perform a leakage test, attach a vacuum pump to the EGR valve. Apply a vacuum of 5 to 6 in-Hg to the valve. The EGR valve should hold vacuum.

9   If access is possible, position your finger tip under the vacuum diaphragm and apply vacuum to the EGR valve. You should feel movement of the EGR diaphragm.

10   Remove the EGR valve and clean the inlet and outlet ports with a wire brush or scraper. Do not sandblast the valve or clean it with gasoline or solvents. These liquids will destroy the EGR valve diaphragm.

11   If the specified conditions are not met, replace the EGR valve.

EGR control system

Refer to illustrations 6.14 and 6.15

12   If a code is displayed there are several possibilities for EGR failure. Engine coolant temperature sensor, TPS, MAF sensor, TCC system and the engine rpm govern the parameters the EGR system use for distinguishing the correct ON time.

13   All systems use an Electronic Vacuum Regulator to control the amount of exhaust gas through the EGR valve. The valve is normally open (engine at operating temperature) and the vacuum source is a ported signal. The PCM uses a controlled "pulse width" or electronic signal to turn the EGR ON and OFF (the "duty cycle"). The duty cycle should be zero percent (no EGR) when in Park or Neutral, when the TPS input is below the specified value or when Wide Open Throttle (WOT) is indicated.

14   To check the EGR vacuum regulator, disconnect the electrical connector to the EGR vacuum regulator, turn the ignition key ON (engine not running) and check for voltage to the solenoid **(see illustration)**. Battery voltage should be present.

15   Next, use an ohmmeter and check the resistance of the EGR vacuum regulator **(see illustration)**. It should be between 30 and 70 ohms.

EGR valve position sensor (1992 through 1996 models)

Refer to illustrations 6.16 and 6.17

16   Check the operation of the EGR valve position (EVP) sensor. This sensor is attached to the EGR valve to provide the PCM with the exact position of the EGR valve pintle. Disconnect the EVP electrical connector and, working on the sensor side **(see illustration)**, install the probes of an ohmmeter into EVP and VREF. Check the resistance of the sensor while applying vacuum to the EGR valve. It should fluctuate between 5,500 to 100 ohms as vacuum is slowly applied.

17   Check for reference voltage to the sensor. With the ignition key on (engine not running), check for voltage on the harness side of the EVP electrical connector **(see illustration)** on terminal VREF. It should be between 4.0 and 6.0 volts. If the test results are incorrect, replace the EVP sensor.

Differential Pressure Feedback (DPFE) sensor (1997 and later models)

Refer to illustration 6.18

18   Check for reference voltage to the DPFE sensor. With the ignition key on (engine not running), check for voltage on the harness side of the electrical connector **(see illustration)** on terminal VREF. It should be between 4.0 and 6.0 volts. If the test results are incorrect, replace the DPFE sensor.

19   Check the operation of the Differential Pressure Feedback (DPFE) sensor. **Note:** *The DPFE sensor on the Differential Pressure Feedback EGR systems have two exhaust lines hooked into the EGR tube.* Check for signal voltage to the sensor. Backprobe the correct terminals and check for a voltage signal while the engine is running first at cold temperatures and then at warm operating temperatures. With the engine cold there should be NO EGR therefore the voltage should be approximately 0.20 to 0.70 volts. As the engine starts to warm and EGR is signaled by the computer, voltage values should increase to approximately 4.0 to 6.0 volts.

Component replacement

EGR valve

20   When buying a new EGR valve, make sure that you get the correct EGR valve. Use the stamped code located on the top of the EGR valve when purchasing an EGR valve.

21   Detach the cable from the negative terminal of the battery.

22   Remove the air cleaner housing assembly (see Chapter 4).

23   Disconnect the EGR valve electrical connector and vacuum hose.

24   Remove the EGR pipe from the exhaust manifold and the EGR valve. **Note:** *On some models it may be necessary to remove the dipstick to gain access to the EGR pipe.*

25   Remove the EGR valve retainer bolts and EGR valve from intake manifold.

26   Remove the EGR gasket, clean the manifold of any remaining gasket material and clean the EGR valve gasket surface if valve is to be reused. On 2005 models, the EGR gasket has a raised ridge in the center. This ridge faces toward the engine during installation.

27   Installation is the reverse of removal.

EGR pipe

28   Remove the EGR valve.

29   Disconnect the EGR pipe at the exhaust manifold, on some models it is necessary to remove the EGR pipe to manifold connector.

30   Installation is the reverse of removal.

EGR vacuum regulator

31   Detach the cable from the negative terminal of the battery.

32   Unplug the electrical connector from the solenoid.

34   Clearly label and detach both vacuum hoses.

35   Remove the solenoid mounting screw and remove the solenoid.

36   Installation is the reverse of removal.

6.40 Remove the DPFE sensor mounting nuts

DPFE sensor

Refer to illustration 6.40

37   Detach the cable from the negative terminal of the battery.

38   Unplug the electrical connector from the sensor.

39   Clearly label and detach both vacuum hoses.

40   Remove the sensor mounting nuts **(see illustration)** and remove the assembly.

41   Installation is the reverse of removal.

7   Evaporative Emissions Control System (EECS)

General description

1   This system is designed to trap and store fuel vapors that evaporate from the fuel tank, throttle body and intake manifold during non-operation or idling, store them in the charcoal canister and then route them into the combustion chamber to be burned during engine operation.

2   The Evaporative Emission Control System (EECS) consists of a charcoal-filled canister and the lines connecting the canister to the fuel tank, ported vacuum and intake manifold vacuum. 1997 and later models are also equipped with a fuel vapor management valve (VMV), a fuel tank pressure sensor, fuel filler cap and fuel vapor valve.

3   Fuel vapors are transferred from the fuel tank, throttle body and intake manifold to a canister where they are stored when the engine is not operating. When the engine is running, the fuel vapors are purged from the canister by a purge control solenoid, which is PCM controlled, and consumed in the normal combustion process. **Note:** *On 1997 and later models, the fuel vapors are purged from the canister by a vapor management valve (VMV) which is PCM controlled, and consumed in the normal combustion process. The fuel tank pressure sensor relays the inside fuel tank pressure to the PCM which in turn regulates the EVAP system purge control system.*

Check

4   Poor idle, stalling and poor driveability can be caused by an inoperative purge control solenoid (1992 through 1996 models), a vapor management valve (1997 and later models), a damaged canister, split or cracked hoses or hoses connected to the wrong tubes.

5   Evidence of fuel loss or fuel odor can be caused by fuel leaking from fuel lines or the throttle body, a cracked or damaged canister, an inoperative bowl vent valve, an inoperative purge valve or VMV, disconnected, misrouted, kinked, deteriorated or damaged vapor or control hoses or an improperly seated air cleaner or air cleaner gasket.

6   Inspect each hose attached to the canister for kinks, leaks and breaks along its entire length. Repair or replace as necessary.

7   Inspect the canister. If it is cracked or damaged, replace it.

8   Look for fuel leaking from the bottom of the canister. If fuel is leaking, replace the canister and check the hoses and hose routing.

Purge control valve (1992 through 1996 models)

9   Apply a short length of hose to the lower tube of the purge valve assembly and attempt to blow through it. Little or no air should pass into the canister (a small amount of air will pass because the canister has a constant-purge hole).

10   With a hand vacuum pump, apply vacuum through the control vacuum signal tube near the throttle body to the purge control solenoid diaphragm.

11   If the purge control solenoid does not hold vacuum for at least 20 seconds, the purge control solenoid is leaking and must be replaced.

12   If the diaphragm holds vacuum, apply battery voltage to the purge control solenoid and observe that vacuum (vapors) are allowed to pass through to the intake system.

Vapor management valve (VMV) (1997 and later)

Refer to illustration 7.14

13   Check the hoses around the VMV for damage or incorrectly routed lines. Correct if necessary.

14   Check the VMV for battery voltage. With the ignition key ON (engine not running), check for battery voltage on the B+ VOLT terminal on the computer side of the VMV harness connector **(see illustration)**. If there is no battery voltage available, have the PCM diagnosed by a dealer service department or other qualified automotive repair facility. If reference voltage is available to the VMV, have the VMV checked using an OBD-II SCAN tool at a dealer service department or other qualified repair facility.

15   The easiest way to check for excess fuel vapor pressure in the fuel tank is simply remove the gas cap and listen for the sound of pressure release similar to a flat tire or air compressor discharge. If the weather is extremely hot, take into account for the extra

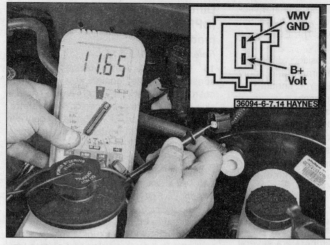

7.14 Check for battery voltage to the Vapor Management valve with the ignition key ON (engine not running)

pressure from the heated molecules. The most accurate test is using the OBD-II SCAN tool. This will run a series of checks using the fuel tank pressure sensor and other output actuators to detect excess pressure. Have the vehicle diagnosed by a dealer service department or other qualified automotive repair facility.

Component replacement

16   Clearly label, then detach, all vacuum lines from the canister.

17   Loosen the canister mounting clamp bolt and pull the canister out.

18   Installation is the reverse of removal.

8   Thermactor systems - operation and checks

Refer to illustration 8.53

General description

1   Thermactor systems are employed to reduce carbon monoxide and hydrocarbon emissions, both a result of incomplete combustion. The thermactor air-injection system functions by continuing combustion of unburned gasses after they leave the combustion chamber by injecting fresh air (from the engine-driven air pump) into the hot exhaust gases at some point after they exit the exhaust ports.

Managed Thermactor Air (MTA) (EEC controlled)

2   The control of the secondary air supply system is totally electronic. After sensing engine demand and operating conditions, the EEC Powertrain Control Module will determine the proper status (vacuum applied or not) for both air bypass and diverter valves and issue the appropriate commands. The integrity of the electrical portion of the control system is constantly monitored by the EEC self-checking system.

Operation

3   Under all conditions, manifold vacuum to the bypass and diverter valves is con-

trolled by the EEC computer (PCM) through two normally-closed solenoid vacuum valves. The Thermactor Air Bypass (TAB) solenoid controls vacuum to the bypass valve and the Thermactor Air Diverter (TAD) solenoid controls vacuum to the diverter valve. The solenoid vacuum switches are supplied continuous power through the EEC-IV power relay. When certain operating conditions are met, the PCM will exercise control over the normally-closed vacuum switches by grounding the power return circuit of the solenoid internally within the PCM. When grounded, the solenoids open, allowing vacuum to be applied to the applicable air control valve. Later models renamed the solenoid vacuum switches as the AIR Diverter (AIRD) solenoid and AIR Bypass (AIRB) solenoid. Their function is identical.

Troubleshooting options

4   The proper operation of thermactor systems can be difficult to judge since in some cases a failure can exist with no outward symptoms or signs. This is particularly true in the case of EEC-controlled systems where many functions occur in response to conditions impossible to duplicate during a test situation. For this reason, the EEC-IV system incorporates a self-check function that monitors the thermactor system during actual operating conditions. If a problem is noted, the EEC-IV will light up the dash mounted "check engine" or "service engine" indicator light and a specific trouble code (DTC) indicating the nature of the problem is generated and stored in the EEC memory.

5   If a concern is raised or if vehicle fails state smog certification, early thermactor systems must be diagnosed in the time-honored, step by step "process of elimination" fashion as outlined in this Section. With the EEC-IV system a second choice is available. The stored trouble codes can be retrieved to aid the technician in troubleshooting several thermactor problems and avoid wasted time spent checking good components and circuits. If you wish to use them, refer to Section 2 for procedures in obtaining and utilizing trouble codes. Otherwise, use operating symptoms to

help guide you through the following step-by-step procedures.

Pump and control valve checks

Air supply pump check

6   Check and adjust the drivebelt tension if necessary and applicable (refer to Chapter 1).

7   Disconnect the air supply hose at the air bypass valve inlet or air pump outlet.

8   The pump is operating satisfactorily if airflow is felt at the pump outlet with the engine running at idle, increasing as the engine speed is increased.

9   If the air pump does not successfully pass the above tests, check the inlet filter or hose for an obstruction. If the inlet tract is free of restrictions, replace the pump with a new or rebuilt unit.

Air bypass valve check (normally-closed)

Caution: *The majority of bypass valves will be normally-closed types recognizable by the top-mounted vacuum port. If you have an early normally-open valve (vacuum port on side), simply reverse the expected value.*

10   Remove the vacuum line from the bypass valve.

11   Disconnect the diverter valve.

12   Start the engine and check for airflow at the bypass valve dump outlet (or ports) while in default state. If no flow is indicated, replace the valve.

13   Using a hand-held vacuum pump (or convenient source of manifold vacuum), apply vacuum to the valve and check the bypass valve at the outlet for airflow. If no flow is indicated or the valve will not hold vacuum, replace the valve.

14   If operating properly, reconnect the hoses and continue to the diverter valve test.

Air diverter valve check (normally-closed)

15   Remove the vacuum hose from the diverter valve and disconnect the upstream (exhaust manifold) and downstream (converter) outlet hoses.

16   Start the engine and check for airflow at the downstream (converter) outlet. If no flow is indicated, verify that input air from the bypass valve is available. If not, proceed to bypass-valve check or vacuum-control check. If input air is available, replace the diverter valve.

17   Using a hand-held vacuum pump (or convenient source of manifold vacuum), apply vacuum to the valve and check the valve upstream (exhaust manifold) outlet for airflow. If no flow is indicated or the valve will not hold vacuum, replace the valve.

18   If operating properly, reconnect the hoses and continue to vacuum-control checks.

Combined air bypass and diverter valve

19   Mark and remove both vacuum hoses from the valve and disconnect the upstream (exhaust manifold) and downstream (converter) outlet hoses. Verify that the proper vacuum port is being used for each test.

20   Start the engine and check for airflow at the dump outlet (or ports). If no flow is indicated, replace the valve. Note: *Airflow should be restricted from both upstream and downstream outlets during this test. If flow is indicated, replace the valve.*

21   Using a hand-held vacuum pump (or convenient source of manifold vacuum), apply vacuum to the bypass vacuum port and check the valve at the downstream (converter) outlet for airflow. If no flow is indicated or the valve will not hold vacuum, replace the valve.

22   Tee a vacuum line from the hand pump (or manifold vacuum line) and simultaneously apply vacuum to both vacuum ports on the valve.

23   Check for airflow at upstream (exhaust manifold) outlet. If no flow is indicated, replace the valve. Note: *Airflow should be restricted from the downstream outlet during this test. If flow is indicated, replace the valve.*

24   If operating properly, reconnect the hoses and continue to *Vacuum control checks.*

Vacuum control checks

Caution: *The following checks assume that the bypass and diverter valve are themselves functional. If in doubt, perform valve checks before proceeding.*

Bypass valve vacuum check

25   Warm the engine to operating temperature.

26   With the engine running, remove and check for vacuum at the bypass valve vacuum hose (on combination valves, remove the hose at bypass port). Vacuum should be indicated at the hose.

27   If no vacuum is indicted, check all vacuum hoses for leaks or obstructions, then check for vacuum with the engine running at the manifold side of the solenoid valve. Repair any vacuum supply problems, if found. If hoses are okay and vacuum is present, the problem could be a vacuum solenoid switch or the electrical circuits. Proceed to the solenoid checks to isolate.

Diverter valve vacuum check (all models)

28   Warm the engine to operating temperature. Turn the engine off and prepare to check vacuum at the diverter valve vacuum hose (on combination valves, at diverter port vacuum hose).

29   Start the engine and begin timing as soon as the engine starts. Observe the vacuum gauge.

30   If the gauge indicates vacuum upon initial start, then sometime after 100 seconds and before approximately 180 seconds vacuum drops to zero, the system is operating properly.

31   If no vacuum is indicated, check all vacuum hoses for leaks or obstructions, then check for vacuum with the engine running at the manifold side of the solenoid valve. Vac-uum should be indicated.

32   If no manifold vacuum is indicated, trace the hose to the manifold source and eliminate any blockage.

33   Repair any vacuum-supply problems if found. If the hoses are okay, manifold vacuum is present, or if bypass vacuum stays high, the problem could be the vacuum solenoid switch or electrical circuits. Proceed to the solenoid checks to isolate.

Solenoid valve checks (TAD/TAB, AIRD/AIRB)

34   Solenoid vacuum valve problems can be physical (blocked, stuck, leaking to atmosphere or internally) or electrical (open/shorted windings). Solenoid valves used in this application are normally closed with a vented outlet (vacuum bleeds from the air control valve when the solenoid is closed). The quickest way to check the solenoid valve is to perform a combination test to each solenoid valve as in the following steps.

35   Disconnect the electrical connector(s) from the solenoid valve(s).

36   Connect a vacuum source on one port and a vacuum gauge on the other.

37   Jumper one solenoid electrical terminal to ground and the other to a known 12-volt source. Caution: *Do not leave the hot (battery) jumper on any longer than necessary.*

38   Apply vacuum and observe the gauge. Release the vacuum, remove the power to the solenoid, and repeat the vacuum test - observe the gauge.

39   The gauge should indicate and hold vacuum in one test but not the other if the valve is operating properly. Replace the solenoid vacuum valve if a failed condition is found. Note: *A very small leakage rate is acceptable.*

40   Apply vacuum to the outlet port of the valve to check venting. Vacuum should bleed. If not, replace the valve. If each solenoid valve passes, the problem must be in the control circuitry.

Reverse flow check valve - check

41   Disconnect the hoses from both ends of the check valve.

42   Blow through both ends of the check valve, verifying that air flows in one direction only.

43   If air flows in both directions or not at all, replace the check valve with a new one.

44   When reconnecting the valve, make sure it is installed in the proper direction.

Thermactor system noise test

45   The thermactor system is not completely noiseless. Under normal conditions, noise rises in pitch as the engine speed increases. To determine if noise is the fault of the air-injection system, detach the drivebelt (after verifying that the belt tension was correct) and run the engine. If the noise disappears, proceed with the following checks. Caution: *The pump must accumulate 500 miles (vehicle miles) before the following checks are valid:*

8.53 Typical location of thermactor system air pump

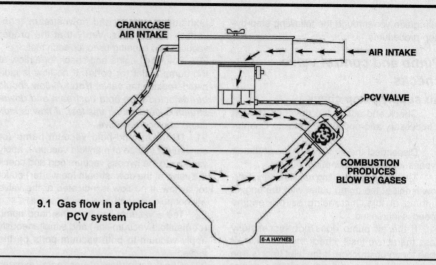

9.1 Gas flow in a typical PCV system

a) *Check for seized pump and replace if required.*
b) *Check for loose or broken mounting brackets or bolts, replace and/or tighten securely if required.*
c) *Check for overtightened mounting bolts (may warp or bind pump).*
d) *Check for leaky, pinched, kinked, or damaged hoses and rework or replace as required.*
e) *Check that the bypass and diverter valves are operating correctly, repair as required.*

Component replacement

Thermactor Air By-Pass (TAB/AIRB) or Thermactor Air Diverter (TAD/AIRD) solenoid

46   Detach the cable from the negative terminal of the battery.
47   Locate the vacuum control solenoid(s) on the engine mounted solenoid bracket assembly.
48   Unplug the electrical connector from the solenoid(s).
49   Label the vacuum hoses and ports, then detach the hoses.
50   Remove the solenoid/bracket screws and detach the solenoid(s).
51   Installation is the reverse of removal.

Air pump and control valves

52   To replace the air-bypass valve, air-supply control valve, check valve, combination air-bypass/air-control valve or the silencer, label and disconnect the hoses leading to them, replace the faulty component and reattach the hoses to the proper ports. Make sure the hoses are in good condition. If not, replace them with new ones.
53   To replace the MTA air supply pump, first loosen the appropriate engine drivebelts (refer to Chapter 1), then remove the faulty pump from the mounting bracket **(see illustration)**. Label all hoses as they're removed to facilitate installation of the new unit.
54   After the new pump is installed, adjust

the drivebelts to the specified tension (refer to Chapter 1).
55   If you're replacing either of the check valves, be sure to use a back-up wrench if connected to a steel air tube.

9   Positive Crankcase Ventilation (PCV) system

Refer to illustration 9.1

1   The Positive Crankcase Ventilation (PCV) system reduces hydrocarbon emissions by scavenging crankcase vapors. It does this by circulating fresh air from the air cleaner through the crankcase, where it mixes with blow-by gases and is then rerouted through a PCV valve to the intake manifold **(see illustration)**.
2   The main components of the PCV system are the PCV valve, a fresh-air filtered inlet and the vacuum hoses connecting these two components with the engine and the EECS system.
3   To maintain idle quality, the PCV valve restricts the flow when the intake manifold vacuum is high. If abnormal operating conditions arise, the system is designed to allow excessive amounts of blow-by gases to flow back through the crankcase vent tube into the air cleaner to be consumed by normal combustion.
4   Checking and replacement of the PCV valve and filter is covered in Chapter 1.

10   Catalytic converter

General description

1   The catalytic converter is an emission-control device added to the exhaust system to reduce pollutants from the exhaust gas stream. A single-bed converter design is used in combination with a three-way (reduction) catalyst. The catalytic coating on the three-way catalyst contains platinum and rhodium, which lowers the levels of oxides of nitrogen (NOx) as well as hydrocarbons (HC) and carbon monoxide (CO).

2   On 2001 and later 4.2L and 4.6L engines, there are two 3-way converters, one in each pipe from the exhaust manifolds. On 5.4L and 6.8L engines, there are three converters, one on each exhaust pipe and one further down after the exhaust pipes merge.

Physical checks

3   The catalytic converter requires little if any maintenance or servicing at regular intervals. However, the system should be inspected whenever the vehicle is raised on a lift or if the exhaust system is checked or serviced.
4   Check all connections in the exhaust pipe assembly for looseness or damage. Also check all the clamps for damage, cracks, or missing fasteners. Check the rubber hangers for cracks.
5   The converter itself should be checked for damage or dents which could affect its performance and/or be hazardous to your health. At the same time the converter is inspected, check the metal protector plate under it and the heat insulator above it for damage or loose fasteners.

Functional checks

Note: *On California models and all 2003 and later models, an extra oxygen sensor, called a monitor sensor, is mounted after the catalytic converter. By comparing the input from the sensors before and after the catalytic converter, the PCM can determine the converter's operating efficiency. If the efficiency is below standards, the PCM will set a diagnostic trouble code and illuminate the CHECK ENGINE light to alert the driver. On these models, a scan tool can quickly determine if the converter needs to be replaced.*

6   Potential converter problems can be associated with two situations, vehicle fails state smog certification check or exhibits low power. Both situations can be caused by a converter that has been overheated and is either non-functional or restrictive.
7   A non-functional converter is difficult to diagnose. If all other engine systems are operating properly, and the converter is relatively cold (this is a judgment call, no specifications

exist, **do not** check by feeling converter) the converter is probably bad.

8   A restricted converter can be checked. If a performance issue is in question, proceed to backpressure check.

Backpressure check

9   Attach a vacuum gauge to a source of manifold vacuum and attach a tachometer to the engine.

10   Set the parking brake and put the transmission in Park.

11   Start the engine and warm it to operating temperature. Turn the engine off and wait for a few minutes (this allows any backpressure to escape).

12   Start the engine and observe the vacuum gauge. Vacuum should be 16 in-Hg or greater on an engine in a good state of tune.

13   Let the engine idle for a few minutes while watching the gauge. Vacuum should hold fairly steady.

14   Increase the engine speed and hold it for one minute at 2000 rpm while observing the vacuum gauge. The vacuum gauge should read continuously high vacuum at the end of one minute with no additional throttle required to maintain rpm. If the vacuum gauge dropped significantly or if more throttle was required to maintain rpm, converter restriction can be suspected. Turn the engine off and proceed to the next operation to isolate the problem further.

15   Let the exhaust system cool, then remove the exhaust pipe at the exhaust manifold(s).

16   Repeat the test. If vacuum is now steady and high in the engine-running test, the converter is restricted. Replace the converter.

Caution: *Although rare, if a restricted muffler is suspected, reconnect the converter, discon-nect the muffler and repeat the test to determine if the muffler is the cause.*

Replacement

17   Do not attempt to remove the catalytic converter until the complete exhaust system is cool. Raise the vehicle and support it securely on jackstands. Apply some penetrating oil to the clamp bolts and allow it to soak in.

18   Remove the bolts and the rubber hangers, then separate the converter from the exhaust pipes. Remove the old gaskets if they are stuck to the pipes.

19   Installation of the converter is the reverse of removal. Use new exhaust pipe gaskets and tighten the clamp bolts securely. Replace the rubber hangers with new ones if the originals are deteriorated. Start the engine and check carefully for exhaust leaks.

Notes

Chapter 7
Automatic transmission

Contents

Specifications

Torque specifications

	Ft-lbs (unless otherwise indicated)
Torque converter-to-driveplate nuts	20 to 30
Transmission pan bolts	See Chapter 1
Torque converter housing-to-transmission case	28 to 40
Transmission-to-engine bolts	40
Transmission mounting	
Mount-to-transmission	
Models through 2000	45 to 60
2001 and later	72
Mount-to-crossmember	60 to 80
Crossmember and gussets to frame	45 to 55
Transmission range sensor retaining screws	62 to 89 in-lbs
Output shaft yoke retaining nut (if equipped)	75 to 110
E40D solenoid body fasteners	80 to 100 in-lbs

1 Automatic transmission - general information

Caution: *All automatic transmissions supplied as original equipment on vehicles covered by this manual are equipped with high-temperature resistant seals. This includes those seals used on the manual and kickdown levers, the O-rings and oil pan gasket. Under no circumstances should older design seals be used on the transmission.*

Econoline vans covered in this manual use several different automatic transmissions. The transmission used depends on the specific options such as engine size and gross vehicle weight.

Other than the number of forward speeds, the main differences between the transmissions are in their maximum torque carrying capacity and their speed and load sensing mechanisms which determine shift points. The C6 and AOD automatic transmissions utilize a governor for speed sensing and

a vacuum diaphragm throttle valve to sense engine load. A throttle kickdown rod is incorporated for operator-forced downshifts upon application of wide open throttle. The E4OD, 4R70W, 4R75W and 4R100 transmissions use various engine and drivetrain sensors and special programming within the electronic engine control (EEC) computer to calculate speed and load conditions, then commands actuators within the transmission to initiate a shift.

The E4OD, 4R70W, 4R75W, TorqShift

and 4R100 transmissions are equipped with a lock-up torque converter known as the torque converter clutch or TCC. The TCC provides a direct connection between the engine and the drive wheels for improved efficiency and fuel economy. These transmissions do not use a throttle valve (TV) system. Instead, the transmission kickdown function normally controlled by a TV cable is controlled electronically. The TorqShift six-speed transmission is a heavy-duty overdrive automatic used only on diesel and V10-equipped vans on 2004 and later models.

Because of the complexity of the clutches and the electronic and hydraulic control systems, and because of the special tools and expertise needed to overhaul an automatic transmission, diagnosis and repair of the transmission must be handled by a dealer service department or a transmission repair shop. The procedures in this Chapter are limited to general diagnosis, routine maintenance and adjustment: replacing the shift lever, replacing and adjusting the shift cable, and similar jobs. Serious repair work, however, must be done by a transmission specialist. But if the transmission must be rebuilt or replaced, you can save money by removing and installing it yourself, so instructions for that procedure are included as well.

2   Diagnosis - general

Note: *Automatic transmission malfunctions may be caused by five general conditions: poor engine performance, improper adjustments, hydraulic malfunctions, mechanical malfunctions or malfunctions in the computer or its signal network. Diagnosis of these problems should always begin with a check of the easily repaired items: fluid level and condition (see Chapter 1), shift linkage adjustment and throttle valve (TV) linkage adjustment. Next, perform a road test to determine if the problem has been corrected or if more diagnosis is necessary. If the problem persists after the preliminary tests and corrections are completed, additional diagnosis should be done by a dealer service department or transmission repair shop. Refer to the Troubleshooting section at the front of this manual for information on symptoms of transmission problems.*

Preliminary checks

1   Drive the vehicle to warm the transmission to normal operating temperature.
2   Check the fluid level as described in Chapter 1:
  a) *If the fluid level is unusually low, add enough fluid to bring the level within the designated area of the dipstick (see Chapter 1), then check for external leaks (see below).*
  b) *If the fluid level is abnormally high, drain off the excess, then check the drained fluid for contamination by coolant. The presence of engine coolant in the auto-*

matic transmission fluid indicates that a failure has occurred in the internal radiator walls that separate the coolant from the transmission fluid (see Chapter 3).
  c) *If the fluid is foaming, drain it and refill the transmission (see Chapter 1), then check for coolant in the fluid or a high fluid level.*
3   Check the engine idle speed and general operating performance. **Note:** *If the engine is malfunctioning, do not proceed with the preliminary checks until it has been repaired and runs normally.*
4   Inspect the manual shift control linkage (see Section 3). Make sure that it's properly adjusted and that the linkage operates smoothly.

Fluid leak diagnosis

5   Most fluid leaks are easy to locate visually. Repair usually consists of replacing a seal or gasket. If a leak is difficult to find, the following procedure may help.
6   Identify the fluid. Make sure it's transmission fluid and not engine oil or brake fluid (automatic transmission fluid is a deep red color).
7   Try to pinpoint the source of the leak. Drive the vehicle several miles, then park it over a large sheet of cardboard. After a minute or two, you should be able to locate the leak by determining the source of the fluid dripping onto the cardboard.
8   Make a careful visual inspection of the suspected component and the area immediately around it. Pay particular attention to gasket mating surfaces. A mirror is often helpful for finding leaks in areas that are hard to see.
9   If the leak still cannot be found, clean the suspected area thoroughly with a degreaser or solvent, then dry it.
10   Drive the vehicle for several miles at normal operating temperature and varying speeds. After driving the vehicle, visually inspect the suspected component again.
11   Once the leak has been located, the cause must be determined before it can be properly repaired. If a gasket is replaced but the sealing flange is bent, the new gasket will not stop the leak. The bent flange must be straightened.
12   Before attempting to repair a leak, check to make sure that the following conditions are corrected or they may cause another leak. **Note:** *Some of the following conditions cannot be fixed without highly specialized tools and expertise. Such problems must be referred to a transmission repair shop or a dealer service department.*

Gasket leaks

13   Check the pan periodically. Make sure the bolts are tight, no bolts are missing, the gasket is in good condition and the pan is flat (dents in the pan may indicate damage to the valve body inside).
14   If the pan gasket is leaking, the fluid level or the fluid pressure may be too high,

the vent may be plugged, the pan bolts may be too tight, the pan sealing flange may be warped, the sealing surface of the transmission housing may be damaged, the gasket may be damaged or the transmission casting may be cracked or porous. If sealant instead of gasket material has been used to form a seal between the pan and the transmission housing, it may be the wrong sealant.

Seal leaks

15   If a transmission seal is leaking, the fluid level or pressure may be too high, the vent may be plugged, the seal bore may be damaged, the seal itself may be damaged or improperly installed, the surface of the shaft protruding through the seal may be damaged or a loose bearing may be causing excessive shaft movement.
16   Make sure the dipstick tube seal is in good condition and the tube is properly seated. Periodically check the area around the speedometer gear or sensor for leakage. If transmission fluid is evident, check the O-ring for damage.

Case leaks

17   If the case itself appears to be leaking, the casting is porous and will have to be repaired or replaced.
18   Make sure the oil cooler hose fittings are tight and in good condition.

Fluid comes out vent pipe or fill tube

19   If this condition occurs, the transmission is overfilled, there is coolant in the fluid, the case is porous, the dipstick is incorrect, the vent is plugged or the drain-back holes are plugged.

3   Shift linkage and cable - inspection, removal, installation and adjustment

Note: *Removal of the shift linkage or cable is a prerequisite to removing the transmission from the vehicle. Although the shift linkage is part of a more complicated steering column shift mechanism, only the linkage removal steps necessary to allow transmission removal will be outlined in this section. In addition, adjustment procedures are provided for use after reinstallation of linkage or for correction of possible performance related problems.*

Inspection

1   Raise vehicle and support it securely on jackstands.
2   Inspect the cable for kinks, dents, thermal damage or any other condition that may hinder smooth operation. Check for a loose transmission cable bracket. Inspect the remaining cable inside the cab under the dash panel for similar problems.
3   Correct any problems found prior to adjustment.

Removal

4   Remove the shift cable end from the transmission lever ballstud.
5   Remove the shift cable from the transmission bracket by releasing the cable body retaining tabs and pulling it out of the bracket. Secure the cable out of the way.

Installation

6   Installation is the reverse of removal, but don't install the shift cable to the transmission lever ball stud until adjustment has been completed.

Adjustment

7   With the engine off and the parking brake applied, place the transmission selector lever at the steering column in the Drive (C-6) or Overdrive (AOD, E4OD, 4R100 and 4R70W) position.
8   Have an assistant hold the selector lever against the stop by applying a bit of down pressure on the lever.
9   Raise the vehicle and support it securely on jackstands.
10   If not already done, remove the shift cable end from the transmission lever ballstud (cable).
11   On AOD, E4OD, 4R100 and 4R70W transmissions, pull down the cable freeplay locking tab on the lower cable body end.
12   Shift the manual lever at the transmission into the Drive position (C6) or Overdrive position (AOD, E4OD, 4R100 and 4R70W) by moving the lever all the way to the First gear position (rear), then forward two (2) detents. Count the detents as the manual lever is rotated.
13   On AOD, E4OD, 4R100 and 4R70W transmissions, with the selector lever and transmission manual lever both in the Overdrive position, snap the shift cable onto the transmission lever ballstud and re-lock the cable freeplay locking tab by pushing the tab back into the cable body. **Note:** *The shift cable locking mechanism on the C6 differs from the others. Instead of a tab, the C6 uses a rotating ratchet type mechanism.*
14   Have your assistant remove pressure from the shift lever knob and check the operation of the shift lever in all positions to make certain the manual lever at the transmission is in full detent in all gear ranges. Readjust the linkage as required.

---

4   Throttle valve (TV) cable (AOD only) - removal, installation and adjustment

---

Note: *Removal of the throttle valve cable is a prerequisite to removing the transmission from the vehicle and only those cable removal steps necessary to allow transmission removal will be outlined in this section. In addition, adjustment procedures are provided for use after re-installation of linkage or for correction of possible performance related problems.*

Removal

1   Disconnect the shift cable end from the transmission lever ballstud.
2   Remove shift cable from transmission bracket by releasing the cable body retaining tabs and pulling it out of the bracket. Secure the cable out of the way.

Installation

3   Installation is the reverse of removal. Proceed to Step 4 and adjust the cable.

Adjustment

4   Verify that the cable routing is free of sharp bends and that the cable operates freely.
5   Place the transmission in N (neutral) and set the parking brake.
6   At the throttle housing, unlock the TV control cable self-adjusting lock mechanism at the end of the cable housing body by releasing the clamp tabs in the housing window and prying the clamp out from the top with a small screwdriver. Verify that the cable housing can be pushed freely towards the cable bracket against the spring tension.
7   From under the vehicle, have an assistant hold the transmission TV lever against it's idle position stop (clockwise as far to the rear as possible) and hold. The cable slack take-up spring will then set the proper cable length automatically. An alternative method is to install a suitable spring (or springs) to hold the lever rearwards with about 10-pounds of force.
8   While still holding the transmission lever against the idle stop, lock the upper cable clamp in place by pushing the clamp back into the cable body until it's flush. **Note:** *Prior to re-locking the cable, verify that the throttle lever is resting on its normal idle stop.*
9   If used, remove the transmission lever retention springs.

---

5   Transmission control switch (E4OD, 4R100, 4R70W and 4R75W) - description, check and component replacement

---

Description

1   Normally, the powertrain control module (PCM) allows automatic shifts from first through fourth gear. When the transmission control switch (TCS) is pressed, overdrive is overridden, and the PCM allows shifts from first through third only. (The PCM also turns on the transmission control indicator lamp (TCIL), an LED which indicates that "overdrive cancel mode" has been activated. If the TCIL flashes instead, there's either a sensor failure or a short in the electronic pressure control cir-

cuit (EPC); in either event, take the vehicle to a dealer to have the system serviced.) When the switch is pressed again, normal operation is resumed.

Check

2   The TCS circuit can be fully tested only at the dealer. However, there are some simple tests you can do to determine whether the switch itself is bad:
   a) *Check fuse 20 (see Chapter 12). Fuse 20 is a 5A fuse.*
   b) *Remove the TCS (see below) and check the resistance of the switch. When the TCS button is pressed and held down (it's a momentary-contact switch, so you have to hold it down to measure the resistance), the resistance should be less than 5 ohms; when the button is released, resistance should be more than 10 K-ohms. If the TCS doesn't perform as described, replace it. If the indicated resistance is within the specified range, go to the next test.*
   c) *Apply battery voltage to the TCS and verify that the TCIL comes on. If it doesn't, replace the TCS. If it does come on, the switch is okay. Take the vehicle to a dealer to have the remainder of the system checked out.*

Component replacement

3   Remove the TCS cover.
4   Remove the TCS.
5   Installation is the reverse of removal.

---

6   Kickdown cable (C6 only) - removal, installation and adjustment

---

Removal

1   Remove the kickdown cable end from the transmission lever ballstud.
2   Remove the kickdown cable from the transmission bracket by releasing the cable body retaining tabs and pulling it out of the bracket. Secure the cable out of the way.

Installation

3   Installation is the reverse of removal. Proceed to Step 4 and adjust the cable.

Adjustment

4   Ratchet the cable self-adjusting mechanism to obtain maximum outer conduit length.
5   Insert a 0.060 feeler gauge between the upper cable conduit body and the cable bracket on the conduit side of the bracket.
6   Set the cable length by opening the throttle to the wide open position. The self adjuster should ratchet as the cable outer conduit shortens in length.
7   Remove the feeler gauge to gain proper cable freeplay.

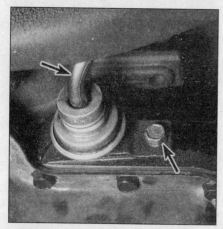

7.2 To remove the vacuum modulator, detach the vacuum line (arrow) and remove the hold-down bolt (arrow)

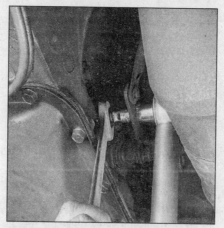

8.2 Adjusting the intermediate band

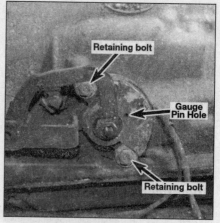

9.1 Neutral start switch adjustment details (C6 models)

7 Vacuum modulator (C6 only) - check and replacement

Refer to illustration 7.2

Check

1   Raise vehicle and support securely on jackstands.
2   Locate the vacuum modulator on rear or side of transmission **(see illustration)**.
3   Detach the vacuum hose from the modulator.
4   Connect a vacuum gauge to the vacuum hose and start the engine. If the gauge does not indicate manifold vacuum, trace the vacuum hose back to the engine to locate the leak or restriction. Repair as required.
5   Remove the bolt from the modulator bracket and remove the valve from the transmission.
6   Using a magnet, remove the control rod from the bore in the transmission.
7   Place the control rod into the modulator.
8   Using a hand-held vacuum pump, apply vacuum to the modulator and observe the rod and the vacuum gauge. The modulator should hold a steady vacuum and the control rod should retract. As vacuum is released, the rod should extend back to its static position. If the modulator fails either check, replace it.

Replacement

9   Check the O-ring on the modulator. If it's cracked, hardened or shows any other signs of wear, replace it with a new one. Lubricate the O-ring with clean automatic transmission fluid before installation.
10   Installation is the reverse of removal. Don't forget to install the control rod prior to modulator installation. Tighten the bracket bolt securely.

8 Band adjustment (C6 only)

Refer to illustration 8.2

1   The intermediate or front band is used to hold the sun gear stationary to produce Second gear. If it is not correctly adjusted, there will be noticeable slip during the First-to-Second gear shift or on the downshift from High to Second gear. The first symptoms of these problems will be very sluggish shifts.
2   To adjust the intermediate band, loosen, remove and discard the locknut on the band adjustment screw (located on the left-hand side of the case). Tighten the adjusting screw to 120 inch-pounds, then loosen it exactly 1-1/2 turns. Install a new locknut and tighten it securely while holding the adjustment screw to keep it from turning **(see illustration)**.

9 Neutral start switch (C6 only) - adjustment

Refer to illustration 9.1

1   With the automatic transmission linkage properly adjusted (see Section 3), loosen the two Neutral start switch retaining bolts **(see illustration)**.
2   Place the transmission selector lever in Neutral.
3   Rotate the switch and insert a No. 43 drill bit (shank end) into the gauge pin holes of the switch. **Note:** *The drill shank must be inserted a full 31/64 inch through all three holes of the switch.*
4   Tighten the switch retaining bolts securely, then remove the drill bit from the switch.
5   Check the operation of the switch. The back-up lights should come on only when the transmission is in Reverse and the engine should start only with the transmission lever in Park and Neutral.

10 Transmission range (TR) sensor (1996 and later) - description, adjustment and replacement

Description

1   The transmission range (TR) sensor, which is located at the manual lever on the transmission, is an information sensor for the powertrain control module (PCM). Among its functions are those normally handled by a conventional park/neutral start switch: it prevents the engine from starting in any gear other than Park or Neutral, and closes the circuit for the back-up lights when the shift lever is moved to Reverse. For information on the TR sensor's other functions, refer to Chapter 6.

Adjustment

Refer to illustration 10.4
2   If the engine starts in any position other than Park or Neutral, the TR sensor is either out of adjustment or defective. First, perform a quick functional check to verify that the sensor is operating properly.
3   Raise the vehicle and support it securely on jackstands.
4   The factory recommends a special transmission range (TR) sensor alignment tool, but there's a quick and easy method to verify whether the sensor is adjusted, and to adjust it if it isn't:
a) *Turn the ignition switch to On, put the shift lever in Reverse and verify that the back-up lights come on.*
b) *If they do, but the engine can't be started in Park or Neutral, or it can be started in any gear other than Park or Neutral, then the sensor is probably defective. The complete sensor check procedure is in Chapter 6.*

10.4 To adjust the transmission range sensor without the special tools: Place the shifter in reverse. Detach the shift cable, loosen the sensor retaining bolts, move the sensor slightly until the back-up lights come on, then tighten the sensor retaining bolts to the torque listed in this Chapter's Specifications and reattach the shift cable

c) *If they don't, detach the shift cable from the manual lever (see Section 6), loosen the sensor retaining bolts* **(see illustration)** *and move the sensor slightly until the back-up lights come on. Tighten the sensor retaining bolts to the torque listed in this Chapter's Specifications and reattach the shift cable.*

d) *If you can't get the back-up lights to come on by moving the sensor slightly, verify that the back-up lights and the back-up light circuit are okay (see Chapter 12 and the Wiring Diagrams at the end of Chapter 12). If the back-up lights and circuit are okay, the sensor is probably bad. Refer to Chapter 6.*

5   Remove the jackstands and lower the vehicle.

Replacement

6   Raise the vehicle and place it securely on jackstands.

7   Unplug the electrical connector from the TR sensor.

8   Detach the shift cable from the manual lever (see Section 3).

9   On vehicles equipped with a 4R70W or 4R75W transmission, remove the manual lever; on models with an E4OD or 4R100, the manual lever is between the TR sensor and the transmission, so it doesn't need to be removed.)

10   Remove the TR sensor retaining bolts **(see illustration 10.4)**.

11   Remove the TR sensor.

12   Installation is the reverse of removal. Be sure to tighten the sensor retaining screws to the torque listed in this Chapter's Specifications and adjust the sensor (see Step 5). Remove the jackstands and lower the vehicle.

---

11   Shift interlock system (1996 and later) - description, check and actuator replacement

Note: *1992 through 1995 models are equipped with a mechanical brake shift lock actuator installed into the steering column. Refer to a dealer service department for information.*

Description

1   The shift interlock system prevents the shift lever from being moved out of the Park position unless the brake pedal is depressed. The system consists of a shift lock actuator mounted on the steering column. When the ignition key is turned to the Run position, the actuator is energized unless the brake pedal is depressed. If the shift lever cannot be moved out of the Park position when the brake pedal is applied, the following series of simple checks will help you quickly pinpoint the problem.

Check

2   The shift lock actuator receives voltage when the ignition key is in the Run position. This circuit energizes the actuator and it prevents you from moving the shift lever out of the Park position. The actuator also receives voltage from another circuit, through the brake light switch, that is closed only when the brake pedal is depressed. It's this second circuit that de-energizes the solid state actuator when the brake pedal is depressed. So first, try to verify that the actuator is working.

3   Get inside the vehicle, close the doors and windows, start the engine, let it settle down to a fully warmed-up idle, put your head under the dash so that your ear is close to the actuator (it's mounted on the steering column), then depress the brake pedal and listen carefully for the sound of the actuator clicking.

4   If you don't hear the actuator click when you depress the brake pedal, check the 10A fuse for the actuator and the 15A fuse for the brake light switch (see Chapter 12). Replace either fuse if it's bad and recheck the actuator.

5   If the actuator and brake light switch fuses are good but the actuator still doesn't click when the brake pedal is depressed, verify that the actuator is getting battery voltage through both circuits (one is hot in the Run position, one is hot only when the brake light switch is closed).

6   If the actuator isn't getting voltage through the first "hot-in-Run-only" circuit, repair that circuit and retest.

7   If the actuator isn't getting voltage through the brake light switch circuit, apply the brake pedal and verify that the brake lights come on.

a) *If the brake lights don't come on, troubleshoot the brake light circuit and determine whether the circuit itself or the brake light switch is defective (see Chapter 9), make the necessary repairs or component replacement, then retest the actuator.*

b) *If the brake lights come on, the brake light switch and circuit are okay. Repair the circuit between the brake light switch and the actuator and retest.*

c) *If the actuator still doesn't work, replace it (see below).*

Actuator replacement

8   Disconnect the cable from the negative terminal of the battery. Remove the left side under-dash panel and the knee bolster behind it. Detach the shift indicator cable and any electrical connectors that may interfere with the lowering of the steering column. Remove the four nuts and lower the column for access to the shift lock actuator.

9   Remove the shift lock actuator bolts.

10   Remove the insert plate and shift lock actuator.

11   Remove and discard the shift lock actuator clip. (The shift lock actuator clip is an assembly aid and doesn't need to be replaced). Separate the insert plate from the shift lock actuator.

12   Installation is the reverse of removal. Tighten the steering column mounting bolts to 156 in-lbs.

---

12   Transmission mounts - check and replacement

Refer to illustration 12.2

Check

1   Raise the vehicle and support it securely on jackstands.

2   Insert a large screwdriver or prybar into the space between the transmission extension housing and the frame crossmember and pry up **(see illustration)**.

3   The transmission should not move significantly away from the insulator. If it does, the mount should be replaced; proceed to Step 5.

4   If the mount is okay, remove the jackstands and lower the vehicle.

Replacement

5   Remove the mount-to-crossmember nuts and the mount-to-transmission bolts.

6   Place a jack under the transmission and raise it enough to allow removal of the mount.

7   Install a new mount and lower the transmission enough to start all fasteners hand tight.

8   Remove the jack and tighten the mount fasteners to the torque listed in this Chapter's Specifications.

9   Remove the jackstands and lower the vehicle.

13 Extension housing oil seal - replacement

Refer to illustrations 13.6 and 13.8

1   Raise the vehicle and support it securely on jackstands.

2   The extension housing oil seal is located at the extreme rear of the transmission, where the driveshaft is attached. If leakage at the seal is suspected, raise the vehicle and support it securely on jackstands. If the seal is leaking, transmission lubricant will be built up on the front of the driveshaft and may be dripping from the rear of the transmission.

3   Refer to Chapter 8 and remove the driveshaft. **Note:** *The driveshaft is balanced as an assembly with the transmission output flange and the pinion flange at the rear axle. Always make matching marks one the mating flanges at each end of the driveshaft before removing the driveshaft.*

4   On circular flange or yoke type output shafts, remove the flange/yoke nut and washer and remove flange/yoke.

5   Using a soft-faced hammer, carefully tap the dust shield (if equipped) to the rear and remove it from the transmission. Be careful not to distort it.

6   Using a screwdriver or prybar, carefully pry the oil seal out of the rear of the transmission **(see illustration)**. Do not damage the splines on the transmission output shaft.

7   If the oil seal cannot be removed with a screwdriver or prybar, a special oil seal removal tool (available at auto parts stores) will be required.

8   Using a large section of pipe or a very large deep socket as a drift, install the new oil seal **(see illustration)**. Drive it into the bore squarely and make sure it's completely seated.

9   Reinstall the dust shield, if equipped, by carefully tapping it into place.

10   On circular flange or yoke type output shafts, clean the yoke splines and lightly lubricate them with multi-purpose grease, then slip the flange/yoke over the output shaft and carefully past the new seal until it bottoms.

12.2 Pry up on the transmission mount and check for looseness.

Coat the nut with a thread locking compound. Install the washer and nut and tighten the nut to the torque listed in this Chapter's Specifications.

11   Lubricate the splines of the transmission output shaft and the outside of the driveshaft sleeve yoke with lightweight grease, then install the driveshaft. Be careful not to damage the lip of the new seal.

12   Remove the jackstands and lower the vehicle.

13   Check/refill the transmission with lubricant (see Chapter 1).

14 Automatic transmission - removal and installation

Refer to illustrations 14.5 and 14.17

Removal

1   Disconnect the cable from the negative battery terminal.

2   If possible, raise the vehicle on a hoist. Alternatively, raise the vehicle to obtain the maximum possible amount of working room underneath, and support it securely on jackstands. Familiarize yourself with the applicable components.

3   Drain the transmission fluid (see Chapter 1). After draining, temporarily install the pan with four bolts to hold it in place.

4   Remove the torque converter access cover and adapter plate bolts from the front lower end of the converter housing.

5   Mark the torque converter and one of the studs with white paint so they can be installed in the same position **(see illustration)**. Remove the driveplate-to-converter attaching nuts, turning the engine as necessary to gain access by means of a socket on the crankshaft pulley attaching bolt. On some models, rubber plugs must be removed in order to access the converter nuts.

6   Rotate the engine until the converter drain plug is accessible, then remove the plug, catching the fluid in the drain pan. Install and tighten the drain plug securely.

7   Remove the driveshaft (see Chapter 8). Place a polyethylene bag over the end of the transmission to prevent dirt from entering.

8   Remove the manual shift linkage (see Section 3)

9   Remove the TV control rod or cable if equipped (see Section 4, AOD only).

10   Remove the kickdown rod or cable if equipped (see Section 5, C6 only).

11   Remove the vacuum modulator hose, if equipped (see Section 6, C6 only).

12   Disconnect the Neutral safety switch electrical connector (C6 and AOD).

13   Disconnect the manual lever position sensor electrical connector (E4OD, 4R100, 4R70W and 4R75W).

14   Remove the two bolts retaining the solenoid body connector heat shield and remove the shield. Disconnect the solenoid body electrical connector (E4OD only).

15   Remove the transmission fluid filler tube retaining bolt and lift the filler tube and dipstick out of transmission housing.

16   Remove the starter (see Chapter 5).

17   Disconnect the oil cooler lines at the transmission and plug them to prevent dirt from entering **(see illustration)**. Use a flare nut wrench to avoid rounding off the nuts.

18   Position a transmission jack beneath the transmission and raise it so that it *just begins*

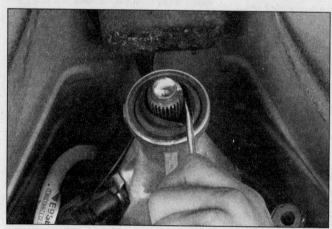

13.6 Use a large screwdriver or prybar to pry the seal out of the transmission extension housing

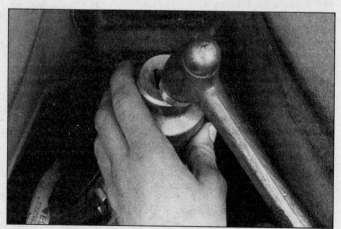

13.8 A hammer and a large socket can be used to drive the new seal evenly into the bore

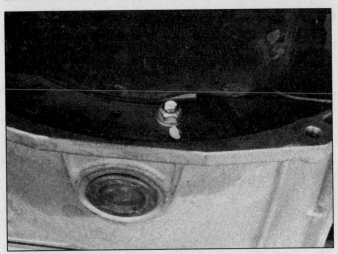

14.5 Mark a torque converter stud to the driveplate to ensure that they're still in dynamic balance when reassembled

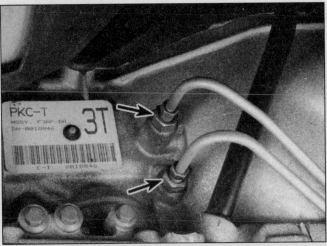

14.17 Remove the oil cooler line fittings (arrows), pull the lines away from the transmission and plug them to keep out dirt and moisture

to lift the transmission weight.

19   Remove the nuts and bolts securing the rear mount and insulators to the crossmember (see Section 12).

20   If right and left gussets are installed between the crossmember and frame rails, remove the gusset attaching nuts and bolts and remove the gussets.

21   Remove any harness ties on the crossmember and the nuts and bolts securing the crossmember to the frame rails, raise the transmission slightly and remove the crossmember.

22   Disconnect the inlet pipe flange(s) from the exhaust manifold(s) (see Chapter 4). On later models, unbolt the exhaust pipe heat shields from the crossmember.

23   Support the rear of the engine using a jack or blocks of wood.

24   Make sure that the transmission is securely mounted on the jack and remove the transmission housing-to-engine bolts.

25   Carefully move the transmission to the rear, down and away from the vehicle. Make sure the converter stays with the transmission.

Installation

26   Installing the transmission is essentially the reverse of the removal procedure, but the following points should be noted:

a) Push in on the converter and turn it to ensure that it's completely engaged with the front pump of the transmission.

b) Rotate the converter to align the bolt drive lugs and drain plug with their holes in the driveplate.

c) Do not allow the transmission to take a "nose-down" attitude as the converter will move forward and disengage from the pump gear.

d) If the torque converter is fastened to the driveplate with bolts, position the driveplate so one bolt hole is in the six o'clock position. Install one bolt, then rotate the engine (clockwise only) and install the other bolts. Don't tighten any bolts until all of them have been installed.

e) Adjust the kickdown rod/cable (see Section 5) or TV rod/cable (see Section 4) and manual selector linkage (see Section 3) as necessary.

f) If the vehicle is equipped with a transmission fluid inline filter, install a new filter. If the transmission is not equipped with a transmission fluid filter, install a fluid filter service kit. Purchase this factory service kit from the dealer parts department.

g) When the vehicle has been lowered to the ground, add sufficient fluid to bring the level up to the Max mark on the dipstick with the engine not running. Having done this, start the engine and check and top-up the fluid level as described in Chapter 1.

Notes

Chapter 8
Driveline

Contents

Specifications

Rear axle type

E-150	Ford semi-floating with integral carrier (8.8 or 9.75-inch ring gear)
E-250	Dana 60 semi floating
E-350	Dana 60 full floating; Dana 70 full floating

Torque specifications

Ft-lbs (unless otherwise indicated)

Rear axle

Dana

Drive pinion nut minimum torque	250 to 270
Drive pinion rotation preload (used bearings)	15 to 20 in-lbs
Pinion shaft lockpin	20 to 25
Cover-to-housing bolts	
Grade 5	35
Grade 8	45
Axleshaft retaining bolts (full-floating axle)	
1992	40 to 55
1993	65 to 85
1994 on	90 to 120
Wheel bearing adjusting nut (full-floating axle)	
Step 1	65 to 75
Step 2	back-off 1/4 turn
Step 3	15 to 20

Ford integral carrier

Drive pinion nut minimum torque	160
Drive pinion rotation preload (used bearings)	8 to 14 in-lbs
Pinion shaft lock bolt (using Loctite or equivalent)	15 to 30
Rear cover screw	25 to 35

Driveshafts

Center support bearing bracket-to-crossmember	30 to 47
U-joint-to-companion flange U-bolt nuts	8 to 15
U-joint yoke-to-circular companion flange bolts	70 to 95

1 Rear axle - general information

The rear axle assembly consists of a straight, hollow housing enclosing a differential assembly and axleshafts. These assemblies support the vehicle's 'sprung' weight components through leaf springs attached between the axle housings and the vehicle's frame rails.

The rear axle assemblies employed on vehicles covered by this manual are of two designs: those with semi-floating axleshafts and those with heavy duty full-floating axleshafts. Full-floating axleshafts do not themselves bear any of the vehicle's weight, can be removed independent of the tapered roller wheel bearings and are designed only to transfer power to the rear wheels. Semi-floating axleshafts are themselves an integral part of the rear wheel support system, bearing vehicle weight as well as transferring power to the rear wheels. Both types of rear end designs use hypoid gears with the pinion gear centerline below the axleshaft centerline.

Due to the need for special tools and

2.2 If a seal removal tool isn't available, a prybar or even the end of the axle can be used to pry the seal out of the housing

2.3 Removing the axleshaft bearing with a slide hammer and puller attachment

equipment, it is recommended that operations on these models be limited to those described in this Chapter. Where repair or overhaul is required, remove the axle assembly and take it to a rebuilder, or exchange it for a new or reconditioned unit.

Always make sure that an axle unit is exchanged for one of identical type and gear ratio.

2 Rear axleshaft oil seal and bearing (semi-floating type) - replacement

Refer to illustrations 2.2, 2.3 and 2.5

1   Remove the axleshaft (see Section 4).
2   Remove the axleshaft seal using a special seal removal tool, a prybar or the end of the axleshaft **(see illustration)**. If seal replacement is all that is required, proceed to Step 4.
3   If both bearing and seal require removal, both can be removed at the same time. Use a slide hammer in combination with a special bearing removal tool or an internal-jaw puller **(see illustration)**.
4   Inspect the inner surface of the housing for any conditions that would prevent the new seal or bearing from fitting into its seat correctly. Remedy any problems of this type such as burrs, galling or rust before attempting to install the new bearing or seal.
5   If replaced, lubricate the new bearing with rear axle lube and install it squarely into the axle housing bore. Using an appropriate bearing/seal driver, tap the bearing into the housing until it bottoms in the bore **(see illustration)**. **Caution:** *Continuously verify that the bearing is being pressed squarely and not being cocked in the bore during this process.*
6   Prior to seal installation, smear a small amount of RTV sealant on the outer edge of the seal (do not allow the sealant to touch the

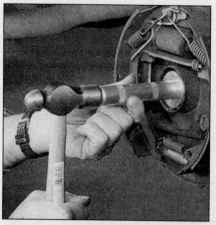

2.5 Install the rear axle bearing into the axle tube using the appropriate bearing driver

sealing lip) and coat the inner sealing lip with multi-purpose grease.
7   Using an appropriate seal driver, tap the new seal into its bore. The seal must receive even pressure around its circumference, thus a tubular drift, large socket or special tool should be used for this. Drive the seal into the housing until it seats.
8   Install the axleshaft(s) (see Section 4).

3 Rear wheel hub bearings and grease seal (full-floating type) - removal, inspection and installation

Refer to illustration 3.4

Removal

1   Raise the rear of the vehicle and place it securely on jackstands.
2   Remove the rear wheels, then remove the axleshafts (see Section 5)
3   Remove the brake drums. All models allow separate removal of the brake drum (E-150, 250) or brake hub with disc (E-350) from the wheel hub assembly, allowing easier removal of the wheel hub. To remove the brake drum, remove the push-on drum retainers, if equipped, and pull the drum off the hub. If the brake drum will not come off easily, it may be necessary to retract the brake shoes slightly (see Chapter 9). **Note:** *If the vehicle is equipped with rear disc brakes, remove the hub and disc assembly (see Chapter 9).*
4   Install a special hub wrench so that the drive tangs of the tool engage the four slots in the hub nut and remove the nut **(see illustration)**.
5   Remove the outer bearing from the hub and pull the hub straight off the spindle.
6   Use a large screwdriver or prybar to pry the seal from the back of the wheel hub. Remove the inner bearing.

3.4 A special hub locknut wrench is required to turn the hub nut on full-floating axles - the drive tangs must fit into the hub nut slots

4.6 Position a large screwdriver between the rear axle case and a ring gear bolt to keep the differential case from turning when removing the pinion shaft lockpin

4.7 Rotate the differential case 180-degrees and slide the pinion shaft out of the case until the stepped part of the shaft contacts the ring gear

Inspection

7   Clean the hub nut and bearings with cleaning solvent; allow the parts to air dry.

8   Clean the inside of the wheel hub to remove all axle lubricant and grease. Clean the axle spindle.

9   Inspect the bearing assemblies for signs of wear, pitting, galling and other damage. Replace the bearings if any of these conditions exist. Inspect the bearing races for signs of erratic wear, galling and other damage.

10   If the bearing races need replacement, drive out the bearing races from the wheel hub with a brass drift. Install the new races with a bearing cup replacer and drive handle or other suitable tool designed for this purpose. Never use a drift or punch for this operation as these races must be driven squarely, seated correctly and can be damaged easily.

Installation

11   Prior to installation, pack the inner and outer wheel bearings with high temperature grease (see Chapter 1) or equivalent. If you do not have access to a bearing packer, pack each bearing carefully by hand and make sure the entire bearing is penetrated with grease.

12   Install the newly packed inner wheel bearing into the hub. Install a new hub inner seal with a suitable drive tool (tubular drift, large socket or special tool) being careful not to damage the seal.

13   Prior to installing the wheel hub, coat the inner seal lip with grease and wrap the spindle threads with electrician's tape to prevent damage to the inner wheel bearing seal during installation. Also, cover the spindle with a light coat of grease.

14   Carefully slide the hub assembly over the spindle, being very careful to keep it straight so as not to contact the spindle with the seal (which would damage it). Remove the electrician's tape.

15   Install the newly packed outer wheel bearing over the spindle and into the wheel hub.

16   Install the hub nut, make sure the tab is located in the keyway with the identification markings facing out. Using the locknut wrench, tighten the locknut to 65 to 75 ft-lbs. Rotate the hub occasionally while tightening the locknut. Back the locknut off 90-degrees (1/4-turn counterclockwise), then tighten it to 15 to 20 ft-lbs.

17   Install the axleshaft (see Section 5) and brake drum. Tighten the axleshaft retaining bolts to the torque listed in this Chapter's Specifications.

18   Adjust the brakes if they were retracted for removal purposes (see Chapter 9).

19   Install the wheel, remove the jackstands and lower the vehicle.

20   Recheck the torque on the axleshaft bolts (see Section 5).

4   Rear axleshaft (semi-floating type) - removal and installation

Refer to illustrations 4.6, 4.7 and 4.8

Removal

1   Raise the rear of the vehicle and place it securely on jackstands.

2   Remove the wheel(s) (see Chapter 1).

3   Release the parking brake and remove the brake drum(s) (see Chapter 9). On models with rear disc brakes, remove the caliper and disc, then wire the caliper out of the way so it won't hang on the brake hose (see Chapter 9).

4   Drain the rear axle lubricant into a suitable container by removing the rear axle housing cover (see Chapter 1).

5   If still in place, discard the gasket.

6   Remove the differential pinion shaft lockpin and discard it **(see illustration)**. **Note:** *It is possible for some Dana semi-floating axles to be equipped with lockpins coated with Loctite (or equivalent), or with lockpins with torque-prevailing threads. The Loctite-*

treated lockpins have a 5/32-inch hexagonal socket head, and the torque-prevailing lockpin has a 12-point drive head. If the axle is equipped with a Loctite-treated lockpin, it must not be re-used. If the lockpin is of the torque-prevailing type, it may be re-used up to four times (four removals and installations). When in doubt as to the number of times the torque-prevailing pin has been used, replace it with a new one.

7   Lift out the differential pinion shaft to gain access to the axleshaft C-locks **(see illustration)**.

8   Push the flanged end of the axleshaft toward the center of the vehicle and remove the C-lock from the end of the shaft **(see illustration)**. **Note:** *On Ford integral carrier axles, make sure not to lose or damage the rubber O-ring which is in the axleshaft groove under the C-clip.*

9   Pull the axleshaft from the housing, making sure not to damage the oil seals. **Caution:** *Do not rotate the differential while the pinion shaft is removed, or the pinion gears and shims can fall out.*

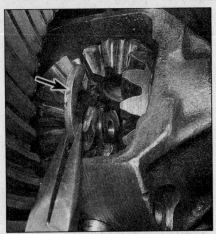

4.8 Push in on the axle flange and remove the C-lock (arrow) from the inner end of the axleshaft

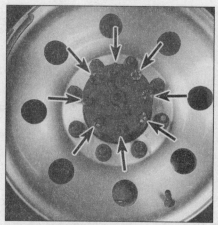

5.1 Remove the axleshaft flange bolts . . .

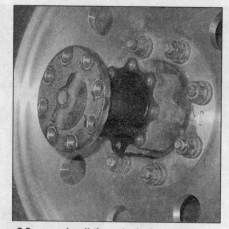

5.2 . . . and pull the axleshaft straight out of the axle housing

5.3 Check the O-ring for cracks or deterioration (it's a good idea to replace it whenever the shaft is removed

Installation

10   Installation is basically the reverse of the removal procedure. Make sure not to damage the axle seal when reinstalling the axleshaft (the splines on the end of the shaft are sharp). Apply a thread locking compound to a new pinion shaft lockpin and tighten it to the torque listed in this Chapter's Specifications. **Warning:** *Failure to correctly install the axleshaft C-locks or lockpin can result in loss of wheel/axle assembly or rear wheel lockup.*

11   Most axle housing covers are sealed with RTV sealant rather than a gasket. Before applying this sealant, make sure the machined surfaces on both cover and carrier are clean and free of oil. When cleaning the surfaces, cover the inside of the axle with a clean lint-free cloth to prevent contamination. Apply a continuous bead of the sealant to the carrier casting face, inside the cover bolt holes. Install the cover within 15 minutes of the application of the sealant and tighten the bolts in a criss-cross pattern to the torque

listed in this Chapter's Specifications.

12   Install the brake drum(s) and adjust if required (see Chapter 9). On models equipped with rear disc brakes, reinstall the disc and the caliper (see Chapter 9).

13   Install the wheel(s) (see Chapter 1).

14   Fill the rear axle with lubricant (see Chapter 1).

15   Remove jackstands and lower vehicle. Test drive and check for leaks.

5   Rear axleshaft (full-floating type) - removal and installation

Refer to illustration 5.1, 5.2 and 5.3

Removal

1   Remove the bolts which attach the axleshaft flange to the hub **(see illustration)**. There is no need to remove the wheel or jack up the vehicle.

2   Tap the flange with a soft-faced hammer to loosen the shaft and then grip the rib of

the face of the flange with a pair of locking pliers; twist the shaft slightly in both directions and withdraw it from the axle tube **(see illustration)**.

Installation

3   Installation is the reverse of removal but hold the axleshaft level in order to engage the splines at its inner end with those in the differential side gear. Always use a new gasket or O-ring on the flange and keep both the flange and hub mating surfaces free of grease and oil **(see illustration)**. Use new bolts, lock washers and/or a thread locking compound and tighten the bolts to the torque listed in this Chapter's Specifications. **Note:** *Final tightening of the axleshaft retaining bolts should be done after the wheel lug nuts have been tightened (if the wheel was removed).*

4   If a loss of fluid is observed, check the differential lubricant level and re-fill if required (see Chapter 1).

5   Test drive the vehicle and check for leaks.

6.4 use an inch-pound torque wrench to check the torque necessary to rotate the pinion shaft

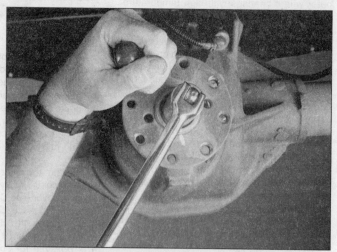

6.6 If you don't have the factory tool to hold the pinion flange while loosening and backing off the pinion flange locknut, use a screwdriver inserted through a hole in the flange and jammed against the top of the reinforcing rib on the differential carrier

6.7 If the pinion flange is difficult to remove, pull it off with a small puller

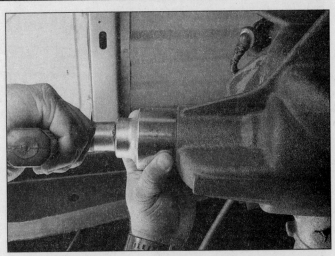

6.10 Lubricate the lips of the new pinion seal and seat it squarely in the bore, then drive it into the carrier with a seal driver or a large socket

6 Rear differential pinion bearing seal - replacement

Refer to illustrations 6.4, 6.6, 6.7 and 6.10
Caution: *If equipped with a Ford integral carrier type rear axle, this procedure disturbs the pinion bearing preload adjustment. Follow the procedure very carefully to reset the pinion bearing preload during reassembly.*

1   Raise the rear of the vehicle and place it securely on jackstands.

2   If equipped with a Ford integral carrier type rear axle, remove the axleshafts (see Section 4 or 5). **Note:** *The removal of the axleshafts is advisable to eliminate the added pinion shaft rotation resistance that otherwise might contribute to a false pinion shaft rotation preload torque value.*

3   Remove the driveshaft (see Section 10).

4   If equipped with a Ford integral carrier type rear axle, using an inch-pound torque wrench (scale from approximately 0 to 40 inch-pounds) on the drive pinion nut, measure and record the torque necessary to rotate the drive pinion in a load-free state **(see illustration)**.

5   Mark the drive pinion-to-companion flange orientation for proper location of flange to pinion upon reassembly.

6   Using a suitable holding tool **(see illustration)** secure the companion flange while removing the pinion nut.

7   Using a two-jaw puller, remove the companion flange from the drive pinion shaft **(see illustration)**. **Note:** *Some fluid loss may occur.*

8   Avoiding contact with the pinion shaft/threads, tap out an edge of the seal using a dull screwdriver. Using Vise-grips or other similar clamping pliers, grip the exposed edge and tap out the seal.

9   Prior to installing the new seal, coat the housing mating surface with RTV sealant and lubricate the seal lip with clean differential lubricant.

10   Clean the seal mating surface and install a new seal squarely in the housing bore. Using an appropriate seal driver if available, drive the seal squarely into the housing until it bottoms **(see illustration)**. If a seal driver isn't available, a large deep socket or section of pipe can be used.

11   Align the companion flange to the pinion marks and gently tap the flange onto the shaft far enough to get several pinion nut threads started. **Note:** *Do not tap on the flange any more than necessary - allow the pinion nut to press the flange onto the shaft.*

12   Using a suitable holding tool, secure the companion flange while tightening the pinion nut to the minimum torque listed in this Chapter's Specifications. If equipped with a Ford integral type rear axle, while tightening, take frequent measurements of rotation torque using an inch-pound torque wrench (see Step 4) until the original free loaded rotation torque is obtained. **Note:** *If the original recorded reading was less than the specified rotation preload torque, continue tightening the drive pinion nut above the minimum torque value (in small increments) to obtain the specified rotation torque. If the rotation reading was higher than specification, stop tightening the pinion nut when the original rotation torque value is obtained again. In no case should the drive pinion nut be backed off to reduce rotation torque, so increase nut torque in small increments and check rotation torque after each increase.*

13   Install the driveshaft (see Section 10).

14   Install the axleshafts (see Section 4 or 5).

15   Install the wheels (see Chapter 1).

16   Check the differential lubricant level and add if required (see Chapter 1).

17   Test drive the vehicle and check for leaks.

7 Rear axle assembly - removal and installation

Removal

1   Chock the front wheels, raise the rear of the vehicle and support it on jackstands placed under the rear frame member.

2   Remove the wheels and brake drums. On models with rear disc brakes, remove the caliper and disc, then wire the caliper out of the way so it won't hang on the brake hose (see Chapter 9).

3   Remove the driveshaft (see Section 10).

4   Disconnect the lower end of the shock absorbers from the axle housing and disconnect the rear stabilizer bar if so equipped (see Chapter 10).

5   Remove the brake vent tube (if equipped) from the brake line junction and retaining clamp.

6   Remove the brake lines from the clips that retain them to the axle and disconnect the brake line fittings from the wheel cylinders. Immediately plug the lines to prevent fluid loss and moisture or contamination from entering the system (see Chapter 9). Disconnect the parking brake cables and remove any clips or fasteners securing the cables to the rear axle housing.

7   On vehicles with rear anti-lock brakes (RABS), be sure to unplug the brake sensor electrical connector (see Chapter 9).

8   Support the weight of the axle on a floor jack and remove the nuts from the spring U-bolts. Remove the bottom clamping plates (see Chapter 10).

9   Lower the axle assembly on the jack and withdraw it from the rear of the vehicle.

Installation

10   The axle assembly is installed by reversing the removal procedure. Tighten all

10.2 Mark the driveshaft-to-companion flange relationship for proper reassembly

13.2 Removing a snap-ring from the bearing cup

fasteners to the torque values listed in this Chapter's Specifications and Chapter 10 Specifications.
11   Connect the brake lines and bleed the brakes (see Chapter 9).

8   Driveshaft(s) - general information

The driveshaft is of tubular construction and may be of a one or two-section type according to the wheelbase of the vehicle.

All driveshafts used to drive the rear wheels have needle bearing type universal joints. Single-section shafts have a splined sliding sleeve at the front end connecting it to the output shaft of the transmission, while two-section shafts have a central slip joint. The purpose of these devices is to accommodate, by retraction or extension, the varying shaft length caused by the movement of the rear axle as the rear suspension deflects.

Where a two-section shaft is used, the shaft is supported near its forward end on a ball bearing which is flexibly mounted in a bracket attached to the frame crossmember.

The attachment of the rear end of the driveshaft to the rear axle pinion flange may be by U-bolt or bolted flange, according to the date of production and model.

The driveshaft is finely balanced during manufacture and it is recommended that care be used when universal joints are replaced to help maintain this balance. It is sometimes better to have the universal joints replaced by a dealership or shop specializing in this type of work. If you replace the joints yourself, mark each individual yoke in relation to the one opposite in order to maintain the balance. Do not drop the assembly during servicing operations.

9   Driveshaft(s) - balancing

1   Vibration of the driveshaft at certain speeds may be caused by any of the following:

a) *Undercoating or mud on the shaft*
b) *Loose attachment bolts*
c) *Worn universal joints*
d) *Bent or dented driveshaft*

2   Vibrations which are thought to be emanating from the driveshaft are sometimes caused by improper tire balance. This should be one of your first checks.
3   If the shaft is in a good, clean, undamaged condition, it is worth disconnecting the rear end attachment straps and turning the shaft 180-degrees to see if an improvement is noticed. Be sure to mark the original position of each component before disassembly so the shaft can be returned to the same location.
4   If the vibration persists after checking for obvious causes and changing the position of the shaft, the entire assembly should be checked out by a professional shop that has the proper equipment, or replaced.

10   Driveshaft(s) - removal and installation

Refer to illustration 10.2
Note: *Where two-piece driveshafts are involved, the rear shaft must be removed before the front shaft.*

Removal

1   Raise the vehicle and support it securely on jackstands.
2   Use chalk or a scribe to "index" the relationship of the driveshaft to the differential

axle assembly mating flange. This ensures correct alignment when the driveshaft is reinstalled **(see illustration)**.
3   Remove the nuts or bolts securing the universal joint clamps to the flange. If the driveshaft has a splined slip joint on one end (either to the transmission or the center carrier bearing) be sure to place marks on the mating flange or shaft to retain proper alignment during reinstallation.
4   Remove the nuts or bolts retaining the straps or universal joint to the flange on the opposite end of the driveshaft (if so equipped).
5   Pry the universal joint away from its mating flange and remove the shaft from the flange. Be careful not to let the caps fall off of the universal joint (which would cause contamination and loss of the needle bearings).
6   Repeat this process for the opposite end if it is equipped with a universal joint coupled to a flange.
7   If the opposite end is equipped with a sliding joint (spline), simply slide the yoke off the splined shaft.
8   If the shaft being removed is the front shaft of a two-piece unit, the rear is released by unbolting the two bolts securing the center bearing assembly. Again, make sure both ends of the shaft have been marked for installation purposes.

Installation

9   Installation is the reverse of removal. If the shaft cannot be lined up due to the components of the differential or transmission having been rotated, put the vehicle in Neutral or rotate one wheel to allow the original alignment to be achieved. Make sure the universal joint caps are properly placed in the flange seat. Tighten the fasteners to the torque listed in this Chapter's Specifications.

13.3a Removing the bearing cups from the yoke using different size sockets on either side of the cup

13.3b Pliers are used to twist the cup completely out of the yoke

11   Driveshaft carrier bearing - check and replacement

Check

1   The carrier bearing can be checked in a similar manner as the universal joints are examined. Check for looseness or deterioration of the flexible rubber mounting.

2   Further examination of the carrier bearing can be made by running the vehicle in gear with the rear wheels raised in the air. However, this should be done with the vehicle supported on a lift and by a dealer service department or other qualified repair facility who can perform the tests safely.

Replacement

3   Remove the driveshaft assembly (see Section 10).

4   With the driveshaft removed from the vehicle and the shaft sections separated at the center bearing, remove the bearing dust shield.

5   Remove the strap which retains the rubber cushion to the bearing support bracket.

6   Separate the cushion, bracket and bearing.

7   Pull the bearing assembly from the driveshaft.

8   Replace any worn components with new ones and reassemble. If the inner deflector was removed, install it to the shaft and stake it at two opposite points to ensure that it is a tight fit.

9   Pack the space between the inner dust deflector and the bearing with lithium-base grease.

10   Carefully tap the bearing and slinger assembly onto the driveshaft journal until the components are tight against the shoulder on the shaft. Use a suitable piece of tubing to do this, taking care not to damage the shaft splines.

11   Install the dust shield (small diameter first) and press it up against the outer slinger.

12   Install the bearing rubber cushion, bracket and strap.

13   Reconnect the driveshafts, making sure the previously made marks are aligned (see Section 10).

12   Universal joints - general information, lubrication and check

1   Universal joints are mechanical couplings which connect two rotating components that meet each other at different angles.

2   These joints are composed of a yoke on each side connected by a crosspiece called a trunnion. Cups at each end of the trunnion contain needle bearings which provide smooth transfer of the torque load. Snap-rings, either inside or outside of the bearing cups, hold the assembly together.

3   Refer to Chapter 1 for details on universal joint lubrication. Also see the routine maintenance schedule at the beginning of Chapter 1.

4   Wear in the needle roller bearings is characterized by vibration in the driveline, noise during acceleration, and in extreme cases of lack of lubrication, metallic squeaking and ultimately grating and shrieking sounds as the bearings disintegrate.

5   It is easy to check if the needle bearings are worn with the driveshaft in position, by trying to turn the shaft with one hand, the other hand holding the rear axle flange when the rear universal joint is being checked, and the front half coupling when the front universal joint is being checked. Any movement between the driveshaft and the front half couplings, and around the rear half couplings, is indicative of considerable wear. Another method of checking for universal joint wear is to use a pry bar inserted into the gap between the universal joint and the driveshaft or flange. Leave the vehicle in gear and try to pry the joint both radially and axially. Any looseness should be apparent with this method. A final test for wear is to attempt to lift the shaft and

note any movement between the yokes of the joints.

6   If any of the above conditions exist, replace the universal joints with new ones.

13   Universal joints - replacement

Refer to illustrations 13.2, 13.3a and 13.3b

1   With the driveshaft removed, mark the location of the joint yokes in relation to each other.

2   Extract the snap-rings from the ends of the bearing cups **(see illustration)**.

3   Using sockets or pieces of pipe of suitable diameter, use a vise to press on the end of one cup to displace the opposite one into the larger socket wrench or pipe. The bearing cup will not be fully ejected and it should be gripped with pliers and twisted completely out of the yoke **(see illustrations)**.

4   Remove the first bearing cup by pressing the trunnion in the opposite direction, then repeat the operations on the other two cups.

5   Clean the yoke and inspect for damage or cracks.

6   Obtain the appropriate repair kit which will include trunnion, cups, needle rollers, seals, washers and snap-rings.

7   Before beginning reassembly, pack the reservoirs in the ends of the trunnion with grease and work some into the needle bearings taking care not to displace them from their location around the inside of the bearing cups.

8   Position the trunnion in the yoke, partially install one cup into the yoke and insert the trunnion a little way into it. Partially install the opposite cup, center the trunnion, then, using the vise, press both cups into position using sockets of diameter slightly less than that of the bearing cups. Make sure that the needle bearings are not displaced and trapped during this operation.

9   Install the snap-rings.

10   Align the shaft yokes and install the other bearing cups in the same manner.

Notes

Chapter 9 Brakes

Contents

Specifications

General
Brake fluid type .... See Chapter 1

Drum brakes
Drum wear limit .... Specified on drum
Minimum lining thickness .... See Chapter 1

Disc brakes
Minimum pad lining thickness .... See Chapter 1
Disc minimum thickness .... Specified on disc
Maximum runout
  Front disc
    E-150, 250, 350 (single rear wheels) .... 0.003 inch
    E-350 (dual rear wheels) .... 0.005 inch
  Rear disc (E-350)
    1996 through 1999 .... 0.008 inch
    2000 on .... 0.0015 inch

Torque specifications

	Ft-lbs (unless otherwise indicated)
Backing plate-to-axle housing nuts	20 to 30
Brake booster-to-firewall nuts	15 to 20
Caliper mounting bolts	
Front caliper	
E-150 (1994 on)	22 to 27
E-250, 350	
1992 through 1994	85 to 100
1995 and 1996	22 to 26
1997 on	16 to 30
Rear caliper (E-350)	27
Anchor plate-to-spindle bolts	
Front brakes	
1995 to 2003	141 to 191
2004 and later	
E150, E250	129
E350	166
Rear brakes (1996 on)	128
Master cylinder-to-brake booster nuts	18 to 25
Wheel speed sensor mounting bolt	
Rear-wheel anti-lock systems	25 to 30
4-wheel anti-lock systems	44 to 53 in-lbs

1   General information

General description

All models covered by this manual are equipped with hydraulically-operated, power-assisted brake systems. All front brake systems are disc type, while the rear brakes are either drum type or disc type. All models are equipped with a rear wheel anti-lock brake system (RABS) and some 1995 and later models may be equipped with a four wheel anti-lock brake system (4WABS). These systems are described in Section 2. All 2004 and later models are equipped with rear disc brakes and 4-wheel ABS systems.

The brake disc and hub on rear disc brake systems are one casting and not available separately. The brake disc and hub incorporate the rear wheel bearings, cups and seals.

All brakes are self-adjusting. The front disc brakes automatically compensate for pad wear, while the rear drum brakes incorporate an adjustment mechanism which is activated as the brakes are applied.

The hydraulic system is a split design, meaning there are separate circuits for the front and rear brakes. If one circuit fails, the other circuit will remain functional and a warning indicator will light up on the dashboard, showing that a failure has occurred.

Master cylinder

The master cylinder is located under the hood, mounted to the power brake booster, and is best recognized by the large fluid reservoir on top. The removable plastic reservoir is partitioned to prevent total fluid loss in the event of a front or rear brake hydraulic system failure.

The master cylinder is designed for the "split system" mentioned earlier and has separate primary and secondary piston assem-blies, the piston nearest the firewall being the primary piston, which applies hydraulic pressure to the front brakes.

The control valve that is built into the master cylinder regulates the hydraulic pressure to the rear brake system.

Parking brake

The parking brake mechanically operates the rear brakes only, through cable actuation. It's activated by a pedal mounted on the left side kick panel. The parking brake cables pull on a lever attached to the brake shoe assembly (drum) or caliper (disc), causing the shoes to expand against the drum (drum brake systems).

Incorporated into the parking brake pedal assembly is a self-adjusting mechanism. Proper tension is maintained on the parking brake cable whenever the pedal is depressed. There are no provisions for adjustment.

Anti-lock Brake System (ABS)

A rear wheel anti-lock brake system (RABS) is used on these vehicles to improve directional stability and control during hard braking. Some models are equipped with a 4-wheel anti-lock brake system (4WABS) that prevents wheel skid at all four wheels.

All 2004 and later models are equipped with rear disc brakes and 4-wheel ABS systems.

Precautions

There are some general cautions and warnings involving the brake system on this vehicle:

a) *Use only brake fluid conforming to DOT 3 specifications.*
b) *The brake pads and linings may contain asbestos fibers which are hazardous to your health if inhaled. Whenever you work on brake system components,* *clean all parts with brake system cleaner. Do not allow the fine dust to become airborne.*
c) *Safety should be paramount whenever any servicing of the brake components is performed. Do not use parts or fasteners which are not in perfect condition, and be sure that all clearances and torque specifications are adhered to. If you are at all unsure about a certain procedure, seek professional advice. Upon completion of any brake system work, test the brakes carefully in a controlled area before putting the vehicle into normal service.*

If a problem is suspected in the brake system, don't drive the vehicle until it's fixed.

2   Anti-lock brake system - general information

Description

Refer to illustration 2.7

The Anti-lock brake system is designed to maintain vehicle maneuverability, directional stability and optimum deceleration under severe braking conditions on most road surfaces. It does so by monitoring the rotational speed of the wheels and controlling the brake line pressure during braking. This prevents the wheels from locking up prematurely.

Two types of systems are used: rear wheel anti-lock brake system (RABS) and 4-wheel anti-lock (4WABS). RABS only controls lockup on the rear wheels, whereas 4WABS prevents lockup on all four wheels.

The rear wheel anti-lock brake system (RABS) consists of the following components and their locations in the vehicle:

a) *Anti-lock electronic control module - located on the instrument panel brace behind the passenger side trim cover.*

**2.7 The hydraulic control unit (A) is located adjacent
to the master cylinder (B) - 4WABS**

**2.13 The ABS speed sensor is mounted on top of
the rear differential (arrow)**

b) *RABS valve - located on the left frame side rail just behind the engine mount front crossmember.*

c) *A single rear axle sensor and sensor ring - located in the rear axle housing.*

d) *ABS amber warning light - located in the instrument cluster.*

The RABS valve consists of an accumulator, dump solenoid and an isolation valve. During normal braking conditions, brake hydraulic fluid from the master cylinder enters the RABS valve and passes through to each of the rear wheels.

When the anti-lock brake control module senses that a rear wheel is about to lock up, the RABS valve opens and closes in mil-second intervals to control the hydraulic fluid to the rear wheel cylinders. This prevents lockup of the rear wheels.

The four wheel anti-lock brake system (4WABS) consists of the following components and their locations in the vehicle:

a) *Anti-lock electronic control module - located next to the fuel filter (early models) or mounted next to the HCU (late models).*

b) *Hydraulic Control Unit (HCU) - located in the engine compartment.*

c) *Two front wheel anti-lock sensors and two sensor rings - located at each front wheel.*

d) *A single rear axle speed sensor and sensor ring - located in the rear axle housing.*

e) *ABS relay - located in the fuse box.*

f) *ABS amber warning light - located in the instrument cluster.*

The hydraulic control unit consists of a brake pressure control valve block, a pump motor and a hydraulic control unit reservoir with a fluid level indicator assembly **(see illustration)**

During normal braking conditions, brake hydraulic fluid from the master cylinder enters the hydraulic control unit through two inlet ports and passes through four normally open inlet valves, one to each wheel.

When the anti-lock brake control module senses that a wheel is about to lock up, the anti-lock brake control module closes the appropriate inlet. This prevents any more fluid from entering the affected brake. If the module determines that the wheel is still decelerating, the module opens the outlet valve, which bleeds off pressure in the affected brake.

Actuator assembly

The actuator assembly includes the master cylinder and a control valve which consists of a dump valve and an isolation valve. The valve operates by changing the brake fluid pressure in response to signals from the control unit.

Control module

The control module for the anti-lock brakes on RABS-equipped models is called the anti-lock electronic control module; it's located inside the center of the dash. The control unit on 4WABS-equipped models is mounted next to the fuel filter on early models or directly under the hydraulic control unit on late models. Either control unit is the "brain" for the system. The function of the control unit is to accept analog voltage inputs from the speed sensors, process that data, and control hydraulic line pressure to avoid wheel lockup.

The control units for both systems constantly monitor the system, even under normal driving conditions, to detect malfunctions. If a problem develops within the system, the control unit illuminates a yellow ABS warning light on the instrument cluster, and may even shut down the anti-lock system if it's a serious malfunction. A diagnostic trouble code will also be stored, which, when retrieved by a service technician, will indicate the problem area or component.

Speed sensor

Refer to illustration 2.13

A speed sensor produces an "analog" (continuously variable) voltage output, which

is transmitted to the control unit, where it's converted to digital information, compared to the control unit's program, and interpreted as wheel rotation speed. On both systems, a single rear wheel speed sensor is located in the top of the differential carrier **(see illustration)**. 4WABS systems also use a front wheel speed sensor in each front steering knuckle.

Brake light switch

The brake light switch, known as the brake on-off (or BOO) switch on these models, signals the control unit when the driver steps on the brake pedal. Without this signal the anti-lock system won't activate. The RABS or RWABS system is de-activated when the brake pedal is released.

Diagnosis and repair

If the yellow ABS warning light on the instrument cluster comes on and stays on, make sure the parking brake is released and there's no problem with the brake hydraulic system. If neither of these is the cause, the anti-lock system is probably malfunctioning. Although special test procedures are necessary to properly diagnose the system, the home mechanic can perform a few preliminary checks before taking the vehicle to a dealer service department.

a) *Make sure the brakes, calipers and wheel cylinders are in good condition.*

b) *Check the electrical connectors at the control unit.*

c) *Check the fuses.*

d) *Follow the wiring harness to the speed sensors and brake light on-off (BOO) switch and make sure all connections are secure and the wiring isn't damaged.*

e) *Use a code reader or scan tool to check for ABS-specific diagnostic trouble codes*

If the above preliminary checks don't rectify the problem, the vehicle should be diagnosed by a dealer service department.

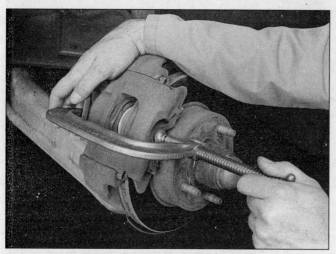

3.6 Push the pistons back into their bores with a C-clamp to provide room for the new brake pads

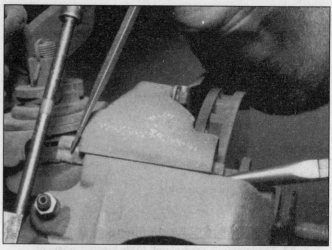

3.7a Use pliers and squeeze the caliper retaining pin while prying the other end until the tabs on the pin enter the spindle groove and . . .

3   Brake pads - replacement

Refer to illustrations 3.6 and 3.7a through 3.7m

Warning: *Disc brake pads must be replaced on both front wheels at the same time - never replace the pads on only one wheel. Also, the dust created by the brake system may contain asbestos, which is harmful to your health. Never blow it out with compressed air and don't inhale any of it. An OSHA approved filtering mask should be worn when working on the brakes. Do not, under any circumstances, use petroleum-based solvents to clean brake parts. Use brake system cleaner only!*

1   The caliper design differs with the various models. The E-150 has a single-piston caliper and all other models have a dual-piston caliper. On 1992 and 1993 E-150 models, the caliper is retained by spring-lock caliper sliding pins. All other models use caliper mounting bolts to retain the caliper to the anchor plate or spindle. Brake pad service is essentially the same for both types of calipers. **Note:** *The following photo sequence illustrates a single piston, front caliper brake assembly. The dual piston assembly mounted on the front and rear of late models is similar.*

2   Remove the cover from the brake fluid reservoir and siphon out about half of the brake fluid.

3   Apply the parking brake and block the rear wheels. Loosen the wheel lug nuts, raise the front of the vehicle and support it securely on jackstands.

4   Remove the front wheels. Work on one brake assembly at a time, using the assembled brake for reference if necessary.

5   Inspect the brake disc carefully as outlined in Section 4. If machining is necessary, follow the information in that Section to remove the disc, at which time the pads can be removed from the calipers as well.

6   Push the piston back into the bore to provide room for the new brake pads. A large C-clamp can be used to accomplish this **(see illustration)**. As the piston is depressed to the bottom of the caliper bore, the fluid in the master cylinder will rise. Make sure it doesn't overflow. If necessary, siphon off some additional fluid. **Caution:** *Don't use a screwdriver or similar tool to pry the piston away from the rotor.*

7   Follow the accompanying illustrations for the actual pad replacement procedure **(see illustrations 3.7a through 3.7m)**. Be sure to stay in order and read the caption under each illustration.

8   When reinstalling the caliper, be sure to tighten the caliper bolts to the torque listed in this Chapter's Specifications. After the job has been completed, firmly depress the brake pedal a few times to bring the pads into contact with the disc.

9   Check for fluid leakage and make sure the brakes operate normally before driving in traffic.

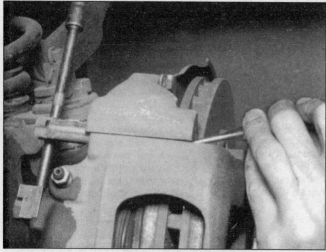

3.7b . . . drive out the pin with a punch and hammer (1992 and 1993 E-150 model)

3.7c If equipped with caliper mounting bolts, remove the bolts (arrows) and . . .

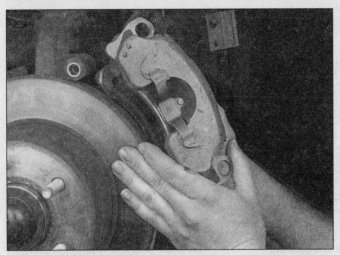

3.7d . . . remove the caliper from the brake disc - on later 2-piston calipers, both pads will stay in the caliper bracket, not the caliper

3.7e If the caliper isn't going to be removed for service, suspend it with a length of wire to relieve any strain on the brake hose

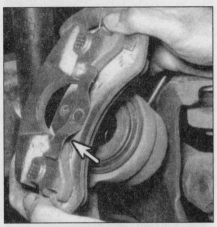

3.7f Release the locking tabs and slide the outer pad from the caliper, then remove the inner pad and anti-rattle clips - on E-150 2-piston calipers, remove the two springs that secure the pads in the caliper mounting bracket

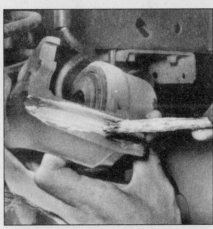

3.7g Prior to installing the caliper, lightly lubricate the V-grooves where the caliper slides into the anchor plate with disc brake caliper slide rail grease or . . .

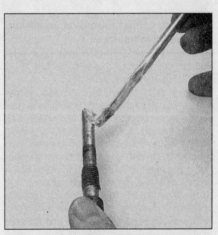

3.7h . . . apply caliper slide rail grease to the sliding surface of the caliper bolts

3.7i Use an eight inch C-clamp and press the piston into the caliper until it bottoms out

3.7j Insert a new anti-rattle clip on the lower end of the inner pad - on 2-piston caliper systems, install both pads in the caliper mounting bracket, and install the retaining clips (E-150 models only)

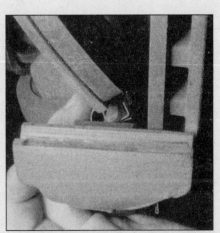

3.7k Make sure the spring tags on the spring clip are positioned correctly and the clip is fully seated

3.7l Compress the anti-rattle clip and slide the upper end of the pad into position - then push the outer pad into position on the caliper mounting ears

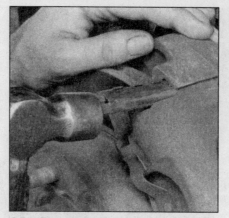

3.7m Place the caliper assembly onto the brake disc, then drive the caliper pins into their grooves or install the caliper mounting bolts (1992 and 1993 models shown)

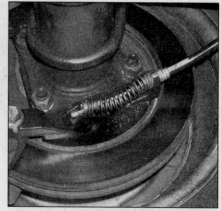

4.4 On rear disc brake systems, retract the spring, pull the cable up and out of the cable stop and remove the cable end from the caliper

4 Brake caliper - removal, overhaul and installation

Refer to illustrations 4.4, 4.6, 4.7, 4.8, 4.13, 4.14, 4.15a, 4.15b and 4.16

Warning: *Dust created by the brake system may contain asbestos, which is harmful to your health. Never blow it out with compressed air and don't inhale any of it. An OSHA approved filtering mask should be worn when working on the brakes. Do not, under any circumstances, use petroleum-based solvents to clean brake parts. Use brake system cleaner only!*

Note: *If an overhaul is indicated (usually because of fluid leakage) explore all options before beginning the job. New and factory-rebuilt calipers are available on an exchange basis, which makes this job quite easy. If it is decided to rebuild the calipers, make sure that a rebuild kit is available before proceeding. Always rebuild the calipers in pairs - never rebuild just one of them.*

Removal

Refer to illustration 4.4

1   Apply the parking brake and block the wheels. Loosen the wheel lug nuts, raise the front/rear of the vehicle and support it securely on jackstands.

2   Remove the front or rear wheels, depending on which set of calipers will be overhauled.

3   Unscrew the brake hose banjo bolt and detach the hose from the caliper. **Caution:** *On 4WABS-equipped models, plug the brake hose immediately to prevent air from getting into the hydraulic control unit (HCU). If air gets into the HCU, you will not be able to bleed the brakes properly at home. On non-4WABS models, cap the end of the hose to prevent fluid loss and contamination.*

4   Refer to the first few Steps in Section 3 to separate the caliper from the rotor - it's part of the brake pad replacement procedure. **Note:** *On rear disc brake systems, disconnect the emergency brake cable from the caliper* **(see illustration).**

Overhaul

5   Clean the exterior of the caliper with brake system cleaner. Never use gasoline, kerosene or petroleum-based cleaning solvents. Place the caliper on a clean workbench.

6   Position a wood block or several shop rags in the caliper as a cushion, then use compressed air to remove the piston from the caliper **(see illustration).** Use only enough air pressure to ease the piston out of the bore. **Warning:** *Never place your fingers in front of the piston in an attempt to catch or protect it when applying compressed air, as serious injury could occur.*

7   Carefully pry the dust boot out of the caliper bore **(see illustration).**

8   Using a wood or plastic tool, remove the piston seal from the groove in the caliper bore **(see illustration).** Metal tools may cause bore damage.

9   Remove the caliper bleeder screw and discard all rubber parts.

10   Clean the remaining parts with brake

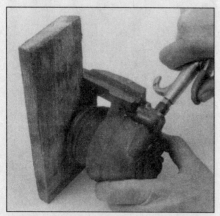

4.6 With the caliper padded to protect the piston, use compressed air to force the piston out of its bore - make sure your hands or fingers are not between the piston and caliper

4.7 Remove the dust boot from the caliper bore groove

4.8 The piston seal should be removed with a plastic or wooden tool to avoid damage to the bore and seal groove

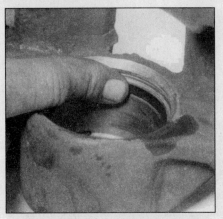

4.13 Push the new seal into the groove with your fingers, then check to see that it isn't twisted or kinked

4.14 Install the dust boot in the upper groove in the caliper bore, make sure it's completely seated

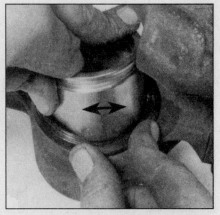

4.15a Insert the piston into the dust boot (NOT the bore) at an angle, then work the piston completely into the dust boot using a rotating motion

system cleaner, then blow them dry with compressed air.

11　Carefully examine the piston for nicks and burrs and loss of plating. If surface defects are present, the parts must be replaced. Check the caliper bore in a similar way.

12　Discard the mounting pins if they're corroded or damaged.

13　When assembling, lubricate the piston bore and seals with clean brake fluid. Install the seal in the groove of the caliper bore **(see illustration)**. Make sure the seal does not become twisted and that it is firmly seated in the groove.

14　Install a new boot in the upper groove of the caliper bore **(see illustration)**.

15　Lubricate the piston with clean brake fluid, insert the piston into the boot **(see illustration)**, then push it squarely into the bore, Use a C-clamp and wood block to press the piston in until it bottoms out **(see illustration)**.

16　Seat the lip of the dust boot in the groove on the piston **(see illustration)**.

17　Install the bleeder screw.

Installation

18　Refer to Section 3 for the caliper installation procedure, as it is part of the brake pad replacement procedure.

19　Install a new sealing washer on each side of the brake hose fitting, then install the brake inlet hose banjo bolt and tighten it securely.

20　Bleed the brakes as outlined in Section 12.

21　Install the wheels and lower the vehicle. Tighten the lug nuts to the torque listed in the Chapter 1 Specifications.

22　Test the brake operation before placing the vehicle in normal service.

5 Brake disc - inspection, removal and installation

Refer to illustrations 5.4, 5.5a and 5.5b

Inspection

1　Loosen the wheel lug nuts, raise the vehicle and support it securely on jackstands. Remove the wheel(s).

2　Remove the brake caliper (see the first few steps of Section 3). It's not necessary

to disconnect the brake hose. After removing the caliper, suspend the caliper out of the way with a piece of wire **(see illustration 3.7e)**. Don't let the caliper hang by the hose and don't stretch or twist the hose.

3　Visually check the disc surface for score marks and other damage. Light scratches and shallow grooves are normal after use and may not always be detrimental to brake operation, but deep score marks - over 0.015-inch - require disc removal and refinishing by an automotive machine shop. Be sure to check both sides of the disc. If pulsating has been noticed during application of the brakes, suspect disc runout. Be sure to check the wheel bearings to make sure they're properly adjusted.

4　To check disc runout, place a dial indicator at a point about 1/2-inch from the outer edge of the disc **(see illustration)**. Set the indicator to zero and turn the disc. The indicator reading should not exceed the runout limit listed in this Chapter's Specifications. If it does, the disc should be refinished by an automotive machine shop. **Note:** *Professionals recommend resurfacing of brake discs regardless of the dial indicator reading to pro-*

4.15b Use a C-clamp and a block of wood to bottom the piston in the cylinder bore - make sure it goes in perfectly straight, or the sides of the piston may be damaged

4.16 Install the lip of the dust boot in the groove in the caliper piston

5.4 Use a dial indicator to check disc runout - if the reading exceeds the maximum allowable runout limit, the disc will have to be machined or replaced

5.5a The minimum thickness limit is cast into the disc (typical)

5.5b Use a micrometer to measure the disc thickness at several points near the edge

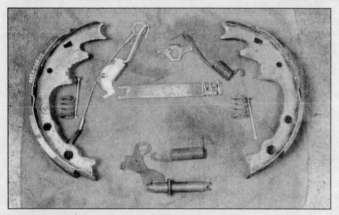

6.1 During removal, lay the parts out in their correct order of removal to keep from getting confused

6.4 Before removing drum brake components, wash them off with an aerosol brake system cleaner and allow them to dry - position a drain pan under the brake assembly to catch the residue - DO NOT use compressed air to blow brake dust from the components!

duce a smooth, flat surface that will eliminate brake pedal pulsation's and other undesirable symptoms related to questionable discs.

5   The disc must not be machined to a thickness less than the minimum refinish thickness. The minimum wear (or discard) thickness is cast into the inner surface of the disc **(see illustration)**. The disc thickness can be checked with a micrometer at several points around the disc **(see illustration)**.

Removal

6   Refer to Chapter 1, Section 26, for the hub/disc removal procedure on front disc brake systems. Refer to Chapter 8, Section 3 for the hub/disc removal procedure on rear disc brake systems.

Installation

7   Install the disc and hub assembly and adjust the wheel bearings.

8   Install the caliper and brake pad assembly.

9   Install the wheel(s), then lower the vehicle to the ground. Tighten the lug nuts to the torque listed in the Chapter 1 Specifications. Depress the brake pedal a few times to bring the brake pads into contact with the disc. Bleeding of the system isn't necessary unless the brake hose was disconnected from the caliper. Check the operation of the brakes carefully before placing the vehicle into normal service.

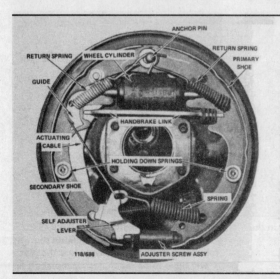

6.5a Components of the rear brake assembly (right side shown)

---

6   Rear brake shoes (E-150 models) - replacement and adjustment

Refer to illustrations 6.1, 6.4 and 6.5a through 6.5y

Warning: *Dust created by the brake system may contain asbestos, which is harmful to your*

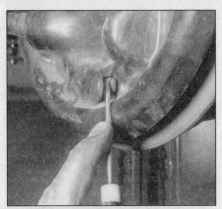

6.5b If, after releasing the parking brake, the drum will not slide off the shoes, remove the rubber plug from the backing plate . . .

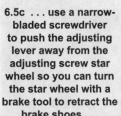

6.5c . . . use a narrow-bladed screwdriver to push the adjusting lever away from the adjusting screw star wheel so you can turn the star wheel with a brake tool to retract the brake shoes . . .

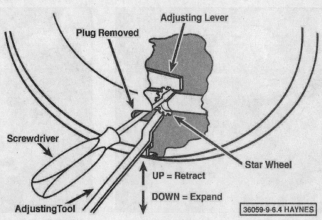

health. Never blow it out with compressed air and don't inhale any of it. An OSHA approved filtering mask should be worn when working on the brakes. Do not, under any circumstances, use petroleum-based solvents to clean brake parts. Use brake system cleaner only!

Caution: *Drum brake shoes must be replaced on both wheels at the same time - never replace the shoes on only one wheel. Whenever the brake shoes are replaced, the retrac-tor and hold-down springs should also be replaced. Due to the continuous heating/cooling cycle that the springs are subjected to, they lose their tension over a period of time and may allow the shoes to drag on the drum and wear at a much faster rate than normal.*

1   To ease installation of the brake assembly, during the removal procedures lay out all parts in an assembled order on a rag near the work area **(see illustration)**.

2   Loosen the wheel lug nuts, raise the rear of the vehicle and support it securely on jackstands. Block the front wheels to keep the vehicle from rolling.

3   Release the parking brake.

4   Remove the wheels. **Note:** *All four rear brake shoes must be replaced at the same time, but to avoid mixing up parts, work on only one brake assembly at a time. Before removing any drum brake components, wash them off with an aerosol brake system cleaner and allow them to dry - position a drain pan under the brake to catch the residue -* **do not use compressed air to blow the brake dust from the parts! (see illustration).**

5   Follow the accompanying photos **(see illustrations 6.5a through 6.5y)** for the inspection and replacement of the brake shoes. Be sure to stay in order and read the caption under each illustration. **Note:** *If the brake drum cannot be easily removed, make sure that the parking brake is completely released, then apply some penetrating oil at the hub-to-drum joint. Allow the oil to soak in and try to pull the drum off. If the drum still cannot be removed, the brake shoes will have to be retracted. This is accomplished by first removing the plug from the backing plate. With the plug removed, pull the lever off the adjusting star wheel with one small screwdriver while turning the adjusting wheel with another small screwdriver, moving the shoes away from the drum.*

6.5d . . . and slide the drum off the axle hub

6.5e Use a brake spring tool to remove the shoe retracting springs

6.5f Pull up on the adjusting cable and disconnect the cable eye from the anchor pin

6.5g Remove the anchor pin plate

6.5h Remove the shoe retaining springs and pins (one on each shoe)

6.5i Pull the shoes apart and remove the adjusting screw

6.5j Remove the primary shoe, then remove the parking brake strut and spring

6.5k Remove the adjuster pawl

6.5l Pull the secondary shoe away from the backing plate

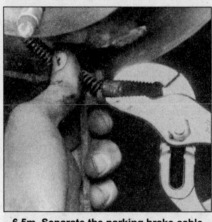

6.5m Separate the parking brake cable and spring from the actuating lever

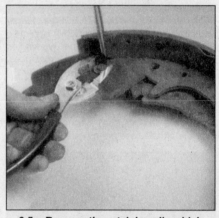

6.5n Remove the retaining clip which holds the parking brake actuating lever to the brake shoe

6   Before reinstalling the drum it should be checked for cracks, score marks, deep scratches and hard spots, which will appear as small discolored areas. If the hard spots cannot be removed with fine emery cloth or if any of the other conditions listed above exist, the drum must be taken to an automotive machine shop for resurfacing. **Note:** *Professionals recommend resurfacing the drums whenever a brake job is done. Resurfacing will eliminate the possibility of out-of-round drums. If the drums are worn so much that they can't be resurfaced without exceeding the maximum allowable diameter (cast into the drum), then new ones will be required. At the very least, if you elect not to have the drums resurfaced, remove the glazing from the surface with medium-grit emery cloth using a swirling motion.*

7   Install the brake drum on the axle flange.

8   Install the wheels, then lower the vehicle to the ground. Tighten the lug nuts to the torque listed in the Chapter 1 Specifications.

9   Make a number of forward and reverse stops to adjust the brakes until satisfactory pedal action is obtained.

10   Check brake operation before driving the vehicle in traffic.

6.5o Install the parking brake actuator lever on the new brake shoe and install the retaining clip

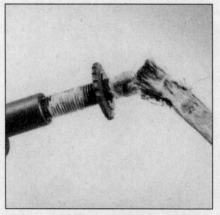

6.5p Lubricate the adjusting screw with high-temperature brake grease

6.5q Lightly coat the shoe contact areas on the backing plate with high-temperature brake grease

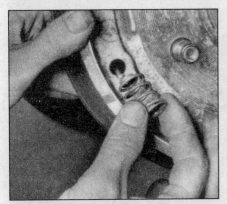

6.5r Position the shoes on the backing plate, insert the retaining pins through the backing plate and shoes and place the springs over the pins

6.5s Install the retaining spring caps

6.5t Make sure the wheel cylinder plungers and the parking brake strut properly engage the brake shoes

7   Rear brake shoes (E-250 and E-350 models) - replacement and adjustment

Refer to illustrations 7.6, 7.9 and 7.22

Warning: *Drum brake shoes must be replaced on both wheels at the same time - never replace the shoes on only one wheel. Also, the dust created by the brake system is* harmful to your health. Never blow it out with compressed air and don't inhale any of it. An OSHA approved filtering mask should be worn when working on the brakes. Do not, under any circumstances, use petroleum-based solvents to clean brake parts. Use brake system cleaner only!

Caution: *Whenever the brake shoes are replaced, the retractor and hold-down springs should also be replaced. Due to the continu-* ous heating/cooling cycle that the springs are subjected to, they lose their tension over a period of time and may allow the shoes to drag on the drum and wear at a much faster rate than normal.

1   To ease installation of the brake assembly, during the removal procedures lay out all parts in an assembled order on a rag near the work area **(see illustration 6.1)**.

2   Loosen the wheel lug nuts, raise the

6.5u Install the adjusting screw with the long end pointing towards the front of the vehicle

6.5v Install the adjusting pawl

6.5w Install the anchor pin plate, cable guide and cable

6.5x Install the shoe guide and adjusting cable eye to the anchor pin, then install the shoe retracting springs

6.5y Connect the cable and spring to the lever, then install the drum and adjust the brake shoe-to-drum clearance

7.6 The parking brake lever is secured in place by the pivot bolt at the top

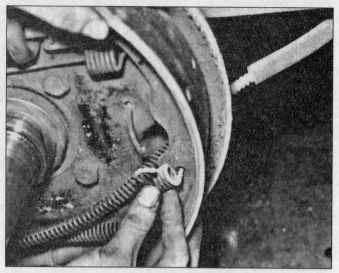

7.9 Remove the brake shoe hold-down springs

rear of the vehicle and support it securely on jackstands. Block the front wheels to keep the vehicle from rolling.

3   Release the parking brake.

4   Remove the wheels and the brake drums. **Note 1:** *If the brake drum cannot be easily pulled off the axle and shoe assembly, make sure that the parking brake is completely released, then apply some penetrating oil at the hub-to-drum joint. Allow the oil to soak in and try to pull the drum off. If the drum still cannot be pulled off, the brake shoes will have to be retracted. This is accomplished by first removing the plug from the backing plate. With the plug removed, pull the lever off the adjusting star wheel with one small screwdriver while turning the adjusting wheel with another small screwdriver, moving the shoes away from the drum. The drum should now come off.* **Note 2:** *All four rear brake shoes must be replaced at the same time, but to avoid mixing up parts, work on only one brake assembly at a time.*

5   Before removing any drum brake components, wash them off with an aerosol brake system cleaner and allow them to dry - position a drain pan under the brake to catch the residue - **do not use compressed air to blow the brake dust from the parts! (see illustration 6.4).**

6   Remove the parking brake lever assembly retaining nut from the back of the backing plate. Remove the parking brake lever assembly **(see illustration)**.

7   Remove the adjusting cable assembly from the anchor pin. Detach it from the cable guide and disconnect the other end from the adjusting lever.

8   Remove the brake shoe retaining springs from both primary and secondary brake shoes. Use a brake spring tool for this operation.

9   Remove the brake shoe hold-down springs from both the primary and secondary brake shoes **(see illustration)**.

10   Remove the brake shoes. The adjust-

ing screw assembly will fall loose at this time. Keep all parts of this assembly together.

11   Clean all of the springs and adjusting components with brake system cleaner.

12   Clean the brake backing plate and hub components left on the vehicle. If the six ledge pads on the backing plate are corroded or rusty, sand them lightly to bare metal. **Note:** *Prior to reassembly, inspect the wheel cylinder for signs of leakage and overhaul or replace a leaking wheel cylinder as required (refer to Section 8).*

13   Apply a light coat of brake lube to the shoe contact areas on the backing plate. Apply a coating of lube to the retracting and hold-down spring contact points on the brake shoes and backing plate.

14   Dismantle and clean the pivot nut, adjusting screw, washer and socket. Take care not to mix these adjusting components from side-to-side as they are built for left-side or right-side installation only. If these components become mixed, the adjusting lever and the socket end of the adjusting screw are stamped with the letter L (left) or R (right).

15   Lubricate the threads of the adjusting screw components with brake lube and retract the adjustment to the smallest dimension.

16   Install the upper brake retracting spring between the two brake shoes and make sure you have the shoes positioned correctly.

17   Place the shoes and spring assembly into position on the backing plate and position the wheel cylinder pushrods into their slots on the brake shoe webbing.

18   Install both brake shoe hold-down springs.

19   Position the brake shoe adjusting screw assembly into place between the bottom of the brake shoes with the slot in the head of the adjusting screw pointed toward the primary shoe.

20   Install the lower brake shoe retracting spring.

21   Install the adjusting lever spring and the

cable assembly to the adjusting lever. Position the adjusting lever onto the proper pin of the secondary shoe.

22   Place the adjusting lever cable into its proper position around the cable guide and hook the cable end to the anchor pin. Make sure the adjusting lever is engaged in the teeth of the adjusting screw **(see illustration)**.

23   Install the parking brake lever and retaining nut.

24   Before reinstalling the drum it should be checked for cracks, score marks, deep scratches and hard spots, which will appear as small discolored areas. If the hard spots cannot be removed with fine emery cloth or if any of the other conditions listed above exist, the drum must be taken to an automotive machine shop for resurfacing. **Note:** *Professionals recommend resurfacing the drums whenever a brake job is done. Resurfacing will eliminate the possibility of out-of-round drums. If the drums are worn so much that they can't be resurfaced without exceeding the maximum allowable diameter (cast into the drum), then new ones will be required. At the very least, if you elect not to have the drums resurfaced, remove the glazing from the surface with medium-grit emery cloth using a swirling motion.*

25   Install the brake drum on the axle flange.

26   Manually adjust the brakes (by turning the adjustment screw) until there is a slight drag on the brake drum, then back-off the adjuster until no drag is heard when the drum is turned.

27   Install the wheels, then lower the vehicle to the ground. Tighten the lug nuts to the torque listed in the Chapter 1 Specifications.

28   Make a number of forward and reverse stops to adjust the brakes until satisfactory pedal action is obtained.

29   Check brake operation before driving the vehicle in traffic.

7.22 Make sure the adjusting lever contacts the adjusting screw as shown

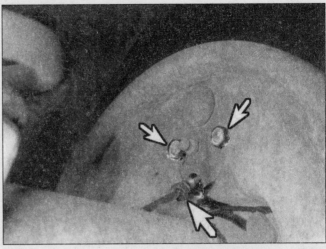

8.4 To remove the wheel cylinder, disconnect the brake line fitting and remove the mounting bolts (arrows)

8 Wheel cylinder - removal, overhaul and installation

Note: *If an overhaul is indicated (usually because of fluid leakage or sticky operation) explore all options before beginning the job. New wheel cylinders are available, which makes this job quite easy. If it's decided to rebuild the wheel cylinder, make sure that a rebuild kit is available before proceeding. Never overhaul only one wheel cylinder - always rebuild both of them at the same time.*

Removal

Refer to illustration 8.4

1   Loosen the wheel lug nuts, raise the rear of the vehicle and support it securely on jackstands. Block the front wheels to keep the vehicle from rolling.

2   Remove the brake shoe assembly (see Section 6 or Section 7).

3   Remove all dirt and foreign material from around the wheel cylinder.

4   Unscrew the brake line fitting **(see illustration)**. Don't pull the brake line away from the wheel cylinder.

5   Remove the wheel cylinder mounting bolts.

6   Detach the wheel cylinder from the brake backing plate and place it on a clean workbench. **Caution:** *On 4WABS-equipped models, plug the brake line immediately to prevent air from getting into the hydraulic control unit (HCU). If air gets into the HCU, you will not be able to bleed the brakes properly at home. On non-4WABS models, cap the end of the line to prevent fluid loss and contamination.* **Warning:** *If the brake shoe linings are contaminated with brake fluid, install new brake shoes.*

Overhaul

Refer to illustration 8.7

7   Remove the bleeder screw, cups, pistons, boots and spring assembly from the

wheel cylinder body **(see illustration)**.

8   Clean the wheel cylinder with brake fluid or brake system cleaner. **Warning:** *Do not, under any circumstances, use petroleum-based solvents to clean brake parts!*

9   Use compressed air, if available, to remove excess fluid from the wheel cylinder and to blow out the passages.

10   Check the cylinder bore for corrosion and score marks. Crocus cloth can be used to remove light corrosion and stains, but the cylinder must be replaced with a new one if the defects cannot be removed easily, or if the bore is scored.

11   Lubricate the new cups with clean brake fluid.

12   Assemble the wheel cylinder components. Make sure the cup lips face in.

Installation

13   Place the wheel cylinder in position and install the mounting bolts.

14   Connect the brake line and tighten the fitting. Install the brake shoe assembly.

15   Bleed the brakes (see Section 12).

16   Check the brake operation before driving the vehicle in traffic.

9 Master cylinder - removal, overhaul and installation

Removal

Warning: *If the vehicle is equipped with the four-wheel Anti-lock Brake System (4WABS), make sure you plug the brake line immediately after disconnecting it from the master cylinder, to prevent air from entering the HCU.*

Note: *On most models, access to the master cylinder is better with the coolant recovery tank out of the way (see Chapter 3).*

1   Push the brake pedal down several times to expel the vacuum from the brake booster.

2   Place newspapers under the master cylinder to catch the brake fluid that will spill out. Remove the brake lines from the primary and secondary outlet ports of the master cylinder. **Note:** *Use a flare-nut wrench, if available, to prevent rounding off the fittings.* Plug the ends of the lines to prevent the entry of dirt and moisture.

3   Disconnect the electrical connector from the fluid level sensor, if equipped. On models with cruise control, disconnect the cruise control deactivator switch connector at the master cylinder.

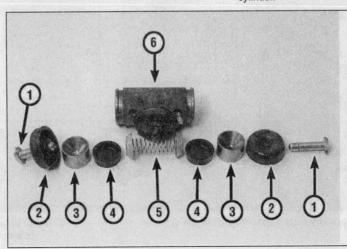

8.7 Exploded view of a typical wheel cylinder

1   Pushrods
2   Dust boots
3   Pistons
4   Cups
5   Expander spring
6   Wheel cylinder

9.6 After you've disassembled the master cylinder assembly, wash all the parts in clean brake fluid, blow them off with compressed air, and lay them out for inspection:

1   *Reservoir*
2   *Snap-ring*
3   *Primary piston/ spring assembly*
4   *Secondary piston/ spring assembly*
5   *Reservoir grommets*
6   *Master cylinder*

9.8 Use a Phillips head screwdriver to push the primary piston into the cylinder, then remove the snap-ring

4   Remove the nuts which secure the master cylinder to the brake booster.

5   Remove the master cylinder from the vehicle. **Caution:** *Brake fluid will damage painted surfaces, so don't spill any on the vehicle.*

Overhaul

Refer to illustrations 9.6, 9.8, 9.9, 9.10 and 9.11

Note: *Before deciding to overhaul the master cylinder, check on the availability and cost of a new or factory-rebuilt unit and also the availability of a rebuild kit.*

6   Clean the exterior of the master cylinder and dry it with a lint-free rag. Remove the reservoir cap and pour out any remaining brake fluid **(see illustration)**.

7   Place the master cylinder in a vise with the vise jaws clamping on the mounting flange.

8   Use a large Phillips screwdriver to depress the piston assembly, then remove the snap-ring from the retaining groove at the rear of the master cylinder **(see illustration)**.

9   Remove the primary piston assembly from the cylinder bore **(see illustration)**. Inspect the seal for damage.

10   Remove the secondary piston assembly from the cylinder bore. It may be necessary to remove the master cylinder from the vise and invert it, carefully tapping it against a block of soft wood to expel the piston **(see illustration)**. Inspect the seal for damage.

11   If fluid has been leaking past the reservoir grommets, carefully pry the reservoir from the body with a screwdriver **(see illustration)**. Remove the grommets and discard them.

12   Inspect the surfaces of the cylinder bore and pistons for corrosion, wear and damage. If these are evident, replace the complete master cylinder assembly. Do not hone the master cylinder bore.

13   If these main components are in good condition, then the original assembly is worth overhauling.

14   If the rubber seals are swollen or very loose on the pistons, suspect oil contamination in the system. Oil will swell these rubber seals and if one is found to be swollen it is reasonable to assume that all seals in the brake system need attention.

15   Purchase a repair kit which contains all the necessary seals and other replaceable parts. Some repair kits will contain a complete primary piston assembly.

16   Wash all the internal components in clean brake fluid or brake system cleaner. Do not use any other type of fluid. Mineral spirits or solvent must never be allowed to come in contact with hydraulic cylinder components.

17   Lubricate the new reservoir grommets with brake fluid and press them into the master cylinder body. Make sure they are properly seated.

18   Inspect the reservoir cap and reservoir for cracks or damage and replace if necessary.

19   Lay the reservoir on a hard surface and press the master cylinder body into the reservoir, using a rocking motion.

20   Lubricate the cylinder bore with clean brake fluid.

21   Dip the secondary piston assembly into clean brake fluid and push the piston into the cylinder, so the spring will seat against the closed end of the cylinder. Ease the seals into the bore taking care that they do not roll over.

22   Reinstall the master cylinder in a vise so that the open end of the cylinder is facing up. Dip the primary piston assembly into clean

9.9 Remove the primary piston assembly from the cylinder

9.10 Tap the master cylinder against a block of soft wood to eject the secondary piston assembly

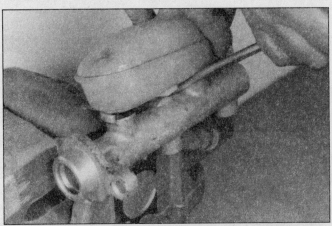

9.11 If you remove the reservoir (to replace leaking seals or a broken reservoir), gently pry it off with a screwdriver or prybar

10.7 Working in the passenger compartment, disconnect the brake light switch and booster pushrod (arrows)

brake fluid and then push the piston, spring end first, into the master cylinder.

23 Depress the piston and install the retaining snap-ring. Make sure it is seated correctly in the bore groove.

Installation

24 Installation is the reverse of removal with the following additions:

a) **Note:** Whenever the master cylinder is removed, the entire hydraulic system must be bled. The time required to bleed the system can be reduced if the master cylinder is filled with fluid and bench bled (see below) before the master cylinder is installed on the vehicle.

b) Insert threaded plugs of the correct size into the cylinder outlet holes and fill the reservoirs with fresh brake fluid. The master cylinder should be supported in such a manner that the brake fluid will not spill during the bench bleeding procedure.

c) Loosen one plug at a time, starting with the rear outlet port first, and use a large Phillips screwdriver to push the piston assembly into the bore to force air from the master cylinder. To prevent air from being drawn back into the cylinder, the appropriate plug must be tightened before allowing the piston to return to its original position.

d) Stroke the piston three or four times for each outlet to ensure that all air has been expelled.

e) Since high pressure is not involved in the bench bleeding procedure, an alternative to the removal and installation of the plug with each stroke of the piston is available. Before pushing in on the piston assembly, remove one of the plugs completely. Before releasing the piston, however, instead of installing the plug, simply place your finger tightly over the hole to keep air from being drawn into the master cylinder. Wait several seconds for the brake fluid to be drawn from the reservoir to the piston bore, then repeat the

procedure. When you push down on the piston it will force your finger off the hole, allowing air inside to be expelled. When only brake fluid is being ejected from the hole, install the plug and go to the other port.

f) Refill the master cylinder reservoirs and install the diaphragm and cap. On 2001 and later models, reinstall the master cylinder with NEW mounting nuts only.

g) Bleed the brake system as outlined in Section 12 and test the brakes carefully before driving the vehicle in traffic.

h) Install new master cylinder mounting nuts. The old nuts are not re-usable.

10 Power brake booster - removal and installation

1 The power brake booster unit requires no special maintenance apart from periodic inspection of the vacuum hose and the case.

2 Dismantling of the power unit requires special tools and is not ordinarily done by the home mechanic. If a problem develops, install a new or factory rebuilt unit.

Removal

Refer to illustration 10.7

Warning: Wait until the engine is completely cool before beginning this procedure.

3 Detach the coolant hoses, remove the coolant reservoir mounting bolts and lift the coolant reservoir from the engine compartment.

4 Remove the nuts attaching the master cylinder to the booster and carefully pull the master cylinder forward until it clears the mounting studs. Don't bend or kink the brake lines. On most models, the coolant recovery tank must be removed to remove the brake booster (see Chapter 3).

5 Loosen the clamp and disconnect the vacuum hose where it attaches to the check valve on the power brake booster. Remove the check valve from the booster.

6 From the passenger compartment, disconnect the electrical connector from the brake light switch.

7 From the passenger compartment, disconnect the retaining pin, then slide the brake light switch, booster pushrod, spacers and bushings off the brake pedal arm (see illustration).

8 Remove the nuts securing the booster to the firewall.

9 Working in the engine compartment, lift the booster unit away from the firewall and out of the vehicle.

Installation

Refer to illustration 10.11

10 Install the booster unit in the reverse order of removal.

11 Before installing the master cylinder to the booster, check the distance from the end of the booster pushrod to the face of the booster assembly, with a force of approximately five pounds applied to the end of the pushrod (see illustration). Turn the pushrod adjusting screw in or out as required to obtain the correct length of 0.995-inches.

12 When adjustment is complete, reinstall the master cylinder and check for proper operation before driving the vehicle in traffic.

10.11 Check the master cylinder-to-booster pushrod clearance

11 Brake hoses and lines - inspection and replacement

1   Brake hoses and lines should be inspected when recommended in the maintenance schedule and whenever the vehicle is raised. See Chapter 1 for inspection intervals and procedures.

Replacement

Front brake hose

2   Using a back-up wrench, disconnect the brake line from the hose fitting.
3   Use a pair of pliers to remove the U-clip from the female fitting at the bracket, then detach the hose from the bracket.
4   Unscrew the inlet fitting bolt from the caliper. Discard the sealing washers.
5   To install the hose, place a new sealing washer on each side of the hose fitting, install the inlet fitting bolt and tighten it securely.
6   Without twisting the hose, install the female fitting in the frame bracket.
7   Install the U-clip retaining the female fitting to the frame bracket.
8   Using a back-up wrench, attach the brake line to the hose fitting.
9   When the brake hose installation is complete, there should be no kinks in the hose. Make sure the hose doesn't contact any part of the suspension. Check this by turning the wheels to the extreme left and right positions. If the hose makes contact, remove it and correct the installation as necessary. Bleed the system (see Section 12).

Rear brake hose

10   Using a back-up wrench, disconnect the hose at the frame bracket, being careful not to bend the bracket or steel lines.
11   Remove the U-clip with a pair of pliers and separate the female fitting from the bracket.
12   Disconnect the two hydraulic lines at the junction block, then unbolt and remove the hose.
13   Bolt the junction block to the axle housing and connect the lines, tightening them securely. Without twisting the hose, install the female end of the hose in the frame bracket.
14   Install the U-clips retaining the female end to the bracket.
15   Using a back-up wrench, attach the steel line fittings to the female fittings. Again, be careful not to bend the bracket or steel line.
16   Make sure the hose installation did not loosen the frame bracket. Tighten the bracket if necessary.
17   Fill the master cylinder reservoir and bleed the system (see Section 12).

Metal brake lines

18   When replacing brake lines be sure to use the correct parts. Don't use copper tubing for any brake system components. Purchase steel brake lines from a dealer or auto parts store.
19   Prefabricated brake line, with the tube

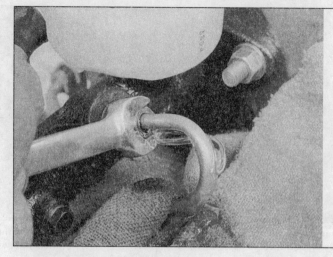

12.7 Have an assistant depress the brake pedal and hold it down, then loosen the fitting nut, allowing air and fluid to escape; repeat this procedure on both fittings until the fluid is clear of air bubbles

ends already flared and fittings installed, is available in standard lengths at auto parts stores and dealers. These lines are not bent to the proper shapes. Remove the damaged section of brake line and using the proper tubing bending tools, form the replacement section to match the original exactly.
20   When installing the new line make sure it's securely supported in the brackets and has plenty of clearance from moving or hot components.
21   After installation, check the master cylinder fluid level and add fluid as necessary. Bleed the brake system (see Section 12) and test the brakes carefully before driving the vehicle in traffic.

12 Brake hydraulic system - bleeding

Refer to illustrations 12.7 and 12.10
Warning 1: *The following procedure is a manual bleeding procedure. This is the only bleeding procedure which can be performed at home without special tools. However, if air has found its way into the hydraulic control unit, the entire system must be bled manually, then with a special scan tool, then manually a second time. If the brake pedal feels "spongy" even after bleeding the brakes, or the ABS light on the instrument panel does not go off, or if you have any doubts whatsoever about the effectiveness of the brake system, have the vehicle towed to a dealer service department or other repair shop equipped with the necessary tools for bleeding the system.*
Warning 2: *Wear eye protection when bleeding the brake system. If the fluid comes in contact with your eyes, immediately rinse them with water and seek medical attention.*
Note: *Bleeding the hydraulic system is necessary to remove any air that manages to find its way into the system when it's been opened during removal and installation of a hydraulic component.*

1   It will be necessary to bleed the complete system if air has entered the system due to low fluid level, or if the brake lines have been

disconnected at the master cylinder.
2   If a brake line was disconnected only at a wheel, then only that caliper or wheel cylinder must be bled.
3   If a brake line is disconnected at a fitting located between the master cylinder and any of the brakes, that part of the system served by the disconnected line must be bled. The following procedure describes bleeding the entire system, however.
4   Remove any residual vacuum from the brake power booster by applying the brake several times with the engine off.
5   Remove the cap from the master cylinder reservoir and fill the reservoir with brake fluid. Reinstall the cap(s). **Note:** *Check the fluid level often during the bleeding operation and add fluid as necessary to prevent the fluid level from falling low enough to allow air bubbles into the master cylinder.*
6   Have an assistant on hand, as well as a supply of new brake fluid, a clear container partially filled with clean brake fluid, a length of clear tubing to fit over the bleeder valve and a wrench to open and close the bleeder valve.
7   Begin the bleeding process by bleeding the master cylinder **(see illustration)**.
8   On models with four-wheel ABS, bleed the lines where they enter the ABS HCU using the same technique.
9   Moving to the right rear wheel, loosen the bleeder valve slightly, then tighten it to a point where it is snug but can still be loosened quickly and easily.
10   Place one end of the hose over the bleeder valve and submerge the other end in brake fluid in the container **(see illustration)**.
11   Have the assistant push the brake pedal slowly to the floor, then hold the pedal firmly depressed.
12   While the pedal is held depressed, open the bleeder valve just enough to allow a flow of fluid to leave the valve. Watch for air bubbles to exit the submerged end of the tube. When the fluid flow slows after a couple of seconds, close the valve and have your assistant release the pedal.
13   Repeat Steps 11 and 12 until no more air is seen leaving the tube, then tighten the

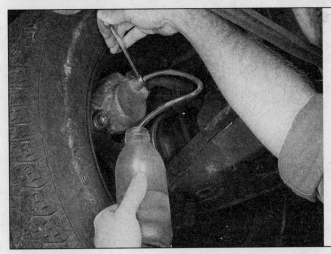

12.10 When bleeding the brakes, a hose is connected to the bleed screw at the caliper or wheel cylinder and then submerged in brake fluid - air will be seen as bubbles in the tube and container (all air must be expelled before moving to the next wheel)

bleeder valve and proceed to the left rear wheel, the right front wheel and the left front wheel, in that order, and perform the same procedure. Be sure to check the fluid in the master cylinder reservoir frequently.

14   Never use old brake fluid. It contains moisture which can boil, rendering the brakes inoperative.

15   Refill the master cylinder with fluid at the end of the operation.

16   Check the operation of the brakes. The pedal should feel solid when depressed, with no sponginess. If necessary, repeat the entire process. **Warning:** *If, after bleeding the system you do not have a firm brake pedal, or if the ABS light on the instrument panel does not go off, or if you have any doubts whatsoever about the effectiveness of the brake system, have it towed to a dealer service department or other repair shop equipped with the necessary scan tool for bleeding the ABS HCU.*

13   Brake pedal - removal and installation

1   Disconnect the cable from the negative battery terminal.

2   Disconnect the electrical connector from the brake light switch **(see illustration 10.7)**. Where applicable, on later models remove the fasteners at the pedal assembly and set the under-dash fuse-relay panel aside.

3   Disconnect the self-locking pin and spacer connecting the brake pedal assembly, brake light switch assembly and master cylinder pushrod together.

4   Remove the brake light switch, bushing and master cylinder push rod from the pin on the brake pedal.

5   Remove the nut from the long bolt.

6   Slide the long bolt out far enough to remove the brake pedal, bushing and spring washer.

7   Remove the master cylinder push rod spacer from the brake pedal.

8   Installation is the reverse of removal with the following additions.

9   Clean, inspect and lubricate the brake pedal bolt bushing with engine oil prior to installation.

Notes

Chapter 10
Suspension and steering systems

Contents

Specifications

Torque specifications

Ft-lbs

Front suspension

Models through 2002

Axle pivot bolt and nut	110 to 150
Axle pivot bracket bolt	80 to 110
Jounce bumper bolt	15 to 21
Lower balljoint stud nut	110 to 150
Radius arm-to-frame bracket nut	81 to 120
Radius arm bracket-to-frame bolt	64 to 88
Radius arm-to-axle arm bolt	188 to 254
Shock absorber-to-front radius arm nut	50 to 68
Shock absorber upper nut	25 to 35
Spring upper retainer bolt	19 to 26
Stabilizer bar bracket bolts	15 to 21
Upper balljoint clamp bolt	64 to 88

2003 and later models

Axle pivot bolt and nut	129
Axle pivot bracket bolt	80 to 110
Jounce bumper bolt	15 to 21
Lower balljoint stud nut	130
Radius arm-to-frame bracket nut	98
Radius arm bracket-to-frame bolt	64 to 88
Radius arm-to-axle arm bolt	221
Shock absorber-to-front radius arm nut	59
Shock absorber upper nut	30
Spring upper retainer bolt	22
Stabilizer bar bracket bolts	18
Upper balljoint clamp bolt	77

Rear suspension

	Ft-lbs (unless otherwise indicated)
Rear leaf spring U-bolt nut	
E-150 models	72 to 98
E-250, E-350 models	109 to 148
Shock-to-lower bracket bolt	
1992 through 1995 models	44 to 59
1996 and later models	51 to 67
Shock-to-upper bracket nut	25 to 34
Shackle-to-spring bolt	
1992 through 1995 models	83 to 113
1996 and later models	
E-150 models	73 to 97
E-250, E-350 models	110 to 150
Spring-to-front bracket bolt	
E-150 models	110 to 136
E-250, E-350 models	240 to 290
Spring shackle-to-rear bracket bolt	
1992 through 1995 models	83 to 113
1996 and later models	57 to 76
Stabilizer bar link to frame	50 to 70
Stabilizer bar link to stabilizer bar	18 to 23
Stabilizer bar retainer to axle	24 to 34

Steering linkage

Drag link-to-Pitman arm nut	51 to 73
Drag link-to-connecting link nut	51 to 73
Tie-rod adjusting sleeve nut	30 to 42
Tie-rod to spindle nut	51 to 84
Pitman arm-to-steering gear nut	170 to 228

Steering system

Airbag module-to-steering wheel nuts (1996 and earlier)	36 to 48 in-lbs
Airbag module-to-steering wheel bolts (1997 and later)	90 to 107 in-lbs
Flex coupling-to-steering gear input shaft bolt	30 to 42
Power steering gear hoses to gear	20 to 25
Power steering gear-to-frame bolts	
Models through 2003	54 to 66
2004 and later	122
Power steering pump-to-bracket bolts	
1992 through 1995 models	30 to 41
1996 and later models	15 to 22
Steering wheel bolt	23 to 33

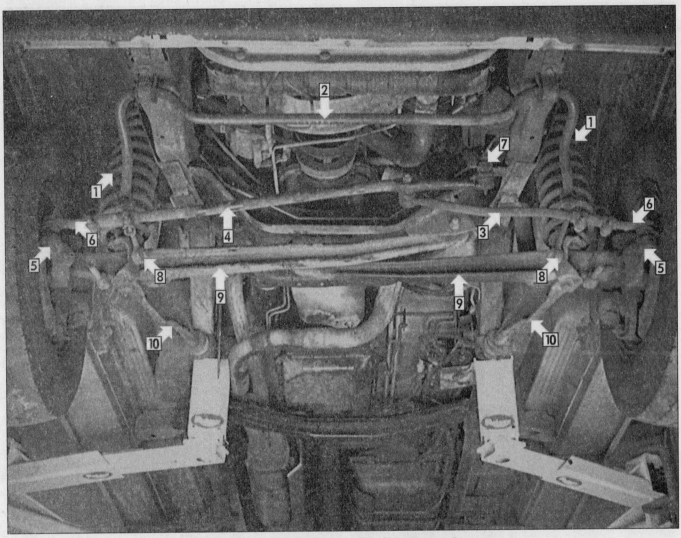

1.1 Front suspension and steering components

1	Spring and shock absorber	5	Front wheel spindle (steering	8	Stabilizer bar link
2	Stabilizer bar		knuckle)	9	I-beam
3	Tie-rod	6	Tie-rod end	10	Radius arm
4	Drag link	7	Pitman arm		

1   General information

Refer to illustration 1.1 and 1.5

The front suspension on the Econoline models covered in this manual is a twin I-beam type, which is composed of coil springs, I-beam axle arms, radius arms, upper and lower balljoints and spindles, tie-rods, shock absorbers and an optional stabilizer bar **(see illustration)**.

The front suspension consists of two independent axle arm assemblies. One end of the assembly is anchored to the frame and the other is supported by the coil spring and radius arm. The spindle is connected to the axle by upper and lower balljoints. The balljoints are constructed of a lubricated-for-life special bearing material. Lubrication points are found on the tie-rods and steering linkage. Movement of the spindles is controlled by the tie-rods and the steering linkage.

Two adjustments can be performed on the axle assembly. Camber is adjusted by removing and replacing an adapter between the upper balljoint stud and the spindle. Toe-in adjustment is accomplished on both models by turning the tie-rod adjusting sleeve.

The hydraulic shock absorbers are of the direct, double acting type that are pressurized by low pressure gas. Both shock absorbers are of the telescoping design and come equipped with rubber grommets at the mounting points for quiet operation. The low pressure gas shock absorbers are sealed and charged with nitrogen gas to reduce shock absorber fade and improve ride. The shock absorbers are non-adjustable. The shock absorbers are not rebuildable and must be replaced as complete assemblies.

1.5 Rear suspension components

1	Rear shock absorber	4	Leaf springs
2	Shock absorber lower mounting bracket	5	Spring U-bolts
3	Axle housing		

The rear suspension uses shock absorbers and semi-elliptical leaf springs **(see illustration)**. The forward end of each spring is attached to the bracket on the side of the frame side rail. The rear of each spring is shackled to a bracket on the side of the frame rail. The rear shock absorbers are direct, double acting units.

Since most procedures that are dealt with in this chapter involve jacking up the vehicle and working underneath it, a good pair of jack-stands will be needed. A hydraulic floor jack is the preferred type of jack to lift the vehicle, and it can also be used to support certain components during various operations. **Warning:** *Never, under any circumstances, rely on a jack to support the vehicle while working under it.* **Warning:** *The manufacturer states that whenever any of the suspension or steering fasten-*

ers are loosened or removed they must be replaced with new ones - discard the originals and don't re-use them. They must be replaced with new ones of the same part number or of original equipment quality and design. Torque specifications must be followed for proper reassembly and component retention.

2   Front shock absorbers - inspection, removal and installation

Inspection

1   The common test of shock damping is simply to bounce the corners of the vehicle several times and observe whether or not the vehicle stops bouncing once you let go. A slight

rebound and settling indicates good damping, but if the vehicle continues to bounce several times, the shock absorbers must be replaced.
2   If the shock absorbers stand up to the bounce test, visually inspect the shock body for signs of fluid leakage, punctures or deep dents in the metal of the body. Replace any shock absorber which is leaking or damaged, even if it passed the bounce test in Step 1.
3   After removing the shock absorber, pull the piston rod out and push it back in several times to check for smooth operation throughout the travel of the piston rod. Replace the shock absorber if it gives any signs of hard or soft spots in the piston rod travel.
4   Prior to installing the new shock absorbers, pump the piston rod fully in and out several times to lubricate the seals and fill the hydraulic sections of the unit.

**2.7 Hold the shock absorber shaft while turning
the top nut (arrows)**

**2.8 The shock absorber lower mount is attached
to the radius arm (arrow)**

Removal and installation

Refer to illustrations 2.7 and 2.8

Caution: *The low pressure gas shock absorbers are pressurized to 135 PSI with nitrogen gas. Do not attempt to open, puncture or apply heat to the shock absorbers.*

5   Loosen the front wheel lug nuts on the side to be dismantled. Raise the front of the vehicle, support it securely on jackstands, block the rear wheels and set the parking brake. Remove the front wheel.

6   The shock absorbers are mounted next to the coil springs.

7   Support the outer end of the axle with a floor jack. Remove the top nut with a deep socket while holding the shaft with an open end wrench **(see illustration)**. Lift off the insulator.

8   Remove the nut securing the shock absorber to the radius arm **(see illustration)**.

9   To remove the shock absorber, slightly compress the shock and remove it from its brackets.

10   Installation is the reverse of the removal steps with the following additions:

a) *Install and tighten the new nuts and bolts to the torque listed in this Chapter's Specifications.*

b) *Install the wheel and lug nuts, lower the vehicle and tighten the lug nuts to the torque listed in Chapter 1.*

3   Front wheel spindle - removal and installation

Removal

1   Remove the front wheel and brake disc (see Chapter 9).

2   Remove the brake dust shield.

3   Remove the cotter pin and nut and disconnect the tie-rod end from the spindle.

4   Remove the cotter pin from the lower balljoint stud nut, then remove the nut.

5   Remove the clamp bolt from the upper balljoint.

6   Mark the exact orientation of the camber adjuster to the spindle. Pry the camber adjuster from the spindle. If necessary, use a two-jaw puller to remove the camber adjuster.

7   Strike the lower yoke of the axle to break the spindle loose from the balljoint studs. **Caution:** *Don't use a fork-type separator to detach the balljoint. This will damage the balljoint seal.*

8   Remove the spindle together with the balljoints.

Installation

9   Before installation, check that the upper and lower balljoint seals were not damaged during spindle removal and that they are positioned correctly. Replace if necessary.

10   Position the spindle and balljoints in the axle arm.

11   Install the camber adjuster on the upper balljoint, making sure it's aligned correctly.

12   Tighten the lower balljoint nut to the torque listed in this Chapter's Specifications, then tighten further until the cotter pin hole lines up. Install a new cotter pin and bend it to secure the nut.

13   Install the clamp bolt on the upper balljoint and tighten it to the torque listed in this Chapter's Specifications.

14   Install the dust shield.

15   Install the brake disc and the front wheel (see Chapter 1).

16   Have the front end alignment checked by a dealer service department or an alignment shop.

4   Balljoints - removal and installation

Removal

1   Remove the spindle (see Section 3).

2   Remove the snap-ring from the lower balljoint. **Note:** *Remove the lower balljoint first.*

3   Using a C-frame type balljoint press and the appropriate size receiving cup on

the lower balljoint, press the balljoint out of the spindle. **Note:** *If the C-frame assembly tool and receiver tool are not available or will not remove the balljoint, take the spindle assembly to a dealer service department or machine shop and have the balljoints pressed out.* **Warning:** *Don't heat the spindle or balljoint to aid in removal since the temper may be removed from the components, leading to premature failure.*

4   Use the same tool setup used in Step 3 on the upper balljoint and press the balljoint out.

Installation

5   Install the upper balljoint with the C-frame assembly, balljoint receiver cup and installation cup. **Note:** *Always install the upper balljoint first since the special tool must pass through the lower balljoint receptacle in the axle. However, on 2004 and later models, the manufacturer recommends installing the lower balljoint first.*

6   Turn the screw in the C-frame clockwise and press the balljoint into the axle until it is completely seated.

7   Install the lower balljoint with the C-frame assembly, balljoint receiver cup and installation cup.

8   Turn the screw in the C-frame clockwise and press the balljoint into the axle until it is completely seated.

9   Install the lower balljoint snap-ring.

10   The remainder of installation is the reverse of removal.

5   Coil spring - removal and installation

Refer to illustrations 5.2, 5.5 and 5.6

Removal

1   Loosen the front wheel lug nuts on the side to be dismantled. Raise the front of the vehicle, support it securely by jackstands placed on the frame rails, block the rear

5.2 With the vehicle supported on jackstands, use a floor jack to raise and lower the front axles

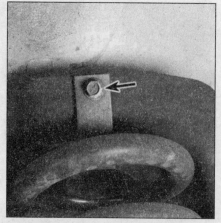

5.5 Remove the retainer bolt and retainer securing the spring to the frame (arrow)

5.6 Loosen the retaining nut at the other end of this bolt at least four full turns - push the bolt up so the lower retainer is free to tip to one side

wheels and set the parking brake. Remove the front wheel.

2   Place a floor jack under the axle to be worked on **(see illustration)**. On 2001 and later models, remove the stabilizer bar (see Section 11).

3   On models through 2004, remove the bolt and nut securing the shock absorber to the radius arm **(see illustration 2.8)**.

4   Remove the brake caliper assembly and suspend it with a length of wire to relieve any strain on the brake hose (see Chapter 9).

5   At the upper end of the spring, remove the retainer bolt and retainer securing the spring to the frame **(see illustration)**.

6   On early models, loosen the radius arm-to-axle nut at least four full turns to allow the spring cup to pivot a little. On later models, just remove the bolt and tab securing the upper end of the spring, then lower the axle and remove the spring.

7   On 2005 models, spray the lower end of the spring with a light lubricant and rotate the spring counterclockwise a half-turn, then remove the spring by tilting it away from the chassis.

8   Tip the lower retainer and lift the spring up and over the lower retainer and bolt. If necessary, use a prybar. Remove the spring.

Installation

9   Make sure the lower retainer and insulator are in place on the front axle and radius arm.

10   Push the front axle down to allow installation of the spring. Install the lower end of the spring into the spring retainer and orient the insulator's "D" shape into the spring's bottom coil.

11   Apply slight pressure on the floor jack and slowly raise the front axle and orient the spring's upper coil into the front spring tower helix in the frame. Raise the front axle until the spring is correctly seated both at the top and bottom.

12   Install the upper spring retainer and bolt. Tighten the bolt to the torque listed in this Chapter's Specifications.

13   Tighten the radius arm-to axle retaining bolt and nut to the torque listed in this Chapter's Specifications.

14   Install the brake caliper assembly (see Chapter 9).

15   Install the bolt and new nut securing the shock absorber to the radius arm. Tighten the nut to the torque listed in this Chapter's Specifications.

16   Install the wheel and lug nuts, lower the vehicle and tighten the lug nuts to the torque listed in Chapter 1.

---

6   Radius arm - removal and installation

Refer to illustrations 6.3 and 6.4

Removal

1   Remove the coil spring (see Section 5).

2   On early models, disconnect the stabilizer bar links. On later models, remove the stabilizer bar from the axle (see Section 11).

3   Remove the bolt, spring insulator, retainer and nut securing the radius arm to the front axle **(see illustration)**.

6.3 Remove the nut and bolt securing the radius arm to the front axle (arrow)

4   From the rear side of the radius arm bracket, remove the nut, washer and insulator **(see illustration)**.

5   Remove the radius arm and remove the spacer, insulator and retainer from the radius arm threaded end.

Installation

6   Install the front end of the radius arm onto the front axle.

7   From above the axle, install the radius arm-to-axle bolt, retainer, insulator and a new nut. Tighten the nut only finger tight at this time.

8   Install the retainer, insulator and spacer onto the threaded end of the radius arm.

9   Install the radius arm into the rear bracket and install the insulator, washer and new nut. Tighten the nut to the torque listed in this Chapter's Specifications.

10   Tighten the radius arm-to-axle bolt and nut to the torque listed in this Chapter's Specifications.

11   On models so equipped, install the through bolt securing the stabilizer bar to the front axle. Tighten the bolt and nut to the

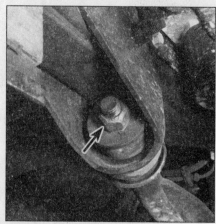

6.4 From the rear side of the radius arm bracket, remove the nut, washer and insulator (arrow)

11.2 Unscrew the nut from the stabilizer bar link (early models)

1   Link
2   Stabilizer bar

torque listed in this Chapter's Specifications.
12   Install the coil spring assembly (see Section 5).

7   Radius arm insulators - replacement

1   Remove the coil spring (see Section 5).
2   Loosen the axle arm pivot bolt.
3   Remove the shock absorber upper nut and compress the shock.
4   From the rear side of the radius arm bracket, remove the nut, washer and insulator **(see illustration 6.4)**.
5   Raise the front axle arm with a floor jack until the axle arm is level.
6   Push the radius arm forward until it is free of the radius arm frame bracket.
7   Remove the radius arm spacer, insulator and retainer from the radius arm threaded end.
8   Installation is the reverse of the removal steps with the following additions:

   a) Install new insulators and a new nut.
   b) Tighten the bolts and nut to the torque listed in this Chapter's Specifications.

8   Front axle arm - removal and installation

Removal

1   Raise the front of the vehicle, support it securely on jackstands, block the rear wheels and set the parking brake. Position the front wheels in the straight ahead position.
2   Remove the coil spring (see Section 5) and front spindle (see Section 3).
3   Remove the front stabilizer bar (see Section 11).
4   Remove the radius arm-to-axle nut, bolt and spring seat (see Section 6).

11.3 Unscrew the stabilizer bar bracket bolts, then remove the stabilizer bar

5   Remove the bolt and nut securing the axle arm to the frame pivot bracket. Remove the axle arm.

Installation

6   Install the axle arm to the frame pivot bracket with a new retaining bolt and nut. Tighten the nut finger-tight.
7   Install the front axle arm onto the radius arm. Install the radius arm-to-axle bolt, nut and spring seat, leaving the nut loose.
8   Install the front spindle (see Section 3) and the coil spring (see Section 5).
9   Tighten the radius arm-to-axle bolt to the torque listed in this Chapter's Specifications.
10   Install the front stabilizer bar (see Section 11).
11   Install the wheel and lug nuts. Lower the vehicle and tighten the lug nuts to torque listed in the Chapter 1 Specifications.
12   Tighten the axle arm pivot bolt to the torque listed in this Chapter's Specifications.
13   Have the front end alignment checked by a dealer service department or an alignment shop.

9   Axle pivot bushing - removal and installation

Removal

1   Raise the front of the vehicle, support it securely on jackstands, block the rear wheels and set the parking brake. Position the front wheels in the straight ahead position.
2   Remove the front spring (see Section 5).
3   Remove the retaining bolt and nut, then pull the pivot end of the axle down until the bushing is exposed.
4   Install the forcing screw, bushing remover and receiver cup or equivalent bushing removal tools onto the bushing. Position the spacer between the walls of the axle, then turn the forcing screw and press the bushing out of the axle.

Installation

5   Insert the bushing in the axle receptacle. Install the receiver cup, forcing tool and bushing replacer onto the axle. Turn the forcing screw and press the bushing into the axle.
6   The new bushing must be flared to prevent movement within the axle. Install the forcing screw, receiving cup and flaring tool, or equivalent. Turn the forcing screw and flare the lip of the bushing.
7   The remainder of installation is the reverse of the removal Steps.

10   Axle pivot bracket (right-side only) - removal and installation

Removal

1   Loosen the front wheel lug nuts on the side to be dismantled. Raise the front of the vehicle, support it securely on jackstands, block the rear wheels and set the parking brake. Remove the front wheel.
2   Remove the coil spring (see Section 5). Remove the axle pivot nut and bolt, pull the axle down and out of the bracket.
3   Remove the bolts and nuts securing the right-side axle pivot bracket to the frame and remove the bracket from the frame crossmember.

Installation

4   Position the front axle bracket onto the frame crossmember. Install the new bolts from within the frame crossmember and out through the bracket, then install the new nuts. After all of the bolts and nuts have been installed, tighten them to the torque listed in this Chapter's Specifications.
5   The remainder of installation is the reverse of the removal Steps.

11   Front stabilizer bar - removal and installation

Refer to illustrations 11.2 and 11.3
1   Raise the front of the vehicle, support it securely on jackstands, block the rear wheels and set the parking brake. Position the front wheels in the straight ahead position.
2   On early models, detach the stabilizer bar from its links **(see illustration)**. On later models, the stabilizer bar ends fit into holes in the axles, without links.
3   Remove the stabilizer bar retaining brackets and bushings, then remove the bar **(see illustration)**.
4   If necessary, use a forcing screw and receiver cup to remove and install the axle arm bushings.
5   Installation is the reverse of the removal steps. Tighten the bolts and nuts to the torque listed in this Chapter's Specifications.

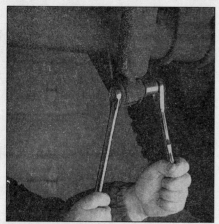

12.3 Remove the shock absorber lower mounting nut and bolt

12.4 Unscrew the upper mounting nut, then remove the shock absorber

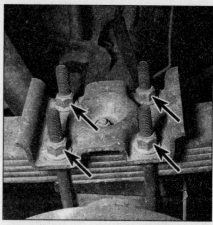

13.4 Remove the four U-bolt nuts

12   Rear shock absorbers - inspection, removal and installation

Refer to illustrations 12.3 and 12.4

Inspection

1   Refer to Section 2 for inspection procedures.

Removal and installation

2   Raise the rear of the vehicle, support it securely on jackstands and block the front wheels. Place a floor jack under the axle adjacent to shock absorber being removed. Apply just enough jack pressure to take the load off the shock absorber.
3   Remove the nut and bolt securing the lower end of the shock absorber to the rear axle **(see illustration)**.
4   Remove the nut and insulator securing the top of the shock absorber to the upper mounting bracket on the frame **(see illustration)**.
5   Installation is the reverse of the removal steps. Tighten the nuts and bolts to the torque listed in this Chapter's Specifications.

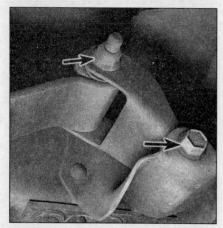

13.5 Remove the spring shackle fasteners

13   Rear leaf spring - removal and installation

Refer to illustrations 13.4 and 13.5

Removal

1   Raise the rear of the vehicle until the weight is off the rear springs but the tires are still touching the ground.
2   Support the vehicle securely on jackstands and support the rear axle with a jack. DO NOT get under a vehicle that's supported only by a jack, even if the tires are still installed.
3   Remove the nut and bolt securing the lower end of the shock absorber to the spring plate. Compress the shock up and out of the way.
4   Remove the nuts from the U-bolts and remove the U-bolts and the spring plate from the spring **(see illustration)**.
5   Remove the bolts and nuts securing the shackle assembly at the rear of the spring **(see illustration)**. Let the spring pivot down and rest on the floor.
6   Remove the spring hanger bolt, nut and retainer at the front of the spring. Remove the spring.
7   Inspect the spring eye bushings for wear or distortion. If worn or damaged have them replaced by a dealer service department or properly equipped shop.

Installation

8   Place the spring in the rear shackle. Install the bolt and nut and tighten them finger-tight.
9   Install the spring in the front bracket. Tighten the bolt and nut finger-tight.
10   Position the rear shackle on the frame. Install the bolt and nut and tighten them finger-tight.
11   Position the axle under the spring and install the spring seat. Make sure the spring tie-bolt is positioned in the hole in the spring, then install the U-bolts and nuts. Tighten the nuts finger-tight.

12   Lower the vehicle to the ground so its weight is resting on the tires. Tighten the spring bracket bolt and nut, shackle bolts and nuts and U-bolt nuts to the torque listed in this Chapter's Specifications.

14   Steering system - general information

The steering system consists of a Pitman arm, drag link, steering connecting link and tie-rods. The Pitman arm transfers the steering gear movements through the drag link and steering connecting link to the tie-rods at each end. The tie-rods move the knuckle (or spindle) and front wheels to the desired steering movement. The tie-rods are equipped with an adjusting sleeve for setting the toe-in.

All models are equipped with steering gear that consists of a belt-driven pump and associated lines and hoses. The power steering pump reservoir fluid level should be checked periodically (see Chapter 1).

The steering wheel operates the steering shaft, which actuates the steering gear through universal joints and the intermediate shaft. Looseness in the steering can be caused by wear in the steering shaft universal joints, the steering gear, the tie-rod ends and loose retaining bolts.

15   Steering wheel and clockspring - removal and installation

Warning: *Some models are equipped with airbags. Always disconnect the negative battery cable, then the positive cable and wait 2 minutes before working in the vicinity of the impact sensors, steering column or instrument panel to avoid the possibility of accidental deployment of the airbag, which could cause personal injury (see Chapter 12).*

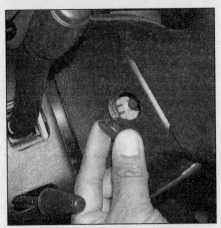

15.2a Remove the access plugs from the steering column cover

15.2b Remove the airbag mounting bolts or nuts

15.2c Pull the airbag module straight out . . .

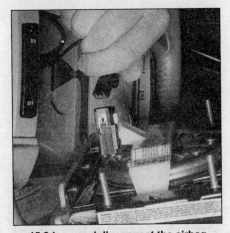

15.2d . . . and disconnect the airbag electrical connector

15.4 There should be factory alignment marks on the steering wheel and column; if not, make your own (arrows)

15.5a On 1996 and earlier models, remove the steering wheel with the puller like the one shown here - DO NOT pound on the wheel to remove it

Steering wheel removal

Refer to illustrations 15.2a, 15.2b, 15.2c, 15.2d, 15.4, 15.5a and 15.5b

1   First disconnect the cable from the negative terminal of the battery, then the positive terminal of the battery. **Warning:** *Wait 2 minutes for the capacitor in the airbag system to discharge. Position the front wheels in the straight-ahead position and lock the steering column.*

2   On models without a driver's side airbag, simply pull the horn pad straight off. On models equipped with a driver's side airbag, lock the steering wheel in the straight-ahead position and remove the airbag module retaining bolts or nuts **(see illustrations)**, lift the module off the steering wheel and unplug the module electrical connector **(see illustrations)**. Set the module aside in a safe, isolated area, with the airbag side of the module facing UP. **Warning:** *When carrying the airbag module, keep the driver's (trim) side of it away from your body, and when you set it down, make sure the driver's side is facing up.*

3   Unplug the electrical connector for the horn and the cruise control, if equipped.

4   Remove the steering wheel retaining

bolt. There should already be an alignment mark on the upper edge of the steering shaft and another mark on the steering wheel hub **(see illustration)**. If not, then mark the relationship of the steering shaft to the hub (if marks don't already exist or don't line up) to simplify installation and ensure correct steering wheel alignment. **Warning:** *Discard the hub bolt. Use a new one during installation.*

5   Use a puller to detach the steering wheel from the shaft **(see illustrations)**. Don't use an impact puller and don't pound on the steering wheel or shaft. Route the contact assembly wire harness through the steering wheel as the wheel is lifted off the shaft.

6   If equipped with cruise control, make sure the slip ring grease is not contaminated. Check the slip ring contacts for wear or damage and make sure they are properly seated.

Clockspring removal

Refer to illustrations 15.11, 15.12 and 15.14

7   If equipped with tilt steering, remove the tilt wheel handle and shank by twisting the assembly counterclockwise.

8   Remove the lower steering column shroud mounting screws and remove the

15.5b On 1997 and later models, remove the steering wheel with a two-jaw puller

shroud from the steering column.

9   Remove the ignition switch lock cylinder (see Chapter 12).

10   Remove the upper steering column shroud by lifting up.

11   Stabilize the service lock on the clockspring by installing a piece of tape across the

15.11 Install a piece of tape to secure the service lock

15.12 Remove the set screw from the key-in-the-ignition warning switch

15.14 Pry the retaining clips (arrows) out to release the clockspring

airbag clockspring **(see illustration)**. Note: *The airbag contact has a service lock that prevents accidental rotation of the clockspring while it is off the steering column.*
12   Remove the key-in-the-ignition warning switch **(see illustration)**.
13   Disconnect the sliding contact connector from the bracket.
14   Pry the retaining clips out **(see illustration)** from the clockspring.
15   Separate the wire from the two retaining clips wrapped against the steering column.
16   Remove the clockspring from the steering column.

Installation

17   Install the clockspring onto the steering column and make sure the electrical harness connector is positioned at 3 o'clock. **Note:** *If the clockspring service lock has been released accidentally, rotate the airbag sliding contact rotor counterclockwise until it reaches its stop. Rotate the assembly from this position two turns clockwise.*
18   Press the retaining clips back in to secure the clockspring.
19   Secure the harness wiring into the clips and install the electrical connectors.
20   The remaining steps are the reverse of the removal.
21   To install the wheel, align the mark on the steering wheel hub with the mark on the shaft and slip the wheel onto the shaft. Install a new bolt and tighten it to the torque listed in this Chapter's Specifications.
22   Plug in the horn connector and the cruise control connector, if equipped.
23   On models with a driver's side airbag, connect the airbag electrical connector and install the airbag module. Tighten the fasteners to the torque listed in this Chapter's Specifications.
24   On models without a driver's side airbag, simply push the horn pad straight on to install it on the wheel.
25   First connect the positive cable, then the negative battery cable.

16 Drag link - removal and installation

Refer to illustration 16.3

Removal

1   Raise the front of the vehicle, support it securely on jackstands, block the rear wheels and set the parking brake. Position the front wheels in the straight ahead position.
2   Remove the cotter pins and nuts securing the drag link to the steering connecting arm and to the Pitman arm.
3   Use a Pitman arm puller and detach the drag link from the Pitman arm **(see illustration)**.
4   Loosen the clamp bolts on the tie-rod adjusting sleeve.
5   Unscrew the adjusting sleeve. Count and record the number of turns it takes to back the sleeve off the drag link.
6   Remove the drag link.

Installation

7   Loosely install the drag link ball stud into the Pitman arm. Position the steering connecting arm ball end into the drag link. Make sure the front wheels and steering wheel are in the straight ahead position. Make sure the ball ends are seated in the taper to prevent

16.3 Use a puller to separate the drag link from the Pitman arm

them from rotating while tightening the nuts.
8   Install the drag link onto the tie-rod adjusting sleeve and turn it the same number of turns noted during removal in Step 4. Tighten the clamp bolts on the tie-rod adjusting sleeve to the torque listed in this Chapter's Specifications.
9   Install new nuts on the studs of the Pitman arm and steering connecting arm and tighten to the torque listed in this Chapter's Specifications. Install new cotter pins and bend the ends over completely.
10   Install the wheel and lug nuts. Lower the vehicle and tighten the lug nuts to torque listed in the Chapter 1 Specifications.
11   Have the front end alignment checked by a dealer service department or an alignment shop.

17 Steering connecting link - removal and installation

Warning: *Whenever any of the suspension or steering fasteners are loosened or removed they must be replaced with new ones - discard the originals and don't re-use them. They must be replaced with new ones of the same part number or of original equipment quality and design. Torque specifications must be followed for proper reassembly and component retention.*

Removal

1   Raise the front of the vehicle, support it securely on jackstands, block the rear wheels and set the parking brake. Position the front wheels in the straight ahead position.
2   Remove the cotter pin and nut from the ball end of the steering connecting link.
3   Use a Pitman arm puller and remove the ball end from the drag link.
4   Loosen the clamp bolts on the tie-rod adjusting sleeve.
5   Unscrew the connecting link from the tie-rod adjusting sleeve. Count and record the number of turns it takes to remove the connecting link from the tie-rod adjusting sleeve.
6   Remove the steering connecting link.

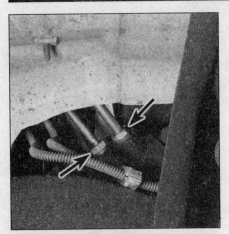

19.4 Remove the power steering gear hose/line fittings from the steering gear assembly (arrows)

19.8 Mark the Pitman arm and the sector shaft, then remove the Pitman arm with a puller

19.9 The power steering gear is mounted to the frame with three bolts (arrows)

Installation

7 Install the steering connecting link onto the tie-rod and turn it the same number of turns noted during removal in Step 5. Tighten the clamp bolts on the tie-rod adjusting sleeve to the torque listed in this Chapter's Specifications.

8 Install the steering connecting link end into the drag link. Make sure the front wheels and steering wheel are in the straight ahead position. Make sure the ball end is seated in the taper to prevent them from rotating while tightening the nut.

9 Install a new nut on the stud and tighten to the torque listed in this Chapter's Specifications. Install a new cotter pin and bend the ends over completely.

10 Install the wheel and lug nuts. Lower the vehicle and tighten the lug nuts to torque listed in the Chapter 1 Specifications.

11 Have the alignment checked by a dealer service department or an alignment shop.

18 Tie-rod ends - removal and installation

Removal

1 Loosen the front wheel lug nuts on the side to be dismantled. Raise the front of the vehicle, support it securely on jackstands, block the rear wheels and set the parking brake. Remove the front wheel.

2 Remove the cotter pin and loosen the nut on the tie-rod end stud. Discard the cotter pin.

3 Disconnect the tie-rod end from the steering spindle with a puller.

4 Loosen the clamp bolts on the tie-rod adjusting sleeve.

5 Unscrew the tie-rod end from the adjusting sleeve. Count and record the number of turns it takes to back the tie-rod end off the sleeve.

6 Remove the tie-rod end.

Installation

7 Install the tie-rod onto the steering adjusting sleeve and turn it the same number of turns noted during removal in Step 5.

8 Tighten the clamp bolts on the tie-rod adjusting sleeve to the torque listed in this Chapter's Specifications. Make sure the tie-rod is positioned correctly in the same position as when it was removed.

9 Make sure the front wheels and steering wheel are in the straight ahead position and install the tie-rod end onto the spindle. Make sure the tie-rod stud is seated in the taper to prevent it from rotating while tightening the nut.

10 Install a new nut on the stud and tighten it to the torque listed in this Chapter's Specifications. Install a new cotter pin and bend the ends over completely.

11 Install the wheel and lug nuts. Lower the vehicle and tighten the lug nuts to the torque listed in the Chapter 1 Specifications.

12 Have the front end alignment checked by a dealer service department or an alignment shop.

19 Steering gear - removal and installation

Refer to illustrations 19.4, 19.8 and 19.9

Warning : *Some models are equipped with airbags. Always disconnect the negative battery cable, then the positive cable and wait 2 minutes before working in the vicinity of the impact sensors, steering column or instrument panel to avoid the possibility of accidental deployment of the airbag, which could cause personal injury (see Chapter 12).*

Removal

1 Set the front wheels to the straight-ahead position.

2 Disconnect the cable from the negative battery terminal.

3 Turn the ignition key to the Run position to unlock the steering wheel. **Warning:**

On models equipped with an airbag, make sure that the steering shaft is not rotated with the steering gear removed or damage to the airbag contact assembly could occur. One method of preventing the steering shaft from rotating is to run the seat belt through the steering wheel and clip the seat belt buckles together.

4 Place a pan under the steering gear. Remove the power steering hoses/lines and cap the ends and the ports to prevent excessive fluid loss and contamination **(see illustration)**.

5 Remove the bolt securing the flex coupling to the steering gear.

6 Loosen the front wheel lug nuts. Raise the front of the vehicle, support it securely on jackstands, block the rear wheels and set the parking brake. Remove both front wheels.

7 Remove the large nut and washer securing the Pitman arm to the sector shaft.

8 Use a Pitman arm puller or an equivalent puller and remove the Pitman arm from the sector shaft **(see illustration)**. **Caution:** *Don't hammer on the end of the puller, as the steering gear will be damaged.*

9 Loosen all three bolts securing the steering gear box to the frame **(see illustration)**. Support the steering gear and remove the bolts and washers and remove the steering gear from the lower steering column shaft.

Installation

10 Make sure the steering gear is centered. Turn the input shaft to full lock in one direction, then count and record the number of turns required to rotate it to the opposite full lock position. Turn the shaft back through one half of the number of turns just counted to center the assembly.

11 Check that the front wheels are in the straight ahead position and that the steering wheel spokes are in a horizontal position. Reposition if necessary.

12 Position the flat on the gear input shaft so it is facing down. Position the flex coupling on the steering gear input shaft, aligning the flat with the flat on the input shaft.

20.6 A power steering pump pulley removal tool is needed to remove the power steering pump pulley - they're commonly available at most auto parts stores

20.10 This tool is used to install the power steering pump pulley (arrow)

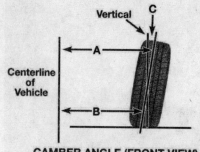

CAMBER ANGLE (FRONT VIEW)

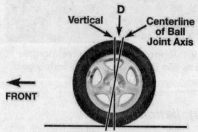

CASTER ANGLE (SIDE VIEW)

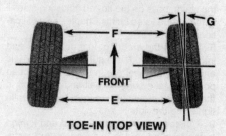

TOE-IN (TOP VIEW)

22.1 Front wheel alignment details

A minus B = C (degrees camber)
D = degrees caster
E minus F = toe-in (measured in inches)
G = toe-in (expressed in degrees)

13   Install all three bolts securing the steering gear box to the frame. Tighten the bolts to the torque listed in this Chapter's Specifications.

14   Align the two blocked teeth on the Pitman arm with the four missing teeth on the steering gear sector shaft and install the Pitman arm. Install the washer and nut and tighten the nut to the torque listed in this Chapter's Specifications.

15   Install the bolt securing the flex coupling to the steering gear input shaft. Tighten the bolt to the torque listed in this Chapter's Specifications.

16   Install the front wheel(s) and lug nuts.

17   Lower the vehicle and remove the floor jack. Tighten the lug nuts to the torque listed in Chapter 1.

18   Connect the pressure and return lines to the steering gear assembly and tighten to the torque listed in this Chapter's Specifications.

19   Turn the ignition key Off and connect the negative battery cable.

20   Fill the fluid reservoir with the specified fluid and refer to Section 21 for the power steering bleeding procedure.

20   Power steering pump - removal and installation

Refer to illustrations 20.6 and 20.10

Removal

1   Disconnect the cable from the negative battery terminal.

2   Remove the drivebelt from the power steering pulley (see Chapter 1).

3   Raise the vehicle and support it securely on jackstands. On models so equipped, remove the splash shield from below.

4   Disconnect the return hose at the pump and drain the fluid into a container.

5   Disconnect the pressure hose from the pump.

6   Remove the drivebelt pulley as follows:

a)   *Install a power steering pump pulley removal tool onto the pulley* (**see illustration**).

b)   *Hold the large nut with a wrench and rotate the screw nut clockwise pulling the pulley from the pump.* **Caution:** *Do not apply excessive force on the pulley shaft as it may damage the internal parts of the pump.*

7   On early models, Remove the bolts securing the pump to the mounting bracket. On later models, the pump is bolted directly to the engine without a bracket.

8   Remove the pump from the mounting bracket.

Installation

9   Place the pump in the bracket and install the mounting bolts. Tighten the bolts to the torque listed in this Chapter's Specifications.

10   Install the pulley onto the pump using a special tool (**see illustration**). Be sure the pulley removal groove is toward the front of the vehicle and is flush with the end of the shaft (within 0.010-inch).

11   Install the pump drivebelt (see Chapter 1).

12   Install the pressure and return hoses to the proper fittings on the pump.

13   Fill the pump reservoir with the specified fluid (see Chapter 1) and bleed the system (see Section 21).

21   Power steering system - bleeding

1   The power steering system must be bled whenever a line is disconnected. Bubbles can be seen in power steering fluid that has air in it and the fluid will often have a tan or milky appearance. On later models, low fluid level can cause air to mix with the fluid, resulting in a noisy pump as well as foaming of the fluid.

2   Open the hood and check the fluid level in the reservoir, adding the specified fluid necessary to bring it up to the proper level (see Chapter 1).

3   Start the engine and slowly turn the steering wheel several times from left-to-right and back again. Do not turn the wheel completely from lock-to-lock. Check the fluid level, topping it up as necessary until it remains steady and no more bubbles are visible.

22   Wheel alignment - general information

Refer to illustration 22.1

Note: *Since wheel alignment requires special equipment and techniques it is beyond the scope of this manual. This section is intended only to familiarize the reader with the basic terms used and procedures followed during a typical wheel alignment.*

The three basic checks made when aligning a vehicle's front wheels are toe-in, caster and camber (**see illustration**).

Toe-in is the amount the front wheels are angled in relationship to the center line of the vehicle. For example, in a vehicle with

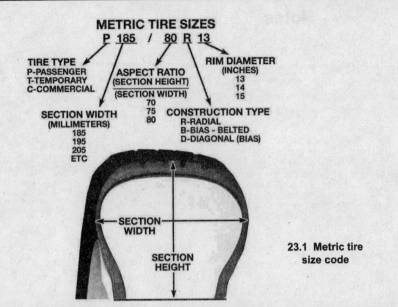

METRIC TIRE SIZES

P 185 / 80 R 13

TIRE TYPE
P-PASSENGER
T-TEMPORARY
C-COMMERCIAL

ASPECT RATIO
(SECTION HEIGHT)
(SECTION WIDTH)
70
75
80

RIM DIAMETER
(INCHES)
13
14
15

SECTION WIDTH
(MILLIMETERS)
185
195
205
ETC

CONSTRUCTION TYPE
R-RADIAL
B-BIAS - BELTED
D-DIAGONAL (BIAS)

SECTION WIDTH

SECTION HEIGHT

23.1 Metric tire size code

zero toe-in, the distance measured between the front edges of the wheels and the distance measured between the rear edges of the wheels are the same. In other words, the wheels are running parallel with the centerline of the vehicle. Toe-in is adjusted by lengthening or shortening the tie-rods. Incorrect toe-in will cause the tires to wear improperly by allowing them to "scrub" against the road surface.

Camber and caster are the angles at which the wheels and suspension are inclined in relation to a vertical centerline. Camber is the angle of the wheel in the lateral, or side-to-side plane, while caster is the tilt between the steering axis and the vertical plane, as viewed from the side. Camber angle affects the amount of tire tread which contacts the road and compensates for changes in suspension geometry as the vehicle travels around curves and over bumps. Caster angle affects the self-centering action of the steering, which governs straight-line stability.

Proper wheel alignment is essential for safe steering and even tire wear. Symptoms of alignment problems are pulling of the steering to one side or the other and uneven tire wear. If these symptoms are present, check for the following before having the alignment adjusted:

a) *Loose steering gear mounting bolts*
b) *Damaged or worn steering gear mounts*
c) *Worn or damaged wheel bearings*
d) *Bent tie-rods*
e) *Worn balljoints*
f) *Improper tire pressures*
g) *Mixing tires of different construction*

Front wheel alignment should be left to a dealer service department or an alignment shop with the proper equipment and experienced personnel.

23   Wheels and tires - general information

Refer to illustration 23.1

All models covered by this manual are equipped with radial tires **(see illustration)**. Use of other size or type of tires may affect the ride and handling of the vehicle. Don't mix different types of tires, such as radials and bias belted tires, on the same vehicle - handling may be seriously affected. It's recommended that tires be replaced in pairs on the same axle, but if only one tire is being replaced, be sure it's the same size, structure and tread design as the other tire on the same axle.

Because tire pressure has a substantial effect on handling and wear, the pressure of all tires should be checked at least once a month or before any extended trips are taken (see Chapter 1).

Wheels must be replaced if they are bent, dented, leak air, have elongated bolt holes, are heavily rusted, out of vertical symmetry or if the lug nuts won't stay tight. Wheel repairs that use welding or peening are not recommended.

Tire and wheel balance are important to the overhaul handling, braking and performance of the vehicle. Unbalanced wheels can adversely affect handling and ride characteristics as well as tire life. Whenever a tire is installed on a wheel, the tire and wheel should be balanced by a shop with the proper equipment and expertise.

Notes

Chapter 11   Body

Contents

1   General information

These models feature a welded body that is attached to a separate frame. Certain components are particularly vulnerable to accident damage and can be unbolted and repaired or replaced. Among these parts are the body moldings, front fender, bumpers, hood, doors and all glass (except the windshield).

Only general body maintenance procedures and body panel repair procedures within the scope of the do-it-yourselfer are included in this Chapter.

2   Body - maintenance

1   The condition of the vehicle's body is very important, because the resale value depends a great deal on it. It's much more difficult to repair a damaged body than it is to repair mechanical components. The hidden areas of the body, such as the fenderwells, the frame and the engine compartment, are equally important, although they don't require as frequent attention as the rest of the body.

2   Once a year, or every 12,000 miles, it's a good idea to have the underside of the body steam cleaned. All traces of dirt and oil will be removed and the area can then be inspected carefully for rust, damaged brake lines, frayed electrical wires, damaged cables and other problems. The front suspension components should be greased after completion of this job.

3   At the same time, clean the engine and the engine compartment with a steam cleaner or water soluble degreaser. **Caution:** *Avoid the direct aim of any high-pressure cleaning solutions to any of the many electronic components placed in the engine compartment and in the frame areas.*

4   The fenderwells should be given close attention, since undercoating can peel away and stones and dirt thrown up by the tires can cause the paint to chip and flake, allowing rust to set in. If rust is found, clean down to the bare metal and apply an anti-rust paint.

5   The body should be washed about once a week (or when dirty). Wet the vehicle thoroughly to soften the dirt, then wash it down with a soft sponge and plenty of clean soapy water. If the surplus dirt is not washed off very carefully, it can wear down the paint.

6   Spots of tar or asphalt thrown up from the road should be removed with a cloth soaked in solvent or kerosene.

7   Once every six months, wax the body and chrome trim. Apply wax only after a thorough washing of the body and trim. Longest-lasting results are obtained when the paint is cleaned with a very mild polish, then waxed with a quality carnuba wax. If a chrome cleaner is used to remove rust from any of the vehicle's plated parts, remember that the cleaner also removes part of the chrome, so use it sparingly.

These photos illustrate a method of repairing simple dents. They are intended to supplement *Body repair - minor damage* in this Chapter and should not be used as the **sole** instructions for body repair on these vehicles.

1 If you can't access the backside of the body panel to hammer out the dent, pull it out with a slide-hammer-type dent puller. In the deepest portion of the dent or along the crease line, drill or punch hole(s) at least one inch apart . . .

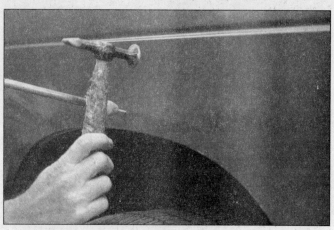

2 . . . then screw the slide-hammer into the hole and operate it. Tap with a hammer near the edge of the dent to help 'pop' the metal back to its original shape. When you're finished, the dent area should be close to its original contour and about 1/8-inch below the surface of the surrounding metal

3 Using coarse-grit sandpaper, remove the paint down to the bare metal. Hand sanding works fine, but the disc sander shown here makes the job faster. Use finer (about 320-grit) sandpaper to feather-edge the paint at least one inch around the dent area

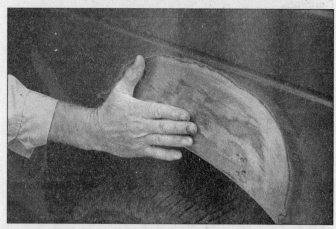

4 When the paint is removed, touch will probably be more helpful than sight for telling if the metal is straight. Hammer down the high spots or raise the low spots as necessary. Clean the repair area with wax/silicone remover

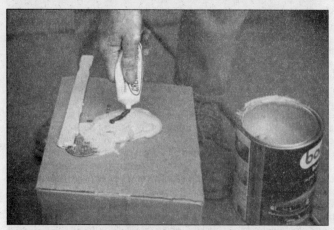

5 Following label instructions, mix up a batch of plastic filler and hardener. The ratio of filler to hardener is critical, and, if you mix it incorrectly, it will either not cure properly or cure too quickly (you won't have time to file and sand it into shape)

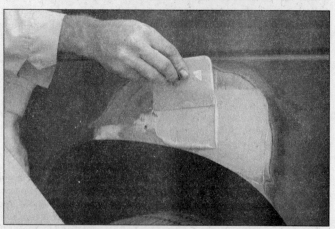

6 Working quickly so the filler doesn't harden, use a plastic applicator to press the body filler firmly into the metal, assuring it bonds completely. Work the filler until it matches the original contour and is slightly above the surrounding metal

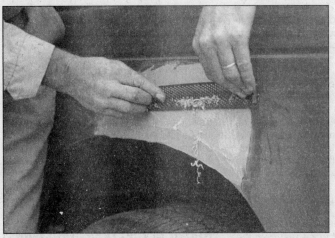

7 Let the filler harden until you can just dent it with your fingernail. Use a body file or Surform tool (shown here) to rough-shape the filler

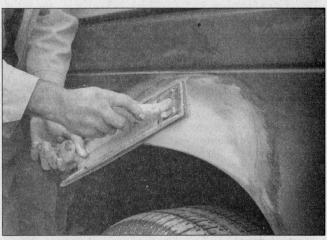

8 Use coarse-grit sandpaper and a sanding board or block to work the filler down until it's smooth and even. Work down to finer grits of sandpaper - always using a board or block - ending up with 360 or 400 grit

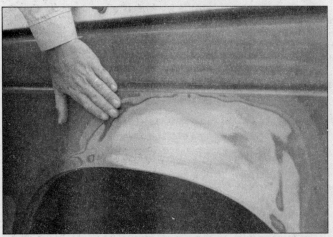

9 You shouldn't be able to feel any ridge at the transition from the filler to the bare metal or from the bare metal to the old paint. As soon as the repair is flat and uniform, remove the dust and mask off the adjacent panels or trim pieces

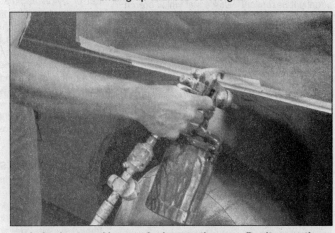

10 Apply several layers of primer to the area. Don't spray the primer on too heavy, so it sags or runs, and make sure each coat is dry before you spray on the next one. A professional-type spray gun is being used here, but aerosol spray primer is available inexpensively from auto parts stores

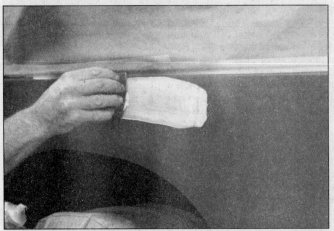

11 The primer will help reveal imperfections or scratches. Fill these with glazing compound. Follow the label instructions and sand it with 360 or 400-grit sandpaper until it's smooth. Repeat the glazing, sanding and respraying until the primer reveals a perfectly smooth surface

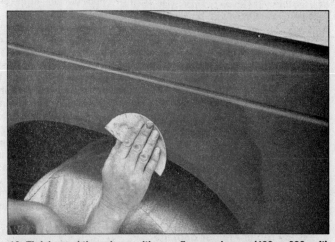

12 Finish sand the primer with very fine sandpaper (400 or 600-grit) to remove the primer overspray. Clean the area with water and allow it to dry. Use a tack rag to remove any dust, then apply the finish coat. Don't attempt to rub out or wax the repair area until the paint has dried completely (at least two weeks)

3   Vinyl trim - maintenance

Don't clean vinyl trim with detergents, caustic soap or petroleum-based cleaners. Plain soap and water works just fine, with a soft brush to clean dirt that may be ingrained. Wash the vinyl as frequently as the rest of the vehicle.

After cleaning, application of a high-quality rubber and vinyl protectant will help prevent oxidation and cracks. The protectant can also be applied to weather stripping, vacuum lines and rubber hoses, which often fail as a result of chemical degradation, and to the tires.

4   Upholstery and carpets - maintenance

1   Every three months remove the floormats and clean the interior of the vehicle (more frequently if necessary). Use a stiff whisk broom to brush the carpeting and loosen dirt and dust, then vacuum the upholstery and carpets thoroughly, especially along seams and crevices.
2   Dirt and stains can be removed from carpeting with basic household or automotive carpet shampoos available in spray cans. Follow the directions and vacuum again, then use a stiff brush to bring back the "nap" of the carpet.
3   Most interiors have cloth or vinyl upholstery, either of which can be cleaned and maintained with a number of material-specific cleaners or shampoos available in auto supply stores. Follow the directions on the product for usage, and always spot-test any upholstery cleaner on an inconspicuous area (bottom edge of a backseat cushion) to ensure that it doesn't cause a color shift in the material.
4   After cleaning, vinyl upholstery should be treated with a protectant. **Note:** *Make sure the protectant container indicates the product can be used on seats - some products may make a seat too slippery.* **Warning:** *Do not use protectant on vinyl-covered steering wheels.*
5   Leather upholstery requires special care. It should be cleaned regularly with saddle-soap or leather cleaner. Never use alcohol, gasoline, nail polish remover or thinner to clean leather upholstery.
6   After cleaning, regularly treat leather upholstery with a leather conditioner, rubbed in with a soft cotton cloth. Never use car wax on leather upholstery.
7   In areas where the interior of the vehicle is subject to bright sunlight, cover leather seating areas of the seats with a sheet if the vehicle is to be left out for any length of time.

5   Body repair - minor damage

See photo sequence

Repair of minor scratches

1   If the scratch is superficial and does not penetrate to the metal of the body, repair is very simple. Lightly rub the scratched area with a fine rubbing compound to remove loose paint and built-up wax. Rinse the area with clean water.
2   Apply touch-up paint to the scratch, using a small brush. Continue to apply thin layers of paint until the surface of the paint in the scratch is level with the surrounding paint. Allow the new paint at least two weeks to harden, then blend it into the surrounding paint by rubbing with a very fine rubbing compound. Finally, apply a coat of wax to the scratch area.
3   If the scratch has penetrated the paint and exposed the metal of the body, causing the metal to rust, a different repair technique is required. Remove all loose rust from the bottom of the scratch with a pocket knife, then apply rust inhibiting paint to prevent the formation of rust in the future. Using a rubber or nylon applicator, coat the scratched area with glaze-type filler. If required, the filler can be mixed with thinner to provide a very thin paste, which is ideal for filling narrow scratches. Before the glaze filler in the scratch hardens, wrap a piece of smooth cotton cloth around the tip of a finger. Dip the cloth in thinner and then quickly wipe it along the surface of the scratch. This will ensure that the surface of the filler is slightly hollow. The scratch can now be painted over as described earlier in this Section.

Repair of dents

Warning: *Some models are equipped with airbags. Always disconnect the negative battery cable, then the positive cable and wait 2 minutes before working in the vicinity of the impact sensors, steering column or instrument panel to avoid the possibility of accidental deployment of the airbag, which could cause personal injury (see Chapter 12).*
4   When repairing dents, the first job is to pull or hammer the dent out until the affected area is as close as possible to its original shape. There is no point in trying to restore the original shape completely as the metal in the damaged area will have stretched on impact and cannot be restored to its original contours. It is better to bring the level of the dent up to a point about 1/8-inch below the level of the surrounding metal. In cases where the dent is very shallow, it is not worth trying to pull it back out at all.
5   If the back side of the dent is accessible, it can be hammered out gently from behind using a soft-face hammer. While doing this, hold a block of wood firmly against the opposite side of the metal to absorb the hammer blows and prevent the metal from being stretched.
6   If the dent is in a section of the body which has double layers, or some other factor makes it inaccessible from behind, a different technique is required. Drill several small holes through the metal inside the damaged area, particularly in the deeper sections. Screw long, self tapping screws into the holes

just enough for them to get a good grip in the metal. Now the dent can be pulled out by pulling on the protruding heads of the screws with locking pliers.
7   The next stage of repair is the removal of the paint from the damaged area and from an inch or so of the surrounding metal. This is easily done with a wire brush or sanding disk in a drill motor, although it can be done just as effectively by hand with sandpaper. To complete the preparation for filling, score the surface of the bare metal with a screwdriver or the tang of a file or drill small holes in the affected area. This will provide a good grip for the filler material. To complete the repair, see the Section on filling and painting.

Repair of rust holes or gashes

8   Remove all paint from the affected area and from an inch or so of the surrounding metal using a sanding disk or wire brush mounted in a drill motor. If these are not available, a few sheets of sandpaper will do the job just as effectively.
9   With the paint removed, you will be able to determine the severity of the corrosion and decide whether to replace the whole panel, if possible, or repair the affected area. New body panels are not as expensive as most people think and it is often quicker to install a new panel than to repair large areas of rust.
10   Remove all trim pieces from the affected area except those which will act as a guide to the original shape of the damaged body, such as headlight shells, etc. Using metal snips or a hacksaw blade, remove all loose metal and any other metal that is badly affected by rust. Hammer the edges of the hole in to create a slight depression for the filler material.
Note: *If replacing the damaged section with a ready-made steel patch panel, do not cut the damaged area out until you have the replacement panel and see how much area it covers. Metal patch panels are generally welded in.*
11   Wire brush the affected area to remove the powdery rust from the surface of the metal. If the back of the rusted area is accessible, treat it with rust inhibiting paint.
12   Before filling is done, block the hole in some way. This can be done with sheet metal riveted or screwed into place, or by stuffing the hole with wire mesh.
13   Once the hole is blocked off, the affected area can be filled and painted. See the following subsection on filling and painting.

Filling and painting

14   Many types of body fillers are available, but generally speaking, body repair kits which contain filler paste and a tube of resin hardener are best for this type of repair work. A wide, flexible plastic or nylon applicator will be necessary for imparting a smooth and contoured finish to the surface of the filler material. Mix up a small amount of filler on a clean piece of glass or sheetmetal (use the hardener sparingly). Follow the manufacturer's instructions on the package, otherwise the filler will set incorrectly.

8.3 Scribe or draw alignment marks on the hood (arrow) to ensure proper alignment of the hinge on reinstallation

15   Using the applicator, apply the filler paste to the prepared area. Draw the applicator across the surface of the filler to achieve the desired contour and to level the filler surface. As soon as a contour that approximates the original one is achieved, stop working the paste. If you continue, the paste will begin to stick to the applicator. Continue to add thin layers of paste at 20-minute intervals until the level of the filler is just above the surrounding metal. While waiting for the filler to harden, clean your metal or glass mixing board with lacquer thinner before the residue hardens.

16   Once the filler has hardened, the excess can be removed with a body file. From then on, progressively finer grades of sandpaper should be used, starting with a 180-grit paper and finishing with 600-grit wet-or-dry paper. Always wrap the sandpaper around a flat rubber or wooden block, otherwise the surface of the filler will not be completely flat. Curved body areas can be sanded by wrapping the sandpaper around a short length of smooth-exterior radiator hose. During the sanding of the filler surface, the wet-or-dry paper should be periodically rinsed in water. This will ensure that a very smooth finish is produced in the final stage.

17   At this point, the repair area should be surrounded by a ring of bare metal, which in turn should be encircled by the finely feathered edge of good paint. Rinse the repair area with clean water until all of the dust produced by the sanding operation is gone.

18   Spray the entire area with a light coat of primer. This will reveal any imperfections in the surface of the filler. Repair the imperfections with fresh filler paste or glaze filler and once more smooth the surface with sandpaper. Repeat this spray-and-repair procedure until you are satisfied that the surface of the filler and the feathered edge of the paint are perfect. Rinse the area with clean water and allow it to dry completely.

19   The repair area is now ready for painting. Spray painting must be carried out in a warm, dry, windless and dust free atmosphere. These conditions can be created if you have access to a large indoor work area, but if you are forced to work in the open, you will have to pick the day very carefully. If you are working indoors, dousing the floor in the work area with water will help settle the dust which would otherwise be in the air. If the repair area is confined to one body panel, mask off the surrounding panels. This will help minimize the effects of a slight mismatch in paint color. Trim pieces such as chrome strips, door handles, etc. will also need to be masked off or removed. Use masking tape and several thicknesses of newspaper for the masking operations.

20   Before spraying, shake the paint can thoroughly, then spray a test area until the spray painting technique is mastered. Cover the repair area with a thick coat of primer. The thickness should be built up using several thin layers of primer rather than one thick one. Using 600-grit wet-or-dry sandpaper, rub down the surface of the primer until it is very smooth. While doing this, the work area should be thoroughly rinsed with water and the wet-or-dry sandpaper periodically rinsed as well. Allow the primer to dry before spraying additional coats.

21   Spray on the top coat, again building up the thickness by using several layers of paint. Begin spraying in the center of the repair area and then, using a circular motion, work out until the whole repair area and about two inches of the surrounding original paint is covered. Remove all masking material 10 to 15 minutes after spraying on the final coat of paint. Allow the new paint at least two weeks to harden, then use a very fine rubbing compound to blend the edges of the new paint into the existing paint, Finally, apply a coat of wax.

6   Body repair - major damage

1   Major damage must be repaired by an auto body shop. These shops have the specialized equipment required to do the job properly.

2   If the damage is extensive, the frame must be checked for proper alignment or the vehicle's handling characteristics may be adversely affected and other components may wear at an accelerated rate.

3   Due to the fact that all of the major body components (hood, front fenders, etc.) are separate and replaceable units, any seriously damaged components should be replaced rather than repaired. Sometimes the components can be found in a wrecking yard that specializes in used vehicle components, often at a considerable savings over the cost of new parts.

7   Hinges and locks - maintenance

Once every 3,000 miles, or every three months, the hinges and latch assemblies on the hood and side and rear doors should be given a few drops of light oil or lock lubricant. The door latch strikers should also be lubricated with a thin coat of grease to reduce wear and ensure free movement. Lubricate the door locks with spray-on graphite lubricant.

8   Hood - removal, installation and adjustment

Refer to illustration 8.3
Note: *The hood is heavy and somewhat awkward to remove and install - at least two people should perform this procedure.*

Removal and installation

1   Open the hood and support it in the open position with a long piece of wood.

2   Cover the fenders and cowl with blankets or heavy cloths to protect the paint.

3   Scribe or draw alignment marks around the bolt heads or hinge perimeter to ensure proper alignment on reinstallation **(see illustration)**.

4   Have an assistant hold onto the hood on one side while you hold the other side.

5   Remove the hood-to-hinge assembly bolts on your side of the hood, then hold your side of the hood while your assistant removes the hood-to-hinge bolts on the other side.

6   Lift the hood off.

7   Installation is the reverse of the removal steps with the following additions:

a)   Align the hood and hinges using the alignment marks made in Step 3.

b)   Be sure to tighten the bolts securely.

Adjustment

8   The hood can be adjusted to obtain a flush fit between the hood and fenders.

9   Slightly loosen the hood retaining bolts.

10   Move the hood from side-to-side or front-to-rear until the hood is properly aligned with the fenders at the front. Open the hood and tighten the bolts securely.

11   Loosen the bolts securing the hood latch assembly. On 2001 and later models, remove the pushpin fasteners and the radiator cover to access the hood latch.

12   Move the latch until alignment is correct with the hood latch striker. Tighten the latch bolt securely.

9.2 Mark the position of the hood latch (arrow) to ensure proper alignment of the latch on reinstallation

9.3 The hood latch is secured by two bolts

9   Hood latch control cable - removal and installation

Refer to illustrations 9.2 and 9.3

Removal

1   Open the hood and support it in the open position with a long piece of wood. On 2001 and later models, remove the pushpin fasteners and the radiator cover to access the hood latch.
2   Scribe or draw alignment marks around the hood latch to ensure proper alignment on reinstallation **(see illustration)**.
3   Remove the bolts securing the hood latch and remove the latch **(see illustration)**.
4   Remove the radiator grille and radiator air deflector (see Section 24).
5   Remove the bolt and disconnect the cable end from the latch assembly.
6   Remove the cable clips from the radiator support bracket and apron.
7   Remove the drivers side cowl side trim panel.
8   Remove the screws that secure the hood release handle.
9   Working in the passenger compartment, remove the cable grommet from the firewall, then pull the cable through the opening.

Installation

10   Installation is the reverse of the removal steps with the following additions:
   a) *Insert the cable through the grommet in the firewall and make sure the grommet is properly seated within the firewall hole.*
   b) *Before closing the hood, operate the control cable and make sure the latch control operates correctly.*

10   Engine cover - removal and installation

1   Move both front seats all the way toward the rear. On 2001 and later models, remove the driver's knee bolster (panel below the steering column). On models so equipped, remove the floor console.
2   Unlatch the four engine cover latches.
3   Lift the engine cover up and remove it through the passenger front door.
4   Installation is the reverse of removal.

11   Front door - removal, installation and alignment

Removal and installation

Refer to illustrations 11.1 and 11.5

1   Open the door. Remove the hinge check-to-door jamb bolts **(see illustration)**. Leave the hinge check attached to the door.
2   With the door in the open position, place a jack under the door or have an assistant hold the door while the hinge bolts are removed. **Note:** *Place thick padding on top of the jack to protect the door's painted finish.*
3   On models so equipped, remove the door trim panel sufficiently to gain access to the electrical connectors, then disconnect the electrical connectors to the door wiring harness.
4   Scribe or paint lines around the door hinges to ensure proper alignment on reinstallation.
5   Remove the hinge-to-door bolts **(see illustration)** and carefully lift off the door.
6   Installation is the reverse of removal. Align the door.

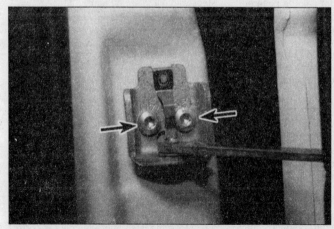

11.1 Remove the two bolts (arrows) securing the hinge check-to-door jamb - leave the hinge check attached to the door

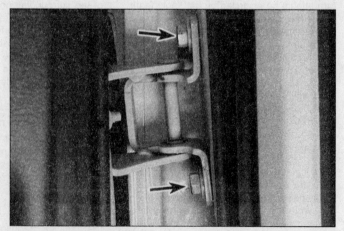

11.5 Remove the door hinge-to-door jamb bolts (arrows) - leave the hinge attached to the door jamb; remove the door

Alignment

7   Check the alignment of the door all around the edge. The door should be evenly spaced in the opening and should be flush with the body.

8   Adjust if necessary as follows:

a) *Note how the door is misaligned and determine which bolts need to be loosened to correct it.*

b) *Loosen the bolts just enough so the door can be moved with a padded prybar. Reposition the door as necessary, then tighten the bolts securely.*

9   The door lock striker can also be adjusted both up-and-down and sideways to provide positive engagement with the lock mechanism (see Section 16).

10   Tighten the hinge-to-body bolts securely.

12 Dual cargo side doors - removal, installation and alignment

Removal and installation

1   Open the door. Remove the hinge check-to-door jamb bolts **(see illustration 11.1)**. Leave the hinge check attached to the door.

2   With the front side door in the open position, place a jack under the door or have an assistant hold the door while the hinge bolts are removed. **Note:** *Place thick padding on top of the jack to protect the door's painted finish.*

3   Scribe or paint lines around the door hinges to ensure proper alignment on reinstallation.

4   Remove the hinge-to-door bolts and carefully lift off the door.

5   Repeat Steps 1 through 4 for the rear side door.

6   Installation is the reverse of the removal steps. Align the doors.

Alignment

7   Check the alignment of both doors all around the edge. The doors should be evenly spaced in the opening and should be flush with the body.

8   Adjust if necessary as follows:

a) *Note how the door is misaligned and determine which bolts need to be loosened to correct it.*

b) *Loosen the bolts just enough so the door can be moved with a padded pry bar. Reposition the door as necessary, then tighten the bolts securely.*

9   The door lock striker can also be adjusted both up-and-down and sideways to provide positive engagement with the lock mechanism (see Section 16).

10   Tighten the hinge-to-body bolts securely.

13 Sliding side door - removal, installation and alignment

Note: *The sliding door is heavy and somewhat awkward to remove and install - at least two people should perform this procedure from Step 5 on.*

Removal and installation

1   Open the door and slide it toward the rear a minimal amount.

2   Remove the upper garnish molding, quarter trim panel and slider door lower latch cover.

3   Remove the body side door lower track stop from the lower body side door track.

4   Remove the center track shield. On 2001 and later models, remove the scuff plate.

5   On early models, slide the door fully toward the rear. Have an assistant hold the door while you tilt the front upper corner in until the body side door upper roller is out of the upper track. On 2001 and later models, slide the door forward all the way and with an assistant outside holding the door, push from the inside to disengage the lower roller. Tilt the door to release the center roller from its track and finally, slide the door rearward and tilt it outward to disengage the upper roller from its track.

6   Place a jack under the door. **Note:** *Place thick padding on top of the jack to protect the door's painted finish.*

7   Lift the body side door lower roller up out of its track.

8   Remove the rear center roller from its track and remove the door.

9   Installation is the reverse of the removal steps.

Alignment

10   Check the alignment of the door all around the edge. The door should be evenly spaced in the opening and flush with the body.

Front upper alignment

11   Loosen the two body side door upper roller-to-body side door bolts.

12   Move the body side door upper roller in or out to obtain a flush fit with the adjacent body panel at the top edge of the door. Tighten the bolt securely.

Front lower alignment

13   Support the sliding door so that it cannot move up or down while making this in-and-out adjustment.

14   Loosen the body side door lower roller-to-body side door bolts.

15   Move the side door lower roller forward to obtain a snug fit with the adjacent body panel and rearward to move it away from the body, at the B-pillar post. Tighten the bolt securely.

Rear, upper and lower edge alignment

16   Open the sliding door - do not slide it toward the rear.

17   Loosen the rear latch striker bolts, then move the striker as required to obtain a flush fit with the adjacent body panel. Tighten the bolt securely.

Up and down alignment

Caution: *The sliding door lower roller must be horizontal to assure hold-open latch function. The door upper roller assembly must not be less than 5/64-inch from the bottom flange of the body side door upper track. The front latch striker must not be used for up or down adjustment of the sliding door. Raise and lower the lower roller if vertical adjustment is required.*

18   Support the door to prevent slippage while loosening the door lower roller.

19   Remove the lower latch cover.

20   Loosen the three bolts securing the door lower roller to the body.

21   Use a soft-faced hammer and tap the lower roller up or down until alignment is correct. Tighten the bolts securely.

14 Dual rear doors - removal, installation and alignment

Removal and installation

Refer to illustration 14.4

1   Open the door. Remove the hinge check-to-door jamb bolts **(see illustration 11.1)**. Leave the hinge check attached to the door.

2   With the door in the open position, place a jack under the door or have an assistant hold the door while the hinge bolts are removed. **Note:** *Place thick padding on top of the jack to protect the door's painted finish.*

3   Scribe or paint lines around the door hinges to ensure proper alignment on reinstallation.

4   Remove the hinge-to-door jamb bolts **(see illustration)** and carefully lift off the door.

14.4 Remove the hinge-to-door bolts (arrows) - leave the hinge check attached to the door; remove the door

Leave the hinges attached to the door.
5   Repeat Steps 1 through 4 for the other rear door.
6   Installation is the reverse of the removal steps. Align the doors.

Alignment
7   Check the alignment of the doors all around the edge. The doors should be evenly spaced in the opening and should be flush with the body.
8   Adjust if necessary as follows:
  a) *Note how the door is misaligned and determine which bolts need to be loosened to correct it.*
  b) *Loosen the bolts just enough so the door can be moved with a padded pry bar. Reposition the door as necessary, then tighten the bolts securely.*
9   The door lock striker can also be adjusted both up-and-down and sideways to provide positive engagement with the lock mechanism (see Section 16).
10   Tighten the hinge-to-body bolts securely.

15   Door hinge - removal and installation

Refer to illustration 15.4
Note: *If both hinges are to be replaced, it is easier to leave the door in place and replace one hinge at a time.*
1   With the door in the open position, place a jack under the door or have an assistant hold the door while the door hinge bolts are removed. **Note:** *If a jack is used, place thick padding on top of the jack to protect the door's painted finish.*
2   On front doors so equipped, remove the door trim panel sufficiently to gain access to the electrical connectors, then disconnect the electrical connectors to the door wiring harness.
3   Scribe or draw lines around the door hinges to ensure proper alignment on reinstallation.
4   Remove the hinge-to-door bolts, then

15.4 Remove the hinge-to-door bolts (arrows), carefully remove the door, then remove the hinge-to-body bolts and remove the hinge

carefully remove the door. Remove the hinge-to-body bolts **(see illustration)** then remove the hinge.
5   Installation is the reverse of the removal steps with the following additions:
  a) *Apply a sealant to the hinge before installing it onto the body panel.*
  b) *Adjust the door if necessary.*

16   Hinged door latch striker - removal, installation and adjustment

Removal and installation
1   Unscrew the door latch striker latch from the door jamb.
2   Installation is the reverse of removal. Adjust if necessary.

Adjustment
3   The door latch striker can be adjusted vertically and laterally as well as fore-and-aft. **Note:** *Don't use the door latch striker to compensate for door misalignment.*
4   The door latch striker can be shimmed to obtain the correct clearance between the latch and the striker. Don't use more than one shim per door.
5   To check the clearance between the latch jamb and the striker area, spread a layer of dark grease on the striker.
6   Open and close the door several times and note the pattern in the grease.
7   Move the door striker assembly laterally to provide a flush fit at the door and pillar or at the quarter panel.
8   Securely tighten the door latch striker after adjustment is complete.

17   Door inner and outer handle and latch assembly - removal and installation

Front doors
1   To remove the inner door handle, remove the screw and the handle cover, then remove the handle-mounting screw and push the handle rearward to remove it. Remove the door trim panel and watershield (see Section 19).
2   Remove the screws securing the door outer handle assembly to the door.
3   Disconnect the handle link from the outer handle and lock cylinder.
4   On models so equipped, drill out the rivet securing the front door remote control and link.
5   Unsnap the front door latch pushbutton rod from the door lock cylinder.
6   On models so equipped, drill out the rivet securing the keyless entry keypad.
7   Remove the three Torx screws securing the latch to the door.
8   Remove the cable clip on the cable from the door inner panel.
9   Remove the latch assembly from the

access hole in the door.
10   Installation is the reverse of the removal steps, plus the following additions:
  a) *If a new latch is being installed, install the rod retaining clips in it.*
  b) *Attach the control rod and lock cylinder rod to the latch before installing the latch.*
  c) *Tighten the latch screws securely.*
  d) *If equipped, replace drilled out rivets with pop-rivets.*
  e) *Check operation of the handles and lock before installing the watershield and door panel.*

Front dual cargo side door
11   On models so equipped, remove the door trim panel and watershield (see Section 19).
12   Remove the screws securing the door outer handle assembly to the door.
13   Disconnect the handle link from the outer handle and lock cylinder.
14   On models so equipped, drill out the rivet securing the front cargo door remote control and link.
15   Unsnap the front door latch push button rod from the door lock cylinder.
16   On models so equipped, drill out the rivet securing the keyless entry keypad.
17   Remove the three Torx screws securing the remote control and latch assembly to the door.
18   Remove the cable clip on the cable from the door inner panel.
19   Remove the latch assembly from the access hole in the door.
20   Installation is the reverse of the removal steps, plus the following additions:
  a) *If a new latch is being installed, install the rod retaining clips in it.*
  b) *Attach the control rod and lock cylinder rod to the latch before installing the latch.*
  c) *Tighten the latch screws securely.*
  d) *If equipped, replace drilled out rivets with pop-rivets.*
  e) *Check operation of the handles and lock before installing the watershield and door panel.*

Rear dual cargo side door
21   On models so equipped, remove the door trim panel and watershield (see Section 19).
22   Push up the lower leg of the keeper and slide the keeper toward the outside of the door to disengage the cable.
23   Push the cable through the handle slot, then open up the handle.
24   Move the inner cable and slide it through the slot in the inner side of the handle assembly. Remove the cable from the handle.
25   Pinch the legs of the cable clip together and push the clip through the hole in the door inner panel.
26   Remove the two screws securing the upper latch, then pull the latch and cable up and remove it.

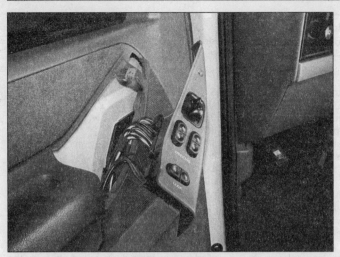

19.2 Lift the window regulator switch plate and slide it forward after removing the screws

19.4 Remove the door inside hand cup after removing the mounting screw

27 Remove the two screws securing the lower latch.

28 Drill out the rivets securing the door remote control assembly. Remove the remote control and pull the lower latch and cable up and remove it.

29 Installation is the reverse of the removal steps, plus the following additions:

a) *If a new latch is being installed, install the rod retaining clips in it.*

b) *Attach the control rod and lock cylinder rod to the latch before installing the latch.*

c) *Tighten the latch screws securely.*

d) *If equipped, replace drilled out rivets with pop-rivets.*

e) *Check operation of the handles and lock before installing the watershield and door panel.*

Sliding door cable latch

Caution: *This procedure should be entrusted to a dealer service department. A spacer block and special adjusting tools are required for proper removal and installation of the sliding door latch cable. Any adjustment without the use of this spacer is not recommended because the rear latch lever could be incorrectly positioned, which could cause a hazard during normal operation of the vehicle.*

Right dual rear door

30 On models so equipped, remove the door trim panel and watershield (see Section 19).

31 Remove the nuts securing the door inner handle assembly to the door. Remove the handle.

32 Remove the four screws securing the door outer handle and license plate holder assembly to the door. Carefully pull the assembly away from the door - remove the double-adhesive seal at the bottom of the frame. Disengage the rod from the door lock cylinder. Disengage the cable from the back door handle and remove the door outer handle.

33 Drill out the rivet securing the door remote control assembly.

34 On models so equipped, drill out the rivet securing the power lock actuator.

35 Remove the three Torx screws securing the remote control and latch assembly to the door.

36 Remove the latch assembly from the access hole in the door.

37 Installation is the reverse of the removal steps, plus the following additions:

a) *Make sure the finger of the handle is positioned under the remote control lever during assembly.*

b) *Install new double-adhesive seal at the bottom of the license plate frame.*

c) *Snap the rod into the lock cylinder lever.*

d) *Tighten the latch screws securely.*

e) *Replace drilled out rivets with pop-rivets.*

f) *Check operation of the handles and lock before installing the watershield and door panel.*

Left dual rear door

38 See Section 12 for this procedure, which is identical for side door pairs and rear door pairs.

18 Door lock cylinder - removal and installation

1 Raise the window all the way.

2 On models so equipped, remove the door trim panel and watershield (see Section 19).

3 Disconnect the door latch control-to-cylinder rod.

4 Use a pair of pliers and slide the cylinder retainer clip away from the lock cylinder and door.

5 Remove the lock cylinder from the door.

6 Install the lock cylinder into the door opening from the outside and push the retainer clip into place. Make sure it's seated correctly.

7 Reconnect the lock cylinder rod-to-door latch control.

8 Check for proper lock operation, then install the watershield and the door trim panel.

19 Door trim panel - removal and installation

Front door trim panel

Hi-series models

Refer to illustrations 19.2 and 19.4

Caution: *Don' try to pry the door trim panel loose from the door as the hook retainers will break off.*

1 Remove the screw and remove the outside rear view mirror mounting hole cover.

2 Remove the screw from the window regulator switch plate. Lift the window regulator switch plate and slide it forward to access the switch mounting screws (**see illustration**).

3 Remove screws and separate the window and door lock switches from the plate. On 2001 and later models, remove the large plastic armrest/handle bezel panel by pulling downward and then sliding it rearward.

4 Remove the screw from the door inside handle cup and remove the cup (**see illustration**).

5 On the drivers side, on models so equipped, disconnect the outside rear view mirror electrical connector.

6 In the area where the door inside handle cup was located, remove the single screw.

7 Remove the screw from inside of the lower trim panel.

8 Remove the screw from the door trim panel upper front corner.

9 Lift the door trim panel straight up and disengage the clips securing the lower edge of the trim panel to the door panel. Remove the trim panel.

10 If necessary, carefully peel the watershield from the door. Be careful not to tear it.

11 Installation is the reverse of the removal steps.

Lo-series models

12   Remove the screw and remove the outside rear view mirror mounting hole cover.

13   Remove the screws and remove the door upper trim panel.

14   Remove the window regulator handle.

15   Remove the screw and the arm rest.

16   Use a screwdriver and turn the door trim panel retainers counterclockwise until they are loose, then remove the retainers from around the perimeter of the door trim lower panel.

17   Lift the door trim panel straight up and remove the trim panel.

18   If necessary, carefully peel the watershield from the door. Be careful not to tear it.

19   Installation is the reverse of the removal steps.

Dual-cargo and dual-back doors

20   Remove the door pull handle screw trim caps, then remove the screws and remove the door pull handle.

21   On Hi-series models, remove the retainers and remove the door upper trim panel.

22   On Hi-series models, remove the screw trim caps and screws around the perimeter of the door trim lower panel.

23   On Lo-series models, use a screwdriver and turn the door trim panel retainers counterclockwise until they are loose, then remove the retainers from around the perimeter of the door trim lower panel.

24   Lift the door trim panel straight up and remove the trim panel.

25   If necessary, carefully peel the watershield from the door. Be careful not to tear it.

26   Installation is the reverse of the removal steps.

Sliding door trim panel

Caution: *Don't try to pry the door trim panel loose from the door as the hook retainers will break off.*

27   Remove the door pull handle screw trim caps, then remove the screws and remove the door pull handle.

28   On Hi-series models, remove the flipper window latch screws and latches. Push the windows out and rest the latch on the outside of the door.

29   On Hi-series models, remove the retainers and remove the door upper trim panel. Remove the screws at the upper corners of the lower trim panel.

30   On Lo-series models, use a screwdriver and turn the door trim panel retainers counterclockwise until they are loose, then remove the retainers from around the perimeter of the door trim lower panel.

31   Lift the door trim panel straight up and remove the trim panel.

32   If necessary, carefully peel the watershield from the door. Be careful not to tear it.

33   Installation is the reverse of the removal steps.

20   Front door window glass - replacement and adjustment

Replacement

1   Remove the door trim panel and watershield (see Section 19).

2   On models so equipped, remove the door speakers (see Chapter 12).

3   Raise the window all the way.

4   Remove the screws and detach the rear glass run retainer from the door and take it out.

5   Remove the inside and outside belt weather strips from the door.

6   Lower the window enough to provide access to the glass bracket and retention rivets. Drill-out the rivets. **Caution:** *Do not try to pry out the rivets as glass damage may occur.*

7   Lift the glass out through the top of the door.

8   Installation is the reverse of the removal steps, with the following additions:

   a) *Lubricate the regulator rollers, shafts and tracks with multi-purpose grease.*

   b) *Raise and lower the window to check its operation before installing the speakers (if equipped), watershield and door trim panel.*

Adjustment

9   Lower the glass two-to-three inches from the full-up position.

10   Loosen the three guide assembly nut and washer assemblies.

11   Push the glass toward the rear until it bottoms out within the door frame.

12   Move the window guide post toward the rear within the retention slot in the door inner panel. Tighten the three guide assembly nuts securely.

13   Raise and lower the window several times and check for proper fit.

14   Install the watershield and door trim panel.

21   Front door window regulator - replacement

Manual

1   Remove the door trim panel and watershield (see Section 19).

2   Remove the window glass (see Section 20).

3   Carefully drill-out the three upper rivets that secure the regulator bracket to the inner door panel.

4   Carefully drill-out the two lower rivets that secure the regulator lower bracket to the inner door panel.

5   Remove the two nut and washer assemblies that secure the window regulator upper bracket.

6   Remove the window regulator through the access hole in the door panel.

7   Installation is the reverse of the removal steps. Replace drilled out rivets with pop-rivets.

Power

8   Remove the door trim panel and watershield (see Section 19).

9   Remove the window glass (see Section 20).

10   Disconnect the power window electrical connector from the regulator control switch.

11   Carefully drill-out the rivets that secure the regulator drive assembly to the inner panel.

12   Remove the motor bracket from the inner panel. Rotate it to gain access to the three screws securing the regulator drive motor.

13   Remove the screws and separate the window regulator drive assembly from the bracket and cable drum housing.

14   Separate the window regulator drive motor from the power window regulator.

15   Remove the two upper nuts and carefully drill-out the two lower rivets securing the power window regulator to the inner panel.

16   Remove the power window regulator and cable assembly through the access hole in the door panel.

17   Installation is the reverse of the removal steps. Replace drilled out rivets with pop-rivets.

22   Hinged glass - replacement

Note: *This procedure pertains to removal of the glass portion of the hinged window only - not the frame.*

1   On the dual rear door, use duct tape and tape the glass panel to the exterior of the door frame.

2   Remove the interior trim panel, if necessary (see Section 19).

3   Remove the three screws securing the latch and latch anchor to the door or inner body panel.

4   Have an assistant hold onto the window from outside the vehicle.

5   Remove the nuts from the top of the glass and the two screws from the window hinge, then remove the glass assembly from the door.

6   Installation is the reverse of the removal steps. To reduce the possibility of wind noise, reinstall all hinge components in their original locations.

23   Windshield and fixed glass - replacement

Replacement of the windshield and fixed glass requires the use of special fast-setting adhesive/caulk materials and some specialized tools and techniques. These operations should be left to a dealer service department or a shop specializing in automotive glass work.

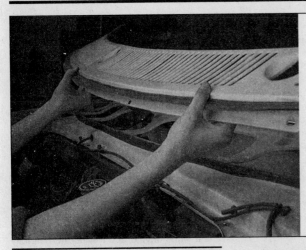

25.2 Remove the cowl panel and set it aside - later models are a one-piece design

24 Radiator grille - removal and installation

Warning: *Some models are equipped with airbags. Always disconnect the negative battery cable, then the positive cable and wait 2 minutes before working in the vicinity of the impact sensors, steering column or instrument panel to avoid the possibility of accidental deployment of the airbag, which could cause personal injury (see Chapter 12).*

1   Open the hood.
2   Remove the two plastic rivets at the lower corners of the grille.
3   On early models, remove the three screws at the top of the grille and detach the grille from the vehicle. **Note:** *On late models (1997 and later), firmly grasp the radiator grille on the bottom section and pull out to disengage the three lower clips.*
4   Installation is the reverse of the removal procedure. Be careful not to over tighten the screws.

25 Cowl panel and vent seal - removal and installation

Refer to illustration 25.2

1   Remove the windshield wiper arms and open the hood.
2   Loosen the cowl panel vents screws and raise the top panels up and off the seal **(see illustration)**.
3   Unsnap and remove the seal from both top panels.
4   Installation is the reverse of the removal procedure. Be careful not to over tighten the screws.

26 Front fender and apron - removal and installation

Warning: *Some models are equipped with airbags. Always disconnect the negative battery cable, then the positive cable and wait 2 minutes before working in the vicinity of the impact sensors, steering column or instrument*

panel to avoid the possibility of accidental deployment of the airbag, which could cause personal injury (see Chapter 12).

1   Remove the grille (see Section 24) and the headlight trim and housing.
2   Remove the two side bolts securing the end of the radiator grill opening panel to the front fender.
3   Remove the three screws at the lower front edge of the fender to the wheel housing.
4   Remove the screw and shim(s) at the rear lower edge of the fender.
5   Open the front door and remove the upper screw and shim(s) from the upper rear edge of the fender. On later models, the upper and lower mounting screws at the rear of the fender are accessed through the door opening.
6   Remove the two screws securing the fender to the radiator support.
7   Remove the three screws and shim(s) securing the top edge of the front fender to the radiator support.
8   Carefully detach the fender from the vehicle.
9   Installation is the reverse of the removal procedure. Don't tighten any of the bolts until they are all installed. **Note:** *Install the same number of shims during installation.*

27 Front bumper and cover - removal and installation

Front bumper

Note: *The bumper is heavy and somewhat awkward to remove and install - at least two people should perform this procedure.*

1   Raise the front of the vehicle, support it securely on jackstands, block the rear wheels and set the parking brake. On models so equipped, remove the pushpins and the condenser air deflector panel.
2   Have an assistant hold onto the bumper assembly, then remove the two nuts on each side securing the bumper to the frame.
3   Remove the bumper and isolators from the frame.
4   Installation is the reverse of the removal steps with the following additions:

a)   *If you're installing a new bumper, transfer the license plate holder and any additional items to the new bumper.*
b)   *Be sure to install the isolators between the bumper and frame.*
c)   *The bumper can be adjusted by repositioning the fasteners in the brackets. Tighten the fastener nuts securely.*

Bumper cover

5   Remove the front bumper from the vehicle.
6   Drill-out the rivets on the bottom of the bumper.
7   Remove the nut on each side securing the front cover to the bumper.
8   Use a pair of pliers, carefully compress the barbs securing the front cover, then carefully remove the cover from the bumper.
9   Installation is the reverse of the removal steps with the following additions:

a)   *Locate the center of the cover and mark with chalk or a piece of tape.*
b)   *Locate the center of the bumper and mark with chalk or a piece of tape.*
c)   *Center the cover on the bumper and press the center cover barb into the hole in the bumper.*
d)   *Carefully stretch the cover along the bumper and install the barbs into the holes in the bumper. If necessary, use a rubber mallet to tap the barbs into the bumper holes.*
e)   *Tighten all fasteners securely.*

28 Rear bumper - removal and installation

Note: *The bumper is heavy and somewhat awkward to remove and install - at least two people should perform this procedure.*

1   Have an assistant hold onto the bumper assembly and remove the two nuts on each side securing the bumper to the frame.
2   If necessary, remove the stone deflector from the body.
3   Installation is the reverse of the removal steps with the following additions:

a)   *Loosely install the bumper fasteners, then adjust the bumper position so there is an even horizontal gap between the bumper and body.*
b)   *Tighten the fasteners securely after adjustment.*

29 Seats - removal and installation

Warning: *Most models are equipped with airbags. Always disconnect the negative battery cable, then the positive cable and wait 2 minutes before working the vicinity of the impact sensors, steering column or instrument panel to avoid the possibility of accidental deployment of the airbag, which could cause personal injury (see Section 24).*

Front seats

1   On models so equipped, disconnect the electrical connector for the power seat. On later models with airbags, disconnect the electrical connectors at the seatbelt pre-tensioners.

2   Remove the stud covers, the nuts and washers securing the seat assembly to the support assembly attached to the floor pan and lift the seat from the vehicle.

3   If necessary, remove the four bolts securing the seat support assembly to the floor pan and remove the seat support from the vehicle.

4   Installation is the reverse of the removal steps. Tighten the retaining nuts and/or bolts securely.

Rear captain seats

5   Disconnect the seat belt from the seat assembly.

6   Pull the handle on the side of the seat to release the seat latch from the floor mounted latch striker plate.

7   Slide the seat toward the passenger side of the vehicle and remove it from the vehicle.

8   Installation is the reverse of the removal steps with the following additions:

a) *Insert the four pins in the support assembly into the four holes in the floor mounted latch striker plate assembly.*

b) *Rotate the handle down and in as far as it will go to lock the seat in place.*

Rear bench seat (quick release)

9   Remove the detachable safety belts and store on rear seat shoulder strap hook.

10   Move the seat to the full rearward position.

11   Disengage the seat from the seat back latch striker.

12   Lift the right and left latch rod hook ends out of the seat latch strikers.

13   Remove the seat assembly from the vehicle.

14   Installation is the reverse of the removal Steps.

30   Seat belt check

1   Check the seat belts, buckles, latch plates and guide loops for obvious damage and signs of wear.

2   Check that the seat belt reminder light comes on when the ignition key is turned to the Run or Start position.

3   The seat belts are designed to lock up during a sudden stop or impact, yet allow free movement during normal driving. Check that the retractors return the belt against your chest while driving and rewind the belt fully when the buckle is unlatched.

4   If any of the above checks reveal problems with the seat belt system, replace parts as necessary.

Chapter 12
Chassis electrical system

Contents

1 General information

Warning: *To prevent electrical shorts, fires and injury, always disconnect the cable from the negative terminal of the battery before checking, repairing or replacing electrical components.*

The electrical system is a 12-volt, negative ground type. Power for the lights and all electrical accessories is supplied by a lead/acid-type battery that is charged by the alternator.

This Chapter covers repair and service procedures for the various electrical components not associated with the engine. Information on the battery, alternator, distributor and starter motor can be found in Chapter 5.

It should be noted that when portions of the electrical system are serviced, the negative cable should be disconnected from the battery to prevent electrical shorts and/or fires.

2 Electrical troubleshooting - general information

Refer to illustrations 2.5a, 2.5b, 2.6, 2.9 and 2.15

A typical electrical circuit consists of an electrical component, any switches, relays, motors, fuses, fusible links or circuit breakers related to that component and the wiring and connectors that link the component to both the battery and the chassis. To help you pinpoint an electrical circuit problem, wiring diagrams are included at the end of this Chapter.

Before tackling any troublesome electrical circuit, first study the appropriate wiring diagrams to get a complete understanding of what makes up that individual circuit. Trouble spots, for instance, can often be narrowed down by noting if other components related to the circuit are operating properly. If several components or circuits fail at one time, chances are the problem is in a fuse or ground connection, because several circuits are often routed through the same fuse and ground connections.

Electrical problems usually stem from simple causes, such as loose or corroded connections, a blown fuse, a melted fusible link or a failed relay. Visually inspect the condition of all fuses, wires and connections in a problem circuit before troubleshooting the circuit.

If test equipment and instruments are going to be utilized, use the diagrams to plan ahead of time where you will make the necessary connections in order to accurately pinpoint the trouble spot.

The basic tools needed for electrical troubleshooting include a circuit tester or voltmeter (a 12-volt bulb with a set of test leads can also be used), a continuity tester, which includes a bulb, battery and set of test leads, and a jumper wire, preferably with a circuit breaker incorporated, which can be used to bypass electrical components **(see illustrations)**. Before attempting to locate a problem with test instruments, use the wiring diagram(s) to decide where to make the connections.

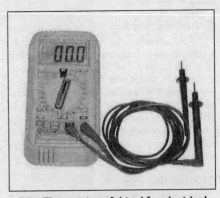

2.5a The most useful tool for electrical troubleshooting is a digital multimeter that can check volts, amps, and test continuity

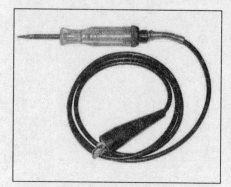

2.5b A test light is a very handy tool for checking voltage

2.6 In use, a basic test light's lead is clipped to a known good ground, then the pointed probe can test connectors, wires or electrical sockets - if the bulb lights, the part being tested has battery voltage

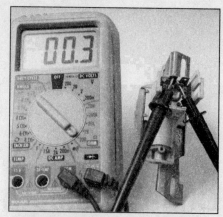

2.9 With a multimeter set to the ohms scale, resistance can be checked across two terminals - when checking for continuity, a low reading indicates continuity, a high reading indicates lack of continuity

Voltage checks

Voltage checks should be performed if a circuit is not functioning properly. Connect one lead of a circuit tester to either the negative battery terminal or a known good ground. Connect the other lead to a connector in the circuit being tested, preferably nearest to the battery or fuse **(see illustration)**. If the bulb of the tester lights, voltage is present, which means that the part of the circuit between the connector and the battery is problem free. Continue checking the rest of the circuit in the same fashion. When you reach a point at which no voltage is present, the problem lies between that point and the last test point with voltage. Most of the time the problem can be traced to a loose connection. **Note:** *Keep in mind that some circuits receive voltage only when the ignition key is in the Accessory or Run position.*

Finding a short

One method of finding shorts in a circuit is to remove the fuse and connect a test light or voltmeter in place of the fuse terminals. There should be no voltage present in the circuit. Move the wiring harness from side-to-side while watching the test light. If the bulb goes on, there is a short to ground somewhere in that area, probably where the insulation has rubbed through. The same test can be performed on each component in the circuit, even a switch.

Ground check

Perform a ground test to check whether a component is properly grounded. Disconnect the battery and connect one lead of a continuity tester or multimeter (set to the ohms scale), to a known good ground. Connect the other lead to the wire or ground connection being tested. If the resistance is low (less than 5 ohms), the ground is good. If the bulb on a self-powered test light does not go on, the ground is not good.

Continuity check

A continuity check is done to determine if there are any breaks in a circuit - if it is passing electricity properly. With the circuit off (no power in the circuit), a self-powered continuity tester or multimeter can be used to check the

circuit. Connect the test leads to both ends of the circuit (or to the "power" end and a good ground), and if the test light comes on the circuit is passing current properly **(see illustration)**. If the resistance is low (less than 5 ohms), there is continuity; if the reading is 10,000 ohms or higher, there is a break somewhere in the circuit. The same procedure can be used to test a switch, by connecting the continuity tester to the switch terminals. With the switch turned On, the test light should come on (or low resistance should be indicated on a meter).

Finding an open circuit

When diagnosing for possible open circuits, it is often difficult to locate them by sight because the connectors hide oxidation or terminal misalignment. Merely wiggling a connector on a sensor or in the wiring harness may correct the open circuit condition. Remember this when an open circuit is indicated when troubleshooting a circuit. Intermittent problems may also be caused by oxidized or loose connections.

Electrical troubleshooting is simple if you keep in mind that all electrical circuits are basically electricity running from the battery, through the wires, switches, relays, fuses and fusible links to each electrical component (light bulb, motor, etc.) and to ground, from which it is passed back to the battery. Any electrical problem is an interruption in the flow of electricity to and from the battery.

Connectors

Most electrical connections on these vehicles are made with multiwire plastic connectors. The mating halves of many connectors are secured with locking clips molded into the plastic connector shells. The mating halves of large connectors, such as some of those under the instrument panel, are held together by a bolt through the center of the connector.

To separate a connector with locking clips, use a small screwdriver to pry the clips

apart carefully, then separate the connector halves. Pull only on the shell, never pull on the wiring harness as you may damage the individual wires and terminals inside the connectors. Look at the connector closely before trying to separate the halves. Often the locking clips are engaged in a way that is not immediately clear. Additionally, many connectors have more than one set of clips.

Each pair of connector terminals has a male half and a female half. When you look at the end view of a connector in a diagram, be sure to understand whether the view shows the harness side or the component side of the connector. Connector halves are mirror images of each other, and a terminal shown on the right side end-view of one half will be on the left side end-view of the other half.

It is often necessary to take circuit voltage measurements with a connector connected. Whenever possible, carefully insert a small straight pin (not your meter probe) into the rear of the connector shell to contact the terminal inside, then clip your meter lead to the pin. This kind of connection is called "backprobing" **(see illustration)**. When inserting a test probe into a terminal, be careful not to distort the terminal opening. Doing so can lead to a poor connection and corrosion at that terminal later. Using the small straight pin instead of a meter probe results in less chance of deforming the terminal connector.

3 Fuses and fusible links - general information

Fuses

Refer to illustrations 3.1a, 3.1b, 3.3a, 3.3b and 3.3c

The electrical circuits of the vehicle are protected by a combination of fuses, circuit breakers and fusible links. The interior fuse/relay panel is located near the lower section of the steering column, while the main fuse-

2.15 To backprobe a connector, insert a small, sharp probe (such as a straight-pin) into the back of the connector alongside the desired wire until it contacts the metal terminal inside; connect your meter leads to the probes - this allows you to test a functioning circuit

3.1a The power distribution fuse panel is located in the engine compartment - to remove the cover, press down above the Ford emblem, slide the cover out of its tabs and lift it off - on later models the panel is just to the left side of the radiator

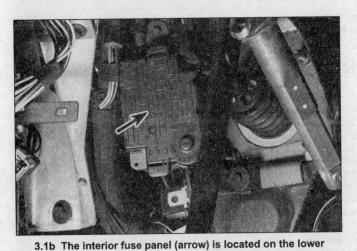

3.1b The interior fuse panel (arrow) is located on the lower portion of the steering column - pull on the tabs and remove the panel for access

3.3a A fuse puller and spare fuses are mounted in the cover of the interior fuse panel

relay panel is in the engine compartment (see illustrations).

Each of the fuses is designed to protect a specific circuit, and the various circuits are identified on the fuse panel itself.

Several sizes of fuses are employed in the fuse blocks. There are small, medium and large sizes of the same design, all with the same blade terminal design. The medium and large fuses can be removed with your fingers, but the small fuses require the use of pliers or the small plastic fuse-puller tool found in most fuse boxes (see illustrations). If an electrical component fails, always check the fuse first. The best way to check the fuses is with a test light. Check for power at the exposed terminal tips of each fuse. If power is present at one side of the fuse but not the other, the fuse is blown. A blown fuse can also be identified by visually inspecting it (see illustration).

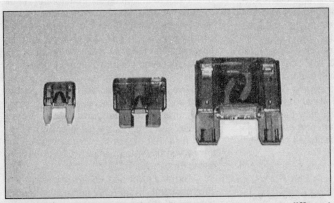

3.3b All three of these fuses are of 30-amp rating, yet are different sizes, at left is a small fuse, the center is a medium, and at right is a large - make sure you get the right amperage and size when purchasing replacement fuses

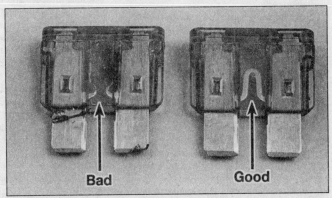

Bad   Good

3.3c When a fuse blows, the element between the terminals melts - the fuse on the left is blown, the one on the right is good

Be sure to replace blown fuses with the correct type. Fuses (of the same physical size) of different ratings may be physically interchangeable, but only fuses of the proper rating should be used. Replacing a fuse with one of a higher or lower value than specified is not recommended. Each electrical circuit needs a specific amount of protection. The amperage value of each fuse is molded into the top of the fuse body.

If the replacement fuse immediately fails, don't replace it again until the cause of the problem is isolated and corrected. In most cases, this will be a short circuit in the wiring caused by a broken or deteriorated wire.

Fusible links

Some circuits are protected by fusible links. The links are used in circuits that are not ordinarily fused, such as the alternator circuit.

The fusible link for the alternator circuit, and other circuits, is located on the right side of the engine, next to the starter relay and battery (1997 and later) or next to the engine compartment fuse panel (1992 through 1996). The link is a short length of heavy wire that can be purchased at a dealer parts department.

To replace a fusible link, first disconnect the negative battery cable.

Although the fusible links appear to be a heavier gauge than the wires they're protecting, the appearance is due to the thick insulation. All fusible links are several wire gauges smaller than the wire they're designed to protect. Fusible links can't be repaired, but a new link of the same size wire can be installed. The procedure is as follows:

a) *Cut the damaged fusible link out of the wire.*

b) *Strip the insulation back approximately 1-inch.*

c) *Spread the strands of the exposed wire apart, push them together and twist them in place.*

d) *Use rosin core solder and solder the wires together to obtain a good connection.*

e) *Use plenty of electrical tape around the soldered joint. No wires should be exposed.*

f) *Connect the negative battery cable. Test the circuit for proper operation.*

4   Circuit breakers - general information and check

Circuit breakers protect certain circuits, such as the power windows and power seats. Depending on the vehicle's accessories.

Because the circuit breakers reset automatically, an electrical overload in a circuit-breaker-protected system will cause the circuit to fail momentarily, then come back on. If the circuit does not come back on, check it immediately.

For a basic check, pull the circuit breaker up out of its socket on the fuse panel, but just

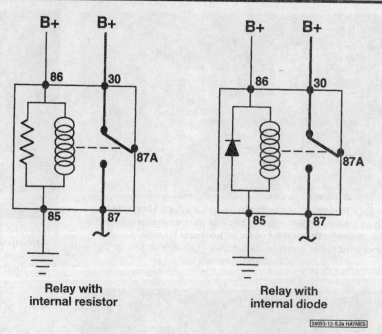

5.2a Typical ISO relay designs, terminal numbering and circuit connections

far enough to probe with a voltmeter. The breaker should still contact the sockets.

With the voltmeter negative lead on a good chassis ground, touch each end prong of the circuit breaker with the positive meter probe. There should be battery voltage at each end. If there is battery voltage only at one end, the circuit breaker must be replaced and/or the circuit repaired.

5   Relays - general information and testing

General information

1   Several electrical accessories in the vehicle, such as the fuel injection system, horns, starter, and fog lamps use relays to transmit the electrical signal to the component. Relays use a low-current circuit (the control circuit) to open and close a high-current circuit (the power circuit). If the relay is defective, that component will not operate properly. Most relays are mounted in the engine compartment and interior fuse/relay boxes **(see illustrations 3.1a and 3.1b)**. The electrical center located below the left end of the instrument panel, also contains several relays. If a faulty relay is suspected, it can be removed and tested using the procedure below or by a dealer service department or a repair shop. Defective relays must be replaced as a unit.

Testing

Refer to illustrations 5.2a and 5.2b

2   Most of the relays used in these vehicles are of a type often called "ISO" relays, which refers to the International Standards Organization. The terminals of ISO relays are numbered to indicate their usual circuit con-

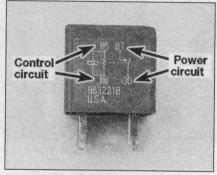

5.2b Most relays are marked on the outside to easily identify the control circuit and power circuit - this one is of the four-terminal type

nections and functions. There are two basic layouts of terminals on the relays used in the covered vehicles **(see illustrations)**.

3   Refer to the wiring diagram for the circuit to determine the proper connections for the relay you're testing. If you can't determine the correct connection from the wiring diagrams, however, you may be able to determine the test connections from the information that follows.

4   Two of the terminals are the relay control circuit and connect to the relay coil. The other relay terminals are the power circuit. When the relay is energized, the coil creates a magnetic field that closes the larger contacts of the power circuit to provide power to the circuit loads.

5   Terminals 85 and 86 are normally the control circuit. If the relay contains a diode, terminal 86 must be connected to battery positive (B+) voltage and terminal 85 to ground. If the relay contains a resistor, terminals 85 and 86 can be connected in either direction

with respect to B+ and ground.

6   Terminal 30 is normally connected to the battery voltage (B+) source for the circuit loads. Terminal 87 is connected to the ground side of the circuit, either directly or through a load. If the relay has several alternate terminals for load or ground connections, they usually are numbered 87A, 87B, 87C, and so on.

7   Use an ohmmeter to check continuity through the relay control coil.

a) *Connect the meter according to the polarity shown in the illustration for one check; then reverse the ohmmeter leads and check continuity in the other direction.*

b) *If the relay contains a resistor, resistance should be indicated on the meter, and should be the same value with the ohmmeter in either direction.*

c) *If the relay contains a diode, resistance should be higher with the ohmmeter in the forward polarity direction than with the meter leads reversed.*

d) *If the ohmmeter shows infinite resistance in both directions, replace the relay.*

8   Remove the relay from the vehicle and use the ohmmeter to check for continuity between the relay power circuit terminals. There should be no continuity between terminal 30 and 87 with the relay de-energized.

9   Connect a fused jumper wire to terminal 86 and the positive battery terminal. Connect another jumper wire between terminal 85 and ground. When the connections are made, the relay should click.

10   With the jumper wires connected, check for continuity between the power circuit terminals. Now, there should be continuity between terminals 30 and 87.

11   If the relay fails any of the above tests, replace it.

---

6   Multifunction switch - replacement

Warning: *Most models are equipped with airbags. Always disconnect the negative battery cable, then the positive cable and wait 2 minutes before working in the vicinity of the impact sensors, steering column or instrument panel to avoid the possibility of accidental deployment of the airbag, which could cause personal injury (see Section 24).*

1   The multifunction switch is mounted on the steering column and controls the function of the turn signals, hazard warning, headlamp dimmer, windshield wiper and windshield washer through the turn signal stalk.

2   Disconnect the negative battery cable, then the positive battery cable.

3   Remove the key lock cylinder (see Section 8). Remove the screws securing the steering column upper and lower shrouds and remove the shrouds.

4   Remove the two electrical connectors from the back-side of the multifunction switch.

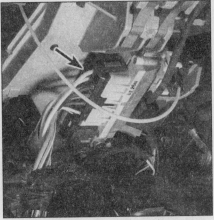

8.4 Location of the ignition switch electrical connector (arrow)

Replacement

5   Remove the screws retaining the multi-function switch the steering column assembly.

6   Installation is the reverse of removal.

---

7   Turn signal/hazard flasher relay - replacement

1   Disconnect the negative cable from the battery.

2   The flasher relay is located in the passenger compartment fuse panel **(see illustration 3.1b)**. Remove the fuse panel cover, then remove the flasher by pulling straight out. On later models, the electronic flasher is located outside the fuse/relay panel, to the left of the steering column or near the top of the brake pedal.

3   Install the new flasher unit. Be sure to line up the metal contacts with the slots in the fuse panel. Press the flasher firmly into place, then reinstall the fuse panel cover.

---

8   Ignition switch and key lock cylinder - check and replacement

Refer to illustrations 8.4 and 8.14
Warning: *Some models are equipped with airbags. Always disconnect the negative battery cable, then the positive cable and wait 2 minutes before working in the vicinity of the impact sensors, steering column or instrument panel to avoid the possibility of accidental deployment of the airbag, which could cause personal injury (see Section 24).*

1   The ignition switch is located on the lower section of the steering column and is actuated by a rod connected to the key lock cylinder.

Check

2   Disconnect the negative battery cable, then the positive battery cable.

3   Remove the steering column shrouds and lower steering column cover. On later models, the key-lock cylinder must be removed before

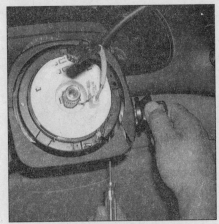

8.14 Ignition key lock cylinder removal details

the column covers can be removed.

4   Remove the bolt securing the electrical connector to the ignition switch, release the clips and remove the connector from the switch **(see illustration)**.

5   Check the mechanical operation of the switch and lock cylinder by rotating the key through all of the switch positions. The movement should feel smooth with no sticking or binding. The ignition switch should return from the Start position to the Run position without assistance (spring return). If sticking or binding is encountered, replace the lock cylinder assembly.

Replacement

Ignition switch

6   Perform Steps 2 through 4 above.

7   Place the ignition switch in the Run position.

8   Remove the ignition switch retaining screws and remove the switch from the steering column.

9   Install the switch aligning the switch pin with the slot in the lock/column assembly. **Note:** *Both the switch and the ignition key should be in the Run position, the slot will align with the index mark in the steering column casting when positioned correctly.*

10   Install the retaining screws and tighten securely. Install the electrical connector.

11   The remainder of installation is the reverse of removal.

Key lock cylinder

12   Disconnect the negative battery cable, then the positive battery cable.

13   Insert the key in the lock and turn it to the Run position.

14   Insert a 1/8-inch drill bit, or similar tool through the hole in the trim shroud directly under the lock cylinder **(see illustration)**. Depress the retaining pin while pulling out on the lock cylinder housing.

15   Install the lock cylinder in the opposite manner. Make sure the cylinder is completely seated and aligned before turning the key to Lock position and removing the key.

9.7 Remove the clip and separate the linkage from the motor drive arm

1 Clip	2 Drive arm

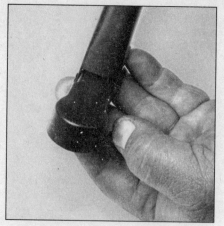

10.2a Lift up on the arm, pull on the side latch and pull the arm off the spindle

10.2b Be sure to pull the latch back far enough to clear the spindle

9   Windshield wiper motor - removal and installation

Refer to illustration 9.7

1   Turn the windshield wiper switch ON.
2   Turn the ignition switch ON and keep your hand on the key. When the wiper arms move to the straight up position, turn the ignition switch OFF.
3   Disconnect the negative battery cable from the battery.
4   Remove the right side wiper arm and blade assembly (see Section 10).
5   Remove the cowl vent and seal at the base of the windshield (see Chapter 11).
6   Use a small screwdriver to unlock the electrical connector tabs, then disconnect the electrical connector at the windshield wiper motor.
7   Remove the windshield wiper adapter and connecting arm clip securing the motor drive arm to the windshield wiper mounting arm and pivot shaft **(see illustration)**. **Note:** *On 2001 and later models, remove a small panel to the left of the wiper assembly that allows access to disconnect the wiper linkage.*
8   Remove the three bolts securing the windshield wiper motor to the front cowl.
9   Installation is the reverse of removal. **Note:** *The wiper motor drive arm must be approximately 180-degrees from the park position during installation, otherwise it will be difficult to install the linkage to the motor.*

10   Windshield wiper arm - removal and installation

Refer to illustrations 10.2a and 10.2b

1   **Note:** *To prevent damage to the windshield and also to make sure the wipers are operating under normal conditions, keep the windshield wet during this step. Prior to removing the wiper arm, turn the windshield wipers switch ON, allow the wipers to travel through several cycles, then turn it OFF. This will ensure that the wiper arm is in the parked position parallel to the base of the windshield.*
2   Swing the wiper arm and blade away from the windshield. Slide the latch away from the wiper spindle **(see illustrations)**, then pull the wiper arm assembly off the spindle.
3   Installation is the reverse of removal with the following additions.
   a) *Position the arm back onto the post in the parked position. Do not position the arm too low as it will hit the base of the windshield during normal wiper operation.*
   b) *Make sure the latch is correctly seated in the groove in the wiper spindle.*

11   Windshield wiper control module - removal and installation

Note: *On most models, the wiper control module is located behind the instrument panel, to the right of the steering column. On 2005 models, it is integrated into the wiper motor assembly.*
1   Disconnect the negative battery cable from the battery.
2   Remove the instrument panel lower trim panel.
3   Disconnect the electrical connector from the windshield wiper control module.
4   Remove the screw securing the windshield wiper control module to the instrument panel lower brace.
5   Installation is the reverse of removal.

12   Windshield washer reservoir and pump assembly - removal and installation

Removal

1   Disconnect the negative battery cable from the battery.
2   Remove the air cleaner intake tube assembly (see Chapter 4).
3   On late models (1997 and later), remove the battery and the battery tray (see Chapter 5).
4   Use a small screwdriver to unlock the electrical connector tabs, then disconnect the washer pump electrical connector.
5   Remove the bolts and nuts securing the washer reservoir and pump motor assembly to the passenger side fender well.
6   Lift the washer reservoir up and disconnect the small hose from the base of the reservoir. Place your finger over the end of the small hose fitting on the reservoir to prevent spilling the washer fluid in the engine compartment. Remove the reservoir assembly.
7   Drain the washer fluid from the reservoir into a clean container. If the fluid is kept clean it can be reused.
8   Use a small screwdriver and carefully pry out the pump motor from the reservoir receptacle. Do not damage the plastic housing during removal.
9   Remove the one-piece seal/filter and inspect for damage or debris.
10   Flush out the reservoir with clean water to remove any residue. Inspect it for any foreign matter.
11   Inspect the reservoir pump chamber prior to installing a used motor into a new reservoir. Clean it if necessary.

Installation

12   Lubricate the inside diameter of the seal/filter with a soapy water solution and insert the seal/filter and windshield washer pump assembly into the windshield washer reservoir. Push the assembly in until it seats completely.
13   Install the reservoir onto the fender well and secure with the bolts and nuts.
14   Connect the hose to the fitting to the reservoir and refill the reservoir with washer fluid.
15   Connect the electrical connector. **Caution:** *Do not operate the pump without fluid in the reservoir, as it could be damaged. After the reservoir is filled, operate the pump and check for leaks.*

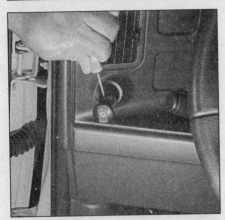

13.6 Insert a hooked tool, depress the spring in the headlight knob slot and remove the knob

13.12 Remove the switch retaining screws (arrows) and pull the switch partially out

13.13 Release the locking tabs (arrow) and disconnect the electrical connector

13 Headlight switch - replacement

Refer to illustrations 13.6, 13.12 and 13.13

Warning: *Some models are equipped with airbags. Always disconnect the negative battery cable, then the positive cable and wait 2 minutes before working in the vicinity of the impact sensors, steering column or instrument panel to avoid the possibility of accidental deployment of the airbag, which could cause personal injury (see Section 24).*

1   Disconnect the negative cable, then the positive cable from the battery. Remove the engine cover.

Models through 2004

2   Pull out and remove the ash tray receptacle.

3   Remove the three screws and remove the ash tray retainer.

4   Remove the snap-in molding on each side of the steering column.

5   Remove the cigar lighter element.

6   Insert a hooked tool into the headlight knob slot and depress the spring, then remove the knob from the shaft **(see illustration)**.

7   Unscrew the switch bezel from the instrument panel finish panel.

8   Remove the screws securing the instrument panel steering column cover and remove the cover.

9   Remove the screws securing the instrument panel finish panel. Unsnap the retainer and pull the finish panel away from the instrument panel. Disconnect all electrical connectors and remove the panel.

10   Pull the headlight switch shaft all the way out to the full ON position.

11   Press on the shaft release button. While holding the button down, pull the shaft out of the switch.

12   Remove the screws securing the switch **(see illustration)**.

13   Pull the switch part way to gain access to the electrical connector, release the locking tabs, then disconnect the electrical connector from the switch **(see illustration)**. Remove the bezel nut and remove the switch from the bracket.

14   Installation is the reverse of removal.

2005 models

15   Pull the headlight switch out to the Headlight ON position. While using a small pin or screwdriver to depress the clip in the knob, pull the knob from the switch shaft.

16   The bezel around the switch can be unscrewed by hand (counterclockwise).

17   If equipped, tilt the tilt column to the down position, apply the parking brake and pull the shift lever to its lowest position.

18   Refer to Section 17 and remove the radio.

19   Refer to Chapter 11 and remove the instrument cluster bezel.

20   Pull out the instrument panel finish panel (which surrounds the cluster and goes all the way to the radio) and disconnect any electrical connectors behind it.

21   With the finish panel off, the bolts securing the switch are exposed. Remove the switch and disconnect its electrical connector.

22   Installation is the reverse of the removal procedure.

14 Headlight bulb - replacement

Sealed beam headlights

Refer to illustration 14.4

1   The headlights on base models are replaceable sealed-beam units. The high-beam and low-beam filaments are contained in the same unit. If one of filaments fail, the entire unit must be replaced with a new one.

2   Open the hood.

3   Remove the two screws securing the headlight trim ring. Pull up on the trim ring and release the two lower locating tabs from the body.

4   Remove the four screws retaining the headlight retaining ring **(see illustration)**. Be careful not to disturb the two headlight adjusting screws.

14.4 Typical sealed beam headlight assembly installation details

5   Pull the headlight out far enough to gain access to the electrical connector, then disconnect the connector.

6   Replace the headlight unit with one of the exact same size and type. Attach the electrical connector to the prongs on the back of the unit. Place the headlight bulb into the adjusting ring with the large number embossed on the lens at the top. Make sure the alignment lugs cast into the unit are positioned in the recesses of the headlight adjusting ring.

7   Install the retaining ring and screws, then install the headlight trim ring. Be sure to correctly position the two lower locating tabs in the body.

Composite headlight bulbs (aerodynamically styled)

Refer to illustrations 14.10 and 14.13

Warning: *Halogen gas filled bulbs are under pressure and may shatter if the surface is scratched or the bulb is dropped. Wear eye protection and handle the bulbs carefully, grasping only the base whenever possible. Do not touch the surface of the bulb with your fingers because the oil from your skin could cause the bulb to overheat and fail prematurely. If you do touch the bulb surface, clean it with rubbing alcohol.*

8   Open the hood.

9   Disconnect the negative cable from the battery.

14.10 Slightly bend back and lift the two black tabs (arrows) while holding onto the front of the headlight assembly

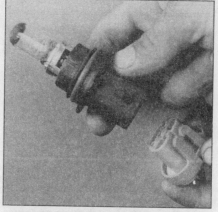

14.13 After removing the headlight bulb from the housing, release the retaining clip and pull the connector straight out of the socket

16.1 Remove the lamp assembly mounting screws (arrows)

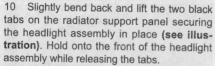

10   Slightly bend back and lift the two black tabs on the radiator support panel securing the headlight assembly in place **(see illustration)**. Hold onto the front of the headlight assembly while releasing the tabs.

11   Carefully pull the headlight assembly out far enough to gain access to the electrical connector, then disconnect the connector from the bulb holder.

12   Rotate the retaining ring about 1/8-turn counterclockwise (viewed from the rear) and slide it off the base.

13   Carefully pull the connector straight out of the socket **(see illustration)**. Do not rotate the bulb during removal.

14   Without touching the glass with bare fingers, plug the connector into the socket of the new bulb. Position the flat on the plastic base up.

15   Align the socket locating tabs with the grooves in the forward part of the plastic base, then push the socket firmly into the base. Make sure the base mounting flange contacts the socket.

16   Slide the retaining ring on. Turn it clockwise until it hits the stop, then connect the electrical connector.

17   Carefully push the headlight assembly into the radiator support panel while aligning

the three adjuster screws. Hold it in place and push the two black tabs down into engagement until you hear them "snap" into place. Make sure the headlight assembly is secured properly, try to pull it forward. If it is loose, remove the assembly and reinstall it.

18   Test the headlight operation, then close the hood.

19   Have the headlight adjustment checked and, if necessary, adjusted by a dealer service department or service station at the earliest opportunity.

Headlight housing assembly replacement (aerodynamically styled)

20   Perform Steps 8 through 13 and Steps 15 through 18 of this procedure for housing assembly replacement **(see illustration 14.10)**.

15   Headlights - adjusting

Note: *The headlights must be aimed correctly. If adjusted incorrectly they could momentarily blind the driver of an oncoming vehicle and cause a serious accident or seriously reduce your ability to see the road. The headlights*

should be checked for proper aim every 12 months and any time a new headlight is installed or front end body work is performed. It should be emphasized that the following procedure is only an interim step which will provide temporary adjustment until the headlights can be adjusted by a properly equipped shop.

1   Sealed beam type headlights have two spring loaded adjusting screws, one on top, controlling up-and-down movement and one on the side controlling left-and-right movement. The aerodynamically styled headlights utilize one outer angle drive mechanism for left-and-right movement and one inner adjusting screw for up-and-down movement.

2   There are several methods of adjusting the headlights. The simplest method requires a blank wall, masking tape and a level floor.

3   Position masking tape vertically on the wall in reference to the vehicle centerline and the centerline of both headlights.

4   Position a horizontal line in reference to the centerline of all headlights. **Note:** *It may be easier to position the tape on the wall with the vehicle parked only a few feet away.*

5   Adjustment should be made with the vehicle sitting level parked 25 feet from the wall, the gas tank half-full and no unusually

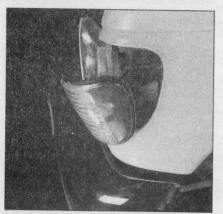

16.2 Pull the lamp assembly straight out from the body

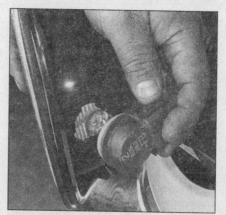

16.3 Remove the socket from the lamp assembly . . .

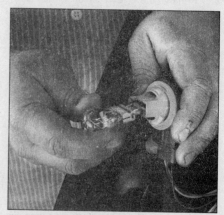

16.4 . . . and pull the bulb straight out of the socket

heavy load in the vehicle.

6   Starting with the low beam adjustment, position the high intensity zone so it is two inches below the horizontal line and two inches to the right of the headlight vertical line. Adjustment is made by turning the appropriate adjusting screw (refer to Step 1) to raise or lower the beam. The other adjusting screw should be used in the same manner to move the beam left or right.

7   With the high beams on, the high intensity zone should be vertically centered with the exact center just below the horizontal line. **Note:** *It may not be possible to position the headlight aim exactly for both high and low beams. If a compromise must be made, keep in mind that the low beams are the most used and have the greatest effect on driver safety.*

8   Have the headlights adjusted by a dealer service department or service station at the earliest opportunity.

16 Bulb replacement

Parking/turn signal/front side marker lamp

Refer to illustrations 16.1, 16.2, 16.3 and 16.4

1   Remove the two screws that secure the lamp assembly **(see illustration)**.

2   Pull the assembly straight out to expose the bulb socket **(see illustration)**.

3   Rotate the bulb socket counterclockwise and remove the socket from the housing **(see illustration)**.

4   Firmly grasp the bulb and pull the bulb straight out of the socket **(see illustration)**.

5   Installation is the reverse of removal.

Rear combination lights (stop, tail, turn and backup)

Refer to illustration 16.6

6   Remove the screws securing the rear combination lamp assembly **(see illustration)**.

7   Pull the housing straight out from the body.

8   Rotate the bulb socket counterclockwise and remove the socket from the housing **(see illustration 16.3)**.

9   Firmly grasp the bulb and pull the bulb straight out of the socket **(see illustration 16.4)**.

10   Installation is the reverse of removal.

License plate bulb

Refer to illustration 16.13

11   Remove the two plastic screws securing the lens.

12   Pull the lens down far enough to access the socket.

13   Twist the socket counterclockwise and remove it from the lens assembly **(see illustration)**.

14   Pull the bulb out of the socket.

15   Installation is the reverse of removal.

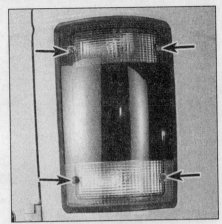

16.6 Remove the lamp assembly mounting screws (arrows)

High mount brake light

Without cargo lamp attached

Refer to illustrations 16.16, 16.18 and 16.19

16   Remove the screws that secure the lamp assembly to the body **(see illustration)**.

17   Lift the lamp assembly off, taking care not to damage the paint.

18   Work the bulb socket out of the lamp body **(see illustration)**.

19   Pull the bulb out of the socket **(see illustration)**.

20   Installation is the reverse of removal.

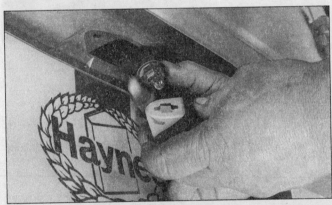

16.13 Rotate the bulb socket counterclockwise and remove the socket and bulb from the lens assembly

16.16 Remove the lamp assembly screws

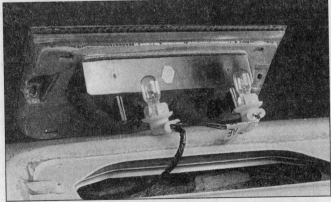

16.18 Remove the bulb socket from the lamp assembly . . .

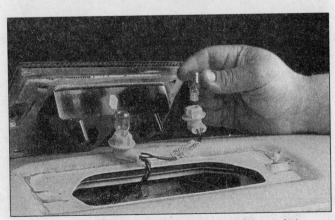

16.19 . . . and pull the bulb straight out of the socket

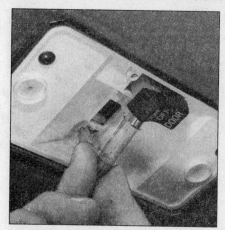

16.28 Carefully pull the bulb from the terminals

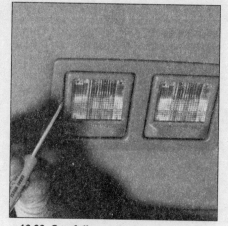

16.30 Carefully pry the lens loose and detach the lens

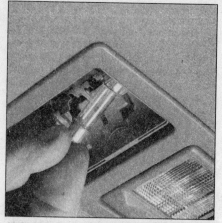

16.31 Remove the bulb from the terminals

With cargo lamp attached

21 Remove the screws that secure the high mount/cargo lamp assembly to the body.
22 Lift the lamp assembly off, taking care not to damage the paint.
23 Remove the two screws and remove the cargo lamp lens.
24 Remove the two screws and remove the cargo lamp from the high mount. Move the cargo lamp out of the way.
25 Remove the miniature bulb from the high mount socket.
26 Installation is the reverse of removal.

Cargo light

Refer to illustration 16.28

27 Remove the screws and cover.
28 Carefully pull the bulb from the terminals **(see illustration)**.
29 Installation is the reverse of removal.

Dome light

Refer to illustrations 16.30 and 16.31

30 Use a small screwdriver and carefully pry the dome light lens away from the base **(see illustration)**. Remove the lens.

31 Pull the bulb out of the terminals **(see illustration)**.
32 Install a new bulb and press it in all the way, then install the dome light lens assembly.

Dome/map combination light

33 Use a small screwdriver and carefully pry the dome light lens away from the base. Remove the lens.
34 Pull the dome light bulb straight out of the socket.
35 To remove the map light bulb(s), remove the screws and remove the lamp assembly from the headliner.
36 Pull the map light bulb(s) straight out of the socket.
37 Installation is the reverse of removal.

Glove compartment light

38 Open the glove compartment and remove the contents.
39 Remove the mounting screw and pull the lamp/striker assembly part way out of the instrument panel.
40 Carefully pull the bulb out of the housing.
41 Installation is the reverse of removal.

16.42 Carefully pry the lens off

Vanity mirror light

Refer to illustrations 16.42 and 16.43

42 Pry the lens off the light **(see illustration)**.
43 Pry the bulb out of its clips **(see illustration)** and push a new one in.
44 Push the lens back into position.

16.43 Pry the bulb out of the clips and push a new one in

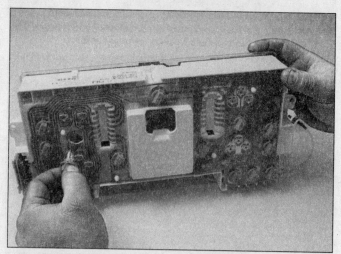

16.46 Rotate the bulb holder counterclockwise and remove it from the instrument cluster

17.2 Insert the tools until they seat, then push outward simultaneously on both tools to release the clips and withdraw the radio from the dash

18.3 Use a small wrench to remove the antenna mast

Instrument cluster bulbs

Refer to illustration 16.46

Note: *The instrument cluster printed circuit board is fragile. Be careful when removing the bulb assemblies.*

45   Remove the instrument cluster to gain access to the bulbs (see Section 20).

46   Grasp the bulb holder, twist 1/4-turn counterclockwise and remove the bulb and socket from the instrument cluster **(see illustration)**. Remove the bulb from the socket and install a new bulb.

47   Installation is the reverse of removal.

17   Radio - removal and installation

Refer to illustration 17.2

Warning: *Most models are equipped with airbags. Always disconnect the negative battery cable, then the positive cable and wait 2 minutes before working in the vicinity of the impact sensors, steering column or instrument panel to avoid the possibility of accidental deployment of the airbag, which could cause personal injury (see Section 24).*

1   Disconnect the cable from the negative then the positive battery terminal. Remove the instrument cluster trim panel (see Section 21).

2   Insert a radio removal tool into the radio face plate **(see illustration)**. Push the tool in about 1-inch to release the retaining clips on each side.

3   Using the special tool, pull the radio partially out of the instrument panel, then disconnect the power, speaker and antenna wires from the radio.

4   Pull the radio assembly out of the instrument panel.

5   Installation is the reverse of removal.

18   Radio antenna - removal and installation

Refer to illustration 18.3

1   Remove the cowl panel vent (see Chapter 11).

2   Reach under the instrument panel, pull straight out and disconnect the antenna from the rear of the radio chassis. **Note:** *On late models, it is possible to disconnect the antenna lead from the antenna base under the fender.*

3   Unhook the two retaining clips securing the antenna lead-in cable **(see illustration)**.

4   Remove the fender inner splash shield. Remove the shield by pulling the push-pins out of the push-pin casings and unlocking the shield from the fender.

5   Remove the antenna mast from the antenna base (turn counterclockwise). Disconnect the antenna cable from the plastic clips along the top of the defroster nozzle.

6   Using a small screwdriver, carefully pry the antenna cap from the base and remove the cap.

7   Remove the screws securing the antenna base to the body and slowly pull the antenna cable out through the body opening. Remove the antenna base assembly and gasket.

8   Tie a piece of string onto the radio end of the antenna cable and the other end to the instrument panel. This will be used to pull the new antenna cable back through the same path as the old one. Remove the antenna cable.

9   Installation is the reverse of removal with the following additions.

a)   Be sure to install a new gasket.

b)   Untie the string and attach it to the new antenna cable. Slowly pull the string and antenna cable back through the body opening. Discard the string.

19   Speakers - removal and installation

Refer to illustration 19.2

Note: *The models covered by this manual are equipped from the factory with a speaker in each front door and on optional stereo equipped models additional speakers are installed in the sliding door or the right-side cargo door and on the driver side interior panel behind the B-pillar.*

1   Remove the trim panel (see Chapter 11).

2   Remove the screws securing the speaker to the door or speaker bracket **(see illustration)**.

3   Lift out the speaker and disconnect the electrical connector at the speaker. **Caution:** *Do not operate the radio with the speakers disconnected.*

4   Installation is the reverse of removal.

19.2 After removing the door trim panel, the speaker retaining screws (arrows) are easy to reach

20.7 Remove the transmission indicator cable loop from the ballstud and the thumbwheel bracket from the steering column (arrows)

20.9 Remove the instrument cluster mounting screws (arrows)

20 Instrument cluster - removal and installation

Refer to illustrations 20.7, 20.9, 20.10 and 20.12

Warning: *Most models are equipped with airbags. Always disconnect the negative battery cable, then the positive cable and wait 2 minutes before working in the vicinity of the impact sensors, steering column or instrument panel to avoid the possibility of accidental deployment of the airbag, which could cause personal injury (see Section 24).*

Caution: *On 2004 and later models, if a new cluster is installed a scan tool must be used to download the original module's data and then install the data into the new module.*

1   Disconnect the negative, then the positive battery cable from the battery.

2   Remove the steering wheel (see Chapter 10).

3   Remove the headlight switch (see Section 13).

4   Remove the screws and steering column opening cover and remove the cover.

5   Remove the screws securing the instrument cluster finish panel.

6   Remove the instrument cluster finish panel by carefully unsnapping it's retaining clips starting at the lower clips and then the upper clips. On 2001 and later models, there are two bolts at the top and two clips at the bottom.

7   Remove the transmission PRND21 indicator cable loop from the ball stud on the shift lever **(see illustration)**.

8   Remove the thumbwheel bracket from the steering column by removing the thumbwheel bracket screws.

9   Remove the four screws securing the instrument cluster **(see illustration)**.

10   Remove the two screws securing the gear selector indicator (PRND21) and cable to the instrument cluster **(see illustration)**. Remove the selector indicator down and out of the cluster. It is not necessary to disconnect the indicator.

11   Carefully pull the instrument cluster assembly partially out from the instrument panel.

12   Squeeze the locking tabs on the printed circuit three electrical connectors, then disconnect them from the printed circuit board **(see illustration)**.

13   Remove the instrument cluster assembly.

Warning: *Always store and place the instrument cluster in the upright (normal in dash) position. Failure to do so can result in loss of gauge anti-vibration fluid and contamination of the gauge face from the fluid leakage.*

14   Replace any failed bulbs as required by twisting the socket from the back of the printed circuit board.

15   Installation is the reverse of removal.

20.10 Remove the gear selector indicator (PRND21) mounting screws (arrows) and remove it from the instrument cluster

20.12 Disconnect the electrical connectors (arrows) by squeezing the locking tabs - then disconnect them from the printed circuit board

21 Brake light switch - replacement

1 The brake light switch is located on a flange or a bracket protruding from the brake pedal support.

2 Disconnect the electrical connector from the switch.

3 Remove the hairpin retainer and spacer securing the switch to the brake pedal arm.

4 Slide the switch, pushrod, nylon washers and bushing away from the pedal, then remove the switch.

5 To install, place the switch with the U-shaped side nearest the pedal and directly over or under the pin. The bushing must be in the pushrod eyelet with the washer face on the side closest to the retaining pin.

6 Slide the switch up or down so the master cylinder pushrod and bushing are trapped, then push the switch firmly down.

7 Install the plastic washer and hairpin retainer.

8 Connect the electrical connector to the switch. Make sure the electrical connector is routed correctly and will travel the full swing of the pedal without binding.

22 Power window system - description and check

The power window system operates the electric motors mounted in the doors which lower and raise the windows. The system consists of the control switches, the motors (regulators), glass mechanisms and the associated wiring.

Diagnosis can usually be limited to simple checks of the wiring connections and motors for minor faults which can be easily repaired. These are:

a) *Inspect the power window actuating switches for broken wires and loose connections.*

b) *Check the power window fuse/and or circuit breaker.*

c) *Remove the door panel(s) and check the power window motor wires to see if they're loose or damaged. Inspect the glass mechanisms for damage which could cause binding.*

23 Power mirrors - removal and installation

1 Disconnect the negative cable from the battery.

2 Remove the door trim panel (see Chapter 11).

3 Peel the watershield away from the upper front corner of the door.

4 Remove the mirror mounting fasteners.

5 Pull the mirror out, disconnect its electrical connector and remove it.

6 Installation is the reverse of removal.

24 Airbag - general information

Most models are equipped with a Supplemental Inflatable Restraint System (SIR), more commonly known as an airbag. This system is designed to protect the driver from serious injury in the event of a head-on or frontal collision. It consists of an airbag module in the center of the steering wheel, two crash sensors mounted at the front and the right side of the vehicle and a diagnostic monitor which also contains a backup power supply located in the passenger compartment.

First-generation airbag systems included only a driver's side airbag, while later models have an optional passenger-side airbag mounted in the right side of the instrument panel. The newest systems also have seatbelt "pre-tensioners" which instantly take up any seatbelt slack in the event of a signal from the impact sensors.

Airbag module

The airbag inflator module contains a housing incorporating the cushion (airbag) and inflator unit, mounted in the center of the steering wheel. The inflator assembly is mounted on the back of the housing over a hole through which gas is expelled, inflating the bag almost instantaneously when an electrical signal is sent from the system. A coil assembly on the steering column under the module carries this signal to the module.

This coil assembly can transmit an electrical signal regardless of steering wheel position. The igniter in the air bag converts the electrical signal to heat and ignites the sodium azide/copper oxide powder, producing nitrogen gas, which inflates the bag.

Sensors

The system has three sensors: two crash sensors, one at the center of the radiator support and the other on the right frame rail and a safing sensor behind the right side cowl kick-panel in the passenger compartment.

The crash sensors are basically pressure sensitive switches that complete an electrical circuit during an impact of sufficient G force. The electrical signal from these sensors is sent to the electronic diagnostic monitor which then completes the circuit and inflates the airbag(s). At least two sensors (one crash sensor and the safing sensor) must be closed to inflate the airbag.

Electronic diagnostic monitor

The electronic diagnostic monitor supplies the current to the airbag system in the event of the collision, even if battery power is cut off. It checks this system every time the vehicle is started, causing the "AIR BAG" light to go on then off, if the system is operating properly. If there is a fault in the system, the light will go on and stay on, flash, or the dash will make a beeping sound. If this happens, the vehicle should be taken to your dealer immediately for service.

Disabling the system

Whenever working in the vicinity of the steering wheel, steering column or near other components of the airbag system, the system should be disarmed. To do this, perform the following steps:

a) *Turn the ignition switch to Off.*

b) *Detach the cable from the negative battery terminal, then detach the cable from the positive battery terminal and wait 2 minutes for the electronic module backup power supply to be depleted.*

Enabling the system

a) *Turn the ignition switch to the Off position.*

b) *Connect the positive battery cable.*

c) *Connect the negative battery cable*

Disabling/enabling 2005 model systems

On these models, remove the cover from the interior fuse/relay box under the instrument panel. With all accessories off and the key Off, remove the 10-amp fuse for the Restraints Control Module. Turn the ignition to the Run position and observe the airbag warning light on the instrument panel. If the light stays on continuously for at least 30 seconds, you have removed the correct fuse. Turn the key Off, disconnect the battery cables and wait two minutes.

To enable the system, turn the key to the Run position (battery still disconnected) and reinstall the RCM fuse. With no one in the vehicle, reconnect the battery cables. Turn the key to the Off position and then back On after 10 seconds and observe the airbag warning light. It should stay on for six seconds after the key is turned On and then go out.

The first time the Key is turned to On, watch the light for at least 30 seconds, while the system self-checks for problems. Problems in the airbag system could be indicated by the airbag warning light: flashing, failing to illuminate, or staying on all the time. If any of these symptoms occur, check the airbag system with a scan tool to check for diagnostic trouble codes.

25 Wiring diagrams - general information

Since it isn't possible to include all wiring diagrams for every model year covered by this manual, the following diagrams are those that are typical and most commonly needed.

Prior to troubleshooting any circuit, check the fuses and circuit breakers to make sure they're in good condition. Make sure the battery is fully charged and check the cable connections (see Chapter 1). Make sure all connectors are clean, with no broken or loose terminals.

1992-94 4.9L & 1995 4.9L (FEDERAL) ENGINE SCHEMATIC

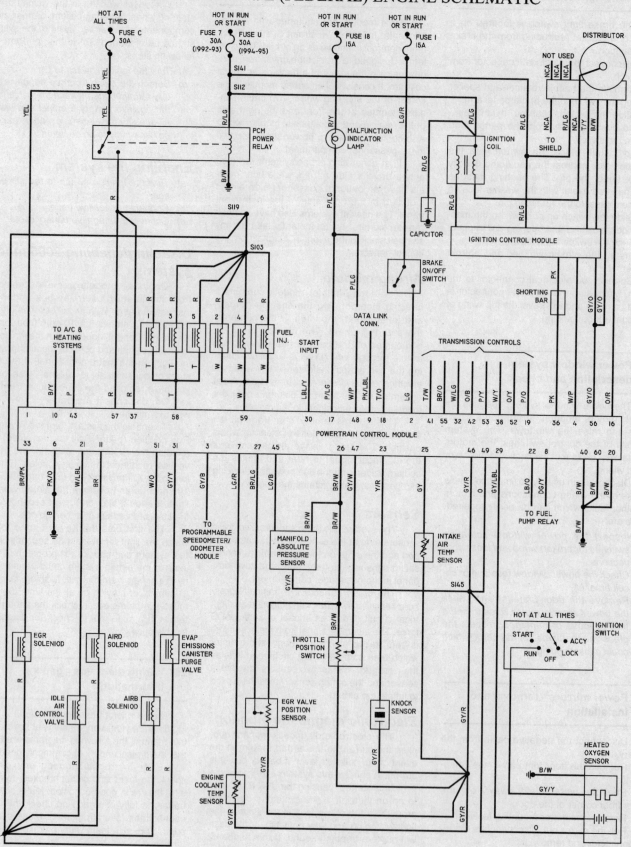

EXTERIOR LAMPS
1992-1996

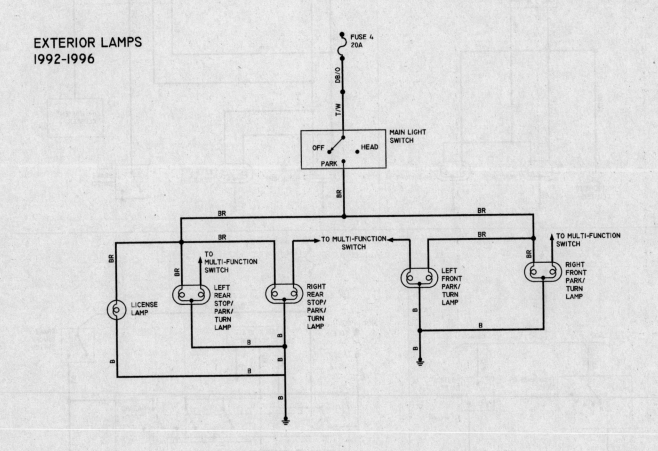

1992-96 CHASSIS SCHEMATICS

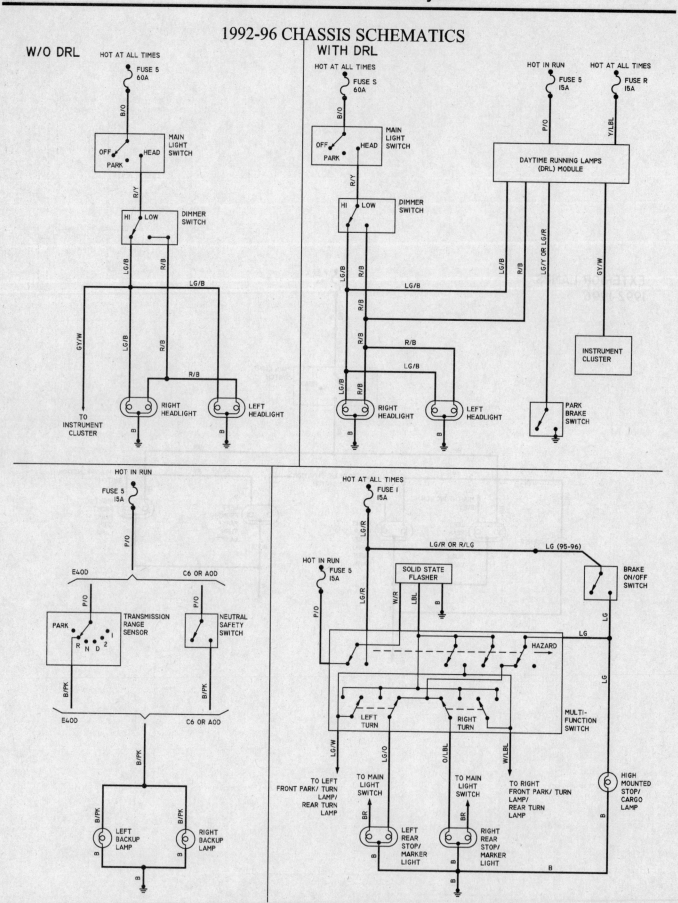

1994-95 7.5L & 1996 7.5L (Federal) ENGINE SCHEMATIC

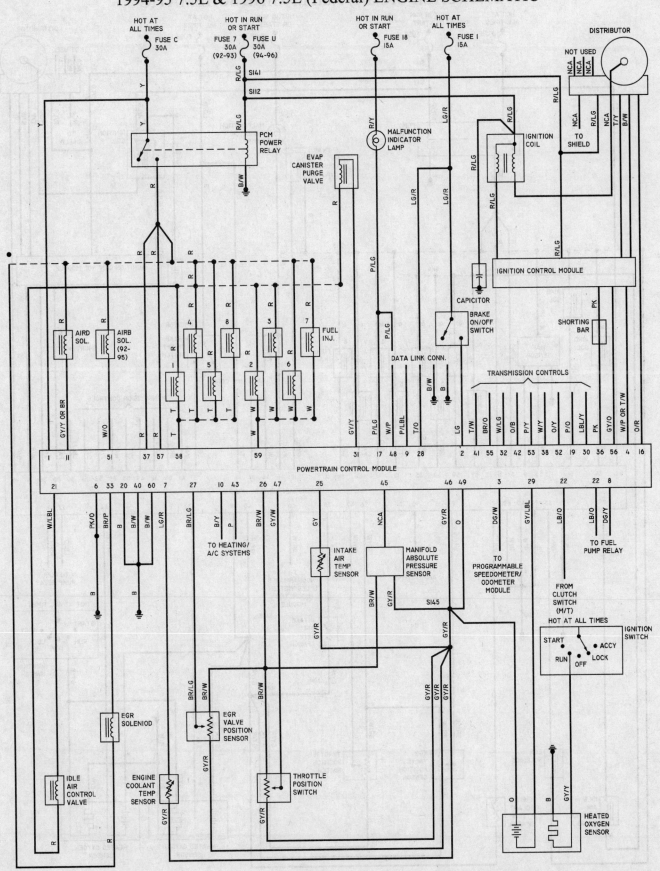

1995 (CALIFORNIA) 5.8L ENGINE SCHEMATIC

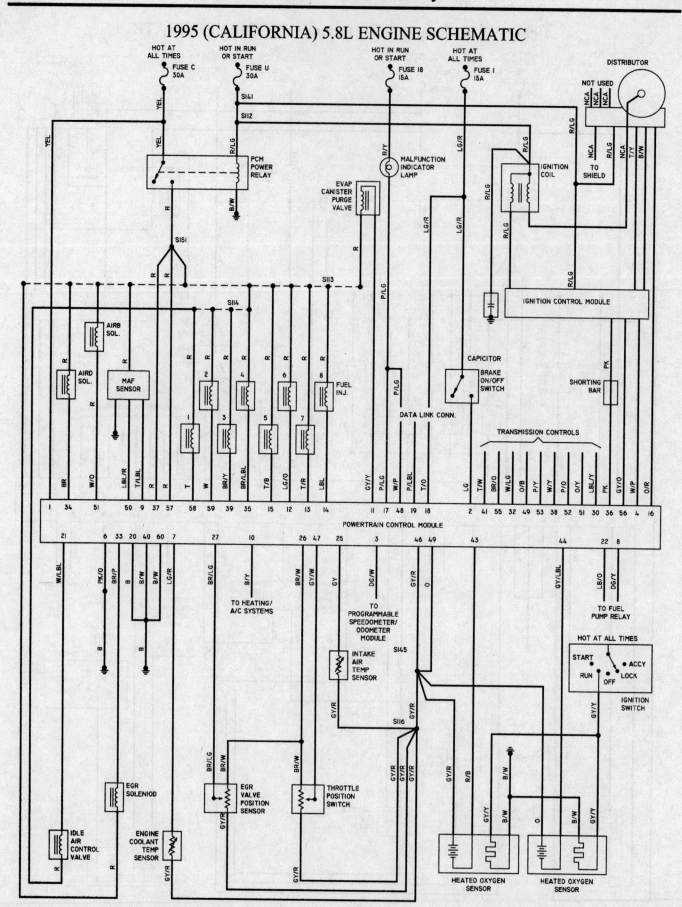

1992 5.0L ENGINE SCHEMATIC

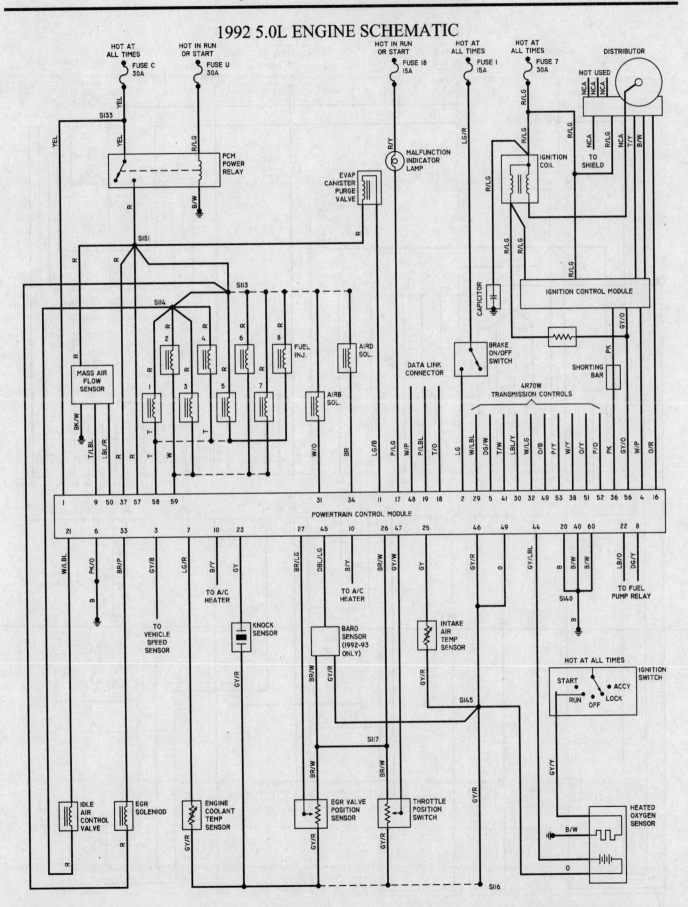

1993-95 5.0L ENGINE SCHEMATIC

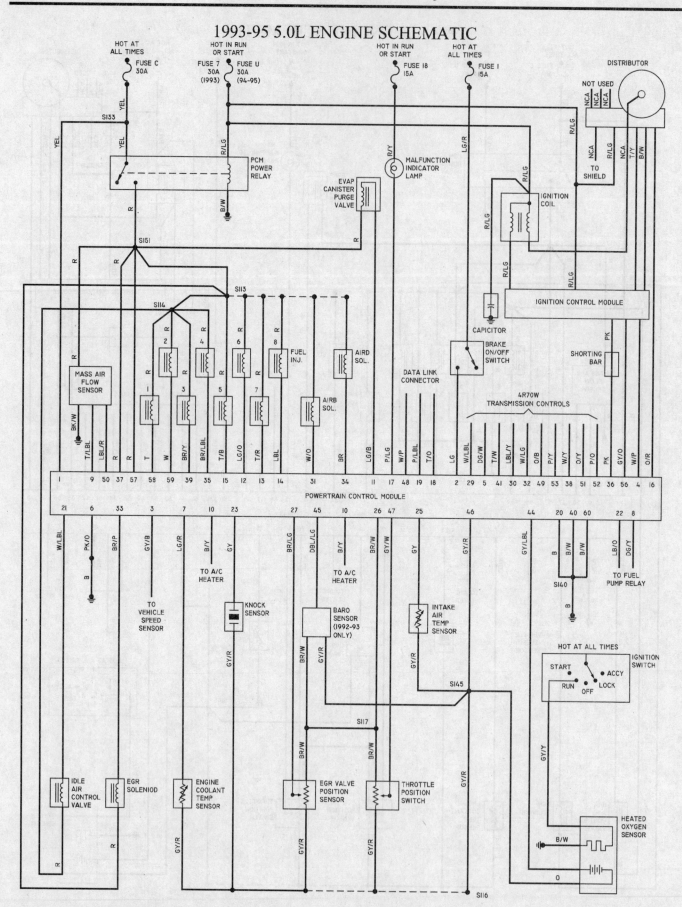

1995 4.9L (CALIFORNIA) ENGINE SCHEMATIC

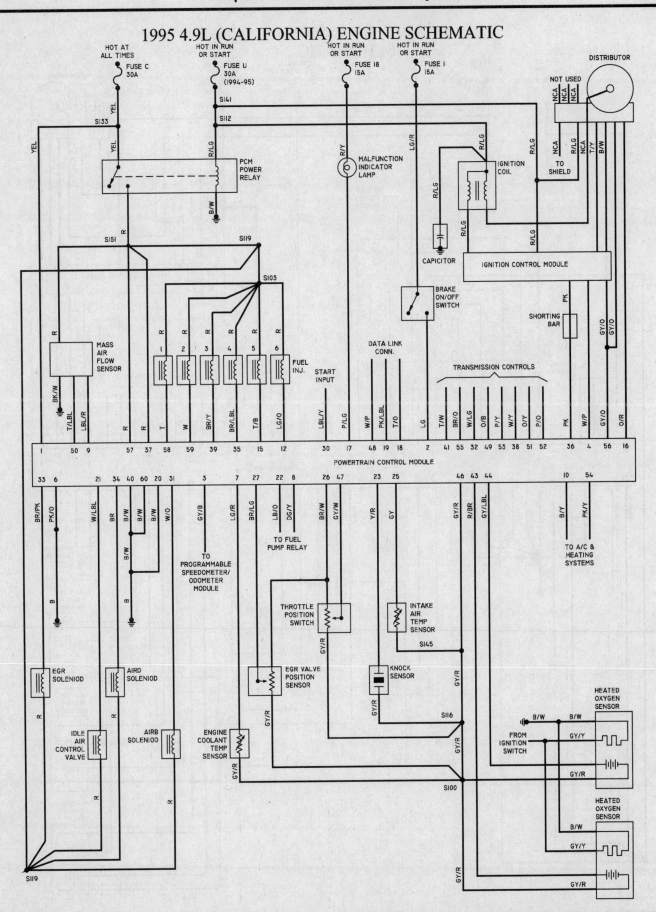

1996 4.9L ENGINE SCHEMATIC

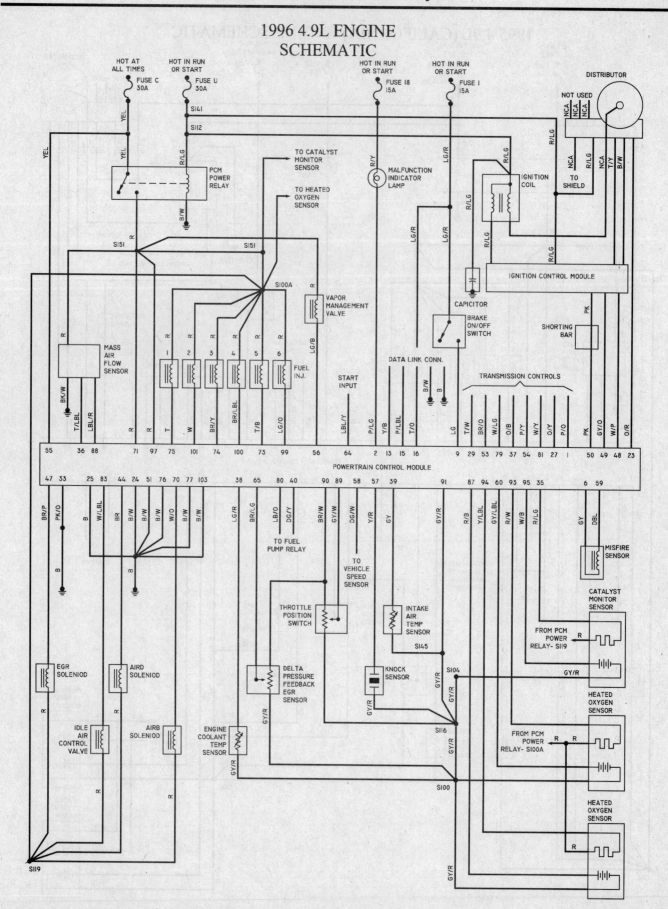

1992-93 7.5L ENGINE SCHEMATICS

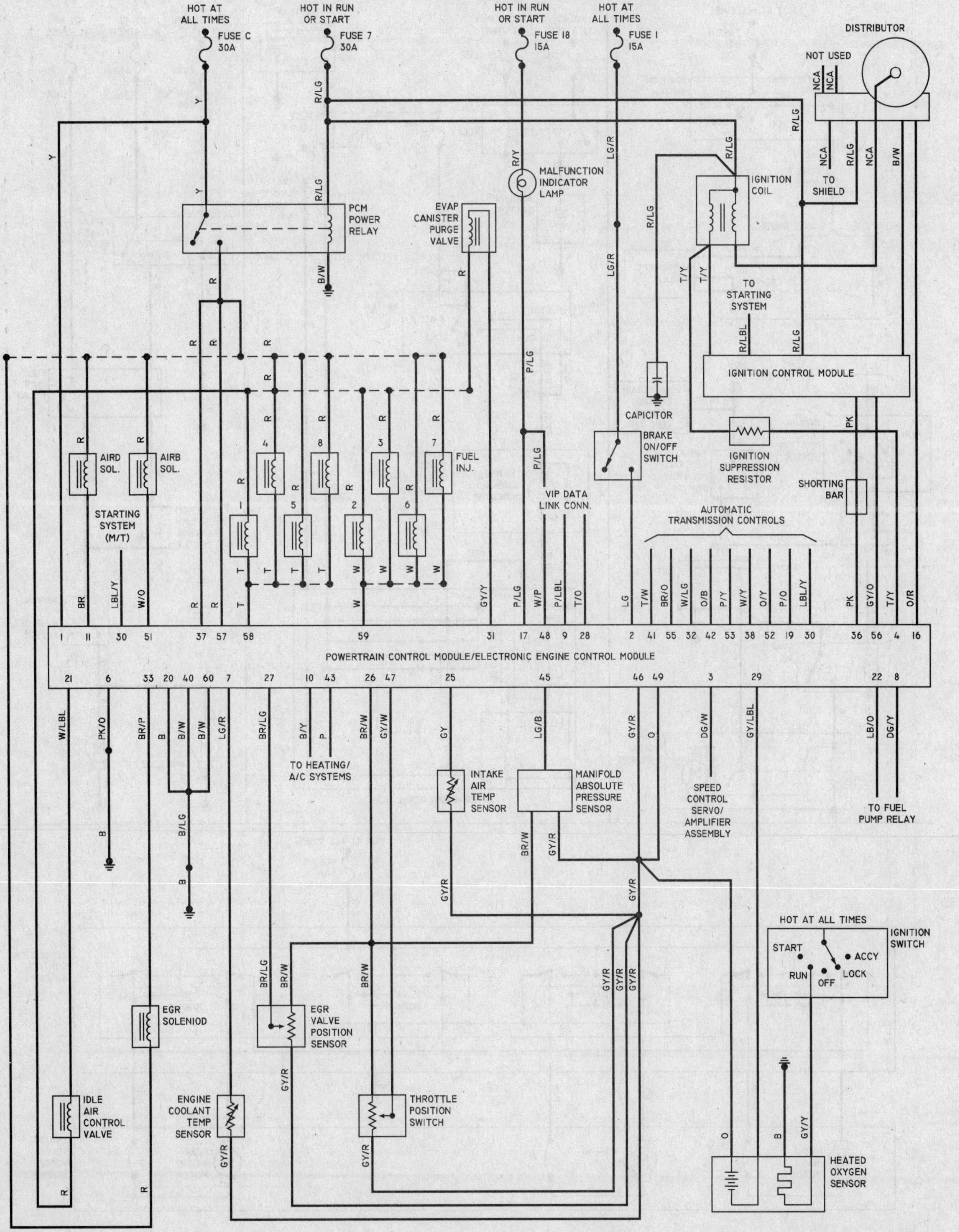

1992-96 CHASSIS (GASOLINE) SCHEMATICS

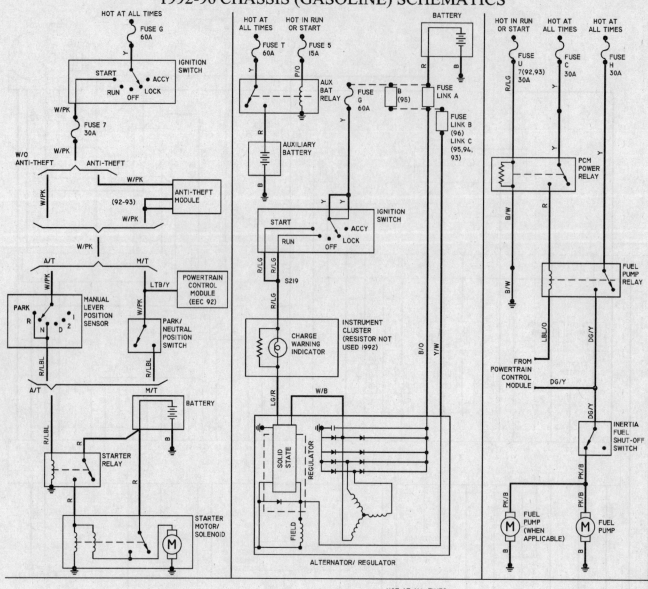

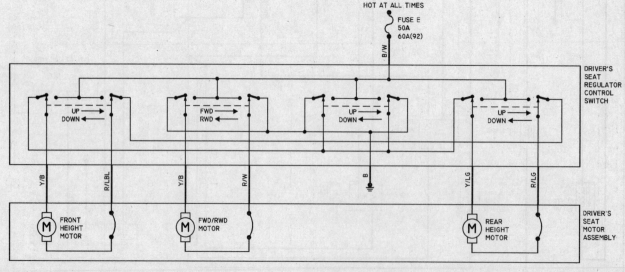

1996 5.0L ENGINE SCHEMATIC

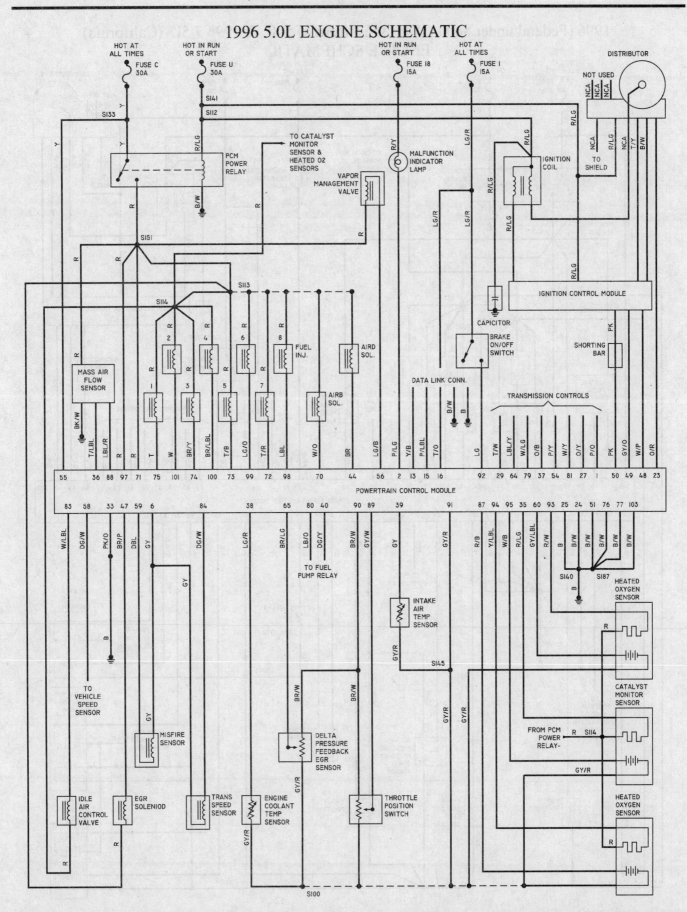

1996 (Federal under 8600 GVW & California) 5.8L & 1996 7.5L (California)
ENGINE SCHEMATIC

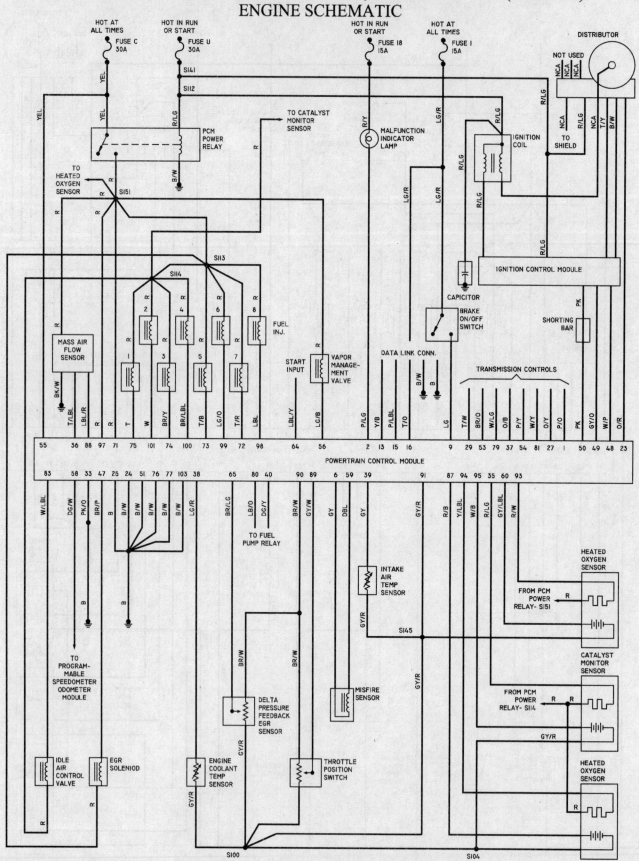

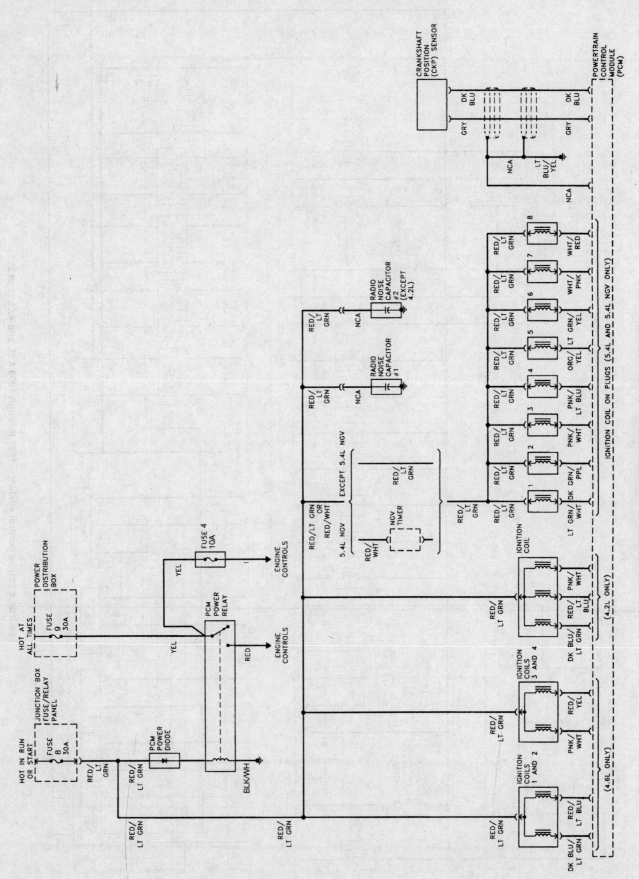

Typical distributorless ignition system circuit diagram

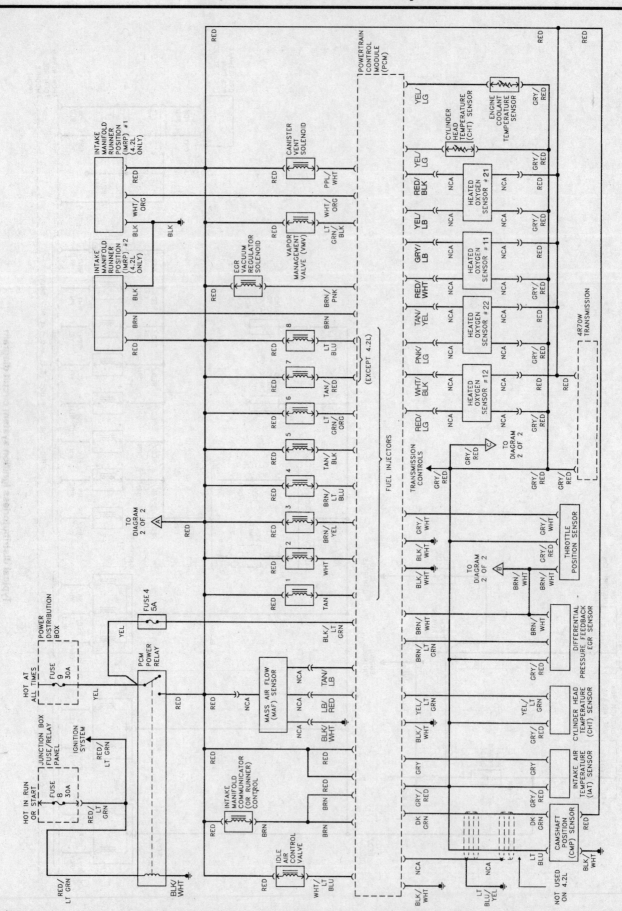

Electronic engine control system – 1997 through 1999 4.2L and 4.6L (1 of 2)

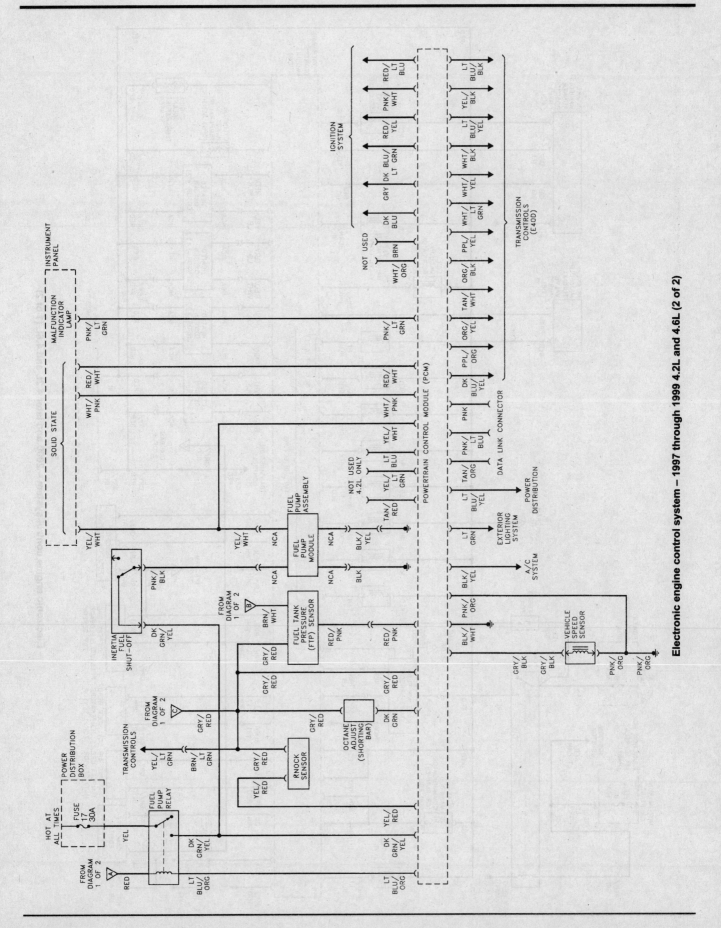

Electronic engine control system – 1997 through 1999 4.2L and 4.6L (2 of 2)

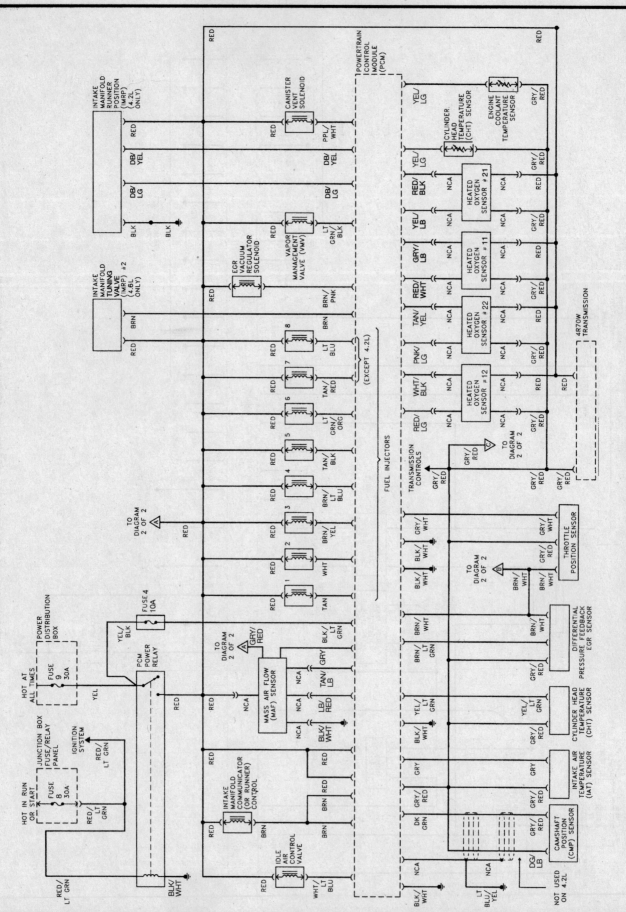

Electronic engine control system – 2000 and later 4.2L and 4.6L (1 of 2)

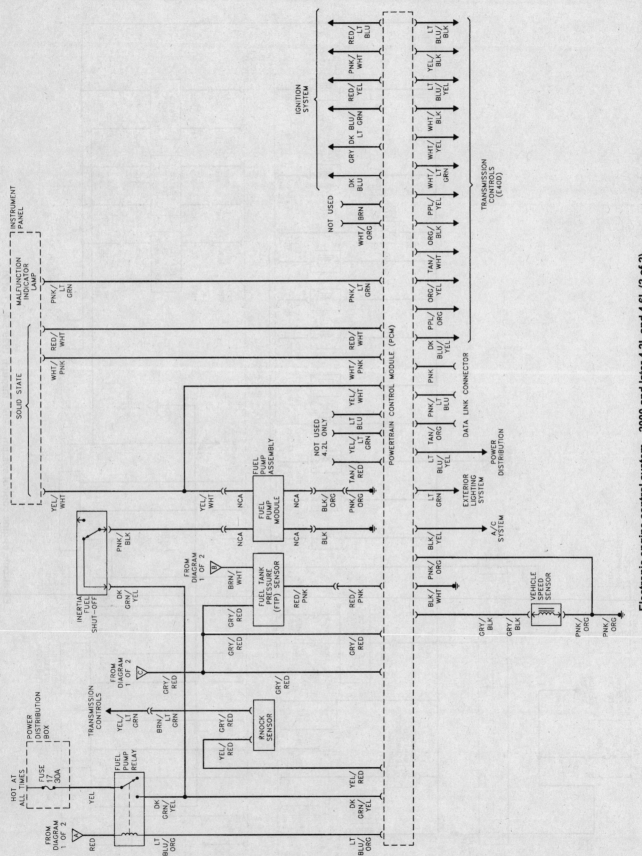

Electronic engine control system – 2000 and later 4.2L and 4.6L (2 of 2)

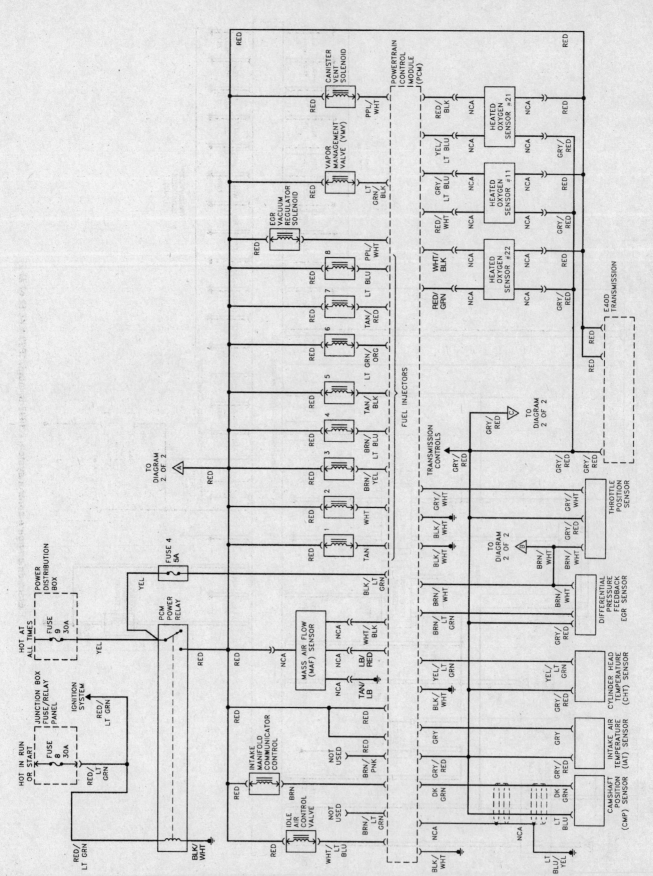

Electronic engine control system – 1997 through 1999 5.4L (1 of 2)

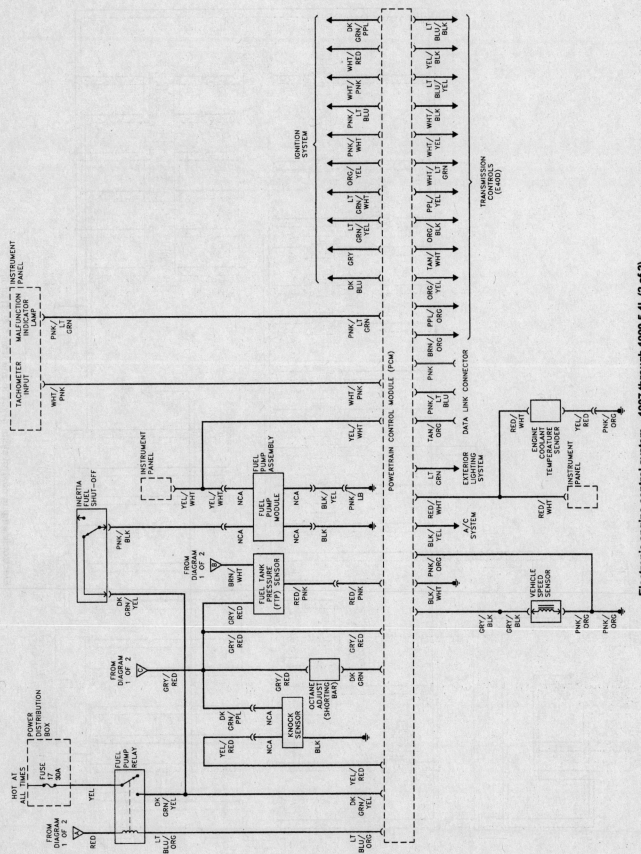

Electronic engine control system – 1997 through 1999 5.4L (2 of 2)

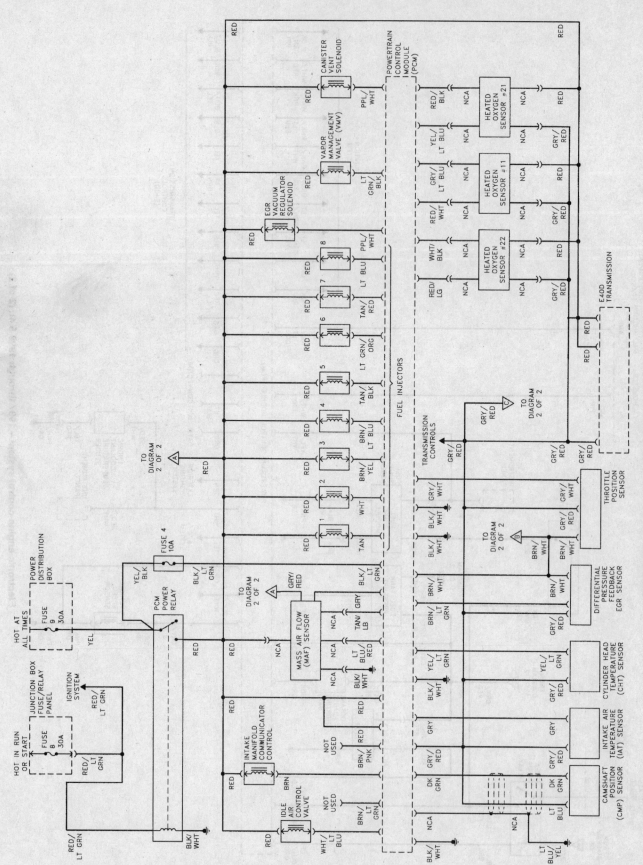

Electronic engine control system – 2000 and later 5.4L (1 of 2)

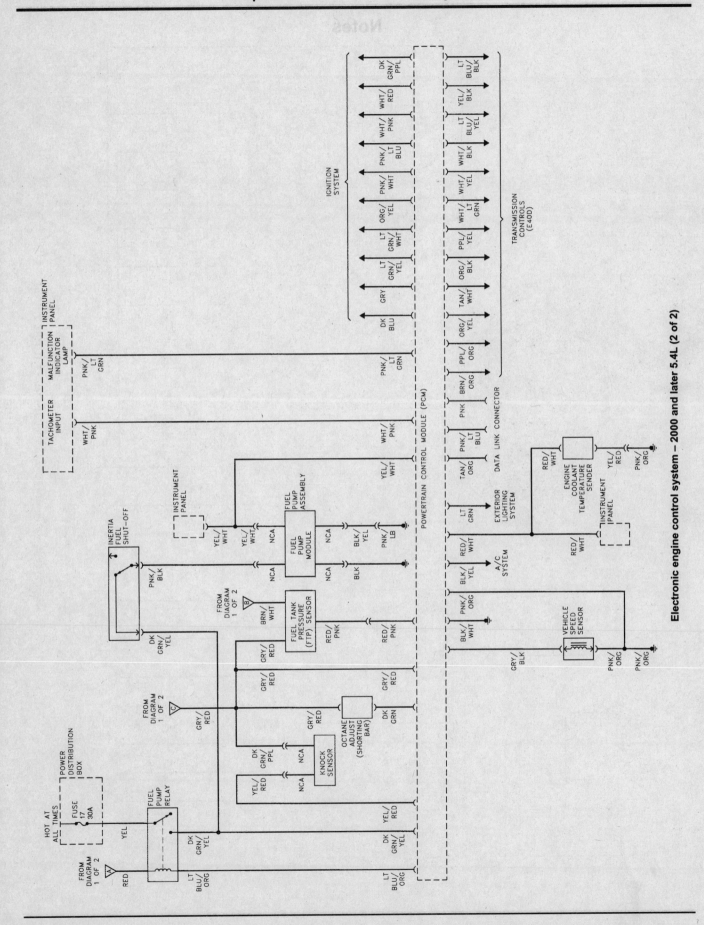

Electronic engine control system – 2000 and later 5.4L (2 of 2)

Notes

Index

Haynes Automotive Manuals

NOTE: If you do not see a listing for your vehicle, consult your local Haynes dealer for the latest product information.

HAYNES XTREME CUSTOMIZING

11101	Sport Compact Customizing
11102	Sport Compact Performance
11110	In-car Entertainment
11150	Sport Utility Vehicle Customizing
11213	Acura
11255	GM Full-size Pick-ups
11314	Ford Focus
11315	Full-size Ford Pick-ups
11373	Honda Civic

ACURA

12020	Integra '86 thru '89 & Legend '86 thru '90
12021	Integra '90 thru '93 & Legend '91 thru '95

AMC

	Jeep CJ - see JEEP (50020)
14020	Mid-size models '70 thru '83
14025	(Renault) Alliance & Encore '83 thru '87

AUDI

15020	4000 all models '80 thru '87
15025	5000 all models '77 thru '83
15026	5000 all models '84 thru '88

AUSTIN-HEALEY

	Sprite - see MG Midget (66015)

BMW

18020	3/5 Series not including diesel or all-wheel drive models '82 thru '92
18021	3-Series incl. Z3 models '92 thru '98
18022	3-Series, E46 chassis '99 thru '05, Z4 models '03 thru '05
18025	320i all 4 cyl models '75 thru '83
18050	1500 thru 2002 except Turbo '59 thru '77

BUICK

19010	Buick Century '97 thru '02
	Century (front-wheel drive) - see GM (38005)
19020	Buick, Oldsmobile & Pontiac Full-size (Front-wheel drive) '85 thru '05
	Buick Electra, LeSabre and Park Avenue; Oldsmobile Delta 88 Royale, Ninety Eight and Regency; Pontiac Bonneville
19025	Buick Oldsmobile & Pontiac Full-size (Rear wheel drive)
	Buick Estate '70 thru '90, Electra'70 thru '84, LeSabre '70 thru '85, Limited '74 thru '79 Oldsmobile Custom Cruiser '70 thru '90, Delta 88 '70 thru '85,Ninety-eight '70 thru '84 Pontiac Bonneville '70 thru '81, Catalina '70 thru '81, Grandville '70 thru '75, Parisienne '83 thru '86
19030	Mid-size Regal & Century all rear-drive models with V6, V8 and Turbo '74 thru '87
	Regal - see GENERAL MOTORS (38010)
	Riviera - see GENERAL MOTORS (38030)
	Roadmaster - see CHEVROLET (24046)
	Skyhawk - see GENERAL MOTORS (38015)
	Skylark - see GM (38020, 38025)
	Somerset - see GENERAL MOTORS (38025)

CADILLAC

21030	Cadillac Rear Wheel Drive all gasoline models '70 thru '93
	Cimarron - see GENERAL MOTORS (38015)
	DeVille - see GM (38031 & 38032)
	Eldorado - see GM (38030 & 38031)
	Fleetwood - see GM (38031)
	Seville - see GM (38030, 38031 & 38032)

CHEVROLET

24010	Astro & GMC Safari Mini-vans '85 thru '03
24015	Camaro V8 all models '70 thru '81
24016	Camaro all models '82 thru '92
24017	Camaro & Firebird '93 thru '02
	Cavalier - see GENERAL MOTORS (38016)
	Celebrity - see GENERAL MOTORS (38005)
24020	Chevelle, Malibu & El Camino '69 thru '87
24024	Chevette & Pontiac T1000 '76 thru '87
	Citation - see GENERAL MOTORS (38020)
24032	Corsica/Beretta all models '87 thru '96
24040	Corvette all V8 models '68 thru '82
24041	Corvette all models '84 thru '96
10305	Chevrolet Engine Overhaul Manual
24045	Full-size Sedans Caprice, Impala, Biscayne, Bel Air & Wagons '69 thru '90
24046	Impala SS & Caprice and Buick Roadmaster '91 thru '96
	Impala - see LUMINA (24048)
	Lumina '90 thru '94 - see GM (38010)
24048	Lumina & Monte Carlo '95 thru '03
	Lumina APV - see GM (38035)

24050	Luv Pick-up all 2WD & 4WD '72 thru '82
	Malibu '97 thru '00 - see GM (38026)
24055	Monte Carlo all models '70 thru '88
	Monte Carlo '95 thru '01 - see LUMINA (24048)
24059	Nova all V8 models '69 thru '79
24060	Nova and Geo Prizm '85 thru '92
24064	Pick-ups '67 thru '87 - Chevrolet & GMC, all V8 & in-line 6 cyl, 2WD & 4WD '67 thru '87; Suburbans, Blazers & Jimmys '67 thru '91
24065	Pick-ups '88 thru '98 - Chevrolet & GMC, full-size pick-ups '88 thru '98, C/K Classic '99 & '00, Blazer & Jimmy '92 thru '94; Suburban '92 thru '99; Tahoe & Yukon '95 thru '99
24066	Pick-ups '99 thru '03 - Chevrolet Silverado & GMC Sierra full-size pick-ups '99 thru '05, Suburban/Tahoe/Yukon/Yukon XL '00 thru '05
24070	S-10 & S-15 Pick-ups '82 thru '93, Blazer & Jimmy '83 thru '94,
24071	S-10 & Sonoma Pick-ups '94 thru '04, Blazer & Jimmy '95 thru '04, Hombre '96 thru '01
24072	Chevrolet TrailBlazer & TrailBlazer EXT, GMC Envoy & Envoy XL, Oldsmobile Bravada '02 and '03
24075	Sprint '85 thru '88 & Geo Metro '89 thru '01
24080	Vans - Chevrolet & GMC '68 thru '96
24081	Chevrolet Express & GMC Savana Full-size Vans '96 thru '05

CHRYSLER

25015	Chrysler Cirrus, Dodge Stratus, Plymouth Breeze '94 thru '00
10310	Chrysler Engine Overhaul Manual
25020	Full-size Front-Wheel Drive '88 thru '93
	K-Cars - see DODGE Aries (30008)
	Laser - see DODGE Daytona (30030)
25025	Chrysler LHS, Concorde, New Yorker, Dodge Intrepid, Eagle Vision, '93 thru '97
25026	Chrysler LHS, Concorde, 300M, Dodge Intrepid, '98 thru '03
25030	Chrysler & Plymouth Mid-size front wheel drive '82 thru '95
	Rear-wheel Drive - see Dodge (30050)
25035	PT Cruiser all models '01 thru '03
25040	Chrysler Sebring, Dodge Avenger '95 thru '02

DATSUN

28005	200SX all models '80 thru '83
28007	B-210 all models '73 thru '78
28009	210 all models '79 thru '82
28012	240Z, 260Z & 280Z Coupe '70 thru '78
28014	280ZX Coupe & 2+2 '79 thru '83
	300ZX - see NISSAN (72010)
28018	510 & PL521 Pick-up '68 thru '73
28020	510 all models '78 thru '81
28022	620 Series Pick-up all models '73 thru '79
	720 Series Pick-up - see NISSAN (72030)
28025	810/Maxima all gasoline models, '77 thru '84

DODGE

	400 & 600 - see CHRYSLER (25030)
30008	Aries & Plymouth Reliant '81 thru '89
30010	Caravan & Plymouth Voyager '84 thru '95
30011	Caravan & Plymouth Voyager '96 thru '02
30012	Challenger/Plymouth Saporro '78 thru '83
30016	Colt & Plymouth Champ '78 thru '87
30020	Dakota Pick-ups all models '87 thru '96
30021	Durango '98 & '99, Dakota '97 thru '99
30022	Dodge Durango models '00 thru '03 Dodge Dakota models '00 thru '03
30025	Dart, Demon, Plymouth Barracuda, Duster & Valiant 6 cyl models '67 thru '76
30030	Daytona & Chrysler Laser '84 thru '89 Intrepid - see CHRYSLER (25025, 25026)
30034	Neon all models '95 thru '99
30035	Omni & Plymouth Horizon '78 thru '90
30036	Dodge and Plymouth Neon '00 thru'03
30040	Pick-ups all full-size models '74 thru '93
30041	Pick-ups all full-size models '94 thru '01
30042	Dodge Full-size Pick-ups '02 thru '05
30045	Ram 50/D50 Pick-ups & Raider and Plymouth Arrow Pick-ups '79 thru '93
30050	Dodge/Plymouth/Chrysler RWD '71 thru '89
30055	Shadow & Plymouth Sundance '87 thru '94
30060	Spirit & Plymouth Acclaim '89 thru '95
30065	Vans - Dodge & Plymouth '71 thru '03

EAGLE

	Talon - see MITSUBISHI (68030, 68031)
	Vision - see CHRYSLER (25025)

FIAT

34010	124 Sport Coupe & Spider '68 thru '78
34025	X1/9 all models '74 thru '80

FORD

10355	Ford Automatic Transmission Overhaul
36004	Aerostar Mini-vans all models '86 thru '97
36006	Contour & Mercury Mystique '95 thru '00
36008	Courier Pick-up all models '72 thru '82
36012	Crown Victoria & Mercury Grand Marquis '88 thru '00
10320	Ford Engine Overhaul Manual
36016	Escort/Mercury Lynx all models '81 thru '90
36020	Escort/Mercury Tracer '91 thru '00
36022	Ford Escape & Mazda Tribute '01 thru '03
36024	Explorer & Mazda Navajo '91 thru '01
36025	Ford Explorer & Mercury Mountaineer '02 and '03
36028	Fairmont & Mercury Zephyr '78 thru '83
36030	Festiva & Aspire '88 thru '97
36032	Fiesta all models '77 thru '80
36034	Focus all models '00 thru '05
36036	Ford & Mercury Full-size '75 thru '87
36044	Ford & Mercury Mid-size '75 thru '86
36048	Mustang V8 all models '64-1/2 thru '73
36049	Mustang II 4 cyl, V6 & V8 models '74 thru '78
36050	Mustang & Mercury Capri all models Mustang, '79 thru '93; Capri, '79 thru '86
36051	Mustang all models '94 thru '03
36054	Pick-ups & Bronco '73 thru '79
36058	Pick-ups & Bronco '80 thru '96
36059	F-150 & Expedition '97 thru '02, F-250 '97 thru '99 & Lincoln Navigator '98 thru '02
36060	Super Duty Pick-ups, Excursion '99 thru '02
36062	Pinto & Mercury Bobcat '75 thru '80
36066	Probe all models '89 thru '92
36070	Ranger/Bronco II gasoline models '83 thru '92
36071	Ranger '93 thru '05 & Mazda Pick-ups '94 thru '05
36074	Taurus & Mercury Sable '86 thru '95
36075	Taurus & Mercury Sable '96 thru '05
36078	Tempo & Mercury Topaz '84 thru '94
36082	Thunderbird/Mercury Cougar '83 thru '88
36086	Thunderbird/Mercury Cougar '89 and '97
36090	Vans all V8 Econoline models '69 thru '91
36094	Vans full size '92 thru '05
36097	Windstar Mini-van '95 thru '03

GENERAL MOTORS

10360	GM Automatic Transmission Overhaul
38005	Buick Century, Chevrolet Celebrity, Oldsmobile Cutlass Ciera & Pontiac 6000 all models '82 thru '96
38010	Buick Regal, Chevrolet Lumina, Oldsmobile Cutlass Supreme & Pontiac Grand Prix (FWD) '88 thru '05
38015	Buick Skyhawk, Cadillac Cimarron, Chevrolet Cavalier, Oldsmobile Firenza & Pontiac J-2000 & Sunbird '82 thru '94
38016	Chevrolet Cavalier & Pontiac Sunfire '95 thru '04
38020	Buick Skylark, Chevrolet Citation, Olds Omega, Pontiac Phoenix '80 thru '85
38025	Buick Skylark & Somerset, Oldsmobile Achieva & Calais and Pontiac Grand Am all models '85 thru '98
38026	Chevrolet Malibu, Olds Alero & Cutlass, Pontiac Grand Am '97 thru '03
38030	Cadillac Eldorado '71 thru '85, Seville '80 thru '85, Oldsmobile Toronado '71 thru '85, Buick Riviera '79 thru '85
38031	Cadillac Eldorado & Seville '86 thru '91, DeVille '86 thru '93, Fleetwood & Olds Toronado '86 thru '92, Buick Riviera '86 thru '93
38032	Cadillac DeVille '94 thru '02 & Seville - '92 thru '02
38035	Chevrolet Lumina APV, Olds Silhouette & Pontiac Trans Sport all models '90 thru '96
38036	Chevrolet Venture, Olds Silhouette, Pontiac Trans Sport & Montana '97 thru '01 General Motors Full-size Rear-wheel Drive - see BUICK (19025)

GEO

	Metro - see CHEVROLET Sprint (24075)
	Prizm - '85 thru '92 see CHEVY (24060), '93 thru '02 see TOYOTA Corolla (92036)
40030	Storm all models '90 thru '93
	Tracker - see SUZUKI Samurai (90010)

(Continued on other side)

Haynes North America, Inc., 861 Lawrence Drive, Newbury Park, CA 91320-1514 • (805) 498-6703

Haynes Automotive Manuals (continued)

NOTE: If you do not see a listing for your vehicle, consult your local Haynes dealer for the latest product information.

GMC
Vans & Pick-ups - *see CHEVROLET*

HONDA
42010 Accord CVCC all models '76 thru '83
42011 Accord all models '84 thru '89
42012 Accord all models '90 thru '93
42013 Accord all models '94 thru '97
42014 Accord all models '98 thru '02
42015 Honda Accord models '03 thru '05
42020 Civic 1200 all models '73 thru '79
42021 Civic 1300 & 1500 CVCC '80 thru '83
42022 Civic 1500 CVCC all models '75 thru '79
42023 Civic all models '84 thru '91
42024 Civic & del Sol '92 thru '95
42025 Civic '96 thru '00, CR-V '97 thru '01,
Acura Integra '94 thru '00
42026 Civic '01 thru '04, CR-V '02 thru '04
42035 Honda Odyssey all models '99 thru '04
42040 Prelude CVCC all models '79 thru '89

HYUNDAI
43010 Elantra all models '96 thru '01
43015 Excel & Accent all models '86 thru '98

ISUZU
Hombre - *see CHEVROLET S-10 (24071)*
47017 Rodeo '91 thru '02; Amigo '89 thru '94 and
'98 thru '02; Honda Passport '95 thru '02
47020 Trooper & Pick-up '81 thru '93

JAGUAR
49010 XJ6 all 6 cyl models '68 thru '86
49011 XJ6 all models '88 thru '94
49015 XJ12 & XJS all 12 cyl models '72 thru '85

JEEP
50010 Cherokee, Comanche & Wagoneer Limited
all models '84 thru '01
50020 CJ all models '49 thru '86
50025 Grand Cherokee all models '93 thru '04
50029 Grand Wagoneer & Pick-up '72 thru '91
Grand Wagoneer '84 thru '91, Cherokee &
Wagoneer '72 thru '83, Pick-up '72 thru '88
50030 Wrangler all models '87 thru '03
50035 Liberty '02 thru '04

KIA
54070 Sephia '94 thru '01, Spectra '00 thru '04

LEXUS
ES 300 - *see TOYOTA Camry (92007)*

LINCOLN
Navigator - *see FORD Pick-up (36059)*
59010 Rear-Wheel Drive all models '70 thru '01

MAZDA
61010 GLC Hatchback (rear-wheel drive) '77 thru '83
61011 GLC (front-wheel drive) '81 thru '85
61015 323 & Protegé '90 thru '00
61016 MX-5 Miata '90 thru '97
61020 MPV all models '89 thru '94
Navajo - *see Ford Explorer (36024)*
61030 Pick-ups '72 thru '93
Pick-ups '94 thru '00 - *see Ford Ranger (36071)*
61035 RX-7 all models '79 thru '85
61036 RX-7 all models '86 thru '91
61040 626 (rear-wheel drive) all models '79 thru '82
61041 626/MX-6 (front-wheel drive) '83 thru '92
61042 626 '93 thru '01, MX-6/Ford Probe
'93 thru '01

MERCEDES-BENZ
63012 123 Series Diesel '76 thru '85
63015 190 Series four-cyl gas models, '84 thru '88
63020 230/250/280 6 cyl sohc models '68 thru '72
63025 280 123 Series gasoline models '77 thru '81
63030 350 & 450 all models '71 thru '80

MERCURY
64200 Villager & Nissan Quest '93 thru '01
All other titles, see FORD Listing.

MG
66010 MGB Roadster & GT Coupe '62 thru '80
66015 MG Midget, Austin Healey Sprite '58 thru '80

MITSUBISHI
68020 Cordia, Tredia, Galant, Precis &
Mirage '83 thru '93
68030 Eclipse, Eagle Talon & Ply. Laser '90 thru '94

68031 Eclipse '95 thru '01, Eagle Talon '95 thru '98
68035 Mitsubishi Galant '94 thru '03
68040 Pick-up '83 thru '96 & Montero '83 thru '93

NISSAN
72010 300ZX all models including Turbo '84 thru '89
72015 Altima '93 thru '04
72020 Maxima all models '85 thru '92
72021 Maxima all models '93 thru '04
72030 Pick-ups '80 thru '97 Pathfinder '87 thru '95
72031 Frontier Pick-up '98 thru '01, Xterra '00 & '01,
Pathfinder '96 thru '01
72040 Pulsar all models '83 thru '86
Quest - *see MERCURY Villager (64200)*
72050 Sentra all models '82 thru '94
72051 Sentra & 200SX all models '95 thru '99
72060 Stanza all models '82 thru '90

OLDSMOBILE
73015 Cutlass V6 & V8 gas models '74 thru '88
*For other OLDSMOBILE titles, see BUICK,
CHEVROLET or GENERAL MOTORS listing.*

PLYMOUTH
For PLYMOUTH titles, see DODGE listing.

PONTIAC
79008 Fiero all models '84 thru '88
79018 Firebird V8 models except Turbo '70 thru '81
79019 Firebird all models '82 thru '92
79040 Mid-size Rear-wheel Drive '70 thru '87
*For other PONTIAC titles, see BUICK,
CHEVROLET or GENERAL MOTORS listing.*

PORSCHE
80020 911 except Turbo & Carrera 4 '65 thru '89
80025 914 all 4 cyl models '69 thru '76
80030 924 all models including Turbo '76 thru '82
80035 944 all models including Turbo '83 thru '89

RENAULT
Alliance & Encore - *see AMC (14020)*

SAAB
84010 900 all models including Turbo '79 thru '88

SATURN
87010 Saturn all models '91 thru '02
87020 Saturn all L-series models '00 thru '04

SUBARU
89002 1100, 1300, 1400 & 1600 '71 thru '79
89003 1600 & 1800 2WD & 4WD '80 thru '94
89100 Legacy all models '90 thru '98

SUZUKI
90010 Samurai/Sidekick & Geo Tracker '86 thru '01

TOYOTA
92005 Camry all models '83 thru '91
92006 Camry all models '92 thru '96
92007 Camry, Avalon, Solara, Lexus ES 300 '97 thru '01
92008 Toyota Camry, Avalon and Solara and
Lexus ES 300/330 all models '02 thru '05
92015 Celica Rear Wheel Drive '71 thru '85
92020 Celica Front Wheel Drive '86 thru '99
92025 Celica Supra all models '79 thru '92
92030 Corolla all models '75 thru '79
92032 Corolla all rear wheel drive models '80 thru '87
92035 Corolla all front wheel drive models '84 thru '92
92036 Corolla & Geo Prizm '93 thru '02
92037 Corolla models '03 thru '05
92040 Corolla Tercel all models '80 thru '82
92045 Corona all models '74 thru '82
92050 Cressida all models '78 thru '82
92055 Land Cruiser FJ40, 43, 45, 55 '68 thru '82
92056 Land Cruiser FJ60, 62, 80, FZJ80 '80 thru '96
92065 MR2 all models '85 thru '87
92070 Pick-up all models '69 thru '78
92075 Pick-up all models '79 thru '95
92076 Tacoma '95 thru '04, 4Runner '96 thru '02,
& T100 '93 thru '98
92078 Tundra '00 thru '02 & Sequoia '01 thru '02
92080 Previa all models '91 thru '95
92082 RAV4 all models '96 thru '02
92085 Tercel all models '87 thru '94
92090 Toyota Sienna all models '98 through '02

TRIUMPH
94007 Spitfire all models '62 thru '81
94010 TR7 all models '75 thru '81

VW
96008 Beetle & Karmann Ghia '54 thru '79
96009 New Beetle '98 thru '00
96016 Rabbit, Jetta, Scirocco & Pick-up gas
models '75 thru '92 & Convertible '80 thru '92
96017 Golf, GTI & Jetta '93 thru '98
& Cabrio '95 thru '98
96018 Golf, GTI, Jetta & Cabrio '99 thru '02
96020 Rabbit, Jetta & Pick-up diesel '77 thru '84
96023 Passat '98 thru '01, Audi A4 '96 thru '01
96030 Transporter 1600 all models '68 thru '79
96035 Transporter 1700, 1800 & 2000 '72 thru '79
96040 Type 3 1500 & 1600 all models '63 thru '73
96045 Vanagon all air-cooled models '80 thru '83

VOLVO
97010 120, 130 Series & 1800 Sports '61 thru '73
97015 140 Series all models '66 thru '74
97020 240 Series all models '76 thru '93
97040 740 & 760 Series all models '82 thru '88
97050 850 Series all models '93 thru '97

TECHBOOK MANUALS
10205 Automotive Computer Codes
10206 OBD-II & Electronic Engine Management
Systems
10210 Automotive Emissions Control Manual
10215 Fuel Injection Manual, 1978 thru 1985
10220 Fuel Injection Manual, 1986 thru 1999
10225 Holley Carburetor Manual
10230 Rochester Carburetor Manual
10240 Weber/Zenith/Stromberg/SU Carburetors
10305 Chevrolet Engine Overhaul Manual
10310 Chrysler Engine Overhaul Manual
10320 Ford Engine Overhaul Manual
10330 GM and Ford Diesel Engine Repair Manual
10340 Small Engine Repair Manual, 5 HP & Less
10341 Small Engine Repair Manual, 5.5 - 20 HP
10345 Suspension, Steering & Driveline Manual
10355 Ford Automatic Transmission Overhaul
10360 GM Automatic Transmission Overhaul
10405 Automotive Body Repair & Painting
10410 Automotive Brake Manual
10411 Automotive Anti-lock Brake (ABS) Systems
10415 Automotive Detailing Manual
10420 Automotive Electrical Manual
10425 Automotive Heating & Air Conditioning
10430 Automotive Reference Manual & Dictionary
10435 Automotive Tools Manual
10440 Used Car Buying Guide
10445 Welding Manual
10450 ATV Basics
10452 Scooters, Automatic Transmission 50cc
to 250cc

SPANISH MANUALS
98903 Reparación de Carrocería & Pintura
98904 Carburadores para los modelos
Holley & Rochester
98905 Códigos Automotrices de la Computadora
98910 Frenos Automotriz
98913 Electricidad Automotriz
98915 Inyección de Combustible 1986 al 1999
99040 Chevrolet & GMC Camionetas '67 al '87
Incluye Suburban, Blazer & Jimmy '67 al '91
99041 Chevrolet & GMC Camionetas '88 al '98
Incluye Suburban '92 al '98, Blazer &
Jimmy '92 al '94, Tahoe y Yukon '95 al '98
99042 Chevrolet & GMC Camionetas
Cerradas '68 al '95
99055 Dodge Caravan & Plymouth Voyager '84 al '95
99075 Ford Camionetas y Bronco '80 al '94
99077 Ford Camionetas Cerradas '69 al '91
99088 Ford Modelos de Tamaño Mediano '75 al '86
99091 Ford Taurus & Mercury Sable '86 al '95
99095 GM Modelos de Tamaño Grande '70 al '90
99100 GM Modelos de Tamaño Mediano
'70 al '88
99106 Jeep Cherokee, Wagoneer & Comanche
'84 al '00
99110 Nissan Camioneta '80 al '96, Pathfinder '87 al '95
99118 Nissan Sentra '82 al '94
99125 Toyota Camionetas y 4Runner '79 al '95

Over 100 Haynes
motorcycle manuals
also available

3-06